PRAISE FOR *OF LIVING STONE*

"For me as a young person in the 1980s and 1990s, Vine was the only stranger I thought of as family. He was funny and heart-stabbingly blunt. So we have Vine Deloria to thank for revitalizing Indigenous knowledge gathering. Inspired by Vine's life work, Anishinaabe people now understand that we learn by listening (*bzindamowin*), observing (*gnawaaminjigewin*), and ceremony (*manidookewin*). We also know it's important to have a LOT of fun (*miiziiwapine*). *Of Living Stone* is both a somber memorial and a raucous celebration of Vine's work."

—**Matthew Fletcher**
(Grand Traverse Band of Ottawa and Chippewa Indians),
University of Michigan, and author of *The Ghost Road*

"This collection of writings on Vine Deloria, Jr. reminds me of the majestic outcroppings across Indigenous lands, waters, and skies—rock beings converging, supporting, and building with one another. *Of Living Stone* sheds critical light on the work of this intellectual giant whose scholarship and activism are foundational bedrock for the field of American Indian and Indigenous studies. Hence it is indispensable reading for all who are engaged in Indigenous resurgence and relationality in and beyond academe—from Indigenous artists, community organizers, and knowledge holders, to language warriors, tribal leaders, and non-Indigenous allies and comrades; for those engaged in liberation struggles and Land Back, climate justice, and movements to protect the sacred; for all of us who seek sustainable pathways and collective futures through indigeneity."

—**Christine Taitano DeLisle**, author of
Placental Politics: CHamoru Women, White Womanhood, and Indigeneity under U.S. Colonialism in Guam

OF LIVING STONE

OF LIVING STONE

Perspectives on Continuous Knowledge and the Work of Vine Deloria, Jr.

Edited by
David E. Wilkins
and
Shelly Hulse Wilkins

Fulcrum Publishing
Wheat Ridge, Colorado

Library of Congress Cataloging-in-Publication Data

Names: Wilkins, David E. (David Eugene), 1954- editor. | Wilkins, Shelly Hulse, editor.
Title: Of living stone : perspectives on continuous knowledge and the work of Vine Deloria, Jr. / edited by David E. Wilkins and Shelly Hulse Wilkins.
Description: Wheat Ridge : Fulcrum Publishing, [2024]. | Includes bibliographical references and index.
Identifiers: LCCN 2023043184 (print) | LCCN 2023043185 (ebook) | ISBN 9781682754665 (paperback) | ISBN 9781682754672 (ebook)
Subjects: LCSH: Deloria, Vine--Criticism and interpretation. | Deloria, Vine--Influence. | American literature--Indian authors--History and criticism. | BISAC: SOCIAL SCIENCE / Essays | SOCIAL SCIENCE / Ethnic Studies / American / Native American Studies
Classification: LCC E90.D45 .O35 2024 (print) | LCC E90.D45 (ebook) | DDC 810.9/897--dc23/eng/20231114
LC record available at https://lccn.loc.gov/2023043184
LC ebook record available at https://lccn.loc.gov/2023043185

Cover design by Kateri Kramer

Unless otherwise noted, all websites cited were current as of the initial edition of this work.

Printed in the United States
0 9 8 7 6 5 4 3 2

Fulcrum Publishing
3970 Youngfield Street
Wheat Ridge, Colorado 80033
(800) 992-2908 • (303) 277-1623
www.fulcrumbooks.com

This book is dedicated to the memories of

Hank Adams (Assiniboine-Sioux),
Senator John R. McCoy (Tulalip),
and
Nazhone Wilkins (Navajo-Lumbee)

CONTENTS

Introduction ... *xiii*

SECTION 1—OAK

Chapter 1. Vine Comes with Responsibility Carved into His Soul ... 3
Tantoo Cardinal

Chapter 2. Vine Deloria, Jr. and the Little Traverse Bay Bands of Odawa Indians ... 6
Frank Ettawageshik

Chapter 3. Vine Deloria, Jr., Whither the Women? ... 13
Sarah Deer

Chapter 4. The Black and the Red: Vine Deloria, Jr. and the Problem of African America ... 20
Kyle T. Mays

Chapter 5. Indigenous Peoples and Imagined Borders ... 25
Rebecca Tsosie

Chapter 6. Nationhood and Race: A Response to *Tribes, Treaties, and Constitutional Tribulations* ... 42
Martin Case

Chapter 7. The Essence of the Treaty Process: A Delorian View of Colonial Diplomacy ... 54
Samuel R. Cook

Chapter 8. Native Veterans, Political Participation, and Cultural Conservation ... 76
Tom Holm

Chapter 9. On Vine's Shoulders....89
Megan Minoka Hill and Norbert S. Hill, Jr.

SECTION 2—WATER

Chapter 10. A Letter to Vine on the Virtues of a Good Blade....101
Cannupa Hanska Luger

Chapter 11. The World We Still Live In (In Hawai'i nei)....105
Noenoe K. Silva

Chapter 12. Knowing the Land....120
Margaret Hiza Redsteer

Chapter 13. Deloria's Philosophy of (Pseudo)Science....134
Kyle Whyte

Chapter 14. God Is All of Those Things....140
Lauren Schad

Chapter 15. Stewardship as Native Teleology: Ceremonial Life and Restoring Right Relations....151
Natalie Avalos

Chapter 16. Revisiting Vine Deloria, Jr.'s Support for Unrecognized Tribes in a Time of Environmental Crises....160
Ryan E. Emanuel

Chapter 17. Seventh Generation: Bringing Forth a Traditional Value into Contemporary Times....175
Jordan P. Lewis

SECTION 3—SKY

Chapter 18. If You Can't Beat 'Em....185
Migizi Pensoneau

Chapter 19. That Time Deksi Vine Came Home to White Swan to Stand with Us and Defend Our Ancestors—and We Won!....190
Faith Spotted Eagle

Chapter 20. Vine Deloria, Jr.'s International Reach: Building Consciousness and Solidarity........202
Édith Patrouilleau with Aurélie Journée-Duez

Chapter 21. From Politicization to Movement Building: Indigenous Media and the New Indigenous Renaissance........213
Melanie K. Yazzie

Chapter 22. Media Plight........225
Mark Trahant

Chapter 23. Vine Deloria, Jr. and Indian Education........228
Gregory A. Cajete

Chapter 24. Building a Bridge from the Ivory Tower to the Woodstove: A Response to "More Ivory Than Red: False Allegiances in Academia"........253
Wendy S. Greyeyes and Tiffany S. Lee

Chapter 25. Deloria's Call for an Indian Education Revolution........268
Cheryl Crazy Bull

Chapter 26. The Sovereign Fruits of Vine........282
Deron Marquez

SECTION 4—STONE

Chapter 27. Memories of Vine........301
Doug George-Kanentiio

Chapter 28. Round Dancing and Counting Coup in Academic Circles with Vine Deloria, Jr.........305
Paulette F. C. Steeves

Chapter 29. Deloria/Des Lauriers: Vine Deloria, Jr.'s Ties to the French........314
Marine Le Puloch

Chapter 30. In the Spirit of Vine Deloria, Jr: Indigenous Kinship Renewal and Relational Sovereignty........321
Gabriel S. Galanda

Chapter 31. List-Making and the Real Pandemic....346
Kiros A. B. Auld

Chapter 32. The Moral Order of Kinship....354
Thomas Biolsi

Chapter 33. Indian Child Welfare, Tribal Sovereignty, and the Preeminence of the Tribal-State Axis....372
Céline Planchou

Chapter 34. Why This Memorial? A Statue Dedication Honoring Community and Friendship in Sheridan, Wyoming, October 9, 2023....385
Vivian Arviso

Chapter 35. *Continuous Knowledge: Of Living Stone*'s Cover Art....391
James Johnson

Acknowledgments....*393*
Appendix....*395*
Notes and Bibliographies....*413*
Contributors....*465*
Index....*487*
About the Editors....*508*

INTRODUCTION

"...[S]tone is regarded as the most perfect form of life since it has a physical integrity in itself."

—Vine Deloria, Jr.,
The World We Used to Live In

In the summer of 2020, the murder of George Floyd in Minneapolis ignited a great movement for justice and change. People across the country fought to reclaim their communities and their rights through direct action. They protested, marched, and toppled statues honoring heroes of white supremacy, refusing to tolerate the hate and violence these monuments symbolized and encouraged. Many so-called great men—traitors and murderers like Robert E. Lee, Juan de Oñate, Christopher Columbus, and Junípero Serra—were unceremoniously dethroned to be melted down, warehoused, or sent to museums where their misdeeds could be studied up close. It was a very good day here in Richmond, Virginia, when a bronze Columbus discovered the bottom of Fountain Lake.

In the midst of these events, *Indian Country Today* asked their readership which Native they believed deserving of a monument to be placed upon those newly unoccupied plinths and pedestals. Standing Rock author, activist, scholar, and philosopher, Vine Deloria, Jr., was at the top of the list of ten they chose for this honor. While we are sure Vine would have been both flattered and amused by the notion of a Vine Shrine, he would have been most taken with the irony of replacing one set of lifeless icons with another.

Non-Indigenous folks have long found it fitting to tear rocks from their places in the Earth and reshape them into idols. They seem to have no understanding of the slow, enduring memory of the stone beings. Like trees in a forest, all stone, from mountain to pebble, relies upon other stone. Melding, stacking, supporting, shifting—there is constant movement as each fragment of the whole seeks to achieve balance. In *The World We Used to Live In*, Vine shared several stories about the power of stones, observing that they "provide a cosmic perspective that the people must always keep in mind." For statue worshippers, this understanding has not merely been lost, but corrupted to such an extent that, for them, stone symbolizes not just permanence, but immobility. The death of growth, change, time, and perspective.

As we literally look up to those idols looming high on their pedestals, we are supposed to feel humility and gratitude for their extraordinary accomplishments. They are also intimidating reminders of who holds the reins of power. But, as we know from Native traditions, there are no new ideas, there are no solitary heroes, and permanence is a fiction. Survival, health, and fulfillment are only attainable through ongoing shared effort and balance. Stories, visions, and instructions for achieving these goals are passed along across generations and modified through discussion, community experiences, and trial and error. Knowledge is not linear, nor is it one-dimensional, and it is certainly not property. Knowledge is community—a shared circle where past, present, and future coexist, evolve, and inform one another. Those of us currently occupying the present adopt what is still useful, repurpose ideas to fit current needs, and build upon what we have been given to meaningfully engage with one another and with the worlds we inhabit.

We can all agree that monuments, by and large, fail to do much to spread ideas, expand knowledge, or further our chances of communal survival. That said, before we further castigate the notion of monolithic tributes to cultural icons, there are, to our minds, two important current exceptions of honoring individual Natives that exemplify and inspire dedication to community within their unique contexts.

The first is the statue of Billy Frank, Jr. (Nisqually, 1931–2014) selected to represent the people of Washington State in the US Capitol's

National Statuary Hall. Frank, a staunch defender of treaty rights and our environment, was a close friend of Vine's. His image replaced a bronze figure of nineteenth-century Indian-hating missionary Marcus Whitman that had represented the state for seventy years. The statement made by this highly public action, set in motion by a law initially sponsored by State Representative Debra Lekanoff (Tlingit) and signed by Governor Jay Inslee, was both a long-overdue acknowledgment of past wrongs and a highly visible commitment to working together for a better future.[1] That said, we think Billy would have had some colorful commentary on being forced to hang around Congress in perpetuity, and would have been delighted to know he had toppled Whitman from the other side.

Elizabeth Cook-Lynn (Crow Creek Sioux, 1930–2023), who recently walked on after a lifetime of good work, was instrumental in creating a monument with a different kind of meaning. Unrelenting in her fight against the disrespect, erasure, and straight-up violence that Native peoples had come to expect from their non-Native South Dakota neighbors, in 2013, she began the effort to create the First Nations Sculpture Garden to call attention to the Indigenous peoples and histories of the northern plains. She spent the next four years in conflict with a hostile city council and other local powers as she fought to reclaim space for an Indigenous presence in Rapid City, where life-sized bronze statues of white leaders are bolted to nearly every downtown street corner.

Because of her efforts, a group of four sculptures by Marilyn Wounded Head (Oglala Lakota, 1952–2019) honoring the lives and works of Charles Eastman, Nicholas Black Elk, Oscar Howe, and Vine Deloria, Jr., now stand in a local park. In an interview with reporter Tom Crash of the *Lakota Times*, Cook-Lynn explained, "We did not come here from somewhere else, we're not going anywhere, we're going to be here, this is who we are and this is where we belong. . . . These faces in this tiny garden are meant to be reminders and memorials for the education in history and culture of all future generations—history matters to all of us."[2]

Reclamation of history is difficult—even these mainstream ways of honoring were only realized after years of unrelenting advocacy. The very concept of history is under threat as, across the country, authoritarian movements gain power and attention by attacking anyone who is nonwhite, non-Christian, nonbinary, or differently abled. Evidence of friendship and community building across societal barriers is erased. Centuries of denigration and displacement have taken a grievous toll, and the virulent backlash against efforts to tell the stories of all peoples within the borders of what is now the United States is increasingly violent.

For non-Native cultures, the very act of creating static monuments is a kind of propagandic death that locks a limited personal story in time. In our combined years of political, legal, and historical research, we have yet to come across this type of so-called honoring by Native peoples prior to European encroachment. Although a statue can symbolize an apology or even an affirmation of Indigenous history and presence, elevation of an individual over community has never been a part of a long-term strategy for Indigenous peoples. Communities honored their relatives by transforming them into the embodiment of the people, a living tribute to collective survival.

The United States was colonized and created by white men of property who have since been lauded as benevolent fathers—visionary geniuses—when, in fact, their special abilities and freedoms were made possible by all those they enslaved, removed, and dominated. Thomas Jefferson, author of the Declaration of Independence (wherein he proposed that all men are created equal before going on to slander Indigenous peoples as "merciless Indian savages") is still widely regarded as the most brilliant of these men. Yet, a visit to Monticello, his home built, financed, supported, and run by the six hundred people he held captive over the course of his long lifetime, reveals the enormous cost of such "genius."

A worn spot on the parquet flooring in one of the marvelously designed rooms marks the place where, over decades, one uniformed enslaved boy after another stood to fan Jefferson as he dined, conversed, and thought his great thoughts. The narcissism and hypocrisy required to justify the barbarity of the years spent by all those children to move the heavy Virginia summer air for one so-called great man is incomprehensible. To then think of the human hours required to maintain all his projects, whims, and desires calls to mind nothing less than a vampire, as he and all the others of his ilk maintained their lifestyles by feeding off the stolen safety, kinship, love, comfort, creativity, freedom, and land of African Americans and Indigenous peoples. Two and a half centuries later, his bankrupt legacy is a largely parasitic culture that still attempts, at great cost, to capture and silence living stone.

So, rather than a statue, we believe Vine would have preferred that his tools—decades of research, writing, and activism—be put to real use; not just parroted or lauded, but strenuously critiqued, and then either modified for current use, or kept as memories of other times. This is the practical way Native peoples have always carried knowledge and traditions forward.

Philosopher and religious scholar Houston Smith once described Vine as a giant oak of a man. Vine did, indeed, stand tall, but his strength and reach were only possible because he was deeply rooted in kinship and community—the antithesis of those like Jefferson whose strength came from standing upon others. While rightly credited for his significant body of work, Vine rarely acted alone—save when he was hunkered down in his basement typing out his latest work, a pack of filterless Pall Malls close at hand. He began his career as one tree in a forest of Native giants, like Billy Frank, Jr., Helen Scheirbeck, Lorraine Loomis, Henrietta Mann, Sam Deloria, Ramona Bennett, Oren Lyons, Hank Adams, Suzan Shown Harjo, Tillie Walker, Clyde Warrior, Joe DeLaCruz, Madonna Thunder Hawk, John Trudell, Janet McCloud, the Bellecourt brothers, Ada Deer, Russell Means, Bernie Whitebear, Floyd Westerman, Dennis Banks, Maiselle Bridges, Robert K. Thomas, and Mel Tonasket, who came of age at a time when Indigenous communities organized to fight for human, civil, and treaty rights, as well as the rights of the Natural World.

Vine was, without question, a unique talent—smart and seemingly fearless, armed with a razor-sharp sense of humor. And he was in the right place at the right time in history with a voice that could not be ignored. While his writings were original and shockingly new to non-Natives, they were rooted in concepts that had been inherited, discussed, and refined with his relatives, friends, and colleagues. As part of something much bigger, created and bolstered by his family and community, he honed these collective ideas, built upon them, and brought them into the broader public arena. This is not to diminish his personal accomplishments, but to put them in context. Vine was human. He was all at once meticulous, brilliant, ambitious, vain, principled, sarcastic, loyal, stubborn, volatile, and courageous. A complex being—just like the rest of us.

When David Wilkins undertook the task of writing *Red Prophet* in 2016, his hope was to distill Vine's mountain of work into a list of ideas and recommendations using straightforward language accessible for those who never had the chance to know him. Even then, momentous cultural shifts were already underway; young people across Indian Country were organizing via social media and inspiring their relatives and allies to protect the Earth and its communities. Then came the pandemic and with it the agonizing loss of Elder knowledge. Since then, climate change has accelerated, threatening already vulnerable Native communities. Societal divisions, driven by those with authoritarian ambitions, have multiplied and led to more violence. It is our urgent responsibility to protect all our relations using tools that have been passed down to us. Vine's legacy of knowledge, energy, and ambition were always part of our collective story and they will remain with us as long as we work together for our common good. This collection of thoughtful and creative perspectives from an eclectic mix of individuals not only gives deeper meaning to Vine's writings, but, perhaps, more importantly, provides an example of ever-living transfers and transformations of traditional knowledge—the continuous flow of information and care that is an antidote to the broader cultural worship of death and endings. This legacy should be accessible and relevant, especially as we are increasingly called upon to differentiate between living knowledge and artificially generated information.

Although Vine's context and focus may sometimes appear narrow—or in some cases even outdated—when compared to contemporary thinking, his ideas can be recalibrated and applied to bolster current movements, both within what is now the US and internationally, such as those related to environmental racism, violence against women, LGBTQIA2S+ rights, law enforcement reform, the Landback movement, belonging, and the ongoing battle against the foundational white supremacy of the United States.

The contributors have provided examples of powerful thoughts and actions based upon or inspired by his work using plain, direct language he would have appreciated. Vine is the common thread in this mix of artists, activists, and academics. Past, present, and future are intertwined and imagined—what might have been and hope for what we could yet become. The diverse and wide-ranging voices reflect Vine's own panoramic interests and concerns. Whether the authors affirm, criticize, or retool his work, each starts from a place of deep respect and commitment. We are honored to help them share their knowledge, recollections, and calls for change.

The four sections are an attempt to categorize the viewpoints and memories of this collective. Section 1, Oak, centers on current approaches to critical issues rooted in traditional knowledge, including Vine's legacy, identifying what has been useful and what is lacking. In Section 2, Water, are found perspectives on mending, reclaiming, and creating what is needed, driven by ceremony and tending relations. Pieces in Section 3, Sky, explore possibilities through the transformative powers of humor, imagination, activism, and education. Finally, Section 4, Stone, connects to the past—both what was and what continues—including reconstruction of pathways to kinship and traditions that encompass all beings.

The legacy of visions, knowledge, and strategies that moved through Vine's prodigious body of works, both collective and unique, are embers kept ready to build the next fire. That flame burned bright in 2020 when the Lakota people stood at the most depraved monument of them all, Mount Rushmore, carved from the living stone of the Six Grandfathers—to protect their sacred lands from being used as a political rally backdrop by then-president Donald Trump. Here, they not only pushed back, they introduced the Landback movement to an international audience. This is knowledge flowing continuously through the present.

These works inspired by ideas inherited from Vine and his contemporaries are testaments to the loyalty, laughter, wisdom, determination, and longevity of Indigenous peoples. Each of us can take up this work. Each of us must take up this work. Together we seek balance as a living monument—close as a forest of oaks, relentless as water, broad as the sky, strong as living stone.

1

Oak

CHAPTER 1

VINE COMES WITH RESPONSIBILITY CARVED INTO HIS SOUL

Tantoo Cardinal

He came, Vine Deloria Jr., with Responsibility carved into his soul
to show the world who we Really are.
In rage with laughter, he proceeded in denial of the images put forward
with boots on our neck telling the world they were justified in this theft,
this crime against our humanity . . . Theft of Land, "Resources" they call
Our Mother's enzymes.
Ridding the vermin. Picking the lice off their Discoveries.
Why, even God knew (Jesus of Nazareth with his blue eyes and
blond hair), they were the Ones who deserved it.

The first ones to create the lie knew it was a lie.
Then they acculturated their generations to come, their minions, to feel
comfortable in the lie, until now they Demand their Truth to be real.
Evidence shows Not.
Evidence shows
They did not and do not know the Truth
The Original Truth of the Land holds.
She is a Body. She is Alive. She Remembers,
and She has Laws that no man-made denial genius will withstand.
We are One with Her
Our Mother Earth.

She preserved us through the Age of Genocide.
She saw us safely to the shore with the bit of mud that holds the blueprint of Our Mother, our Existence with enough breath left to blow upon it for the generations that slowly, surely, determinably found our way out from under the blanket of Genocide.

We had Keepers of the Dawn.
Vine Deloria, Jr. was one.
He knew where the riches to survival were kept.
He knew where the riches to thriving were kept . . . Within the chest most maligned—in Ceremony, in Prayer, in the Ways/Culture, in Language of Natural Force . . . picking up a weapon—the Language of Those Who Intend to Smother, to weave a protective frock for the ones coming behind through the passageway gnawed open with Ceremony, Prayer, Family, Community, Relationship, Education—Knowledge—of Truth, Soul, Heart.

We saw you from the hillside
Peering through the gel of jealousy and disdain Creating Oppression,
That short-lived glory.

Now we stand
Among the pillars of those who came before us having built
our shelters, now our wings. It is our time
Destiny and Fate beckon.
The oppressors' children are beginning that whimper Our Mother will respond to Only when it is time.
"Tell the Truth," she will say. "How did you get that thing you say is yours?
That domain you say is yours. Didn't you say you were going to share?
You signed an agreement, a promise, with a pen, not with your heart.
Go back now to your heart
Where Truth never sleeps."

Truth is
These Men came and created their own story of Favor and Superiority while Woman carried the Greatest Gift of Creation. Shamelessly they attacked women and children at the outset, knowing the power base, and blurred Man's responsibility under the blindfold of Colonialism.
They were slippery
And Vine, with his Ancestors on his shoulders and his allies at his side found the rudder, the buttons to shift directions, to help us see who and what we came to be, the Elder Children of Our Mother who remember Her stories and will not let Her wishes die.

Happy Indigenous Day
Keep your sleeves rolled up
Mother is watching
And Listening
And Guiding
And Cheering us on.

CHAPTER 2

VINE DELORIA, JR. AND THE LITTLE TRAVERSE BAY BANDS OF ODAWA INDIANS

Frank Ettawageshik

As I am writing these words, my Tribe, Waganakising Odawak, the Little Traverse Bay Bands of Odawa Indians, is just completing a general election. It has now been twenty-seven years since President Bill Clinton signed our reaffirmation legislation PL 103-324 into law. There are many individuals whose efforts over several generations made this possible: Margaret Boyd, Andrew Blackbird, Jonas Shawandase, Sam and Charlie Keway, and Bob and Juanita Dominic, to name a few. Many modern-day Tribal leaders and consultants were also part of the effort. In addition, we were aided by the involvement of Vine Deloria, Jr. This story recounts how our Tribe's and my own relationship with Vine came to be, and is about how Vine's writings, scholarship, and personal intervention aided us in ending a 120-year struggle with the United States over our Tribal existence.

My introduction to Vine Deloria, Jr. was when I read *Custer Died for Your Sins* attending the University of Michigan in Ann Arbor in 1969. The 1960s was a very turbulent time on college campuses in the United States. At the time I was exploring many ideas and philosophies and acclimating to the larger world. My high school graduating class of forty-four in rural Michigan had not prepared me for suddenly being in the midst of nearly forty thousand students. This was before the Native students' organization was formed. There were few Indians, and we most often were invisible in the larger university population. I was raised knowing my clan and my traditional name. I understood the broad strokes of our family and Tribal history. However, reading *Custer Died for Your Sins* took me to a new perspective on my heritage, and this helped form the background for the work that I later took on as a Tribal leader.

I left Ann Arbor in 1972 and began teaching pottery at the Keweenaw Bay Indian Tribal Center in Baraga, Michigan. For several years I was involved in the art world, making stoneware pottery and beginning my efforts to regain the woodland Indian pottery skills of my ancestors. Eventually my path led me to increased involvement in my Native heritage and in Tribal affairs. In 1989, I went to a Tribal meeting to listen and offer my assistance. I left the meeting being elected vice chair and thus began a career in Tribal politics, during which I served fourteen years as Tribal chairman.

At the Little Traverse Bay Bands of Odawa Indians, we were working on fixing a historical wrong that caused us to not be on the list of federally recognized Tribes. Although we were signors to a series of treaties going back to pre-Revolutionary times, the US did not recognize us. During the years following 1855—the year we signed our last treaty with the US—we had attempted to remedy the bureaucratic errors that had created this situation. Our efforts included letters, petitions, and legal actions, spanning decades. By 1989 this culminated in our seeking Administration for Native Americans (ANA) grant funding for status clarification, which we first received in 1990. The grant was to prepare for the federal acknowledgment process at the Department of the Interior, Branch of Acknowledgement and Research.

In addition to this administrative track, we also sought and were successful in getting draft reaffirmation legislation written and sponsored in the US House of Representatives. The legislation was for two Tribes: The Little Traverse Bay Bands of Odawa Indians and The Little River Band of Ottawa Indians, both Tribes from our traditional territories along the shores of Lake Michigan. As part of this effort, we sought resolutions of support from the state of Michigan, local units of government, recognized Tribes from the Great Lakes, and across the United States. We gradually built up a collection of support resolutions. One that we sought was from the National Tribal Chairman's Association. We were told that they would not support any "new" Tribes because any new Tribe would just divide up the already inadequate federal funding into smaller amounts.

We also were working on meeting the objectives of the ANA grant, one of which was to hold a conference on sovereignty and constitution development, to assist us in preparing for federal recognition. In conversations with our Tribal attorney as we were looking for speakers for the conference, we talked about Vine's book *The Nations Within*. We wanted someone who could speak to the information in the book. After some discussion, someone said, "Why don't we just ask Vine?" Initially, we had not thought about going directly to Vine, but we decided to go for it, and we sent an inquiry. To our surprise, he said yes. Grand Traverse Band of Ottawa and Chippewa Indians, a neighboring federally recognized Tribe, offered to contribute by paying Vine's transportation to northern Michigan and piggybacking an event at their Tribal offices with our conference.

The conference, held in April 1992, was a success. As we spoke about our 120-year struggle with the United States, Vine became aware of and interested in our work. During this conference, Vine stressed that our revised constitution should recognize inherent rights and that all governance authority emanates from our Tribal citizens. Through the constitution, the citizens delegate authority to the Tribal government, reserving the right through amendment to give more authority to the government or to take some away. The Tribal government is not the Tribe; rather, the Tribal government serves the Tribe. He also explained how the constitution lays out the interface between the Tribe and other sovereigns with whom the Tribe has relationships.

In parallel efforts, while we were working on the documentation for a petition for federal acknowledgment, we were working on moving our legislation in the US Congress. The sponsor of our legislation in the

House was now Congressman Dale Kildee of Michigan. He spoke to us of the importance of the US Constitution, Article 1, Section 8, the Commerce Clause, stating, "Congress shall have the power to Regulate Commerce with the foreign Nations, and among the several States, and with the Indian Tribes." In the supremacy clause, the Constitution goes on to say in part that "this Constitution and the Laws of the United States made in Pursuance thereof, and all Treaties made, or which shall be made, under the Authority of the United States, shall be the supreme Law of the Land." We understood that the US Constitution acknowledged the preexistent sovereignty of Tribal governments to the United States, and that our treaties were considered "the supreme Law of the Land." We now had the benefit of guidance regarding the workings and powers for our constitutional development from Vine and from the US Constitution.

A congressional hearing on our legislation was scheduled for July of 1992. Vine offered to testify. It was more than we could have hoped for, and we accepted his offer. We told him of the resolutions of support we received, and we told him of the reluctance of many existing federally recognized Tribes to support our efforts, due to limited federal funding being divided up into even smaller portions.

Several weeks after his offer to testify, Vine sent me a copy of a letter he sent to the Great Plains Tribes. In the letter he reminds the Tribes that they seek to hold the United States to its treaty obligations to them. He then provides a copy of a treaty that predates the United States, brokered by, but not signed by, Great Britain, between the Anishinaabeg at Michilimackinac and the Lakota, Nakota, Dakota Nations.[1] According to Vine's scholarship, this 1781 treaty was the first between Indian nations written in English. His argument was that to hold the US to their obligations, it is necessary to live up to the obligations in other treaties that Indian Nations have made. Since the federally recognized leaders were hesitant to support our efforts, Vine took his request to the traditional leaders. Our request to them was based on the treaty we both had signed. After some discussion, the traditional leaders agreed and adopted a resolution in support of our federal recognition efforts.[2]

At that first hearing for our legislation in the US House, Vine testified about the problems of the federal recognition process. He outlined the obstacles that the bureaucracy creates, complicating an already onerous struggle. He went on to highlight that his Tribe had signed a treaty with our people before the United States came into existence. His testimony included a copy of the resolution he secured from the traditional leaders on our behalf.

Vine later provided written testimony at a second hearing in the US House. Having a person of his reputation and notoriety on Indian issues provide testimony for our Tribe was a significant boost to our efforts, which led to passage by both the House and Senate. The bill was signed by President Clinton on September 21, 1994, in an Oval Office ceremony, becoming PL 103-324.

The Little Traverse Bay Bands of Odawa Indians' and the Little River Band of Ottawa Indians' federal statuses were now achieved. After securing interim funding and getting into the federal budget cycle for subsequent funding, we then each had to implement the legislation by developing a formal roll of our citizens and complete the work on our revised constitution in preparation for a secretarial election. The roll was prepared and certified on March 31, 2003. In a long process involving review of other Tribes' existing constitutions and repeated public meetings and mailings to our Tribal citizens, the draft revised constitution was completed and submitted to the Bureau of Indian Affairs for review for an election to adopt it. The lessons we learned from Vine were incorporated within the draft constitution. A separation of powers constitution incorporating legislative, executive, and judicial authorities in balance with each other was adopted by secretarial election, the results of which were announced on February 1, 2005.[3]

In the years following the passage of the reaffirmation legislation, we kept up our communications with Vine. When Vine's son Philip became a member of the University of Michigan faculty, my wife and I attended a reception at the multicultural center at Trotter House in Ann Arbor. I brought my copy of Vine's book *The Metaphysics of Modern Existence*.

When I presented it to him to sign, he said, "Frank! You must be one of the nine people who read this book. And one of them was my mother!" Since that time, the book has had several reprints and is used in many college and university classes across the nation.

Later, while I was living in East Lansing, Michigan, for a couple of years around 2000, Vine was the speaker at a large dinner meeting for the Michigan State University Native students. I was able to attend and heard many inspirational thoughts from him in response to questions posed by the students. After several had asked him for assistance with an impending issue, Vine paused and then told this story. He said that Custer was about to attack the village. The young people were all coming to their Elders and saying "Help! Custer is about to attack the village!" Vine then took a long pause and looked across all the eager young faces. "You are coming to us Elders to take up the fight," he said. "We are tired and old. It's your damn turn to deal with these issues!" And then he smiled. I was impressed that he was challenging the next generation, that he was supportive, but as an Elder and not as the frontline warrior.

A year or so before Vine passed, he came again to visit our Tribe as a guest speaker. He sat on a stool in the commons area of our recently built Tribal Governmental Center. Our new center was built around a large octagon-shaped meeting room with a wooden-beamed, vaulted ceiling and a firepit in the center. The room was lined with tables and chairs filled with Tribal citizens and employees. Vine's visit was part of a cultural immersion lecture series arranged by the Little Traverse Bay Bands Tribal Court.

Vine spoke about three visits to our Tribe and of the progress he witnessed for our community since he first became acquainted with us. His first visit was one he had not talked about to us before. In the early 1960s, along with Ben Quigno of the Saginaw Chippewa Tribe in Mt. Pleasant, Michigan, he came to Little Traverse Bay. Amongst the Indians he visited were some living in cars in the woods and having outhouses for plumbing. The poverty and lack of development was obvious. There was substandard housing, no federal recognition, no Tribal office building, no economic enterprises, few jobs, and inadequate health care.

In 1992 he visited a second time to attend the conference on sovereignty and constitution development that we hosted using ANA funds. He told us that seeing the changes from his first visit, seeing the organizing work that we had done in securing an office and grant funding, seeing all the work in progress contributed to his desire to testify in Congress on our behalf.

And now he had returned a third time and could see how much progress we had made. Since the passage of PL 103-324, we had adopted a constitution based on inherent rights of our people, we had built several office buildings, and were operating a casino resort. We created nearly one thousand jobs in our community and offered a full spectrum of Tribal government services. We moved from seeking donations to rent a meeting hall to meeting in our own hotel conference room and having an annual government budget of nearly $30 million.

One of my treasured photographs was taken at the Newseum in Washington, D.C., following a speech that Vine gave in 2005. After the speech, Vine, Billy Frank, Jr., and I were sitting talking together in the front row of the emptying auditorium. Both men had inspired and educated me as I worked in leadership of my Tribe. I was filled with awe and gratitude being able to share this moment with men who meant so much to my development as a leader.

Vine spent a lifetime thinking and writing, supporting Tribal sovereignty and Tribal governments. His work laid the groundwork for a whole new generation of leaders. But his work also educated a whole generation of more enlightened Tribal citizens who expected more from their leaders and governments, and who were better equipped to demand respect for their traditional lifeways and the exercise of sovereignty. The coming generations are being built upon and supported in part by the continuing effects of the words and life of Vine Deloria, Jr., and nowhere is this more evident than for the citizens of the Waganakising Odawak, the Little Traverse Bay Bands of Odawa Indians.

CHAPTER 3

VINE DELORIA, JR., WHITHER THE WOMEN?

Sarah Deer

I was born at 3:03 a.m. on Thursday, November 9, 1972, in Silver Spring, Maryland. Just six days prior and twenty miles away, members of the American Indian Movement and their allies had taken over the Bureau of Indian Affairs (BIA) building as part of a radical activist effort known as the Trail of Broken Treaties. Later in the afternoon of my birthday, the occupation ended. I am indeed a part of generation X—those who were born during the late 1960s and early 1970s but were not witnesses to the powerful and controversial activism that took place during that time period.

Moreover, my father, Montie Deer—originally from Kansas—was not in the Washington, D.C., region for purposes of radical activism. Instead, he had joined forces with the likes of Ladonna Harris and Barney Old Coyote to support the American Indian National Bank Project just after graduating from law school. At the time of the BIA occupation, he was on the Hill seeking congressional support for the proposed bank. I gather that Deloria straddled the chasm between the more radical activists and the establishment Indians. Perhaps that is why I am so drawn to his writings.

The corpus of Vine Deloria's work has been a primary way that someone of my generation has learned about the critical activist interventions of Indian people during that perilous period that included Alcatraz, the

BIA occupation, and the standoff at Wounded Knee. But, of course, as Vine fans know—his intervention was marked by a deep commitment to bring an intellectual angle to these pernicious problems. His quick wit served him well—particularly in response to expected reactions from white folks. So, of course, these were the kinds of books I wanted to read once college began.

I am someone who loves vintage books and bookstores. Used bookstores are becoming rare these days, but anytime I'm in a new city, I seek one out and go straight to the Native American section. As a result, I have collected first-edition paperbacks of Deloria's most famous books, including *Custer Died for Your Sins*, *God Is Red*, *We Talk, You Listen*, and *Behind the Trail of Broken Treaties*. Most are in very poor condition (especially my copy of *God Is Red*, which I have wrapped in a rubber band to keep the pages from falling out). Some of them have been inscribed with the name of the original owner. Somehow, the fact that these books were physically acquired and read during the 1970s makes me feel closer to understanding the time and place in which the books were written. I have a hard copy of his 1979 book, *The Metaphysics of Modern Existence*, one of his less accessible titles. I was a philosophy major as an undergraduate, but I still admit that I have found *Modern Existence* a very challenging read. I also still have my copy of *American Indians, American Justice*, coauthored with Clifford M. Lytle, which I was assigned to read in law school by Seneca scholar Robert Odawi Porter. Since I graduated law school in 1999, there has been a plethora of textbooks and articles about Tribal law, but at the time I took Tribal Law and Policy at the University of Kansas in 1997, the Deloria and Lytle book was the go-to book for understanding the relationship between federal Indian law and Tribal governments. There is no doubt that Deloria's writings formed the foundation of how I understand twentieth-century Indian activism.

Now—to critique Deloria's writings? I feel like that is an ominous task for a generation X person. From what I know of his character, he would have laughed off any suggestion that his work was flawless and needed no criticism.

So, here goes:

I'm a self-identified feminist. From my standpoint, one of the biggest deficiencies in Deloria's writings is a failure to adequately address the struggle of Native women and children during the tumultuous era of the 1960s and 1970s. "Gender," "sexuality," and "child rearing" were not part of his lexicon; I have found very few examples where Deloria mentions Indian women and/or children. In the early stages of *Custer Died for Your Sins*, he does talk about the era of Indian boarding schools as part of his discussion of laws designed to "conform to white institutions." And his August 1977 *Los Angeles Times* op-ed discusses concerns about sterilization of Native women in Indian Health Service facilities. But other than that, Deloria rarely wrote about gendered issues.

Was Deloria sexist? I have no evidence to suggest that he was, and I don't want this critique to suggest that he disrespected women in his day-to-day life. But his writings suggest that the fight for Indian rights was *NOT* a gender-neutral movement—it was a masculine movement. Indeed, many of the academic books about the Red Power movement seem to be written by men, for men. This is slowly changing as historians revisit this period of time and have unearthed fascinating perspectives of the Native women who orchestrated the takeover of Alcatraz, the occupation of the BIA building, and the standoff at Wounded Knee.

Deloria was a reflection of his time, as are we all. Even the mainstream, white feminist movement was in its nascent stages. And many Native women rejected the approach of white feminists, some finding it completely irrelevant to their lives. Perhaps Deloria felt that he could not adequately articulate the needs of Indian women because he was a man. But the few books published by Indian women during the 1960s and 1970s have long since been overshadowed by Deloria's contribution to the intellectual lives of Indian activists. That's why today's Native feminists must fill this void with our own histories.

About two years ago, I opened my dusty copy of *Custer Died for Your Sins* and noticed on the publisher's page that Chapters 1 and 4 were originally published in *Playboy* magazine. Keep in mind that I was a child of the 1970s and 1980s. Growing up, *Playboy* was the only "dirty" magazine that I knew about. And while I heard once in a while that men bought the magazine "for the articles," I thought that was just a veiled excuse to look at dirty pictures. "Ah-ha!" I said to myself. Here is an example of sexism: Deloria published articles in a pornographic magazine. Surely that proves he was chauvinist! But after doing some of my own research (just a simple Google search, actually), I learned more about the authors who published in *Playboy* during the same time period—including feminist writers Margaret Atwood, Ursula Le Guin, and Joyce Carol Oates. In 1965, *Playboy* published a transcript of a conversation between Alex Haley and Martin Luther King, Jr. I learned that Jimmy Carter nearly torpedoed his own presidential campaign by granting a wide-ranging interview to *Playboy* in 1976. So, I now better understand the claim that the articles could be as stimulating as the pornography itself. Publishing in *Playboy*—at least during that time period—is not necessarily evidence of sexism. (Hugh Hefner himself is another story altogether.)

The first and only time I had a personal conversation with Deloria was on Friday, December 10, 2004 (less than a year before his passing). I was helping organize a huge national conference for my employer, the Tribal Law and Policy Institute on the Agua Caliente Indian Reservation in southern California. The conference focused on victims of crime in Indian Country, and it was funded by the Department of Justice. Conference attendees included crime victim advocates, Tribal law enforcement officers, Tribal prosecutors, and victims of crime themselves. It was my idea to invite Deloria to the conference to deliver a keynote at the event. During the many months of planning the conference, I learned that, earlier that year, Deloria had refused an honorary doctorate from the University of Colorado (his alma mater) because of a scandalous cover-up of sexual assaults committed by football players on campus. I viewed his decision through the lens of victims' rights and was impressed that the premier public Indian intellectual had taken such a strong stance against the university's cover-up.

I reached out to one of Deloria's former students, and she was able to get me in contact with him. I figured it was a long shot, but he agreed to come and provide a keynote presentation over the noon hour on December 10. I made sure he got a first-class ticket.

The morning of the day of his keynote, I had the opportunity to spend about an hour with him on the hotel patio, talking about what he might be able to say to this particular audience. Of course, he was chain-smoking the whole time. I was initially thoroughly intimidated and scared, but he was more down-to-earth than I had expected. I told him that his refusal to accept the honorary doctorate was a strong message to victims that they should be believed. This came as somewhat of a surprise to him; I don't think he realized the importance of that action. I told him that many of the Tribal crime victim advocates in the audience were looking forward to hearing about his decades of work to ensure safety and security for Indian lives. At about 11:50, I suggested that we start heading toward the podium area where he would deliver his speech. He looked at his watch and said, "Don't we still have ten minutes?" He then lit another cigarette and indicated that we would not be heading to the podium until he had finished smoking it.

Deloria's keynote was powerful indeed, and the conference host retains a copy of the transcript. In explaining why he refused the honorary doctorate, he said, "I felt [the University of Colorado] should have spoken for the needs of the three women who were raped by football players. What was really sad, was that I couldn't find anyone on the campus who would speak up with me." He also shared his perspective on traditional criminal law practices, noting that "when I grew up in South Dakota, each reservation seemed to be dominated by one or two older women who could read the riot act to their relatives and people in the community, and they pretty much kept things in check." He encouraged the audience to bring those principles back, noting that "we need to look seriously at establishing certain prestigious positions within the Tribal community, one of which would be an elderly woman. They should have the power to intervene as a moral presence in whatever is happening in tribal institutional life." It was a wonderful contribution to the conference.

After his speech, I had the opportunity to sit next to him for the lunch. I brought along copies of two Tribal law textbooks that I had recently coauthored: *Introduction to Tribal Law* (with Justin Richland) and *Tribal Criminal Law and Procedure* (with Carrie Garrow). I offered these two books to him as gifts. I didn't know if he already had copies. He looked briefly at the covers, opened them, and then passed them back to me. He said, "I can't accept these books." My heart sank. Had he already read the books and disliked them? Had I angered him in some way? Was he concerned about packing books in his luggage? A moment passed, and then he winked at me and said, "They're not signed." I let out a gasp of relief. Then I signed the books, and he accepted them.

That was the first and only time with this intellectual giant. I regret that I did not get a picture with him, and I was devastated to hear the news of his passing the following November. His words and presence during our meeting stayed with me. When I read his writings today, I think about how fearless a writer he was. When I met Ada Deer (no relation) a few years later, she impressed upon me the kind of risk-taker that she had to be during her heyday as an activist and secretary of the BIA. I asked her how she convinced federal officials to include all of the Alaska Native villages in the BIA list of federally recognized Tribes. She quipped, "I didn't ask them. I just did it."

I decided to start asking myself, "What would Ada do?" and "What would Vine do?" when encountering twenty-first-century challenges in my own writings and activism. I was riffing off evangelical Christians' question, "What Would Jesus Do?" A few years later, when I traveled to Washington, D.C., for the release of the Amnesty International Report, "Maze of Injustice," my coworkers made up a special custom T-shirt for me that read "What Would Vine Do (WWVD)?" I wore it on the plane to and from the event. I figured it would give me inspiration to "take no prisoners" as I introduced the findings of the report at the National Press Club.

Vine Deloria, Jr. was not divine; he was not perfect. From my angle, I believe that had he provided more critique of the federal government's treatment of Indian women, it would have jump-started conversations that came later. But it was a different place, a different time, and he was only one person, after all. I'll continue collecting first editions of Deloria's books whenever I find them. Though I did not experience the Indian rights movement in the 1960s and 1970s, I feel I have a better understanding of the kinds of conversations that were happening. And this is an invaluable gift to those of my generation.

CHAPTER 4

THE BLACK AND THE RED

Vine Deloria, Jr. and the Problem of African America

Kyle T. Mays

Introduction

I've often imagined sitting down with Vine Deloria, Jr., the great Indigenous intellectual, and asking him straight up, "So, Professor Deloria, what do you actually think about Black people and the future of Black America?" I don't ask this question because I believe that Deloria was anti-Black. I have no evidence of that, and from his writings, it seems he was very much invested in helping Black folks get their freedom through nationalism. Also, this exercise is futile because there is obviously no way to sit down with Deloria. All I have are his thoughts written down in books forty years ago. But I think the question is worth exploring anyway. Because I have two questions that I can't ask Deloria, I can't help but to ask some direct, hypothetical questions from the perspective of an urban, Afro-Indigenous person today.

What would Deloria think of the relationship between the Black American struggle for freedom and Indigenous sovereignty? Would he rethink his position, which many Native people have found conclusive, that African Americans are fighting for civil rights, or integration into the US democratic project, and Native Americans are fighting for sovereignty, or simply to be left alone? Using the historical example of Stokely Carmichael (Kwame Ture) and contemporary forms of activism, I contend that Deloria often flattened Black radical history and would likely rethink his positions on most African Americans only seeking integration.

Deloria's Position

Deloria believed that the political goals of African America were so categorically different from Native Americans that they should hardly be compared. He argued that African Americans sought civil rights, or integration into society. Black people were not treaty people, and therefore they sought to be included into the nation-state, even though he believed that a fruitless—if not foolish—effort. He believed that Native Americans wanted nothing more than to be left alone. They simply wanted the US to honor the treaties. If the US government simply honored the treaties and let Native people control their own destinies and not meddle, Tribal Nations would thrive because they would control their own destinies. He outlined this position most explicitly in *Custer Died for Your Sins: An Indian Manifesto* but also in *Behind the Trail of Broken Treaties*.

In *Custer Died for Your Sins*, he argued that US policy wanted to exclude African Americans and include Indigenous Nations because they wanted Indigenous land and because they didn't want to share resources, culture, and space with African Americans. Though even that formulation ignores the fact that the US very much wanted to exploit Black labor for the benefit of capitalists. Nevertheless, Deloria supported parts of Black power, writing, "Black power, as a communications phenomenon, was a godsend to other groups" because it "allowed the concept of self-determination suddenly to become valid."[1] Furthermore, Deloria wrote, for Native people calling for more sovereignty, "Stokely Carmichael was the first black who said anything significant."[2] Deloria didn't respect African American calls for civil rights, but he certainly respected sovereignty and self-determination.

In *Behind the Trail of Broken Treaties*, Deloria opined, "Minority groups were often astounded to learn that the Indians were not planning to share the continent with their oppressed brothers once the revolution was over. Hell, no. The Indians were planning on taking the continent back and kicking out all the black, Chicano, Anglo, and Asian brothers who had made the whole thing possible."[3] This quote always makes me wonder what my great-grandmother, who had Afro-Saginaw Chippewa children, and raised them in Detroit, a predominantly Black city, would have thought of such a proposition. Even beyond my own family, what then do we do with the Freedmen of the Five Tribes who continue to be in the limbo of citizenship? Or other Afro-Indigenous peoples for that matter? Anyhow, I agree that Indigenous people should be able to choose how they incorporate others into their land, which would require new arrangements, treaties, and so forth. Moreover, Deloria seems to take a shot at Stokely Carmichael (who would later change his name to Kwame Ture), who was well respected by at least a few Native activists up until his death. During the occupation of the Bureau of Indian Affairs' office in 1972, Ture went up there to see what everything was about. Deloria remarked on this attempt at solidarity: "Stokely Carmichael, the popularizer of Black Power from several years back, visited the building and pledged his all but invisible support."[4] My question to Deloria would be, "What in the hell did you expect him to do?" Seriously, should Ture have broken a window or stolen some files? Sometimes, all you need is for people to show up—that's it. Moreover, this critique doesn't hold up well, given that Ture was very much aware of his relationship to Native peoples' land.

In the winter of 1974, in St. Paul, Minnesota, Ture made clear that he was on the side of Native Americans seeking sovereignty. He was there speaking in solidarity with American Indian Movement members who were on trial (for what?). He was one of the few Black activists who unambiguously stated that the US was not Black land. This statement is profound and unique for the time. As Deloria argued, many Black folks wanted to reform US democracy. Ture wanted to leave it. For him, Africa was his homeland. In his speech, he stated, "Anybody who thinks seriously about working on behalf of the red man must deal with this truth.

The land on which we live, on which we inhabit, which we exploit—that land belongs to the red man. He must come first in any dealings with the land."[5] In this statement, it is clear that Ture was not invested in the US democratic project continuing in its settler-colonial, business-as-usual self. He respected that this was Indigenous land, and that fact was the basis on which anyone, including African Americans who wanted to work in solidarity with Native people, must accept. This statement also suggests that Deloria certainly misunderstood the history of Black radicals rejecting the whole idea of the US democratic project. But Ture's comments did not only center on land. He also framed the Black and the Red connection in their stances against capitalism.

Ture argued that "all of us must struggle against capitalism."[6] He further contended that "the red man is struggling to build socialism. So is the black man. Poor whites in this country have to struggle against capitalism. The difference is that the black man and the red man are conscious of their oppression. The poor white man is not conscious of his oppression."[7] For Ture, the connection that bound African Americans and Native Americans was capitalism. The development of modern US capitalism was built on enslavement and land expropriation, and for this reason we must think about how the afterlives of anti-Black and anti-Indigenous sentiments continue to structure the everyday lives of Black and Indigenous peoples. Finally, Ture remarked, "Our people know that we will get his land back."[8]

In September 1991, Ture appeared in Libya along with Clyde Bellecourt, a cofounder of the American Indian Movement. Bellecourt was there to receive the Gaddafi Prize for Human Rights on behalf of Indigenous peoples in the Americas. They appeared on a panel to discuss the past and contemporary forms of activism. There, Bellecourt showed Ture love because he remains one of the few people of African descent who showed explicit forms of solidarity with Indigenous peoples. I also think Ture admired Indigenous activism, even their struggle for sovereignty, because he was looking for something—perhaps trying to reclaim his lost Indigenous roots from Africa. Ture showed all of us how solidarity with Indigenous peoples should work. First, it was predicated on assuming that Indigenous people will reclaim their land. And second, that the goal is to support a cause without worrying about how it will be reciprocated; reciprocation will come in time when you need solidarity for your own struggle.

So, what can we learn from this brief example? First, I think Indigenous Nations might continue to find ways to make room for the descendants of enslaved Africans. Whatever their protocols are for guests could be updated to create relations with Black people (and perhaps other groups forced to come to the US because of the United States' neoliberal wars across the globe!). If we are truly to center sovereignty, and create relations and further nation building in the aftermath of white supremacy and settler colonialism, working with other oppressed groups like African Americans might further both of our desires for freedom and sovereignty. These are just some thoughts; I hope we can get there soon.

CHAPTER 5

INDIGENOUS PEOPLES AND IMAGINED BORDERS

Rebecca Tsosie

I am honored to contribute to this volume honoring Vine Deloria's intellectual legacy. I am inspired by the book's vision, which calls for us to reach back into the rich repository of Deloria's work, to "repurpose ideas to fit current need, and build upon what we have been given *to create living paths forward*." Creating a "living path forward" is a vital need for all contemporary societies. The COVID-19 pandemic showed us that we simply are not sustainable, as nations or as individuals, without others. Yet, as I write this, there are continuing divisions and controversies that impact our ability to see ourselves as distinctive but *interdependent* Nations, to commit to a pathway that facilitates life, and to honor the promises that were written down more than a century ago by political leaders who were attempting to create justice between nations.

This essay explores how Vine Deloria's work illuminates the potential transboundary application of treaty rights and Indigenous human rights to effectuate the right of self-determination. What real and imagined borders must be challenged to realize this promise? How can nineteenth-century treaties inform the construction of meaningful political consent for Indigenous Nations? Can cultural sovereignty promote collaborative governance? As I work through these questions, I will look at the clashes on the US–Mexico Border and those that affect sacred places on "public" lands within the US. These are two of the most vexing areas for Indigenous peoples because they test the political and legal boundaries of Tribal sovereignty, and they also challenge the "self-determination" of Indigenous peoples as "peoples."

I. Indigenous Peoples and the "Borderlands"

This essay is about borders, both the ones that are constructed across international boundaries—such as the US–Mexico Border—and the ones that are constructed within our minds. The "imagined borders" are perhaps even more powerful than the political ones because they incorporate categories of meaning that become "real" as we unconsciously accept them. In his many writings, Deloria challenged simplistic understandings of complex terms, such as "sovereignty" and "self-determination." He also challenged the artificial lines that construct western "theology," separating it from "philosophy," and the ways in which we trick ourselves into thinking that the "law" is, in fact, an instrument of "justice."[1] All of these categories are relevant to the ways in which we construct borders.

Within an Indigenous metaphysics, as Deloria noted, the categories are inseparably linked, given the relational understanding of the Universe that most Indigenous peoples have. Moral principles ensure survival across generations, while political principles guide our social and economic interactions within each generation. For this reason, Deloria wrote, treaties are important constitutive documents. They are created by governments and fit the circumstances of a particular time and place, but the principles are binding upon the descendant nations and their citizens. Justice between nations is the foundation for treaties, just as our Constitution is the foundation for civil rights between and among citizens.

To explore these themes further, I will examine the ways in which Indigenous peoples' rights are understood on the northern and southern borders of the United States. Indigenous peoples preexist all of the governments that now claim national status in North America, and yet their rights are understood contextually, as if they were rooted within these modern nation-states.

II. Indigenous Peoples and the Southern Border

The US–Mexico border has a complex history, rooted in the nineteenth-century politics of Manifest Destiny. Following the conclusion of the US–Mexico War, the two nations entered into the 1848 Treaty of Guadalupe Hidalgo, and the United States expanded its domestic territory by one-third, to encompass all or part of what is now Arizona, California, Colorado, Kansas, New Mexico, Nevada, Oklahoma, Texas, Utah, and Wyoming. In 1854, the United States negotiated the Treaty of La Mesilla, which enfolded an additional twenty-nine thousand square miles of Mexico's land into the United States, incorporating what is now southern Arizona and New Mexico. Through the "Gadsden Purchase," the United States acquired a region marked by extensive and violent conflict. The Mexican government had attempted to hold the United States liable for damages to Mexican citizens that it alleged were caused by bands of Apache and Comanche Indians, asserting that these "uncivilized" Tribes were under the political control of the United States. The US contested that, and the damages claims were later resolved in the Treaty of La Mesilla.

The traditional territory of the Western Apache people extended throughout what is now Sonora, Mexico, and northeast into Texas, New Mexico, and Arizona. Some of this ancestral territory also overlapped with that of the O'odham people, who are also organized within several bands across what is now northern Mexico and Arizona. In the Treaty of Guadalupe Hidalgo, the United States agreed to take responsibility for the "uncivilized" Tribes and bands within its national boundaries, while also recognizing the rights of "civilized" Indigenous persons to hold land rights and citizenship.[2] The Pueblo Nations of New Mexico were regarded as civilized by Spain and also by Mexico. The Pueblo Nations held land grants from the King of Spain, and the Mexican government recognized their citizenship in Mexico, as well as their property rights. The Treaty of Guadalupe Hidalgo required the United States to protect the civil rights of Mexican citizens who were annexed into the United States, including their rights to religious freedom. The Mexican government was aware of the racial restrictions that the US placed on "citizenship," and the treaty required the US to extend equal treatment to the Mexican citizens who chose to stay on their land and become incorporated into the US.

The US–Mexico Border separated many Tribes in the Southwest region, rendering those on the Mexican side virtually invisible.[3] Today, some of the Apache and O'odham groups on the US side have federal recognition, but other bands do not, even though they are culturally distinctive and have a deep ancestral presence in this region. Although this essay focuses on the Western Apache and O'odham peoples, there are many other Indigenous peoples in the Borderlands region, including the Yaqui, Kumeyaay, Kickapoo, and Cocopah, and each of these peoples has a distinctive history and set of associations with the land. The concept of Indigeneity posits an ancestral connection between people and place, and that connection is not severed by removal. The concept of place has an associated metaphysics within Indigenous thought, as Deloria pointed out in his writings.[4] Origin places endure, as do sacred places and burial sites. However, today, that metaphysics and association with Indigenous peoples eludes our national consciousness.

As a national society, we are fixated on the perceived threat of "illegal immigrants" storming "our" southern border. The Trump administration undertook the rapid construction of more than four hundred additional miles of the border wall, suspending relevant environmental and cultural resource protections in the process. The environmental impacts of the wall have been severe. Within southern Arizona, the border wall bisected a flourishing ecosystem that is home to endangered species, including the Mexican Jaguar, and where life depends upon the natural flow of the San Pedro River and the natural springs that dot the land.[5] Since construction commenced in 2018, contractors have installed impassable steel barriers that block wildlife from traversing the area, and scientists fear that this may result in the permanent loss of some species. In this arid region, water is essential to life. The federal contractors also pumped water from the river as they constructed the wall, which dried up many natural springs and replaced the gentle flow of water with dry gullies and a gravel streambed.

The environmental impacts are visible, but the impacts on Indigenous peoples often are not because the political identity of many Indigenous peoples is "split" by the international border. If the impacts fall upon those on thc "US" side, they may trigger a cognizable Tribal interest. The Tohono O'odham Nation is the beneficial owner of a large reservation that sits on the border, and sixty-two miles of the border wall are located on that reservation. The Nation filed an amicus brief in a case litigated by the Sierra Club to enjoin construction of the wall in protected areas of the Organ Pipe Cactus National Monument and the Cabeza Prieta National Wildlife Refuge, both of which contain extensive cultural sites as well as plants and animals that are culturally important to the O'odham people.[6] The case was ultimately unsuccessful, but it is instructive to note that the best way for Indigenous peoples to get their claim into court is often through *environmental* actions. The courts understand environmental harm, but they often fail to understand cultural harm. In addition, many of the impacts of the border wall are completely disregarded because the harm is understood to fall upon "Mexicans."

In August 2020, the La Posta Band of Diegueno Mission Indians, a federally recognized Tribal government, filed a lawsuit in a California federal district court seeking to block the construction of the border wall along California's southern border.[7] These are the traditional lands of various bands of Kumeyaay Indians, and there are burial sites and sacred sites throughout the area. About a month earlier, the construction crew encountered a burial site with ancestral human remains, but the US Customs and Border Protection Department refused to halt construction or give cultural leaders access to the area during the exhumation so that they could perform the required practices. The Tribe's motion for a temporary injunction was ultimately denied, and similar desecrations occurred for the O'odham people on the Arizona–Mexico border. In both cases, the federal officials were informed about the presence of burial sites and sacred sites but failed to engage in formal consultation or engage in a mitigation strategy. The Tribes' traditional and customary practices have been impacted because the border wall bisects their cultural sites, precluding Tribal practitioners from accessing sacred places and impairing their religious freedom.

On the US side of the border, Indigenous peoples enjoy the political protection afforded by federal recognition as well as US citizenship. On the Mexican side of the border, all bets are off. There was a limited consultation with the federally recognized Tribal governments in Arizona about construction of the border wall but no consultation with Indigenous groups that lack federal recognition.[8] The cultural harms, like the environmental harms, impact the entire area as a whole and they cannot be limited to a certain group.

The United States has been unwilling to acknowledge liability for human rights abuses on the southern border, such as mass incarceration of immigrant families, separation of children from parents, overcrowded holding facilities, and the violent militarization of the border region. All these practices were justified by the vitriolic political rhetoric of the Trump administration, which depicted "Mexicans" as lawless freeloaders, trying to "jump" the border in order to gain the goods of our democratic society. The wall is now a political embarrassment for the Biden administration because it embodies a set of harms that are widely seen as unacceptable because of the disproportionate impacts on women, children, families, Indigenous peoples, cultural and spiritual values, and the environment. It also embodies an ugly and dehumanizing racial politics among states such as Texas that believe they have the power to police the border if the federal government backs away from "immigration enforcement."

In sum, we have not moved much beyond the conflict that characterized the southern border in the years following the Treaty of Guadalupe Hidalgo. The area is still heavily militarized, and the United States asserts a national security interest that overrides basic civil rights. The rights of federally recognized Tribal governments ought to be protected under US law, but as the *La Posta* case demonstrates, cultural rights and environmental rights are subordinated to national security, so consultation is more of a procedural nod to the Tribal governments than any enforceable system to protect their land rights or cultural rights. Indigenous peoples on the Mexican side of the border are viewed as Mexican nationals. They have no right to be in the United States as citizens, and they are not identified as holding any ancestral rights that are recognized by the United States.

III. Indigenous Peoples and the Northern Border

Interestingly, there is a recent case from the Supreme Court of Canada about Indigenous rights on the northern border. In *R. v. Desautel*, the Supreme Court of Canada held that an American citizen who is a member of a US federally recognized Tribe could not be prosecuted for hunting Elk within the portion of the Tribe's traditional use area that is now in British Columbia.[9] The defendant, a member of the Colville Tribe, asserted an aboriginal use right to hunt in the traditional territory of his ancestors, the Sinixt people, and the Court agreed that aboriginal rights "arise from prior occupation of the land now forming Canada's provinces rather than modern day citizenship or residency within Canada's borders." The Court attributed the displacement of the Indigenous peoples across national borders to colonization and not any voluntary action by the Indigenous peoples, meaning that the defendant had not voluntarily surrendered those ancestral rights.

Importantly, Canada's Constitution Act of 1982 provides that "the existing aboriginal and treaty rights of the aboriginal peoples of Canada are hereby recognized and affirmed." In this case, the court held that the "aboriginal peoples of Canada" include members of groups that were involuntarily pushed across the border with the US, and that "aboriginal rights" include the right to hunt for Elk within the aboriginal territory.

The *Desautel* case aligns with international human rights law. The UN Declaration on the Rights of Indigenous Peoples, for example, specifically counsels nation-states to accommodate the rights of transborder Indigenous peoples to freely associate with one another and to continue their traditional practices.[10] Indigenous human rights are not dependent upon national citizenship. In the United States, there is a tendency to conflate "Indian" status with federal recognition and US citizenship, and this can negate the human rights claims of Indigenous peoples and jeopardize their cultural survival.

As the *Desautel* case demonstrates, treaty rights and aboriginal rights are distinct categories, although in some cases they might overlap. In Canada, both sets of rights enjoy status as "constitutional rights," which is not true in the United States. In the United States, treaty rights are protected so long as the federal government has not abrogated these rights.[11] Aboriginal rights *might* receive legal protection in some cases, but the law constructs these rights narrowly within each of the various categories, including usufructuary rights, water rights, and land rights (framed as rights to "use and occupancy").

There is some compatibility between the Indigenous rights structures of Canada and the United States, but virtually no compatibility between the equivalent structures in the US and Mexico. Instead, the ongoing politics on the southern border has a distinctive racial character, where "Mexican immigrants" are constructed as uncivilized, lawless, and dangerous, and dehumanizing policies, such as separating women and children in federal detention centers are quite similar to the genocidal practices of the nineteenth-century Indian wars.

IV. Sacred Places on Public Lands: The Case of Oak Flats

To explore the connection between "borders" and "sacred places," I will return to the story of what happened to the Western Apache people after they were annexed into the United States. After the Treaty of Guadalupe Hidalgo was signed in 1848, the United States entered the 1852 Treaty of Santa Fe with several Apache leaders to secure peace and friendship.[12] The United States sought to forge a political allegiance that would assist it in its effort to exert control over the newly acquired territory. After the Gadsden Purchase, however, the United States did not engage in further treaty-making with the Apache Bands. Rather, it undertook a genocidal campaign against the Western Apache people that culminated in their removal from most of their traditional lands, and their relocation onto smaller reservations under the control of the US Army. Although there were political and cultural differences among the Bands, and some had actually assisted the US military, the United States treated all Apaches as "wards" and placed them under military control.

In 1886, the United States sent more than five hundred Apaches who were deemed "hostile" to US interests to a federal prison at Fort Marion, Florida. The Apaches were held for a total of twenty-seven years as prisoners of war, although they were subsequently transferred to other federal prisons, ultimately ending up at Fort Sill, Oklahoma. Geronimo was one of the Apache leaders sent to Fort Sill, where he died in 1909, still a prisoner of war. The Fort Sill Apache ultimately gained federal recognition as a separate Indian Tribe in Oklahoma. Today, the Fort Sill Apache Tribe's website explains that "Fort Sill Apache Tribal members are descended from 81 former Prisoners of War, who received allotments in Oklahoma after their release." The Tribe is "comprised of the descendants of the Chiricahua and Warm Springs Apaches who lived in southwestern New Mexico, southeastern Arizona, and northern Mexico until they were removed from their homelands" and imprisoned by the United States.

The Apache–US conflicts within the Borderlands ultimately resulted in the historic and ancestral Bands being divided up among different states. Today, the federally recognized groups in Arizona are located on different reservations. Those that lack federal recognition are invisible, although many still live in the Borderlands region. Some Apaches still live on the Mexican side of the border and are understood to be "Mexicans" even though both the Mexican government and the United States engaged in genocidal military campaigns against them.

All the Western Apache Bands share a language and set of cultural associations. One of the most significant sacred sites to the Western Apache people is at Oak Flat in southeastern Arizona. Oak Flat, or Chich'il Bildagoteel, is held to be the origin place of at least eight Apache Bands, and it has always been, and continues to be, a place of prayer and ceremony for the Apache people. The site is currently on federal public land, managed by the US Forest Service. Generations of Apache people have accessed the site for religious practices and for gathering traditional medicines, foods, and plants. The site sits over a vast copper deposit, which was "discovered" in 1995. After many years of political wrangling in Congress and opposition by Tribal governments and environmental groups to any land transfer, the late senator John McCain attached a rider to a must-pass defense appropriations bill minutes before the deadline in 2014.[13] This so-called "midnight rider" slipped through Congress as the "Southeast Arizona Land Exchange and Conservation Act," authorizing the transfer of lands under the jurisdiction of the US Forest Service and inclusive of Oak Flat to the Resolution Copper Corporation, which is a subsidiary of Rio Tinto/BHP. Resolution agreed to transfer several parcels of its private lands in Arizona to the federal government in exchange for the lands with this valuable copper deposit. President Barack Obama signed the bill into law.

By transferring the lands out of federal ownership, Resolution could mine without adherence to the panoply of federal environmental and cultural resource laws that pertain on public lands. Some of those laws protect Tribal cultural interests and burial sites, but they often require an expensive and cumbersome set of surveys and Tribal consultations. Instead, the Forest Service was required to undertake an assessment of the proposed impacts and issue a Final Environmental Impact Statement (FEIS), which would trigger a sixty-day period that would culminate with the final transfer.

In the last days of the Trump administration, the US Forest Service issued the FEIS, which resulted in three separate lawsuits seeking to halt the transfer.[14] The San Carlos Apache Tribe is the federally recognized Tribe that is closest to the site, and that Tribal government filed an action on behalf of the Western Apache people, as did Apache Stronghold, a nongovernmental organization composed of Western Apache cultural leaders, their supporters, and even some of the direct descendants of the Apache leaders who had signed the 1852 Treaty of Santa Fe. The Arizona Mining Reform Coalition filed a third lawsuit, seeking to prevent some of the extreme environmental impacts to the land and water that will result from the construction of this vast open-pit copper mine. The petitioners sought a preliminary injunction barring the transfer, but the federal district court denied their claims on the grounds that the federal government had the lawful authority to effectuate the land transfer, and that petitioners should seek relief in Congress.

In March 2021, the Biden administration directed the Forest Service to temporarily rescind the FEIS, thereby averting the final action. Although appeals were pending in the Ninth Circuit, that court dismissed the actions as premature after the Forest Service rescinded the FEIS. As of the current date, there has not been a final resolution of this issue. Oak Flat remains within the ancestral territory of the Western Apache people, and it is a site that has been continuously used for religious and cultural purposes for generations. As such, it merits protection under international human rights law. In particular, Article 25 of the UN Declaration on the Rights of Indigenous Peoples recognizes that "Indigenous peoples have the right to maintain and strengthen their distinctive spiritual relationship with their traditionally owned or otherwise occupied and used lands [and] territories . . . and to uphold their responsibilities to future generations in this regard."

This human rights principle is reinforced by the text of the Treaty of Guadalupe Hidalgo, which required the United States to uphold the religious freedom of those who were incorporated into the United States, which arguably would include the bands of Western Apache people. In 1986, a federal district court in New Mexico found that the Treaty of Guadalupe Hidalgo protected the religious rights of Pueblo Indians, including their right to possess eagle feathers for religious purposes.[15] The Pueblo Nations are under the trust protection of the US as federally recognized Tribal governments. Although they do not have separate treaties with the United States, the *Abeyta* court held that the Treaty of Guadalupe Hidalgo specifically protected religious rights, including those of the Pueblo Indian nations. It would be inconsistent with contemporary principles of international human rights law to deny equal protection for religious liberty to other Indigenous peoples who were involuntarily annexed into the United States. Therefore, the Apache people might have a contemporary treaty claim under the reasoning of the *Abeyta* case and in association with Article 25 of the UN Declaration.

The Treaty of 1852 is also potentially relevant, although the United States has long maintained that general treaties of peace and friendship with Indian Tribes do not confer property rights. The Treaty of 1852 does, however, acknowledge a political relationship between the Western Apache people and the United States, and, at a minimum, that relationship should require a duty of good faith and fair dealing.[16] Oak Flat was "taken" by a midnight rider, after legislative attempts to pass similar bills in Congress failed. The US political process was circumvented by this action, as was the protection of US historic preservation law. Oak Flat was designated as a Traditional Cultural Property under the National Historic Preservation Act in 2010, and its unique cultural and historical value should preclude a land transfer that would render this the "private property" of Resolution Copper.

In sum, the Oak Flat case raises treaty claims and other political and legal issues for purposes of US law. It also raises a host of international human rights claims that become visible when we remove the imaginary boundaries that limit and qualify Indigenous rights.

V. Indigenous Peoples in the Borderlands: The Role of Cultural Sovereignty, Treaty Rights, and Collaborative Governance

Vine Deloria gave life and meaning to the concept of Indigenous self-determination long before the UN General Assembly adopted the Declaration on the Rights of Indigenous Peoples.[17] Self-determination is an inherent moral and political right that resides in all "peoples." The UN Declaration expressly recognizes that Indigenous peoples have the same right to self-determination as all other peoples, and this right to autonomy must be recognized by the nation-states. The right to self-determination can be effectuated in many different ways: by recognizing the sovereignty of an Indigenous government, by comanagement of shared resources, or even by participatory rights exercised by members of Indigenous groups in their capacity as "citizens."

The United States recognizes the political rights of federally recognized Tribes, and this domestic sovereignty model is one way to secure Indigenous self-determination. The US Supreme Court has constructed a rather limited conception of Tribal political sovereignty as a "domestic dependent nation."[18] Federal Indian law asserts that the sovereignty of Tribal governments is qualified by the overriding authority of the United States, which ultimately led to the Supreme Court to conclude that Tribal sovereignty could be "implicitly divested" by virtue of their "dependent status." In particular, the Court doubted that Tribal governments could fairly exert jurisdiction over non-Indians. The Court therefore held that Tribal governments lack criminal jurisdiction over non-Indians[19] and that they have only limited civil jurisdiction over non-Indians, particularly on fee lands within the reservation.[20] This parsimonious account of Tribal jurisdiction, of course, had nothing to do with Tribal legal systems or the essence of Tribal sovereignty.

One of Deloria's most profound jurisprudential contributions was his nuanced understanding of Tribal sovereignty as both "political" and "cultural." Specifically, he believed that Tribal political sovereignty must be located within an "internal, culture and community-based model of sovereignty." The orientation of Tribal societies toward the "collective" interest ensures cultural survival, in comparison to the radical individualism of US politics, which often favors short-term economic gain and corporate interests. In an article that I coauthored many years ago with Comanche Tribal chairman Wallace Coffey, we drew on Deloria's work to assert that Tribal "cultural sovereignty" is the "effort of Indigenous nations to assert their own norms and values as they structure their collective futures."[21] Cultural sovereignty is the core of Tribal "inherent sovereignty," and it contains the moral vision that has always guided the people as they structured their social, political, and cultural institutions.

Political and cultural sovereignty are both vitally important. The political sovereignty of federally recognized Indian Tribes secures their right to exercise jurisdiction over trust lands on the reservation and to otherwise protect Tribal interests. Cultural sovereignty, however, has allowed many Tribal governments to survive devastating events, such as termination of their trust status. Even if the United States does not extend federal recognition, or if it later withdraws that protection, an Indigenous nation can survive as a collective government within its territory.

In the context of the transborder rights of Indigenous peoples, it seems fitting to envision the collective rights of the "people" as they have existed through time, and certainly prior to colonization. Indigenous self-determination predates European colonization, and current national boundaries should not negate ancestral rights. The Canadian Supreme Court's effort to acknowledge ancestral rights, even for Indigenous persons who are now citizens of another country, acknowledges the traditional relationship between people and place that is the cornerstone of Indigenous identity. The citizenship that matters for purposes of honoring Indigenous human rights is embedded within the traditional relationship between people and place.[22]

VI. Cultural Sovereignty: Governance of Sacred Places

Vine Deloria's pathbreaking scholarship on Tribal religions and sacred places illuminated the spiritual relationship between Indigenous peoples and their traditional territories, which today are often located on federal "public lands." As Deloria noted, the US Constitution doesn't protect Indigenous land-based religious practices, nor does the American Indian Religious Freedom Act. There have been incremental steps to accommodate Indigenous cultural practices, such as the designation of a Traditional Cultural Property under the National Historic Preservation Act. In addition, federal agencies must now transfer Indigenous remains excavated on federal land to the culturally affiliated federally recognized Tribal governments or lineal descendants pursuant to the Native American Graves Protection and Repatriation Act, rather than designating the ancestral remains as "federal property" for purposes of the Archaeological Resources Protection Act.

Yet, as the Oak Flat case demonstrates, there is no enforceable protection for an Indigenous sacred site under US law, and cultural practitioners are free to "believe" that a site is sacred, but they cannot prevent the government from developing—or destroying—"its" property.[23] As the *La Posta* case demonstrates, the federal government can waive its duty to consult with Tribal officials prior to excavation of a burial site if there is an overriding national interest. Religious freedom for Indigenous peoples is still in jeopardy, and yet they continue to exercise their "moral responsibility" to protect their sacred places, which is the essence of "cultural sovereignty." What mode of protection is possible for Indigenous peoples and sacred places in the twenty-first century?

VII. Recognition of Indigenous Nationhood: Is There a Need for New Domestic and International Treaties?

In their comprehensive work, *Tribes, Treaties, and Constitutional Tribulations*, Professors Vine Deloria, Jr. and David Wilkins undertook a thorough analysis of the US Constitution and demonstrated that this document does not provide legal rights for American Indians, and they concluded that the treaty-making process was the only way to effectuate justice between nations.[24] The US may continue to rely upon outmoded notions of its "overriding sovereignty" within the "domestic, dependent nation" model of Ttribal sovereignty, as it has in the past when it abrogated Tribal treaty rights.[25] However, in an era of "self-determination," we should call for a higher standard.

The United States engaged in treaties and other constitutive agreements with Tribal governments as political sovereigns throughout the nineteenth century and beyond, shifting to the use of negotiated "agreements" after the end of treaty-making in 1871. As Deloria observed, Indigenous "nationhood" calls for adherence to the norm of consent.[26] The principle of consent is a "wholly political principle," and it is not a "legal doctrine."[27] The current federal "consultation" model of engaging Tribal governments is primarily procedural and does not align with the political model of consent that is operative among nations. The UN Declaration on the Rights of Indigenous Peoples offers several provisions that can be used to design a domestic benchmark for the United States as it aligns its national law to recognize the human rights of Indigenous peoples.[28]

Within the Borderlands, the principle of self-determination requires the recognition of Indigenous peoples as tied to place. The Canadian Supreme Court's approach aligns with this human rights construction, and this model could be extended to other transborder groups. The Inuit people, for example, are now located within several different countries, including the United States, Canada, and Greenland. They have organized themselves, as an Indigenous people, within the Inuit Circumpolar Conference. Today, their relationship with their ancestral territory is jeopardized by climate change. Using a narrow lens, the rights of Inuit people are dependent upon whatever services the nation-state can afford to its citizens who lose their homes to flooding or other climate events. Government assistance will vary, depending upon which country the Inuit people reside in. Using the broader lens, all the nation-states share a collective duty to the Inuit people to allow them to protect their cultural existence as a *people* within their *territory*. Inuit territory sits on top of all those nation-states, just as the Navajo Nation sits on top of three different states. The boundaries of Indigenous territory do not map onto the political lines drawn by contemporary nations or states. It may be time for new political agreements that involve Indigenous peoples as treaty partners with nation-states, articulating the terms of a collaborative governance of territory. Importantly, the concept of territory is inclusive of rivers, watersheds, and forests, and the Indigenous place names for these features often show the linkages as well as the ethical duties that are required to care for them.[29]

This collaborative governance model is currently being explored within domestic US policy. For example, the Bears Ears National Monument in southern Utah acknowledges the role of five Tribal governments in the shared management of the monument along with the federal agencies. Tribal traditional knowledge is explicitly mentioned as core to the purpose of the monument. The Tribal Coalition has a governance role that is distinctive and draws upon the historical relationship of each Tribe to the lands within the monument.

In July 2020, the Supreme Court issued its historic decision in *McGirt v. Oklahoma*, finding that the Muscogee Creek Nation's Treaty reservation had never been disestablished under federal law and that criminal jurisdiction must follow the statutory rules applicable to "Indian country."[30] The borders of the Muscogee Creek Nation's reservation had been "invisible" to many Oklahoma citizens for over a century. The reservation borders were still there, but, after statehood, Oklahoma assumed jurisdiction without legal authority to do so, until most people came to believe that the reservation had been extinguished. This is the power of "imaginary" borders, and it took a courageous majority of the US Supreme Court to correct the injustice to the Muscogee Creek Nation and "hold the Government to its word."

This instruction could also apply to correct injustices that are occurring on the southern border. Of course, the international application of cultural sovereignty and collaborative governance will be contested on the southern border due to the racial politics of "immigration." It is instructive to remember that Congress is held to have constitutional "plenary power" over immigration and over Indian affairs. This gives the US government the opportunity to apply political principles, where necessary to achieve justice. Of course, plenary power can also be used to cause extreme injustice, and that was the lesson of the nineteenth-century "plenary power" cases in federal Indian law that upheld unilateral treaty abrogation, dispossession of Indigenous land, and other human rights abuses.[31] Will the US government choose to use its power in a principled manner as we move further into the twenty-first century? The UN Declaration on the Rights of Indigenous Peoples recognizes the moral and political right of Indigenous peoples to exercise self-determination. Moreover, there is a legal foundation for this approach within the Treaty of Guadalupe Hidalgo, the 1852 Treaty of Santa Fe, and the political accords with Indigenous peoples that have been negotiated over nearly two centuries in the Borderlands region. In sum, we can choose to construct a more just future as we create "a living path forward."

CHAPTER 6

NATIONHOOD AND RACE

A Response to *Tribes, Treaties, and Constitutional Tribulations*

Martin Case

In their book *Tribes, Treaties, and Constitutional Tribulations*, Vine Deloria and David E. Wilkins examine the "the manner and circumstances under which the Constitution of the United States was applied to American Indians . . . and to their lands, treaties, and rights." They offer a harsh and clear-eyed critique of the inconsistent manner in which the US has applied—or ignored—its own political and moral principles in relations with Indigenous nations. The authors' premise is that "Federal Indian law," stripped of the hypocritical veneer given to it by law professors, has become a hodgepodge of personal grudges, ad-hoc policies, inconsistent judicial decisions, and a general exercise of ignorance about Indians, framed in statutory language.[1]

At first glance, their critique of the US legal system might seem to be an occasion for which critical race theory was invented. Originating at the intersection of race, law, and history, critical race theory focuses on how racism in the US legal system underlies, frames, and maintains inequities. It's a powerful critical tool. Deloria and Wilkins, however, stay grounded in a different position; the topic of race is not even mentioned in the index to their book. Instead, they demonstrate cultural and intellectual integrity in adhering to Indigenous sovereignty and identity, rather than a colonialist-fabricated formation of race, as a point from which to critique the incoherence of US Indian policy.

This is not to say that their position is *opposed* to the premises of critical race theory. In fact, the very opening of their book is a powerful indictment of the trumped-up controversies in which right-wing reactionaries have mired critical race theory in the past several years:

> Almost every known human society bases its beliefs and institutions upon historical precedents, seeking to remain within the boundaries originally established by its founding ancestral line. Nevertheless, in the course of national existence human memory fades and mythological interpretations of the beginnings of human society take hold in the popular imagination. Eventually the past, in spite of all efforts to the contrary, becomes idealized in our view of national origins, and the hard facts of history, in particular those incidents and activities of which a nation is not proud, become deeply buried in the national psyche. Present views of reality are believed to have always prevailed, and bringing a corrective viewpoint to prominence is seen as disruptive and often heretical, as if the past existed only to reflect current prejudices.[2]

Tribes, Treaties, and Constitutional Tribulations, like critical race theory, examines structural inequities in US law and jurisprudence. But the view of that subject changes when Indigenous sovereignty and national identity move from the wings of public discourse to share center stage with the US Constitution. The work of Deloria and Wilkins is a powerful contribution to the arsenal of approaches that, like critical race theory from another direction, demand coherent consideration and consistent, moral action from "American" society.

The function of modern race formation was to supplant the diverse national identities of Indigenous people with a blanket racial identity, and then to excise that identity from colonialist societies. One of the strengths of the critical approach from Deloria and Wilkins is that it yields no ground to the colonialist mindset that gave rise to today's racial categorizations in the first place. The authors, occupying intellectual territory informed by Indigenous sovereignty, nationhood, and identity, resist the very impulse of race formation.

Racism is typically presented as an illustration of the distance between the ideals of the US (equality and freedom) and its social realities. Critical race theory, for instance, examines how the forced *presence* of enslaved people in the economic life of the nation created an institutionally reinforced legacy of inequity. Deloria and Wilkins, in contrast, are dealing with the legacy of forced *removal*. They are not interested in the distance between colonialist ideals and realities within a non-Indigenous system; they are interested only in the realities. "Instead of saying what the branches of government are *supposed* to do," they write, "we will examine vignettes of what they have *actually* done when dealing with American Indians."[3]

Racism has profoundly affected US-Indian relations, certainly; the legacy of white supremacism simmers just below the surface of *Tribes, Treaties, and Constitutional Tribulations*, as the authors wind their way through the bewildering inconsistency of US "Indian policy." But at the intersection of Indigenous sovereignty and the Constitution, where Deloria and Wilkins stand, racism cannot be teased out of the fabric of US-Indian relations to be examined on its own. It is an inherent and *foundational* quality of US Indian law. Deloria and Wilkins deal with the result, the aftermath, of racism's inextricable incorporation into the body of US institutions, and in particular into US "Indian law" and related jurisprudence.

Racism in the US is sometimes presented as a source of irony. "Thomas Jefferson wrote that all men are created equal, yet he enslaved three hundred people at a time. Isn't that ironic?" Irony depends on the subversion of assumptions. If you assume that Jefferson believed in equality, his slaveholding was ironic; if you assume he was a racist slaveholder, "all men are created equal" is ironic. Centuries of effort have been devoted to reconciling such apparent ironies.

Yet white supremacism in fact is not ironic. It is incoherent; its supposed ironies are irresolvable. And the most incoherent expressions of white supremacism anywhere—literally, anywhere—are found in the territory that Deloria and Wilkins must traverse in tracking the application of constitutional principles to the rights of Indigenous peoples. In particular, the Doctrine of Discovery—one of the world's great monuments to racist incoherence—forms the very foundation of both the US property system and the assertion of Indigenous sovereign rights within the context of US law. There is no path around that for the authors.

Chief Justice John Marshall's opinion in the Supreme Court case *Johnson v. M'Intosh* is the entry point through which the Doctrine of Discovery became lodged at the heart of the US political and economic system.[4] His reasoning followed what the authors call a "strangely logical sequence," which included the idea that property titles in the US consist of two rights: the right of dominion (what nation will control the territory?) and the right of occupancy (who gets to live on the land?). Indigenous peoples originally enjoyed the right of occupancy in their territory; even a delusionist such as Marshall could not deny that. But the right of *dominion*, in Marshall's world, was created through the *discovery* of a territory by a European power, regardless of who inhabited the territory at the time. Indigenous Nations could dispose of their right of occupancy only to a colonialist nation that had dominion over a territory. By gaining both the right of occupancy (most often through nation-to-nation treaties with Indigenous peoples) and the right of dominion, colonialist powers could perfect their title and distribute territory to whomever they wanted.

The ideology behind the doctrine is clearly white supremacist, but Deloria and Wilkins choose to critique Marshall's opinion on the basis of internal inconsistencies. (After boarding his train of culturally biased assumptions, Marshall rode it for sixty jaw-dropping pages, contradicting his own reasoning at several stops along the way.)

One of the absurdities that stems from Marshall's Doctrine of Discovery is the idea that Indigenous nations cannot have dominion over the territory they inhabit, simply because they were already here when Europeans arrived. Even Marshall, at the conclusion of his opinion, acknowledges how shaky that idea is, writing,

> However extravagant the pretension of converting the discovery of an inhabited country in the conquest may appear, if the principle has been asserted in the first instance, and afterwards sustained; if a country has been acquired and held under it; if the property of the great mass of the community originates in it, it becomes the law of the land, and cannot be questioned. So, too, with respect to the concomitant principle, that the Indian inhabitants are to be . . . deemed incapable of transferring the absolute title to others. However, this restriction may be opposed to natural right, and to the usages of civilized nations, yet, if it be indispensable to that system under which the country has been settled, and be adapted to the actual condition of the two people, it may, perhaps, be supported by reason, and certainly cannot be rejected by courts of justice.

These closing words of Marshall's opinion in *Johnson v. M'Intosh* present a final, farewell absurdity that is too petty to attract the attention of the authors: if "the law of the land" "cannot be rejected by courts of justice," why does the Supreme Court exist?

In recent years a growing number of institutions—and particularly churches with a social justice bent—have "repudiated" the Doctrine of Discovery because of its racist construction. Repudiation is a political statement, a rhetorical device, and on its own doesn't do much to affect the status of the doctrine. But since the first publication of *Tribes, Treaties, and Constitutional Tribulations*, though, the United Nations passed its Declaration on the Rights of Indigenous People; churches typically include in their repudiations a call to consider the implications of that UN document.[5]

The Declaration "addresses both individual and collective rights; cultural rights and identity; rights to education, health, employment, language, . . . to remain distinct and to pursue their own priorities in economic, social and cultural development" (UN Office of High Commissioner for Human Rights). Unfortunately, when it was approved in 2007 the declaration was supported by 111 nations and opposed by four: the US, Canada, Australia, and New Zealand, the only four countries that base their property systems on the Doctrine of Discovery (though, since then, even those countries have endorsed it). Perhaps the UN Declaration can serve as a roadmap to addressing global political and economic inequities at some point in the future.

In the meantime, churches and other repudiators of the Discovery Doctrine must face the same fact that Deloria and Wilkins faced. While there may be some institutions from which racism might be excised, ameliorated, or negated by social change, by changing laws, or by constitutional amendments, the Doctrine of Discovery presents a harder challenge. Thanks to Marshall, the doctrine is hardwired into constitutional law as the foundation for all US property titles.

The motivation of churches to repudiate the Doctrine of Discovery arises from their own historical role in US Indian Affairs. Organized religions played an outsized part in the government's century-long project to "civilize" Indigenous peoples. Deloria and Wilkins trace the beginning of this project to a "humanitarian impulse," a response to the devastating effects of US expansion on the Indigenous population. This impulse led to legislation offering government relief to Indigenous Tribes in 1819, which included instruction in European-rooted models of agriculture. But over the course of its history, the focus of "civilization" efforts expanded to include moral instruction in Christianity. The Bureau of Indian Affairs relied increasingly on institutions from fiercely competing denominations to do its work.

The goal of "civilization" programs was the total assimilation of Indigenous peoples into white society. It was one impulse behind US Indian policy, which in a typically inconsistent manner also pursued the goal of complete removal of Indigenous people from white society. By 1828, Superintendent of Indian Affairs Thomas L. McKenney questioned whether "civilization" could work *without* Indian removal: "*What are humanity and justice, in reference to this unfortunate race?* Are these found to lie in a policy that would leave them to linger out a wretched and degraded existence, within districts of country already surrounded, and pressed upon by a population whose anxiety and efforts to get rid of them are not less restless and persevering than is that law of nature immutable, which has decreed that, under such circumstances, if continued in, *they must perish?*" (emphasis in original).[6]

Missionaries, as advocates of assimilation, narrowly lost the political battle against the 1830 Indian Removal Act. But their work was far from over. Churches took an ever more prominent role in the "civilization" effort as it moved west with the Tribes. By 1872, the western Indian agencies, where US Indian policy was administered to local Tribes, were under the "exclusive or near-exclusive control" of missionaries; Deloria and Wilkins present, from the report of the commissioner of Indian Affairs for that year, a list of thirteen denominations that ran agencies, and the Tribes that those agencies "served." Starting eleven years later, and continuing for nearly a hundred years, the practice of Indigenous religions was criminalized and punished with prison terms. This attempt at cultural ethnocide is the legacy that drives the repudiation of the Doctrine of Discovery today.

Deloria and Wilkins point out that nothing in the Constitution grants authority to the federal government to civilize people, and that the establishment of Christianity as the only permissible religion for Indigenous people was inarguably unconstitutional. But they do find in the Doctrine of Discovery a kind of backdoor construction linking this effort to the very foundation of the US property system. When Marshall laid out his doctrine in 1823, he claimed that Indigenous nations were compensated for their loss of dominion over the land they inhabited, not in a monetary sense but in the cultural advantages that Europeans brought to North America: "The character and religion of its inhabitants afforded an apology for considering them as a people over whom the superior genius of Europe might claim an ascendancy.... They made ample compensation to the inhabitants of the new [world], by bestowing on them civilization and Christianity in exchange for unlimited independence."[7]

The authors' comment on Marshall's statement resonates as the central point of conflict between Indigenous Nations and the United States. "Here," they write, "sovereignty and land proprietorship are regarded as the same thing, an idea that certainly originates in the feudal system of land tenure in Europe."[8]

In pursuit of property, the US initially was compelled to enter treaties with Indigenous nations, because this was the doctrine-approved method of perfecting land titles. As the authors point out, "Without question the first generation of American statesmen believe the treaty-making power was the primary constitutional authority for dealing with Indian tribes."[9] By contrast, the Indigenous nations of North America based their land tenure on many forms of land tenure that are often generalized and shorthanded as "kinship relationships." Those nations never equated sovereignty with proprietorship. Their treaty-making was an expression of sovereignty, but beyond the context of land acquisition.

From the colonialist perspective, this was a flaw. As Commissioner of Indian Affairs Elbert Herring reported in 1832, "The absence of *meum* and *tuum* [mine and yours] in the general community of possessions, which is the grand conservative principle of the social state, is a perpetual operating cause of the *via inertiae* of savage life."[10] And Herring's successor, T. Hartley Crawford, latter opined that,

> Unless some system is marked out by which there shall be a separate allotment of land to each individual . . . you will look in vain for any general casting off of savagism. . . . Common property and civilization cannot co-exist. . . . At the foundation of the whole social system lies individuality of property. It is, perhaps, nine times in ten the stimulus that manhood first feels. It has produced the energy, industry, and enterprise

> that distinguish the civilized world, and contributes more largely to the good morals of men than those are willing to acknowledge who have not looked somewhat closely at their fellow human beings. With it come all the delights that the word hope expresses; the comforts that follow fixed settlements are in its train, and to them belongs not only an anxiety to do right that those gratifications may not be forfeited, but industry that they may be increased.[11]

In 1787, a year before the US Constitution was ratified, Congress passed the Northwest Ordinance. This legislation (which was renewed after the Constitution went into effect) laid out the first terms by which the country would expand across the continent. One of its most notable passages relates to Indian relations:

> The utmost good faith shall always be observed toward the Indians; their lands and property shall never be taken from them without their consent; and in their property, rights, and liberty, they shall never be invaded or disturbed, unless in just and lawful wars authorized by Congress; but laws founded in justice and humanity shall, from time to time, be made, for preventing wrongs being done to them, and for preserving peace and friendship with them.[12]

Despite this passage, Congress was already attempting to make treaties that would clear Indigenous peoples out of the Northwest Territory. In fact, the same ordinance sets out plans to divide the territory's two hundred sixty thousand square miles into states for white settlement, even though Indigenous people controlled the entire area. Within fifteen years, the US had overcome its ambivalence about maintaining a permanent military by establishing a standing army, not to fight the British or French but to fight the Native confederacy that was opposing US expansion.

The Northwest Ordinance, then, at the very beginning of the US colonialist enterprise, reflects the contradictions that would mark US Indian policy for 150 years, including the contradictions of removal and assimilation, and the "inconsistent judicial decisions" of Indian law. Beneath these contradictions, though, the US approach to Indian Affairs was animated by a remarkably consistent vision: *the absence of Indigenous people*. Whether by full-scale war, by removal from their homelands, or by assimilation that would end their cultural identity, US policies historically assumed no future for Indigenous people.

Months before the Louisiana Purchase opened a vast new area for US expansion, Thomas Jefferson wrote to William Henry Harrison (governor of Indiana Territory) to explain the purpose of commerce with Indigenous nations: "The decrease of game rendering their subsistence by hunting insufficient, we wish to draw them to agriculture. . . . They will perceive how useless to them are their extensive forests, and will be willing to pair them off from time to time. . . . They will in time either incorporate with us as citizens of the United States or remove beyond the Mississippi. The former is certainly the termination of their history."[13]

Jefferson was not expressing any joy at the prospect of this termination, but as Deloria and Wilkins write, "As Indians have become less of a military threat and own considerably less land, the perspective of people serving in the respective branches of government has become harsher and more contemptuous."[14] The following passages are two examples out of many to be found in reports from commissioners of Indian Affairs that express a vision of the end of Indigenous people.

In 1848, Commissioner William Medill wrote,

> I have the honor to lay before you . . . the latest and most authentic information respecting the condition and prospects remnant of remnants of an interesting people, who once held undisputed sway over the territory we now occupy, but who have gradually melted away before the advance of civilization, or, in broken groups, been swept westward by the

> pressure and rapid extension of a more intelligent and enterprising race. While, to all, the fate of the red man has, thus far, been alike unsatisfactory and painful, it has, with many, been a source of much misrepresentation and unjust national reproach. Apathy, barbarism, and heathenism must give way to energy, civilization, and Christianity; and so the Indian of this continent has been displaced by the European; but this has been attended with much less of oppression and injustice than has generally been represented and believed. If, in the rapid spread of our population and sway, with all their advantages and blessings to ourselves and to others, injury has been inflicted upon the barbarous and heathen people we have displaced, are we as a nation alone to be held up to reproach for such a result? Where, in the contest of civilization with barbarism, since the commencement of time, has it been less the case with us; and where have there been more general and persevering efforts, according to our means and opportunities, than those made by us, to extend to the conquered all the superior resources and advantages enjoyed by the conquerors?[15]

The "remnants of an interesting people" to whom he refers were at that point in control of half the current continental US. Four years later, Commissioner Luke Lea expressed a similar sentiment, in similarly racist language:

> When civilization and barbarism are brought in such relation that they cannot coexist together, it is right that the superiority of the former should be asserted and the latter compelled to give way. It is, therefore, no matter of regret or reproach that so large a portion of our territory has been wrested from its aboriginal inhabitants and made the happy abodes of an enlightened and Christian people. That the means employed

> to affect this grand result have not always been just, or that the conquest has been attended by a vast amount of human suffering, cannot be denied. Of the Indian's wrongs there is, indeed, no earthly record. But it will not be forgotten, by those who have a correct understanding of this subject, that much of the injury of which the red man and his friends complain has been the inevitable consequence of his own perverse and vicious nature. In the long and varied conflict between the white man and the red—civilization and barbarism—the former has often been compelled to recede, and be destroyed, or to advance and destroy.[16]

The idea that Indians would not survive the presence and expansion of the US was the one constant assumption beneath the greatest contradictions of US history.

That assumption was irretrievably wrong. The longest-abiding nations on the continent are still here, though their sovereignty is conscribed in the current moment. Given the extent of environmental and civil degradation that unfettered individualism has engendered, it is more probable that Indigenous nations will remain intact in some meaningful way longer than the US will.

What do US-Indian relations look like when stripped of the fallacy on which they have been predicated? Indigenous sovereignty is the enduring centerpiece, and not merely a contingency recognized by the US when expedient. That sovereignty remains extra-constitutional in its origin and operation and requires a nation-to-nation relationship. Nothing has to be reinvented. The future must be a return to the original relationship between the US and Indigenous nations, the simple (but not easy!) relationship asserted by Deloria and Wilkins in the postscript to *Tribes, Treaties, and Constitutional Tribulations*:

"The treaty process is viable and remains the most appropriate, most fair, and certainly the clearest manner in which to identify and demarcate the rights of tribal nations."[17]

CHAPTER 7

THE ESSENCE OF THE TREATY PROCESS

A Delorian View of Colonial Diplomacy

Samuel R. Cook

On April 15, 1716, the French traveler John Fontaine observed a meeting between Saponi leaders living at Fort Christanna in Brunswick County, Virginia, and Governor Alexander Spotswood. The Saponies and many of their kinspeople of the Monacan Alliance who had been displaced as a result of colonial pressures had agreed to settle at the fort and serve as a buffer against powerful Tribes to the southwest in return for protection from further settler incursions. On this occasion, the Saponi leaders sought Spotswood's assistance in a retaliatory raid against an Iroquois party that had invaded the fort and killed fifteen of their citizens. The meeting began with an exchange of gifts, a customary element of Indigenous diplomatic protocol—followed by a long moment of silence, after which Fontaine noted one of the leaders began to speak "after they had spit several times on the ground."[1]

Fontaine reported on the discharge of saliva as if it were a casual, crude habit, of no relevance to the forthcoming dialogue. In reality, spitting was a common and sacred ritual for many peoples of the Southeast who were about to engage in negotiated agreements. It could signify both a purging of the mind and words, and a commitment of oneself to the Earth—an act of "grounding."[2] This is significant because the Saponies and their Siouan kinspeople are often portrayed as living in a state of tutelage under British protection, having been weakened by settler encroachments, disease, and warfare with both Europeans and hostile Indian Nations. What it actually signifies is that the leaders of the Monacan Alliance understood any prior agreements with the English to be organic compacts, necessarily subject to renegotiation, reaffirmation through substantive gestures of allegiance and support, and above all sacred bonds.

If this vignette seems insignificant in the realm of contemporary Indigenous law, it underscores one of the most critical flaws that Vine Deloria, Jr. (Standing Rock) saw in American Indian law and policy: namely, that while the laws governing Tribal-settler relations in North America were purportedly born of diplomacy between Indigenous leaders and colonial authorities, the law itself is framed through the selective interpretive lens of non-Indigenous policy makers. Unfortunately, few scholars have followed Deloria's lead in scrutinizing the vast lexicon of diplomatic discourse, including treaties—colonial, post-Revolutionary, ratified and unratified, or otherwise—and other expressions of diplomatic discourse that should be understood as the basis for federal Indian law and policy. Scholars and practitioners instead rely on an ambiguous body of law that largely stems from Felix S. Cohen's seminal *Handbook of American Indian Law*. Yet Deloria reminds us that "no Indians were participants in writing the *Handbook*, or even in gathering the data to be included in it."[3] Indeed, Deloria devoted considerable time to collecting original documents and accounts of treaty negotiations, meetings between Tribal leaders and colonial officials, and related records to illuminate the extent to which Indigenous peoples were active agents in the diplomatic exchanges that laid the foundation for Indian law and policy. The lasting dynamic that is all too often ignored in the policy-making process and ensuing analyses is that Tribal leaders have always engaged in *negotiation* in articulating and challenging policies that impact the lives of their constituents most profoundly.[4]

This essay provides a brief history of Indigenous and non-Indigenous diplomatic relations in what became the Commonwealth of Virginia to argue that Indigenous agency, while taking various forms, has always influenced state and federal policies. Empowered by the federal government's recent recognition of its relationships with these Tribes, they have begun to assert this influence in new and powerful ways. This has become abundantly clear as the seven federally recognized Tribes located within Virginia's current-day boundaries[5] are now negotiating with the state to produce a Tribal Nations-Commonwealth Sovereignty Accord, which purports to level the playing field between Tribal, state, and national polities in normalizing government-to-government relations in a crucible of mutual consent and respect. This dialogue is not novel. It reflects a historical continuum of negotiation that has been obscured by selective settler legal traditions but should not be isolated from international principles for intergovernmental relations.

Foundations of Indigenous Diplomacy

Indigenous peoples were not helpless recipients of rights construed through treaties by colonial authorities on behalf of European sovereigns; rather, they were active agents in the process of diplomacy, and if they did not fully comprehend European protocols, neither did Europeans adequately grasp Native diplomacy. Nonetheless, Europeans *did* engage in diplomatic relations with Tribes because they had little choice, regardless of motive. As David DeJong notes, "Of the Indian treaties secured during the colonial period, more than three-fourths—roughly 300—were for military alliance or friendship . . . and fewer than six dozen directed toward land cessions."[6] For whatever reasons Europeans and their progeny negotiated treaties with Indians, these documents formed the core of what we know as Indian law and policy today. Yet as Deloria and DeMallie note, we should rightly include the entire corpus of diplomatic records, documents, and proceedings as equally important legal grounding for diplomatic policy.[7] This includes any records of Indigenous dialogue and negotiation during the treaty-making process, and any actions—ritual or otherwise—intended to reaffirm or clarify the nature of diplomatic relations and agreements.

Indigenous diplomacy was—and remains—an integral part of the historical treaty-making process, and the broader lexicon of diplomacy is as relevant as any treaty. Furthermore, colonial treaties that predate the American republic remain valid covenants that must be reassessed in defining the ongoing relationship between Indigenous peoples, the contemporary American republic, and all subsidiaries of the latter, especially states. This is evident in the way treaties and other colonial-era documents and transactions of diplomacy provided the foundation for federal Indian law and policy as we know it today, which is indisputably a unique and anomalous realm of national—if not international—jurisprudence that requires clarification. This is because diplomacy is a multiparty endeavor. While Indigenous peoples have faced countless barriers in efforts to contribute to the legal narrative, they remain actors nonetheless and continue to influence policy at both national and international levels. Indeed, Natives are the only group that might be collectively considered an ethnic or racial group with an entire title of the *United States Codes* (Title 25 USC) devoted to them. That, however, accentuates the fallacy of treating them simply as ethnic minorities and of ignoring their political status as sovereign nations beyond the pale of the federalist system.

Finally, Indigenous diplomacy must be considered as a continuum of reciprocity where all parties must renew their alliances and revisit the conditions thereof on a regular basis. From this perspective one can understand that Native interactions, transactions, and exchanges with federal authorities constitute acts of diplomacy rooted in a philosophy of sovereign responsibility and are not simply lobbying activities. The emerging sovereignty accord between the Commonwealth of Virginia and the Tribal Nations within its boundaries provides a perfect example.

The Evolution of Treaty-Making

Scholars and practitioners who analyze and evoke Indian treaties in the context of federal law and policy tend to emphasize those treaties negotiated after the advent of the American republic. The US State Department maintains a cumulative list of all treaties in which the United States has been a party, or treaties negotiated by English colonies in North America prior to the American Revolution that had a formative impact on US diplomacy. Interestingly, although the State Department is the executive agency charged with overseeing diplomatic relations, actual oversight duties are assigned to the Interior Department. The first treaty on that list is the The Great Treaty of 1722, also known as the Treaty of Albany, between the Five Nations of Iroquois and the Colonies of New York, Virginia, and Pennsylvania.[8] This treaty probably marked the first diplomatic effort of multiple colonies to deal collectively with a powerful Indigenous polity; it also marked a profound shift in the dynamics of treaty-making that would form the backbone of a centralized Indian policy in the British colonies, then the United States.

Previously, the colony of Virginia engaged Tribes in a rather piecemeal system of diplomatic relations with individual Tribal polities, or Indigenous leaders purporting to represent numerous Tribes (although that was rarely the case). The 1646 and 1677 treaties laid a uniform framework for establishing militarily weakened Tribes as "tributaries"[9] to the governor of Virginia as agent to the Crown, although this status may well have been misconstrued as an act of subservience on the part of Indigenous parties involved. Notably, some of these treaties and agreements called on the Tribes involved to serve as a buffer between the colony and so-called hostile Tribes on the frontier. Such was the case with the agreement establishing the Siouan settlement at Fort Christanna.[10] But by 1722, although these Tribes were represented in treaty negotiations in Albany and Fort Henry, British emissaries were more concerned with securing peace with the powerful Five Nations of Haudenosaunee in order to pave a less turbulent road for western expansion.

The 1744 Treaty at Lancaster, in fact, marked a clear move away from colonial diplomacy with the Tribes associated today with Virginia. While it had at least involved solicitations from various Indigenous leaders from Virginia, it was predicated on a number of previous agreements with and between tributary Tribes who found the colonial government's protection of their territories from settlers and enemy Indian nations inconsistent at best. By 1744, the Tribes historically considered tributaries were no longer on record as parties in diplomatic relations. And while the 1722 treaty had secured a solemn agreement on the part of the Haudenosaunee (Iroquois) that they would not cross east of the Blue Ridge into Virginia—implying that they had previously laid claim to some of that territory—in the Lancaster Treaty the Six Nations (now including the Tuscarora) agreed to a "Disclaimer and Renunciation of all their Claim or patence [*sic*] of right whatsoever" of remaining lands in western Virginia."[11] The Iroquois effectively gave land that was the ancestral territory of some of the western polities of the Monacan Alliance to the English Crown without clear consent from the former. As a result, English settlers wasted no time surveying and staking claims across the Blue Ridge, which would necessitate more treaties of peace as these settlers encroached on lands of the Cherokees, Shawnees, and other Tribes to the west.

The English concentration on diplomacy with the Six Nations created a great deal of tension with other Indian Nations, which, in turn, nearly cost the British their victory over the French in the ensuing Seven Years War. The 1752 Logg's Town Treaty (negotiated by the colony of Virginia) foreshadowed this tension. It brought the Iroquois, Shawnees, and various other Algonquian nations together to ease the claims of the Ohio Land Company that clearly transcended the nebulous boundaries for British expansion described in the Lancaster Treaty.[12] Nonetheless, most of the Tribes involved in that treaty—with the exception of the Iroquois—found the English commitment to the covenant to be weak and insincere, and most cast their allegiance with the French in 1755. The Seven Years War, or French and Indian War, made it very clear to the British Crown that inconsistent diplomacy with Indian nations was a dangerous venture, particularly when individual colonies tended to deal with Tribes on their own terms and often in contradictory ways.

Thus, following the Peace of Paris in 1763, the Crown reorganized Indian affairs under two—and ultimately one—department, to maintain a single, consistent policy. This centralization of Indian affairs was intended to prevent individual colonies from taking license, and required any western expansion, settlement, trade, or any other form of interactions with Indigenous peoples to only take place under the authority of a central agency representing the Crown.[13] This centralized system provided the blueprint for the nascent American Confederation as the Revolutionary War broke out.

The Revolutionary War was a turbulent watershed in the evolution of treaty-making with Indian nations in North America, as it effectively marked the last time that western polities could compete against each other in vying for alliances with Indigenous peoples. Previously, Indigenous diplomats could counter English terms of agreement with more generous French offerings, and vice versa (and occasionally other European powers were involved, but decreasingly so by the mid-eighteenth century). The Revolution brought about a complex situation, as the Continental Congress adopted a policy very similar to the centralized British policy. With the conclusion of that war and the withdrawal of British authority over the territories that became the United States, Tribal Nations lost a profound amount of bargaining power in diplomacy.

Legal Foundations and Political Motivations for Treaty-Making

It is important to understand precisely why European powers—and later the United States—made treaties with Tribes in the first place. The simple answer is that treaties provided a convenient way to gain access to North American lands without the expense of warfare and in the midst of situations where colonists were at a military disadvantage. There was, however, a fairly well established ethical (at least from a western perspective) and legal basis for making treaties with Indigenous nations that ultimately formed the core of international law as we know it. In 1532, the Spanish cleric Francisco de Vitoria (who is sometimes considered the father of international law) offered a statement on the Doctrine of Discovery. Issued in 1493, the now infamous papal bull attempted to define and justify the right of conquering power to claim lands of original inhabitants. Vitoria wrote, as other clerics had determined, that Indigenous peoples were human beings with souls—and capable of conversion—and their lands could not be taken without their consent or through the process of "just war."[14] His interpretation of the infamous papal bull became an accepted tenet of western international law for the next two centuries, although theft of Indigenous lands by no means came to a halt. As Deloria and Lytle point out: "Treaty-making became the basis for defining both the legal and political relationships between the Indians and the European colonists."[15]

Europeans nation-states, however, sought various channels for circumventing the agreed upon international conventions of consensual land cessions and "just" warfare. This became eminently clear with the close of the American Revolution, when the Continental Congress and executive branch of the American Confederation took a hardnosed approach to how treaties would be made and interpreted. Bearing in mind that the new nation was built on the spirit of frontier expansion (indeed, the 1763 Royal prohibition against crossing the Allegheny Crest had only catalyzed revolutionary sentiments), Americans were not simply interested in peace with Indian nations. Land cessions, particularly in the Northwest Territory—a vast area that encompassed the present-day states of Ohio, Michigan, Illinois, Indiana, Wisconsin and eastern Minnesota—were the driving concern in Indian affairs.

Engagement with the United States

After the Revolution, the Continental Congress espoused the philosophy that the British had ceded not only authority but also the lands claimed by the Crown, including those territories occupied and retained by the Tribes. By this logic, Indians—in particular those who had sided with the British—should be prepared to give up lands with no compensation. Fortunately, most representatives in Congress understood how costly war with western Tribes could be and encouraged a policy that may have presented a posture of eminent domain over Tribes but used treaties as a mechanism for defusing Indigenous challenges to the taking of land.

The idea was that as more settlers moved west peacefully, the scarcer game would become, and the farther Indians would retreat into extinction.[16] This brutally pragmatic rationale was expressed by George Washington himself in a 1783 letter to Congressman James Duane when he stated: "The gradual extension of our Settlements will as certainly cause the Savage as the Wolf to retire, both being beasts of prey tho' they differ in shape."[17]

Washington at least advocated a conciliatory approach to Indian land cessions. Nonetheless, three major treaties with the Six Nations and other Tribes, seeking to secure American domination of lands across the Ohio, were negotiated—at least from an American perspective—under the premise that these lands had already been ceded to the United States by virtue of its having defeated the British. The 1784 Fort Stanwix Treaty with the Six Nations set the tone, when commissioners informed the Haudenosaunee sachems that the latters' claims west of Pennsylvania already belonged to the United States "by right of conquest."[18] During negotiations at Fort McIntosh the following year, when leaders of various Algonquian Nations stated that they were pleased that the Six Nations had agreed to cede some of their lands, American commissioners bluntly stated that "it is quite the contrary. We have given the hostile Six Nations some of the country which we conquered from them."[19] And the ratified Fort Finney Treaty with the Shawnees bluntly stated that the lands of the Shawnees who remained west of the Miami River were "allotted" to them.[20]

A similar set of treaties was negotiated at Hopewell, South Carolina, in November 1785 with the Cherokees, Choctaws, and Chickasaws. Article IV of the Cherokee Treaty boldly referred to their territory as "the boundary allotted to the Cherokees for their hunting grounds,"[21] ignoring the sophistication of Cherokee civic organization and surplus agriculture. Like the three previous treaties, Article III stated: "That said Indians for themselves and their representative towns do acknowledge all the Cherokees to be under the protection of the United States of America, and no other sovereign whosoever."[22] While this provision seems reminiscent of colonial tributary treaties, it does not necessarily reflect the Cherokee diplomats' understanding of what it meant to be under the "protection" of the United States; nor does it explicitly deny the sovereign status of the Cherokee Nation itself.

A deeper examination of the Indigenous contributions to negotiations in all of these treaties would very likely reveal a serious breach in communications between US emissaries and Indigenous leadership, as well as a questionable rendering of the ratified treaties as the Indigenous diplomats would have understood them. Indeed, as these treaties may appear, as Reginald Horsman suggests, to have been "dictated,"[23] Indigenous backlash was, not surprisingly, eminent. Hostilities on the northwest frontier escalated. The Shawnees almost immediately repudiated the Fort Finney Treaty, and certain Haudenosaunee leaders began to unify Indian nations of the northwest against the Americans.[24] The fact that there was still a formidable British presence on the continent made it abundantly clear that unilateral diplomacy was a losing hand for the Americans.

The raw hubris that surrounded the negotiation of these questionable treaties, however, also helps to elucidate the numerous ethical, cultural, and legal contradictions that have historically framed Euro-American attitudes in negotiating and interpreting what should be considered solemn compacts. Indeed, as the confederation began transitioning into a republic, Secretary of War Henry Knox reiterated the concerns of some of his contemporaries that Indian wars would be costly, and potentially unsuccessful, *and* that treating Indian Nations on equitable terms was a matter of national honor.[25] In his June 1789 report on the state of Indian affairs in the Northwest, Knox asserted: "It is presumable that a nation solicitous of establishing its character on the broad basis of justice, would . . . reject every proposition to benefit itself, by the injuring of any neighboring community, however contemptible and weak it might be."[26] The matter of honor, in fact, became the framing principle for the policy—at least on paper—that would guide the nascent republic on the eve of the implementation of the US Constitution. The Northwest Ordinance of July 13, 1787, was intended to facilitate the orderly acquisition and Euro-American settlement of lands from the Ohio to the Mississippi. Yet Article Three stated in no uncertain terms:

> The utmost good faith shall always be observed towards the Indians; their lands and property shall never be taken from them without their consent; and in their property, rights and liberty, they never shall be invaded or disturbed, unless in just and lawful wars authorized by Congress; but laws founded in justice and humanity shall from time to time be made, for preventing wrongs from being done to them, and for preserving peace and friendship with them.[27]

The Northwest Ordinance, though not statutory law, expressed the intent of Congress, even if it masked multiple motives. Hence, the US Constitution provided a clear framework for diplomacy with Indian Nations in two explicit instances that remain unchanged to date.

Article I, Section 8, Clause 3 of the Constitution gives Congress exclusive authority "to regulate commerce with foreign nations, and among the several states, and with the Indian tribes." In so doing, the Constitution makes it explicit that Indian affairs is exclusively a federal matter over which states can exercise no influence unless otherwise granted such authority by Congress. This was initially implemented and elaborated through a number of trade and non-intercourse acts, beginning in 1790.

Article II, Section 2, in delineating powers of the executive branch, states the president "shall have Power, by and with the Advice and consent of Senate, to make treaties, provided two-thirds of the senators present concur." This clause automatically makes the president subject to congressional oversight in diplomacy, and although Indians are not explicitly mentioned, the treaty-making process with Indian nations was the same as with foreign nations until Congress unilaterally terminated the practice of making treaties with Tribes in 1871. This termination, however, did not abrogate preexisting treaties, and, in accordance with Article XI, Clause 2 of the US Constitution, "All treaties made, or which shall be made under the Authority of the United States, shall be the supreme law of the land."

These provisions in the Constitution have not changed since its ratification. Why, then, are Indian treaties not given serious consideration as documents of diplomacy in national and international politics?

Settler Privilege: The Unilateral Interpretation of Treaties

Contemporary scholars and activists of Indian affairs find themselves repeating terms such as "erasure" and "settler colonialism" as harbingers of antagonism. In fact, colonial policies were always designed to erase Indigenous peoples, even in their most benign renderings. The idea that Indigenous peoples are "vanishing" is so deeply rooted in the western psyche that it permeates the way Natives are represented in the landscapes of education and media as relics of the past. Indian treaties, as documents that remind both policy makers and an uninformed public of the existence of Indigenous peoples as agents, are no exception. As Deloria and DeMallie point out, "Federal and state courts . . . in an effort to reconcile the interpretation of treaties with prevailing public sentiments of the time, often twisted language [of treaties] beyond its meaning to fit predetermined results."[28]

"Interpretation" is the operative term. The system of checks and balances established in the US Constitution gives the courts much greater power than most people realize in determining policy. Once a decision has reached its highest possible forum for arbitration in the justice system—which is ideally, but not always, the US Supreme Court—it effectively becomes the law until reinterpreted by a higher court or overturned by Congress. This places Indian Nations in a precarious position, as they seem to find little recourse in international forums.

While one would assume that the US Constitution would provide a steadfast compass, Indian affairs has often been treated as an archaic vestige of the American legal tradition, as if the mere passage of time has diminished that sphere of constitutional rights and diplomacy. Yet as Deloria and Wilkins point out, the same people who make such assertions "would not, under any circumstances, suggest that the progress in human rights and economic benefits that the majority has made over the past two centuries, due primarily to the expansive interpretation of the same constitutional clauses, be reduced, negated, or eliminated."[29]

Revitalizing Indigenous-US Diplomacy

There is no question that colonial treaties had some very negative impacts on Indigenous peoples, particularly in facilitating cultural genocide and land alienation. Indeed, some of the most salient scholars of American Indian treaties—notably, Francis Paul Prucha[30]—have adopted a pessimistic view of treaties as western impositions that not only became more authoritarian in nature with the progression of time but were often negotiated and ratified without Indigenous peoples fully comprehending or being aware of the actual provisions of the codified documents. However, Indigenous scholars and their allies have always pointed out that Tribal leaders were neither oblivious to the art and concept of diplomacy, nor without their means of preserving a record of diplomatic agreements.[31]

In his compelling book, *Linking Arms Together*, Robert A. Williams (Lumbee) reminds us that diplomacy was neither a foreign concept to Indian Nations before the coming of Europeans, nor was it conducted in a state of ignorant bliss, even if European diplomats assumed the concessions they made toward Indians were only temporary inconveniences for overcoming "obstacles to manifest destiny."[32] Williams encourages us to critically review the record of Indigenous-European diplomacy, including council proceedings, accounts of ceremony and dialogue surrounding these events, and any accounts of Indigenous activity related directly to diplomacy, because: "In a rapidly changing world of human diversity and conflict, American Indians sought to apply their traditions to the problems of achieving law and peace on a multicultural frontier."[33] Williams's book helps illuminate the depth and sophistication of Indigenous diplomacy in North America in terms of forging and sustaining agreements between diverse peoples by examining multiple facets of treaties as legal texts, as dynamic stories, and as sacred narratives that required regular reconfirmation of commitments by all parties involved. He focuses primarily on Haudenosaunee diplomacy in the Encounter Era, in large part because records of Iroquois diplomacy are more ubiquitous. Nonetheless, the European willingness to engage in such rituals of diplomacy is a good indicator of the military prowess of the Haudenosaunee Confederacy at the time. And even if Europeans assumed that such strength would diminish over time, the endurance of Indigenous parties beckons a new consideration of these records of Indian and non-Indian relations as discourses of multilateral diplomacy.

Vine Deloria, Jr. made this a cornerstone of his scholarly activism for most of his career, which manifested itself in his two-volume collection of *Documents of American Indian Diplomacy* (coedited with DeMallie). Since many treaties were negotiated but not ratified, and since codified treaties under the American republic reflected only those terms presented to Euro-American policy makers in the Senate and executive branch, Deloria and DeMallie conclude that an Indian treaty "should include the narratives of the negotiations and any prior or any subsequent form of negotiation conducted according to traditional Indian procedure."[34]

Such an undertaking could fill countless volumes, but Deloria and DeMallie bring up some very important points of consideration for the project at hand. First, do we include colonial treaties in this assessment? This beckons the deeper question of whether the United States should have assumed responsibility for the diplomatic relationships circumscribed by colonial Virginia treaties. In the realm of international law, *The Vienna Convention on the Succession of States in Respect of Treaties* (1978) defines state succession as "the replacement of one State by another in the responsibility for the international relations of a territory."[35] While this principle certainly has roots in the Doctrine of Discovery, it has yet to be adequately understood or clarified, as it does not answer the question of whether a succeeding state assumes all treaty responsibilities that the retiring state held prior to succession. In some cases, it is explicit in treaties of succession.

In the United States, for instance, both the treaty authorizing the Louisiana Purchase in 1803, and the Treaty of Guadalupe Hidalgo (1848) at the close of the Mexican-American War contain explicit provisions acknowledging the responsibility of the United States to maintain treaty obligations with Tribes that the respective states claiming sovereignty over those territories had negotiated.[36] On the other hand, the Peace of Paris, concluding the Revolutionary War and transferring territorial sovereignty from Britain to the United States, was conspicuously absent of references to Indigenous peoples and treaties. It might be argued that the "doctrine of universal succession," which is one of two major doctrines used to formulate and interpret articles of state succession, would have to prevail since the other doctrine, the "Clean Slate Doctrine" did not formally exist until the late nineteenth century.

Universal succession implies that the succeeding state assumes *all* prior obligations in international relations, while the Clean Slate Doctrine basically acknowledges a state's prerogative to define its own terms for territorial succession.[37] As noted earlier, the United States as it existed under the Articles of Confederation seemed to take a clean-slate approach to diplomacy with Indians, assuming absolute sovereignty over territory by right of conquest. Nonetheless, Indigenous resistance proved that such an approach was imprudent at best.

In fact, the Indigenous people within the boundaries of Virginia have consistently argued the point of universal succession through their words and actions, if not in those precise terms. While colonial treaties have often been treated by non-Indians as outdated conveyances, many of those treaties have "succession clauses" stating that the Tribes involved acknowledge their relationship with any sovereign entities who succeed the British Crown. This is true of the 1677 Treaty of Middle Plantation, and all the later treaties between Governor Spotswood and various Indian nations in 1714.[38] Indeed, the Cheroenhaka Nottoway Tribe very clearly states on its website, "Our tribal government contends that the Successor Clause [in the 1714 Treaty with the Nottoway] meant that the recognized relationships that the Tribe had with colonists from 1713 to 1775 continued with the Commonwealth of Virginia beginning in 1776 and with the Federal Government in 1781 to the present time."[39] To that end, the Cheroenhaka leadership has since 2012 reinstated the practice of delivering three arrows to the governor of Virginia each year in compliance with their tributary obligations under the treaty. As with many Tribes, this practice was preempted, if not abandoned for several years, because the Commonwealth, Crown, and their successors failed to uphold their treaty obligations.

This brings up a second important point from Deloria and DeMallie concerning the inclusion of subsequent forms of Indigenous negotiation in the lexicon of diplomacy. Tribes such as the Pamunkey and Mattaponi, whose reservations are the oldest within the United States, have consistently presented the governor of Virginia with tribute in the form of game every year since the 1677 Treaty of Middle Plantation. This is not simply a tradition; it is clear evidence that Virginia Tribes have sustained diplomatic discourse since before the founding of the United States, and continue to do so. This is why the majority of Tribes in Virginia continued to pursue federal recognition in spite of the state's ongoing attempts to eradicate and erase them. The success of recognition petitions and bills is often attributed to anthropologists and lawyers collecting and compiling data, and to congressional advocates who advance the legislation. However, Tribes enlist such specialists because they carry the burden of proof. The very evidence used to illustrate claims of legitimacy of Tribal identities is, in truth, part of a historical discourse of diplomacy. Not only do these data demonstrate historical assertions of the Indigenous mantra that "we're still here," but they very often elucidate moments when Tribal leaders have actively attempted to engage state and federal governments.

Modern Nation-to-Nation Relations: Federal Recognition as a Diplomatic Act

The provisions of the Thomasina E. Jordan Federal Recognition Act of 2017 confirming federal acknowledgment of six Tribes located with the boundaries of the state of Virginia—Chickahominy, Chickahominy Eastern Division, Upper Mattaponi, Monacan, Nansemond, and Rappahannock—is replete with diplomatic language.[40] While the first section of each of the six titles begins by summarizing historical evidence of the continuous existence of each Tribe, these sections accentuate the diplomatic relations and activities of Tribal leaders throughout history. Not only does each title mention all treaties with which respective Tribes were involved, but also includes moments when Tribal leadership actively engaged federal, state, and local policy makers to assert Tribal sovereign rights.

Section 101, for example, chronicles various moments of correspondence between Chickahominy leadership and Commissioner of Affairs John Collier during the 1930s and 1940s, indicating that the head of the Indian Bureau was sincerely interested in working with that Tribe in whatever capacity he could. In various sections the act also chronicles the efforts of representatives from several of these Tribes to challenge their racial designation during World War II, often facing prosecution for resisting the draft when they were placed in "colored" regiments.[41] These, and related actions regarding census enumerations during the eugenics era, must be understood as diplomatic activism rather than civil rights stances, as Tribal leaders and representatives were asserting a political identity. Regardless of who penned or introduced these bills, a thorough reading of the act reveals that it bears the imprint of the Indigenous leaders who sought its passage as an article of diplomacy.

In fact, the very act of pursuing federal recognition is at its essence an act of diplomatic engagement. While the burden of proof is on the Tribe, it is a mistake to assume that Tribal leaders and constituents pursue such recognition simply because they believe they will get special benefits. The onerous process of pursuing recognition is enough to dissuade that kind of thinking. Rather, it must be understood as an engaged effort on the part of Indigenous polities to assert control over inherent sovereign powers that were never relinquished voluntarily. This is not simply a matter of self-preservation; rather it is an assertion of responsibility within Indigenous communities and toward those outside. Which brings us to the proposed Tribal Nations-Commonwealth Sovereignty Accord.

Formal Establishment of Twenty-First-Century Government-to-Governments Relations

"Since negotiation is the essence of the treaty process," wrote Vine Deloria, "and today reflects the modern government-to-government policy, we have here a procedure that stands well within the historic tradition of give and take that once characterized the federal relationship."[42] Although addressing inconsistencies in federal Indian policy that could potentially be mitigated through a new treaty-making process, Deloria was also acknowledging the preconstitutional roots of this process and the fallacy of assuming that Indigenous leaders ever totally relinquished their inherent ability to negotiate with other polities. As previously stated, Tribal Nations within the boundaries of what is now Virginia have historically maintained discourses of diplomacy, even when colonial, state, and federal polities were slow to respond or altogether unresponsive.

Since 2020, the seven federally recognized Tribes within the Commonwealth, with Chief Anne Richardson (Rappahannock) at the vanguard, have used their sovereign status to leverage deeper diplomatic commitments with the state. During the first wave of the coronavirus pandemic, the leaders enlisted David Wilkins (Lumbee) and Shelly Hulse Wilkins, scholars with both knowledge and expertise in Tribal-state relations, to frame a guiding document, The Tribal-Commonwealth Accord: An Agreement between Tribal Nations and the Commonwealth of Virginia (see appendix), that would establish a formal foundation of mutual respect and cooperation between the federally recognized Tribes and the executive branch of state government. Such an agreement would usher in an unprecedented chapter in government-to-government relations at the levels where relations have historically been the tensest. The leaders convened via Zoom to review the accord, giving their final, unanimous approval in April 2021. On September 24, 2021, these leaders hosted a Sovereign Nations of Virginia Conference to introduce the proposed agreement through a series of panels that provided historical context and a proposed structure for the exercise of modern-day diplomacy in

Virginia. The accord provides a blueprint for coexistence in a complex society; the operative term is "responsibility."

Although the US Constitution gives Congress exclusive authority over Indian affairs, the extent to which Tribal and state governments should interact with each other in their respective sovereign capacities has yet to be clarified. However, federally recognized Tribes located throughout the United States have, at least since the 1980s, initiated relationships of cooperation with their non-Indian neighbors over issues of critical and mutual concern. These include the negotiation of compacts for cross-deputization of law enforcement agencies when crimes transcend both state and reservation boundaries, extradition, and so forth.[43] In recent years, Tribal governments have been at the forefront of advancing sovereignty accords with state governments as instruments expressing covenants of mutual responsibility. These are not articles of separation but rather understandings of mutual respect, expectations, and cooperation.

The preamble of the draft Tribal-Commonwealth Accord states that the agreement is intended to "establish the basis for lasting government-to-government relations bound by respect, deep understanding, and consent that is free, prior and informed." While the draft accord systematically lays out the rights of all parties involved, it is fundamentally a covenant of mutual responsibility that necessarily requires all parties to interact on a continuing basis and to reassess and reconfirm their interrelatedness. The accord also contains a section on protocols and principles that details how both state and Tribal governments are expected to uphold commitments to this agreement. This includes the establishment of a permanent, executive cabinet level Office for Tribal Relations, led by a director tasked with the coordination of all executive agencies under the governor's direction. This is to ensure that policies and procedures impacting Indigenous peoples will not fall prey to willful ignorance or neglect but will instead be conducted smoothly and professionally in good faith. The accord is also quite explicit in outlining Tribal governmental responsibilities, such as establishing and maintaining systems of accountability.

As Indigenous legal scholars have pointed out for generations, one of the most salient differences between Indigenous political discourse and western legal traditions is that the latter places primacy on *rights*, and especially individual rights, while the former places paramount importance on responsibility—individuals' responsibilities to each other, governments' responsibilities to their constituents and to other governments, and human responsibilities to other forms of life and to the world in general.[44] In the former case, this is deeply seated in worldviews that do not privilege human beings over other forms of life and posit that any society must function as—if not be consciously part of—an ecosystem.[45] The Tribal-Commonwealth Accord offers the opportunity for Indigenous and non-Indigenous agents to come together and rekindle the multilateral spirit of diplomacy.

As promising as this accord may be, the timing of its introduction came during a transition for the Virginia state government. It was introduced to outgoing governor Ralph Northam and other state lawmakers just a few weeks before elections that saw both executive and legislative majorities shift from Democratic to Republican control. Thus, it has yet to become a mutually endorsed covenant or officially implemented policy. Perhaps the incoming leaders will recognizethe nonpartisan benefits of continuing pursuit of an agreement. The Tribal-Commonwealth Accord could provide a pathway for transcending partisan politics and a mutually beneficial path forward for all those residing within the state's boundaries.

Conclusion

On November 18, 2021, Virginia governor Northam issued Executive Order 82, "Consultation with Federally Recognized Tribal Nations for Environmental and Historic Permits and Reviews."[46] While this order basically affirms the state's commitment to existing federal laws requiring consultation with federally recognized Tribes, such as the Native American Graves Protection and Repatriation Act[47] and Tribal-specific provisions of legislation such as the Clean Air Act,[48] it is the first sign of the Commonwealth's commitment to the proposed accord. However, the future of any order or agreement issued by an outgoing Democratic administration in a state that transitioned to a Republican majority is uncertain given the divisive political atmosphere endemic throughout the country. During his first weeks in office in 2022, the new governor, Glen Youngkin, removed all references to EO 82 from his official website, an action that seems to indicate his administration is not likely to formalize these commitments.

The Chiefs of these seven federally recognized Tribes are the primary agents advancing the draft Tribal-Commonwealth Accord and subsequent dialogue. This may draw scrutiny from those who assume that federal recognition places these leaders in a privileged position; however, I would argue that it instead places them in a position of extreme responsibility. Nonetheless, Indian policy is, more often than not, an affair of bipartisan ignorance or nonpartisan competence in as much as policymakers who have made the effort to learn about Indian law realize that it is rooted in diplomacy and not the politics of race or identity. It is the persistence of Indigenous leaders that has usually prompted such education.

Glen Coulthard, a Canadian Dineh scholar, echoes the concerns of many Indigenous scholars and activists that the politics of recognition "in its contemporary liberal form promises to reproduce the very configurations of colonialist, racist, patriarchal state power that Indigenous peoples' demands for recognition have historically sought to transcend."[49] Coulthard's critique is based on broader historical analyses of the impact of colonialism on the consciousness of Indigenous peoples, and certainly underscores the efficacy of "divide-and-rule" tactics in many circumstances. It is important to realize, however, that at various points in time many Indigenous communities have pursued tactics of invisibility, what Edward Spicer called "cultural blind spots," in order to survive.[50] This is largely the case with most Tribes located within Virginia. Even those who could not be deliberately invisible—such as the Pamunkey and Mattaponi Tribes—used ingenious means of preserving traditional institutions within western institutions, such as churches and legal mechanisms regarding land trust. Their willingness to now actively engage in the politics of recognition is grounded in generations of experience. The pursuit of recognition—which does not end with the legal conveyance of Tribal status but continues as Tribes continuously assert their sovereign rights—means being recognized as true partners at the table.

Considering that the campaign to attain federal recognition through legislation took more than two decades for the six Tribes acknowledged in 2018—and even longer for the Pamunkey Tribe's success through administrative recognition—there is reason to have faith in the tenacity of Tribal leaders. As is almost always the case in Indian affairs, the burden of educating policymakers and the public is on Indigenous delegates. These leaders had to convince multiple administrations and legislative constituencies that such recognition was no threat to the Commonwealth in order to gain support from congressional delegates and sponsors. Some of these leaders have openly endorsed both Democratic and Republican candidates in specific elections, and many know the intricate nuances of Virginia lawmaking and procedural implementation better than most freshman lawmakers.

As Deloria pointed out, "negotiation is the essence of the treaty process,"[51] and for Tribal leaders within Virginia it has never been extinguished, regardless of policies deliberately and openly crafted to do just that. Thus, in a time when scholars of Indian law and policy are once again attempting to "restate"[52] Indian law and policy as a coherent and organic canon based on mutual respect, the Tribal-Commonwealth Accord may evolve beyond a movement and into a blueprint for normalizing government-to-government relations in a manner that is designed to include Indigenous diplomatic discourse.

CHAPTER 8

NATIVE VETERANS, POLITICAL PARTICIPATION, AND CULTURAL CONSERVATION

Tom Holm

In the not-too-distant past, I was discharged from the US Marine Corps and immediately enrolled at the University of Oklahoma in Norman. I became involved in the Sequoyah Club, the OU chapter of the National Indian Youth Council (NIYC) and the local branch of the Vietnam Veterans Against the War. Before I arrived in Norman, NIYC and the members of the Sequoyah Club had protested the football team's mascot known as Little Red and began a campaign against displaying Native remains at the Stovall Museum. As a consequence of my involvement in these organizations, I was able to hear, meet, and shake the hands of Muhammad Ali, Carter Camp, Vernon Bellecourt, and John Kerry. Later, while in graduate school there, my friend Jerry Bread got me involved in establishing an American Indian Studies program and an American Indian Graduate Student organization. It was quite a time in the early 1970s.

My second teaching job was at the University of Wisconsin–Milwaukee. While there, I met Irene Mack, Wallace Pyawasit, and John Boatman, all of whom have passed on but who left the Native people of Wisconsin with a sense of pride in their heritage and the fact that they played a great part in developing Native American studies and programs for the benefit of Native people outside the university. I heard John Trudell speak, and one of my students at the time told me that Trudell was also a veteran of Vietnam, serving in the US Navy.

The experience in Milwaukee was pivotal because a number of Native activists—especially urban Indian activists—passed through there. One was especially important to me: Vine Deloria, Jr. In late 1979, Vine asked me to come to the University of Arizona. Because a blizzard had just hit Milwaukee, I immediately said yes to his offer. My wife, Ina, packed up the kids and off we went by way of Oklahoma to Tucson, arriving there on the afternoon of January 1, 1980.

For a year or so, Vine and I worked closely together in the Political Science Department as part of the MA program in American Indian Policy and Law that he inspired and bulldozed through the faculty and dean's office. After Scott Momaday, Leslie Silko, and Robert K. Thomas were recruited, we worked on a stand-alone program in Indian studies featuring an interdisciplinary MA.

Vine was quite a taskmaster in the MA program. I served more or less as the complaint department—probably because I was around the same age as our graduate students. At one time, he suggested that I do a comprehensive study of the Indian Appropriation Acts, not only to see how much was spent over the years on Indians but also to look into added-on provisions, such as ending treaty-making in 1871. I was already heavily involved in doing research on Native veterans, especially of the Vietnam War, and had to put off the appropriations inquiry to some other time. I never got around to it.

As a result of my research and background, I was asked to serve on two Veterans' Administration Commissions, a workshop on Native veterans at the National Congress of American Indians conference, and to testify before a Senate subcommittee on Indian affairs. At that time, academic departments were a bit more congenial than today. We went to lunch, played poker, and often met informally to talk over ideas and policies. Vine once brought up the question of whether Indian veterans were more politically active in Tribal government than nonveterans. He also pointed out that I, as a Marine veteran, was advocating change in the Veterans Administration to include more Native veterans in VA programs. He added, jokingly, that he thought I was "mad because you didn't get a parade" upon my return from Vietnam. I did get back at him by reminding him that he was a Marine veteran with his own extensive activism on behalf of Indian people. I, also jokingly, added that I thought he was mad because the Marine Corps didn't make him a drill instructor so that he could make some poor recruit's life miserable.

Vine Deloria, Jr. was a scholar-activist who, as I mentioned, was a fellow veteran of the US Marine Corps. He liked to use his gruff, Marine Corps voice at times, and I think I was the only one who noticed. But more importantly, Deloria spoke for those of us who felt deeply the cognitive dissonance of joining a branch of the military service even as we were marginalized and robbed of our lands, treaty rights, and cultural heritage. Whether or not he was a fighter as the Marine Corps had taught him to be is irrelevant; he was a champion of Native rights and cultural conservation.

In addition to looking into PTSD (post-traumatic stress disorder) among Native veterans and how they have fared since going off to war, I decided to note those veterans who were politically active and/or deeply involved in preserving their Tribal cultures. I also looked at those who were active in arts and letters and who, like Deloria's own writings, advocated for Native American cultural preservation, Tribal sovereignty, and US policy change. I found a long list of veteran contributions in those particular arenas.

Among the firsts, inevitably, is the late Billy Frank, Jr., a citizen of the Nisqually Nation in Washington State. Even before Frank enlisted in the Marine Corps, he had been arrested while exercising his own Tribal fishing rights. That arrest set him on the path of protesting and asserting the treaties his people made with the federal government, especially fishing the rivers and streams of the state of Washington. Frank's activism and willingness to be incarcerated for a cause would eventually lead to the series of Washington state "fish-ins." Without detailing all of the actions and court cases that were a part of the Tribes' fight to exercise their right to fish the rivers of the state, Frank, along with Hank Adams and support from a number of organizations, and big names, like Marlon Brando, sparked the movement. Frank would go on to say that he had been arrested more than fifty times since 1945, but his numerous detentions did not deter him. Ultimately, the Washington versus Native American fishing fight led to the filing of *United States v. Washington*, which resulted in the Boldt decision and a reaffirmation of Native treaty rights—or at least a decision not to interfere with those rights. Frank passed away in 2014, and the next year he was posthumously awarded the Presidential Medal of Freedom by President Barack Obama.[1]

One of the most famous Native war veterans took an active part in a heated controversy in Los Angeles in 1947. Early that year, Superior Court Judge Ruben S. Schmidt ruled against a Native woman who had been sued on the basis that she and her husband had violated the perpetual deed restriction that forbade occupancy by a person or persons of non-Caucasian decent. Isabel Crocker, a Seneca Indian originally from Pennsylvania, along with her three daughters, were ordered to vacate their home. Her husband, Harry, was allowed to stay because he was of French and English ancestry. The Crockers had argued that Isabel was three-fourths Seneca, and that the deed restriction violated public policy, the state constitution, and the Fourteenth Amendment to the Constitution of the United States.[2]

The racism involved in the Crockers' case stirred the ire of one prominent Native American veteran. Will Rogers, Jr., who had served in the US Army and was wounded in Europe, took up the cause and helped organize the American Indian Citizens' League (AICL). Several Hollywood actors with Native backgrounds joined, including Chief Thundercloud, who played Tonto at one time, and character actor Monte Blue, a heartthrob in silent movies and who claimed Cherokee and Osage descent. To support the Crockers, Rogers and the AICL organized a large rally on March 24, 1947, at Hollywood High. Ira Hayes, an Akimel O'odham from the Gila River Indian Community and one of the Marines in the famous Joe Rosenthal photograph of the flag raising on Mount Suribachi during the terrible fighting on Iwo Jima, was recruited to give a speech at the rally. Hayes and Henry Reed, a survivor of the Bataan Death March, even met with Mayor Fletcher Bowron of Los Angeles to plead the Crockers' case. Ultimately, the restrictive deeds were made, more or less, void in the seminal court case *Shelley v. Kraemer*, in which the Supreme Court ruled that under the Fourteenth Amendment to the Constitution a state cannot void a person's property rights based on race.[3]

Hayes would be involved in advocacy on several levels, including advocating that the Bureau of Indian Affairs be compelled to stay out of his own reservation's politics. In his time in Washington, D.C., Hayes pleaded with the federal government to restore Akimel O'odham water rights.[4]

Veteran activism on behalf of treaty rights, good government, cultural preservation, and Tribal sovereignty continued throughout the 1950s through the 1970s. By and large, the earliest Native protests of that era revolved around the controversial federal policies of termination and relocation. The fish-ins of the 1960s led to more militant protests during the 1970s. Both the civil rights movement and the war in Vietnam seemed to spur a renewed, and even more righteous and expanded advocacy of political and social change. As Paul C. Rosier wrote: "As during the 1950s, when Native leaders promoted themselves as "First Americans" more patriotic than government officials, a new generation of Native activists emerging from the crucible of Vietnam took the moral high ground to exemplify American national honor at a time when it was eroding at home and abroad, especially among newly recognized Third World nations, articulating the notion that treaties are sacred international documents that know no temporal or spatial limits."[5]

Native Vietnam veterans were well-represented in all of the seminal Native American protests of the late 1960s and early 1970s: The Alcatraz occupation, the Trail of Broken Treaties, and the Wounded Knee occupation. An Apache Vietnam veteran, Anthony Garcia, organized the first landing on Alcatraz, and several other Vietnam veterans related their combat experience in Vietnam with the struggle for Native rights at home.[6] Woody Kipp, a Blackfeet Marine Vietnam veteran, dealt with this idea in his fine autobiography, *Viet Cong at Wounded Knee*. Kipp, while serving as an engineer in the war, came to know first-hand the Vietnamese battle for self-determination and sovereignty. He took part in the occupation of Wounded Knee with the understanding that he had become the insurgent—like the Viet Cong—enemy of the United States. Kipp viewed himself and his fellow Native activists as comrades in arms besieged in Wounded Knee as partisans fighting against colonial rule. Eventually, Kipp became an instructor at Blackfeet Community College.[7]

The Vietnam veteran contingency at Wounded Knee II was large indeed. Oglala veteran Buddy Lamont was killed just a day before the agreement to end the siege of Wounded Knee. Former Oglala president, the late Enos Poor Bear, lamented the fact that his son, a paratrooper who was wounded in Vietnam, was shot during the siege by federal marshals. *Akwesasne Notes*, a Native newspaper of the day, summed up the connection between Vietnam and Wounded Knee II:

"The young men defending Wounded Knee are militarily skilled and trained. Almost all are Vietnam veterans. . . . In Southeast Asia, they learned about guerilla warfare, courtesy of the U.S. Government, and now they are using what they learned for their people."[8]

Their willingness to endure gunfire once again could have to do with cognitive dissonance. They had served in the military and had seen combat in Vietnam. To come home, take part in a protest against how their people have been treated, to be surrounded by men in uniform with military-type vehicles, and to be fired on by those uniformed men must have induced a level of anger that was not easily shaken off.

One of our colleagues at the University of Arizona, Robert K. Thomas, once described colonialism as the deprivation of experience. Deloria, in one of our discussions, explained the idea further. Essentially, the deprivation of experience is, or was, the inability of a people to experience change on their own terms. Colonialism replaces a group's language, substitutes another version of history, forces a change in the way humans relate to one another, compels adherence to a different system of religious observances (ceremonial change), and attempts (and too often succeeds) to reduce the size of the colonized peoples' national territorial expanse. All too often the colonized group has to struggle simply to maintain their national identity. The conflict, then, narrows to simple survival, both individually and collectively. And it is this conflict that forced some Native American servicemen to rethink their ideas of patriotism and service and identify with the Vietnamese and their desire to throw off French and American interference in determining their own national political destiny.

Other veterans focused their talents on challenges within their nations. For example, Apesanakwat, a Marine Vietnam veteran, was not only an actor of repute and an originator of the Indian Gaming Regulatory Act, he also served as Tribal chairman of the Menominee Nation for a record eight terms. My own old friends, Richard Allen and the late Rogan Noble, both Marine Vietnam veterans, served the Cherokee Nation for many years. Allen was a policy analyst for Chief Wilma Mankiller and Noble was the first director of the Cherokee Nation's veterans' services.

Native veteran writers, like Woody Kipp, stand out as both humanist contributors to literature and activists determined to preserve their cultures. Perhaps the perfect example of a writer/poet/cultural activist is the late Jim Northrup. He was another Marine Vietnam veteran who returned home to his Fond du Lac Anishinaabe reservation to write seven books. Northrup's prose and poetry were humorous, but his subtle critiques of society in general, his stint in Vietnam, and his understanding of his people's history and culture were both enlightening and highly readable. He was a teacher of the Ojibwe language and actually practiced his traditional ways with ricing, maple syrup harvesting, and basketry, and he certainly liked the idea of being a storyteller in the old way. He once wrote in his self-deprecating way: "I used to be known as a bullshitter, but that didn't pay anything. I began calling myself a storyteller—a little better, more prestige—but it still didn't pay anything. I became a freelance writer. At first it was more free than lance."[9]

Northrup's short critique of the Indian boarding school experience—he attended Pipestone Indian School—is not only succinct but biting and ironic: "There's an expression in Ojibwe, pronounced 'hai.' It's like showing sympathy. As I was getting off the bus [to attend the Pipestone School] for the first time, I said that to someone who tripped. I got slapped by the matron, who said, 'You don't use that kind of language here.'"[10] The matron's particular words were likely reserved for putting a stop to the use of profanity. Yet Northrup's ironic story suggests that the matron was inferring that the Ojibwe language was vulgar, blasphemous, and sacrilegious.

Simply looking over what a few Native veterans have contributed to either their home communities or to Native issues generally led me to undertake what became a rather fruitless survey of more than one hundred Native Tribal governments. I asked, on a single sheet of paper, how many veterans served as members of the Tribal council or the judiciary, and whether their Tribal chairperson was a veteran. This survey took place in 2002, so it would still be hopelessly out of date even if the Tribes had rewarded me with returning the filled-out surveys.

Yet the nineteen surveys that were returned produced some interesting information. There was enough, in fact, that the notion deserves further study. In seven out of nineteen Tribal councils, more than half were veterans. The judiciary systems were seemingly packed with veterans. There were veterans who served as cultural advisors to the courts as well as judges in the highest courts. At that time, nine out of the nineteen had a veteran serving as the Tribal chairperson, governor, or chief administrative officer. Four Tribes had vice or assistant executives.

If nothing else, the survey begs the question of why veterans are seemingly overrepresented in Tribal government, activist groups, and in the use of prose and poetry to advocate for Native rights, sovereignty, and cultural conservancy. Perhaps they are not really disproportionately represented. What I have found over the years is that, compared to non-Natives, Native Americans serve in the military in numbers far exceeding their proportional population. During the Vietnam War, for example, non-Native draftees and enlistments totaled around 3 percent of the total population. Native Americans, during the war, enlisted or were drafted at a rate of nearly 10 percent of the total Native population—more than three times the percent of non-Native to their population. It stands to reason, then, that Native Tribes have more veterans per capita to pick from to fill Tribal political and judicial positions. Likewise, there are more veterans to write about or take part in cultural conservation or political activism.

If Native Americans enter military service in disproportional numbers relative to their population, the question that must be asked is: Why do Natives sign up in the first place? Many fought in World War I even when they were not citizens of the United States. And during the Second World War, Nazi radio broadcasters thought it strange that Native people would fight for their oppressors.

There are numerous reasons underlying the Native American seeming propensity to serve in the US military. In 1981, Cynthia Enloe published her excellent study entitled *Ethnic Soldiers: State Security in a Divided Society.* Enloe demonstrated that settler and colonial state elites recruit for, or simply allow, Indigenous or ethnic people to join the state military services according to two general criteria. The first is whether the ethnic or Indigenous group is politically reliable—that is to say, safe. The second criterion concerns a group's perceived military proclivities. In the 1850s, the British coined the term "martial race" to designate those groups in India that had maintained a kind of warrior spirit and, of course, had rebelled against British colonial rule. In short, a martial race was fearsome and not politically reliable. The martial race had to be tamed before it could be useful to the colonizers.[11]

Native Americans, almost from the start of the European invasion of North America, fell into the category of the martial race. In American folklore Indians have attacked peaceful wagon trains, dashed out the brains of white children, toasted hapless frontiersmen at the stake, raped hundreds of beautiful white women, scalped innocent pioneers, and treacherously murdered and mutilated thousands of gallant soldiers in unprovoked ambushes. Native Americans became part of the white man's mythos of a great blood sacrifice that ultimately spread "Western Civilization" across the continent. Of course, Europeans made peace and friendship treaties with Native peoples and, for the most part, failed to enforce them. Meanwhile, the Native Nations, because of the utter failure of the whites to abide by their agreements, were forced to embrace militarism simply to protect their national territories and cultures. In the minds of the colonizing Europeans, Native Americans were a so-called martial race. And since the founding of the United States, Native nations, as a result of treaties, were deployed as allies and auxiliaries of the American state. Native Americans fought against other Native nations, against the British in the Revolution and in the War of 1812, and in the Mexican War. Natives also fought with both Union and Confederate troops during the Civil War. The Indian Scouting Service was formed in 1866, and there was an attempt to form several companies of Native Americans in the US Army during the 1890s. Natives charged up San Juan Hill with Teddy Roosevelt and went in pursuit of Pancho Villa with General Pershing. If any group of people has developed a military tradition in the United States, Native Americans have to be placed at the top of the list.

By the end of the nineteenth century, whites began to view Native Americans as having been pacified, either by military force, a precipitous decline in population, or by the effects of a policy to assimilate Native peoples into the mainstream of society. This pacification process supposedly turned Native Americans into a politically reliable, or at least a safe, minority group. Still, this extensive service does not fully explain why Native Americans, who have been so ill-served by the United States, enter the military is such high numbers.

I have been looking into this phenomenon for more than forty years and can offer only a few ideas. Several Native veterans have asserted that poverty drove them into the service. "Three hots and a cot," said one. Another offered, "First time I had a pair of pants what weren't passed down." Some referenced family traditions. A few I interviewed for my *Strong Hearts, Wounded Souls: Native American Veterans of the Vietnam War* could trace US military service from their fathers who served in World War II, to grandfathers who served in World War I, and to ancestors who served in the Indian Scouting Service. Two Vietnam veterans even mentioned their treaty obligations in their decision to join the service.

But a healthy majority of the veterans I've talked to over the years alluded to the idea that they had cultural or traditional incentives to enter military service. From the perspective of many modern scholars, some Tribes had no real warrior traditions. The Hopi people, for example, are often depicted in the literature on the matter as complete pacifists. Yet the Hopi recognized the Twin War Gods, the grandsons of Spider Woman, as major deities, as did the Zuni. They are depicted as young men who were the protectors of the people. The Pueblo peoples and many sedentary peoples are viewed as basically peaceful, like the Akimel O'odham and many of the Indigenous peoples of what is now California. I would contend that this is simply a modern stereotype based on the western concept of warfare rather than on Native American notions of why, how, and when human beings should take part in organized violence. Some Tribes practiced highly ritualized forms of warfare. Many Tribes raided others for goods and even for captives to replace the dead, both spiritually and physically (mourning war). Most Tribes had ceremonies that helped their people cross the line between war and peace and back again, whether to honor the warrior's bravery or to purge the combatant of the trauma and the malignant spirits that might emerge from the chaos and death of combat.

Warriorhood was almost universally part and parcel of the societal expectations of young men. In many societies there are few ways for young males to gain high status except in war. Older men can have political, economic, and even spiritual influence in society. According to historian Gwynne Dyer, Native American battles were "not lethal, nor even very destructive . . . individuals get killed, a few at a time—mostly young males, who are both biologically and economically the most dispensable of the tribe—but the society itself survives intact."[12] Or, as Creek Micco Efau Harjo said in 1802 during a treaty negotiation: "There is among us Four Nations [Creek, Cherokee, Choctaw, and Chickasaw] old customs, one of which is war. If the young men, having grown to manhood, wish to practice the ways of the old people, let them try themselves at war, and when they have tried let the chiefs interpose and stop it. We want you to leave us alone."[13]

Turning once again to Cynthia Enloe's *Ethnic Soldiers*, she outlines several ideas about why minority members of a given settler or colonial state might enter military service. The first explains this willingness as a desire on the part of the ethnic soldiers to become fully accepted members of the state. Simply put, if one is willing to serve, then one has status even within a stratified, and frankly racist, society. The Japanese American entrance and record of valor in the US Army during World War II is an example of this desire.[14] Another explanation is what might be called the Gurkha experience in the British military. The Gurkhas are a group of people who live in several mountain villages in Nepal. The British recruit the young men from these villages to serve in special Gurkha units with distinctive uniforms, military rituals, and even weapons. They join because their fathers before did so, and they send part of their paychecks back to their home villages. In short, they contribute to their village economies and the maintenance of their local customs. They typically return to their homes and are given valued status and often become leaders within their communities.[15]

I have argued that the Native American experience in the US military services leans toward the Gurkha example. A very solid number of veterans take part in ceremonies that either honor or attempt to rid them of the trauma of war. Retirees contribute to their local ceremonial cycle and, as has been demonstrated, take an active role in local politics and the maintenance of Tribal custom.

They, too, are, in many cases, given valued status, and, if they have demonstrated the traditional virtues of generosity, humility, honesty, and courage, they will attain leadership roles. Even when the war itself was not looked upon favorably, Native peoples seemed to honor their sacrifice above all else. The warrior was more important than the war. As one Lakota woman put it, "Most people here don't like the war at all, but they don't like those Indians boys who are draft dodgers either."[16]

It seems that Native American veterans can and do take pride in being accepted in their communities as "warriors" in the Tribal sense of the word rather than as soldiers or sailors or airmen who served their time in the US armed forces. Native communities, in turn, acknowledge their service in terms that the veterans fought for their people rather than a government. The veterans' willingness to endure the exigencies of combat gives them value as knowledgeable individuals worthy of becoming leaders. As a Ho-Chunk Elder said at a powwow in Wisconsin nearly a half century ago, "We honor our veterans for their bravery and because by seeing death on the battlefield they truly know the greatness of life."[17]

CHAPTER 9

ON VINE'S SHOULDERS

Megan Minoka Hill and Norbert S. Hill, Jr.

In 1978, Vine participated in a moderated discussion at the University of Arizona called "Words and Place: A Conversation with Vine Deloria, Jr."[1] With horn-rimmed glasses, cigarette in hand, he reflected on ideological and practical mismatches between the white and the Indian worlds. The white world, he explained, could not bear the realities of the Indian world and was singularly bound to its own cultural worldview. Because of this, Indians and Indian ways of thinking were sidelined as convenient stereotypes and tropes that conformed to the mainstream narrative. To feel safe, white America preferred non-Indian experts to tell them about Tribes, the truth lost in translation and often resulting in disastrous federal Indian policies. He'd come to realize that the only way to confront this marginalization was to attack the foundations of white ethos. In doing so, Vine called for a generation of well-educated Indians who could "tear social sciences to pieces"—a generation, firmly grounded in their own Indian identities and cultures, who could introduce new questions and bring nonlinear interpretations of world history forth to both set the record straight and chart the future.

Vine was forty-five years old at the time of the interview, and Indian Country was on the cusp of an Indigenous political renaissance in the United States, propelled, in large part, by the ideas he set forth in *Custer Died for Your Sins: An Indian Manifesto* and *Behind the Trial of Broken Treaties: An Indian Declaration of Independence*. These books set the stage for the passage of the Indian Self-Determination and Education Assistance Act (PL-638) in 1975, yielding greater governing power to Tribal governments to achieve their own priorities, on their own terms.

Vine was a truth-teller. With piercing wit, he observed and exposed hypocrisy and patterns of inequity, lighting the way forward. His messages put language to the Indian experience, unveiling truths and realities that weren't yet conscious. He invited us to rethink structures and systems and reject so-called universal truths. While Vine's books and interviews are locked in time, Indian Country collectively stands on his shoulders, his ideas resonating even more strongly than when he first shared them.

Today, we find Indian Country on the threshold of a new and potentially significant transformation. With COVID-19 federal relief funds from the Coronavirus Aid, Relief, and Economic Security Act and the subsequent $32.5 billion in American Relief Plan Act (ARPA) funds designated for Tribal governments, Tribes have an unprecedented opportunity to build and transform their nations in ways that simultaneously benefit their citizens and uphold cultural values. Large-scale, long-lasting, and desperately needed investments in infrastructure are possible and could significantly improve both standards of living and life outcomes for generations of Native people.

With this opportunity, however, comes responsibility. To achieve the greatest long-term impact from these funds, Tribal leaders must think strategically, their vision benefiting from the Haudenosaunee seventh-generation principal, which asks leaders to base their decisions on the potential impact hundreds of years in the future. As leaders determine how to best invest the relief funds, they have an additional opportunity and duty to reclaim their foundational governing documents in ways that reflect who they are as Indian people, operating in a contemporary world, and also to invest in the next generation of leadership who can continue to reframe the past, understand the present, and create the future informed by Indigenous values.

There is great hope. Since Vine's seminal work, Tribe after Tribe has exercised their sovereignty and expanded their self-governing powers to serve their people, their actions implicitly answering a question Vine posed in an article for *Indian Country Today* that strikes at the very core of nation-building efforts throughout Indian Country. In it, he asked, "Are we building nations or are we dissolving communities?"[2]

A Marshall Plan for Indian Country?

When the coronavirus began to encroach upon Indian lands in the early spring of 2020, Tribal Nations immediately enacted orders to keep their citizens and their regions safe. They were the first governments in the country to issue stay-at-home orders, shuttering schools and businesses. Yet they still experienced both the highest COVID-19 infection and death rates compared to all other US populations.[3]

Outbreaks of coronavirus in Indian Country mirrored outbreaks anywhere in the world with hotspots associated with super-spreader events, be they religious or social. The key difference for Indian Country was its starting place; the pandemic added extreme stress to an already stressed situation. Research found that the high rates were due in large part to several infrastructure-driven factors, including access to potable water, adequate housing, linguistically and culturally relevant communications, and broadband connectivity. Of course, underlying all this, were abysmal chronic health disparities, reflecting generations of persistent underinvestment and underfunding of health-care systems compounded by the legacy of colonialism and institutional racism.[4]

At its core, the COVID-19 pandemic has revealed the weak points of many nations, including Tribal Nations. The crisis has highlighted systems that aren't working, have been long ignored, and have been Band-Aided over for generations. Almost four decades ago, with the release of *The Nations Within: The Past and Future of American Indian Sovereignty*, Vine observed a need for governments to update their structures and services to meet the current needs of their citizens, saying, "Tribal governments, like cities and counties, are facing a time when radical changes in the structure of government must take place. The town square, main street, and agency headquarters have all become vestiges of the past. New ways of providing services, and indeed new services, are required."[5] Unfortunately, for many governments, cities, and Tribes alike, radical updates were not initiated, and arguably the impact of the virus was exacerbated by both inaction and inertia.

Indian Country cannot afford to look the other way anymore. More crises will come; it is not a matter of *if*, it is *when*. More than ever, it is important for Tribal Nations to engage in nation building, exercising their self-determination, building key infrastructure, revising their governing institutions, and growing the next generation of leaders in ways that are culturally aligned and sustainable. The time is now, and so is the opportunity.

On March 11, 2021, ARPA was signed into law. It is not just another federal grant program that will cycle back around in a year or two. Amounting to $32.5 billion and aimed at assisting Tribes recover from the pandemic, it is a potential Marshall Plan for Indian Country. It is the largest infusion of federal funding into Indian Country in the history of the United States. The funds present a once-in-a-lifetime chance for Tribal governments to invest, build, and transform their nations.

This funding is long overdue. Decades of underinvestment have created a quagmire of need, which, as noted earlier, directly resulted in Tribal Nations aggregately experiencing the highest infection and death rates of COVID-19 in the US. With ARPA funds, Tribes can update water systems, build necessary housing, and develop effective broadband infrastructure.

It is too early to know if Indian Country will take full advantage of the promise of ARPA. Like drinking from a fire hose, Tribal leaders are tasked with pivoting quickly and spending the funds by the US Treasury's deadline. Although not contradictory to the Treasury's spending guidelines, it is concerning to observe Tribes directing significant portions of these funds as per capita payments to their citizens. While it is unquestionable that individuals have suffered tremendous human and financial loss during the pandemic, distributing the rescue package funds on a per capita basis may be short-sighted. If history is a teacher, these individual distributions will only offer short-term relief. Instead, if, as Vine suggested, Tribal governments assess, invest in, and update their services and the systems that deliver services, it may seed a long-lasting environment of opportunity, abundance, and sustainability for their citizens.

Given the possibilities ARPA offers, Tribes must continue to update and refine their governing documents and especially their criteria detailing who is and who isn't a citizen, to ensure they position and strengthen their governments in ways that can meet the moment today and tomorrow.

A Chicken Pot Pie

What do you get when a Potawatomi and a Chippewa have a child? A Potato Chip! How about a Chickasaw, a Potawatomi, and a Paiute? A Chicken Pot Pie! This is a joke comedian Charlie Hill often told at his gigs. Native audiences would roar with laughter, tears running down their faces. Charlie, like Vine, had a gift for truth-telling. Simultaneously funny and biting, these jokes laid out the most serious challenge to the survival of Tribes in the US today. Continuing with the food metaphor, unwinding and bringing clarity to the complexities of Tribal citizenship was once likened to a bowl of spaghetti by Vine in a 2005 interview.[6] Love and connection notwithstanding, children resulting from mixed unions pose a problem of Indian survival, especially when many Tribes continue to use blood quantum as the primary measurement of citizenship. It is a complex challenge with no clear solution, but one that has revealed itself to be central to the future survival of Native people throughout the US. Today, Tribes must reevaluate citizenship and naturalization and what it means to be Native.

Identifying who a nation's citizens are (or aren't) is the most sovereign act a government can undertake. With mortality rates increasing due to an aging population and low birth rates, the number of recognized Tribal citizens is on the decline. Given these trends, blood quantum has become the most compelling issue this century for Indian Country. Initially imposed by the federal government and now internalized by many

Tribal Nations as the primary mechanism to define Tribal citizenship, measures of blood have shaped Native identity, unilaterally deciding "Who is an Indian?" While most Natives can agree that blood quantum is not sustainable over time, agreeable solutions remain evasive. Addressing these changing demographics is a race against time.

The good news is that across Indian Country, many Tribes have heeded Vine's call to reevaluate and update their governing structures. From Ysleta del Sur Pueblo[7] to the Citizen Potawatomi Nation,[8] Tribes are relying on their core values to rewrite constitutions and enact contemporary citizenship policies to reflect and sustain their nations. Yet still, too many Tribes remain bound by the 1934 Indian Reorganization Act (IRA) constitutions and measurements of blood quantum. Not surprisingly, these constitutions were not written to assist Tribes govern. In both word and action, these documents shrank the governing powers of Tribes, disrupting not only traditional ways of governance but also traditional ways of determining citizenship that had thrived for millennia. Without changing these imposed, foreign, and short-sighted citizenship criteria, any investments in Indian Country are futile; without citizens, Tribal Nations, which have survived millennia, will disappear and be relegated to footnotes in history books.

My dad (and coauthor of this chapter) tells the story of his first job interview. Sitting in front of a panel, he was asked, "Norbert, why are you an Indian?" Without skipping a beat, he replied, "It came with the body." It was an inappropriate question to ask in a professional interview, even in 1971. Yet, it is a good question and perhaps a good place to start when reimagining Tribal citizenship criteria. Tribal Nations can only benefit by reflecting on and processing targeted questions on collective and individual identities to reframe criteria. We might ask, what does it mean to be Indian? What does it mean to be a citizen of a nation? What is a citizen's responsibility to that nation? What are the ways language, land, and culture factor into identity and citizenship? What is the role of *benefits*? What is the result of doing nothing? And, ultimately, why does it matter?

Succession or Serendipity?

As a tenured university professor with advanced degrees in theology and law, Vine was acutely aware of the limitations and even casualties of earning a western education as a Native person. He often spoke and wrote about the ways the US education system stripped away Indigenous ways of thinking. Politically, he wondered how such degrees prepared Indian students to exercise self-determination and lead their nations when their preparations were led and certified by non-Native expectations. He worried that without interventions to contextualize the education of Native people in Indigenous worldviews, "we will find that we are basically agreeing to model our lives, values, and experiences along non-Indian lines."[9]

Of course, that was the point. General Pratt's *Save the Man, Kill the Indian* mantra fueled the Indian boarding school era. Children were torn away from their families, some at gunpoint, to any number of schools dotting the country. Forbidden to speak their language or practice their traditions, these children faced untold cruelties as they were indoctrinated into western society, turning them into farmers and domestics. Today we are starting to learn of the magnitude of those traumas, with heartbreaking images of rusty, toddler-sized handcuffs populating our social media feeds along with painful stories of abuse, amplified by the relentless unearthing of schoolyard cemeteries.

While the boarding school era has ended, reverberations of those assimilationist policies remain alive in school curricula today, prioritizing revisionist history and locking Natives in a convenient, one-dimensional past. Thankfully, this is changing and with the noted expanded investments in infrastructure fueled by ARPA, Tribes also have an invitation to reconsider leadership succession planning thoughtfully.

Already, Tribal governments are exercising their self-determination, reclaiming lesson plans and challenging state standards to tell their truths. Examples are multiplying from the Chickaloon Native Village's Ya Ne Dah Ah School,[10] which elevates Ahtna Athabascan cultural practices by integrating traditional teachings into all classes from math to science to social studies—to the Agua Caliente Band of Mission Indians' People Curriculum[11] that spearheaded a unique partnership between the Tribe, the school district, and the district's foundation to reclaim and rewrite curricula for third, eighth, and eleventh graders, teaching each the region's Indigenous truth—to the Akwesasne Freedom School,[12] an intergenerational language immersion school, which opens the day with the Haudenosaunee Thanksgiving Address and conducts all classes in the Mohawk language.

Each of these programs imbue education with Indigenous ways of being and are creating learning environments that reveal and reinforce identities and connection to each other and their respective Tribal Nations. These programs, and others like them, are just the beginning. While an essential start, succession planning doesn't end with the decolonization of education. Indian Country must also decolonize succession planning if we are to grow the cadre of prepared, future leaders that Vine hoped for.

The sad truth is that sometimes many of us in Indian Country aren't good at building each other up; we are good at pointing out mistakes and remembering those shortcomings. Perhaps unsurprisingly, this isn't a winning model for effective succession planning. What if, instead, Tribal governments and organizations reclaimed their own leadership systems, informed by core values, to build a pipeline of both knowledge and experience? In Haudenosaunee country, there is a version of this called Ohero:kon, "Under the Husk" Rites of Passage.[13] Over the course of seven years, Ohero:kon revives traditional, intergenerational coming-of-age teachings that nurture Mohawk identity and leadership as their youth become adults. The Leadership Institute at the Santa Fe Indian School[14] also mentors their youth to foster leadership from within, in ways that are firmly rooted in pueblo ethos, critical thinking, and service. Programming bridges participants' sacred responsibility to their pueblos and to themselves as they grapple with and transcend modern demands. At minimum, both programs offer inspiration to other Tribal Nations as they develop their own succession pipelines, and at most, they offer lessons that can be teased out, adapted, and applied to their own context, reflecting their own cultural values. Given the diversity of Indian Country, there is no one way to effectively implement succession and leadership planning. Yet Tribal Nations have a responsibility to encourage and grow their youth in healthy and uplifting ways so that they have the tools to become the leaders they were born to become. Too much is at stake. Succession planning cannot be left to serendipity, otherwise, Indian Country may be left to rely on accidental leaders.

Last Thoughts

Vine's ability to put words to reality continues to offer Tribal Nations the courage and inspiration to chart their own futures on their own terms. The interviews and writings he left behind remind us to honor and prioritize Native ways of being to question and reframe certainties set forth and blindly accepted by the mainstream. With this foundational grounding, the business of Indigenous nation building has a firm foundation on which to flourish. And with it, Indian Country is positioned to make the most of opportunities, like the ARPA relief funds, to build and upgrade infrastructure to better serve community and weather the next crisis. This foundation also sets the footing for Tribal governments to take a hard look at their governing documents, especially those that determine citizenship, and update them to reflect Tribal identities, realities, and future sustainability, including opening opportunities for the young leaders. Vine's work is done, but his shadow is long and Indian Country stands tall on his shoulders.

2

Water

CHAPTER 10

A LETTER TO VINE ON THE VIRTUES OF A GOOD BLADE

Cannupa Hanska Luger

Dear Vine,

We have never met, and yet through the mysteries of genetic memory, my grandfather's cells, in my body, spark recollection in your words.

I couldn't shake the sensation, while reading your books, that I was a child in the living room lying in my grandfather's giant reclining chair pretending to sleep just outside of the kitchen doorway covered in one of my Norwegian grandmother's star quilts overhearing a conversation spoken between sips of weak coffee, the sort that could be drunk well into the night without much disturbance of sleep.

I can smell Old Gold 100s wafting out of the kitchen where these sorts of conversations would happen regularly. The gentle tinkle of spoon and sugar stirring across the rims of Grandma's china perforate the conversation at twenty-minute intervals. The old chairs creak under the weight of these stories as your bodies search for comfort in uncomfortable discussions.

To be transparent, I was born in 1979, a year after our ceremonial life was granted access to religious freedom in America and therefore cannot make sense of this sensation as it seems so real to me and also impossible. I was told by my mother that you did visit my grandparents' place to have conversations with my grandfather Carl.

Perhaps it was the radical imagination of your generation that swept across Indian Country and bloomed in the minds of many men in positions of standing. I was raised on these ideas and still tend the garden beds of their germination. There are a lot of weeds here, rampant patriarchy, intergenerational trauma, and gaps of connection between the generations, ironically due to advancements in communication, and so it goes.

However, in the first chapter of *Custer Died for Your Sins*, you state something that we still face: “The more we try to be ourselves the more we are forced to defend what we have never been”—primarily American. This country is contracting from the pangs of an identity crisis. It has believed too long in a myth of its origins and has been treading across the land like a hoard of amnesiac zombies. As a nation it remains displaced. There is a hole in the environment the shape of human beings, and the people here believe the hole is in themselves.

As a species we have an innate desire to belong to place, but as an experiment this country decided to abolish that desire and force place to belong to it. Most Indigenous people retain that sense of belonging and therefore are immune to the doctrine of American society. Our cultures exist as a mirror that reflects America without its comfortable distortion; this clarity is unnerving and strikes fear in the shallowness of American culture.

I am an artist, a social engineer, building bridges across the chasms of divergent minorities in America to reinforce our intersectional experiences. I came to this position wading across the Indian art market. This market was conceived outside of Indigenous culture and the result commodified our culture to a desperate American population.

Their desperation is a result of the lack of a deep time relationship with place, and so it consumes our history and converts that to anecdotal evidence of their own historical rhetoric. Rename the mountains, rename the rivers. Settler moves to innocence. They fill the curio cabinets of their museums with our lives and deem them dead. We have to navigate dimly lit rooms of the academy to conspire with our relatives sequestered in glass. We demand the opportunity to feed them and maintain them and are hobbled by their efforts to preserve us in stasis.

That level of preservation is pervasive in our own identity. We have, in the minds of the populace, become relics. Honored only as warriors, braves, hyper-masculine tropes of the Super Indian, the medicine man, the shaman—impossible one-dimensional entities forever foreign in the land of our creation, *other.* That honor leaves us reduced and distilled in the mind of America as a simple and brutal word: "enemy." Our existence threatens their wealth as it is by and large extracted from the land they cannot belong to. Our relation to more than human kinships was long ago declared as primitive and yet today co-opted by green industries without acknowledgment of Indigenous protocol or meaning.

You wrote, "The corporation forms the closest attempt of the white man to socialize his individualism and become a tribal man . . . the unfortunate outcome of that tribalism is that it never considered learning from the indigenous tribal communities and instead became the monsters of its own imagination. American corporations have become the 'merciless Indian Savages.'" We are spoken of this way in the Declaration of Independence, and our present population remains the enemy.

And so, we fight to sustain and maintain our cultural values against an industrious Tribe, one that has converted the population to a cargo cult, worshipping gods without names. Set poised at the altars of media screens, the American population on average spends six hours a day muttering their prayers and are rewarded for their time and devotion with belongings, instead of *belonging.* In the same breath they demonize cultures with blood rituals and then demand human sacrifice to oil and sugar.

There is something nefarious in our effort to confront these atrocities; which is, we reinforce the stigmata of the settler colonial gaze. We become enemy, combatants, warriors, and to do this we have to be braves. This time we strive to be warriors by our own definitions. Warriors not out for personal glory but to put themselves in harm's way for the seven generations.

So, I find myself again a child drifting off to sleep in a time that never happened. Overhearing a conversation and commitment to my well-being by my elders. I hear my grandfather say, "It is hard to be an Indian, we value our people more than we value ourselves, we put them first and know that if they are cared for we will be cared for in return. This is contrary to the white man's society in every way, and it surrounds us and that is why it is hard to be an Indian."

Many nights I fell asleep on my grandfather's chair listening to conversations held at that round table in the kitchen where we shared meals with guests that would arrive unannounced. There was always a plate for them. Our generosity is limitless, and that reminds me of a metaphor I use to treat the trauma passed through our genes.

The first knife was created not for combat but for sharing. To divide the harvest carefully for everyone. And how you make a good knife is with heat and pressure. Our people have experienced heat and pressure. My ancestors and I are the tempered spine, and my children are the fine-honed edge of that blade. This reflection helps me find reverence for the suffering of the previous generations—your generation, Vine.

CHAPTER 11

THE WORLD WE STILL LIVE IN (IN HAWAI'I NEI)

Noenoe K. Silva

The World We Used to Live In, one of Vine Deloria, Jr.'s last books, is a tour de force and a provocation to all of us who would like to understand the epistemologies and ontologies of our Indigenous ancestors. Using accounts from a variety of eyewitnesses across North America over several centuries, and by Indigenous persons themselves, he reports on and analyzes relationships and communications that American Indians had with the spirit world, animals, plants, rocks, elements, and sacred places.[1] In our world, Kānaka Hawai'i of the past and present also have analogous relationships with similar entities. In this chapter, I take Deloria's work as a springboard to consider some of the recent twentieth- and twenty-first-century accounts of such relationships. These include calling Pele (the volcano deity) to begin an eruption; having relationships with shark and mo'o (reptilian) ‹aumākua (deified ancestors); and communications and interventions by ‹aumākua, akua, and/or kūpuna o ka pō (ancestors) in the fight to save Maunakea.[2] I draw on personal accounts from the Hawaiian language newspapers, radio interview recordings, written accounts in English, and recent scholarship by Kānaka 'Ōiwi (Native Hawaiians).

In the concluding paragraph to *The World We Used to Live In*, Deloria expresses hope that "Indians will read these stories and know that many powers are available through the ceremonies and rituals of the tribes, and that the powers can be applied to our daily lives to enrich our well-being and enhance our understanding of life in the physical world."[3] We naturally worry that too much knowledge was lost and is now unrecoverable, but our recent ancestors also tell us that they can convey knowledge through dreams and other means.[4] The advances in scholarship that I refer to at the end of the chapter will also help us in this effort and will, no doubt, inspire further work in this endeavor.

Calling Pele to Awaken

Kānaka in the past had a close relationship with Pele, the akua of the volcano. She is considered an akua nui, a major god in the pantheon of four hundred, four thousand, four hundred thousand akua.[5] She is also affectionately called Tūtū Pele, Grandmother Pele. She is both feared and respected, especially when she sends out her destructive burning lava over inhabited land (to create new land), as she did most recently and spectacularly in 2018. Not surprisingly, she is the subject of many mo'olelo (stories), and the epic of her youngest sister, Hi'iakaikapoliopele, is one of the mo'olelo with the most versions published in 'ōlelo Hawai'i.[6]

In the twentieth century and until today, many Kānaka continue a reverent relationship with Pele. People travel on māka'ika'i (journeys to honor *akua* or land) to offer her their gifts, prayers, and kānaenae (chants of supplication or affection). Here I present two twentieth-century accounts of individuals who asked Pele through kānaenae to display her fires and lava, to which she immediately responded affirmatively.

The first is an account of a November 1929 visit to Kīlauea, the crater that contains Pele's home crater of Halema'uma'u. The author is Z. P. Kalokuokamaile, a prolific contributor to the 'ōlelo Hawai'i newspapers in the early to mid-twentieth century, whose knowledge of the language, history, and culture of Kānaka Hawai'i was highly regarded. Kalokuokamaile was a native and lifelong resident of Nāpo'opo'o in South Kona, born there in 1850. He was educated in 'ōlelo Hawai'i in the Calvinist mission primary school and selected to attend secondary school at the mission seminary, Lahainaluna, on Maui, where instruction was also in ʻōlelo Hawaiʻi. He graduated, returned home, and taught school nearby in Keʻei. He was a dedicated member of the Calvinist church and taught Sunday school for decades.

When he was a child he learned from his father and various kāhuna (specialists in various fields) how to build houses in the old Kānaka way; how to carve canoes, including selection and felling of the right trees; how to fish and to make many different kinds of fishing nets; how to grow kalo and other foods; and a vast knowledge of plants and their uses. Between 1914 and 1923, Kalokuokamaile (a.k.a. Kawaikaumaiikamakaokaopua) wrote articles giving names and details of various plants, birds, seaweeds, and shore fish, and details of the construction of the heiau (worship site) Hikiau, as well as several multipart series describing the old ways of canoe carving, house building, and making fishing nets.[7] It was because of these and many other contributions in the papers that he became known as an authority on ʻōlelo Hawaiʻi and mea Hawaiʻi (things Hawaiian).

In 1929, Kīlauea volcano was erupting. Kalokuokamaile wrote his account of the mākaʻikaʻi he took with a friend and members of his family to Kīlauea. I will paraphrase his account, and include a translation of some parts here. On today's highway, the distance between Nāpoʻopoʻo where he was living and Kīlauea is about eighty-two miles, but it was much longer in 1929 before the highway was built. Kalokuokamaile relates that a friend offered to drive them but they couldn't start until four p.m. He thought that was late and worried when they might arrive since the road was known to be "*inoino*," or very bad. His friend didn't pick them up until five p.m, which he grumbled about. And indeed it took them until ten p.m. to reach Kīlauea. When they arrived, the eruption had slowed or stopped; there was nothing much to see. He writes:

Ninau aku la wau ia Mana, he wahi makana kanaenae no ka oukou ia Pele? Hoole like mai la ka poe kanaka e kuku ana ame na wahine, a nui wale aku, ame na poe kaikamahine hookani pila. Aole no nae i hookani i na pila a lakou e paa ana.	I asked Mana (a young man there from Kohala), did any of you offer a gift of a kānaenae (a chant/prayer of praise or supplication) to Pele? All the many men and women crowded around there said they did not. And there were some girls with musical instruments there but they had not played.

He then asked everyone to be quiet while he chanted a *kānaenae* to Pele. He includes in his account an excerpt of what he chanted/prayed.

I ka pau ana o keia mau pauku i ke kanaenaeia, (oia na pauku e kau ae la maluna), ua hoomaka ke ahi e a hanini iwaho o ka lua, a ikeia aku la he kanaka elemakule e haawe ana he ukana ma ke kua, a olelo mai la kekahi poe ia'u, e nana aku oe i kela kanaka e nana mai la ia oe. Aole i liuliu iho, iho ana ka ihu o ka manu a kau ma ka waha o ka lua, a hele ke kino i ka loa o umi kapuai ka loa, a pela no hoi na eheu, hele i ka laula. Aole i nalowale iki keia manu, a ninau mai la ia'u kekahi poe. Heaha la ka manao ame ka hana a keia manu? Ua olelo aku la wau, ua aeia ka kakou pule, a ua hoomaikaiia mai kakou	When these verses were offered, the fire began and the lava flowed out of the crater. An old man carrying a bundle on his back was seen. Some people said to me: "Look at that man who is looking at you." Then the beak of a bird descended and landed on the mouth of the crater; its body was ten feet long and so was its wingspan. It stayed there, and some people asked me, "What is the meaning and the action of this bird?" I replied, "Our prayer request has been granted, and we have been thanked."

He goes on to describe the sight of the lava flow; apparently, it looked like a line of cars (but because they had taken a long and perilous journey in a car, this could also be his sense of humor):

Akahi no a ke ahi a pii pu me ka uwahi, a a-a hoi na kaa oto a ka Luahine Hookalakupua o ka Lua e ku lalani ana, me he mea ala ua hoonohonoho likeia e ka makai.	The fire started to burn and rose up with smoke, and the automobiles of the Magical Old Woman of the Crater were burning, standing in a line as if they had been lined up by an inspector.
A ua helu aku wau a ehiku, e a-a like ana, aole oi o kekahi a emi hoi kekahi. Eia no ka manu ke okuu mai nei, oia mau no ia. Eia no ke ahi ke pii nei, a kani hoi ka pila a kamaliiwahine, pii hou ke ahi. He nani mai hoi kau; make-pono ka hele ana o ka loa. O keia paha ka helu ekahi o na mea i hoikeia e ka Luahine. Oia mau no ka manu ame ka elemakule. Pau ka hora 12 o kela po Poaono la 29 o Nowemapa, hoi okoa makou a kau i kaa oto.	I counted seven of them, all burning the same, none more or less than another. The bird stayed crouched there. The fire was rising up, and when the girls played their instruments, the fire rose higher. It was very beautiful; the long journey had been worth it. This is perhaps the best that has been displayed by the Old Woman (Pele). The bird and old man continue on. At midnight of that night, Saturday, the 29th of November, we all got back in the car and went home.

Kalokuokamaile is like a lot of Kānaka then and now; although they are churchgoers, there is no conflict when it comes to their relationship with Pele and sometimes with their *ʻaumākua* (deified ancestors) and other continuing elements of our ancestors' spiritual beliefs and practices. Note, however, that he does not use the word "akua" for Pele; that word he likely reserved for the Christian god. He calls her "ka wahine" (the woman), "ka Luahine Hookalakupua o ka Lua" (the Magical Old Woman of the Crater), "Luahine" (Old Woman), and her name. But not only is there no conflict in the mind of the Sunday school teacher, he writes this account to be published in the newspaper in order to teach people how to properly engage with Pele. It seems to me he is telling Kānaka we shouldn't act like malihini (tourists) and just go to look. Instead we should engage in *māka'ika'i* in which we prepare a gift of *kānaenae*, or music, or something else appropriate. After all, all Kānaka are related to the akua in our world. We should address Pele and not be afraid to, in his words: "E nonoi ae . . . i ka lokomaikai o Pele e hoike piha mai i kona nani apau i keia anaina nui," "Ask of the generosity of Pele to fully show all of her beauty to this big audience." He even provides the text of an appropriate kānaenae in case the reader doesn't have it from another source.

The second account of calling to Pele to show her fires was given by Robert Kamohoali'i Plunkett at the 1956 annual meeting of the Bishop Museum Association.[8] The entire program was in 'ōlelo Hawai'i. The emcee was a very young Rubellite Kawena Kinney, later to become *'ōlelo* Hawai'i Professor Rubellite Kawena Johnson. Here is the little I know about Kamohoalii Plunkett: he was born in 1882 in Pe'ahi, Maui. He graduated from the Kamehameha Schools in 1902, and was living in Hau'ula on O'ahu when he died in 1969.[9] He may have been a kalo farmer and poi supplier, since a 1922 newspaper column reported that a poi supplier in the area named Robert Plunkett had reduced his prices and made people happy.[10]

Kamohoali'i relates his story of traveling to the island of Hawai'i with a friend. Everywhere they went, whether ma uka (inland) or ma kai (seaward), they would see the arching of rainbows. As they neared Kīlauea, his friend told him that these rainbows are appearing because you are Kamohoali'i. Kamohoali'i is the name of a brother of Pele who takes the form of a shark, but who also is a "paia pali kapu" or sacred cliff wall at Kīlauea.[11] When they arrive at Kīlauea, Kamohoali'i offers a long chant to Pele. When he is finished, the fires start burning and the lava flows.

On the same recording, just before Plunkett tells his story, Kaleohano Kalili offers a *kānaenae* (chant of appeal) to awaken Pele. It is different from Kalokuokamaile's, but the intent, action, and result are the same. The pairing of the two must be intentional. This account is almost thirty years later, and Plunkett and Kalili were born more than thirty years after Kalokuokamaile, but the knowledge continued. Kamohoaliʻi emphasizes his genealogical and familial relationship to the volcano Pele. On his mākaʻikaʻi he does not just share Kamohoaliʻi's name; in some sense, he is Kamohoaliʻi. This is attested to by the rainbows appearing whether they are looking inland or seaward. Those are hōʻailona, messages from relatives in the spirit world, who, in this case, are the *akua* of the volcano.

Although I cannot know his intent for certain, it seems to me that both he and Kalili are teaching about how to approach Pele. They are telling the audience: we recognize our relationships with akua and we should know these pule and oli, these kānaenae, in order to properly conduct our relationships with them. They demonstrate with their voices and this moʻolelo how powerful our language and our relationships with the elements of our world can be.

Sharks

In the following section, I will give some twentieth-century examples of continuing relationships with sharks, some of which are ʻaumākua. The first is from John Dominis Holt's heartrending *Recollections: Memoirs of John Dominis Holt 1919–1935*. Holt is from an illustrious family of high Chiefs; *haole* historical figures like John Young, whom Kamehameha I took in to instruct on firearms and British ships, and who was treated as a high Chief; and wealthy landowners and capitalists. Born in 1919, Holt experienced the full impact of attempted forced assimilation to American culture, but remained interested in and engaged in Kānaka ways. He was a writer who articulated this conflicted state in novels, poetry, stories, a play, and a celebration of the Native art of featherwork.[12] His most famous work is probably *On Being Hawaiian*, a short book that is widely regarded as kicking off the Hawaiian renaissance.[13] It is a beautifully angry and necessary screed against racist representations of Hawaiians common in the media of the day (1964) that includes discussion and photos of his ancestors.

Holt begins *Recollections* with his earliest memories. The first paragraph begins:

> Kawela Bay was a treeless, wind-blown place, with a matchless sand beach. . . . In the outer reaches of the bay, among coral reefs and stone outcroppings, reef fish of all kinds abounded. . . . Sometimes a lone shark found its way through the coral and rocks to the edge of the beach where we swam. We watched one once, swimming with her young safely hovering under her belly. As they approached shore, she seemed to regurgitate her brood to allow them to wiggle in the sand as the waves swept up and down the beach.[14]

This foreshadows the huge role that sharks will play in this chapter about his childhood. While at Kawela, Holt became close to the property caretaker, Kaiʻa, who "was from an old family of that area, so he knew the land and sea extremely well, one of the last of the elder Hawaiians whose life was spent from birth to death on the north shore of Oʻahu."[15] Kaiʻa took him up to see the ancient burial caves in the cliffs above Kawela, which were also "'Home o nā ʻaumākua,'—home of the family gods."[16]

Then, "After we were companions for some weeks, he told me about the sharks living under the ledge that sloped down into the water to the sand below the reef. As we stood on the coral, he pointed out the dark area, saying that in the deepest corner were the sharks, whole families of them."[17] Kaiʻa soon afterward offered to take Holt down into the sharks' abode. Kaiʻa taught him how to hold his breath for a long time, and carried the five-year-old on his back while he dived into the water. "Kaiʻa . . . had dived all of his life and knew how to get down to the bottom quickly. . . .

I saw brilliant fish scattering in all directions around us. Kaiʻa . . . pulled his way to the bottom, following the steep ledge. Then I saw these great living things lying on the bottom, rolling slowly from side to side in the lolling current."[18]

Kaiʻa took Holt to visit the sharks many times, and told him about the "aliʻi makua—the old sharks that had been living in the bay for ages and ages." "Sometimes, with me on his back, Kaiʻa would go down and come up close to the older sharks and reach out slowly with a hand to pick off barnacles that had encrusted their eyes."[19] The sharks trusted the fishermen of Kawela, and would even up come up to the surface to get ʻawa (kava), which the fishermen used "to pacify them in order to prevent them from interfering with the fishing boats."[20] Those folks felt no need to kill sharks; they did not need to fear them and instead developed relationships with them.

Unfortunately, "years later there would be events that would shatter the memory of the innocent pleasures of the bay. . . . My father and his friends carried out shark hunts in the outer reaches of the bay's deep water. . . . Using high-powered rifles, my father and his friends slaughtered sharks by the dozens at close, shooting directly in the eyes—eyes that I had watched Kaiʻa delicately clean."[21] This is one of many such tragic events brought on by American values becoming more widespread in Hawaiʻi. Holt attributes it to the advent of modernity, but it is clear to me that it is a facet of settler colonialism.

Mary Kawena Pukui tells a somewhat similar but less tragic story. Pukui was the leading scholar of Hawaiian language, culture, and music between around 1930 to 1980. She was raised as a Native speaker of ʻōlelo Hawaiʻi but was also bilingual with English and displayed intellectuality at an early age. She was a consummate translator of Hawaiian histories, legends, and mele (poetry and song), and contributed to the work of the folklorists and Hawaiian ethnographers at the Bishop Museum for decades.

During World War II, Pukui was conscripted to work at Pearl Harbor supervising the dyeing of camouflaging material. Perhaps working daily at Pearl Harbor, whose name is properly Puʻuloa, prompted her memories of childhood days spent there. She wrote "Ke Awa Lau o Puʻuloa: The Many-Harbored Sea of Puʻuloa," during this time.[22] She and her family had lived there for a time near a fishpond called Kapākule. She writes: "There were times when the sharks were caught in the pond at low tide, but no Hawaiian there ever dreamed of molesting them. Never shall I forget the day when a haole guest of Mikalemi went to harpoon one of the sharks in the pond. My uncle shouted for him to get away from there and swore as I had never heard him swear before. Those sharks were as dear to him as a relative, and he did not want to see them speared any more than he wanted us to be hurt in the same way."[23]

She then writes that at age twelve, she was taken to the cave of the guardian shark, Kaʻahupāhau. "Most of the cave was deep under water." Pukui relates various stories about Kaʻahupāhau and her brother, Kahiʻukā. One is how Kaʻahupāhau became the guardian of people and forbade sharks from harming them. A young woman stole a lei from an older woman, which angered Kaʻahupāhau, who sent a shark to kill her. "Kaʻahupāhau soon recovered from her anger and became very sorry. She declared that from henceforth all sharks in her domain should not destroy, but protect the people round about. As flowers were the cause of the trouble she forbade their being carried or worn on the waters of Puʻuloa. From that time all the people of that locality and the sharks in the lochs were the best of friends."[24]

She relates further: "It was said that when the nets of the fishermen, used as an entrance barrier, were torn by an enemy shark, Kaʻahupāhau made a net or barrier of her own body which none was able to tear through. Never would she let any monster of the deep destroy her people. She loved them and they loved her."[25]

She also attests to people riding the sharks:

> Because the sharks, though numerous, were not harmful anywhere within the Pearl Lochs, the natives used to have fun mounting on their backs and riding them as cowboys ride horses. To turn them around, a little pressure was used just

> back of the eyes. Is this a tall fish story of men riding sharks? No, it is not. My uncle said that it was true and so did the historian Kamakau.[26]

She tells the story of how the US Navy built a dry dock right over the home cave of Kaʻahupāhau's son, despite being warned by the "old timers." "When the crash came and the dock well built though it was, fell shattered and broken, it was no surprise to the old timers. In spite of the disaster, no life was lost, for Kaʻahupāhau did not delight in the loss of human life."[27]

Many families have stories about their ʻaumākua, some of whom are sharks, but most of us no longer know their names, how to recognize them, or where to find them. In the old days, people knew their shark ʻaumakua, would feed them, and could rely on them for help if they got into trouble in the ocean. The same is true for other ʻaumākua, who can be pueo (owls), moʻo (lizard-like deities), Pele herself, or any number of any other animals or elements. In the next section we will consider Kānaka relationships with ʻaumākua and akua (deities) today.

ʻAumākua

From 1972 to 1988, Larry Lindsey Kauanoe Kimura hosted a radio show at the University of Hawaiʻi where he interviewed mānaleo, Native speakers of ʻōlelo Hawaiʻi. In 1980, his uncle Joseph (aka Iokepa) Makaʻai was a guest on the show and related a story of his own encounter with his family ʻaumakua. When he was young, he was out fishing with his grandfather in Kona, island of Hawaiʻi. His grandfather noticed that bad weather was about to arrive, so they turned and headed back to shore. Along the way, their canoe was bumped from below, and Iokepa did not know what caused it. His grandfather explained that it was the shark ʻaumakua who was helping get them to shore. That ʻaumakua was actually Iokepa's uncle, his father's older brother, who had apparently undergone the kakuʻai transfiguration process, in which a deceased person is transfigured into an ʻaumakua.[28] Makaʻai doesn't give a date when this occurred, but it was obviously within his father's lifetime. He says that he is never afraid when he is on the ocean along the Kona coast because he knows his ʻaumakua is there. He repeats several times that he was shown how to recognize his ʻaumakua uncle by a white stripe along the shark's underside. The young guest and guest host (Kalā Enos and Kīʻope Raymond) that evening spend a long time asking him about the conflict they obviously were feeling with their Christian faith, but Makaʻai says repeatedly that his religion, LDS, has not prohibited his belief in his ʻaumakua. He also says repeatedly that he doesn't want to tell anyone what to believe, and doesn't usually talk to young people about this, but he thinks everyone has an ʻaumakua, and they should pray to Iesū (Jesus). He also relates that his grandfather (and perhaps others) would clean limu kala (a seaweed) from this shark's body from time to time.[29]

Ceremonies Today

In her dissertation on the Makahiki and the akua Lono, Kalei Nuʻuhiwa describes the makahiki ceremonies of old in detail, based on all available sources in both ʻōlelo Hawaiʻi and English. The ceremonies marked the change to and from the wet season. The wet season is governed by Lono and the dry season by the akua Kū. She then describes the advent of the new makahiki ceremonies that began on Kahoʻolawe as part of the movement to stop the bombing of the island and to heal it.

> The PKO [Protect Kahoʻolawe ʻOhana] shared the moʻolono [leaders of the Lono ceremonies] and the Makahiki ceremonies with other communities, which quickly spread to other communities on the other islands. People who also wanted to heal their lands or their communities reached out to the moʻolono for assistance. The modern Makahiki ceremonies gave Hawaiians a response to triumph over the generations of trauma inflicted by those who sought to disconnect Hawaiians from our own environment, from our own practices, and from our own akua. The Kanakaʻole Makahiki created for the

> PKO continues to assist others in healing the ʻāina spiritually and also assists in recognizing Lono within their own communities. [It] continues to uplift and empower Hawaiians today.[30]

More recently, Nuʻuhiwa and others have revived another Makahiki ceremony as described by nineteenth-century authors Davida Malo and John PapaʼĪʼī.[31] Using the old system of timekeeping, they conducted the ceremonies on the appropriate nights, and observed the phenomena that our kūpuna described, including the rising of Makaliʻi, the Pleiades, at the expected time. Lono appeared as a pūnohuʻula, a type of rainbow in a red sky. Nuʻuhiwa testifies: "The kuapola ceremonies we conducted on Hikiau and Keʻekū heiau made me realize yet again that Hawaiian forms of knowledge do not need confirmation by Eurocentric academia or western science and that there is no need to justify Hawaiian knowledge to anyone else but ourselves."[32]

On the basis of their intimate relationship with and close observation of their island world, over countless generations our intellectual ancestors came up with a system for the study of the same, which is also the modality by which our akua make themselves known. Pualani Kanakaʻole Kanahele has revitalized this system of study, which she terms "Papakū Makawalu." Nuʻuhiwa uses this system to study Lono and chants for Lono. A key method is to identify the phenomena in a chant (e.g., storms, volcanic eruptions, flora, fauna) and then go out and observe it. This approach allows us to more fully understand ancestral ontology and epistemology and consequently their spiritual belief system.

In *Ka Poʻe Moʻo Akua: Hawaiian Reptilian Water Deities*, Marie Alohalani Brown provides another huge leap toward understanding that system. In addition to her comprehensive documentation and cataloguing of the moʻo akua, she relates stories of past and contemporary engagements with the moʻo akua and moʻo ʻaumākua. She writes:

> During the course of a *Ka Leo Hawai'i* broadcast, Jonah Kamalani, a kama'āina of North Kohala, Hawai'i, told Kimura that his kupuna wahine could understand mo'o and would often speak with their mo'o 'aumakua. It would give her news, such as if a visitor would arrive the next day or if trouble was coming, which she would then share with the family. If someone in their family killed a mo'o, she would be angry because their 'aumakua was a mo'o.[33]

She cites Kawena Pukui's report of a friend who prayed to her moʻo ʻaumakua in the 1970s. Brown also relates her own experience of offering a chant to the moʻo guardian of Kaloko fishpond in Kona, Hawaiʻi.[34]

Importantly, in the epilogue, Brown documents some of our collective efforts to continue and revise our ancestral ceremonies, prayers, and relationships to the spiritual world for our continued welfare. She describes the ceremonies people conducted while protecting Maunakea:

> Mauna a Wākea has been a catalyst for the resurgence of Ho'omana [our traditional religion]. Each day, kia'i [protectors] participate in or lead 'Aha (religious ceremonies) four times a day. As a consequence, hundreds of 'Ōiwi have, for the first time in their lives, the opportunity to practice our religion together in public. Because thousands of visitors have witnessed or participated in these 'Aha and because the 'Aha have been videoed and made available to the public on the Pu'uhonua o Pu'uhuluhulu website, there is a growing awareness around the world about Ho'omana and the fact that it is a living religion. These 'Aha manifest protective mana through prayer chants and hula (in this case, a form of kinetic prayer).[35]

One instance of protection sent in response to prayer was the stalling of two police vehicles on the first day of these acts of protection of the Mauna in July 2019. Noelani Goodyear-Kaʻōpua captures the essence of the relationship in her poem, "On the Cattle Guard," her remembrance of being chained to the cattle guard on the road to the summit of Maunakea in order to stop construction vehicles from going up. She notes that their arrests were thwarted when two police vehicles died on their journey to Maunakea, and attributes this to the power of kiaʻi prayers and the discipline of kapu aloha, in which aloha prevails as a protective force.[36]

We all experienced many other instances of responses to our ceremonies and prayers. While many—if not most—of our ceremonies and prayer practices are based on, but differ substantially from, those recorded by nineteenth-century writers, we are the continuation of our ancestors and we are finding life, Kānaka life, in reclaiming and creating ceremonies and prayers that connect us to those ancestors and to the ʻaumākua and akua who take the forms of elements, plants, and animals in the world that surrounds us.

I think, I hope, that Vine Deloria would be heartened by the ability of today's Kānaka to reclaim our ancestral ways, to experience without anxiety the connections to our ancestors and their akua, and to do so to enrich our lives, and as Kalei Nuʻuhiwa says, without feeling a need to justify Kānaka knowledge to anyone but ourselves.

Many thanks to David and Shelly Wilkins for inviting me to contribute this chapter. Mahalo a nui to Marie Alohalani Brown and Jonathan Goldberg-Hiller for their reading and valuable suggestions.

CHAPTER 12

KNOWING THE LAND

Margaret Hiza Redsteer

> Regardless of what Indians have said concerning their origins, their migrations, their experiences with birds, animals, lands, waters, and other peoples, the scientists have maintained a stranglehold on the definitions of what reliable human experiences are. The Indian explanation is always cast aside as superstition, precluding Indians from having an acceptable status as human beings, and reducing them in the eyes of educated people to a pre-human level of ignorance.
>
> —Vine Deloria, Jr, *Red Earth, White Lies*[1]

The year 2020 was a year in which many inequities became clearer, as Indigenous Americans in the United States died from COVID-19 at twice the rate of white Americans. Policing and discrimination also become harder to ignore with the advent of social media: the public has witnessed the callous treatment of people dying directly at the hands of those with power (such as the video showing the death of George Floyd, and the death of Clint John in Farmington, New Mexico). Issues of uneven justice have long been evident in reservation border towns as well as larger urban areas, and these events prompted the visit of Louis Farrakhan, a former acolyte of Malcolm X from the Nation of Islam, to the Navajo Nation in July 2020. Farrakhan's visit was controversial because of the history of the Nation of Islam in the life of Malcolm X and his revolutionary political movement. The visit to the Navajo Nation was to express solidarity during a momentary glance at those whose history remains for the most part unseen.

For people of color who have careers in the sciences, as I do, this momentary glance at the challenges we face offers hope that the scientific community will come to terms with the inequities we experience. Reservations and their borderlands are part of the landscape I work in as a scientist and are also where I grew up and raised a family. These concerns about scientific research are embodied in that quote from Vine Deloria, Jr., and his concerns over the science narratives that pertain to Indigenous people remain germane. Current challenges point to how science is acknowledged and informs our lives, who practices it, what it focuses on, and how it is funded.

Scientists continue to be predominantly white and male despite forty years of various efforts to encourage people from diverse backgrounds to pursue science careers.[2] The inequities in the geological sciences, where I have staked my career, is one of the most exclusively white and male of all. The scientific rationality and technical expertise used by the white males endowed with these practices measures success by its detachment from the commonplace parts of society (meaning women and nonwhite others).[3] As science "progresses," it promotes a moral detachment from the interests of, needs of, and responsibilities to the flourishing of women, communities, and environments that is equated with objectivity, while promoting materialism.[4] Questions over how science is practiced continue as we, as a global community, contend with a once-in-a-century pandemic. Some politicians and political groups around the globe have spurned epidemiologists' public health advice that has been learned over centuries of observation and instead have embraced vaccines and other technological remedies for those with the means, allowing society to ignore why some groups are so much more vulnerable.[5]

The scientific community—and science in general—is also in a crisis that is partly understood as a workforce diversity issue, one that shows

Native American representation in science fields to be very low indeed—in some cases nonexistent.[6] E. M. O'Brien's 1992 federal study provided information on Native American science degrees and representation in science as well as the importance of a Native presence for a viable science workforce in the twenty-first century.[7] This report suggested that at least an elevenfold increase in American Indian doctorate degrees in STEM fields would be needed for adequate representation in a globally competitive workforce. Since then, however, views have changed about whether science or technology is more important for economic competitiveness and security.[8] Moreover, the federal scientific workforce in the United States has also lost many scientists to what some see as a concerted effort to eliminate them. According to the Union of Concerned Scientists, "Officials have overruled the recommendations of scientific experts, dismissed independent science advisors, and hindered data collection and public access to scientific information."[9] As many challenges that require scientific information have been looming on the horizon—even before the pandemic—science continues to be under attack. Many of these scientists are in climate change and environmental studies. Decades of increasingly alarmed climate scientists have published warnings. Various attempts to communicate emergency conditions include admonitions about global warming, climate change, global heating, and the climate crisis in hopes that changing the phrasing would underscore the need for urgent action. However, the countries that have contributed significantly to this crisis (including the US) have continued to emit more greenhouse gases and develop more fossil fuel resources and extraction technologies than in the past. (See, for example, the numerous reports produced by the Intergovernmental Panel on Climate Change.)

As many critics have observed, sciences that have benefited political, corporate, cultural, colonial, and racist interests are more likely to be wholeheartedly embraced and their agendas researched.[10] As our exploitation of the Earth's systems reach critical limits and biodiversity plummets, the lines of inquiry that regard natural systems required for our mutual survival need further study to be accepted. At the same time, those from Indigenous communities who observe the land and the weather from day to day have contributed to the essential scientific understanding of natural systems as the climate changes.[11]

Under these circumstances, reopening the dialogue of one of science's most articulate critics, Vine Deloria Jr., is useful in thinking about the role of science in our world. Many of Vine's critiques of science were bound to his thoughts on the ethical implications of how science is utilized and the myriad of potential consequences, from the precolonial narratives about Indigenous people and their rights to the land to who has control over information and power. The long history of climate change research and our need to adapt to the ongoing climate crisis provides a glaring example of why Vine's criticisms should be revisited, even though he did not live to see the mounting evidence of climate-change impacts occurring in Indigenous communities.

My views about science are different from Vine's because I am an Earth scientist and believe it is a powerful practice with the potential to inform and enrich. Yet many of the criticisms of scientific practices he wrote about not only resonate but also highlight what is critical to understanding the problems in science research today. Additionally, his thoughts and actions about knowledge dissemination were focused on fortifying those who worked toward maintaining Native lifeways while government and corporate forces were unraveling them. His proposal for a Native American Research Institute could be a vital mechanism for addressing the pressing needs in Native communities because research by and for Indigenous communities is linked to their survival. Vine enriched the Native American community and understood that Native people needed to be supported in their own efforts by building a unified collaborative network rather than using knowledge for competitive individual advancement. One of the meaningful ways that Vine contributed to Native American thought while avoiding the spotlight was to organize traditional knowledge gatherings about specific topics. I have been lucky in some ways as I was around when many important, as well as less-known, Elders were with us and attended a traditional gathering about geology that was spearheaded by Vine Deloria, Jr. before he walked on. It was the last one.

Although Vine Deloria, Jr. was not a scientist, he was an articulate critic of science and what has been termed "western science" (i.e., the conventional theoretical sciences of European origin). In fact, he thoughtfully discussed the scientific method approach in his analysis by asking pointed questions after careful consideration of his observations. In a class at the university where I teach, my students learn about the scientific method that includes my perspective as a researcher. It is often seen as a six-step process, but there are seven steps that I teach from experience as a publishing scientist. First is Observation, followed by the Question posed by the scientist, as precursors for a developing Hypothesis, Prediction, Experiment, Results, and my addition: Analysis. To my students, I underscore how much the perspective of a person or researcher can influence the questions they ask. They learn about different methods of measurement and how they influence the questions posed and the problem that is recognized. I also stress that analysis is needed to think about whether the information collected was meaningful, biased, or if a correlation in the data could be the result of something additional that was not included or measured.

Scientific investigations depend upon the intent of the researcher; methods and analysis are supposedly followed based on the recognition that an observation is subject to a person's perceptions and biases. A clear example of the differences in questions and perspectives scientists put forward, and how they interpret evidence, is demonstrated by research on Rapa Nui (Easter Island). Here, one set of researchers unearthed what they considered to be weapons of clan warfare, while other scientists interpreted the same artifacts as farming implements.[12] In Vine's writing, it was clear that he, too, was intimately familiar with the ways that data could be interpreted or disregarded.

Vine's perspective about "western science" came from the position of an insightful observer but also as a person who understood the political implications of being seen as a subject of research, rather than a researcher, and "the impact of scientific doctrine on the status of Indians in North America."[13] In his 1973 book *God Is Red*, he discussed a "fundamental cleavage of information about Indians and information by Indians."[14] Vine provided examples, including the paradox of the scientist who was interested in Native history and culture and who excavated burial sites in what he and his colleagues considered a "respectful" enterprise. He also discussed non-Native historians who were not likely to understand or recount the struggle of Navajo and Hopi people pitted against coal development brokered by the Tribal governments and the Bureau of Indian Affairs on their behalf. These examples show the intended or unintended impacts of western science when the goals of the researcher are not aligned with the needs and histories of local Indigenous communities. He hoped that researchers would not only ask the questions he wanted to answer, but also that they ask them from a framework of recognizing the equal humanity of the Indigenous inhabitants of North America.

Twenty-four years later, in *Red Earth, White Lies*, Vine compellingly critiqued "western science" hypotheses regarding the pre-Columbian history of the Americas, the hotly debated yet accepted scientific views regarding the Pleistocene megafauna extinction in North America, and the "Clovis-first" peopling of the continent about 11,500 years ago. This theory involves the migration of people from Asia to North America, based on the premise that no Indigenous people could have been in the Americas before the age of specific stone artifacts (described by scientists working in Clovis, New Mexico). The work to maintain a specific scientific view of the late arrival of Indigenous people solidified a narrative that Indigenous people were also newcomers, and therefore not entitled to their homelands and American continents.[15] Vine analyzed, wrote, and spoke about studies related to the ancient history of the Americas eloquently and unsympathetically. He was familiar with many dismissed examples that undermined a Clovis-first hypothesis. Unfortunately, he did not live long enough to learn about how the accumulation of research and observations from scientists finally overwhelmed the Clovis-first dogma. As research and findings from Idaho, Oregon, Washington, Ohio, Delaware, Maryland, Texas, New Mexico, and British Columbia continued to be published, and iconic places such as Monte Verde, Chile, and Bluefish Caves in the Yukon are now recognized as archaeological evidence of a human presence in both North and South America, the scientific community has acknowledged a pre-Clovis presence.

The recognition of pre-Clovis sites has greatly advanced the scientific understanding of the history of Indigenous people in North America. It has also redeemed the careers and reputations of archaeologists who accidentally uncovered artifacts that were too old.[16] However, it is difficult to ignore the many decades when our understanding and knowledge could have been enriched if these questions about a deeper history of the Americas were a suitable line of inquiry. How much have we not learned, given the questions remaining about what is an acceptable understanding of Indigenous history in the Americas now? This question remains important. Central to Vine's criticism of science is that it embraces hypotheses and protects them from scrutiny rather than allowing continued analysis and data collection. In Vine's arguments, without the consideration of data and observations that may not fit accepted paradigms, those paradigms become cultural and religious viewpoints and influence the questions that are topics of continued research.[17]

Vine also expressed concerns that Native people, after becoming part of academia, would not be able to examine how their role in research related to the welfare of Indigenous communities.[18] What Vine could not articulate, because he did not experience it, are the problems and concerns of scientists such as those outlined in the 2018 Union of Concerned Scientists Report on recent science censorship. The reality is that science research is limited based on who has access to laboratory space, analytical equipment, and research staff. Topics of research depend on what is funded and set forth by federal agency research guidelines and the priorities of agency directors, in addition to funding allocations from Congress and the National Science Foundation. Although there are cases of outright censorship in recent years, reports about it are rare. Science is controlled by access to resources, and this access can be cut off at key points without accountability, such as by slowing an editorial review process or even blocking a research publication that may present data counter to a prevailing view.

To describe and understand the Earth is a goal among Earth scientists and was for a time the mission statement of the US Geological Survey, a federally funded research agency. To understand the Earth is a goal of mine as well, but my questions (and motivations) are different from many. As a young mother of three children living on the Navajo Nation in northeastern Arizona, I heard a lot of stories about the land and how it had changed. There were other experiences, too. In the summertime, whether traveling from Tolani Lake, Arizona, to Flagstaff, or from Crow Agency, Montana, to Billings, the relief from excessive heat was astounding when departing from reservation boundaries. In many places on the reservation in Arizona there was no running water or refrigeration for relief from this heat. Water quality, whether in Birney or Crow Agency, Montana, could be accessed from the tap, but no one in their right mind would contemplate drinking it, because it was brown, fetid, and often destroyed plumbing fixtures. These experiences change the types of questions one might ask if they happen to take up science as a career. After obtaining a PhD in geochemistry in 1999, I was hired by the US Geological Survey and started work to answer these questions when my own research project was funded a few years later. Since then, I have published papers that include how the location of reservation boundaries must be considered when examining the vulnerability of reservation populations to climate change.[19] I have also included the accounts of Tribal Elders and their observations of the land.[20]

While conducting research and directing a research project, I was able to focus on bringing science back to Native communities (for Native people who have been and are, in many cases, practicing science). The work focused on the land and providing information about the many environmental issues on the Navajo Nation. It also provided communities with a formal set of data from Tribal Elders and acknowledgment of land use issues for community resource and hazard planning. Native student interns participated and built research connections to the community. It was an opportunity for them to learn science and do research that was meaningful for them and their families. Some of these students completed bachelor's, master's, and doctorate degrees and have science careers now. Unfortunately, this work was not funded by the incoming Trump administration when they reset federal priorities in 2017. I resigned from the US Geological Survey at that time.

Recognition of Indigenous people in global climate change sciences has similarly been gradual with limited participation. As far back as 1896, Swedish chemist Svante Arrhenius predicted that carbon dioxide (CO_2) emitted from humans burning coal into the atmosphere could raise the Earth's temperature.[21] But it would take many more decades of research to understand the consequences of what we now understand as the climate crisis; the Earth's climate is governed by a wide range of factors that are interlinked in a complex web of physical and biological processes. Yet as Vine wrote in 1973, "The lands wait for those who can discern their rhythms. The peculiar genius of each continent, each river valley, the rugged mountains, the placid lakes, all call for relief from the constant burden of exploitation."[22]

After the creation of the Intergovernmental Panel on Climate Change (IPCC) in 1988, the US Global Change Research Act of 1990, and the UN Conference on Environment and Development (Rio 1992 Earth Summit), which adopted the UN Framework Convention on Climate Change (UNFCCC), the world's attention concentrated on areas sensitive to climate change impacts. These areas include small tropical islands, high mountains, tropical forests, desert margins, and polar regions, where today's Indigenous peoples commonly reside.[23] Despite broad international attention to Indigenous peoples' lands as harbingers of the planetary change, somewhat undiplomatically referred to as "canaries in the coal mine,"[24] Indigenous people were initially excluded from the climate change discussion.[25] The United Nations Framework Convention on Climate Change divided historic Indigenous lands among "countries" or "parties."[26] The Second IPCC Report in 1996 made only a cursory reference to Indigenous peoples in polar regions. Moreover, Indigenous peoples were not represented at the annual UNFCCC Conferences of the Parties until 1998, and only since 2001 were Indigenous peoples' organizations officially recognized as constituencies in climate change negotiations.[27]

Nevertheless, in North America, Arctic Indigenous peoples and scientists worked collaboratively and voiced warnings about the growing impact of climate change. Awareness of climate change hotspots emerged: low-lying coastal areas, tropical islands, and mountainous and arid lands. Information on impacts to Indigenous communities across North America evolved as the number of scholarly papers, conferences, research initiatives, special journal issues, and books on Indigenous peoples and climate change grew. Acknowledging the lack of significant engagement with Indigenous groups in the first two US National Climate Assessments, the most recent assessment included more information about Indigenous peoples.[28] Then, after initial exclusion, the Fifth Assessment Report from IPCC Working Group II concluded that traditional knowledge must be considering in climate change adaptation. As the report's Technical Summary stated:

> Indigenous, local, and traditional knowledge systems and practices, including indigenous peoples' holistic view of community and environment, are a major resource for adapting to climate change (robust evidence, high agreement). Natural resource dependent communities, including indigenous peoples, have a long history of adapting to highly variable and changing social and ecological conditions. But the salience of indigenous, local, and traditional knowledge will be challenged by climate change impacts. Such forms of knowledge have not been used consistently in existing adaptation efforts. Integrating such forms of knowledge with existing practices increases the effectiveness of adaptation.[29]

Clearly, recognition of the traditional knowledge (gained as land management know-how accumulated through generations of subsistence living in a particular environment) and that Indigenous people and Native Americans know the land they live on has grown. This important acknowledgment has been celebrated, but it also leads to new challenges for Native people who see this as a recognition that Indigenous people have an important role in future climate change discussions.[30] While this role is now recognized, students who participated in the work I led to examine climate change impacts on the Navajo Nation, and who subsequently completed science degrees, have not become researchers of their own studies. In hindsight, it has only just become apparent to me how rare the opportunity was to conduct research to benefit people in a reservation community that I knew, on lands that I know and still consider my home no matter how far away my profession takes me now. Yet during science meetings, my work is sidelined with questions about Native culture, and my contribution to legitimate science becomes a kind of tokenism that disregards the hard work necessary to conduct research, whether or not that research happens to be on Tribal lands.

There are few resources and avenues available even though community-based research has become popular in academia. Native Americans with doctoral degrees in science are considered adequately educated to be Tribal liaisons for the Department of Interior Climate Science Centers but have not been hired as research scientists. The current paradox in addressing climate change on Native lands is that some researchers actively look for ways to bring traditional knowledge into natural resource management without empowering those who know the land, the birds, the fish, and all our relatives. As reservations lose populations due to poor living conditions that are exacerbated by climate change, Native people will need science resources so that they can sustain the land themselves.

In this critical time when the connection between our future and our present could not be so evident, it is good to be reminded of models that Vine Deloria, Jr. suggested as paths forward. He viewed the role of a scientist in Native communities being like that of scouts. In other words, scientists could provide "critical and detailed information to their communities and leadership, to equip them with the knowledge to make appropriate decisions."[31] The concept of a Native Research Institute as Vine proposed comes to mind. As Kyle Whyte points out, although Tribal colleges, Indigenous archaeology, and other efforts to bring conventional science together with local and traditional knowledge exist, the resources necessary to address our need to find a sustainable future in a changing world require thinking about the (unmet and in some cases unestablished) needs of Indigenous communities.[32] A research centered on Indigenous needs will have to be bolstered as an independent body that is seen as credible and legitimate by all parties involved. It will need to include scientific, Earth system–based information connected to place and to be shared and communicated in understandable ways. Finding a livable future in a changing world will require thinking about our relationship to existing science and knowledge structures in more systemic ways, just as we have begun to do with racism. This is a necessary shift in our framework of thinking because the systems in place will not provide Tribes with the information needed to implement a paradigm of "Free, Prior and Informed Consent." Consenting requires having the information needed to understand and study what would result from an agreement over something such as energy development or mining.

Vine Deloria, Jr. frequently remarked about the spiritual aspects of the Earth and that the worldview of Native people did not regard the Earth as an object. He spoke for many when he accused the scientific community of viewing the Earth not as spiritual but rather as a resource for material things. As the ecological and environmental sciences become more interdisciplinary, there has similarly been an effort to recognize ecosystem services to account for the market failures resulting from an economy and society that do not recognize—let alone measure—the benefits and necessity of maintaining healthy ecosystems for human survival. Over time, research has come to describe many interconnected systems that act to move matter and energy, such as the carbon cycle and the nitrogen cycle, that manifestly connect soil, sediment, and living organisms through the biosphere, atmosphere, hydrosphere, cryosphere, and lithosphere. We have learned that the center of the Earth is the source of intense heat, and that this circulation of heat energy within the Earth has been critical to the formation of the atmosphere and hydrosphere in addition to the structure of the Earth itself. Currently, many would argue that with the advent of climate change we are also testing the limits of the feedbacks among these systems and may push current system equilibria beyond the thresholds that support human life as well as other forms of life on Earth.[33] Yet, our larger US society and popular media continue to focus on scientific advances that require extravagant funding, such as the many remote missions to explore Mars, rather than what is required for a safe and sustainable life on Earth. It is hard to see how the relatively small number of Native American students completing the pipeline of STEM education can be sufficient to address the issues raised by the destruction of life-sustaining ecosystems. Much more will be needed than placing an ever-increasing burden of expectation on the youth of today, who by themselves cannot overcome the systems we inhabit. The end of the pipeline itself needs to be questioned given the priorities of mainstream society and its economic paradigm.

As Vine reminds us, we cannot become the subjects of attentive research, we need to be the researchers ourselves because there are significant political and legal ramifications to not having our own recognized place in the world. How much meaning does traditional knowledge have without the societies and lifeways that create it? Indigenous knowledge depends on continuous observation and experiences to know the land in an ever-changing world. As in geology, learning about the rocks and the soil also requires something different from book knowledge. Those who wish to use Indigenous knowledge to solve the problems of climate change adaptation should recognize that some forms of knowledge do not fit neatly on a data sheet in the way conventional western science is compiled. Indigenous knowledge involves community networks and landscapes in an accumulated experience of living and observing.[34] There is deep knowledge in oral histories from Elders who are the ones who keep Native culture and traditions and teach us about who we are. They have sung the songs that describe the homes of the Holy People. They have also studied and practiced and known the land for many years, and it is this experience that is their knowledge, and they are the ones who we need to keep it if Native lands are to remain viable homelands.

The questions articulated by Vine Deloria, Jr. over the inequities in science, including whose expertise is accepted, reminds us that understanding our origins, our migrations, and our experiences matter and should be recognized. What is valued and experienced by people is closely connected to how scientists as human beings practice science and the basic questions that we ask.

CHAPTER 13

DELORIA'S PHILOSOPHY OF (PSEUDO)SCIENCE

Kyle Whyte

Among the wide range of topics that Vine Deloria, Jr. engaged with over the course of his career includes the nature of science, which will be the subject of this essay. Deloria participated in scientific debates—such as over the land bridge theory of Native American origins—he critiqued different scientific methods, and he uplifted Indigenous peoples' knowledge and scientific systems in contrast to dominant forms of science emanating from Europe and European diasporic settler nations like the US.

His work on science has several reputations. One holds Deloria as a revered professor invoking dominant mainstream academic standards to defend Native peoples' sovereignty and knowledge. In many of Deloria's writings, he is quick to point out the flaws of various scientific methodologies. One of Deloria's earlier contributions of this kind is his chapter on anthropologists in *Custer Died for Your Sins* (1969). In it, Deloria addresses the problems of methodology and colonial desire in anthropological studies of Indigenous peoples. The chapter is both a trenchant critique and a humorous account of anthropological follies and blunders.

A very different Deloria reputation emphasizes his fascination with pseudoscience, uplifting questionable epistemic practices to critique dominant scientific traditions. Deloria, especially in *Red Earth, White Lies*, disregarded scientists' well-established knowledge on evolution, the age of the Earth, and the existence of dinosaurs. Deloria was fascinated by philosophers of science like Paul Feyerabend, who is considered to hold fringe views about the nature of science.

In terms of the latter's reputation, at least some Native intellectuals have expressed concern about the rigor of Deloria's research and analysis. It's not uncommon for me to hear scholars claim that Deloria's earlier writings were indeed cogent, but that later on he slipped into a more unaccountable and less rigorous form of scholarship.

Is this the best way to remember Deloria's philosophy of science? I would like to investigate whether there are potential philosophical reasons why Deloria sought to push the boundaries of science by invoking pseudosciences or other seemingly unrigorous claims. Without seeking to defend any of Deloria's claims that are simply indefensible, I will offer an account of Deloria's philosophy of science that is both reasonable and anticipates trends that occurred later in fields like science and technology studies.

Going back to Deloria's earliest published writing, he espoused a particular philosophy of science that anticipated later research by non-Native scholars on the social dimensions of science and technology. Deloria's critique of anthropology does more than call out the falsity of the method. He describes the institutions, protocols, and customs that anthropological methodology is governed by, even though anthropologists themselves argue that their work is governed strictly by empiricism. Deloria calls out anthropologists' institutions, protocols, and customs as egotistical, ritualistic, and organizationally illogical.

In the essay on anthropology, then, Deloria pushes the critique of science beyond what many sociologists of science were doing in the 1960s. He was discussing science as itself a social and cultural formation. In so doing, Deloria provides an ethnography of anthropology, demonstrating the bankruptcy of the peer-review and rewards systems of the field. This chapter anticipated, by some years, the move in science and technology studies to turn the ethnographic gaze onto scientific processes themselves.

Yet anthropology itself was a familiar science to Deloria as an Indigenous person, as someone whose family included anthropologists, and whose community had been subjected to anthropology. What anthropologists actually did, in terms of their methods, was readily apparent to the Indigenous persons who experienced it firsthand. There is no black box on anthropology, at least for Native people, with the exception—as Deloria points out in the chapter—that no one really knows how anthropologists take what they've learned and translate it into the most absurd concepts and ideas that they eventually publish to great acclaim.

Other scientific fields, including paleontology, biology, physics, and ecology, are ones that have less publicly accessible methods. Each of them operates in some form of a black box. People with a healthy respect for science take for granted the truth of the conclusions that experts in the fields express academically and publicly. Experts in the aforementioned fields have arrived at conclusions that have been problematic for Indigenous peoples in different ways. Scientists who proclaimed Native people came on a land bridge from Asia were playing into or intentionally bolstering political tensions set to undermine the basis of Tribal sovereignty in the US. Scientists who held up fields like ecology as the primary keepers of environmental knowledge were wholly excluding living Indigenous knowledge systems that were often much more rigorous in peer review and sophisticated in their analysis of variables of annual and long-term environmental change.

One way of interpreting Deloria's work is as a response to such scientific judgments that have negative ramifications for Indigenous peoples. The problem is that in the description I gave in the previous paragraph, it sounds like I am suggesting that political or social concerns and values should drive scientific research. This suggestion, of course, is one that cannot serve the purpose of critiquing science or pointing out the problems with experts or scientific studies. The suggestion would be dismissed as coming from someone who believes that nonepistemic values should govern science.

Deloria's strategy for criticizing such problematic forms of science has at least two reasonable dimensions to it. First, and most clearly, Deloria sought to demonstrate that there is no such thing as "value-free" science. Deloria's criticisms of the land-bridge theory, for example, demonstrate how the entire edifice of social science rests on assumptions that validate colonial conquest, the dismissal of Indigenous peoples' knowledge, and standards of peer review that are not fully transparent or rigorous. Deloria sought to show that all the fuss about being objective in certain scientific fields was betraying the real values that underwrite scientists' true desires and motivations for the studies they create and the claims they make.

When Deloria contrasts Indigenous peoples' knowledge systems with European and American science, he does *not* claim that Indigenous science is value-free. Rather, Indigenous science has a more mature relationship with the inevitability that values are integrated across all stages of knowledge production. Indigenous knowledge systems are truly ones where the relationship between *science and society* has been worked out. For Indigenous knowledge keepers, the idea of objectivity or rigor does not serve to obscure the values that are operative in the scientific methods and reward systems.

Second, and more to the challenge of the argument in this essay, Deloria's fascination with pseudoscience and the arts provides its own lessons for today's readers. In interviews and writings, he stated his fascination with obscure "sciences" and suggests the power of poetry for conveying knowledge against scientific modes of writing. He espoused views of how the world works and of history that defy core truths in dominant scientific traditions in Europe, the United States, and other parts of the world.

Deloria's pushing of epistemic boundaries is a strategy for putting in high relief the cultural, religious, and economic assumptions of dominant academic science. While he is known for espousing the strategy of beating non-Native people at their own game, at the same time he understood that waging debates between knowledge claims held to be equally credible by all interlocuters would only validate the assumptions of dominant academic science. Deloria instead uses pseudoscience side by side with more widely and dominantly accepted scientific claims that have negative consequences for Native persons and Tribal Nations.

Deloria's use of pseudoscience has a heuristic effect. Pseudoscience and the arts are generally *not* imbricated within the institutions, protocols, and customs of dominant science. They are knowledge claims and forms of expression that—regardless of their epistemic merits—are knowledge claims that do not owe their genesis to attempts to satisfy cultures and reward systems of fields like ecology or archaeology. They are knowledge claims governed by different institutions, protocols, and customs. They have not been sanitized by dominant scientific fields.

When Deloria considers pseudoscience, it serves to suspend our assumptions about the cogency of dominant scientific fields. He pushes readers to actually come up with a clear and concise explanation for why a scientific verdict is obviously correct. Exactly how do some experts establish the Earth is billions of years old? Exactly how do we know large megafauna or dinosaur-like beings were not witnessed a few generations ago? What exactly is the evidence base suggesting that Native people migrated across a land bridge? For Deloria, if we accept that the pseudoscience is absurd because it looks like a magic trick pulled out of a hat, can we do any better in our defenses of knowledge when we seek to establish the veracity of certain dominant scientific claims?

For Deloria, when we seek to defend dominant science against pseudoscience or even the arts (or narrative traditions), we find that dominant science is itself a storytelling practice, and one that is replete with its own insecurities, interests in maintaining its accountability to elite and powerful institutions and interests, and desire to shroud the true values that govern its methods and rewards. Dominant science fields are *not* accountable to Indigenous peoples, for they cannot grapple openly and maturely with their inevitable relationship to societies—societies like Indigenous peoples.

Deloria's argument then about science can be pushed beyond the idea of whose epistemic claims are superior. In a place like the US where Indigenous peoples' research and educational institutions were largely upended by colonialism, scientists in dominant universities and federal research institutions have assumed they are the authorities on Native peoples' history, current affairs, and the very land the US has only recently exercised authority over. Deloria demonstrates that such scientists are not suitable experts for Indigenous peoples. They have not worked out the balance between method and social accountability. In this essay, I do not want to apologize for every bizarre claim that Deloria seems to accept in his writing. But I do want to highlight that one lesson we can learn is how, ironically, certain scientific fields fall short of their own ideals when confronting examples of the most dismissible pseudoscience.

We can interpret Deloria's philosophy of science in terms of its complex relationship to the goal of empowering Indigenous knowledge systems. By demonstrating to scientists in dominant fields the social dimensions of their methods and expertise, he had two purposes. The first was to offer a critique of dominant scientific claims. The second was to normalize the relationship between science and society, thereby opening up space for discussing Indigenous knowledge systems as rigorous science in their own right. Deloria's philosophy of science operates as both an evaluation of dominant science and a set of arguments about the strengths of Indigenous knowledge systems. Given the connection between Deloria's philosophy of science and his advocacy of sovereignty, his philosophy of science combines epistemology, social relevance, and political stakes.

CHAPTER 14

GOD IS ALL OF THOSE THINGS

Lauren Schad

Beginning in 1969, renowned activist, author, and lawyer Vine Deloria, Jr.'s literary work analyzed—but was not limited to—dissecting the relationships between Indigenous peoples and the Eurocentric world. Through various compositions, Deloria presented his findings in no other manner than being blunt and honest, with a touch of traditional Indian humor thrown in throughout. Although at times seemingly controversial, his forward thinking allowed an authentic and personable narrative into Indigenous literature that was historically dominated by non-Indigenous writers. Not only did his work break down systemic barriers for the next generation of Indigenous peoples to be heard in the scholastic domain, it also opened the dialogue between contrasting communities that was oftentimes ignored.

In Deloria's *God Is Red*, the relationships between Christianity and other denominations are paralleled to that of Indigenous religion and spirituality. It is under a microscope that we begin to read openly and critically, to ask ourselves whether Deloria's logic and philosophy hold true in modern generations. With the intention to understand and predict the evolution of this religious intersectionality, we must examine the ongoing oppression of Indigenous peoples; the views and thoughts of the urbanized Native on whether structured, colonized religion and traditional spirituality are able to coexist in a harmonious way; how this affects the prosperity of Indigenous culture as a whole; and the importance of place and ancestral territories to Indigenous belief systems. In the words of Maya Angelou, "You can't really know where you are going until you know where you have been."[1]

Throughout Deloria's work we are left to wonder what the true definition of religion is. Is it an organized group of people that follow one specific deity and creator? Is it a strict doctrine that we must follow to guarantee our salvation after death? Is it the land we walk on, the air we breathe, the water we consume, and the communities that surround us? Or, is the overall goal a scheme to monopolize territory and people, creating an idealized notion that by doing so, we are following the divine path of God? Regardless of how an individual chooses to interpret religion, it's hard to disprove what religion is not, as there are examples throughout history that reinforce all these statements. Where we find the main differences between these faiths is how these examples are prioritized and how they conduct their livelihoods according to those values.

We learn that within Indigenous culture, the priority of spirituality and faith falls upon our interconnectedness with Mother Earth and her surroundings; respect for our community is a driving force in our betterment as individuals. When looking at the sanctity of time and reference to the beginning, middle, and end, there is no dispute concerning the importance of these timetables. "For many Indian tribal religions, the whole creation was good, and because the creation event did not include a 'fall' the meaning of creation was that all parts of it functioned together to sustain it."[2] In reference to Deloria's ideas on what Tribal religion was and wasn't, the whole remains consistent. Not only have Indigenous peoples started to reclaim their Indigenous identity, they have also begun healing the trauma that was enforced on them at the hands of western religion.

In contrast, westernized religion, historically, finds exploitation and monetizing the religious experience sitting at the forefront of finding one's redemption. The disconnect between person and Earth allows the land to be viewed as something to be monopolized and profited from, rather than sustained and respected. If the church "returned to the intended meaning of religion"[3] one might find a unified community living by principles that lead to a life of worth and salvation. Yet these intricate interpretations of the Bible allow for discrepancies between denominations, causing severance at the promise of unity. How then, we may ask, is a world made up of entirely different people and sacred experiences supposed to follow one exclusive religion? The answer is simple: we're not. We must conclude that commonality in the shared experience of deities and meanings of life should be sufficient in respecting our counterparts. Having said that, of course this idea is seen as ludicrous and a bit naive because the demand for religious hierarchy in western religion continues to overrule reason in the face of diversity.

In a survey conducted for this essay, Organized Religion's Modern Impact included forty-two Indigenous peoples between the ages of eighteen and fifty-one years old. It was found that out of this demographic, 34.1 percent claimed westernized religion as a lifetime practice, as opposed to the 70.7 percent who admitted to practicing Indigenous religion and spirituality. Although not surprising, the real unforeseen results presented themselves when questioning those who practiced both. When asked how they apply these two doctrines, whether it be in conjunction with one another or independently, 75 percent reported practicing them separately. Now one might think that where two religions exist in the same household, they would at least share a collective experience based on the very nature of devotion. Yet, this ceased to be the case. To further analyze these findings, we dove deeper into how these two religions could cohesively parallel one another without ever intersecting or diminishing the other. What we found was that for those individuals who shared the two experiences, they shared them in a limited manner. This is not to discredit the holistic and sacred practices of those individuals but rather to interpret and find the consensus between these experiences. Overwhelmingly, those who responded stated that when the two religions came together, it was by practicing Indigenous religion in a westernized religious location or church, or singing hymns and speaking prayer in their Indigenous language. What we can infer from this is that, although held together in one household or individual, the overall assumption is these two religions may rarely encounter one another outside of spatial or logistical means.

How we choose to interpret this data is subjective at best, but as Deloria has previously stated, "Both religions can be said to agree on the role and activity of a creator. Outside of that specific thing, there would appear to be little that the two views share."[4] It would seem Deloria's reasoning in reference to the blatant inconsistencies between the two religions is in fact supportive of the current idea that they are practiced rather independently and cannot coexist in a religious cohesion. Our next question then must be how, as Indigenous peoples, we came to adopt such drastic doctrines into our everyday lives if said ideals were in profound opposition to our views. To answer this, Indigenous or non-Indigenous peoples must be willing to acknowledge the brutal reality of maltreatment towards the Indigenous communities—found particularly in the residential school system—and how this impacted or influenced the upcoming generations.

In addressing an 1892 convention, Captain Richard A. Pratt, founder of Carlisle Indian Industrial School, said:

> It is a great mistake to think that the Indian is born an inevitable savage. He is born a blank, like all the rest of us. Left in the surroundings of savagery, he grows to possess a savage language, superstition, and life. We, left in the surroundings of civilization, grow to possess a civilized language, life, and purpose. Transfer the infant white to the savage surroundings, he will grow to possess a savage language, superstition, and habit. Transfer the savage-born infant to the surroundings of civilization, and he will grow to possess a civilized language and habit. These results have been established over and over again beyond all question; and it is also well established that those advanced in life, even to maturity, of either class, lose already acquired qualities belonging to the side of their birth, and gradually take on those of the side to which they have been transferred.[5]

Like many others during his time, Pratt was not the only individual who believed in extreme actions to fix the so-called "Indian problem."[6] Rather than finding worth and investing in the extensive knowledge the Indigenous Tribes possessed, the goal was to eradicate all traces of ancestry and culture. Devoted to assimilating these Tribes and nations, the US as well as the Canadian governments began funding—whether through grants or agreements—the Catholic Church in establishing residential or industrial schools for Indigenous children. This became an ongoing relationship between the two, helping institutionalize the assimilation of children over the course of 125 years.[7] During this time, more than 150,000 children were forcibly removed from their homes and placed into residential schools within Canada.[8] The total number of children forcibly removed in the US is less clear. With 60,889 children in boarding schools by 1925, it was predicted that by 1926, 83 percent of Indian school-age children were attending these schools in the US.[9]

Maltreatment in this context might be a brash understatement. There are no better words to describe what happened in these schools other than aggressive attempts at cultural genocide strictly imposed on the Indigenous identity and psyche. The last of these schools closed in 1996. Fast forward to today, these atrocities are now beginning to unveil themselves—atrocities that were inflicted on Indigenous communities on an international scale. Up until now, these had been widely ignored and discredited in school curricula. Those who had knowledge of these crimes were limited to the Indigenous people and those families directly impacted by the intergenerational trauma imposed on them by the Catholic Church and governments sworn to protect them. Therefore, the influence of westernized religion, outside of any individual's own desire to explore, would be woven into the fabric of Indigenous identity, warranted or not.

On June 1, 2021, Tk'emlúps te Secwépemc First Nation announced that they had discovered the remains of 215 children—as young as three years old—at the former site of the Kamploops Indian school in Canada.[10] Not only was there an overwhelming demand for justice from the communities but it was also the first time residential schools, or any Indigenous wrongdoing, would be put under the microscope on a global scale. By the time three weeks had passed, the number of children's remains had surpassed fifteen hundred, with a total of only seven schools so far being reported. To put this into perspective, in Canada 150 residential schools were fully recognized while the US doubled this number for a total of more than 350 schools in operation.

Not only is this a beginning to a painful yet necessary and overdue discovery, we have also found ourselves at the core of an era where accountability is the leading factor in the pursuit of healing past wounds. Much as with the Age of Enlightenment, where the belief of a superior being existed with boundaries of philosophical and scientific reasoning, society is entering and navigating our way through a newly formed era. Thanks to technological advances and the modern generation's intimate relationship with social media, the age of accountability has proven itself to be nothing short of a liberation to those communities historically oppressed. This gruesome discovery resurfaced a long-debated issue within Indigenous communities on the standings of western religion.

In the previously mentioned survey, 92.1 percent of the subjects acknowledged westernized religion contributing to the oppression of Indigenous peoples. When asked if they believed the relationship between westernized religion and Indigenous communities evolved into something positive or negative over time, 36.6 percent answered negative, 24.4 percent answered positive, and 40 percent were inconclusive. Within those who voted inconclusive, one recognized western religion as a coping mechanism in response to the atrocities inflicted on the Indigenous communities. Multiple voters also came forward to mention that this perception of western religion falls solely on the individual and their families. Rather than categorizing it as negative or positive, it is how one chooses to mitigate and heal from these events. Lastly, one respondent reported that evolution is not, in fact, possible when the history and persecution of Indigenous peoples has never been addressed by either side.

For example, despite the prime minister of Canada Justin Trudeau's best efforts in demanding the pope and Catholic Church issue a formal apology concerning the uncovering of these graves, an issuance of or effort toward reparations has yet to be made. Deloria previously mentions that "one aspect of Christian history that is so appalling is the almost continuous warfare between Christians."[11] Deloria elaborates this dividing difference further by stating:

> The response of many Christians to the reminder that their religion has failed to bring peace on earth, or even a semblance of it, has been that the people who committed the numerous sins filling the pages of western and world history were not acting in a Christian manner. If we eliminate those perpetrators of criminal activity from the western world, we are left with a very small percentage of people who were really Christians. Why did these people remain silent while the various abuses were being committed in the name of their religion? There is apparently no answer to that question unless we conclude that there have never really been any outstanding Christians since the early days.[12]

Oftentimes when we see these demands by higher-up officials, such as Trudeau who identifies as being Roman Catholic, we must look at the hypocrisy and irony that lie beneath the surface to these calls of action. Trudeau, allegedly adamant on his request to the Catholic Church, does little to recognize and help solve the contemporary issues and overflow of mistreatments of Indigenous Nations taking place under his current administration. We see this superficial theme throughout political campaigns and politicians' promises to mend the relationships with the Indigenous peoples as having no authentic merit. Politicians are merely making a theatrical demand for justice without acknowledging their own wrongdoings simply because of the pressure from the grieving communities. Deloria understood that when looking at western religions, those who identified themselves as practicing such faith and concealing themselves behind such strict doctrine would then be unintentionally exposing themselves to the flaws in their teachings. If we are to take the literal translation of Deloria's book *God Is Red,* one might understand that the historical trauma seen in 2021—being but one example of suffering caused by westernized religion—does indeed prove that God is, by definition, very red. However, Deloria often scoffed at interpretations that were taken far too literally, whether it be in a westernized or Indigenous religion, and one must not get too carried away on the details.

Although these crimes against humanity are currently being broadcast, over the years the overall portrayal and thoughts on Indigenous religion has shifted from something to be ashamed of and evidence of an uncivilized community to one of fetishization. The traditions and ceremonies found in Indigenous culture became a monetized industry for non-Indians to participate in commonly resulting in some type of soul-searching experience. There are instances of corruption within our own communities by those willing to sell sacred practices and knowledge to those outside of the Tribe. Whether it be from those falsely claiming ancestry, or from individuals within a recognized Tribe, the demand for these experiences continued to expand. Whether or not non-Indigenous peoples sought out medicine men or shamans with no cultural ties to Indigenous religion, the determination toward self-actualization waited for no one.

The abnormally cruel joke of this phenomenon was that the specific ceremonies they were appropriating and profiting from were the very practices that they had so recently punished us for exercising. Whether it be sports mascots depicting red face, sexualization of our regalia during Halloween, the use of our headdresses at festivals, or the mass foraging of our traditional medicine being used on an industrial scale, it seemed that we had reached a time when being Indigenous was suddenly trending. Nevertheless, this created rightful outrage from Indigenous communities as they witnessed profits being made in the name of their practices without any proper accreditation. In short, Indigenous peoples were not allowed to be Indians, but it was made impossible to become white.[13]

While all Indigenous traditions and religions cannot be generalized to fit into one box—especially given that there are currently 574 federally recognized Tribes and nearly 300 currently pursuing federal recognition within the US alone—we still find similarities between different Indigenous religious practices. In the way Deloria defined Indigenous religion, it would be illogical not to include the significance of land and ancestral ties to further assist in our predictions:

> The vast majority of Indian tribal religions, therefore, have a sacred center at a particular place, be it a river, a mountain, a plateau, valley, or other natural feature. This center enables the people to look out along the four dimensions and locate their lands, to relate all historical events within the confines of this particular land, and to accept responsibility for it. Regardless of what subsequently happens to the people, the sacred lands remain as permanent fixtures in their cultural or religious understanding.[14]

The question surrounding ancestral land and religion is substantive. How can a religion be actualized in the confines of four walls and not in nature? And yet, Indigenous practices of spirituality and the manifestation of religion are usually one and the same. Concluding our survey, we asked our participants three questions about land significance: (1) Do they find specific landmarks and places to be spiritual and sacred? (2) Do they find these places and landmarks to be of monumental importance within their Indigenous community? and (3) Do they believe these sacred landmarks and places should be protected under law? With an overwhelming response, the first two questions rated in the ninetieth percentiles in answering yes. With regard to whether these spaces should be protected under the law, the group was unanimous for the first and only question in the survey, acknowledging that these places should be federally protected.

Historically, however, there has been a disconnect between Indigenous and non-Indigenous peoples regarding sacred spaces. Churches and shrines are found at the top of the social stratum when it comes to the maintenance of institutions. When the Notre Dame Cathedral in Paris caught fire on April 15, 2019, an influx of supporters rushed in to restore and protect the sacred space. Within two days, the Notre Dame restoration fund had brought in roughly 900 million euros, a direct reflection of the monument's significance within French and global history.[15] In contrast, the Dakota Access Pipeline protests, which had only occurred three years prior to the cathedral burning, shows the mass inconsistencies found in availability of monetary investments and support from the public. The corporate owners of the pipeline in question not only failed to consult the members of the Tribe regarding direct impacts to their water source, they also failed to acknowledge the inevitable damage and disturbance of sacred sites located close to the river. At face value, the sites in question could be seen on separate spectrums, and some might argue that the historical context of Notre Dame holds superiority over the Indigenous peoples' threatened and desecrated lands. Yet this is an issue that cannot and should not be debated. One is created by humans and found to be holy based on the practices that inhabit the space and another found sacred in and of itself with archaeological artifacts; one cannot make comparisons between the two. The individual experience found in both spaces remains constant in the core of the psyche. This is in no way saying that Notre Dame was not deserving of the support it received, but rather acknowledging that structures built by the very stone the Earth provided should not be the only sacred spaces that deserve support and recognition.

How, then, do we begin to change this systemic mentality that pits one sacred space against another, with one coming out as more important? As it turns out, this task, to motivate non-Indigenous peoples, may no longer be put on the Indigenous Nations but rather within the massive changes seen in the environment as a consequence of climate change. The geological shifts throughout the years are proving to be impossible to ignore and even harder to adapt to, meaning that if we want to maintain our ways of living, perhaps the answer is to return to the sustainable and traditional practices found within Indigenous culture; recognizing that we are not in competition with the Earth and that for us to prosper, we must maintain an extensive relationship with one another, for one another.

In reference to the ability to adapt and progress toward an equilibrium between communities, Deloria stated, "There probably is not sufficient time for the non-Indian population to understand the meaning of sacred lands and incorporate the idea into their lives and practices. We can but hope that some protection can be afforded these sacred places before the world becomes wholly secular and is destroyed."[16] In respect to Deloria, he is right when he states there is not sufficient time for the non-Indigenous population to understand. Because what we find, in attempting to change the mindset of individuals who hold close to their preconceived notion of Indigenous people, is failure.

We must instead work toward impacting the future generations and showing them a world that is worth conserving. If we as Indigenous populations can lead by example in acknowledging our pasts and stopping the intergenerational trauma inflicted on us at the hands of the church, who is to say non-Indigenous folk are unable to yield to the intention of true religion? Was it not the very same religion that was founded all those years ago to follow these principles in the hope of finding meaning within this life and dedicating oneself to the servitude of others? It is a heavy trust that we must put into our fellow equals, but if Deloria has taught us anything, it is that the essence of faith is rooted at the heart of the community.

Therefore, God is capable of being whoever, whatever, we choose them to be.

CHAPTER 15

STEWARDSHIP AS NATIVE TELEOLOGY

Ceremonial Life and Restoring Right Relations

Natalie Avalos

In Vine Deloria, Jr.'s *The World We Used to Live In*, he calls for Native peoples to consider the ethical value but also metaphysical veracity of traditional ceremonies. In this world, Native Elders discerned an orderly process through empirical observation of the natural world and its expression of spiritual power. Birds, animals, and stones came to people in dreams to offer friendship and advice. Medicine people developed spiritual insights through these experiences that would ultimately benefit others in the Tribe. Deloria wrote about ceremonial life because it was the experiential field for all human inquiry but also the primary vehicle for human maturity. For Deloria, the development of a functional social world—one that centers the needs of the land and the spiritual power immanent in it—depends on what he called the completion of relationship—in short, the moral commitment to care for others.

In this essay, I discuss how contemporary Native reclamations of ceremony in the context of stewardship movements, but also transnational religious expression, can heal historical trauma. These moves to reorient self/community to the spirit world not only facilitate human development but also restore right relations with the larger social body of human and other-than-human persons. Moreover, the return to ceremonial life not only articulates an intersubjective teleology that is agentive and healing but also contributes to a larger metaphysical process of decolonization that can transform the relations of power in our social world.

In *The World We Used to Live In*, Deloria critiques the overall western fascination with materialism and its attendant nonbelief, not just in spiritual power but in all forms of respect for the numinous, that which exists beyond human comprehension. He says: "The secularity of the society in which we live must share considerable blame in the erosion of spiritual powers of all traditions, since our society has become a parody of social interactions lacking even an aspect of civility. Believing in nothing, we have preempted the role of the higher spiritual forces, by acknowledging no greater good than what we can feel and touch."[1]

Settler colonialism has produced a desacralized world, one devoid of any coherent morality where only material life and its consumption matters. Maori scholar Linda Tuhiwai Smith tells us the imperial move to dispossess Indigenous peoples of their lands, resources, and labor operates at the level of epistemology; Native peoples were deemed primitive in contrast to the "civilized" and superior west.[2] In the US colonial order, Native religious worlds were condemned as heathen, even evil. The first settlers were Christians who theorized that Indigenous peoples had no religion, no legitimate metaphysic from which they could justify their polity and claims to land.[3] This initial epistemic violence eventually morphed to deem Native peoples as superstitious and unscientific as an anthropological logic replaced a religious one.

The civilizing projects imposed on Native peoples, forced education and missionization, aggressively disrupted their relationships to the sacred world and their attendant ontologies. Anticolonial theorists like Frantz Fanon and Aimé Cesaire frame the colonial relation as ontological, as it reshapes the subjectivities of both the colonized and the colonizer. Deloria frames this catastrophic rupture as primarily metaphysical, a question of differing worldviews but with similar results. He says:

> The change of living conditions experienced by Indian people in the last century also has a great deal to do with the erosion of our spiritual powers. Wrenched from a free life where the natural order had to be understood and obeyed, confined within a foreign educational system where memorization and recital substitute for learning and knowledge, each generation of Indians has been moved farther and farther away from the substance of the spiritual energy that once directed our lives.[4]

Knowledge is produced, but it is often compartmentalized and desacralized, failing to recognize the intersubjective relationships between all phenomena. Deloria interprets the loss of this sacred reality as existential estrangement. The erosion of ceremonial life and covenants with spiritual powers can leave Native peoples lost, philosophically adrift without the community directives that the spirit world can provide.

For Deloria, building a relationship with spiritual power is a critical component of Native identity but also individual and collective purpose. In *Power and Place: Indian Education in America*, a volume cowritten with Daniel Wildcat, Deloria links knowledge production to the possibilities of human flourishing. In this world, knowledge is explored experientially and driven by a principle of correlation, not causation. In this way, it is not linear. Long-term observation enabled our Indigenous ancestors to trust that the relationships between things have a logic to them that will eventually be known. In a chapter titled "American Indian Metaphysics," the authors describe this world as having "a social reality, a fabric of life in which everything had the possibility of intimately knowing relationships because, ultimately, everything was related."[5] The intersubjective relationships between plants, animals, and the greater cosmos are possible because they are all expressions of the same essential life force, or spiritual power. The relationships between all things are also meaningful and serve some sort of purpose, even if this meaning is not readily apparent. The holistic and intersubjective nature of this world conveys its teleological arc.

Here, Deloria asks us to consider the world as a "spiritual universe that has taken on a physical form" instead of a material one that has "accidently produced personality," intimating that the immaterial world *is* the fundamental ground of reality.[6] The material world acts as a conduit for spiritual power, the life force that is a greater source of intelligence. It is these personas, or spiritual powers, residing in places that humans must come to know and be accountable to in order to learn what kind of behavior is appropriate and even expected in such places. In this context, spiritual power is understood to provide first instructions, which not only include ceremonies that support human wellness and flourishing but also those that care and nourish places and their inhabitants, the land more largely. The mutuality built into these relationships calls for what he terms their completion, meaning their reciprocity. Intersubjective relationships have a moral dimension. As human actors recognize their coextensive relationships to the larger social body of human and other-than-human persons over time, they actualize their identities. Individual and collective power and agency is mediated by one's ability to carry out and honor one's responsibilities not only to the collective but also to the spirit world. In essence, this world operates optimally when persons come to recognize their responsibilities to the spiritual power immanent in lands.

Deloria returns to this theme in *The World We Used to Live In*, arguing that this intersubjective experience reflects the unfolding nature of reality that is now beginning to be understood in the world of quantum physics:

> Judging the exploits of medicine men by reference to the physical Newtonian universe is completely irrelevant today with the advances in knowledge of the universe achieved by quantum physics and microbiology. If we were to measure the medicine man's powers by the criteria and beliefs advanced by these two sciences, we would discover that every story in this collection is well within the probable boundaries of a new and

> emerging vision of the universe. Time, space, and substance are not ultimate entities in the quantum universe, but merely handy concepts that apply when we investigate nature from our point of view. They vanish or dissolve into each other at subatomic levels of activity. In the same way, time, space, and substance do not have ultimate values in a ceremony. They appear as a function of the ceremony, not as a border or boundary beyond which it is not possible to go.[7]

For Deloria, time is more than mere chronology, it is the possibility for the "growth of all beings towards maturity."[8] In short, it is these intersubjective relationships that provide the ground for human and other-than-human becoming. Ceremony is neither a finite and bounded concept nor experience. It is an experiential field one enters with humility due to a deep recognition that through it time, space, and substance could be altered—ideally, on your behalf. In this way, it is the ultimate expression of human agency—again, an agency that is coextensive. The experience of intersubjective power makes this greater purpose of stewardship experientially clear. In it, one comes to *know* that they *are* (a material expression of) the universe, ontologically. Deloria theorizes a teleology here that has no chronology but is instead driven by a sense of perennial mutuality. Because it is intrinsic, the ethics of this telos come to be known primarily through the body in sacred or ceremonial contexts. Here, one's identity as a steward is impressed upon them on a cellular level.

While Deloria's observations in *The World We Used to Live In* seem fatalistic, the state of Indigenous religious life in Turtle Island varies widely. The existential estrangement from this intersubjective ground has been catastrophic for many Native peoples because it not only forecloses opportunities for inner knowing, it also denies access to this larger teleological goal of becoming.

For those who have been estranged from ceremonial life, the introduction or return to this world could be profoundly healing. In my experience doing ethnographic fieldwork with urban Indians in Albuquerque and Santa Fe, New Mexico, what constitutes ceremonial or religious life is also quite varied. It may look like a Lakota-style sweat lodge shared by an intertribal veterans' group, being a Roadman and active engagement in "Big Tipi" ceremonies, making yearly pilgrimages to a queer women of color Sun Dance, being a water protector, making clay pottery, or even tending to the variegated life of your garden. While some of these folks grew up in a ceremonial context, others did not and experienced a period of striving to reconnect both to community and sacred worlds. Renya Ramirez's work on urban Indians tells us that Native identity is maintained through two-way cultural flows from reservation and city spaces.[9] However, there are some urban Indians who have no ties to reservations and have been living as refugees from their people for two or more generations. Ceremonial life may or may not be accessible to these people. Despite this, many have built a relationship to an intersubjective reality—the sacred world—in the ways described above. Developing a deep relationship with this sacred world is dire for the bulk of those I spoke to, particularly those who struggled with the impacts of historical trauma.

Native peoples are actively working to ameliorate the effects of historical trauma—an aggrieved form of PTSD that is compounded by continued forms of structural violence. Historical trauma is a relational wound. It is a wound that results from the unjust use of power, such as acts of genocide, but also from the ontological ruptures of epistemic dispossession. Thankfully, healing historical trauma is also relational. Since Native peoples understand themselves as members of a larger social body, Native clinical researchers have generally treated it through the restoration of healthy relationships to self and others, human and other-than-human.[10] In short, the restoration to an intersubjective metaphysic. Transnational, intertribal spaces meet personal needs to connect with others who share a similar worldview, values, and experiences but also provide a sense of solidarity. Native Americans represent roughly 2 percent of the US population. Urban Indian intertribal spaces assert to the greater world that they are still here, despite their social and political marginalization, and that they will honor their own Native-specific lifeways, even if they are illegible to the majority population. It is this combination of actions that exemplifies the collective right to exist *as Native peoples* that Leanne Betasamosake Simpson calls resurgence—the generative culture making that takes place when you carve out a space to honor and celebrate who you are in ways that also signal your sovereignty.[11]

Indigenous peoples operationalize religious action as an expression not only of survivance but also refusal—a refusal to give up their lifeways and claims to their lands in the face of ongoing settler colonialism. This refusal is most powerfully expressed when Indigenous populations defy racialized characterizations of their lifeways and continue to live and act in ways that accord with the ethics and realities embedded in their respective metaphysical worlds. These refusals affirm their humanity in the face of colonial dispossession and also reorient them to an intersubjective metaphysic (and teleology). Deloria was interested in Indigenous metaphysical worlds because he knew they were a critical source of personal and collective power. They act as a generative site for decolonial possibility in Native and Indigenous life. Directed acts of propitiation can transform material conditions. When we think of decolonization in these terms, as not just material but instead mediated by the immaterial, the possibilities for healing and resurgence are exponential.

In recent years, Indigenous peoples have reemerged as a critical voice waging environmental wellness and protection. As the descendants of the original inhabitants of lands now dominated by others, they are often entangled in ongoing struggles to protect their lands and sovereignty. From nineteenth-century expressions like the Ghost Dance to the sacred goals of the American Indian Movement, contemporary forms of Native protest have woven together these historical strands with new expressions of ceremony as protest. In 2012, the First Nations–led Idle No More movement agitated against threats to treaty dissolution by the Canadian state through public facing ceremony. Round dances transformed malls and town squares to spaces of collaborative protest, exploding across

Indian country via social media. Within days, Native-led round dances sprang up in the US, acting in solidarity with Indigenous relatives to the north to publicly decry the continued abuses of settler colonial regimes.[12]

2012's Idle No More Movement was the first national Native movement to gain international attention in several years; however, it was the 2016–2017 #NoDAPL movement at the Standing Rock Reservation in North and South Dakota that brought Native sovereignty efforts back into the national consciousness again. One of its major impacts was the visual narrative it provided: Native peoples on horseback or lined up in prayer in front of dozens of tipis, facing off against hyper-militarized police forces. These images recall the last major standoff between the state and American Indian Movement activists at Wounded Knee in 1973. While the 1973 Wounded Knee occupation used news media as a virtual shield protecting them from outright extrajudicial execution, Idle No More and #NoDAPL used social media as a means to organize support from a growing number of allies and Indigenous peoples around the world.

Protecting sacred places is important because it ensures the future life and well-being of the people. While the people act as stewards, they do this because they know they, too, will be stewarded and they, too, will be led and protected. The spirit world responds dialectically to minute (and concentrated) propitiations by the people to effect change on their behalf. While Red Power–era activism catalyzed a renaissance in ceremonial life, these more recent articulations of protest center religious activity in ways that are distinct. Members of these movements position themselves as "protectors," citing a sacred responsibility to care for the land—protecting and nurturing the life force within it. This ethic was most clearly articulated at the Sacred Stone Camp at Standing Rock where ceremony was held continually. Centering religious praxis communicated that the fight to protect the water is about ensuring the future life and well-being of the people—all peoples, human and other-than-human. The Oceti Sakowin (Lakota/Dakota) peoples' opposition to the Dakota Access Pipeline was a sovereignty issue. By responding with ceremony, the people affirmed their sacred relationships to the lands and the spiritual power within them that make them sovereign. Inspired by these acts of refusal, Indigenous peoples from all over the Americas (and beyond) gathered at the camp to collectively honor these religious lifeways and the source of all life. Together, they supplicated the spirit world and coalesced their spiritual power. They sang, danced, and prayed this protection into being.

Here, religious praxis engenders a coextensive experience of the world and thus access to what can be understood as a Native teleology, or sacred purpose. This teleology is driven by the somatic *knowing* that results from reorienting one's self to the spirit world in ceremonial or sacred contexts. Knowing the universe experientially, through the body, enables an ontological process of becoming with and through the greater universe. It is the cellular understanding that you are its expression. Deloria may be heartened to know that all is not lost. The worlds that he chronicled in *The World We Used to Live In* are still here and growing all the time. They are needed to support the process of becoming human—living in right relationship to the greater cosmos. As these metaphysical traditions are regenerated, Native peoples heal the ontological wounds of settler colonialism. This healing acts as an expression of metaphysical decolonization, or the decolonization that returns one to living and being not as an individual in an inert world but a person that is coextensive with all other expressions of life.[13] In this way, religious praxis becomes decolonial praxis, rebuilding persons, communities, and possibilities for living from the inside out.

CHAPTER 16

REVISITING VINE DELORIA, JR.'S SUPPORT FOR UNRECOGNIZED TRIBES IN A TIME OF ENVIRONMENTAL CRISES

Ryan E. Emanuel

Throughout his career, Vine Deloria, Jr. called on the United States to establish formal relationships with unrecognized groups of Indigenous people.[1] Deloria argued that unrecognized Native American Tribes, especially those in the eastern United States, had been targets of discrimination by the federal government and sometimes even by other Native American Tribes.[2] He blamed the present, precarious position of unrecognized Tribes on the "haphazard" dealings of colonial powers with Indigenous peoples in historic times.[3] Even though Deloria was a sharp critic of the federal government's recognition process, he viewed formal acknowledgment of unrecognized Tribes as a critical step toward justice for Indigenous peoples in the United States.[4]

Deloria and others emphasized the importance of federal recognition and at the same time acknowledged that Native American Tribes are inherently sovereign.[5] Deloria, in particular, observed a distinction between Tribal sovereignty as a legal construct, affirmed through treaties and other instruments, and inherent sovereignty, marked by what he described as "continuing cultural and communal integrity."[6] I think a fair expansion of his view is that inherent sovereignty not only creates and maintains Indigenous community and culture, but it also flows from these structures. In other words, sovereignty is part of a self-reinforcing cycle; its exercise strengthens communities and cultures, and these structures facilitate the further exercise of sovereignty.

Federal recognition does not confer inherent sovereignty, but it can strengthen this self-reinforcing cycle by enabling practical expressions of sovereignty. Perhaps this is why many academic, political, and everyday discussions around federal recognition and sovereignty are framed in terms of economic development, improvements to education and healthcare, and cultural preservation.[7] All of these are practical expressions of sovereignty. Each plays a role in holding together Indigenous communities and ensuring the well-being of human and nonhuman relatives.

Discussions of Tribal sovereignty and federal recognition are not always explicit about the need to protect and steward landscapes, waterways, and other places that are sacred to Indigenous peoples. Yet these sacred places often serve as wellsprings of Indigenous culture and community.[8] To protect and steward these places—and to preserve them for the benefit of future generations—are important acts of sovereignty.[9] For that reason, environmental stewardship and protection are implicit themes in many, if not most, conversations about Tribal recognition, even if they are not articulated outright.

In the present era of accumulating environmental catastrophes—including climate change, pollution, and unsustainable development—Indigenous peoples everywhere face tremendous challenges to protecting and maintaining relationships with places that are important to their communities, cultures, and collective identities.[10] Despite serious flaws in dealings between the United States and Native peoples, Tribes that are presently unrecognized can benefit from federal recognition to the extent that recognition broadens their access to legal, financial, and other tools to protect their territories, preserve place-based knowledge, and maintain place-based cultural traditions.

With that in mind, I consider Deloria's calls for federal acknowledgment of unrecognized Tribes in the context of today's global environmental crises. I begin by telling about his interactions with my own Tribe, the Lumbee, to highlight his fervent belief in federal recognition as an empowering tool for Tribal Nations. The Lumbee Tribe has experienced one of the most exhaustive and contentious journeys to federal recognition in the history of the United States, and Deloria walked alongside the Tribe for decades as an advocate. I then consider his views on recognition in the context of present-day environmental crises. Pollution, climate change, and other environmental issues threaten all Tribes, regardless of recognition status, but unrecognized Tribes are frequently invisible in the realm of environmental governance. Invisibility and the risks that it carries make Deloria's calls for federal recognition seem sharper and more urgent than before.

In late 1974, a bill to amend Public Law 84-570, the so-called Lumbee Act of 1956, languished in the US Senate. Nearly twenty years prior, the Lumbee Act of 1956 had partially recognized the eponymous Native American group clustered in and around Robeson County, North Carolina. Scholarly consensus and local knowledge in the 1970s held that remnants of several contact-era Indigenous groups coalesced amid the wetlands of present-day Robeson County during the eighteenth century following regional wars, epidemics, and episodes of land expropriation.[11] After decades of externally imposed identifiers—which included "Croatan," "Cherokee," and "Siouan"—the group chose to name itself after the Lumbee River, a dominant and culturally significant feature of their home in the Coastal Plain of North Carolina.[12]

The 1956 Lumbee Act affirmed that Lumbee people were Indigenous, and acknowledged the Tribe as a sovereign polity, but it did not establish formal, government-to-government relations between the Tribe and the United States. Congress passed the Lumbee Act during termination, an era in which the federal government actively sought to reduce its formal responsibilities to Tribal Nations and even severed relationships outright with some Tribes.

Recognizing a Tribe in the 1950s swam against the policy currents of the time. On one hand, it is remarkable that anything like the Lumbee Act of 1956 emerged during a period of concerted efforts by Congress to force the assimilation of Indigenous people into white-dominated society.[13] On the other hand, the Lumbee Act was indelibly marked by key objectives of the termination era, which included eliminating federal oversight of Tribes and ending the legal status of Native Americans as trust beneficiaries of the United States.[14]

The legislative history of the Lumbee Act is well known. In 1956, the House of Representatives passed a bill to recognize Lumbees as an amalgamation of Indigenous peoples who survived early waves of colonization. The Senate Committee on Interior and Insular Affairs, concerned about creating new responsibilities (and new financial obligations) toward Native Americans, appended a single sentence to the House version of the bill: "Nothing in this act shall make such Indians eligible for any services performed by the United States for Indians because of their status as Indians, and none of the statutes of the United States which affect Indians because of their status as Indians shall be applicable to the Lumbee Indians."[15]

The full Senate approved the addendum and sent a revised bill back to the House of Representatives for concurrence. President Dwight Eisenhower signed the bill into law in June 1956. With passage of the Lumbee Act, many Lumbees believed that after nearly seventy years of petitioning Congress, the Tribe had finally achieved the same standing as other Tribal Nations.

Within a few years, however, it became clear to many Lumbees that the language added by the Senate disqualified the Tribe from a formal, government-to-government relationship with the United States. The 1956 Lumbee Act also excluded the Tribe from many of the emerging opportunities tailored to promote Tribal self-determination and sovereignty. In particular, the "Nothing in this act" clause made Lumbees ineligible for most of the federal Tribal programs that arose as termination gave way to Richard Nixon's self-determination policies. Thus, in the early 1970s, Lumbee leaders returned to Washington to seek redress through an amendment to the Lumbee Act. The 1974 amendment bill proposed to remedy the Tribe's situation by striking the disqualifying clause from the 1956 Lumbee Act.

Deloria supported an amendment to the 1956 Lumbee Act, a law that he viewed as "an anomaly in Federal Indian legislation."[16] The House of Representatives also recognized a need to amend the Lumbee Act. North Carolina representative Charlie Rose first introduced the amendment bill, and the House passed it in early October 1974. But a companion bill, sponsored by North Carolina's junior senator, Jesse Helms, still lacked a final vote. As the Senate bill languished, Deloria wrote to Sam Ervin, North Carolina's senior senator. In this letter, he criticized Ervin's lack of leadership on the issue and urged him to push for final action on the bill.[17]

Deloria wrote on the heels of a lobbying campaign against the amendment bill by the United Southeastern Tribes (USET), a coalition of (at the time) seven federally recognized Tribes. In October 1974, shortly before the letter to Ervin, the group mailed its own materials to Tribal leaders throughout the United States and also to federal lawmakers and executive branch officials. The mailer included a letter and position paper warning that removal of the disqualifying clause from the 1956 Lumbee Act would grant Tribal recognition to a "possibly non-Indian, multi-racial group of people."[18] USET asserted that Lumbees lacked a common land base, their own language, and markers of "Indian tradition or culture," criteria that were—in USET's view—requirements for Indigenous identity.[19] Some assertions were disingenuous or objectively false, including a claim that the Lumbee population had grown from twenty-two people in the 1930s to fifty-five thousand people in 1974.[20]

Soon after circulating the letter and position paper, USET led an effort to secure opposition to the amendment bill from the National Congress of American Indians (NCAI), a powerful intertribal voice.[21] A resolution introduced by the coalition's members at the 1974 NCAI annual convention framed Lumbee indigeneity as "the subject of substantial doubt and controversy."[22] On the whole, USET's strategy was to paint the Lumbee Tribe as a non-Indigenous group looking to capitalize on resources that were newly available to Tribes during the self-determination era. Lobbying materials cautioned that "the lure of monies is producing a movement of various groups of people, who have long debated their identity, to suddenly determine that they are Indian."[23]

Lumbees disputed USET's assertions vigorously, based in no small part on racial discrimination that they had faced since at least the 1830s, when the North Carolina government revoked many of their civil rights. During the 1974 NCAI convention, Lumbee delegates walked out in protest over the USET-sponsored resolution. Delegates from other unrecognized Tribes joined their protest. Back in Robeson County, James H. Woods, chair of the Lumbee Regional Development Association (the Tribe's governing body at the time), authored a point-by-point response to what he described as a "smear attack" by USET, and he circulated the response to Tribal leaders who were targeted by the campaign.[24]

It is unclear whether Deloria wrote to Senator Ervin as part of a large, Lumbee-led response to this situation, or if he decided to wade into the issue on his own. In any case, Deloria was aware of USET's campaign and brought it up in his letter to the senator. Deloria reminded Ervin that some of the Tribes lobbying against the bill had, until recently, faced similar attacks on their own identities. He pressed Ervin not to side with "narrow and bigoted members of Indian communities who do not know their own history enough to have sympathy and offer to support the Lumbees during this time."[25]

Deloria would later elaborate that he believed opposition to Lumbee recognition to be veiled anti-Black racism. In a 1977 report for the Field Foundation, he observed that several Tribes seeking federal recognition at the time had "notably mixed ancestry," but only Lumbee and other Tribes who had African as well as Native and European ancestry were subject to treatment that was "discriminatory, simplistic, and without precedent in Indian policy, and against the basic values of both Indians and non-Indians."[26] Academics who testified alongside Deloria in later years were even more explicit in condemning anti-Black racism embedded in lobbying campaigns against bills to amend the 1956 Lumbee Act. In particular, William Sturtevant, ethnologist at the Smithsonian

Institution and editor of the multivolume *Handbook of North American Indians* condemned a 1992 report commissioned by the Mississippi Band of Choctaw Indians that concluded Lumbees did not constitute a Native American Tribe because their ancestors were Native Americans from various contact-era communities as well as Black and white people. Sturtevant highlighted the argument's illogic, noting that "no present Indian Tribe would or could claim that some non-Indian ancestry disqualifies a group, since essentially all modern Tribes have some (often much) white ancestry."[27]

A copy of Deloria's letter to Ervin found its way to the principal Chief of the Eastern Band of Cherokee Indians, John Crowe. Deloria, who believed the Eastern Band to have played a key role in USET's lobbying effort, had named the Tribe in his letter to Ervin. Crowe sent a heated response that accused him of distorting the Eastern Band's position on the issue. Crowe asked, "Who the hell are you to label us 'narrow and bigoted'?"[28]

Deloria responded to Crowe, reiterating that he believed the Eastern Band's stated opposition to be a smokescreen for other motives. Deloria also warned that USET's reasons for questioning Lumbee identity may have unintended consequences for all Tribes. He lamented,

> I can only take sorrow in the grounds upon which you are disguising your attacks on the Lumbees. These very arguments, lack of a language, sparsity of Indian blood, tribal rolls, and tribal history, will someday undermine a great many of the federally recognized Tribes because some of them are not on solid ground in these areas and we have managed to look the other way about it. But now that you are making these issues the important issues to tear the Indian community apart, who is next? The Colvilles? Rosebud? San Carlos Apache? Which Tribe and which criteria are we going to use to claim who are the real Indians?

He went on to warn, "One day . . . some smart conservative Congressman is going to start looking at the Indian blood of some of the Tribes and discover that there are no full bloods left and what then? The Eastern Cherokees themselves will have it on the record that this phenomenon means that the people are no longer Indian."[29]

Throughout the fierce exchange, both Crowe and Deloria held tightly to their original position; Crowe believed Lumbees to be illegitimately vying for federal resources and resented Deloria's intervention, and Deloria believed Crowe's position to be disingenuous and potentially damaging to sovereignty for all Native nations.

In the end, these efforts were not enough to spur the Senate bill forward. Neither Ervin nor Helms pressed for action, and the attempt to amend the 1956 Lumbee Act died in the Senate. Factors besides USET's opposition likely determined the fate of the bill. The purpose of this story is not to vilify USET or its member Tribes (although disingenuous arguments warrant deconstruction).[30] I tell the story, rather, to highlight Deloria's support for unrecognized Tribes, and to illustrate his bold fusion of scholarship and advocacy.

Deloria continued to back attempts to amend the Lumbee Act. During the 1980s and 1990s, he worked closely with Lumbee Tribal leaders and strategists, including Arlinda Locklear, a prominent Lumbee attorney who for decades led the Tribe's legislative efforts. For his part, Deloria petitioned legislators and testified in Congress alongside anthropologists, ethnologists, and historians. His testimony leaned on federally commissioned studies, including research by his aunt, anthropologist Ella Deloria, who had worked with Lumbees in Robeson County during the 1940s. He also traveled to Robeson County to make firsthand observations. In 1988, Deloria testified to a Senate committee that he believed Lumbees' community structure to be more authentically "Indian" than any Tribal government created by the federal government (inserting a barb that such manufactured Tribal governments were often designed to cheat Native peoples out of their lands and resources).[31] He detailed the Lumbee habit of recalling kinship and family history, describing the practice as "archetypically Indian."

In 1994, writing to his own senator, Hank Brown of Colorado, Deloria blamed the Lumbee Tribe's present status on their historical isolation in remote swamplands and other "quirks of fate."[32] He pressed the senator to support an amendment bill that had passed the House of Representatives a few months prior and urged him to ignore opposition to the bill, writing, "The tactic generally used by the Bureau of Indian Affairs and the Tribes opposing the Lumbees has been to spread fear that the Lumbees will take up a big budget. This claim, I would suggest, is wholly spurious since the Bureau of Indian Affairs wastes more money on inefficiency than it would spend if you made all the Southeastern states into federal Indians. I doubt if the greed of other Tribes should be regarded as a worthy motive for opposing the federal acknowledgment of the Lumbees."[33] In one fell swoop, Deloria appealed to the Republican senator's fiscal conservatism and targeted the federal bureaucracy with characteristic wit. Still, the bill met the same fate as five other attempts between 1974 and 2020; it passed the House of Representatives but died in the Senate.

Deloria's advocacy for federal recognition extended beyond the Lumbee Tribe. He supported efforts to recognize the Stillaguamish, Tunica-Biloxi, and others, and he encouraged unrecognized Eastern Tribes to organize en masse given that many of them, including the Lumbee, shared a history of poor colonial documentation and erasure through racist policies of the nineteenth and twentieth centuries.[34] All the while, Deloria harshly criticized the federal government's treatment of unrecognized Eastern Tribes, excoriating bureaucratic dealings with Indigenous peoples in eastern states. In the 1999 collection of essays *Spirit and Reason*, he used Carl Seltzer's well-documented visit to Robeson County as an opportunity to lampoon the federal bureaucracy, recounting,

> When they visited Pembroke, North Carolina, during the 1930s to identify the ancestry of the Lumbee Indians who lived in that vicinity, BIA anthropologists used a foolproof method of verifying Indian ancestry. Using a study of the

> Blackfeet Indians that gave the average measurement of their heads, the BIA anthropologists, after much work measuring Lumbee craniums, announced that twenty-two Lumbees qualified as Indians because their measurements perfectly correlated with the average Blackfeet skull. Recognizing that these people could not possibly be Blackfeet, the BIA pronounced them to be lost "Tuscaroras," and they were formally recognized as Indians.[35]

Twenty-five years after his correspondence with Senator Ervin and Principal Chief Crowe, Deloria continued to stress historic injustices against Lumbee people and the federal government's inept dealings with the Tribe.

Deloria's advocacy for Lumbee and other unrecognized Tribes exemplifies scholarship and activism working hand-in-hand, over the arc of a multidecade career, to promote justice for Indigenous peoples. The story of his interventions on behalf of the Lumbee Tribe also illustrates what Lumbee political scientist David Wilkins describes as Deloria's "keen awareness of the policy and culture of Indian Country and their context within the larger society."[36]

For me, as a Lumbee person and an environmental scientist, Deloria's efforts underscore the urgent need to recognize Indigenous sovereignty as all inhabitants of Earth find ourselves in an era of global environmental crises. These crises include climate change, air and water pollution, and patterns of development that disregard important relationships between Indigenous peoples and the specific places that help define and maintain their collective identities. Although environmental crises raise the stakes for all Indigenous peoples (and, really, for all of humanity), I am particularly interested in the implications for the Lumbee and for other unrecognized Tribes. Are these Tribes uniquely vulnerable because of their recognition status? If so, is it time to foreground environmental governance and environmental protection in bids for federal recognition of Tribes? Simply put, I believe the answers are "yes, they are" and "yes, it is." However, It is worth examining in more detail the vulnerability of unrecognized Tribes. I believe their vulnerable situation stems from public policies, institutional limitations, and ongoing discrimination against them—including discrimination that is sometimes led by other Native peoples.

Unrecognized Tribes are vulnerable in part because they are largely invisible within governance systems that were created, ostensibly, to deal with unsustainable development, pollution, climate change, and other threats to places held sacred by Indigenous peoples. These governance systems include state and federal agencies that review environmental and cultural impacts of development activities, and they also include bodies that deal with policy issues surrounding food, water, and energy. Individuals working within these systems may be committed, personally, to amplifying voices and perspectives of unrecognized Tribes, but make no mistake—the systems themselves are steeped in colonialism, the goal of which has always been to separate Indigenous peoples from the places that empower and sustain them. Today, the accumulating and accelerating effects of climate change, extractivism, and other threats shift colonialism's work into overdrive.[37]

To be fair, unrecognized Tribes occasionally receive treatment as interest groups alongside clubs, nonprofits, or business associations, but they are generally denied opportunities to participate as governments that represent Indigenous values and perspectives.[38] One promising exception involves the state of California, which amended state environmental law in 2014 to allow all California Tribes—regardless of their federal recognition status—to participate in environmental reviews within their territories. Notably, California's amended rules declare that a substantial impact to a Tribe's cultural resource will count as a "significant" environmental impact—a designation that cannot be brushed aside easily during regulatory processes.[39]

Unrecognized Tribes can sometimes exercise their inherent sovereignty outside of regulatory systems and other frameworks that render them invisible. Tribes may cooperate (or refuse to cooperate) with corporations and other parties who apply for environmental permits. They may partner with nongovernmental organizations or advance their goals in other ways. Still, Tribes are often forced to channel their efforts to protect the environment through governmental frameworks that condition Tribal engagement on recognition status.[40] With that in mind, federal recognition remains an important tool for Tribes that hope to participate meaningfully in efforts to protect their own sacred places or want to participate in broader policy discussions.[41] Thus, even as threats from pollution, climate change, and other crises fall on Native American Tribes regardless of their recognition status, unrecognized Tribes remain especially vulnerable because of the invisibility created by their status. To be clear, governmental frameworks are often (and deservedly) criticized as ineffective for advancing Tribal priorities related to the environment, but they offer a modicum of legal and regulatory visibility to federally recognized Tribes.[42]

I see at least two policy issues that reinforce the invisibility of unrecognized Tribes in environmental governance. First, the United States has no statutory duty to consult formally with unrecognized Tribes in the development of environmental policies or in permitting actions related to the environment. Federal policies and executive orders aimed at amplifying Tribal perspectives in environmental arenas routinely omit unrecognized Tribes, as well. Second, unrecognized Tribes do not have authority under federal laws (e.g., Clean Air Act, Clean Water Act) to act as states in regulating air and water pollution. Federally recognized Tribes have been granted this authority, and some have used their authority to establish culturally relevant standards for environmental protection. One inspiring example is the Swinomish Indian Tribal Community's practice of incorporating the historical and cultural significance of certain plants in its regulatory assessments of wetlands.[43]

The policies that render unrecognized Tribes invisible are made worse when Tribal institutions lack the capacity to tackle threats from environmental degradation. Institutional capacity can include, for example, professional staff responsible for reviewing policies and regulatory proposals and taking appropriate actions on behalf of the Tribe. Institutional capacity can also include repositories of Tribal knowledge about historical events and cultural activities, many of which are linked to specific places or environmental phenomena (e.g., migrations, agricultural cycles).

Institutional capacity is especially important considering the resources required to collect and recall historical and cultural knowledge for decision-making purposes. Such knowledge may not exist in digital archives or libraries that can be queried at a moment's notice; it may not even be in written form. Although this situation is not unique to unrecognized Tribes, the condition is likely more severe among these Tribes because they are ineligible for many funding and training opportunities aimed at building institutional capacity around cultural and historic preservation. It is also possible that Tribes with active bids for federal recognition have placed most or all of their resources behind these efforts, or they may be hesitant to become involved in "controversial" environmental issues because of potential political implications on their recognition bids.[44]

Finally, it is important to highlight the role of racial discrimination in sustaining the invisibility of unrecognized Tribes in the arena of environmental governance. Deloria and the scholars who advocated alongside him for amendments to the 1956 Lumbee Act believed that opposition by other Native peoples to Lumbee recognition stemmed partly from anti-Black racism—specifically from beliefs about Lumbees that were rooted in eugenics and race science.[45] As Deloria observed in *A Better Day for Indians*, efforts to delegitimize unrecognized Eastern Tribes based on their mixed racial ancestries are not only focused on Lumbees. Tribes in the eastern United States have been targeted going back at least a century, when eugenicist Walter Plecker ordered alteration of birth certificates and other vital records of Native Americans in Virginia.[46]

Whether their intentions are rooted in racism or other factors, it is sufficient to point out that when Native people and organizations oppose federal acknowledgment of unrecognized Tribes such as the Lumbee, they prevent these Tribes from accessing resources needed to participate meaningfully in environmental governance. Ultimately, these actions result in fewer Indigenous voices that are backed by statutes and policies often needed to force environmental decision-makers to take seriously the concerns of Tribal Nations.

As unrecognized Tribes continue to languish in a state of invisibility, they may witness further degradation and loss of sacred places linked to history and culture. This loss is not guaranteed, but it seems likely when decision-makers have no obligation to involve these Tribes in decisions about culturally and historically important places.[47] The steady march of climate change also makes degradation and loss virtually certain for many Tribal communities, particularly coastal communities whose lands are being lost, quite literally, to rising seas.[48]

If the ability of Tribes to exercise sovereignty is part of a self-reinforcing cycle that strengthens community and cultural structures—including structures that protect sacred places and environments—then the inability of unrecognized Tribes to exercise sovereignty in the realm of environmental governance creates a cruel and circular tragedy: without federal recognition, Tribes lack access to regulatory and procedural tools—inadequate as they are—to participate in decision-making about the environment. They also lack access to capacity-building resources to carry out this work on their own. It is possible that with each passing year, the odds of recognition become slimmer for these Tribes, not because the federal acknowledgment process requires connections to ancestral lands and waters remain intact (it does not) but because rapid and destructive environmental changes disrupt relationships between people and place that allow Indigenous peoples to survive as sovereign collectives. If recognition strengthens the self-reinforcing cycle, then lack of recognition may lead to its breakdown.

Such vicious circularity could be used to frame the Lumbee story: denied formal, government-to-government engagement on many issues that affect their ancestral lands and waters, the Tribe as a body politic is often reduced to passively observing environmental degradation. Two specific examples include the Tribal government's inability to regulate air and water pollution from industrialized livestock that have proliferated in Lumbee communities since the 1980s, and the federal government's lack of consultation with the Tribe during the environmental review of the now-canceled Atlantic Coast Pipeline, a shale gas pipeline that energy companies had hoped to construct through the Tribe's territory.[49]

My grim perspective admittedly discounts the Tribe's other, successful exercises of sovereignty in areas related to education, housing, cultural renewal, and more. However, I think it is a clear-eyed and necessary view. As Lumbee people, we sometimes call ourselves People of the Dark Water, which signifies our relationship to the blackwater river that flows through our home.[50] What does it mean to be in relationship with a place that we cannot protect through formal action as a Tribal Nation? Lumbee people have not yet answered this question, and it has not been articulated, explicitly, in half a century of efforts to amend the 1956 Lumbee Act.

Environmental governance rarely appears at the front and center of calls for federal recognition of Tribes in Congress, but perhaps it should. Of more than one hundred Tribal recognition bills filed between the 94th Congress (1975–1976) and the present, only the Mono Lake Kutzadikaª recognition bill (H.R. 8208, 116th Congress) mentions environmental governance in the text of the bill.[51] Environmental protection may be implicit in recognition efforts, but it is time to be more explicit about goals in these areas.[52] Given the current state of our planet, the time is ripe for all Tribes to foreground environmental issues in discussions of recognition and sovereignty.

Tribal recognition is not a panacea, of course, but under the current system of environmental policy and regulation, it most certainly catalyzes the self-reinforcing cycle of sovereignty, community, and culture. Even so, before placing too much stock in recognition, it is helpful to reflect on Vine Deloria, Jr.'s faith in the power of Indigenous people to persist—against all odds—as inherently sovereign peoples. Writing for a collection of essays on Tribal economic development, he observed, "so long as the cultural identity of Indians remains intact no specific political act undertaken by the United States government can permanently extinguish Indian peoples as sovereign entities."[53]

CHAPTER 17

SEVENTH GENERATION

Bringing Forth a Traditional Value into Contemporary Times

Jordan P. Lewis

Introduction

Indigenous societies abide by cultural values and practices that govern behaviors and actions by community leaders and members. One of the well-known values is honoring and respecting our Elders, which is instilled in Indigenous people from a young age and is a steadfast value throughout our lives. One of the Indigenous teachings we learn as we age is taking care of the seventh generation and being cognizant of how our actions and behaviors today will influence our children and grandchildren, as well as the future generations. In addition to being aware of our actions, our priorities and needs shift as we age. As youth we learn from our Elders, we grow up and raise our families, and as we enter older adulthood and Eldership, we step into roles of leaders, mentors, and knowledge keepers. Elders fill specific roles within their family and community and not only focus on the well-being of community members, but also passing on their knowledge and experiences to help youth grow up into healthy community members and be stewards of the land and water. This way, the future generations are able to flourish and have strong connections to the land and community.

The seventh generation, when its meaning and cultural teachings are applied to similar western teachings, is related to Erik Erikson's seventh stage of psychosocial development of generativity versus stagnation.[1] There is very little written on the Indigenous view of the seventh generation, but given the focus on ensuring a healthy future for generations to come, there is a direct link to Erikson's seventh stage of generativity and an older adult's desire to pass on their teachings and experiences. This ensures that youth have opportunities to become healthy older adults with the same vision and commitment to the seventh generation. The United Nations has also recognized the relevance of promoting intergenerational relationships so we can achieve a "society of all ages." Is it a coincidence that Erikson's seventh stage of generativity, concerned with passing down knowledge to the youth, has a similar goal and purpose of the Iroquois notion of the seventh generation?

To explore this connection between Erikson's seventh stage of psychosocial development and the seventh generation, this essay begins with Vine Deloria's perspective on the Indigenous principle of the seventh generation and then discusses how this Iroquois teaching can be applied to aspects of human development, exploring their similarities and differences.

Seventh Generation—Its Origins and Meaning

The seventh generation is a concept believed to have originated with the Iroquois—Great Law of the Iroquois—which urges the current generation to live and work for the benefit of the seventh generation in the future. That is, we need to decide whether the decisions we make today will benefit children two hundred years from now. It is frequently associated with the modern, popular concept of environmental stewardship or sustainability but it is much broader in context. Oren Lyons, Chief of the Onondaga Nation, writes: "We are looking ahead, as is one of the first mandates given us as chiefs, to make sure and to make every decision that we make relate to the welfare and well-being of the seventh generation to come. What about the seventh generation? Where are you taking them? What will they have?"[2]

Oren Lyons presented in his speech at Pace University that our mandate is to serve not only our generation, but to serve the seventh generation. What he meant by this is that Tribal governments, councils, Elder councils, and Tribal Nations need to think not only about themselves, their own family or community, or even their generation. They need to make decisions on behalf of the seventh generation coming. It is important for us to defend and protect them so they may enjoy what we have today, but even better. We need to begin to have these discussions about responsible leadership, responsibility, and long-term thinking and decision-making, or we will not survive all the crises the world is facing now. If we do not defend what we have today, the seventh generation will struggle.

Vine Deloria, Jr.'s Thoughts on the Seventh Generation

The concept seventh generation is heard in conversations across Indian Country, yet very few of us stop to reflect on its meaning and how we can put its meaning into practice. Vine Deloria, Jr. spoke of the popular use of seventh generation in very practical terms and spoke of the romanticism of the concept and its relationship to the mysticism and magic of Native peoples. As explained to him, the generations we are sworn to protect are the seven generations we are connected to. To illustrate Deloria's point, it is possible that many of us have known or will know our great-grandparents, grandparents, parents, our children, grandchildren, and great-grandchildren. Even if we are not fortunate enough to have been in the physical presence of those who came before us, we usually have stories, songs, and photos so that we feel a connection. We also want to make sure our kids and grandkids are healthy, safe, and aware of where they come from; this contributes to their healthy development, sense of identity, and feelings of connectedness. Based on Deloria's critique of this concept, if we count our own generation—ourselves, siblings, and cousins—we are accountable to those seven generations, not some imagined future mythical peoples two hundred years down the road.

Deloria's articulation of the seventh generation makes sense on a human scale and debunks the destructive myth of mystical, all-seeing, and all-knowing Native people. According to stories from our Elders, Native people were visionary, prophets of what was to come, traditional healers, medicine people, and counselors, but not in the New-Age way commonly believed by non-Native people. The belief behind the seventh generation is that each generation is responsible to teach, learn, and protect the three generations that had come before it, its own, and the next three. In this way, we have maintained our communities for millennia and will continue to do so for rest of the time.

While looking to the future and dedicating efforts to ensure we leave the world a better place for our seventh generation, we need to dedicate even more resources and energy to our current seven generations, teaching them our cultural values, teachings, and how to live as healthy, productive, and caring Native people so they can grow up to be Elders, leaders, and stewards of the land for their descendants. This strong desire among older adults to pass on their skills, knowledge, and experiences as a legacy to help younger people have a healthy future, is referred to as "Indigenous cultural generativity."[3] Passing on our knowledge to the youth is a cultural value we all learn as Native people but is a common psychosocial development stage of adulthood defined as generativity.

Generativity and Indigenous Communities

The idea of generativity is grounded in Elders teaching their grandchildren and other youth. Generativity, defined by Erikson, is "the concern in establishing and guiding the next generation."[4] Generative adults pass on knowledge and experiences to their youth to help them develop and thrive, which can include technical skills, cultural values and beliefs of their family and community, and other lessons and experiences important to their legacy.[5] Cultural generativity, passing on and keeping of culturally relevant symbolic systems, such as their ideals and values, and the passing of cultural aesthetics, ideas, and values to succeeding generations so their cultural heritage is nourished and preserved for current youth and the seventh generation.[6] For older adults to engage in generative acts, they must have generative concern, or the concern for the welfare of the younger generations.[7] For example, there is generative concern that American Indian and Alaska Native youth are lacking interactions with their Elders, disconnected from their cultural values and traditional foods, and not learning the history of their Native communities. Given the current world issues with climate change, technological advances, and disconnect between generations, I believe our ancestors would be concerned for the seventh generation.

It is important to ensure there are opportunities in which Elders can be active in sharing their knowledge with youth to enable them to continue experiencing benefits of generativity, including cultural and technical generativity. Erikson explains old people can and need to maintain a grand-generative function, for there can be little doubt that the discontinuity of family life contributes greatly to the lack of involvement in old age—an involvement that is necessary for staying mentally and physically active.[8] Rural communities are experiencing their own form of discontinuity of family life with the outmigration of families, and this trend directly affects the role of elders in both their families and communities. The ability and opportunity to share their knowledge and wisdom of living a traditional lifestyle with their family was an important aspect of aging successfully, but it also ensured that youth grew up in a healthy community and world where they would be able to age successfully. When asked about who is aging successfully, an Elder shared, "Ones that like to give advice to others and help direct the right way by talking." Another Elder shared, "As they age, they like to share about awareness and acknowledge what obstacles they are facing."

Human societies demand older and more experienced members to take responsibility for younger and less experienced members. Adults in midlife are asked to provide support to younger generations as parents, mentors, teachers, leaders, or volunteers.[9] Indigenous Elders fill specific roles in their community, such as mentoring others and teaching how to be good stewards of the land, which contributes to their sense of generativity, or consideration of the seventh generation. This concept is a cultural value among Indigenous Elders and communities and continues to be taught to the younger generations. This idea of leading and caring for the next generation, or the seventh generation, has been documented among other minority and Indigenous groups, and has a direct impact on the Elders' sense of purpose as well as builds community capacity. There are many opportunities for families and communities to use Elders' knowledge and skills in invaluable ways, enabling them to pass on legacies to the next generations.[10]

This notion of feeling needed by your family and community is directly related to Elders' feelings of worth and optimism. Having a role in one's family and community and believing things will improve through conscious decisions to live a healthy and productive life are key to successful aging, and teaching the younger generation—future generations—contributes to the feeling that your life has meaning. One aspect of generativity is the behavior older adults exhibit when they express concern for passing on something that will have a positive influence and be helpful for the younger, or seventh, generations.[11]

Generativity and the Seventh Generation

As we have seen, generativity focuses on the person's concern for the future generations, passing on their legacy through teaching and mentoring so their grandchildren and future generations live in a better world. While the seventh-generation concept is less formal and not a theory or formal area of study, there are similarities between generativity and the seventh generation as they both focus on ensuring a healthier world for current and future generations. In the traditional Arapaho lifestyle, there was a type of knowledge and way of communicating passed down by the Elders that is appropriate for each stage of life.[12] As we progress through life stages, there are specific lessons and terms relevant for each stage the Elders teach us; these lessons instruct us in how to be healthy and eventually step into the role of Elder. Similar to the belief that our actions will benefit the seventh generation, there must be a belief in the species,[13] such as your community and family, in order for older adults to be generative.

Within the field of generativity is the idea of passing on something helpful to guide the younger generations,[14] but there is another equally important aspect of generativity: leaving a positive legacy, or succession, to the next generation, referred to as an intergenerational buffer.[15] Adults try to absorb and avoid passing on to their succeeding generations the negative experiences they've faced during their life course, so that the young generation need not experience that same pain and discomfort, which Kotre referred to as the intergenerational buffer.[16]

Older Indigenous Australians feel they have an important role as cultural knowledge bearers, which they transmit to younger generations. They also provide guidance and advice, based on their own life experiences, to family and community youth, including those who exhibit risky behaviors.[17] For example, this could include not sharing or exhibiting negative behaviors because of negative experiences (e.g., historical trauma, past abusive relationships, or substance disorders) to stop the cycle and pass down a positive legacy. Some highly generative older adults shift their narrative of trauma or negative events into lessons learned and growth, referred to as redemptive narratives.[18] These redemptive narratives are ways for the older adults to improve the future, or seventh generation, and leave a stronger, healthier, legacy.

One of the challenges impacting Indigenous ways of knowing in guiding the future generations and ensuring we care for the seventh generation is "generative mismatch." This is where the knowledge and experiences held by Elders do not align with the knowledge sought by the youth. Respect for Elders is a value shared among American Indian and Alaska Native cultures. However, little research has been done to evaluate the relevance of generativity in caring for Elders,[19] or how the desire to engage in these behaviors with respect to the seventh generation impacts the health and well-being of both young and older generations. The older adults benefit from engaging in generative behaviors and acts and the youth learn the history, culture, and skills from their Elders that will help them thrive and be healthy.

Conclusion

"The seventh generation" is a term heard frequently in speeches by Tribal leaders, community members, and others who wish to leave the world a better place. They tend to use this term to justify their actions and behaviors and help them accept their own existence because it will continue in the lives of others in the future;[20] this enables them to transcend their own mortality.[21] The key to generativity is "binding each generation to those that gave it life and to those for whose life it is responsible": the future, or seventh, generation.[22]

Vine Deloria, Jr. envisions a genuine intertribal, intercultural, and interdisciplinary inquiry that draws upon western and Indigenous pathways toward understanding the unifying reality and knowledge that underlies all existence.[23] Whether you are basing your actions on the seventh generation, or wanting to be generative in your mid-to-later years, to believe in your fellow human is to place hope in the advancement and betterment of human life in succeeding generations.[24] Erikson thought generativity was a universal phenomenon given that its principle—regardless of culture and background—makes people care for the next generation and accounts for the transmission of cultural values and practices from older to younger.[25] Oren Lyons stated, "We change, but our principles do not." The goal of generativity, and that of our past, current, and future ancestors is to perpetuate humankind and at the same time advance personal development.[26]

The next time you hear a Tribal leader or community member speak of the seventh generation at a conference or meeting, rather than think of past or future generations you may or may not have met or meet, think about what you want to pass along to make the world a better place. Which of your experiences will help future generations survive and thrive? The survival and continuance of a society, including American Indian/Alaska Native communities, depends on the willingness of its members to invest resources into future generations—to behave in a generative way for the seventh generation.

3

Sky

CHAPTER 18

IF YOU CAN'T BEAT 'EM

Migizi Pensoneau

There was a lot of mulling and ruminating and musing. But once the decision came, it took hold quickly, and I realized that it was the best course of action, given the continued and seemingly never-ending disparity of privilege in this particular country. Now, I recognize that I'm a cis, fairly hetero man, and am fully abled, mentally and physically. There's some inherent societal power in that, just in itself. But the fact of the matter is that I'm a brown man. In particular, I'm a "Native American." That offsets any power I have pretty quickly, and I found myself consistently poor—of finances, of health, and of heart. I was discontented with the kinds of opportunities I was given in the job market. More importantly, as I rounded the corner of forty years, I realized that soon, statistically, I'd be living on borrowed time. When you're poor, and don't eat well, and don't exercise, and you know, colonization . . . well, you don't live very long.

So, what to do? As fate would have it, I caught a piece on Rachel Dolezal, and it was then I knew, and I shouted it out loud, to the bemusement of my girlfriend and the indifference of both my cats: I would become a white man. I was going to be SO insanely white. That was my goal. To be white enough to refer to myself as Hwhite. That ridiculous breathy "H" on the front of "white" really adds a certain something. Simple.

There's a difference between simple and easy, though. See, it's a simple choice to say you are going to be white. But this wasn't going to be some Dolezalian half-measure of co-opting a look and struggle, then hoping nobody noticed. See, being Native isn't a racial identity. It's a political one. We're sovereign nations, and we're citizens within those nations. So, I wanted to go deeper. I wanted to make sure this was a full-on legal change. In ten years, at the age of fifty (an age I hwas now confident I'd make it to, hwhat hwith being Hwhite and everything), I'd be filling in a different circle on my census form.

According to a DNA test, I have at least one-fourth non-Native blood coursing through the ol' veins. Blood quantum has given me citizenship in my Native Nation, the cutoff being one-eighth. If a quarter is good enough for my Tribe, then I felt it stood to reason that I should be able to lay claim to my whiteness as well. One-quarter blood quantum would be more than enough.

The first stop I made in making myself a Hwhite was the formal renunciation of my citizenship to my Tribal nation. Again, simple versus easy. The Tribal switchboard is a labyrinth of bureaucracy, purposeful ignorance, and stated exasperation (on both ends of the phone). First, I called the Tribal nation switchboard and asked to be transferred to my Tribal enrollment office, only to be stuck in a conversation with my auntie, who did not work for the Tribe. She told me she wished I would come home to visit more, but that it was okay, and she understood I must be so busy out there in the big city. How insidious is that? What passive aggressive guilt! In any case, after promising to come home for my cousin's wedding that I know is doomed to fail, I finally hung up the phone and forgot what I was doing for the rest of the day.

When I called back the next day, I was transferred to the wrong department but was able to apply for a grant that I didn't know existed, though I had to send the application by either fax or snail mail, and therefore never submitted it. The day after that, I was finally transferred to the correct department, but they were out to lunch. I left a message, and they called me back the following evening, but I was eating dinner and didn't notice my phone was ringing. I tried again the following day, but it was a Saturday. When Monday finally rolled around, I was connected to the enrollment office but was told that there was no such thing as disenrollment, and what did we look like, Cherokees? After we shared a laugh, I explained that no, really, I would like to be taken off the rolls. There was an awkward pause, and when the enrollment officer said they've never done this before, I said well then, we're trailblazers. We had a little brainstorm session and finally we came to a strange idea. See, my blood quantum comes from my father's side of the family. If I could get them to disown me, then maybe we could look at my being stricken from the rolls. This poor enrollment officer was worried about the precedent we were setting. We might get various families disowning each other all the time now. But I didn't care. Soon, they wouldn't be my people anyway. I was excited. I was going to be Hwhite.

So, I called my aunties and uncles for a small get together and proceeded to insult them in ways that I knew would get me smacked and yelled at. To my uncle, I told him he wasn't a very good basketball player in high school. He got angry and tried to prove otherwise on the little driveway hoop. But when I remained stalwart in my opinion and that, further, I never wanted to hear about how he almost took state that one time, he ended the conversation with a wave of his hand. To my cousin, within earshot of his new girlfriend, I told him I didn't like this one as much as the last girlfriend he brought around. When I woke up from his knockout punch, I moved inside. To my other cousin, I told him that just 'cause he's not drinking anymore, it doesn't mean he can't be fun. To another, that her beadwork was looking shoddy lately, and that a little effort goes a long way. The hardest part was telling my auntie that her cooking sucked. That drew a collective gasp, but it had the desired effect, and I was finally properly shunned. I repeated this process all over the rez. Took about a week. My annoying cousin Bug thought it was hilarious. He kept following me around and cackling when I would insult our extended family. Amused him to no end, the happy prick.

Finally, I'd made it through all the family but him. But Bug refused to hate me. I called him every name under the sun, and he just laughed. I talked about everything I knew about him, which was a lot. Threw it in his face. He just kept laughing. He told me if I'm ever going to do a tour like this again, he's totally game. In particular, he loved seeing the look on my uncle's face when I revealed he didn't have the same mom as my other uncles and aunties. And that was Bug's own father I was insulting. Oh, well. I told him I wouldn't be doing this again, and he reiterated that if I needed anything, to holler. Happy, sunny, positive, optimistic little prick.

In any case. My work was done. I had recorded each family gathering, so I had the proof. I no longer had family here. I'd been disowned. Somewhat informally, to be sure, but it was definitive. My ties were cut. I played the recordings for the enrollment officer, and he heard so many variations of "You're no nephew of mine" in such a short span of time that it took a bit of an emotional toll, and he sat down in shock. It was the most un-Indian thing that'd ever happened to him.

But there was one more hurdle. One more way in which my name was tied to the Tribe. I had to get my name off the trust land that I had inherited. See, there's a complicated system of land ownership on a lot of Native reservations:

Around the time the Indian wars ended, the government decided to change reservation land from a communal Tribal ownership to singular parcels. And because they still saw Indians as simple heathen children, they decided to keep that land "in trust," never fully allowing Natives to control their own territorial destinies. The end goals were assimilation, separation, land grabbing, and, of course, termination. That means the death of all that makes us Native, which means the death of all of us.

Huh. I guess it's not that complicated.

In any case, I had to get my name off my fractionated land, and I had just pissed off all my aunties and uncles and cousins. They weren't going to buy me out. I couldn't just sell it outright to some individual. First, it was just a small fraction of a parcel. And second, it was held in trust, so I couldn't really gain money on it from a bank, say. It's not actually an asset. I could sell to the Tribe, but I think my whiteness was coming on strong, because the idea of that irked me. That felt too close to the neo-war cry of "land back." I shuddered at the thought.

So, what to do. . . .

Then I remembered Bug. He'd take it off my hands. I'd put the land in his name, then finally be free of this ridiculous place and run off to live my dream of being, finally, Hwhite.

When I got to my uncle's place, I found out Bug had collapsed in the kitchen a couple days prior. Apparently, he had some sort of undiagnosed heart problem and was hospitalized for the last couple days. He had just passed that morning. The stupid, idiot, dumbass, sunny, happy, beautiful prick.

My uncle, despite what I recently revealed to him about not being blood related to all of us, asked me to be a pallbearer at Bug's funeral, and could I maybe sing some of our old songs and help keep the fire going during his wake and pour water during sweat and watch over Bug as he made his journey to the next place.

Of course, I agreed.

I realized then that I would never be Hwhite. Not because of the political stuff. That's only part of being Native. See, you can renounce your Nativeness, and rail against your societal condition. You can bemoan all the procedural machinations at work that purposefully keep you downtrodden as a people. You can spend a whole life being forced to learn the concepts and values of the very people who've spent the last five hundred years or so actively trying to kill your people and then benefiting off it. But as I stared into the fire that was lighting Bug's way to the next place and sang and heard the songs that have been sung in this spot for THOUSANDS of years, I realized that as much as I tried, I would never be Hwhite. Because I could never unlearn these things. They were an intrinsic part of my being. And I breathed a sigh of relief that that's the case.

But damn if I didn't have a lot of apologizing to do.

CHAPTER 19

THAT TIME DEKSI VINE CAME HOME TO WHITE SWAN TO STAND WITH US AND DEFEND OUR ANCESTORS—AND WE WON!

Faith Spotted Eagle

This is the oyakapi (story) of when the Ihanktonwan won an okicize (battle) along the Mni Sose (Missouri River) and sent the US Army packing in the winter of 2000. The battle was *Yankton Sioux Tribe vs. USACOE* whereupon we stopped the Mni Sose for six weeks to rebury our ancestors in a respectful cultural manner and location. Our story is a dramatic hard-fought historic chapter in the application of the Native American Graves Protection and Repatriation Act (NAGPRA) (enacted in 1990) on the front line of our people. We applied what Deksi Vine recommended: "Line up federal law, an act of Congress and spiritual law and you can't go wrong." Wopida Deksi, it worked, and we still hear your words.

It was our journey in learning and successfully applying NAGPRA. We further obtained a rare foreclosure from the Advisory Council on Historic Preservation of the Programmatic Agreement on the Missouri River. This required Tribal input for a new programmatic agreement (PA), which took several years (the PA is quite imperfect, but that is another battle). The foundational protection that gave us the ammunition to win this round was the enacted Native American Graves Protection and Repatriation Act, which was through the legislative activism of my Deksi (uncle) Vine Deloria, Jr.; Suzan Harjo; Tim Mentz; and many, many others across Turtle Island. Senators Daniel Inouye and John McCain were crucial supporters of this much needed legislation.

In our Dakota language, the word "Nagiksapa" means that we have an inner knowing that tells us of upcoming crises or the need to be ready. Some elders say that it is really the sicun, the inner spirit in the wombs that we came from in the spirit world before we entered our earthly bodies. So, on December 10, 1999, my "Nagiksapa" surfaced as I crossed the Ft. Randall Dam on my way home to an emergency General Council meeting at Ihanktonwan, traveling from my other homeland, Rosebud, South Dakota. I felt a sense of sadness and foreboding and looked sadly to the west where our old village of White Swan had been destroyed through an act of environmental racism with the building of six mainstem dams on the Missouri in six Native communities, which was no accident.

As I arrived at the meeting at the Tribal casino, I heard my name being paged by an elected Tribal leader, Mr. Ben Gonzales. Ben asked me: "Faith, doesn't the Brave Heart Society involve themselves in taking care of Tribal relatives in burials?" I told him yes, our role in the old days was to respectfully take care of the dead by raising them on scaffolds and on the battlefield. I then asked why. He said: "The Corps of Engineers called and said our relatives' bones are lying all over across the river bottom and we need to go view them."

Nothing could have prepared us for the trauma of viewing the Tribal relative bones scattered across the frozen ground, now dry with frigid winter winds causing snowdrifts over them, including a whole row of baby burials, probably laid to rest from the diseases that ravaged our people when we were restricted to containment camps. The tears fell and froze as we felt the presence of our immediate relatives. Everyone began to weep in the presence of forty-five or more disrespected relative remains. As we viewed the disrespect, primarily in the vicinity of the St. Philip's Episcopal Church Cemetery, we knew from our oral history that there were people buried outside of the church burials because they followed the traditional religion path and did not practice Christianity. The

Corps documented that there were twenty-five to thirty grave sites and casket parts in a three-hundred-thousand-foot area, but we knew there were more, as the Missouri River Trench is one of the richest archaeological and cultural sites in the country.

Systemic Hierarchical Violence

On a hot summer day of fishing along the former location of old White Swan, my father told me I would have to do something about the taking of our village someday. My reply: "I am only twelve years old, what can I do?" His reply: "You will figure it out m'girl." That cold winter day, I knew what he was talking about.

I drove to the US Army Corps Office and talked to the district commander, who will remain nameless, and demanded that the Corps hold the river back while we took care of our ancestors, as it was the humane thing to do. He told me it was beyond his control, and that Omaha would raise the river the following Friday—I had until then to do something. My red rage came out as I told him the bodies were frozen into the ground. I turned and left before I became violent.

The following night as I returned to my home in Rosebud, I sat by the phone crying and praying, and suddenly I was moved to call my dear Deksi Vine Deloria and ask for guidance. It was late, but he took my call as I told him of our sad dilemma. As I sobbed out my story, my beautiful gruff uncle said: "Stop your crying now, there are things to be done." As I sniffled, he said: "Find yourselves an attorney and get a TRO, temporary restraining order, in federal court and then figure out what to do. You can stop that river." Then he said good night and I sat there blinking, but I had a sense of calm. He told me to check in with him often.

So, we did just that, we stopped the river. At that point and in the following months, I knew nothing about NAGPRA and other federal historic preservation laws, but we followed the "spirit, prayers, and ceremonies" and somehow followed the laws to the "t" and beyond. All I can think is the spirits knew federal historic preservation laws too! During the mid-nineties Deksi Vine had thrown his heart and mind into developing NAGPRA with other leaders across the country, just in time for White Swan.

Preparing to Walk with the Ancestors

We convened an official Tribal General Council to inform the people of this crisis. The primary feeling that came out was rage and anger, of course. Once again, even in death our people were being disrespected as the Corps denied leaving the burials down there. We had to get the point across to the courts, so we took a video of the desecration and showed it to the people. The majority realized the urgency of doing this, although a few were upset. But we assured them we would destroy the video once we got the necessary court protection. And we did destroy the video once we were able to get court action in our favor. I knew the ancestors understood why we did that. Some people told us we were "causing bad luck" for messing with our relatives, but it did not make sense to leave them there to be further disrespected by the Army Corps of Engineers and non-Native archaeologists. They were our relatives.

What helped guide me was a story told to me by my Kunsi Isnana Waste Win (Blanche Oldman Spotted Eagle) who departed from this world at the age of 104 in 1976. She said there were two men going across the prairie who came upon a pile of scattered bones. One of the men dismounted his horse, knelt down, said a prayer, and reinterred the bones. The other relative laughed, kicked the bones, and said if the individual had been careful he wouldn't have died. That night as they lay in their lodge, the disrespectful individual heard the cries and laughing of the departed spirit and he became terrified, as the ghost rider repeatedly tormented him. The one who had respectfully reburied the bones slept peacefully through the night. I am eternally grateful for the wise stories that my precious little Isnana Waste Win taught me. I know we are supposed to take care of all relatives, dead or alive, so we moved on.

Some of our people had previous experiences with reburials and were reluctant to be involved. We understood. Never in our history did we have to keep reburying. It was caused by the colonizers. We knew that our intentions were sincere, and whenever we faced doubt or criticism we began to feel the presence of the ancestors in a strange, comforting way that I cannot explain. It was a good, warm feeling. They needed help to continue their journeys and Deksi Vine encouraged us by reminding everyone that many of them were our actual relatives and they had been disturbed. That is why he fought for NAGPRA legislation along with another Tribal relative early on, Ms. Maria Pearson. We were living the reason for NAGPRA.

Uncle Vine made personal financial donations to us for food, gas, and miscellaneous costs. Never did anyone profit from this trauma, cold weather, mourning, and complete social injustice. The majority of the Tribal leadership and the Yankton people were completely in support of our actions. Madame Chairwoman Madonna Archambeau gave unending support, in both words and actions, to our strategy. The chairwoman was a strong-heart woman who placed her belief in the White Swan Negotiation Team formed by General Council to protect our relatives and take necessary spiritual and legal actions to represent our Tribe in this awful situation. It eventually evolved into the Cultural Committee as there was no Tribal Historic Preservation Office at this point in Tribal government. We developed that later. The casino manager, Mr. Ron Archambeau, provided a large meeting room to function essentially as a "war room" for daylong and sometimes nightlong meetings as the crises continued into the long cold winter. Several news teams, including the *New York Times*, came out to cover the blatant disregard of the Army Corps.

A tipi Spirit Camp was erected along the shore at the burial area with the approval of the inherent General Council of the Ihanktonwan, a very old traditional form of government. It was occupied by men and women who were primarily descendants of old White Swan. The camp lasted for six to eight weeks in order to ensure that the remains were taken care of in spite of -26 degree winter weather. A sacred fire was started and maintained throughout the entire fight for our ancestors lasting into February of 2000, until the reinternment was complete. Throughout the camp we were mysteriously but warmly welcomed by the ancestors in numerous other-world encounters who were clearly appreciative.

The Battle with the Army Corps of Engineers

As the Tribe prepared to battle for the respectful handling of the ancestral remains, Tribal attorney Mary Wynne (Sicangu) was hired to work with our Ihanktonwan Oyate (people) and the relatives of White Swan. On December 22, 1999, an emergency General Council Meeting was called at the Ft. Randall Casino with the agenda, "Reburial of Remains from Old White Swan Community." Following much emotional discussion, it was decided to pursue court action to protect the departed relatives. A motion was made to file an injunction or restraining order (as Deksi Vine had recommended) preventing the Corps from allowing the Missouri River to rise further so that we could relocate the remains. The evening of the action, spiritual leader Galen Drapeau, Jr. and elder women society members conducted purification for attorney Ms. Wynne and Elders in preparation for the ensuing court battle.

On the morning of December 23, 1999, while other people were preparing for Christmas, Tribal attorney Mary Wynne and Chair Madonna Archambeau arrived in federal court in Sioux Falls, South Dakota, on icy roads to file a complaint against the Corps of Engineers before Judge Lawrence Piersol. The complaint was filed under the Yankton Sioux Tribe. Further, an affidavit was filed with the signatures of Glenn Drapeau (Business and Claims Committee member) and Faith Spotted Eagle (White Swan descendant and member of Negotiation Team) on behalf of the Yankton Sioux Tribe officially claiming ancestry and connection to the surfaced relatives and remains, as required by NAGPRA. The complaint alleged that the defendants, the US Army Corps of Engineers, violated and continued to violate NAGPRA regulations after inadvertently discovering Native American remains and not ceasing activities. A temporary restraining order was granted on December 23, 1999, that prohibited the Corps from raising the water level higher than the 1,340.3 feet above sea level. A hearing date was set for January 3, 2000, until which time the restraining order would remain in effect.

On the morning that the restraining order was issued, Sharon Drapeau and I were at the White Swan site with district Corps commander Tom Curran. We knew that court documents were being filed, but we remained silent until the result was known. We encouraged Mr. Curran to resolve this issue in a respectful way, when suddenly his phone rang, and he stated he had to excuse himself to go to Sioux Falls. We knew the court battle was beginning as the following day the situation hit the newspapers, and calls all across the nation began coming in.

As things proceeded in federal district court in Sioux Falls, the White Swan Negotiation Team continued to lead the action to protect the remains and to guide necessary spiritual and legal action to represent our Tribe in this terrible situation. The team worked in cooperation with those who were already working on the issue; others that stepped forward included local spiritual leaders, women from the Brave Heart Society, Tribal veterans, members of old White Swan, and relatives of those buried at White Swan. The team was composed of sixteen members and was given approval of the Ihanktonwan on February 2, 2000. The team worked closely with Tribal attorney Mary Wynne and Chair Madonna Archambeau, and it became the forerunner to the Cultural Committee established for this purpose. A few years later, the committee would obtain a Tribal Historic Preservation Office grant.

The Corps arguments submitted to the federal court argued against the restraining order, stating that they were afraid of repercussions to the dams as we approached the year 2000. The judge quickly dismissed those fears as unfounded.

The Outcry from the Oceti Sakowin and the Nations

Immediately after Judge Pierson issued the temporary restraining order, the Yankton Sioux Tribal phone began ringing off the hook (obviously, this was a time before most people had cell phones). A letter from Congressman Patrick J. Kennedy, dated January 12, 2000, admonished the Corps of Engineers for allegedly being insensitive to the Yankton Sioux

Tribe regarding White Swan. The congressman was concerned, among other things, about the Corps' proposal for DNA testing of the remains and also about the Corps' unwillingness to provide land for the reburial of the disturbed remains.[1]

Several Tribes stepped forward at this sad time in defense of Yankton ancestors. In January 2000, the Lower Brule Sioux Cultural Resource Elder Advisory Committee sent a "Letter of Support" for the Yankton to respectfully handle our common relatives located on lands known as White Swan landing, which includes the area of St. Philip's Episcopal Church Cemetery.[2] This elderly advisory board came in several vans to pray and bring food and encouragement to the White Swan Spiritual Camp. Chairman Mike Jandreau spent several days at the site, citing relatives of his that were buried there. These Elders also attended explosive meetings between the Corps and the Ihanktonwan as a measure of support and outrage at the US government, represented by the Corps.

Councilman Jerry Flute of Sisseton arrived at the site during a snowstorm to bring a large box of tobacco. He knew that the tobacco would be needed for the many people that would be coming to pray with the ancestors. The Buffalo Women's Society from Sisseton Oyate also arrived with offerings for the spirits and the camp.

Rosebud council member Tom Frederick of Okreek, South Dakota, brought buffalo meat for the spiritual camp, voicing Sicangu support and presence. The Rosebud Sioux Tribe passed Resolution No. 00-05, January 11, 2000, in support of the Yankton Sioux Tribe's effort of protection at White Swan. Terry Gray of the Rosebud also was present to provide moral and technical support and serve as a supportive witness at the federal court hearings.

Chief Arvol Looking Horse, nineteenth Generation Keeper of the Sacred White Buffalo Calf Pipe, offered encouragement for the Ihanktonwan, and in a subsequent court case at North Point, offered supportive testimony.

The Ponca Tribe of Nebraska declined to join the Yanktons in their legal action, but they did support their efforts to preserve and protect cultural sites and remains.

Resolution No. 10-07 was passed by the Winnebago Tribe on October 19, 2000, supporting the Yankton Sioux Tribe "from those who would despoil it."[3] Tribal Historic Preservation Officer from Standing Rock, Tim Mentz, arrived to voice encouragement to the Ihanktonwan people and to attend meetings held with the Corps of Engineers. His mother, Alma Mentz, as an Elder, strongly voiced her outrage to the Corps of Engineers for actions both at White Swan and at Standing Rock. Spiritual Elder George Ironshield and other Elders came to provide support, encouragement, solidarity, and guidance for the Yanktons.

On January 27, 2000, the Seminole Tribe of Oklahoma contributed $1,000 for the White Swan Spiritual Encampment and voiced their technical assistance and encouragement.[4] The Seventh Generation Fund, through the advocacy of Rosalie Little Thunder (board member) surfaced to support the White Swan Camp with a $2,000 donation for food, fuel, supplies, tents, blankets, equipment, and miscellaneous needs. She spoke of the vision of deceased Tribal Hunka relative Reuben Snake of the Winnebago Tribe, a founding member of the Seventh Generation Fund who was victorious in a battle with the Corps of Engineers in regaining land for Winnebago.

During the exhausting weeks of watching over the ancestors, the White Swan Negotiation Team reached out to the Advisory Council on Historic Preservation (ACHP) which is a presidentially appointed advisory group that oversees Tribal cultural resources and other national historic preservation issues. They came in full body on-site and were appropriately horrified. After late night meetings, I received a call from Mr. Allan Stanfield of the Denver ACHP, stating that a startling decision had been made. Due to the extensive difficulties encountered in the White Swan Case, the ACHP had decided to "foreclose" the Programmatic Agreement on the Missouri River, and it was severed. Instructions were given that it would have to be renegotiated.

Those heated renegotiations eventually led to an agreement that the relatives' remains would be left on-site for the thirty-day NAGPRA requirement, but not without a skirmish. The remains were gathered on a cold, blizzardy day with local combat veterans and Brave Heart Women Society members gently wrapping them into large red felt bundled with sage and prepared for reburial. During the gathering of remains, the Corps made a last-ditch attempt to place the remains in a railroad car that was pulled onto the site area, but they were forbidden to do so in a Yankton standoff that was resolved in a tipi over a hot bowl of soup and Indian bread. The Corps' colonel in charge was clearly affected by the emotional and surreal experience of walking with the ancestors and gave consent to leave the remains to be watched over by Yankton Tribal members without contacting his superiors. They had been attempting to move the remains to a secure site determined by them. We told them we were the secure site. We knew we had won this round.

That night, the remains were taken up to a newly constructed scaffold on a hill above the burial area under the light of an eerie red moon, coyotes howling in the background. Back at the "war room" the next day, I sat by Chair Archambeau who took a call from South Dakota governor Bill Janklow. She listened and then I heard her say, "No, thank you, Governor, we are taking the whole hill area for the reburial but thanks for calling." Apparently, Governor Janklow had called and offered thirty-some feet in the taken area for a reburial area, but Chair Archambeau took the whole hill for the Tribal reburial. What a matriarch!

After the thirty-day NAGPRA notification requirement was met, a well-attended reburial from bands of the Oceti Sakowin was held in support on the hills above old White Swan of the Yankton Sioux Tribe. Tribal folks from all over the Oceti and the country came to help rebury the ancestors with love, ceremony, support, caring, and honoring of our noble ancestors who lived in a different time of beauty, freedom and goodness. It was like being in the circle of a time ship that traveled back to honor them for their sacrifice. Deksi Vine helped us achieve a great victory, and this historic time will always be on our Wintercount, never to be forgotten. We walked proud with the ancestors, and they helped us also.

Following our historic reburial at White Swan, we were greeted with the news of a similar situation at Mad Bear Camp in Standing Rock, which they also fought for. During this period of time, we were told in ceremony that many of our ancestors were showing themselves to signal to us and others that the extreme disrespect that was occurring was unacceptable, and it was time for us to stand up against the disruptions and disrespect. There is much to battle.

This long dark winter of 1990–2000 was further dampened with the enactment of the 1999–2000 Water Resources Development Act, which was a land deal between the governor of South Dakota and South Dakota Game Fish and Parks, which intervened through federal legislation and transferred the taken areas along the Missouri River and transferred them from federal control to state control for parks and habitat areas.[5] Peter Caposello talks about it extensively in his book on the river.[6] According to the Surplus Property Act, taken areas no longer used by the Corps should have been transferred back to Yankton in areas that we occupied. It was another settler-colonial act that took more of our land but that we never fail to believe we will regain some day. We are the ultimate case of die-hard and will never relinquish our rights and presence along our beloved Missouri River. She takes care of us, and we will always take care of her.

There are, however, some bright spots in our constant fight to live along our sacred river. After we lost the areas due to the destructive Water Resources Development Act of 1999, I and members of our Cultural Committee exerted Presidential Executive Order 13007, which states that Native Americans have the right to access areas that they have had use of for many years.[7] Through the assistance of a visionary in the Corps, Ms. Linda Walker of the Portland Army Corps of Engineers office, we were able to convince the Omaha Corps Office to allow the Yankton Cultural Committee and the Brave Heart Society to utilize areas in west White Swan for the purpose of a ceremonial grounds for women's ceremonies, the Isnati Awica Dowanpi, and other designated ceremonies. This area was in fact an area where an altar had existed that belonged to the Deloria Family, through Unkanna, grandfather "Saswe." This was officially approved, and usage of the area officially began during the tenure of Chair Archambeau and the acting Corps commander. We continue to utilize this area for our ceremonies.

And today, we continue the work of being one with the Mni Sose, by developing a Cultural Bioregion, called the MNI WIZIPAN WAKAN (Sacred Water Bundle) that we are seeking to comanage on a 150-mile stretch of the Missouri River from Lower Brule Bottoms to Yankton, South Dakota. We will most certainly tell you about that in the near future. Deksi Vine still watches over and guides us. The water knows that we will succeed.

CHAPTER 20

VINE DELORIA, JR.'S INTERNATIONAL REACH

Building Consciousness and Solidarity

Édith Patrouilleau with Aurélie Journée-Duez

I was invited to contribute to this anthology by "following my instinct, writing down my feelings, and focusing on the idea of international solidarity." David Wilkins gathered from our conversations in Paris that I had "direct experience with the ways Vine's work has influenced activism in France." I hope to bring to life—or at least shed some light—on the story of how solidarity with Indigenous peoples began half a century ago in European countries, as both a witness and an activist from the early seventies until now.

International solidarity in France with Native peoples took its first tentative steps at the Université Paris 7 (Diderot), today known as Université Paris Cité. Headed by the engaged anthropologist Robert Jaulin, a short-lived American Indian Movement (AIM) French support group was set up in 1974 in the wake of the first Standing Rock International Treaty Conference that laid out the international strategy leading to the United Nations Declaration on the Rights of Indigenous Peoples (UNDRIP).[1] That same year, Swiss human rights organization Incomindios was founded to advocate for the rights of Indigenous Peoples worldwide with a special focus on North, Central, and South America.[2]

Custer Died for Your Sins was published in French in 1972. Ironically, the title for the French edition, *Peau-Rouge*, translates literally as R*d S**n.[3] Sadly, to date, it is Vine's only book to have been translated into French. Although Jaulin released a documentary film in 1976 entitled *We Talk . . . You Listen*, the book on which it was based was never translated.[4] Thus, for us, the body of Deloria's work remains in the original English, depriving most French speakers of direct access to the wealth of his writings. He is mainly read behind the doors of academia, so it has been up to academics to share this knowledge.

For those of us lucky enough to read them, *Custer Died for Your Sins*, *We Talk, You Listen*, *Of Utmost Good Faith*, *God Is Red*, and *The Trail of Broken Treaties* were the books that tore off the veil of lies and American myths that had been fed to us by the French school system and the media. That is when "Indians" began to become our contemporaries rather than ghosts of the past animated by delusions. As we well know, multiple Indigenous voices have followed in Deloria's footsteps—inspired by his seminal work—rewriting history, sharing with the world.

Vine Deloria, Jr. laid the foundations that have guided solidarity work, relentlessly asserting the inalienable sovereign rights of Tribal Nations as the rightful inheritance of every passing Indigenous generation. He demanded respect of the more than 371 treaties signed between Native Nations and the US government as the highest law of the land, advocated for reclamation of a land base that would sustain thriving Native communities, acknowledged the sacredness of the land, exposed the myths and lies hailed as historical facts by every US government, and exposed never-ending attempts to eradicate the presence of the original peoples of the land whether by genocidal or assimilationist policies. As he explained at length, Native Nations have specific, inherent rights that they have possessed and exercised since time immemorial.

I met Vine in 1974 when he agreed to be a member of the panel to hear my thesis defense. My subject was "Indian Government Policy and Indian Nationalism in the United States—The Struggle for Self-Determination." He was well acquainted with my thesis director, and I was so happy when he agreed to review my work. Vine and his family welcomed me at their home in Boulder, Colorado, fed me, and took care of the twenty-four-year-old I was. Standing with him outside his home as he practiced cracking a whip is an indelible memory. The thesis defense panel was never convened—life sometimes takes interesting turns. But I saw him then as a giant, which he will always remain for me and so many others.

Years later, reading *Singing for a Spirit*, which unravels his personal family lineage and stories, was an eye-opener to some complex history.[5] AIM and the Red Power movement had become part of the worldwide liberation movements of the 1970s that many of my generation embraced. Vine was certainly my inspiration and that of many others, along with AIM, when the siege of Wounded Knee caught the world's attention. It caught mine in Mombasa, Kenya, where it made the front page of the *Mombasa Times*.

Personal histories intertwine with the collective. In 1977 I coauthored *Nations Indiennes Nations Souveraines* (*Indian Nations, Sovereign Nations*), published by Editions François Maspero, a renowned publisher at the forefront of the French anti-imperialist movement.[6] It was the brainchild of photographer Jean François Graugnard who was covering social insurgencies taking place in France and who had literally bumped into the realities of Indian Country while on a tobacco-picking trip in Canada in 1975 and at the third International Indian Treaty Council Standing Rock conference a few months later. The book was released one week before the opening of the UN's 1977 Geneva conference (the meeting now remembered for the first Indigenous Peoples' Day proclamation) so it could be presented to the North American Indigenous delegations and contribute to making Indigenous perspectives and struggles visible to French-speaking media and readers. It was a bold title at the time; much ground has been covered since then.

The Final Resolution of the 1977 Geneva Conference stated:

> The representatives of the indigenous peoples gave evidence to the international community of the ways in which dis-

> crimination, genocide and ethnocide operated. While the situation may vary from country to country, the roots are common to all: they include the brutal colonization to open the way for the plunder of their land and resources by commercial interests seeking maximum profits; the massacres of millions of native peoples for centuries and the continuous grabbing of their land which deprives them of the possibility of developing their own resources and means of livelihood; the denial of self-determination of indigenous nations and peoples destroying their traditional value system and their social and cultural fabric. The evidence pointed to the combination of this oppression resulting in the further destruction of the indigenous nations.[7]

A new era was unleashed.

Danielle Faure had come across *Nations Indiennes Nations Souveraines*, and gotten in touch with us, and we then traveled to Turtle Island with her nine-year-old son to meet with mothers from the Haudenosaunee clans at Akwesasne. We also visited the survival schools in Minneapolis, Minnesota, and pushed on to Rapid City, South Dakota, to attend the Women of All Red Nations rally.[8] I participated in the Longest March from within the AIM camp from Minneapolis toward Washington, D.C., documenting along the way, and turning it into another book, *Les Chemins de la Survie* (*Paths of Survival*), self-published.[9] I had been welcomed at Akwesasne and Ganienkeh. On all counts, we were impressed by the role of women, a reality that was not evident from media reports then. These watershed moments laid the groundwork for action, and when we returned to France, we decided to form CSIA-Nitassinan (Committee in Solidarity with Indigenous Peoples of the Americas) in France under the nonprofit association law of 1901. Our mission was to put an end to the isolation imposed upon Native peoples by the US and the colonial governments of the continent. "Nitassinan" was added at suggestion of Gilbert Pilot, a young Innu activist who, along with traditional Elder Matthieu Mestanapeu André, was a respected knowledge keeper. In Innu-aimun, "Nitassinan" means "our sacred land we cherish" and refers to the ancestral territory of which they are the guardians.

The first point of the 1977 Geneva Conference final resolution resolved "to observe October 12, the day of the so-called 'discovery' of America as International Day of Solidarity with the Indigenous Peoples of the Americas." We answered the call and have held such a day every single year without fail since 1982. I wish I could speak the names of every Indigenous person from across the Americas who accepted our invitation to fly across the ocean and be a guest speaker, as on each October 12 International Solidarity Day we gather French audiences around their testimonies and calls for action. Since I can't go over it all, I choose to share a few of the uplifting moments we were blessed to witness.

We are proud to have become the first support group for the American Indian political prisoner Leonard Peltier at the international level (1978). Sylvain Duez-Alesandrini, our Corsican brother and strategic member of the CSIA, was instrumental in organizing this effort. I recall the joint statement I had the honor to read to the Human Rights Council in Geneva on July 12, 2013, at the meeting of the Expert Mechanism on the Rights of Indigenous Peoples. Leonard Peltier's case was examined as an emblematic case at the Expert Seminar on Indigenous Peoples and the Administration of Justice, organized by the Office of the High Commissioner on Human Rights in Madrid in November 2003. The rights and protections of political prisoners are critical issues, and Leonard and many others are important to us.

In 2006, Evo Morales appointed Luzmila Carpio, a traditional Aymara-Quechua singer and composer, to serve as ambassador of the Plurinational State of Bolivia in Paris. CSIA had first met Luzmila upon her arrival in exile in France in the mid-1980s, a time when singing in Quechua was not an option in Bolivia. In 2007, she opened International Solidarity Day and welcomed the brothers and sisters who had come to take part: Mapuche from Chile, Wayuu from Venezuela, Maya K'iche from Guatemala, and Lakota from Pine Ridge. Then came the unforgettable moment when she improvised a song accompanied by Henry Red Cloud on his hand drum. "Singing is a political act," she said, "brothers and sisters, we are living victorious moments, but we still have a long way to go and our greatest victories are yet to come; the first steps have been taken. And I feel a strong emotion when, with the past in my heart and my eyes set on the horizon, I see how we have maintained the course we set for ourselves and that each day we are getting stronger and stronger."

Fast forward to 2024. What seemed so far away is occurring. That is to say the numbers of those who listen when Native peoples talk are growing. We acknowledge with gratitude that Indigenous people lead in this common struggle for future generations and Mother Earth. We have become allies, accomplices. We educate ourselves.

International solidarity comes in many guises. CSIA acts to provide space for the voices of Indigenous defenders to resonate and be provided the opportunity to be heard by a French or even the broader European public. As a French organization, we are keenly aware of our responsibilities in solidarity with the Indigenous peoples still under French domination: the Kali'na, Teko, Wayampi, Wayana, Paykweneh, and Lokono in Guiana. Campaigns are launched at the request of active Indigenous members of the resistance on the ground. We operate from the International Center of Popular Culture born in 1976 from a political will to put material and human means at the disposal of nonprofits supporting national liberation struggles, defending human rights, and showing solidarity with migrant workers. We share a small and crowded office with Échanges Solidaires, a nonprofit that distributes organic coffee produced by Zapatista cooperatives in northern Chiapas communities. We work in partnership with sister organizations, setting up partnerships with relevant nongovernmental organizations around specific issues. It involves translating, facilitating meetings, and working as a link with government agencies, the European Parliament, and the UN Educational, Scientific, and Cultural Organization.

When a Mohawk delegation stopped by in Paris to take part in International Solidarity Day 2008 on their way to Geneva, Kenneth Deer and a small group of them needed the French government to let them enter the country on their Haudenosaunee passports. Just three years before, Tom Deer (Teiowí:sonte) had been jailed for one night at the Paris airport as the border police would not let him use his nation's passport to travel through France on his way home from Geneva. He had to buy new tickets through Amsterdam to return home. "In contemporary times, a national passport exists as the ultimate expression of identity," he stated. We are proud to have made the right connections so that *let pass* documents has been granted on a case-by-case basis since then. We are hopeful that the policy can soon be permanently changed to allow every Indigenous person to travel with their nation's passport as a matter of course. We're not quite there yet but have taken an important step in the right direction and will continue to advocate.

CSIA followed the developments of the recognition of Indigenous peoples' rights leading to the adoption by the General Assembly of UNDRIP in September 2007 at the presessional Working Group on Indigenous Populations of the Sub-Commission on the Promotion and Protection of Human Rights and at the Commission on Human Rights. Effective participation of Indigenous players has been greatly facilitated since 1978 by the Indigenous Peoples' Center for Documentation, Research and Information (DOCIP), as initiated at the request of the 1977 delegations, which has been instrumental in providing support to Indigenous representatives who take part in sessions working on Indigenous issues. Its database contains all the interventions collected from Indigenous delegates and other non-Indigenous international or government participants during international conferences. DOCIP also offers translation and interpretation services to Indigenous delegates in English, French, Spanish and Russian, and provides meeting rooms and working spaces. Since 1985, we have also been a member of the European Alliance for the Self Determination of Indigenous Peoples, which emerged from a network of several independent European support groups and human rights organizations from Germany, France, Austria, and Switzerland.

We've also taken part in the Sacred Runs for Land and Life of the AIM Anishinaabe, participated in the Continental Campaign "500 Years of Indigenous, Black and Popular Resistance," and worked on the successful campaign to award the Nobel Peace Prize to the Mayan representative of Guatemala, Rigoberta Menchu Tum (1992). We stood with the Mohawks during the Oka/Kanesatake crisis (1990) and have supported the Zapatista struggle since the uprising in Chiapas (1994). We mobilized alongside the Indigenous Environmental Network and Honor the Earth during the Paris Climate Conference, or the 21st Conference of the Parties (COP21) (2015), and many more actions in solidarity throughout the years. That is who we are.

At this point we're focused on transition. Talented and determined youth who move fast are joining us. They are eager to contribute their passion and their skills. Time is running short, so this is good. I work closely with one of these new leaders, Aurélie Journée-Duez, president of CSIA since 2017. We spoke at length about the Deloria legacy and influence on French activism. I have included her thoughts and experiences here.

Aurélie: Transmission of knowledge is ongoing and it's an honor for me to share a part of this long story of international solidarity with Indigenous peoples of the so-called Americas. Édith, you and I met at Standing Rock in November 2016 thanks to ethnohistorian Joelle Rostkowski and Patsy Phillips (Cherokee). At the time I was interning at the Museum of Contemporary Native Arts in Santa Fe, New Mexico, and working on my PhD. Édith recommended that I read *Custer Died for Your Sins*, so I it was one of the first books I bought in an old bookstore when I got back to Santa Fe. I remember the day I was reading it as I was riding the bus to work at the museum. A white cowboy kept staring at me like I was doing something wrong. He asked: "Do you know what you're doing?" "Yes," I replied, " I am reading a book." "Do you enjoy it?" He was not friendly. I understood then that the book had power.

I also saw how Deloria's work impacted not only Indigenous scholars and activists but also Indigenous artists who graduated from the Institute of American Indian Arts. I quickly came to understand that in order to write or speak about Native lands and territories, histories, and worldviews, it was definitely necessary to immerse myself into his work. *God Is Red* helped me analyze and understand some Indigenous artistic practices that I was working on, such as the way the artists visualized their cosmologies and how they wanted to put them into images.[10] We cannot talk about Indigenous futurisms without thinking about space and time. Deloria helped me think about these two concepts that have been colonized the same way as entire epistemologies have been colonized by western theories and approaches. As he explained, "The western preoccupation with history and a chronological description of reality was not a dominant factor in any tribal conception of either time or history. Indian tribes had little use for recording past events; the idea of keeping a careful chronological record of events never seemed to impress the greater number of tribes of the continent."[11]

I also remember the way Deloria described "anthropologists and other friends." It still makes me smile as I have recently obtained my PhD in anthropology. I love this: "Indians are equally certain that Columbus brought anthropologists on his ships when he came to the New World. How else could he have made so many wrong deductions about where he was?"[12] Irony permits us to reflect upon how we write, what we write, and for whom. We all make mistakes or hesitate, as scholars and/or activists, I think. But the most important thing is not only to apologize, but to go beyond, and forward.[13]

Aurélie's words should give us all hope for the future, as up-and-coming leaders like her know it is essential to study and listen to Indigenous people, particularly Elders, activists, leaders, and scholars like Vine Deloria, Jr. as they take up this hard work.

I feel it's what has been done all these years at CSIA. Instead of making assumptions, this organization followed paths drawn by so many Indigenous friends and partners. During the 2015 Paris Climate Conference, officially known as the 21st Conference of the Parties to the United Nations Framework Convention on Climate Change, we were involved in divest campaigns organized by Indigenous Environmental Network, Women's Earth and Climate Action Network, and the Climate Coalition. The collective work that was accomplished at that time made it possible for us in 2016 to confront BNP Paribas Bank together with Tara Houska (Anishinaabe) and Kanahus Manuel (Secwepmec Nation). In October of that year, Cannupa Hanska Luger (Mandan, Arikara, Hidatsa, Lakota), agreed to join us after we had met in Santa Fe, to speak about Indigenous art and politics. It was an honor for me to organize artistic workshops with him and Romani young people from Romania that created relationships and highlighted commonalities between situations of discrimination and oppression from different parts of the world.

From Standing Rock, we had brought back artworks that were done at camp by Indigenous friends dealing with issues of repression because of their dedication to the defense of their lands and territories. We also had the chance to welcome hip-hop artist and Water Protector Nataani Means (Oglala Lakota, Diné) and sing with him to celebrate the resistance. In October 2018, we continued to honor Indigenous resistance with folk singer and Water Protector Raye Zaragoza (Akimel O'odham, Pima/Xicana). With each initiative, CSIA followed the path Indigenous activists and artists identified as the right way to spread the word and share their frontline struggle.

We cannot speak about Indigenous movements for lands and territories without speaking about the power of Indigenous women. In 2019, CSIA dedicated our annual gathering to them. The most important thing was highlighting Murdered and Missing Indigenous Women issues. Violence against the Earth is violence against women. This was powerfully said by Michelle Cook (Diné) who spoke about colonization and decolonization, artist and activist Daiara Tukano (Tukano, Brazil), and by the filmmaker Kim O'Bomsawin from the Abenaki Nation. She directed *Quiet Killing*, a vibrant documentary about the silence that remained for such a long time about the violence Indigenous children suffered.[14] Joyce

Echaquan was another young Indigenous victim of racism in Canada, and it was important to pay her tribute in 2020.[15]

That same year COVID-19 hit the world, and Indigenous peoples suffered, in particular. Once again capitalism and the western economic system brought viruses. Fortunately, we were able to hold our 2020 gathering, reflecting on how this pandemic should force all of us to change our way of life as Indigenous movements of resistance have tried to do since the advent of colonization.

I believe Vine would have been very pleased to see how anthropologists, activists, and other friends have been inspired by his work to together build a New World, a true New World, decolonized this time, for this sentence is true: "Decolonization is not a metaphor."[16]

International solidarity is about us all and this new world is coming.

Gratitude, Édith

CHAPTER 21

FROM POLITICIZATION TO MOVEMENT BUILDING

Indigenous Media and the New Indigenous Renaissance

Melanie K. Yazzie

Analog Politics

I grew up in the 1980s before the internet was invented and social media consumed our lives. We had five channels on our TV, a radio, and some cassette tapes—and a decent record collection my parents had amassed over the years. My mom, a product of the counterculture of the 1970s, refused to let us watch corporate television or movies made by capitalist media machines like Disney. Like most everything else in our small house, she commandeered the television, making us watch the only channel that had educational and political content—PBS. So, I watched *Sesame Street. The MacNeil/Lehrer Report. Masterpiece Theater*. My sisters and I would sometimes get up at the crack of dawn to sneak a few hours watching cartoons on Saturday mornings, quietly dragging our blankies to the living room so we wouldn't wake up my parents. These were the only moments when we got to watch corporate television, when my mom's eagle eyes were averted by exhaustion.

I dreaded the six o'clock news. Why was there so much war and death, and why did everyone talk so blandly about such horrific things?

I expected more outrage. At least my mom was outraged; she obsessively watched the news even though it upset her. I often wondered why she so faithfully did something that upset her so much. When I finally figured it out—that she had a sense of duty to know what was happening in the world, even though most of it was terrible—I started to force myself to watch, too.

It took a bit longer for me to realize that my mom's commitment to watching the news was also a form of distress from witnessing a lifetime of injustices, on the news and in her own life. She had a habit of calling our local congressional representatives and chewing them out on the phone for supporting US wars abroad or slashing public spending at home. She talked about politics constantly, often with rage. Her persistence wore off on me; I became politicized before I reached ten years of age. I remember the moment I felt that same rage. One night we were watching the news; footage of US-led coalition forces bombing Baghdad flashed across our television screen. The first Gulf War had begun. The news reporter—I think he had a British accent—was scared and somber, sometimes having to yell above the din of bombs as they devoured their targets in a burst of orange flame. The extraordinary expanse of night on our television screen lit up only when bombs arced across the sky. I remember thinking they looked like shooting stars.

Witnessing this historic event changed me. I was uneasy, imagining what Baghdad's people were going through; how many of them were dying or injured, engulfed in flame and darkness. No matter what may have driven the United States to bomb Iraq (I didn't really understand at the time), it just didn't feel right watching hundreds of people die and an ancient city razed to the ground. I felt helpless in the face of a great injustice.

I finally understood my mom's outrage.

That was January 17, 1991, and I was nine years old. Images of war and injustice continued unabated throughout the decade. Two years later, I remember watching the Rwandan genocide play out on live television. And a few years after that, the United States bombed Serbia and invaded Kosovo. I remember news about Irish Republican bombs in Belfast, the bloody and triumphant struggle to end apartheid in South Africa, the Alfred P. Murrah federal building in Oklahoma City torn in half, and more genocide—this time Bosnian. Other than the Monica Lewinsky scandal, which seemed more like gossip than a significant world event, everything else bled into one steady stream of mass violence that shocked and despaired. That fury-inducing sense of injustice grew inside me as the decade wore on.

I was shaped for life by that decade of news about war, genocide, and death. Maybe it wasn't extraordinary compared to other decades, but it was the decade when I came of age and began developing my sense of identity in the world. By the time I graduated from high school in 2000, I wanted to become a foreign war correspondent or a documentary filmmaker—a hard-hitting journalist reporting stories of great suffering and heroism from war zones and front lines. Even Princess Diana's death affected me. I secretly admired her willingness to reject the elitism of British aristocracy and go to front lines of suffering to help the world's downtrodden in the manner of Mother Teresa and Nelson Mandela, both of whom featured prominently alongside Princess Diana as protagonists of major social, environmental, and economic justice efforts in the 1990s. I wanted to bring stories of the oppressed (and their champions) to the world, believing if people knew what was happening, they, too, would be outraged by the injustice in the world and compelled to act.

I didn't become a foreign war correspondent or a documentary filmmaker. After earning my bachelor's degree in political science (which was the closest to a degree in politics I could find at my college), I spent the better part of a decade pursuing my commitment to justice in the Native nonprofit world before I became disillusioned by the lack of material change I saw in that industry. Nonprofits did little to advance my political growth beyond the watershed moments of my youth; mostly, I was disgusted by their obsession with maintaining enormous operating budgets at the expense of creating sustainable programs for our people. Politically speaking, all I learned during that time is what not to do if you want to organize for real change. Somewhat embittered, I went back to school, and, after eight years, earned a PhD in the most social justice–oriented field I could find: American studies. Six years into graduate school, I began to engage in grassroots community organizing about Indigenous issues, becoming more politicized (and radicalized) by direct advocacy work. The uprising at Standing Rock in 2016 occurred at the end of my PhD journey, punctuating this second chapter of my political journey. I say "second chapter" because education alone never politicized me, no matter how many classes I took on feminism, queer politics, critical race theory, or settler colonialism as an undergraduate or graduate student. I've always been a very action-oriented person and cite my on-the-ground experience, whether this be through coordinating projects for nonprofits or organizing on grassroots front lines, as my greatest moments of politicization. I remember defending my dissertation—which itself was about Navajo politics and grassroots resistance—into my committee, mere days after helping to organize a major supply run and caravan to the No DAPL frontlines, which I visited in person two months later once I had turned in the final draft.

Having frontline experience at Standing Rock and elsewhere—and being the subject of many interviews and news stories about these various Indigenous resistance campaigns—changed my perceptions of media. I've had to deal with many ignorant (white) journalists who require an entire Indian 101 history lesson before they are capable enough to tackle complicated interview questions. I have also repeatedly experienced deception and censorship by (white) journalists. The typical scenario is as follows: I take the time to commit to a one-hour (usually hard-hitting) interview. When the story comes out a week later, I discover that the journalist has chosen benign sound bites to bolster some predetermined angle, typically portraying me (and Native people in general) as idiots or criminals (without consent, of course). Often these sound bites are taken out of context and distorted to seem more sensationalist. I see this common practice of white journalists who report on Indigenous movements as a form of whitewashing, where they (or their editors) aggressively edit comments to make Native people less threatening to their largely white audience. This is so common that I've begun to treat interactions with journalists as a type of combat, which is infuriating but also sort of entertaining. Those reading this are likely familiar with the racism in media I'm describing. Who can forget the racist "Something Else" debacle on election night 2020 as CNN reported voting statistics according to racial group, or the firing of Rick Santorum from CNN in May 2021 for ignorantly claiming "there was nothing here" during a private speech one month earlier?[1] These tiresome media habits are part-and-parcel of the vilification and erasure that has always defined America's stance toward Native people. And when it comes to Indigenous political movements, mainstream media is particularly cunning at portraying Indigenous movements and organizers as criminals, another racist (and tired) trope.

Apparently, these habits are hard to break. In *The Indian Historian*, Vine Deloria, Jr. argued that Native people must be more judicious with how they work with mass media to avoid this type of exploitation and reinforcement of negative stereotypes. That was 1972. Fast forward to 2024 and the same problems persist. As in the early 1970s, when Red Power emerged as a modern-day Indigenous political renaissance, 2020 represents, for me, a particularly momentous year after almost a decade of Indigenous uprisings at Standing Rock, Oak Flat, Mauna Kea, Unist'ot'en, and elsewhere—the renaissance of our generation. Despite the presence and impact of these movements, mainstream journalistic representations of the uprisings (or of Indians more broadly) didn't change. Rather, the Indigenous freedom fighters of today, the water protectors and land defenders of our current movement, face the same techniques of soft war counterinsurgency from corporate media, a war of representation that previous generations faced when they similarly refused to accept genocide and US colonial aggression: defamation as violent terrorists in the media, or, portrayed as impoverished wretches in need of (white) salvation.

However, while this type of anti-Indianism in corporate media—particularly the news—has remained relatively intact, within a few short years we have witnessed a remarkable cultural revolution when it comes to representation. We saw the toppling of monuments to colonization, the retirement of anti-Indian mascots like the Washington football team, and the replacement of holidays like Columbus Day with Indigenous Peoples' Day in 2020. Native-written television shows like *Reservation Dogs* and *Rutherford Falls* have gone mainstream. In 2022, *Prey*, the blockbuster fifth film in the Predator series, starred Amber Midthunder (Fort Peck Assiniboine and Sioux) and made a serious, if flawed, attempt to re-create a precontact Comanche society with a Native cast. Most recently, Martin Scorsese consulted with the Osage Nation to make *Killers of the Flower Moon*.

These hard-won victories are the culmination of decades of Indigenous resistance and movement building that has blossomed alongside frontline confrontations to defend land and protect water. I believe these victories prove that Native-led political organizing must also target the realm of culture, whether this be pop culture, museums and monuments, or sports teams, for culture is the battleground in which the war of ideas plays out most centrally. This is likely why the right is attacking critical race theory and other so-called radical ideas in education; they know what's at stake in waging a culture war. After witnessing these events, however, it would seem Indians have gained some ground in the culture war against US imperialism and colonialism. This is good news.

Given the power and momentum of this cultural revolution, it seems worth considering how we can redirect our political organizing toward the cultural arena that remains intractable in the face of this larger tide of historical change: mainstream news. Turning toward media (or perhaps back to media) is a sort of coming-of-age shift for me; I have always focused on on-the-ground organizing. While this still takes center stage in my political activity, my experiences as a social and historical actor in the contemporary Indigenous renaissance I describe here generated a certain critical awareness about media coverage—its biases, limitations, utility, and role—when it comes to Indigenous movements. Alongside a handful of committed Indigenous comrades and relatives, I have thus begun to build what I hope is a robust Indigenous media presence in

North America that is aligned with the interests of Indigenous-led social movements for justice, decolonization, and self-determination. I talk more about this project, which we call Red Media, in the last section of this essay. However, before I turn to that topic, I would like to talk briefly about another type of media—social media—that mediates and, in many ways, commands our relationship with politics and news, oftentimes to dubious ends when it comes to movement building.

Digital Politics

The media of my childhood was categorically different from what youth consume today. In my day, it was the news (and my mom). Today, teens are politicized largely by what they encounter on social media. Sometimes the content is news, but often it's predigested sound bites tailored and curated for social media circulation—infographics, Twitter threads, memes, Instagram slides, or minute-long TikTok explainer videos. Belonging to the only generation that knew the world both before and after the internet (this generation is sometimes called the Xennial generation, which is sandwiched between gen X and millennials), I'm fortunate to have witnessed—and grown up with—these two dominant forms of media that play a role in politicizing youth. I've not only consumed and written the former, analog news, but I've also created and shared every type of social media soundbite I list above. Despite their differences, both serve the same purpose for their respective generation: politicization.

Whereas the analog news of my youth years used technology to help deliver information, social media as a form of digital news exists entirely in the world of the internet. This means digital news is largely self-referential, existing exclusively on the internet and relying solely on corporate-owned tech giants like Facebook and Google not only for circulation but also creation. In this sense, digital news is one step removed from material conditions. It doesn't purport to use technology to deliver the news; rather, it is considered the news. Every post, hot take, tweet, or rant—regardless of its basis in reality, fact, or research—is treated as news. Even analog media outlets now cite these sound bites as news (how often have you seen a tweet in a report on CNN or when Trump was president, Fox featuring one of his tweets as fact?). This general culture regarding news on social media likely led to the fake news phenomenon that grew during Donald Trump's presidency. Since everything may be considered a fact, so, too, can nothing be considered a fact. Everything—including reality—is open to question.

From what I can tell, this has had a mixed impact on not only the news but also on Indigenous movements (and how Indigenous organizers engage with media as a tool of movement building). Most of what's been written on Indigenous political organizing and social media argues that social media has increased Indigenous people's "ability to create international solidarity as well as elevating Indigenous issues to a global platform," viewing social media as a favorable and beneficial addition to political organizing.[2] Scholars also argue that social media allows Indigenous users to imagine alternatives and "destabilise colonial power," thereby contributing to decolonization.[3] There is certainly evidence to support this view, as there is a long history of Indigenous movements utilizing media for their own purposes. As Marisa Duarte notes, the Ejercito Zapatista de Liberación Nacional—more commonly known as the EZLN—is "widely cited as the first social movement to effectively use digital tactics for collective organizing."[4] Following a short period of armed confrontation with the Mexican state that led to a ceasefire, the EZLN shifted their resistance strategy to a war of "ink-and-Internet."[5] Organizers of major Indigenous uprisings like #IdleNoMore and #NoDAPL have been similarly successful in utilizing social media to elevate the political messages of those struggles, contributing to the larger war of ideas I mention earlier.

However, I have yet to see Indigenous scholars (or organizers) seriously discuss the drawbacks of social media for Indigenous movements. For one, mass migration to social media means that news is now largely made up of editorials, which are produced by millions of users and shared and reshared until they go viral—the holy grail of social media relevance. At one time limited to one section of a newspaper or magazine, which would regularly publish multiple types of journalism like investigative reports, essays, analysis, beat news, and photography, sound-bite social media editorials now dominate the entire news cycle. This is the "hot take" industry of social media news, where users opine about current events (or share raw content, like videos recorded on iPhones) in a rapid sequence of tweet, posts, and replies, developing angles (takes) within a matter of hours and recruiting others to agree with them. This user-driven frenzy creates newsworthiness; a hot take that goes viral assumes an almost infallible veracity due simply to its popularity, which itself often depends on a user's agreement (or not) with the personality or politics of the person sharing the hot take (rather than the information itself). Indeed, a single tweet is now taken as fact and circulated, cited, and regurgitated in a closed feedback loop that gains power every time it's shared. Quantity equals facticity in the viral ecology of social media editorials. While Trump is likely the most famous offender when it comes to this phenomenon, it's necessary to point out that Indigenous and left activists—as well as everyday people who use social media for political purposes but are not necessarily active in social movements—participate in this online culture as willingly and heartily as Trump.

Social media is so congested with these fast-paced sound-bite editorials that I often cannot find actual news about a particular current event. Instead, when searching a hashtag or keyword associated with an event, I typically wade through a labyrinth of hot takes and hyperniche navel gazing aggressively curated by algorithms. This isn't to say corporate news doesn't have an angle or agenda—of course media equals power and the hot takes of the ruling class have been rammed down the throats of every American for decades. But I seriously question if the hot-take industry of social media "news" challenges the hold on structural power that corporations still have. The very medium we use to create information is owned, controlled, manipulated, and censored by some of the wealthiest people in human history. Anishinaabe intellectual Leanne Betasamosake Simpson sums it up well: "I have no ability to structurally intervene [on social media]. Yet, almost more than any other structure, the Internet has structurally intervened in my life."[6]

In addition to its relative futility as a method for challenging structural power, much of what is considered activism and movement building on social media is really just a form of highly mediated and biased politicization. This is as true for the left—and Indigenous politics—as it is for the right. To be clear, I recognize and acknowledge that social media plays an undeniable role in shaping our political worlds. In this sense, I agree with organizers and scholars that we should continue to harness its power to advance struggles for Indigenous decolonization and self-determination. However, politicization is only one aspect of political organizing and should not be confused with movement building. In *As We Have Always Done: Indigenous Freedom through Radical Resistance*, Simpson discusses the limitations of social media for Indigenous movement building. Citing her first-person experience organizing for the Idle No More uprising of 2012 and 2013 in Canada, she says that she "began to realize that Idle No More wasn't a movement that we could sustain. Most of my comrades I had never met in person. While there were small groups of people meeting and strategizing about specific actions and events, we had no mechanism to make decisions as a movement because at this point social media had replaced organizing . . . because we had shallow cyber relationships, instead of real-world ones, the larger structure fell apart quickly."[7] She goes on to argue that movement building may not be able to happen online primarily because it is removed from the material relationships that have always been necessary for successful movements. She states, the "movement building step is critical in all movements, but it is particularly crucial to think this through in the age of the Internet.[8] I wonder if this [the internet] creates further alienation . . . from the Indigenous material world. I wonder if this is a digital dispossession from ourselves because it further removes us from grounded normativity."[9]

Simpson cites Glen Coulthard's notion of grounded normativity, which describes the pivotal role of Indigenous relations with land in movements for decolonization. Simpson draws from Anishinaabe oral histories about traveling to describe what Indigenous movement building looks like when based on grounded normativity: "Indigenous agitators of the past . . . spent large amounts of time, years in fact, movement building. Movement building is relationship building, and it involved traveling large distances to create a physical connection with other human and nonhuman beings."[10] This tradition of traveling is the opposite of digital dispossession because it pulls us from the unreality of social media into real relations with each other and our other-than-human relatives. Like Simpson, I worry that well-meaning people confuse their online political activity—whether this be engaging in political debates, hot-take journalism, call outs, content sharing, or forum hosting—with movement building, becoming even more alienated from actual movements built through relationships.

What does this mean for media work and Indigenous movements? I believe social media is beneficial for movement work when it's used as a digital tool to amplify and report on material conditions. The EZLN model is worth studying and updating for our current day and age. However, social media is harmful—dare I say counterrevolutionary—when we mistake politicization for movement building, replacing the slow, purposeful work of building movements and relationships with the shallow relationships and hot-take grandstanding that counts for much of online activism. Digital politics cannot and should not take the place of real politics forged in relation—and in struggle—with others. All movement-oriented media ought to emerge from and nourish actual resistance struggles and offline political relationships. I turn to this in the next section.

A New Indigenous Media

While I sometimes enjoy the biting political analysis offered by hot-take journalists on social media, such practices seem to have eclipsed other types of movement-oriented media. What is the antidote to this challenging situation? I believe it starts with bringing analog news—slow news might also be a good term—back into Indigenous politics by reporting on movements in person and offering a broad spectrum of journalism, writing, and filmmaking on them, regularly and with an impeccable degree of integrity and excellence. I would also argue that trained journalists (it should go without saying these journalists should be Indigenous) who are themselves active in movements ought to lead this charge because only those who understand movements from the inside out—often from direct participation—can accurately report on them and build trust with other movement actors. In other words, we need Indigenous journalism by and for movements—journalism produced by fellow travelers with their feet planted firmly in the Earth. I've recently had the opportunity to help build one such media project called Red Media. By design, Red Media is neither social-media oriented, nor did it arise from social media. To the contrary, we started as a movement, arising from the revolutionary work of an Indigenous grassroots organization I cofounded in 2014. Red Media focuses on developing slow media like books, investigative journalism, and podcast news shows. All our content is produced by Indigenous people and the organization is run entirely by Indigenous people. While we do produce editorial content, we strive to balance it with news and never turn to social media to write hot-take editorials; instead, we host a podcast series that fulfills this purpose through conversation-based political analysis featuring rotating commentators, most of whom are organizers and intellectuals.

It's also worth noting that Red Media refuses to exist on the margins, an inadequate and racist space Indigenous content producers are familiar—and fed up—with. Like other Indigenous journalists and writers, we, too, expect to be taken as seriously as the movements we cover. Per Deloria's 1972 provocation, how do we move from the margins to the center without losing our message or being co-opted? The answer seems pretty clear: we must be grounded in movements and real-world relationships, treating social media with a cautious and perhaps more utilitarian stance, and building a powerful Indigenous media presence without apologies. We are primed in this historical moment to harness recent cultural revolutions into a sustained, well-organized, and Native-run media presence. I imagine such a project might elicit a nod of approval from Deloria.

CHAPTER 22

MEDIA PLIGHT

Mark Trahant

Does the media have its own plight? Something the dictionary defines as a "dangerous, difficult, or otherwise unfortunate situation."

"Unfortunate" covers a lot of media ground. It's unfortunate when five Indigenous members of Congress (at 0.93 percent) is significantly better than the number of Native writers and producers in national news organizations (estimated at two-tenths of 1 percent and zero for broadcast).

Vine Deloria, Jr. didn't write a lot about press performance. That's too bad. There are so many great stories he could have examined.

His distaste for mainstream media was clear in many of the pieces he did write. "Our foremost plight is our transparency," Deloria wrote in *Custer Died for Your Sins*. "Experts paint us as they would like us to be. Often we paint ourselves as we wish we were or we might have been."

This contradiction is certainly true for colonial media, painting us as they would like it to have been.

Many years ago, I had a conversation with Vine about media coverage and gaming. We talked about the changes swiftly taking place regarding both subjects. When the Indian Gaming Regulatory Act was under consideration by Congress, the proposed 1988 law was seen as a rollback of a Supreme Court victory in the *Cabazon* case.[1] We were both speaking at an anniversary for the Newberry Library in Chicago, on September 13, 1997.

At that point I had ten years' worth of coverage about Indian gaming, starting at the *Arizona Republic* in the 1980s.

This is how the story began in the mainstream press. As the *Philadelphia Inquirer* reported on September 19, 1988: "Gambling on Indian reservations, a booming business of bingo parlours and small casinos, would be subject to federal and state regulation under a bill passed by the Senate last week."

Subject to new regulation—federal and state regulation. An assault on sovereignty.

Then, less than a decade later, the mass media story had changed. A September 1997 story by *Forbes* magazine carried the new narrative. "It was a soft-headed idea from the start. Hoping to appease a poor and politically embarrassing minority and their liberal allies, Congress in 1988 set parameters allowing American Indians to run casinos. Gambling would be the new 'buffalo' for impoverished tribes."

Just like that, Congress "gave" Indians casinos. That one paragraph let Congress off the hook and it undermined Tribes at the same time. Instead of a story about a Tribe coming up with its own regulatory structure, the premise of the *Cabazon* litigation, it became Congress taking that away . . . and then gifting Native people an economic engine. The new buffalo.

I like to think of gaming in terms of a ten-thousand-year arc. We have stories about gaming from time immemorial, a narrative that is backed up by a rich archaeological record. Gaming is not a new activity for Indigenous people. (I love that the stick game or bone game has "devices" from centuries ago for a game that is still played today.)

There is another idea worth exploring. In 1983, Deloria wrote about the need for sophistication by the Native press. Too many reprint what is said about us by others. "One can only conclude that it has not been access to news that has been the deficiency," he wrote. "Rather it has been the interpretation of the information that has been sadly lacking. Indians seem to know what's happening. However, they seem to be badly handicapped in interpreting what events, policies, and personalities really mean in their lives."

He suggested, "a generation of people who can interpret the meaning of events for their people, we will have made a very great stride toward determining our own futures." We are on the same track (and it's something that Vine heard me talk about at the Newberry.) And it's very much a press context.

In 1947, a group of scholars came up with the idea that context is the essential link between journalism and democracy. The Hutchins Commission said:

> The account of an isolated fact, however accurate in itself, may be misleading and, in effect, untrue. . . . The country has many groups which are partially insulated from one another and which need to be interpreted to one another. Factually correct but substantially untrue accounts of the behaviors of members of one of these social islands can intensify the antagonisms of others toward them. A single incident will be accepted as a sample group action unless the press has given a flow of information and interpretation concerning the relations between two racial groups such as to enable the reader to set a single event in its proper perspective. If allowed to pass as a sample of such action, the requirement that the press present an accurate account of the day's events in a context which gives them meaning has not been met.

My context was about mainstream media. It was the intellectual "why" to the story about the gaming narrative. But it's also a measure of how often the press gets it wrong.

And now that Vine is gone we should take this notion and apply it to our own media, including social media. Why do we share on social media stories about us that are totally done without us?

There are so many stories about Indian Country that are factually incorrect and substantially untrue. So over time these accounts fail to report the complexity of water rights, crime and justice, child welfare, or even gaming.

The call here is to raise the standards of our own journalism. It's time to get better at nuance and uncovering the roots, adding context that gives the story meaning.

CHAPTER 23

VINE DELORIA, JR. AND INDIAN EDUCATION

Gregory A. Cajete

Introduction

I first met Vine Deloria, Jr. at Cal State–Sacramento where I had been invited by my cousin to give a talk for their Annual American Indian Week. Vine was the keynote speaker, and I was one of several other invited presenters at the conference. Running late due to a flight delay and happy to see that a few students had waited for me, I entered the meeting room and started my slide presentation immediately. I did not at first notice that Vine was sitting in the back of the room. I talked about my work at the Institute of American Indian Arts developing a curriculum that integrated western science with art and the cultural histories and stories of Native Science. I showed slides of Native cultural histories of science and my work with students learning about their own histories. I shared what they learned about western science and ultimately how they presented this knowledge through their own artistic expression.

After the presentation, Vine introduced himself, and we had a conversation about Native Science that lasted more than two hours. He was excited that I was a Native teacher, teaching Native Science to Native students in a Native school. Of course, I had read some of his books, and I remember asking him for guidance about writing my first book, *Look to the Mountain: An Ecology of Indigenous Education.*[1] He gave me great advice, and we had several conversations about the book thereafter. When I completed the manuscript in 1994, he graciously consented to write the preface. Thus began my personal relationship with Vine that lasted almost two decades until his untimely passing.

During that time, we had many conversations by phone, letters, and in person. Our talks were wide-ranging—the existence of Native giants and little people and their frequent mention in traditional stories; what if traditional forms of Native education that included "Native Science" had not been interrupted by colonization; the state of Indian education and the impact western education has had on Native people. We also had deep discussions about the continued sustainability of Native culture, communities, and lands as well as Native philosophy and the role it might play in a global context of informing a more environmentally sustainable future for all people.

Vine's Thoughts on Indian Education

Although Vine was a master of historical and social/political analysis, especially as it pertained to Indigenous peoples, he was also a visionary, theologian, philosopher, and deeply spiritual person. He had an astute ability to have deep dialogue, to listen carefully and observe the social, political, and cultural activities of people. These traits, combined with his tenacious scholarship, terse writing, and reflective orations that cut to the essence of a situation or issue, gave him the ability to provide profound insights to the dynamics of both Native and American history, politics, law, and social contexts.

In many ways he was applying what he had learned growing up and observing Elders. Deloria reflects on this early upbringing that grounded his perception by saying: "Growing up on a reservation makes one acutely aware of the mysteries of the universe. Medicine men practicing their ancient ceremonies perform feats that amaze and puzzle the rational mind. The sense of contentment enjoyed by older Indians in the face of a lifetime's experience of betrayal, humiliation, and paternalism stuns the astute observer. It often appears that Indians are immune to the values which foreign institutions have forced them to confront. Their minds remain fixed on other realities."[2]

In terms of practical solutions to the problems he perceived in Indian education, Vine argued that Indians, Congress (and the States) needed to return control of Indian education to Indian communities so they could appropriately focus on their traditions, language, and core values. This implied a grassroots orientation of community schools that would allow both students and teachers to explore their Indigenous world, past, present, and future. He also urged creating a space for more direct involvement of knowledge holders by allowing students significant time to learn ways, traditions, and stories in the authentic setting of their community and place. At the same time, he wanted students to have a practical education so they would be able to realistically experience the world they would have to interact with when they grew up and became adults.[3]

He wanted an education that allowed students to explore their own cultural roots to engender a true appreciation for how the cultural and lived experience of their peoples could form a foundation for their identity and the work they could do in their communities. To this end, he advocated for "a year of real Indian education" in which Indian youth at the end of their elementary grades could be sent to live in an Indian community with Elders to experience an education in an authentic way. A similar experience would be afforded at the time of graduating or entrance to college where students of that age could reaffirm the traditional basis of their learning and at the same time prepare for entry into a non-Indian world.[4]

In this way, Vine was advocating for a mimicking of historic traditional Indian education and rites of passage processes in the contemporary setting of modern schools. While many may have dismissed this notion as impractical and undoable, his ideas were based on solid experience and astute observations of the current dilemma of Indian education and practical and direct ways to address it.

In *God Is Red*, Vine creates a historical analysis of Native religions, now more than fifty years old, that urges revival of Native thought and engaging its potential for guiding visions for our life in the twenty-first century.[5] Vine's historical analysis of Indigenous encounters with Christianity during the past five hundred years parallels the history of Indigenous encounters with western education. They are intimately related since early on, Catholic, and later Protestant, schools engaged the education of "Indians" so that they would become good Christians. Government and public schools came later and were predicated on an institutionalized version of Captain Pratt's infamous adage, "Save the man, kill the Indian."

Historically, the first attempts at introducing Euro-American schooling to Indians were met with suspicion, apathy, and indignation. However, once education became viewed as an essential aspect of adapting to modern society, it rapidly evolved into an indispensable key to personal and Tribal success in direct proportion to the assimilation or adaptation of core American cultural values. This general scenario was played and replayed for each Tribal community.

He wrote in his foreword to *Look to the Mountain*,

> From the beginning of contact with European culture until the present, education has been a major area of conflict and concern. Early efforts of the Spanish were directed at transforming the Indian culture into an exact replica of church-dominated, administratively controlled villages, cities and provinces that could be understood as an improved version of European Spanish society. The French saw their task as creating a new society, half indigenous, half European. So, while they educated Indian children in the ways of the church, they encouraged leading families to send their children to Indian villages to live as part of the headman's family and absorb Indian ways. The English system from whence American education efforts with Indians were derived, sought only to provide Indians with sufficient familiarity with their culture, particularly their economic system, so that educated Indians could fit into the rural Protestant agricultural milieu.[6]

As Vine explained,

> Early treaties provided that churches would establish schools for Indian children at their respective missions in exchange for a tract of land for their denomination. As education became more important to white Americans, and public secularized education became the norm, the federal government began to include education, at least a teacher and a school building, as a regular part of treaty provisions. Richard Pratt, experimenting with Chiricahua Apache and Cheyenne at Ft. Marion, conceived of the idea of mass, forced, off-reservation educating that, it was supposed, would sweep away barbarism of Indians in one generation. Unfortunately, the transition from a life of freedom and a healthy diet to regimented uniforms, bland and civilized diet of fats, isolation from their families for years at a time proved fatal to many Indian children who were put into the government boarding school system. Those who did survive this ordeal and returned to the reservation had no way to make a decent living and quickly reverted to traditional ways to feed themselves and re-establish family ties. Some graduates of federal boarding schools eventually found employment in the expanding federal bureaucracy that controlled the reservations and helped to create the lethargic administrative apparatus we today call the Bureau of Indian Affairs.[7]

In *Look to the Mountain*, I built upon Vine's statement from an article entitled "The Perpetual Indian Message" in the Tribal College magazine *Winds of Change* to prime the notion of exploring an alternative message for Indian education that is grounded in essence of Indigenous relational philosophy. In the article he provides the following insight:

> A pervasive problem facing the contemporary vision of American Indian education is that its definition and evolution have

> always been dependent on American politics. Much of what characterizes Indian education policy is not research predicated on American Indian philosophical orientations, but the result of Acts of Congress, the history of treaty rights interpretation through the courts, and the historic Indian/white relations unique to each Tribal group or geographic region. Historically, the views guiding the evolution of modern Indian education have not been predicated upon assumptions that are representative of Indian cultural perspectives.[8]

Despite this history and policy orientation, traditional educational processes have continued within the context of many Indian families and communities. And, while there has been some progress in inclusion of Indian content based on policies and congressional acts in the past sixty years, such as the Indian Self-Determination and Education Assistance Act in 1975 and the Tribally Controlled Community College Assistance Act in 1978 as well as other programs such as Head Start and the American Indian Languages preservation and Revitalization Act, the integration of traditional and western approaches into Indian education continues to be a conflicted contemporary dilemma.

Like Vine, I advocate for the exploration of "culturally informed alternatives," which include a context for the expression of traditional understandings of the educational process as viewed from the perspective of traditional thought. I believe that relevant sources of thought, research, and educational philosophy be considered to fully illuminate the future possibilities of a contemporary education system that mirrors Indigenous thought and its primary orientation of relationship with the natural world. This includes exploration of Indigenous teaching methods, which may be viewed as archetypes of human learning and as part of the psyche of all peoples and cultural traditions. Native language and cultural programs can provide a vehicle to create pathways for this aspect of a return to tradition-inspired education for youth in Tribal settings.

Traditional American Indian Education

Education, including Indigenous education, is always in the process of being rebuilt from the stones and upon the foundations of prior structures. The examples that follow describe the basic infrastructure of Indigenous education and some of the "stones" that make up its foundations.

> It is singularly instructive to move away from Western educational values and theories and survey the educational practices of the old Indians. Not only does one get the sense of emotional stability, which indeed might be the impact of nostalgia, but viewing the way the old people educated themselves and their young gives a person a sense that education is more than receiving information, that it is the very purpose of human society and that human societies cannot really flower until they understand the parameters of possibilities that the human personality contains.[9]

Holistic learning and education had been integral to traditional Indian education and socialization until relatively recent times. Holistic teaching and learning were natural outcomes of living in close communion with the natural world. A major purpose of exploring traditional forms of education is to reintroduce the idea of holism and integrated learning in an interactive social environment such as the school or community. The intent is to make education for Indian students related to other learning situations and interdisciplinary activities and a more culturally interactive process than it has been in the western school environment.

Traditionally, teaching and learning occurred within communal, high-contextualized social situations with the lesson and the learning of the lesson interwoven within the life and environment of the learner. Native Americans taught what needed to be taught in the context they thought it should be taught and at the most opportune and appropriate time to teach it. The situation provided the incentive to teach or learn, and all learning and teaching referenced daily life processes. This involved a huge amount of daily interaction.

This pedagogical style is in direct contrast to that of many schools in western societies where normal education is predominately low-context and becoming increasingly so. Times for teaching and learning are scheduled and specific. Education occurs in the very low-context environment of the school surroundings, and interaction between peers and a few adults occurs in a highly formalized relationship. Low-context situations by their nature are specific, and transfer of information occurs in fixed arrays and structured patterns. Low contexts have a minimized flexibility of output of information due to the narrow perspective inherent in their structure.

Native teaching and learning of earlier times took place within high contexts, which are, by nature, open situations in which different things happen at once, at many different levels. A variety of patterns of information are transferred simultaneously. The learner's living place, as well as parents, grandparents, brothers and sisters, extended family, social group or clan, community, and immediate environment provided the context, as well as the tutors for learning. Every situation was a potential learning opportunity. Basic education was not separated into specific categories or in any way disassociated from such things as the natural, social, or spiritual aspects of everyday living.[10]

The goal was self-knowledge and "seeking life" through understanding the creative process of living, sensitivity to and awareness of the natural world, knowledge of one's role and responsibility in the social order, and receptivity to the spiritual essences of the world. Because such goals required continuity of knowledge, perception, experience, and wisdom, cultivation of all one's senses and creative exploration were valued. Verbal ability in the form of storytelling, oratory, and song was highly regarded, yet respected only when the teller or performer had something meaningful to share based upon personal experience and place within the community.

Formal learning and sacred knowledge usually took the form of initiations that occurred at graduated stages of growth and maturation. Important initiation ceremonies and accompanying concentrated education coincided with such times as the end of early childhood (six to nine years), puberty, young adulthood, middle adulthood, late adulthood, and old age. The introduction to sacred knowledge, then, was informally graduated and programmed in such a way that the individual was presented with a new level of knowledge when it was felt he or she was ready. The concept of "lifelong" learning, the call word of modern adult education, was practiced by most Tribes long before adult education in the contemporary sense existed.[11]

The contexts and mechanisms through which teaching and learning occurred included: experiential learning (learning by doing and seeing), storytelling (learning by listening and imagination), ritual/ceremony (learning through initiation), dreaming (learning through the unconscious and imagery), the master/apprentice (learning through apprenticeship), and artistic creation (learning through creative synthesis).

Ritual and ceremony infused every aspect of traditional life. The spirit and the spiritual were the living dynamic at the center of each human being and all that made up the universe. Through ritual and ceremony, teaching and cultivation of the spirit and the spiritual was engendered, from simple symbolic acts of recognizing one's relationship to the spiritual to highly organized, high-contextual events which involved all the people of a particular Tribe for several days.

A ritual's main purposes was to provide a focus of reflection upon the great mystery in one or more of its manifestations and to help revitalize the individual and the group connection to themselves and the world. Through the symbolic use of prayer, song, dance, and communal activity, Native peoples developed highly creative techniques for guiding social behavior and ethics. The social psychology inherent in ritual and ceremony provided powerful group empathy and cohesion, which reinforced the social self-image of each individual participant. Ritual and ceremony formed a major foundation for the socialization of children in all Native American cultures. The important initiations at different stages of the life cycle helped internalize the knowledge inherent in each activity. Every individual needed to be in touch with the spiritual throughout life in order to live fully. In every Native American language there is a phrase that is said or implied in ritual and ceremony. It has variations from Tribe to Tribe; however, it is usually translated to mean "to find our life" or "in search of our life." For Indian people, this phrase describes a main goal or quest of learning and teaching. Indeed, "to find life" and understand its manifestations within each individual self was an essential goal for many forms of traditional education.

In ritual and ceremony, participants re-created an important part of their historic selves and in a metaphoric sense retraced their steps as a social group of people in process. In Jungian terms, this re-creation and reenactment of the cultural creation myth allowed for the expression of the mythical self and all the archetypes therein. The mythical self was fully realized as an integrator of "the spirit within" by Tribal societies and played an important role in traditional Indian education.

Because Native American cultures have changed a great deal since the time when these methods were extensively used, and because modern schooling has usurped their functions and the contexts in which they were applied, many of these methods are no longer as viable as they once were. This does not mean, however, that they are not still highly effective teaching methods. They can be adapted in a variety of ways to modern educational contexts and teaching requirements, as they parallel many of the new methods espoused in holistic education. Their synthesis and application present both a challenge and a vital component of relevancy for the educator of Native Americans. What is required is an openness to the methods and an understanding of their role in the total educational process.

The Contemporary Dilemma of American Indian Education

> Education today trains professionals, but it does not produce people. It is, indeed, not expected to produce personality growth . . . the goal of modern education is to produce people trained to function in an institutional setting as a contributing part of a vast social/economic machine . . . the separation of

> knowledge . . . is an insurmountable barrier for many Indian students and raises severe emotional problems as they seek to sort out the proper principles from these two isolated parts of human experience . . . in traditional Indian society there is no separation . . . the goal is to ensure personal growth and then develop expertise. [12]

The basis of contemporary American education as it has been defined by the prevailing political, social, and economic order of vested interests is the transfer of academic skills and content that prepares the student to compete in the social, economic, and organizational infrastructure of American society. Modern educational theories include little substantial ethical or moral content regarding the means that are used to achieve its ends. Thus, the ideal curriculum espoused by American education ends up being significantly different from the experienced curriculum internalized by students and the real workings of much of American society. The American society that many American Indian students experience is wrought with contradictions, politics, hypocrisy, narcissism, and discriminatory predispositions at all levels, including the schools. As a result, there have been educational conflicts, frustration, and varying levels of alienation experienced by many Indian people resulting from their encounters with mainstream education.

In reflecting on the impact of western education on Indian people, it is important to mention the four contemporary expressions of American Indian education today. First, most Indians have accepted modern education as a way to participate, get ahead, and live the American dream. Indeed, this is the institutionalized pathway for success in a modern society that is acknowledged and supported financially and socially to make a good living and participate in the western economic and social world. It is also sanctioned and legitimized by government and the American public as the way to be an American. Second is the group of Indians who participate in alternative education as opposed to public, parochial, or government-sponsored education. These alternative forms of education can take the form of other holistic forms of western education but are usually offered in private schools and do not necessarily include American Indian cultural content in their curriculum. They are also expensive, which significantly decreases the number of Indian people that can afford their tuition costs. Third are Tribal schools where community members have formed community schools around culture and language as a focus for cultural and community revitalization. These schools have had some success in achieving a cultural-informed alternative that serves the cultural needs of a community. The fourth group are those Indians who still practice their specific traditional forms of education in their extended family, clan, or community. These alternatives, with the exception of the fourth, present what Michele Sam, Ktunaxa Indigenous Canadian researcher terms "intractable conflict" in terms of what is taught and how it is taught and by whom.[13]

Native American peoples, through the expressions and ecological understanding of their educational processes, evolved a natural response to the reality of "other," that other being the natural world, and allowed the other to define itself to them, rather than their imposing purely intellectual meanings and relationships. As a result, Indian people lived with as little impact on the natural state of the land as possible. They allowed the land to be, taking from it only the resources necessary for their survival but always remembering and understanding that it was given to them as a gift. The natural world was appreciated and understood in its significance to a Tribe's continuation as a people in relationship to other entities and natural forces.

It is important to reflect on the changes that have occurred. This is especially true for the changes that Native American people and communities have had to accommodate in their relationship to their natural environments and the educational processes, which allowed them to establish their essential relationship to their "Place." The arrival of Europeans ushered in what could only be called a prolonged period of warfare; persecution; social, cultural, and individual oppression; and deprivation, echoed even to this day in spirit, if not in actuality, in Indian–white relationships. Today the bulk of our traditional systems of governance have been replaced with what one could call a "federally prescribed" government, the primary purpose of which has been to establish, within the context of American Indian societies, a system with which the federal government could administratively enforce control. This prescribed government diminishes or renders the Indigenous forms of government—in which the ecological framework and understanding of relationship with the natural environment was contexted—nonoperative.

Traditional expressions of educating have been all but eliminated in favor of institutions founded on the psychological premise of behavior modification, command, and control. These institutions continue to adhere to a primarily Eurocentric orientation to life and resist any real attempts to consider and integrate the truths and understandings that come through cultural diversity. To survive, Native people, for the most part, have been forced to give up their traditional livelihoods in favor of working within the American eight-to-five technocratic system of economics. The vestiges of our remaining social structures are rapidly disappearing with each generation. Extended families are being replaced by nuclear or single-parent families, resulting in the modern abuses and dilemmas in which fragmented families find themselves.

Along with the disappearance of the extended family and the communal system of clans, the ravages of alienation, expressed through alcoholism, drug and child abuse, and a host of other abuses, are becoming all too apparent when one visits Indian communities today. Every area of traditional Native thought and spirit has suffered grievously. Despite such a dire history and the highly visible impact on Native communities, Native thought continues to reflect a way of life that can present a model for the possibility of a new kind of society. Such thought, in its variations of expression surviving in Indigenous groups around the world, presents the kind of deep ecological philosophy, the deep understanding of relationships to the natural world, so much needed to balance the overarching homogenizing, techno-social paradigm. This orientation also forms an "intractable conflict" with the underlying orientation of American education.

The modern paradigm is founded primarily on the western-mechanistic philosophy of control of nature and the idea that homogenization allows for greater freedom. It is also based upon a body of accepted theory that underpins modern society's assumptions of reality and considers that reality the only reality. This reality is considered the foundation of the only firm answers; it is considered "the real world." This is what is communicated in a variety of ways in the modern education process. This paradigm so guides the consciousness of American mainstream education that it forms the very nature of thought, research, and education and motivates the views, methods, and solutions that are a result of that education. The result has been a kind of "colonization of the mind" with effects and repercussions of a magnitude almost beyond description. One can only understand such a colonization of the mind by realizing that there are alternative cultural realities, honoring their presence, and learning from them. Modern knowledge is not the only legitimate knowledge, and indeed it blocks us in many instances from establishing the kind of relationship that must be set up within this next generation if we are to survive the ecological crises that are beginning to unfold.

Relational Education

To really understand how we are connected to all things, and how understanding those connections can make us healthier and more whole, we can best understand through the epistemologies and ways of doing through Indigenous language and practices. Deloria believed that one way to begin to create a place for tradition in modern education of Indians was to acknowledge that the Indian mind and the western mind perceive the world in entirely different ways.

In his book *Metaphysics of Modern Existence* (1979), Deloria states:

> The fundamental factor that keeps Indians and non-Indians from communicating is that they are speaking about two entirely different perceptions of the world. . . . In a white man's world, knowledge is a matter of memorizing theories, dates, lists of kings and presidents, the table of chemical elements, and

> many other things not encountered in the course of a day's work. Knowledge seems to be divorced from experience. Even religion is a process of memorizing creeds, catechisms, doctrines, and dogmas—general principles that never seem to catch the essence of human existence. No matter how well educated an Indian may become, he or she also suspects that Western culture is not an adequate representation of reality . . . the trick is somehow to relate what one feels with what one is taught to think.[14]

As Deloria put it: "Western people don't have a problem—they don't seem concerned with the ultimate truth of what they are taught—Knowledge is correlated with a higher status employment. . . . Indian customs and beliefs were regarded as primitive, superstitions, and unworthy of serious attention. . . . So, the question of the validity of knowledge contained in Indian traditions was eliminated before any discussions of reality began."[15]

There are several reasons for the difficulty of integration of Indigenous and western forms of education. First is the fact that they are indeed embedded in distinctly different worldviews. Indigenous worldviews are relational and focus on the dynamic balance of relationships within a perceived multiverse. In traditional thought, *axiology* (highest value) lies in the balance between humans, other beings, and spirits of the past, present, and future. *Epistemology* (coming to knowledge) occurs through active learning, symbolic imagery, songs, stories, and dance. *Logic* (cognitive orientation): all elements and beings of the multiverse are linked together. *Process* (understandings that underlie methods for obtaining and application of knowledge): all things are dependently interrelated in the harmony and balance of the multiverse. In Western *axiology*, the highest value lies in the object or the acquisition of the object. *Epistemology* is primarily cognitive, and one knows through counting and measuring. Western *logic* is either/or and *process* is focused on technology and repeatability and reproducibility.

This is also an "intractable conflict"—a fundamental obstacle to cross-cultural communication continues to revolve around significant differences in cultural orientations to the world and to the fact that Indian people have been forced to adapt to an educational process and associated worldview that is not of their own making. Traditionally, Indians view life through a different cultural metaphor than that of mainstream America. This is the frame for the exploration of the Indigenous educational philosophy presented in this chapter.[16]

Traditional Indian education represents an anomaly for the prevailing theory and methodology of western education since what is implied in the application of "objectivism" is the assumption that there is one correct way of understanding the dynamics of Indian education, one correct methodology, one way of understanding the reality of Indigenous educational philosophy, and that there is one correct policy for Indian education. And that *one way* is the way of mainstream America. The mindset of objectivism, when applied to the field of Indian education, excludes serious consideration of the relational reality of Indian people, the variations in Tribal and social contexts, and the processes of perception and understanding that characterize and form its expressions.

Objectivist research has substantial limitations in addressing the multidimensional, holistic, and relational reality of the education of Indian people. It is the affective elements—the subjective experience and observations, the communal relationships, the artistic and mythical dimensions, the ritual and ceremony, the sacred ecology, the psychological and spiritual orientations—that have characterized and formed Indigenous education since time immemorial. These dimensions and their inherent meanings are not readily quantifiable, observable, or easily verbalized and, as a result, have been given little credence in mainstream western Eurocentric approaches to education and research. Yet it is these very aspects that form a profound orientation for learning through exploring and understanding the multidimensional relationships between humans and their inner and outer worlds.

For Indian educators, a key to dealing with the conflict between the objective and relational orientations, the cultural differences and systemic bias in perception, lies in the kind of open communication and creative dialogue that challenges the "tacit infrastructure" of ideas that have guided contemporary Indian education.

Education is essentially a communal social activity. Educational research that produces the most creatively productive insights involves communication within the whole educational community, not just the "authorities" recognized by mainstream educational interests. Education is a communication process and plays an essential role in every act of educational perception. There must be a "flow" of communication regarding the educational process among all educators as a result of individual internal dialogue, interactions among educators, publication, and discussion of ideas. Unfortunately, a serious blockage of communication and fragmentation of educational thought continues to be the rule rather than the exception, and communication related to Indian education is no exception.

Many ideas based on the established "tacit infrastructure" of mainstream American education have been embraced religiously by most educators. This situation, as it pertains to Indian education, limits creative acts of perception. A free play of thought and opening of the field, which is not restricted by unconsciously determined social pressures and the inherent limitations of the currently established paradigms of Indian education, needs to occur. It is only after recognition and critique of this "tacit infrastructure" that a high level of creative thought regarding the possibilities and potentials of Indigenous educational philosophy can take place. And only in realizing that American Indian perceptions of education have traditionally been informed by a different metaphor of teaching and learning can more productive insights into contemporary Indian education be developed.[17] These traditional metaphors of education derived their meaning from unique cultural contexts and interactions with natural environments. In turn, the collective experience of Indian people and their elegant expressions of cultural adaptations have culminated in a body of shared metaphors and understandings regarding the nature of education and its "essential ecology."

The exploration of traditional forms of Indigenous education attempts to develop insights into the community of shared metaphors and understandings specific to Indian cultures, yet reflective of the nature of human learning. Ultimately, an exploration of traditional Indian education is an exploration of nature-centered philosophy. *Traditional Indian education is an expression of environmental education par excellence.* It is an environmental education process that can have a profound meaning for the kind of modern education required to face the challenges of living in the world of the twenty-first century. It has the potential to create deeper understanding of the collective role as caretakers of a world that Americans have been largely responsible for throwing out of balance. There are perceived needs that can be summarized as follows:

1. The need for a contemporary perspective of American Indian education that is principally derived and informed by the thoughts, orientations, and cultural philosophies of Indian people themselves. The articulation and fulfillment of this need is, I believe, an essential step in Indian educational self-determination.
2. The need for exploration of alternative approaches to education that more directly and successfully address the needs of Indian populations during this time of "educational and ecological crisis." During such a time, it is essential to open up the field and to entertain the possibilities of new approaches in a creative quest for more viable and complete educational processes.
3. The need to integrate, synthesize, organize, and give a strategic and imaginative focus to the enormous body of accumulated materials from a wide range of disciplines about Indian cultures and education, moving toward the evolution of a contemporary philosophy for Indian education that is Indigenously inspired and ecologically based.

The purpose of contemporary American Indian education, as it is currently interpreted, has been to assure that Indian people learn the skills necessary to be productive—or at least survive—in the midst of the postindustrial American society. Indians have been taught to be consumers in the tradition of the "American dream" and all the concept entails. We have been encouraged to use modern education to "progress" by being participants in the "system." We have been conditioned to seek the rewards and benefits that modern education purportedly provides. We are enticed from every direction to pursue careers in law, medicine, business, and the sciences that form the pillars of western thought and conditioning.

Despite the many Indian people who have succeeded by embracing western education, we must question the effects modern education has had on our collective cultural, psychological, and ecological viability. What has been lost and what has been gained by participating in a system of education that neither stems from nor honors our unique Indigenous perspectives? How far can we go in adapting to such a system before that system literally educates us out of cultural existence? Have we reached the limits of what we can do with mainstream educational orientations? How can we re-vision and establish once again the "ecology of education" that formed and maintained our Tribal societies?

Ironically, creative western thinkers have embraced what are essentially Indigenous environmental-education views and are vigorously interpreting Indigenous concepts to support the development of their own alternative models. For example, cultural historian and philosopher Thomas Berry proposes a new context for education that is essentially a reinvention of the roles and contexts inherent to Indigenous education:

> The primary educator as well as the primary law giver and primary healer would be the natural world itself. The integral earth community would be a self-educating community within the context of a self-educating universe. Education at the human level would be the conscious sensitizing of humans to the profound communications made by the universe about us, by the sun, the moon, and the stars, the clouds, the rain, the contours of the earth and all its living forms. All music and poetry of the universe would flow into the student, the revelatory presence of the divine as well as insight into the architectural structures

> of the continents and the engineering skills whereby the great hydrological cycle functions in moderating the temperature of the earth, in providing habitat for aquatic life, in nourishing the multitude of living creatures would be as natural to the educational process. The earth would also be our primary teacher of sciences, especially biological sciences, and of industry and economics. It would teach us a system in which we would create a minimum of entropy, a system in which there is no unusable or unfruitful junk. Only in such an integral system is the future viability of humans assured.[17]

Berry's comments mirror what might be termed a contemporized exposition of the Indigenous education processes of Tribal societies. It is exactly within the light of such a vision that *this story* must unfold for Native and non-Native alike. If our collective future is to be one of harmony and wholeness, *or* if we are to even have a viable future to pass to our children's children, it is imperative that we actively envision and implement new ways of educating for ecological thinking and sustainability. The choice is ours, yet paradoxically we may have no choice.

Vine's Thoughts on the Future of Indian Education

Vine predicted that the current generation of Indian youth would move beyond the boundaries for self-determination established after the non-Indian pattern and bring something entirely new to the process of applying western scientific knowledge to Indian problems. He perceived the beginnings of a transformation and the making of a new path for Indian education . . . he perceived Indian professionals moving through and beyond existing educational institutions to form their own businesses and organizations and research centers, where they would work on projects important to Indian communities while at the same time reviving and extending their traditional Tribal practices. He perceived Indian students in colleges creating and navigating their own unique programs of study to address their needs for a relevant education and to gain skills for addressing pressing needs of Indian people and community. He perceived Tribal colleges coming into their own in integrating a modern Tribal form of education with appropriate western higher education and playing an increasingly important role in Tribal political, economic, social, and environmental problems. He perceived Indian students, seeing the shortcomings of western thought and university training, would start to derive the meaning of their education through the lens and context of their own Tribal traditions. He perceived the next generations of Indian students leaving the culture shock of colonization and emerging on the other side of the current western worldview to, once again, control their own fates and carry the traditions and thought of their peoples into the next millennium. One might say that these perceptions are prophetic with a heavy dose of hope and a dash of optimism.

I share these perceptions with Vine. Throughout history human societies have attempted to guide, facilitate, and even coerce the human instinct for learning toward socially defined ends. The complex of activities for forming human learning is what we call education today. Human societies have evolved a multitude of educational forms to maintain their survival and as vehicles for expressing their unique cultural mythos. This cultural mythos is the genesis of that culture's guiding vision; that is, a peoples' story of themselves and their perceived relationship to the world. In its guiding vision, a culture sets forth a set of ideals that guide and form learning processes. These are manifested as qualities and behaviors considered essential to instill in its members. Generally, this set of values is predicated on knowledge and skills considered central to its survival.

An Indigenized Expression of Contemporary Indian Education

The cultural ideals from which the learning, teaching, and systems of education of Native America evolved provide an important foundation for a contemporary Indigenized expression of Indian education.

As such, these ideals present a mirror for reflecting on the critical dilemma of American education. For, while the legacy of American education is one of significant scientific and technological achievement resulting in abundant material prosperity for some, the ultimate, aggregate cost has been inconceivably high. American prosperity has come at the expense of the environment's degradation and has resulted in unprecedented exploitation of human and material resources worldwide.

American education is in crisis as the country finds itself faced with unprecedented challenges in a global community of nations desperately struggling with massive and profound environmental, social, economic, and cultural change. American education must find new ways of helping Americans learn and adapt in a multicultural, twenty-first-century world. It must come to terms with the conditioning inherent in its processes and systems of educating that contribute to the loss of a shared integrative metaphor of Life. The loss of such a metaphor, which may ultimately lead to a social-cultural-ecological catastrophe should be a key concern of every American.

The orchestrated "bottom-line, real world" chorus sung by many in business and government has become the all-too-common refrain of those who announce they lead the world. Yet, what underlies the crisis of American education is the crisis of modern identity and a collective cosmological disconnection from the natural world. Those who identify most with the "bottom line" suffer from image without substance, technique without soul, and knowledge without context. The cumulative psychological results of which are usually unabridged alienation, loss of community, and a deep sense of incompleteness.

In contrast, traditional education historically occurred in a holistic social context that developed a sense of the importance for each individual as a contributing member of the social group. Essentially, Tribally contexted education worked at sustaining a life process. It was a process of education that unfolded through mutual, reciprocal relationships between one's social group and the natural world. This relationship involved all dimensions of one's being while providing both personal development and technical skills through participation in the life of the community. It was essentially an integrated expression of environmental education.

Understanding the depth of relationships and the significance of participation in all aspects of life are the keys to traditional American Indian education. "Mitakuye Oyasin" (all my relatives) is a Lakota phrase that captures an essence of Tribal education because it reflects the understanding that our lives are truly and profoundly connected to other people and the physical world. Likewise, knowledge is gained from firsthand experience and then transmitted or explored through ritual, ceremony, art, and appropriate technology. Knowledge gained in these ways are then used in the context of everyday living. Education becomes education for life's sake. Education is, at its very essence, learning about life through participation and relationship to community, including not only people, but plants, animals, and the whole of Nature.

This ideal of education directly contrasts with the predominant orientation of American education that continues to emphasize so-called objective content and experience detached from primary sources and community. This conditioning for being a marginal participant and perpetual observer involved with only objective content is a foundational element of the crisis of American education and the alienation of modern humans from their own being and the natural world.

In response to such a monumental crisis, American education must forge educational processes that are for "Life's Sake" and honor the Native roots of America. A true transition of today's American educational orientations to more sustainable and connected foundations requires serious consideration of other cultural, life-enhancing, and ecologically viable forms of education. The unfolding catastrophic impacts of climate change and the social equity movement in education spurred on by Black Lives Matter, environmental justice, and immigration may act as catalysts for such a systemic change, but probably in only a few more enlightened schools and educational institutions. The sustainability and social justice education movements have promise to be catalysts for transformation and change. However, American education, as it exists today, is so vested with corporate and political interests that change is unlikely to occur soon. If change happens it will come from the outside, from the margins, from the alternative realms of human society. And these catalysts are gaining momentum.

In this context, traditional American Indian forms of education must be given serious consideration as conceptual wellsprings for the "new" kinds of educational thought capable of addressing the tremendous challenges of the twenty-first century. Tribal education presents examples of models and universal foundations for the transformation of American education and the development of a "new" paradigm for curricula that will make a difference for "Life's Sake" in the world of the twenty-first century.

Final Thoughts

American Indians have struggled to adapt to an educational process, with its inherent social, political, and cultural baggage, that is not their own. Yet, American Indian cultural forms of education contain seeds for new models of educating that can enliven American education as well as allow American Indians to evolve contemporary expressions of education tied to their cultural roots.

For American Indians, a new circle of education must begin that is founded on the roots of Tribal education and reflective of the needs, values, and sociopolitical issues as Indian people themselves perceive them.

Such a new circle must encompass the importance Indian people place on the continuance of their ancestral traditions, emphasize a respect for individual uniqueness in the diversity of expressions of spirituality, facilitate a strong and well-contexted understanding of history and culture, develop a strong sense of place and service to community, and forge a commitment to educational and social transformation that recognizes and further empowers the inherent strength of Indian people and their respective cultures.

To understand how to accomplish this, Indian people must begin to exploit all avenues of communication open to them and establish a reflective dialogue about a contemporary theory for Indian education that evolves from the collective experience of Indian people.

In the past, Indian education has been defined largely by non-Indian educators, politicians, and institutions through a huge volume of legislative acts at the state and federal levels, which for decades have entangled Indian leaders, educators, and whole communities in the morass of the federal government's social and political bureaucracy.

Indeed, Indian education stems more from the US government's self-serving political-bureaucratic relationship with Indian Tribes than any truly culturally contexted process rooted in Tribal philosophies and social values. In fact, what is called Indian education today is really a collection of competing American education ideas adapted to Indian contexts for the purpose of assimilating Indians into mainstream American society.

Traditionally, for Indian people, learning has always been a creative, life-centered activity. Indeed, we are continuously engaged in the art of making meaning and creating our world through the unique processes of human learning. Learning for humans is instinctual, continuous, and simultaneously the most complex of our natural traits. Learning is also key to our ability to survive in the environments that we create and that create us.

It is time for Indian people to define education in their own voices and in their own terms. It is time to explore and express the richness of their collective history that has always included a visionary expression of life. Indigenous education has been, and continues to be, a grand story, a search for meaning, an essential food for the soul.

Note to Reader: In this chapter, I use the terms "Native American," "American Indian," "Indigenous," or the term "Indian," which Vine used in his writing. Although these may not be the current terms of preference, they are used by most "Indian" people when talking among themselves.

CHAPTER 24

BUILDING A BRIDGE FROM THE IVORY TOWER TO THE WOODSTOVE

A Response to "More Ivory Than Red: False Allegiances in Academia"

Wendy S. Greyeyes and Tiffany S. Lee

As Native American Studies professors, we have drawn from and incorporated much of Vine Deloria, Jr.'s scholarship into our courses and research. In this chapter, we offer our insights and experiences in Native American Studies (NAS) in response to Vine Deloria, Jr.'s assertion (as cited in Wilkins) that many Native academics have a stronger allegiance to their disciplines than to their own people.[1] We use the metaphor in our title of building a bridge from the ivory tower to the woodstove because of our experiences growing up in Diné homes among our family. We come from family traditions where discussions, celebrations, feasting, and meetings were held around the woodstoves of our homes. Indigenous intellectual traditions were fostered there and have imprinted fond memories from our childhood to today. As Wilkins notes in his chapter "More Ivory Than Red: False Allegiances in Academia,"[2] Deloria challenged Indigenous intellectuals to analyze the multitude of problems impacting Native Nations rather than theorizing and debating academic concepts in the halls of the university. We have taken up this charge in NAS at the University of New Mexico (UNM). Our chapter will first respond to Deloria's critique and then offer our successes and challenges for addressing the complex issues of our Native communities within the structures of a western academic institution and from our woodstoves.

Deloria's criticism of the culture of ivory tower aspirations began with anthropology, which is a discipline focused on the study of culture. Deloria developed a provocative outline and critique regarding the early work of anthropologists. He was extremely critical of academe's publish-or-perish mentality that too often fueled careless and shallow efforts. In Deloria's seminal work, *Custer Died for Your Sins: An Indian Manifesto*, he asserts that white anthropologists are the vultures of Indigenous communities. Their annual summer migration to Native American reservations to observe Indigenous people working and living in their communities is the fodder for their publications.[3] Academe's need to socially construct and reconstitute the Native American was damaging. In his view, anthropology's pursuit for the truth was to construct generalizable claims about culture. This project of generalizing Native Americans damaged our own conceptualizations of our identity as Indigenous peoples. The books, workshops, and lectures fueled misguided stereotypes about Native Americans. Although anthropology attempted to theorize about Native Americans, to find truths about their realities through "OBSERVATIONS" (all caps in the original), their interpretations fell victim to the westernized interpretation of human evolution and placed Native Americans upon the trajectory of "development" and "civilization." Their work constructed concepts of their perceived understanding of the vanishing Native. In their perception, anthropology was saving the Native American through recordings and documentation. In Deloria's view, anthropologists constructed generalizations of Native Americans to place them on an evolutionary path, although it became evident that anthropology was about reaffirming the supremacy of western knowledge systems. In Deloria's assessment, the anthropologist became anti-Indigenous. He often used satire in his writing and described the anthropologist in this way: "He will have the instruments of his discipline—a camera, tape recorder, a hula hoop, and life jacket hanging from his elongated frame . . . this creature is the anthropologist."[4] Deloria's comical description of anthropology and its construction and impact in understanding the "Indian problem" demonstrates his early arguments regarding how anthropology aimed to deconstruct and insert Native Americans into the architecture of western knowledge. In the same piece, Deloria links the devastating effects of this reimagining of Native Americans by anthropologists to how young Native Americans came to perceive themselves. Deloria writes, "Not even Indians can relate themselves to this type of creature who, to anthropologists, is the 'real' Indian."[5]

The transfer of conceptualizations of Native Americans is described by Deloria as creating an entire class of puppets who perpetuate this canon of theorization and generalizability of Native American.[6] In effect, it created a class of Native Americans who have bought into the imagined vanishing Indians stereotype, according to Deloria. By reimagining ourselves into a place of romanticism, we have disconnected ourselves from the realities of our identity as Native Americans.[7] Also ignored are the true lived experiences of our communities, which devalued the teachings from the woodstove. We have, in essence, replaced our worldviews with western concepts instead of clarifying our own intellectual canons within our communities. Specifically, Wilkins asserts that "Deloria challenged Indigenous intellectuals to analyze the numerous problems impacting Native Nations rather than discussing and redefining, in the halls of academe, concepts like hegemony, colonialism, self-determination, and sovereignty."[8] These concepts are powerful tools to understand the systems of powers but do not easily translate into conversations about solution building within communities. The question we then ask is, "What does this entail in terms of problem-solving in our communities?" Deloria is not arguing that Native Americans disassociate themselves from institutions of higher education but rather become more cognizant of their contributions to canons of knowledge that have no true meaning or relevance for our Indigenous communities. Instead, Native scholars should strengthen skills and research that are necessary to validate Indigenous knowledge. In this case, Wilkins states, "Given his understanding of the validity, vitality, and value of Indigenous knowledge about cosmology (star knowledge), biology (plant and animal knowledge), family life (kinship patterns), criminal jurisdiction (warrior societies as the most effective agents of maintaining peace and order), and music (the role that it plays in health and plant growth), he was concerned that Native peoples were not doing a better job of explaining and describing the inherent benefits of all this knowledge."[9]

Institutions of higher education must create and build a new class of problem-solvers and agents of change for our Native communities as it is imperative for our future. The intellectual realms of academe, which argue that they value science as being objective and pure, creates disillusionment for young Native scholars. As Deloria argued on the topic of Native education, Native students are further misled by outrageous claims made by science that suggest that the various fields of inquiry represent the total sum of human knowledge. Deloria continued to challenge the perception of inquiry and pointed out that "in fact, almost all of western science is reductionist in nature and seeks to force natural experience and knowledge into predetermined categories which ultimately fail to describe or explain anything."[10] This conception of the university's ideology and irrelevance has been taken up within the field of Native Nation building. The project of deconstructing western academic approaches and reconstructing/clarifying an Indigenous approach to studying Indigenous peoples is essential and constitutes the work of NAS, American Indian Studies, and/or Indigenous studies, which are constructing new models and best practices that serve Native Nations and peoples. In Table 1, we show how the contrast between academic approaches and outlooks plays a pivotal role in shaping the design and framework for Native studies. The table provides a sketch of Deloria's reconceptualization of academia and his rebuke of western approaches as compared to Indigenous approaches.

Table 1. Academic critiques and approaches to Indigenous studies (According to Deloria)

	Western approaches to Indigenous studies	Indigenous approaches to Indigenous studies
Epistemology (theory of knowledge)	Theorization of hegemony, colonialism, self-determination, sovereignty	Theorization of cosmology, plant/animal knowledge, kinship, peace, woodstove knowledge
Praxis (application)	Publications, defense of discipline, tenure	Contributions to the community (exercise of sovereignty, problem- solving)
Heuristics	Scientific method, objectify people and nature, control group	Inward gaze, people and nature as living, relational; be present; reality as fluid
Research philosophy	Rationality, objectivity	Community based, community engaged
Pedagogy	Pedagogy of objectivity, rationality, individual performance	Pedagogy of community, listening, conversations, communal spirit

In considering this tremendous project, many Indigenous scholars have voiced the same principles in their own work.

Extending from the dialogue on the approaches in Indigenous studies, Native Nation building literature argues that institutions of higher education are a critical factor for the larger agenda of Tribal Nation building. However, a warning has been put forth by scholars, who argue that "for although indigenous students may be interested in going to college to gain skills and knowledge in areas that may benefit their nation, ultimately, these skills are of little use to them if they lack firsthand knowledge of Native institutions, communities and values."[11] In essence, if graduates do not learn these additional skills to complement their university education, they will have a difficult path in returning to their communities to give back, thus continuing the brain drain impacting many Tribal Nations throughout the country. It is critical that institutions of higher education, especially Tribal colleges and universities, push back and resist against the norms of education that value western knowledge over Indigenous ones.

In this next section, we aim to address Deloria's critique of Native academics who, he asserts, sacrifice a focus on their people in place of their allegiances to their disciplines[12] by demonstrating our approach in NAS at the UNM. Deloria challenged Indigenous intellectuals to go beyond debating and lecturing and instead to focus on analyzing the challenging issues impacting Native Nations as a way to apply their knowledge to real-world problems in Native communities. He also critiqued the purpose of mainstream education when he asserted that "education today trains professionals but it does not produce people."[13] In this sense, the role of developing human beings who contribute to their communities, which is a primary purpose in Indigenous education,[14] is lost. He also said that Native academics still have much work to do at teaching non-Native people about Native issues, communities, experiences, and knowledge.[15] The public consciousness has remained ignorant about the history and contemporary experiences of Native peoples in this country. As Wilkins noted, Deloria strongly encouraged

Native Nations to establish their own research institutions in order to inform policy and to educate from their own place of knowledge and learning. These ideas and assertions are exactly the goals of Native American Studies at the UNM. Coauthor Lee has argued that Indigenous studies and NAS programs have been growing and evolving across the world during the past forty years, with each program focusing on goals related to their contexts and interests.[16]

Many universities have begun to articulate the need for community-based research, sometimes under the guise of service. In this case, anything outside of scholarship or teaching is placed under this category of service and is not viewed as scholarship. Instead, there needs to be a reevaluation of service as it integrates with community-engaged and community-based research practices. Models of these strategies are important for the future of Native American Studies. In creating the department's philosophical core, Native academics and departments should not operate in a state of constant resistance or reaction to the academy. The project of resistance is exhausting for faculty and those responsible for implementing the department's philosophical core. Instead, the philosophical core should focus on community-engaged research and community-based scholarship. This reshapes the philosophical core to an entrenched engagement with our communities. Tackling an entire institutional canon, "the ivory tower," is a battle that has few results. Instead, the canon of Indigenous knowledge must build from its foundational roots, the woodstove of knowledge.

Epistemology—Woodstove Knowledge

Native American Studies embraces knowledge exchange and transformative action as it occurs around the woodstove. It places supreme value around the woodstove as a metaphor for Indigenous knowledge. The stove is a space in which we have conversations and exert our oral stories, the stories that form the basis of our history, language, and culture. Our stories are our theories. Institutions of Higher Education (IHE) must consider these domains not as "new forms of knowledge"

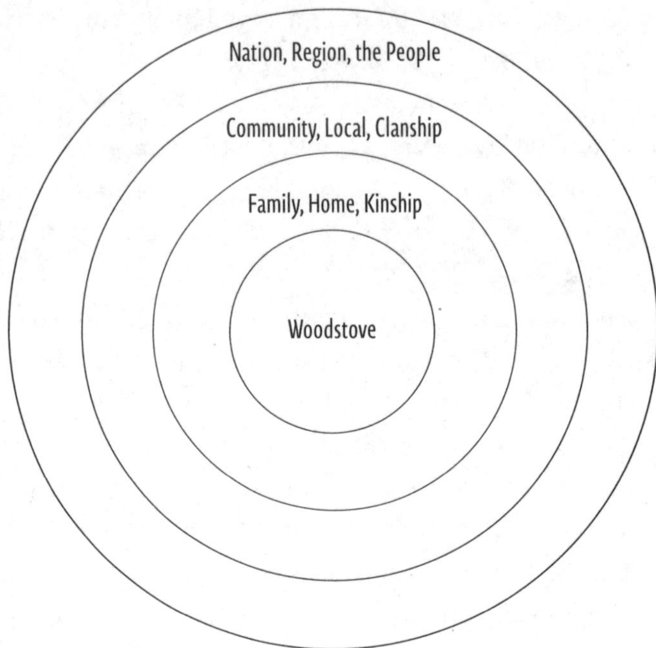

but rather as valued spaces of learning and understanding. The "ivory tower" is a metaphor for IHE because it is disconnected and distant from the people and the communities. It has an aura of superiority towering over those below. Instead, NAS focuses upon honing the meaning of bringing the woodstove Indigenous knowledge systems to the core of our intellectualism.

Praxis—Exercising Sovereignty

The practice of sovereignty is an important component of all of our work in NAS. We revised our NAS Promotion and Tenure guidelines at UNM to recognize the importance of sovereignty through our collaborations with Native communities. Our guidelines state that *Community engagement* impacts communities in transformative ways. It can occur across teaching, scholarship, and service and is rooted in reciprocity, respect, relationships, and relevance. The guidelines also clarify that *Community-based scholarship* is the collaboration with community in research, which produces scholarship that directly benefits community, organizations, or entities. Community engagement and community-based scholarship are highly valued and privileged in NAS as they respond to needs and interests among Indigenous peoples. In our guidelines, this type of scholarship and publication is given equal weight to the western tradition of publishing in peer-reviewed journals and books.

In terms of the application of this work, our faculty approach these two strategies to community work in different ways. I (coauthor Greyeyes) believe my work fulfills both components. The Navajo Nation's Department of Diné Education and the Navajo Nation Board of Education have put out a call for transformative efforts to rebuild an education system that has the equivalent of a state education agency. At the present time, the Navajo Nation does manage its own unified school system, but it is at the mercy of decisions by state public school boards that have become powerful local entities that often challenge the Navajo Nation's sovereign authority. Navajo Nation has long sought out strategies to strengthen their decision-making within these spaces. In my work, I have had the great honor and privilege to research what it means for the Nation to become a state education agency. I had the honor of serving as the lead consultant to unite educators and leaders to lay out a plan for the future. This work has come at the expense of traditional western academic publications but was a significant continuous engagement with the Navajo Nation. Relationship building and continually engaging the dialogue is imperative for this type of work to succeed. Meetings, work sessions, public hearings, newsletter writing, and organizing radio discussion are vital to address these issues of education and to raise community awareness in diverse ways. The portion of transformative change that is not understood by academia is relationship building and continuous engagement. This is critical for ensuring this project of educational transformation occurs. I have also learned that much of transformative change is listening more than speaking. I recognize that all our NAS faculty have approached this component in their own unique ways.

Heuristics—Storytelling

Our department places value upon stories as a valid form of knowledge collection and understanding. In our heuristic move toward knowledge and understanding, we conduct our work in ways that do not objectify our people or communities. This is especially evident in our teaching for our master's degree program. In my courses (coauthor Greyeyes), I require students to develop engagement with their communities by recognizing an element from Linda Tuhiwai Smith's work. In the section titled "On Being Human," she points out that Indigenous people were not viewed by society as inventors, institution makers, history creators—the features of practicing civilization.[17] Our community members are agents of change and it's through their stories that we recognize our community members are change makers of humanity and of civilization. To capture the essence of this reality, it is essential that we rely on storytelling as narratives of truths and a valid element of history. Storytelling is a critical part of my own work and research.

This statement and perception of knowledge also does not discount the use of theory in the field of NAS. The work of Audra Simpson and Andrea Smith in *Theorizing Native Studies* challenges Deloria's argument that our rising academics should make a shift from western theory. The authors synthesize and critique Deloria's conception that theory is Christian based and falls into the domain of temporality, meaning everything and everyone is consumed by this omniscient and Eurocentric act.[18] It is important to note that stories carry a theory, a truth, an understanding of life and patterns of experiences that are used to theorize and tell stories about our being. In this reconfiguration of our truths through storytelling, we do not intend to diminish the need for many forms and elements of theorizing. We believe that recentralizing what truth means, where it comes from, and how it perpetuates itself into the everyday flow of our thinking shapes new meanings of truth.

The project of public hearings is a great example of storytelling and raising concerns about the future of Navajo education. In the transformative project of educational reform, public hearings were recorded, and members from different agencies spoke about their understandings of education and told stories of their personal experiences. In these stories, we learned to engage and refine our philosophy around deep listening. In this case, we had to listen to uncover the public concerns of massive educational reform and the lack of confidence the public had in relation to our central Tribal government. These stories were pivotal in refining the need for clarifying public input in Tribal educational reform; it became apparent that the systems in place did not value the humanity of education. In essence, storytelling is a powerful form of engaging and revaluing our community's input.

Research Philosophy—Positionality

Positionality means to identify your background and your purpose for your research or community policymaking. Identifying yourself and helping others understand why you pursued the specific research topic helps community members and researchers recognize your commitment to the topic. Deloria points out that anthropologists would come into a community and do their observations. After they departed, they were never seen or heard from again. This approach did not provide the accountability necessary to ensure that researchers and policymakers would give back to the people. In other words, identifying one's positionality and philosophy builds trust and ensures stories would be exchanged for help with issues in the community. In many of our students' and faculty's work, we have made it a central part of our job to identify our background and our intentions with our research.

In our methods and policy courses, we ensure that our students clarify and define their positionality within their work. Positionality begins with an introduction of your name, community, influences in your life, your outlook and conceptions of research, and most importantly, how the researcher intends to give back to their community.

In the design of coauthor Greyeyes's community building and policy course, I have constructed a community-engaged policy framework to help my students include a researcher philosophy. The philosophy includes these elements, but ultimately it fulfills this idea of a relational accountability. This means that through the research and work, the researcher must clarify their intentions and their commitment to give back to the community.

Pedagogy of Community

Our teaching portfolios ensure that our students are learning in a manner that centralizes the community as a place of learning, a place of value, and a place we return to. The community work that happens is in direct alignment with our teaching philosophy. We recognize, as Deloria points out, that in Indigenous practices, people are not objectified in order to value rationality over relationality. Instead, we recognize that our communities are alive and are empowered to make social change and to create social movements. We cannot discount the value of community and, therefore, we create collective pedagogical tools and resources for our students to ensure they honor and respect communities.

We have included these pedagogical goals into our rubrics of growth for our department. In many cases, the rubric replaces westernized concepts of "beginner, proficient, excelling" with "seedling, sprouting, harvesting, and regrowth." The project of ensuring that the student is viewed as being a contributor and giving back through "reproduction" acknowledges that they uphold their relational responsibility but also recognizes the value of community within their research and work.

NAS at UNM has made its purpose to provide an education that is community-oriented and facilitates students' roles and connections to community. Practicing a pedagogy of community requires confronting the challenges of recognition and legitimacy as a discipline in academia and among our own Native peoples. It requires stimulating critical consciousness of Native peoples' history and experiences that shape contemporary life in Native communities. In our effort to practice a pedagogy of community, we revised our mission statement to affirm,

"We will honor Indigenous experiences and the strengthening of Native Nations and sustainable communities through academic excellence." Our mission is our driving force for practicing a pedagogy of community. We also developed a rubric that aligns with our mission as one way to measure how our courses, assignments, and activities line up with the components of our mission. However, implementing such a pedagogy in western-influenced institutions of higher education presents challenges.

Next, we share how our department aims to deliver a master's degree program through the practice of a pedagogy of community while meeting the expectations of the university.

NAS is contributing to the discipline by centralizing our communities' knowledge, experiences, and perspectives. Our department has struggled to resist the ivory tower's expectations for western-style research. Instead, we have argued that our people and our communities should be considered and respected from our woodstoves in research, which means from our Native perspectives and lived experiences. Through listening, conversations, debate, and action, our Native American Studies Department challenges western academic norms by developing our own models of community-based and community-engaged research, teaching, and service. Our rubric and mission articulate our own norms and vision of a successful student and embrace the growth of a community-conscious scholar.

Our major effort to inspire a community-conscious scholar is through our Project of Excellence (POE). The POE is similar to a master's degree thesis requirement, but it prioritizes a collaboration and relationship with a community partner. The goal of the POE is to demonstrate the student's accumulation of an NAS theoretical (storytelling) foundation that can be successfully applied to address a target topic or issue relevant to a particular Native Nation, community, inter/national audience, or Indigenous group or organization. The POE is based on a student-led and initiated project combining all prior NAS coursework that will be used in the development of a finished project through a process of evaluative reciprocity with a community partner and NAS faculty advisor. Our stated purpose and goals for the POE include the following: the project must be realistic yet imaginative and conceive of Indigenous ways to understand Native Americans in the twenty-first century; the project shall employ the idea of promoting a systemic change with the intention of remembering Indigenous knowledge that is relevant and useful for Indigenous peoples while also a benefit to society at large; and the project is also a way to reclaim Indigenous representational authority in ways benefiting Native/Indigenous communities.[19]

Our MA degree launched in the fall of 2018, and we graduated eighteen MA students in December 2023. Their POEs provide excellent examples of the outcomes from practicing a pedagogy of community. One Diné student who holds her bachelor's degree in agriculture expanded on her passion for contributing to Indigenous food security and sovereignty through a garden to school project. She worked with her grandmother on their land to do the hard work of tilling the soil, fencing, and creating a garden. Her grandmother's land is near the local elementary school, where she established a grant-funded collaboration with the school's leadership to connect them to her garden. She interviewed local Diné traditional knowledge holders about Diné traditions of and beliefs about growing food. She was able to write an academic paper about her project and continue the collaboration after her graduation to see the project to fruition.

Another MA student was a teacher at a high school that has a majority of Native students and whose mission is to integrate Indigenous perspectives and knowledge into their curriculum and pedagogy. Their school was the beneficiary of a donation of a large area of land in the mountains to the east of the school. This student's POE was to work with a team of teachers and leaders from the school to develop their philosophy of land-based learning and to create land-based curriculum for teachers to implement. This work required her to facilitate "out of the box" thinking regarding the development of educational experiences for the students. It centered Indigenous philosophies of education to align with relationships and learning from the land. These two examples demonstrate one way NAS is transforming education within a western academic institution to address and impact issues of importance to our Native communities.

Conclusion

The future of our department is to continue building and testing new strategies to create a program that fulfills Deloria's vision. We envision a future to build a PhD program that continues to embed the framework we described. So far, across the United States, there are only three other universities with a PhD program in Native or Indigenous studies: University of California–Davis Department of Native American Studies; University of Arizona, American Indian Studies Department; and University of Alaska–Fairbanks, Indigenous Studies.

Before we began this major undertaking, we included community input by conducting a survey in February 2019 during the American Indian Studies Association conference at UNM. We received an astonishing 114 responses from attendees. In addition, we distributed a petition and gathered 438 signatures. And finally, we received support letters from chairs with the College of Arts and Sciences and from other New Mexico colleges, Tribal colleges, and universities. This approach was in line with our value for community engagement, a pedagogy of community, and our sense of responsibility to community. Native American studies is moving in the direction Deloria called for with a stronger focus on integrating Indigenous knowledge, reclaiming our role and purpose in western academic institutions, and recentering our work from the woodstoves of knowledge.

CHAPTER 25

DELORIA'S CALL FOR AN INDIAN EDUCATION REVOLUTION

Cheryl Crazy Bull

This essay examines whether governments, education institutions, and education infrastructure fulfill Deloria's call for Indian education to address Tribal histories and epistemologies and to prepare Tribal citizens for the future. In the nearly fifty years since Deloria made this call, Tribally controlled education in the form of Indigenous early childhood education, Tribal K–12 schools, Tribal Colleges and Universities (TCUs), and Indigenous studies programs at predominantly white institutions (PWIs) have evolved to serve diverse Tribal priorities. The establishment of these institutions and programs focus on the substantive qualities of Indigenous Nations that describe their peoplehood—relationships and kinship; preservation of Tribal languages and cultural practices; political, economic, and governance systems; history; contemporary ways of knowing and living; and religious and spiritual practice. Examining how institutions and education infrastructure fulfill (or do not rise to the level of intended success) Deloria's call for an Indian education revolution brings his philosophy and vision into sharp focus in the context of complex social challenges faced by Tribal Nations.

Tribally Controlled Education

Deloria's commitment to education demonstrated itself not only in his chosen profession as an academic but also in his roles as philosopher, advocate, scholar, and writer. Deloria believed that higher education,

Indian culture, and Indian control of educational institutions were likely to have the greatest impact on Native life,[1] so he made several recommendations intended to influence the actions of Natives in and outside of academia. Among those recommendations, according to Wilkins,

> 1974—Religion and Revolution Among American Indians
> Three central areas of future: Higher education, culture, and Native control of educational institutions. Education should address Tribal histories and epistemologies, as well as preparation for a larger world. One-year breaks at intervals are needed to allow for cultural and spiritual growth.
>
> 1980—Congressional Testimony
> Control of Indian education must be returned to local communities and focus on the content and substance of Indigenous traditions.[2]

While there are many innovations that have occurred in the last fifty years in support of Indigenous sovereignty and self-determination in the education arena, there also remain many of the same challenges that Deloria identified in both his writing and in speeches that he gave during his lifetime. The need for education to focus on the self-determination and identity of Tribes is understood by Native scholars and leaders throughout higher education and the K–12 system. The ability, however, of Tribes and educational institutions to intentionally focus on the characteristics and experiences of self-determination is often undermined by the very government—the federal government—charged with supporting Tribal priorities and initiatives. Most Native students attend public schools and colleges, so state governments through their legislation and their statewide education boards along with local school boards greatly influence their access to culturally relevant, meaningful education.

Deloria believed Tribes should have the greatest influence over access, but an examination of the past fifty years of Tribal education shows that their ability to influence is undermined by complex relationships with local, state, and federal agencies and legislatures. Further, Deloria's experience in academia showed him that Indigenous scholars were often forced to comply with institutional expectations to attain job security and to be influential in terms of policy, practice, research, and pedagogy. Those challenges, such as the continued emphasis on accreditation of Tribally controlled schools and colleges through western processes or the pressure on Indigenous scholars to teach and publish about issues deemed "relevant" to their colleges, undermine the progress that Native people have made with restorative education.

Perhaps unintentionally, because Deloria believed in the role of the federal government in education due to treaties, and throughout his lifetime advocated for the federal government to increase its investment in Indian education, the federal government has emerged as a domineering and often adversely catalytic partner in Indian education. This trust relationship grounded in treaties, while necessary to uphold treaty obligations as well as civil and inherent rights in education, is often detrimental to the authority and intentions of Tribes to restore Tribal ways of living and knowing using formal and informal educational structures and processes. Government funding, though critically important to the delivery of education, often comes with rules and regulations that hamper appropriate instruction, creating an environment in which Tribal citizens must rely on federal—and sometimes state—funding to maintain an even rudimentary formal education system.

Over the years, diverse Tribal engagement with the development of alternative and language immersion schools has been a means for Tribal citizens to work together to attempt to overcome the education systems that federal and state governments impose. These efforts are often successful for short periods of time, but insufficient financial support and goodwill from the federal and state governments mean that they rarely survive the lack of investment. Although Wilkins doesn't identify specific recommendations to federal and state governments regarding education, Deloria's intention appeared to be that the federal government would provide the funding needed by Tribes for them to operate their own educational institutions while also staying out of the way of Tribal priorities and decisions about education.

If the evidence of federal support is both funding and deregulation, the federal government has failed in its duty to support education as a foundational path to Tribal self-determination. The move to Tribal grant schools, the autonomy of TCUs, and the development of less restrictive contracting and grant mechanisms between Tribes and the federal government improved the ability of Tribes to foster more meaningful educational experiences for their citizens. But those acts did not remove federal intervention, nor did they reduce the regulations that control federal purse strings. Two examples that come to mind are the funding for bilingual education programs for Tribally controlled schools and the tying of participation in federal grant programs at TCUs to regional accreditation established through the US Department of Education. Both of those funding streams are subject to the Bureau of Indian Education in the Department of Interior and the US Department of Education programming and funding priorities. Often bilingual education is seen as a tool to promote English as a second language programs for non-English speaking immigrants and is therefore not structured to restore Tribal languages. It is seriously underfunded. While there are other pathways to developing Tribal language programs, such as the Esther Martinez Native Languages Preservation Act, the places where restoration of language can have the most traction— in schools and colleges—are not the places where full funding of restorative Native language education occurs.

TCUs have long sought the independence of having their own accreditation processes. Accreditation is a peer-reviewed model that is intended to affirm, for the public, that an institution is fulfilling its mission and operating with transparency, integrity, and sufficient strategic resources. It has been difficult for the leadership of TCUs to fully engage with the US accreditation system because it is generally intended to foster compliance with agreed upon western standards (agreed upon by the majority non-Tribal institutions) developed outside of Tribal nation building, and focused instead on the individualistic, economy-driven goals of education in the United States. Because TCUs and other Tribally controlled institutions were emergent at the time of Deloria's initial recommendations and because many of the challenges in the relationship between Tribally controlled education institutions only became evident as resources were developed, it is useful to examine the ways that Deloria's recommendations for the role of Tribally controlled education and higher education have come to fruition.

As Deloria developed his understanding of the role of education in restoration of Tribal self-determination, the rise of Tribally controlled education was occurring. Leaders throughout Indian Country identified that the failures of American education were deeply rooted in the assimilation and acculturation policies of both federal and state governments. Young people were rejecting those policies by their failures to achieve in K–12 systems and their lack of participation in higher education. To remedy these failures, grassroots leaders affirmed that their Tribal peoples had the inherent right to educate and socialize their own children and youth. As Tribal leaders connected the authority of their Tribal governments to the right to education, there was a related movement toward civil rights for all peoples occurring in the United States. This movement resulted in the Civil Rights Act of 1964 and contributed to the passage of the American Indian Religious Freedom Act in 1978. Through a series of events, the sovereign right of Tribes to develop educational institutions was being reinforced. The Indian Citizenship Act of 1924, also known as the Snyder Act, served as the basis for creating federal laws that recognized the rights of Tribes to self-determination—the 1934 Indian Reorganization Act and the 1975 Indian Self-Determination and Education Assistance Act.

Those acts created mechanisms and funding to promote Tribal self-rule. While the context for creating those acts is important to understanding them, most important to this discussion is that those acts of Congress were intended to fulfill Deloria's recommendations in all aspects of Indian peoples' lives, from health to education to infrastructure to housing. An interesting aspect of this is that the development of the first Tribally controlled institutions emerged with the very support of the institutions that had opposed Tribal people receiving an education that was not about assimilation. This included the Catholic Church and other Christian churches, and public higher education institutions including land-grant institutions, whose very existence came from the taking of Native peoples' lands for state-sponsored education.

Deloria specifically recommended Indian control of education:

> 1980 Congressional Testimony
>
> "Control of Indian education must be returned to local communities and focus on the content and substance of Indigenous traditions."

The first Tribally controlled education institutions were the Rough Rock Demonstration School and Navajo Community College on the Navajo Reservation. Nearly simultaneously, Tribes in the northern Plains and a group of activists in northern California established their own Tribally controlled institutions. The activism of Indigenous people at the same time (late 1960s, early 1970s) meant that groups of Tribal citizens in various locations established schools intended to immerse young people in their cultures and languages. These schools were the result of community-based leadership and family activism and often had little to do with the formal mechanisms of school establishment primarily run by state actors.

Tribal schools evolved over time from the already established Bureau of Indian Affairs and Christian-operated schools on Indian reservations. These schools were primarily funded by federal and private dollars until an increase in public school development emerged as populations on Indian reservations became increasingly diverse, and more non-Natives began to demand state-sanctioned and -funded schools.

Deloria believed that education served as the means of reinforcing Tribal identity and preserving Tribal sovereignty. It appears that there are strands of that reinforcement evidenced in the curriculum and teaching practices of many schools that serve Native populations, but most Native children and young adults still participate in educational systems that blur their identity through multicultural approaches or that completely ignore their identities. There have been efforts at the state level to implement laws that require the teaching of Tribal history and culture to all children, usually at specific grade levels, but the success of that implementation seems to be dependent on the goodwill of school administrators and teachers and on the investment in training and materials by the state. Two illustrations of this effort are the passage of the Since Time Immemorial: Tribal Sovereignty in Washington legislation in Washington State in 2005, amended in 2015 and required for all schools in the state, and the passage of Indian Education for All in the State of Montana passed in 1999 to enforce a provision in the state's constitution that required American Indian history be taught to all children in Montana schools. In 2021, a group of Montana citizens along with the American Civil Liberties Union and Native American Rights Fund sued the state over its lack of enforcement of Indian Education for All.

Deloria also understood the strong link between education and Tribal economic development. Although he often noted that an overemphasis by the federal government on Tribal economic development undermined the need for investment in self-governance, law, health, and education, he understood that the complexities of Tribal life required complex solutions. Deloria also emphasized the role of research, noting in several of his recommendations that Tribes needed to develop policies to govern research, should expect researchers to generate resources for the Tribes in exchange for their access, and should use research in a restorative manner supporting Tribal identity and cultural revitalization.

It is interesting to note that in many of his recommendations, Deloria specifically focused on the participation and inclusion of young people, perhaps identifying that revitalization would be more meaningful and lasting if young people were given access to Tribal Elders and were encouraged to learn more about kinship and family relationships. Since kinship is so foundational to the philosophies of

Tribes, it makes sense that Deloria would see kinship knowledge as vital to Tribal self-determination. Deloria also advocated for close ties to place—insisting that creating strong bonds between reservation and urban Native populations was necessary for all Tribal people to thrive, with an emphasis on building stronger homelands and even encouraging migration back to homelands to revitalize those places. Education, particularly Tribally controlled education, is the means to achieve all those recommendations—exposing young people to curriculum inclusive of the teaching of Tribal Elders, building kinship ties through language instruction and cultural classes, and developing the strong sense of place rooted in the missions and purposes of Tribally controlled schools and TCUs. Even in Native studies programs at PWIs, the curriculum, while often adapted to teach non-Native students about Natives, is also rooted in the history and culture of all Tribes—and, in particular, frequently of Tribes within the geographic range of the higher education institution and/or of relevance to the citizenship of the Indigenous scholars working at the institutions.

Through their adoption of Tribal Education Codes, Tribes have also made inroads in creating the legal and structural framework that enforces the educational goals of Tribal social and religious identity and an understanding of Tribalism that Deloria advocated for. Among the first Tribes to do so, the Rosebud Sioux Tribe in South Dakota asserted that it, as a Tribal government, had inherent authority over formal education and among other purposes, had the goal to "preserve, protect, and perpetuate tribe."[3] The Tribe went on to describe how it would accomplish its purposes through a variety of local school requirements. A significant number of Tribes now have Tribal Education Codes and departments.

With the establishment of the first Tribally controlled institutions, a parallel but equally vital path was being forged by mostly public education institutions that saw themselves as addressing burgeoning Tribal relationships and civil rights concerns by supporting the establishment of Native studies programs.

Indigenous Early Childhood Education, K–12 Systems, and Higher Education

While still under-resourced and often absent in discussions about Indian education pathways, early childhood education has been identified as essential to restoration of cultural lifeways and intact families. Although Deloria spoke of education and youth, during his heyday of education writing, he rarely considered the details of education beyond his experiences at the postsecondary level. His seminal work about education, *Power and Place: Indian Education in America*, coauthored with Daniel Wildcat, infrequently mentions early childhood education. In the list of recommendations of Deloria's outlined in *Red Prophet*, Wilkins doesn't identify any references to early education. While recognizing that education is part of the metaphysical understanding that all things are interactive and related, Deloria and Wildcat in *Power and Place* prescribe most educational interpretations as being rooted in the educational experiences of adults.[4] It could be argued that adults must facilitate changes that expand education resources and opportunities, but Deloria's failure to be inclusive of such an argument begs the question of relevance beyond the obvious postsecondary focus. Because the socialization role of Tribal families is critical to maintenance of cultural identity and kinship, an expanded view of how to actualize self-determination through family engagement in support of the learning and development of young children is a necessary expansion of Deloria's recommendations.

There is widespread emphasis on the experiences of Native children and youth in K–12 systems. While the graduation of Native youth from high school remains abysmally low, there has been progress in the development of curriculum and school structures focused on Indigenous people. We can safely say that although Deloria's commitment to education was particularly focused on higher education, he advocated for a systemic approach to what we would call today as the indigenization of education—the remaking of education into a system that promulgates Tribal identity and knowledge and provides a frame for the creation and sharing of new knowledge. We see some efforts on the part of Tribal schools to mediate culture by providing students with place-based experiences that teach the stories and practices of their ancestors—albeit in a modern context and within infrastructure (schools) that are decidedly western in their organization. Deloria believed that Tribal governments needed to proactively approach the restoration of family systems and cultural practices and would undoubtedly find the disconnect between the authority of Tribes to establish and support Indian schools and the lack of widespread success of those schools in the education of our youth to be disheartening. Tribal schools have made some progress, and certainly immersion schools that are focused on language and cultural restoration are beacons of hope. But the lack of widespread improvement and restructuring despite federal, state, and Tribal laws, attributable at least in part to being severely under-resourced, could be seen through Deloria's lens as discouraging.

For Deloria, Tribally controlled K–12 schools and TCUs epitomize the intended role of education in strengthening Tribal self-determination. Foundational in Deloria's understanding of the relationship of Tribal governments to education is affirmation of the authority of Tribal Nations to establish and manage their own educational systems, represented by the charters and governing structures of Tribally controlled institutions. Deloria goes beyond the governance of these institutions to examine the choices that are made about curriculum and course content. He believed that Tribal Nations must be willing to examine their history from a Tribal perspective, gathering knowledge from the oral traditions of community members—especially Tribal Elders—and contextualizing that knowledge as a resource for Tribes to be more progressive with decisions and allocation of resources that impact the well-being of their communities and the effectiveness of their governance and its systems. Although successful attainment of high school and postsecondary degrees can be elusive in Tribal settings (due to socioeconomic disparities and issues of access), Tribally controlled institutions do offer place-based curriculum, engage Tribal Elders and cultural informants, and train and hire Native people for paraprofessional and professional positions. Wilkins noted Deloria's testimony to the Congressional Subcommittee on Elementary, Secondary, and Vocational Education affirming his advocacy for the inclusion of traditional knowledge education as necessary to more meaningful education for Native students. He also advocated that teaching in particular replicates the approach to education used by Tribes—small numbers of children with numerous teachers with expertise in relevant areas of instruction. His advocacy for Native people included access to a balanced approach to education that incorporated both traditions and modern knowledge, as he saw the necessity of adapting to modern life.

Deloria also emphasized the importance of finding ways to bring people together to capitalize on diverse intellectual contributions. He was well-known for convening Indigenous people from diverse communities to discuss traditional knowledge, Tribal common law, science, governance, and religion. These types of convening also replicated what Deloria must have a viewed as a more traditional, oral, and inquiring approach to teaching and learning.

Throughout his academic career, Deloria asserted his independence as an educator. His advocacy for predominantly white institutions to be more proactive and deliberate in their engagement with Native scholars, students, and Indian Tribes is well documented. In a 1999 interview with the *Tribal College Journal*, Deloria called schools of education "the worst thing that ever happened to American education" because subject matter was not the focus on teacher education; techniques were the focus.[5] He went on to share his concern that Native people had adopted the language of the colonizer and needed to find a way to reground themselves in the language of their people, not only to communicate more competently but also to capture the traditional knowledge that needs to be shared to be known.

Wilkins notes that in *Power and Place: Indian Education in America*, another recommendation about education emerged:

> 1994—Indian Education in America
>
> Native students must gain an understanding of their own knowledge systems and Native academics should work with their communities to create scenarios to resolve pressing community problems. Every Native youth should be taught family genealogy.[6]

Despite his criticism of American higher education, Deloria also believed that there was an important role for Native scholars, many of whom would be affiliated with predominately white (mainstream) institutions. He called upon scholars to lead the way in learning about and documenting not only the traditional knowledge of Tribes but also to examine the impact of historical events on how Tribal lifeways evolved. Deloria proposed that among the most direct paths to Tribal self-determination was the path of education grounded in Tribal values. He saw the influence of federal and state policy in the emphasis on the rules and regulations associated with consultations and at Indian education conferences.

Did a Revolution in Indian Education Happen?

Certainly, it should be argued that there has been significant progress in the last fifty years in the development of Tribally controlled education institutions, Native language restoration, Native teacher education, and curriculum considering the five hundred–plus years of colonization of Indigenous peoples' educational systems. The progress that has occurred through the dedication of Tribal educators and their communities deserves to be celebrated. Crazy Bull and Guillory advance the role of TCUs as revolutionizing higher education through the creation of place-based, culturally focused institutions that were otherwise unheard of in higher education, especially in the United States.[7] They also align the development of Native studies programs at PWIs with the advent of TCUs, forcing a broader and more comprehensive response by public higher education institutions to the needs of Tribal citizens and Nations. There has been progress made in curriculum development and the pedagogy of teaching and learning for Native people. This progress is greatly aided in the increased number of Native teachers, especially those educated by TCUs and cohort-based programs at PWIs.

Many Tribes have developed comprehensive Native language resources, produced place-based, age- and grade-appropriate curriculum, and many have produced a variety of multimedia resources aimed at families and school systems. Of course, a challenge is that often this curriculum is viewed as an "addition" to the existing western curriculum of schools and colleges, and because of limited time and resources it may be completely left out of the educational experiences of Native children as well as other children who would benefit from a more diverse education. This lack of inclusion is systemic and structural, so improving formal access to an appropriate education for Native children means that schooling at all grades and age levels must be reformed to achieve the goals set forth by Deloria. This requires increased investment, support for Tribes to exercise decision-making control over educational resources, and an emphasis on reinforcing Tribal ways of knowing and identity.

There are clearly several areas where there has been progress toward achieving Deloria's recommendations, such as the development of Native history and culture curriculum, Native language programs, and the increases in the number of Tribally controlled education institutions. TCUs are models for inclusive, traditional, and place-specific education, while Native studies at PWIs are models for developing more diverse and comprehensive approaches to the social, economic, and cultural challenges faced by Tribes. Deloria emphasized in an essay in the *Tribal College Journal* in 1993 that Tribal colleges because of their access to community informants and their place-based missions could serve as the authority about Tribal knowledge, providing mechanisms for restoring and teaching knowledge that is vital to Tribal identity as well as the well-being of society in general.[8] Crazy Bull and Lindquist emphasized that TCUs have found ways to sustain their Tribal spirituality despite the western structures in which they operate.[9] Also, critical to achieving comprehensive and meaningful change in Tribal education is the continued development of language nests, immersion schools, and Tribally chartered schools despite limited resources. These approaches demonstrate the continued commitment of educators and communities to providing education embedded with Tribal ways of knowing. This progress is hampered by the weight of federal policy and the lack of a comprehensive approach to education reform. Deloria's call for Tribal government reform can easily serve as the umbrella for a related call for education reform. Deloria also recognized that Native people live in rural, reservation, and urban settings and attend public, private, and Tribal schools and higher education institutions. The right to a meaningful education and to be socialized into the ways of one's Tribe is an inherent right of Indigenous people, but it has become a right that is clouded by the geographic, cultural, and economic diversity of Tribes and by the myriad of often confusing, underfunded programs that are intended to "help" Native people.

Deloria's call for Tribal Nations to adopt more comprehensive understanding of the "seven generations" construct, to develop their "ability to maintain and adhere to cultural needs and standards that utilize traditional mechanisms," and for institutional reforms that create influential, interdisciplinary, and inclusive opportunities for affirmation of Tribal sovereignty and self-determination, strengthens Indigenous education. This strengthening can break down the remaining barriers to Tribal-controlled education in all its forms—formal and informal—regardless of delivery mechanisms and location. Indigenous education would continue its generative powers of inclusion and opportunity and would be that foundation of transformative change that Deloria believed it was.

CHAPTER 26

THE SOVEREIGN FRUITS OF VINE

Deron Marquez

> But the Indian task of keeping an informed public available to assist the Tribes in their efforts to survive is never ending, and so the central message of this book, that Indians are alive, have certain dreams of their own, and are being overrun by ignorance and the mistaken, misdirected efforts of those who would help them, can never be repeated too often. Every generation of Indians will have to assume this burden which all divergent minorities bear.
>
> —Vine Deloria, Jr., *Custer Died for Your Sins*[1]

The writings of Vine Deloria, Jr., with his panoramic vision and critical depth style, are as alive today as they were in 1969. I had not arrived on Earth yet, but when I was finally introduced to Deloria's *Custer Died for Your Sins*, I felt like he was writing to me, and that was about twenty years after he introduced his manifesto to the world. As I embarked on my Deloria journey, little did I know that in ten years I would be putting his thoughts, teachings, and wisdom into practice. In October of 1999, I was installed as chairman of my Tribe during a time of hyperpolitics and positive economic struggles. The gaming question had been answered in 1987 by the highest court in the land and was then authorized by Congress the following year. States, however, did not want to participate in good faith and worked instead to capitalize on the high ground erroneously bestowed upon them by the congressional act. Tribes that had been in gaming operations for more than a decade faced unprecedented challenges because of states' interference, and in California, the struggle came to a tipping point toward the end of the millennium, just as I became chairman.

This is not an essay on gaming—a multitude of papers and books have been composed on the subject—rather it is an essay on my experiences of *playing leader* for my people. It was then that I began to utilize the Deloria guidebook to maneuver the federal-state-local poli-paradox, whereby all three outside entities were confident they each had the right to dictate to Tribal Nations. Deloria provides the ingredients for survivability and promotes the kindled path, but he does not say how to execute, as those actions are most effectively developed and undertaken as acts of sovereignty by the Tribes who best understand their situations.

It is important to remember that, to this day, many non-Indians remain ignorant of Tribal issues (some willfully) and refuse to acknowledge Tribal rights to freedom of governance over their lands and communities. In 1977, just a few years before gaming dramatically changed the balance of power for many Tribes, the American Indian Policy Review Commission's Final Report was issued by Congress. It explored the situation within Indian Country and came up with questions, findings, and recommendations very similar to those Deloria had already written about twelve years earlier.[2] The report also offered some insights into mainstream attitudes about Natives, particularly through the lengthy dissent of committee member Lloyd Meeds of Washington who wrote: "The fundamental error of this report [the Final Report] is that it perceives the American Indian Tribe as a body politic in the nature of a sovereign as that word is used to describe the United States and the States, rather than as a body politic which the United States, through its sovereign power, permits to govern itself and order its internal affairs, but not to the affairs of others."[3]

This language, implying that Tribes were not sovereign and lacked all essential means to be so, captured the general public's animosity toward

Tribal communities. It is interesting to note that Meeds served as vice chairman of the American Indian Policy Review Commission and had introduced the resolution creating the commission. In fact, during most of his time in office, he had proven to be an Indian Country ally, instrumental in the passage of the Alaska Native Claims Settlement Act of 1971 and supportive of the Boldt Decision's unequivocal affirmation of treaty rights.[4] It was widely believed that this public support of Tribes in his home state had nearly cost him his seat in 1974 and ultimately led to his decision to retire in 1977.[5] Given his previous record on Native issues, it would be reasonable to assume that in this dissent the congressman provided the commission with a way to acknowledge widely held negative public opinions about Indians. It is also possible that his defense of the language was in response to political pressures of the time, and he felt compelled to convey the views of his majority anti-Indian constituency.

> "Geez, Victor . . . I guess the warrior look doesn't work every time."
>
> —Thomas Builds-the-Fire, Smoke Signals[6]

In 1977, at the conclusion of a two-year study, the American Indian Policy Review Commission submitted its final report to Congress.[7] Though this essay is not an exploration of that report or the Commission's overall work, the Meeds dissent continues to resonate, reflecting the ongoing ignorance and animosity still held or represented by many non-Tribal leaders regarding the exercise of Native sovereignty. Nearly half a century later, negative perceptions of Indian Country remain stubbornly entrenched and the so-called culture wars debate we have today are only the latest version of a larger societal reluctance to incorporate uncomfortable or unprofitable realities into the American story. The dissent's repetitive language emphasizes a familiar theme; there are only two sovereigns identified within the US Constitution, the federal government and state governments, with the federal holding supremacy over Indian Country.[8] This federal-state binary framing continues to be used to this day and still bolsters non-Native beliefs, typically based on ignorance or racism, that Indians were receiving preferred treatment. That such ignorance was based on improper education of history, law, and culture needs no explanation. But, taken as a whole, the commission's findings all relate to the fluidity of sovereignty. This differs from the 1928 Meriam Report, which attached each of its recommendations to agency and validation of Native self-rule.[9] Ultimately, the 1977 commission's findings were not surprising, and thus the emerging era demanded not just empowerment, but Tribal action.

The 1969 release of *Custer Died for Your Sins* provided a powerful counternarrative to individuals like Congressman Meeds and inspired within Native Nations the hope and possibility of *sovereign* expressions that were ready to be unleashed throughout Native America. The inherent sovereignty that Deloria spoke of had been practiced by Native peoples long before the creation of the American republic. As Bartelson aptly noted in his 1995 study, sovereignty has become "rigorously interlinked with the foundations of modern political knowledge, it cannot easily be disentangled and analyzed; because sovereignty is so profoundly involved in the naturalization and reification of political reality, it is a difficult object of political knowledge. Indeed, to the extent that sovereignty constitutes the unthought foundation of political knowledge, it is beyond the scope of that knowledge."[10]

Deloria, who knew Meeds from his many appearances before the Indian Affairs Sub-Committee, challenged him to defend his dissenting position, and their April 1978 public debate at San Diego State University was recorded and published later that year.[11] He felt strongly that Indians had to be vocal, to educate both themselves and non-Indians. In rebutting Meeds's assertion that challenging the larger cultural view of Indians would result in a backlash that would be "totally destructive to Indian culture and heritage," Deloria said,

> When Congressman Meeds complains in his dissent that you can't rewrite four hundred years of history, I think what he is

> really saying is that a certain version of history has become so deeply ingrained in Americans' consciousness that it is virtually impossible to change it by legislative action. What we're talking about is a very long-term, well-concentrated educational process. It may take a hundred years to correct the inaccuracies that have crept into American history to become the basis for doctrines that tear away at the hearts of Indian communities.[12]

Courageous leaders like Deloria inspired Indian Country to understand and protect their inherent sovereignty. So, in spite of that considerable non-Indian animosity, over the subsequent ten years, Tribal nations exercised rights in a feverish and unprecedented manner on many fronts, and governmental rights to conduct gaming would surpass all expectations on all levels of sovereignty. That work showed that sovereignty, from an Indigenous perspective, is not something to be debated but rather is an established and inherent force that every Native community wields and practices every day. Every page of *Custer* is dedicated to the notion that sovereignty is vital and is the font of Indigenous cultural and political identity.

Chief Justice Thurgood Marshall, in the foundational case *Worcester v. Georgia* in 1832, acknowledged this reality about sovereignty and identified it as the basic anchor for Native self-governance when he stated, "A weak state, in order to provide for its safety, may place itself under the protection of one more powerful, *without stripping itself of the right of government, and ceasing to be a state*."[13] Because of the unique sovereign Indian-Federal binary form, Tribal nations' actions are equal to all Indians, a truism that is both positive and negative. "The large Tribes cannot seem to understand that a precedent of law set against a small Tribe means one for the larger Tribes as well," which carries the same weight in reverse.[14] Many Tribal governments have become proficient in understanding the broadness and depth of their actions and how those actions could influence Indian Country. Plus, the steady stream of dialogue across Tribal governments has been more abundant than ever before, leading to a casual consultation of best practices. The point is simple: each Tribal nation has its own unique, authentic sovereign platform, but each is only as strong as the weakest platform. Yet, when unified, these sovereign powers can be relentless and successful in multiple spheres. Tribes working together have garnered respect at all levels of government—Tribal, local, state, and federal.

The strong desire for Tribal nations to interact on multiple levels *with each other* has had a profound impact for Indian Country, which was a common theme in *Custer* and served to advance Tribal nations. The Indian sovereign union was (and is) critical. Non-Indians and members of Congress, regardless of political party, may be like Mr. Meeds, who stated that "in our Federal system, as ordained and established by the United States Constitution, there are but two sovereign entities: the United States and the States. . . . The blunt fact of the matter is that American Indian Tribes are not a third set of governments in the American federal system. They are not sovereigns. [Congress] has permitted them to be self-governing entities but not entities that would govern others."[15] Within ten years, this notion would change.

In his coauthored book, *The Nations Within*, Deloria (with Clifford Lytle) traversed new territory, ranging from governmental reforms to federal-state relations, in a chapter called "The Future of Indian Nations." Change is typically ushered by some sort of means; a catalyst that was unforeseen and unpredictable. He begins a chapter titled "The Future of Indian Nations" with, "Self-determination and self-government are not equivalent terms, yet they can describe the same social reality, simply in different contexts."[16] This sentence had a profound effect on me, and I understood that self-government and self-determination must cooperate if a Tribe is finally to reconstitute itself. These few words encompass so much—their profound meaning greatly surpassing the 1977 Final Report's 624 pages. Why? Indian gaming, serving as that catalyst, changed and reconstituted many Tribal and non-Tribal communities. Tribes who could not compete for federal funding due to community size capitalized on and ushered in this new empowerment phenomenon.

Gaming was first introduced in the late 1970s by Seminoles (Florida) and the Penobscot (Maine), but it was the Seminoles who had their rights challenged by Broward County and the state of Florida. These challenges, though not known during those contentious moments, launched an economic juggernaut for many Tribal communities. The federal appeals court, in 1980, established the binary distinction of "civil-regulatory" versus "criminal-prohibitory."[17] This distinction was followed in both Wisconsin and California.[18] In these early days, "high stakes bingo" was the game states sought to close, even though states themselves were operating various games and permitted charity bingo games. According to Wilkins, "By the late 1970s," Indian Country's political self-determination advancement "provoked a backlash among disaffected non-Indians," with reaffirmations and attachments of rights that included fishing, activism and gaming.[19]

Deloria noted, "Finding the solution to Indian economic problems is a desperate task," and, incredibly, these economic problems were solved for some with the implementation of gaming.[20] Sovereign acts by these activating-agent Tribes and individuals fueled Tribal governments to expound on their sovereignty. Gaming was an economic engine sought by Tribal societies desperately needing one and by doing so, it forced upon those Tribal governments to engage governmental spheres that many were not accustomed to dealing with, especially when the state-federal mindset was dominant. The Seminoles were one of the first Nations to lead the movement and to "express pride that they were the first American Indian Tribal nation to launch high-stakes casino gaming, that their legal activism opened the door for a gaming revolution that spread across Indian Country, and that gaming improved their daily lives."[21] Even as the state of Florida was seeking to close the doors, the Seminoles realized the impact, pressed forward, and assisted other Tribal Nations. In 1985, a team from Seminole arrived at the Yuhaaviatam of San Manuel Nation (at that time known as the San Manuel Band of Mission Indians) located in Southern California and assisted in establishing a high-stakes bingo operation.

Gaming allowed these and many other Tribal communities to shed dependence on the federal government and become self-sufficient. With their new engines, they were also able to build a microeconomic environment that created jobs and community engagement. Perhaps most profoundly of all, they produced a new level of intergovernmental self-governance that provided great mutual benefits for surrounding non-Tribal communities that had always abused them or had even sought to eradicate their very existence.

Wilkins observes, the conception and ability of self-rule, the ability to control and govern, does carry an economic burden.[22] "Self-government is probably a farce without some steady form of Tribal income to support it," Deloria said, regarding the leasing of Indian resources, but he furthered his truism with a diagnosis of "reservation economy of most Tribes today is wholly artificial and could not survive but a few weeks without a transfusion from outside the reservation."[23] Some of the most successful Tribal government operations are located on very small reservations with little to none of the extraction-related resources typically linked with wealth. These small, land-based Tribal nations, who received very little federal funding, were able to craft an exploitation of law and external cash infusion on a different level of self-determination and governance than has ever been seen before in Indian Country. The gaming phenomenon ushered in a new era, throwing the old states and federal governments "world order" off-balance.

The Bureau of Indian Affairs (BIA) realized the "potential economic benefits of Tribal gaming operations, and a policy quickly emerged which supported Tribal bingo enterprises as an appropriate means by which Tribes could further their economic self-sufficiency, the economic development of their reservations, and Tribal self-determination."[24] The scenario set the stage for a state, congressional, judiciary, executive, and Tribal government *sovereign* showcase. The Fifth Circuit Court of Appeals ruled in favor of the Seminoles, as noted.[25]

States were troubled by the gaming boom and felt their rights were threatened and diminished. Many state and federal agencies took a combative stance against Tribal governments. While in reality they feared the prospect of newly empowered Tribes, they chose to fight against them through public relations campaigns that relied heavily on racism, calling up the specter of organized crime that they claimed would encroach upon reservations and into border communities. As states and the federal government were attempting to come to terms with gaming enterprises, so were Tribal communities.

Long isolated and lacking many elements of modern society, Tribal Nations, especially the smaller communities, quickly found themselves outnumbered by non-Indians on Indian lands. As Deloria noted, "fishing, ranching and agriculture" were *newer normal activities* for Tribal people, but "recreation and resort management seem strange and out of place for many Indians whose Tribe has developed this kind of economic activity."[26] The 1977 Final Report addresses the traditional economic ventures of human resources, land use, timber, agriculture, water, and mineral resources but does not meaningfully examine enterprise development. Small land base Tribes did not (and do not) have the landscape to engage *newer normal activities* like large land base Tribes. However, small Tribes, like those located in California, bordered large population centers and so enterprise development was key—maximizing square footage to the greatest capital output. Though not a "natural extension" of activities, gaming did (and does) "maximize the use of the land in as constructive a manner as possible."[27]

Though Congress injected states into the internal affairs of Tribal government via mandatory compacts, the explosion of these enterprises was unmatched, and the challenges mounted against Tribal governments were a continuation of years long past. In these modern times, Tribal leadership had to engage a multiprong counter to reaffirm rights that were guaranteed by the high court, acknowledged by Congress, and, in the same congressional breath, curtailed. Tribal governments were thrust into *Deloria engagement realms* that he professed Tribes *must* incorporate into their daily actions. The path to economic stability had to include the use of media, Tribal political allies, non-Tribal political allies, lobby groups and firms, coalitions, lawyers, and mass social outreach.

Because of these economic engines, in the eighties and nineties, Tribal communities were finally able to play politics at a level that countered their antagonists. Tribal societies had to battle not only the state but also the federal government, local governments, other Tribal governments and their legal teams, as well as local communities. The use of the media and public outreach served to educate the masses by using what was so well known to Tribal communities but unknown to outsiders. The strongest messaging—using a media term—was not a fabrication, it was the use of Tribal culture, tradition, and history to tell the truth about self-reliance for Tribal governments. In "Rethinking Tribal Sovereignty," Deloria prescribed this action—using Tribal social and cultural traditions in order to "preserve internal sovereignty"—and this action had a profound impact on "external sovereignty."[28] During this campaign, the term "sovereignty" was replaced with "self-reliance," a conscious choice made by the leadership due to the simple fact that the term "sovereignty" was a complex construct and did not resonate with the non-Indian community.

Bartelson wrote that the constructed "relationship between the very term sovereignty, the concept of sovereignty and the reality of sovereignty is historically open, contingent and unstable" and with it, difficult to comprehend.[29] Thus, Tribal leadership understood the importance of the term, reshaped it to meet the needs of the moment, and deployed the message to face the challenges that were presented to Tribal communities.[30] Tribes led the movement to change the state of California's constitution, a feat never attempted before, and conducted a massively successful campaign, not once, but twice.[31] Tribal societies no longer "failed to impress American society with the uniqueness of either [Tribal] culture, [Tribal] treaty rights, or [Tribal] feelings" or the historical facts within California; Tribal communities possessed the ability to control their history, tell their story, and place it in the minds of millions.[32] With securing the economic engines on reservations, Tribes became true masters of their destinies, no longer relying on external funding sources to fund internal programs, which by monetary connection, crafted internal sovereignty.[33]

For many Tribal governments of that era, these economic engines provided the ability—though not at a national level—as Deloria wrote in 1974, to "protect lands and resources, to educate young people, and provide employment and housing" as planned and executed by a Tribal government on their own terms.[34] The 1977 Final Report stated that the Economic Development Administration found the "highest success rate [were] Tribally owned resource based industries" when compared to non-Tribally owned industries, thus proving that the more consecrated internal controls Tribal governments execute, the more successful Tribes *could* become. Tribal governments are only as strong as *permitted by community*, and along this line of reasoning, it is extremely critical, as Deloria pointed out in 1979, that a unified "self-disciplined community" 'possess[es] sufficient sovereignty to confront and resolve any difficulty," but without support of "the overwhelming majority" the "political entity . . . cannot function for long."[35] With the advent of a new economic era, Tribal communities needed leadership that could confront both internal and external *poli* realms.

> "This ain't *Dances with Salmon* you know!"
> —Victor Joseph, *Smoke Signals*, 1998

As stated before, this is not all about gaming, but gaming does illustrate the Deloria road map. Through battles of securing economic rights, that action gave birth to securing Tribal-to-multigovernment relationships. Compacts became the new form of agreements across Tribal, state, and federal governments. Though not treaties (that process technically concluded in 1871), agreements between Tribes and states with approval by the federal government established a new order for Tribal communities. Tribal Nations' strongest sphere of sovereignty is internal, the boundaries and citizens of the land. As reservations were encountering more non-Indians daily, new challenges forced a deeper commitment to sovereignty by Tribal leadership. Often, sovereignty is linked to legal constructs from treaties, court cases, laws, governmental acts, and the like. Those elements are an extension and, at times, a byproduct of sovereign threads that, woven together, complete sovereign *meaning*.

Robert Jackson provided grounded ideals of "state" by referring to three example areas: (1) territory (2) population, and (3) government authority.[36] Possessing these three elements does not make you a sovereign unless you hold supreme authority, according to Jackson, but it does establish an interesting prelude to claiming sovereign status under a Euro-based paradigm. In 1964, E. H. Carr, writing about the time period of 1919 to 1939, predicted that the "concept of sovereignty is likely to become in the future more blurred and indistinct than it is at present."[37] For many, the term "sovereignty" does not clarify any of its distinct characteristics, but when a sovereign state seeks to curtail the sovereign traits of its community or that of another sovereign, then those acts serve to highlight and define those unique characteristics.

Wishing not to traverse down a rabbit hole, I pondered various inquiries regarding sovereignty during my years as a leader. Does any "state," that can claim those three elements also claim supreme authority? And what is supreme? Supreme authority surely cannot diminish or deny "natural rights?" Then, what is freedom and how free is free? Who decides what freedom is and what it should look like? Can you lose your freedom by diminishing your *individual* sovereignty? Can sovereignty be deflated with more freedom? Sovereignty and freedom are mutual constructs but neither provide the weight of clarity. In my search for an answer, I began to focus on the idea of *responsibility*, a concept extracted from Deloria as it relates to actions, as the most absolute and important code of leadership. It was critical in my mind to avoid the trap of *hollow sovereignty*, whereby a superficial, exploitative treatment of tradition and culture is used to create a sovereign facade. Without true community grounding and commitment to a shared purpose, there is no depth or longevity to a Tribe's internal workings or structure. Instead, we have to exercise *responsible sovereignty* that treats each aspect of our shared culture, traditions, development, security, and preservation with respect. Though its method of practice varies and is best determined by each Tribal society, what remains constant for all Tribes is respect for the course of action. The wielding of responsible sovereignty must be understood, appreciated, and, most of all, held sacred. Without these communal attributes, the term "sovereignty" and acts executed in the name of sovereignty are truly hollow with no generational soul and no attached authenticity. Simply stated by Deloria, "Indian Tribes must act like Indians. That's the only justification for preserving internal sovereignty."[38]

The goals of Tribal leadership have not evolved much over the years. Preservation, advancement, security, and survival have always been essential. Leaders must find ways to uphold these essential elements, and finding those ways is the responsibility of the supreme Tribal community. Deloria said, "The [Indian] people only followed a course of action if they were convinced it was best for them. This was as close as most Tribes ever got to a formal government."[39] Integrity in leadership was a trait, he points out, that must be present. I once wrote that a leader's integrity must emanate from the community, and that leader must then be sustained by the Tribal society's collective ancestral voice. A leader's acts should be based on *what is right for the community*, and that leader must be willing to forge ahead for their community. Leadership, because of present-day complexities, must engage many *poli* spheres and levels without abandoning *leadership integrity*. Because of these complexities, leadership is no longer a "one size fits all" style; it has become situational. Yet every style of leadership must be grounded in Tribal community integrity.

Leadership, like the concepts of sovereignty, freedom, and state, occupies the same "space and time" of two worlds (non-western and western) where tradition, culture, customs, land, law, and time fend off western encroachment of law, manufactured assimilation, distorted boundaries, and detrimental force. Modern-day leadership honors the same great leaders Deloria honors in *Custer* by adhering to their Tribal community integrity. Tribal leaders can maintain their seats, provided the leader "produces, or at least appears to produce, for this Tribe."[40] This paradoxical attachment, because of exposure to external forces, risks the creation of leadership that does not adhere to traditional intent; to ignore or suspend cultural and traditional integrity is the guaranteed way to lose some elements of sovereignty.

Those in Indian Country have real cause for concern if their Tribal leaders start to become *politicians* and register their primary allegiance to entities that do not serve the *whole* Tribal community, whether those entities be internal or external. That is not to say that Tribal leaders who choose to align with outside political parties and/or use their Tribal leadership positions for advancement should be feared. Such individuals can and have played important roles in the development and improvement of intergovernmental relations. However, the community needs to make sure their needs are primary and hold those leaders to account. A weak Tribal politician will be more concerned with gaining a following by favoring a select cohort that assures power retention, thus meeting the first rule of politics: self-preservation. A politician will more likely act in a "representative sovereignty" fashion where only a select cohort (50.1 percent) is represented versus the whole sovereign. Modernity infiltration within Indian Country should not be viewed as a negative; it can only become so if the true sovereign of Tribal society allows its leaders to become unauthentic leaders.

Gaming has exposed Tribal leaders, with all their talents, to new non-Indian sectors, and this strong external pressure to succeed may influence the direction of entire Tribes as leaders seek to attach themselves to an outside national platform. That platform may, indeed, include elements that align with a Tribal society's values or needs, but ultimately the document will lack the overall intent of the actual Tribal platform. As Tribal peoples are elected to represent their state and congressional districts, care must also be given when an Indian speaks. The public will push to make those spoken words be *words for Indian Country*, which will not be true; Indian Country is as diverse as any other collective. Tribal individuals excelling within other forms of governance should be seen as positive advancements, but those individuals must not attempt to speak for Indian Country and only speak for the district they were chosen to represent.

"Now you're wasting your time, Sandy. You see, my red, it don't wash off."

—Buddy Red Bow, *Powwow Highway*, 1989[41]

The Peter Parker Principle—"With great power comes great responsibility"—could also be included in this conclusion, but the simple fact is this: no matter what happens, Indians must always remain Indian. With the emergence of multibillion-dollar operations on reservations, responsibility to one another must be paramount. Tribal communities should always be the primary engagement, first at home, then across the country. This current surge of power that began in the late seventies is limited. It is limited by time, law, and envy. Great care should be given to how it is nurtured and crafted to fit many sovereign spheres. Calculations must be performed before advancing sovereign acts. As Deloria, quoting Walt Kelly's *Pogo* comic strip, noted in 1973, "We have met the enemy and it is us."[42] With great advancement comes an increased chance of greater fragility. Indian Country is only as strong as the weakest link. The weakest link is not a reference to the stability of a Tribal government but instead to the actions taken by any Tribal government that may have, foreseen or unforeseen, negative effects. Unfortunately, these adverse episodes transpire before most of Indian Country has had a chance to weigh in, so Tribes end up reacting to these events and to the actions taken by the federal government, typically by the judicial system.

Currently, Tribes are engaged in two areas of great concern: disenrollment and the Indian Child Welfare Act (ICWA). Both these topics have received coverage, but the genesis of the two are vastly different. Disenrollment is a Tribal government termination policy that removes Tribal citizens off the roles and marks them as *reservationless-Triballess* Indians, no longer under the protection of a Tribal government and in some cases, like ICWA, no longer under federal laws that were designed for their assistance and protection. It is truly unfathomable that in the new millennium Tribal societies would replicate a federal practice of termination, but these actions, despite great strides of Tribal collaboration, were foreseen by Pogo and Deloria. I can only hope some sort of conscious awakening will spur action for reconsideration, preferably Tribal actions and not a federal reaction. Perhaps a collection of Tribes could collaborate and assist these groups of disenrolled Indians. As they obviously have already met the criteria of belonging to a federally recognized Tribe, help could be provided to establish them as Tribal governments, with full weights and measures, recognized by the US government. As members of an amalgamated Tribe they would regain the kinship and status they once enjoyed. Only time will tell what will happen, but it is up to Indian Country to make this right. Only responsible sovereign acts will counter hollow sovereign acts.

The ICWA was crafted to assist Tribal governments and communities in making sure Indian children were not systematically removed from Indian communities by state subsections. The act curtailed these movements, and Indian children remained with Indian families based on a political-society legal standing. Today, non-Indian actors are seeking to undo this category and transition Indian status as a race-based issue, thus pushing the legal battle to a race-based conversation. This underhanded reframing is a blatant attempt to redefine the act as favoring one race and thus open its constitutionality to question. That slippery slope encourages the notion that Tribes are simply a "race" and not a third sovereign, continuing in the vein of Mr. Meeds's 1977 dissent. Tribes are united and pushing back with correct legal arguments and resisting the onslaught of states' rights activists. The irony here is, if Tribes are truly a political society, and if individuals are terminated via disenrollment by Tribal governmental procedures, those Tribal governments' only concern is *poli* Indians and not the individuals making up the Indian race.

We know time stops for no one, and America will not hesitate its progress as noted in 1973 by Deloria: "To the degree that we recognize our relationship with that pace of existence we will be able to renew our communities."[43] Tribal communities across the country have made great strides in strengthening their social-economic status but are still behind the rest of the United States. Remaining active in the advancement front today is different from the activism of pre-1973, but it is equally as important in world where "what is relevant remains seen" in social media platforms. As Deloria put it so well, "If we can now have the courage and humility to join together in search of a modern Indian life, the future will be much better than the past. But such a task is frightening. We will have to eliminate many of our organizations, institute new customs, search for new religious meanings, and come to grips with our contemporary existence, leaving behind myths of yesterday. We are faced with the task of becoming 'honest Indians' again. And, hopefully, we will succeed."[44] I hope so. . .

4

Stone

CHAPTER 27

MEMORIES OF VINE

Doug George-Kanentiio

In 1986 I was asked by the Mohawk Nation Council to assume the duties of editor for *Akwesasne Notes*, then the largest aboriginal news journal in North America and *Indian Time*, the local newspaper for my home community.

My position entailed total dedication to disseminating hard news along with commentary on the most pressing events of our time. We were the only Native-owned publication that carried stories on Indigenous concerns from central Siberia to the highlands of Peru. We printed many articles about the Miskitos of Nicaragua and the Mayans of Guatemala

For *Indian Time*, we printed stories about births, deaths, sports, government operations, weddings, and graduations; those occurrences that were deemed vital to the Akwesasronon, the people of Akwesasne.

As editor, I was determined to follow the trail cleared by Vine. He wrote extensively about the viability of traditional knowledge and the hard sciences that were the basis for Native life precontact. He refused to compromise to the misconceptions and lies upon which western civilization was built with the most flagrant distortions applied as matter of course.

As he did with his books, we did in our periodicals. In most Native homes in those days, one found *Custer Died for Your Sins* along with the latest edition of *Akwesasne Notes* with our centerfold poster-sized photographs taped to living room and college dorm walls.

It was that experience of advocacy that led Vine to call me in 1995, three years after I left *Notes*, to consider joining the Board of Trustees for the National Museum of the American Indian (NMAI).

I had written a story about Rolland Force, the last director of the American Indian Museum (AIM), then located in far upper Manhattan. The facility was isolated and its warehouse falling into serious decay. Visitation was very low, and it seemed on the edge of New York City's cultural venues. In my early nineties article, I agreed with Dr. Force that unless quick action was taken much of the cultural patrimony held by the AIM would be compromised. It was also clear to me that his tactics had created opposition to his desire to be appointed director of a new museum which went to the Cheyenne attorney Richard West.

A few years later Vine's call came, and I told him that since all trustees had to undergo a background check by the federal government I would not, given my active part in many protests and other acts of defiance, be cleared to join the board. Vine said for me not to worry, that he would make sure I was accepted.

I became a board member in January 1996 when the NMAI had minimal staff and a budget that seemed at risk every year primarily because of the opposition of then US representative Newt Gingrich. Part of our task as trustees was to counter his "zero" allocation by lobbying other members of Congress. The late US senators Daniel Inouye and Ben Nighthorse Campbell saved many a day and kept us afloat.

On the board itself it was Vine who was at the tiller, refusing to make compromises in our founding ideals. He asked if I would chair the Collections and Repatriation Committee. That job was to oversee the return of that part of Indigenous culture considered sacred and essential for the spiritual well-being of the nations. This policy was considered heresy by the Smithsonian Institution, of which the NMAI was part. Despite intense opposition by the Smithsonian, we pressed ahead and enacted the most aggressive repatriation initiative in American history. We gave things back when it was set in stone that what museums collected, they did not return.

We also did a complete inventory of what the NMAI actually had. It took months, but we found more than 850,000 items, ranging from canoes to copper bracelets. It took five years to move the collection from the warehouse in Brooklyn to the new resource center in Suitland, Maryland, at two tractor trailers a week, uninterrupted.

I was given yet another job by Vine: to help organize a series of events called "Traditional Knowledge," in which he selected a topic and had Indigenous speakers address the issue at a series of gatherings beginning in Boulder, Colorado, and ending at Frank's Landing in Washington State. Vine designed these conferences, of which there were five in all, to completely end the great fantasies used to qualify Native people.

He began, in 1996, with a session addressing where and when humans entered the hemisphere. Speakers from the Anishinaabe, Maya, Iroquois, Tewa, Inuit, and others were precise in their knowledge, and not one referred to the Bering Strait "theory" as anything more than a demonstrable lie. The speakers followed a common thread and used precise details as to topography, flora, and fauna to describe their respective journeys and all pointed to a common place of origin—but not one presenter said anything about crossing an ice bridge.

Other gatherings discussed plants, animals, stars, giants, and little people. The stories were remarkable given that they were passed on orally and had survived centuries of active suppression. The sixth conference was to be entitled "Dinosaurs and Indians." Vine planned to show, from stories and other forms of evidence, that Native people knew of, and hunted, great lizards and other gigantic animals. That session was to take place in 2007, but Vine died before it could happen.

The last time I was with him was at a Native law conference at Syracuse University, a year after the NMAI opened its doors in 2004. He was glad to be on Onondaga Territory, the capital or "central fire" of the Haudenosaunee Confederacy. He looked at ease with friends such as Oren Lyons, sitting on a stone wall outside on a warm night, his teasing of the Iroquois gentle and provocative.

He wrote to me a couple of days before he died, after he agreed to write the foreword to my book *Iroquois on Fire*. He mentioned that he had been having a stomach problem and was scheduled to visit a doctor to find the cause but otherwise was okay. We later learned that the ailment was an aneurism that would take his life. Our friend, the bison chief of his time, was on his way to the stars.

CHAPTER 28

ROUND DANCING AND COUNTING COUP IN ACADEMIC CIRCLES WITH VINE DELORIA, JR.

Paulette F. C. Steeves

Round Dancing is a form of community solidarity; counting coup on enemies was the highest honor earned in battle by Indigenous warriors of Turtle Island. Thinking of Vine Deloria, Jr. and the path he walked, I see him round dancing, an act of solidarity, hand in hand with many communities. I see him counting coup in many academic circles. Honest words, sharp intellectual mind, and Indigenous humor were his coup clubs. No academic could raise their voice against him with any strength. Western academics had never come up against such a strong, honorable, and educated academic Sioux scholar. Specifically, generations of western archaeologists who had spent years as handmaidens to the nation-state, working to erase Indigenous people, histories, community, lands, and humanities. Vine Deloria, Jr. wove paths of reclaiming, reviving, and healing that opened the way for future generations of truth-tellers. He lit fires of resistance and retelling in the hearts and minds of people on a global scale.

"North American anthropology can be divided into two ages: BD and AD—Before and After Deloria," Don Stull, 1999.[1]

My fondest memories of my undergraduate education are held on a cool, dark, northwestern Arkansas night. My visions of that night are in a permanent gallery of memories hung in the peaceful halls of my mind. I can still smell the sweetgrass weaving throughout the chanting and shifting feet of the round dance, reclaiming Indigenous ways of being, doing, and knowing and reclaiming joy, spirit, songs, laughter, and solidarity after centuries of oppressive colonization.

The Native American Student Association at the University of Arkansas organized a round dance, inviting students, dancers, and singers from the many Indigenous communities in nearby Oklahoma. The round dance was held at night on the lower edge of the campus; fires were lit around the dance area, turtle shell shakers wound around the dancers' legs, creating a rhythm of solidity as dancers joined hands and hearts and wove throughout each other's spirits and lives. The singers' voices were strong, vibrant, and clear and carried on the wind to ancestors and spirits across the land. The laughter was unlike any I have ever heard, so free, so honest, and so full of love. I can still feel my happiness of that night twenty-five years later.

As an Indigenous child growing up in a colonized land, I had missed out on cultural events, ceremonies, and grandparents, aunties, and uncles. Growing up in the fifties, sixties, and seventies in Canada, we had to hide our Cree-Metis background. My mother had lost two children to the government agents in Alberta in the late forties; she was terrified that if they knew we were Cree-Metis, they would take us away from her too. When you grow up during a time of colonization and forced acculturation, masking your identity, forgoing ceremonies, and fearing who you are, small acts of reclaiming make you feel like the luckiest and richest Indian in the world.

Vine Deloria, Jr. was and remains a strong voice for the rights of Indigenous people. His wisdom, honesty, and sharp Indian humor brought fires of reclaiming and reviving to my spirit, soul, and being. Settler people have no clue about Indian comedy, but it comes naturally to Indigenous people, a good way of dealing with colonization, racism, and hatred. If you don't have a sense of humor, the anger and pain would burn you up, just like Thomas Builds the Fire's relations in the movie

Smoke Signals.[2] Following in the footsteps of Vine Deloria, Jr., I learned to think deeply about racism and ongoing colonization, to do the work necessary to make changes for the next generations. I learned to let the hatred and anger flow over my head and past my heart so I would not be consumed by fires of racism. As a Red scholar in a White academia, the weight of racism and hate would have buried me in a deep grave if I did not remember to confront it, then sidestep it leaving racism to flow into the deep abyss of neverland.

I learned this life-saving skill of reclaiming and sidestepping from Vine Deloria, Jr. I let his knowledge, humor, and spirit waft from the pages of his books into my mind, wearing it all like a second skin. His laughter was my sustenance, his strength my guide, his spirit my best friend. Though I did not know it then, this man I would never have the honor to meet would change my life forever. That I never met him is okay. I know him well from his writing, books, articles, and videos. I have a deep and lived understanding of Indigenous peoples' experiences in a colonized world, both historical and ongoing; I live this experience daily. I honor all Indigenous scholars and knowledge holders who have worked tirelessly to open doors and weave paths in western academic worlds for those of us who follow.

I never grew up wanting to be a scholar, a professor, or an archaeologist. No one ever encouraged me to think about higher education; I had no role models and support, and I did not know to dream. I quit high school in grade eight to go to work in the city and send what I could to my mom, who was very ill with cancer. No one in my family had gone to college, and very few had ever completed high school. However, some were gifted and intelligent, surviving colonization, world wars, residential schools, and forced acculturation. I have come to understand that the creator has a way of leading us to the places he wants us to be, to work, to what we have been given to do, and to people like Vine Deloria, Jr., who will guide and inspire us to Pimatisiwin, to live a good life.

By the 1960s, Indigenous scholars had confronted the colonizers' dehumanizing master narrative of Indigenous people and the erasure of their histories. Deloria critiqued cultural presuppositions used by western scholars to legitimize outmoded stereotypes of Indigenous peoples. Stereotypes inflicted violence and harm in many ways, keeping Indigenous scholars outside academic circles. I knew of no Indigenous faculty at my undergraduate institution; I was never required to read an article or book authored by an Indigenous scholar during my undergraduate studies from 1996 to 2000 at the University of Arkansas in Fayetteville. Though I did meet Carrie Wilson, a Quapaw scholar and anthropologist who worked independently as a Native American Graves Protection and Repatriation officer for the Quapaw Tribe in Oklahoma, and she became a sister to me. She mentioned Vine Deloria, Jr. publications a few times, and I began to find his books and articles—*Red Earth, White Lies, Custer Died for Your Sins, God Is Red, Spirit and Reason*.[3] His words infused my mind, heart, and spirit with hope, smiles, and paths to critical thought. According to Deloria, "The constant drumbeat of scientific personalities who manipulate the public's image of Indians by describing archaeological horizons instead of societies, speaking of hunter-gatherers instead of communities, and attacking Indian knowledge of the past as fictional mythology, had created a situation in which the average citizen is greatly surprised to learn that Indians are offended by racial slurs and insults."[4]

It was not until I entered graduate school at the University of New York that Vine's spirit rose in me like a fire consuming the air that fed it. I never thought I would be a threat to anyone in academia. In graduate school, I had my own area of archaeological study that no other student or faculty was researching. But the anger and hatred directed at me in classes and hallways were over the top. In classes, I had always prepared, read the articles and books, and had an informed opinion. It was as if none of the students, all settlers, had ever heard an Indian talk before; they were often shocked, their expressions sometimes ashamed, sometimes stunned, always supporting their angry peers in their silence. One day a student jumped out of her desk, pointed at me in anger, and told me, "You better watch what you are saying." I don't even remember what I said that made her so angry; I was telling my truths. In times like these, the spirit of Vine Deloria, Jr. and his Indian humor covered me with sweet cedar and sage and kept me safe.

Deloria came from an educated and prominent family of Sioux scholars. He had grown up with strong role models. His grandfather, Reverend Philip J. Deloria, was an Episcopal priest and the leader of the Yankton band of the Dakota Nation. His father became an Episcopal archdeacon and a Standing Rock Indian Reservation missionary. Renowned Native American anthropologist and ethnographer, Ella Deloria, was his aunt.

In his book *Red Earth, White Lies*, he critiqued western archaeologists' interpretation of the Indigenous past—rightfully so, as I have discovered. Here is where, during my graduate studies, I began to round dance with Vine. Our critical thought joined forces and counted coup on many western academics, disrupting western discourse of the Indigenous past. In dreams and vision quests, we burned hateful words and dehumanizing textbooks; we critiqued western scholars for creating the First People of the Western Hemisphere (the Americans) as recent immigrants from Asia—as nature, not culture—as mysteriously disappearing from their homelands leaving no descendants.[5] In *Red Earth White Lies*, he highlighted the pseudoscientific assumptions of anthropologists regarding the Bering Land Bridge theory of initial migrations, which have been embedded in general discourse and knowledge production as scientific facts.[6] He exposed many areas of the western interpretation of the Indigenous past that were not supported by scientific data, and, as I read, I began to wonder about the scientific validity of the Bering Land Bridge theory and the dates of late (on a global scale) initial human migrations into the Western Hemisphere.

I asked Steve Holen, an archaeologist at the Denver Museum of Nature and Science, if he knew of any archaeological sites in the Western Hemisphere that dated earlier than eleven thousand to twelve thousand years before the present.[7] He emailed me a list of ten places that predated the so-called Clovis people dates (10,800–11,200 YBP). He also warned me, "Don't tell anyone what you are researching; they are just going to call you crazy." However, when your research is your dissertation, you must publicly discuss and publish it. However, Steve made an important point with his advice to not tell anyone what I was researching. Vine Deloria, Jr. discussed the history of evidence on how every archaeologist who had published on older-than-Clovis-dates archaeological sites in the Americas had been severely critiqued and publicly humiliated.[8] That was another burning question—why? When the goal of archaeology is the understanding and pursuit of the human past, why were archaeologists who published on sites older than 11,200 years before the present in the Americas so aggressively critiqued and demeaned?

I studied the published academic literature on the ten pre-Clovis archaeological sites, the names of which I had received from Steve Holen. I began building a database from the published articles and books on these sites. I asked what I thought was a simple question: How many archaeological sites that date to earlier than 11,200 YBP are there? Maybe thirty or forty. I stopped adding to the database after two weeks when I had added more than three hundred archaeological sites that dated to earlier than 11,200 YBP. I was shocked to find that many pre-Clovis sites. I was also astounded by the level of academic violence leveled at settler archaeologists who published on pre-Clovis sites and the denial of many sites' legitimacy by some American archaeologists.

I realize now that Deloria's critiques, his counting coup on western archaeologists, laid the foundations for what is now known as Indigenous archaeology. Deloria was a much-needed mirror of self-reflection in American academia, one that many anthropologists conveniently avoided in their work of creating histories of the first people of North America. My experience, a decade of working in archaeology from 1998 to 2008, made it clear that archaeologists in the US did not often, if ever, consult with Indigenous people. Archaeologists were ordered to consult with Tribes regarding excavations on Tribal lands after the implications of the Native American Graves Repatriation and Protection Act of 1990.[9] However, on land outside of Tribally controlled areas, archaeologists and archaeological firms I worked for throughout the US avoided Indians like the plague. Worse yet, none of the field archaeologists I worked with had ever taken a course on Indigenous history to earn their archaeology degree, allowing them to work as archaeologists in the Americas. Racism, misinformation, ignorance, and disrespect for Indigenous people were blatant and rampant in archaeological fieldwork and cultural resource management in North America. However, to appease those archaeologists who have vocally demanded that if I critique archaeology, I have to talk about the nice things they do, I offer this.

Not all archaeologists avoided Indians like the plague; some have actively sought out Indigenous communities' support for research, which was also a part of furthering their careers. A few archaeologists became good friends of Indigenous communities and authored publications on their histories, though I do not know if any ever shared their royalties with specific communities whose histories they researched. A few western universities have hired Indigenous archaeologists, though not those who carry coup clubs and actively do the work of decolonization by discussing colonization within academia and archaeology. There are a few western archaeologists who have critiqued their field.[10] I call them truth-tellers, and for their honesty, I am deeply grateful. Deloria's critiques of academic knowledge production forced anthropologists to acknowledge that their craft was not a neutral pursuit based on solid science.

In *Red Earth, White Lies*, Vine Deloria, Jr. had suggested that maybe we need our Indigenous archaeologists to go and excavate archaeological sites. He discussed the dehumanization and erasure of Indigenous people in western accounts of the Indigenous past and present.[11] I agree that this erasure denies Indigenous people a place in world history that accords them full humanity and denies knowledge of the past known from oral traditions and the material record.

After reading that book, I thanked Vine for his words and wisdom. I began reviewing the published literature on Pleistocene-age archaeological sites in North and South America. It became evident that there was an enormous wealth of evidence that Indigenous people were in the

Western Hemisphere for thousands of years before the end of the last glacial maximum eleven to twelve thousand years before the present. The book on my research, inspired by Vine Deloria Jr, was published July 1, 2021: *The Indigenous Paleolithic of the Western Hemisphere.*[12] In my research and book, I reclaim and rewrite the deep Indigenous past of the Western Hemisphere and discuss hundreds of pre-eleven-to-twelve-thousand YBP archaeological sites and Indigenous histories on the lands of North and South America. The title of my book is a bit of Indian humor, as many settler archaeologists always have and to this day still deny there was ever a Paleolithic (old stone age) in the Americas. However, there are many western archaeologists who have risked their careers and reputations to publish academic articles on pre-Clovis-age archaeological sites in North and South America and to them all, to Vine Deloria, Jr., I owe a great debt of gratitude.

Deloria wove paths through battlefields of academia, counting coup on many enemies; he wove paths of truth-telling and reclaiming from the margins to the center of academia for generations of scholars.

Daniel Wildcat put it so well when he wrote,

> I have been profoundly influenced by Vine Deloria, Jr.; I have benefited enormously from his activism, his teaching, his scholarship, his mentoring, and, above all, his friendship. What my encounter with the man and his work revealed most clearly to me was perhaps his most important virtue—his honesty. I see in his work and in his life, not just theories and models but an exercise of spirit and reason, an exercise requiring a dedication to speak honestly—something a good number of those in the academy today, as Deloria has pointed out, ought to take more seriously.[13]

Vine Deloria, Jr. cleared paths into the heart of academia for many Indigenous scholars. However, it has been my experience that many coups still need to be counted in western academia, specifically in archaeological circles. As I continue to experience racism, fear of the truth, and hypocrisy in academic archaeological circles, I realize the work he started is the beginning of the journey. The sea of western academic discontent with Indigenous truth-telling has only just begun to rock. Thus, truth-tellers in academia must continue their work of confronting the master narrative and the roots of deceit that support ongoing colonization. Truth-tellers will continue to round dance with Vine Deloria, Jr., using his words and wisdom as coup clubs, while round dancing through academic circles and weaving paths of healing and Pimatisiwin.

CHAPTER 29

DELORIA/DES LAURIERS

Vine Deloria, Jr.'s Ties to the French

Marine Le Puloch

Peau-Rouge (which translates literally as R*d Sk*n) was the title selected by the French editors of the 1972 translation of Vine Deloria, Jr.'s *Custer Died for Your Sins*. The back cover lauds this special edition as "the first book published in France about Indians that was written by an Indian, a Sioux: Vine Deloria." Fifty years ago, this racist, provocative title was meant to appeal to the sensibilities of a broad French audience of the time, evoking the myth of the proud, free, and brave Lakota warrior riding the Plains on horseback—their societal archetype of the legend of the West. The cover goes on to portray the book as "the story of the conquest of the west, of westerns . . . seen from the other side, by those who suffered from expansion . . . no longer viewed as a saga but as a defeat, the story of a genocide."[1]

This sensational repackaging of *Custer* into *Peau-Rouge* might have sold books but, other than the fact that the author was Native, it bore little resemblance to the actual work. As "the central message of the book," wrote Deloria in the 1988 edition, "[is] that Indians are still alive."[2] Hardly a story of defeat and genocide. The book, indeed, conveys what Anishinaabe scholar and writer Gerald Vizenor coined "Native survivance," which he described as "an active sense of presence" and the renunciation of "dominance, tragedy, and victimry,"[3] at odds with the presentation of *Peau-Rouge*.

At that time, the concept of Red Power was widely publicized in the US, but in France only a few activists and academics had begun to perceive the history of the American Indians as one of unjustly treated peoples standing up for their rights after centuries of oppression. The French public was largely unaware of the 1969 occupation of Alcatraz Island, and the 1972 Trail of Broken Treaties, culminating with the sack of the Bureau of Indian Affairs in Washington, D.C. So, if *Peau-Rouge* immediately caught their attention, it was not so much because people were aware of renewed Native resistance but more likely because of fetishism—and of the commercialization of "spiritualism" that too often goes with it—stemming from the myth of the "noble savage": Deloria the Lakota had lessons to teach the "civilized man." Thus, in the preface to the book, Yves Berger (a popular writer of the time selected for his fame but not much appreciated by the intellectual elite) claims that in *Peau-Rouge*, the "defeated," but noble and wise "R*d sk*ns" "speak as one voice: Listen, White man."[4]

Given those times, *Peau-Rouge* was not such an improbable title as, of course, it was meant to capture the attention of the public and sell books. A few found it offensive; others took it as nothing but a blunder. The average French reader, however, understood the expression as an old term for "Indian" that they erroneously attributed to the face paint some Natives wore. For them, there was no negative meaning, despite the obvious stereotype the term conveys. In 1972, in most French people's minds, induced by the myth of the American West, "R*d Sk*n" simply meant American Indian. For them, the use of a biased term was not meant as an offense but rather suggested a sense of exoticism, romance, and adventure.

At any rate, there is no record of Deloria's thoughts on this title. Although he himself used the term in *God Is Red*, and certainly the Red Power movement was alive and well at the time *Peau-Rouge* was published, turning a stereotype into one's advantage is a common and often powerful practice. Deloria himself wrote in the 1988 edition of *Custer Died for Your Sins*[5] that if "commercialization of the Indian tradition . . . influence[d] people to deal more kindly with the earth and the various life forms on it, then there should be few complaints about its impact on people's lives and practices."[6]

I was curious about the number of copies of *Peau-Rouge* sold in France but could not find existing data to accurately evaluate this. Suffice it to say that the book was very popular and is the basis for the general acceptance that Deloria has always been embraced in France, even when he was not yet famous in the US.[7] In France, Deloria was perceived differently by activists who supported American Indians' rights and resolutely acclaimed him,[8] and by the average academics who—for those who say they respected him—usually considered him somehow too radical to be used as a reference. Historian Elise Marienstras said in a recent interview that she realized upon reading him that she shared his concepts on the rights of minorities, as well as on the role of nations and states in the process of colonization.[9] She saw his work as a predecessor to the "New Indian History" of the early 1970s that focused on the Natives' point of view on the invasion of their territories,[10] but Marienstras did not directly address the events of the 1970s until the last chapter of her 1980 book *La Résistance Indienne aux Etats-Unis.*[11] But the French public of 1972, inspired by romantic views of Native people, was already prepared to listen to what Vine Deloria had to say. In short, if the choice of the title was awkward, to say the least, Deloria's message was clear: American Indians should stop focusing on the "glorious past," and instead start a vast program to strengthen and consolidate their powers as Nations.[12] This, in brief, was what mattered to Deloria, and French readers understood the essence of the book, whatever the title, preface, or back cover.

What was Deloria's "glorious past" would then inquire a historian? Vine Deloria, Jr. was the descendant of a Lower Yankton Lakota woman and a French fur trader named Des Lauriers. In focusing on his French heritage, this essay was first aimed at analyzing the relationship between French and Native peoples in the past in light of Deloria's reception in France, but the pursuit proved unworkable. It made little sense to try to relate Deloria's early renown in France to his French background, since most of those who might have guessed he had a French ancestor by the sound of his name, the English pronunciation of "Des Lauriers," seem never to have taken the trouble to further examine the circumstance.

In *Singing for a Spirit*, Deloria recounts the family oral history, starting in the 1750s in the Lower Missouri, far into the interior of New France, when a young *coureur de bois*, a French boy involved in fur trade[13] named Des Lauriers was saved from starvation by a band of Lower Yankton Dakota, who adopted him. It was the reign of fur trade in New France, and Des Lauriers "became a valued member of the tribe because he could speak French, a commonly used trade language on the [Missouri] river," the area where the band lived.[14]

Generally speaking, intermarriages between French *coureurs de bois*—as Des Lauriers—and Native women were often meant to seal commercial alliances and military coalitions starting in the late seventeenth century. Vine Deloria's French ancestor will serve as a test case with which, using the "regressive method" (*méthode régressive*) "from the best to the least known" (*du mieux au moins bien connu*),[15] to investigate into the heritage French fur traders passed down to their *métisses* children. Vine Deloria's French heritage is in fact rooted in the history of the frontier—the margin between European settlement and Native controlled territory, the "Middle Ground"[16] in which elements of Native and French cultures intermingled and which prospered on fur trade.

Known as "*coureurs de bois*," "*truchements*," or "*voyageurs*," fur traders were the most influential Frenchmen in the so-called New France throughout the seventeenth century and were still considerably influential on the frontier well after the demise of the French empire in North America in 1760.[17] By the time Des Lauriers was adopted by the Dakota, the French had long been on good terms with the Natives. Apart from persuading Native peoples to collect and trade fur, the *coureurs de bois* had no reason to disrupt Indians' ways of life, hence the groups established ways to work together. The *coureurs de bois* acted as interpreters for trading companies, lived with the Natives, and encouraged them to trade with the companies employing them or directly with them when they were working as independent traders. Often sent to live among Native peoples as young teenagers—the age when Des Lauriers was adopted by the Dakota—to learn their language and customs, the *coureurs de bois* quickly embraced the life of their adopted people, and took "country" wives among them.[18] Work of this sort was a source of income and experience that would have allowed a young man of humble background to better himself within French society, and many *coureurs de bois* never truly identified their interests with those of the Native peoples they lived, traded, and intermarried with.[19]

Des Lauriers's circumstances were different. Indeed, unknown numbers, fully assimilated as he was, became what French historian Philippe Jacquin coined "White Indians,"[20] just like today the Guarani Indians of Dourados in Brazil designate "lighter skinned" Guaranis.[21] They were incorporated fully into Native societies, and little is known of them for lack of records; thus, most went largely unnoticed. Des Lauriers is unique in that as a "White Indian" who remained a member of the band all his life, he left traces in the family oral history, as well as in "personal papers identifying the young French boy" Des Lauriers, which Saswe—Vine Deloria, Jr.'s great-grandfather—carried in a medicine bundle around his neck.[22]

In societies without writing, "historical tradition is an oral one, involving legends, stories and accounts handed down through the generations in oral form."[23] In Canada, the Supreme Court validated Indigenous oral history in 1997 as judicial evidence, and placed it on the same footing as historical documents in the *Delgamuukw* case:

> Notwithstanding the challenges created by the use of oral histories as proof of historical facts, the laws of evidence must be adapted in order that this type of evidence can be accommodated and placed on an equal footing with the types of historical evidence that courts are familiar with, which largely consists of historical documents.[24]

In the case of Des Lauriers, oral tradition corroborates the papers preciously preserved by the family, expanding on his life, that of his *métisses* children, and of his later descendants.

The pejorative terms "mixed-blood" and "half-breed," as well as the commonly used *métisses* and later Métis, referred to the children of the fur trade and their descendants. Early on, in inclusive societies such as many of the Natives' for which adoption was a crucial societal practice, no distinction was made between these people and other members of the Tribe. It was still true in the Dakotas in the 1750s when Des Lauriers became a Dakota. Hence, like his children, many *métisses* became full members of their mother's people, sometimes with no trace remaining of their French father's heritage save for their name: Beaulieu, Bonnin, Pelletier, Deloria for Des Lauriers. Like their father and their mother's people, the *métisses* were involved in the fur trade, trapping, collecting, and transporting furs along the water routes to trading posts, sometimes reaching Montréal and Québec on the Saint Lawrence River, the major artery leading into the heart of the country rich in furs. *Métisses* are blood-kin, yet they are seldom mentioned in the sources, as is the case with "White Indians."

It was not until the 1840s that some *métisses* identified as a distinct Native Nation, the Métis. Historian Gilles Havard, author of the popular, thrice award-winning book *L'Amérique fantôme* on the topic of the *coureurs de bois*, ends his study with this decade, when European settlers started invading the West.[25] The Métis lived off buffalo hunting on horseback, and provided fur traders with pemmican, their staple food when on the move. Catholic in faith, they spoke *métchif* (or *mitchif*), from "*métisse*"—a mix of French, Cree, Ojibwa, and other Native languages—and they lived in the vicinity of Red River, in today's southern Manitoba, a settlement established by Lord Selkirk in 1817 for retired employees of the fur trade Hudson's Bay Company and their mixed families. The Métis eventually fought two wars against the new Dominion of Canada—the so-called Métis rebellions—in 1869 in Manitoba, and in 1885 in northern Saskatchewan where they had taken refuge after 1869. The wars were provoked by the Dominion's decision to move settlers into the West, killing and displacing Native peoples in preparation for the exploitation of the area's vast natural resources. This policy ended the age of fur trade when it was in everyone's best interest to alter Natives' ways of life as little as possible.

The French had long shared friendship and kinship bonds with Native peoples when Des Lauriers met the Dakota in the 1750s, and interactions and mixed marriages sometimes meant the total assimilation of *coureurs de bois* such as he. Closely linked to the Natives they traded and intermarried with, it was not uncommon for the French to adopt an Indigenous way of life, wholly integrating into a new society. In France, it was not until 2019, more than 150 year later, with the publication of the aforementioned *L'Amérique Fantôme* that the larger French public was made aware of that reality.

In conclusion, it seems the longtime alliances between the French and the Natives from which Vine Deloria, Jr. stems are unlikely to have been the cause of his early fame in France. It is difficult to pin down exactly why Deloria was better known at the beginning of his career in France than in the US. In the 1970s, the popular image of the "Indian" was (and still is) largely romanticized in both countries and renewed Native militancy at the time when *Peau-Rouge* was published remained relatively undiscussed in France until the early 1980s. It was not until the 2010s that life as it was for Deloria's French ancestor was made known to a wider French audience. Given this lack of understanding of the political and human realities faced by Natives of the time—either due to dearth of information or willful ignorance—the most plausible explanation of Deloria's early fame might simply be the enduring power of the myth of the "noble savage." In the 1970s, the French couldn't have cared less that Deloria had a far distant French ancestor; they embraced him because he was a Dakota, "the Indian warrior" of modern times. In short, while Des Lauriers was valued amongst the Dakota because he spoke French, Deloria was welcomed amongst the French because he was Dakota.

CHAPTER 30

IN THE SPIRIT OF VINE DELORIA, JR.

Indigenous Kinship Renewal and Relational Sovereignty

By Gabriel S. Galanda

"Imperialism leaves behind germs of rot which we must clinically detect and remove from our land but from our minds as well."

—Frantz Fanon[1]

Vine Deloria, Jr. was a realist. He was not afraid to describe the Indigenous condition as it really was. He conceded that Native Nations were no longer "the pristine and stable societies that existed in the remote past."[2] He admitted that by the late twentieth century, Native Nations increasingly emulated white governments that violated human rights.[3] Pointing to the federal Indian reservation system and the Indian Reorganization Act (IRA), in particular, Deloria was sober about the fact that white society's ways infiltrated Indigenous kinship societies long ago.

As he and Clifford Lytle observed in *American Indians, American Justice*: "Many of the old customs and traditions that could have been restored under the IRA climate of cultural concern had vanished during the interim period since the Tribes had gone to reservations. The experience of self-government according to Indigenous traditions had vanished."[4] But Deloria also proposed a solution to the elitism and corruption plaguing Native nations: Indigenous kinship renewal.

In 1978, the US Supreme Court laid bare the historic deterioration of Indigenous kinship in *Santa Clara Pueblo v. Martinez*.[5] That decision foreclosed Tribal citizens' access to federal courts for Tribal civil rights violations; it sounded victory for Tribal sovereignty but accelerated the destruction of Indigenous kinship via Tribal neocolonialism. *Santa Clara Pueblo* has since become the most destructive Indigenous human rights decision ever rendered by the Supreme Court. That decision has sanctioned harm to Tribal citizens that would not befall any other Americans.

As Deloria and Lytle observed in *The Nations Within*, Tribal politicians across the country took *Santa Clara Pueblo* "to mean that they were baldly underestimating the actual powers they possessed as sovereign nations and that they could be considerably bolder in their actions before either Congress or the courts would rein them in."[6] There was next to nothing that would legally or politically stop Tribal autocrats from violating their own relatives' human rights. They could fire, evict, or exile their kin and strip their property, medical, or voting rights, and federal authorities would shrug off the atrocity as an "internal matter" according to *Santa Clara Pueblo.*

Expounding upon Deloria's writings, Dr. David Wilkins explains how "a number of elected tribal officials . . . grabbed hold of the idea of tribal 'self-determination' not to enrich their peoples' lives but rather to 'increase their own personal power over tribal members'" and prevent any "movement within the tribe of more democratically based programs and ideas."[7]

But neither Deloria nor anybody else foresaw the most extreme form of Tribal "self-determination" post-*Santa Clara Pueblo*: the disenrollment of approximately ten thousand Tribal citizens from nearly one hundred Tribes—more than 15 percent of all federally recognized Tribes today—and the denial of enrollment to generations of a great many more Tribes.

To Deloria, "the simple fact of being born establishes [one's] citizenship."[8] Indigenous belonging is axiomatic. According to Indigenous kinship tradition, any relative's "orphanage" was foreign to Deloria.[9] It was seemingly unthinkable to him that Tribal politicians would orphan anybody born unto their people. In his infinite wisdom, however, he did foretell of the destructive, assimilative force that underpins both disenrollment and enrollment moratoria today.

Nearly a half century ago, Deloria warned of the harms associated with Tribal per capita dollars. In a 1980 *Los Angeles Times* column, Deloria predicted that member per capita entitlement would someday sound the death knell for Indigenous kinship systems, predicting: "Per capita distribution . . . would be a clear signal that [our] people have adopted the white man's wasteful ways, and demand everything now in defiance of their responsibilities to coming generations."[10]

That reality has come to pass, especially since 1988, when the federal Indian Gaming Regulatory Act accelerated what is now a $40 billion Tribal gaming economy that spins off annual seven-figure "per caps" on some reservations. Throughout Indian country, an unquenchable thirst for the control and receipt of unearned per capita income has "become an indomitable force in Tribal policy and governance, to the detriment of Indian political stability and self-governance."[11] Tribal per capitalism has decimated Indigenous kinship.[12] As it turns out, Tribal per capita monies are also what precipitated the insidious *Santa Clara Pueblo* decision.

The first part of this chapter deconstructs *Santa Clara Pueblo* and exposes its distinctly economic underpinnings. The second part outlines a legal and political path toward Indigenous kinship renewal and relational sovereignty. Relational sovereignty is a paradigm through which modern Native nations self-govern in fulfillment of Indigenous kinship systems and rules. Within that paradigm, Native nations rule themselves in ways that exalt and protect Indigenous human existence and revive reciprocal obligations and duties within the People.

Santa Clara Pueblo v. Martinez: A Patriarchal Cash Grab

Santa Clara Pueblo is believed to have been formed around AD 1300 in what today is northern New Mexico. The Pueblo was customarily organized into two kiva moieties, the Winter People and the Summer People.

Each moiety was led by a male religious leader known as a cacique. Over time the moieties divided into villages or clans and were led by governors appointed by the caciques. Santa Clara Pueblo traditionally adhered to religious rather than secular laws.

The Pueblo of the Santa Clara reservation was formed in 1905 by Executive Order, including land granted from the Spanish and confirmed by the US Congress in 1858. Land claim litigation plagued the Pueblo from the 1890s to 1920s, resulting in Congress' passage of the Pueblo Lands Act in 1924 and, in turn, the federal payment of land and water settlement monies to the Pueblo. By the 1930s, the Pueblo and its moieties splintered into factions over "dual governors," specifically whether a moiety governor "should be an older, highly respected man who was well versed in the traditional ways, or a younger man, educated in Anglo-American schools, who could speak English and would be able to deal more effectively with non-Pueblo society."[13]

The Pueblo's leadership dispute was resolved in 1935, after a federal census was taken by the Bureau of Indian Affairs (BIA) to identify members of each moiety and faction, which resulted in the Pueblo's adoption of the IRA and a constitution and bylaws. The Pueblo's new government, composed in chief by a governor and council, was "neither wholly traditional nor wholly anglicized."[14] Divisions reemerged amid congressionally appropriated land and water settlement disbursements to Santa Clara pursuant to the Pueblo Lands Act, specifically over per capita payments to members listed on the federal census but who had moved away from the Pueblo.

By the 1930s, Indian per capita dollars had fissured Indigenous nations for nearly 150 years. Many early treaties called for monetary payments to be made to individuals, and US Indian agents began creating Indian "payment rolls" in the late eighteenth century.[15] A circa 1790 payment roll appears to be the first federal roll of Indians, if not the birth of Tribal per capitalism.[16] An 1835 Cherokee treaty introduced the "per capita" or "personal" apportionment of federal monies and benefits to Cherokee families and individuals who wished to remain east of the

Mississippi as "citizens of the States."[17] An 1847 Congressional statute empowered the president to pay treaty annuity monies to "heads of families and other individuals" because, according to Francis Paul Prucha, those "funds were often siphoned off by the chiefs and their friends for purposes that did not necessarily benefit the tribe as a whole."[18] A 1907 companion statute to the Dawes Act authorized the interior secretary to grant Tribal members a "pro rata share of any Tribal or trust funds on deposit in the Treasury of the United States."[19] Those federally authorized monies caused Tribal elitism and factionalism on many reservations, including the Santa Clara Pueblo.[20]

Prior to 1935, there were no written Santa Clara Pueblo membership rules. The Pueblo's original constitution and bylaws codified membership, extending it to four groups of people: (1) all persons of "Indian blood" whose names appeared on the 1935 census roll; (2) all "persons born of parents both of whom are members of the Santa Clara pueblo"; (3) all "children of mixed marriages between members of the Santa Clara Pueblo and nonmembers, provided such children have been recognized and adopted by the council"; and (4) all "persons naturalized as members of the pueblo." There were no gender distinctions in the Pueblo's IRA constitution.

In 1939, the Pueblo's all-male council adopted an IRA membership ordinance that allowed enrollment to only two groups: "all children born of marriages between members of the Santa Clara Pueblo" and "children born of marriages between male members of the Santa Clara Pueblo and non-members." The ordinance declared that "children born of marriages between female members of the Santa Clara Pueblo and non-members shall not be members." Children born of marriages between male Pueblo members and non-members remained eligible for membership.

Although the 1939 membership ordinance was unconstitutional insofar as the 1935 constitution did not forbid the enrollment of children born to Pueblo women of mixed marriages, the Pueblo's constitution bestowed "judicial power" upon the same all-male council that passed the ordinance, rendering any constitutional challenge futile. The councilmen also made political exceptions to the ordinance. As late as 1942, a parent could pay a fee to the Pueblo to enroll children born to females of mixed marriages. Santa Clara belonging had become transactional.

Prior to 1939, children to female members of mixed marriage were granted membership. But a rise in mixed marriages, combined with the infusion of federal settlement monies since the 1920s, changed things. As the Tenth Circuit Court of Appeals explained in *Santa Clara Pueblo*: "It was, then, in response to the economic consequences of mixed marriages that the Pueblo Council determined that the offspring of female line mixed marriages would be denied membership while the offspring of male line mixed marriages would be admitted."[21]

More precisely, Santa Clara's male leaders wanted to maximize per capita distributions of the Pueblo's federal settlement funds for existing members. As plaintiff Julia Martinez's counsel explained to the US Supreme Court, the Pueblo Council passed the 1939 membership ordinance "to limit membership to keep the amount of the per capita payments that the government was making to the tribe [the same]. . . . It is clear that what the council had in mind when they passed this rule was keeping those per capita payments up, nothing more, nothing less."[22]

Two years later, "full-blooded" Santa Clara member Julia Martinez attempted to enroll her daughter Audrey Martinez with the Pueblo. Julia was married to Myles Martinez, a "full-blooded" Navajo Tribal member and World War II veteran. They resided on the Pueblo. They gave birth to Audrey in 1941 and Julia immediately attempted to enroll her. But under the 1939 ordinance, Audrey—despite also being "full blooded"—was denied enrollment, because she was born from a marriage between a female Santa Clara member and a male nonmember Navajo. The Martinez family continued to live on the Pueblo, where they reared eight children, including Audrey. They taught them all to speak Tewa and participated in Santa Clara religious and ceremonial traditions. Audrey and her seven siblings were "culturally, for all practical purposes, Santa Clara Indians."[23]

Julia resumed her attempts to enroll Audrey and her other children in earnest in 1963; her efforts were "vigorous and constant" for the next fifteen years.[24] She allied with other Pueblo mothers with children of mixed marriages to form a committee, which unsuccessfully petitioned the Pueblo's Council to enroll their children.

By 1972, Julia and Audrey, who by then was an adult, had exhausted all available remedies within the Pueblo. They were left with no option but to file suit in the US District Court in New Mexico to compel Audrey's enrollment. They sued the Pueblo and its governor for prospective injunctive and declaratory relief, seeking to invalidate the 1939 membership ordinance. They did not sue for money. They claimed the law violated their right to equal protection as guaranteed by the federal Indian Civil Rights Act (ICRA). Plainly, the ordinance was sexist.

ICRA was passed in 1968 amidst the American civil rights movement, in reaction to growing civil rights abuses by Tribal politicians. By the 1960s, according to Deloria and Lytle, Indigenous societies that historically "had no concept of civil rights because every member of the society was related, by blood or clan responsibilities, to every other member" began to mirror southern states and other white governments that violated individuals' civil liberties.[25]

Tribal human rights violations date back to at least to the establishment of reservations in the early to mid-1800s. According to Dr. Stephen Cornell in *Return of the Native*: "Reservation containment raised the stakes and narrowed the means of dispute resolution. Now there were central positions of limited power to be won or lost and diminishing resources to be controlled."[26] Corruption and injustice ensued almost immediately.[27]

As Stephen Pevar explains, Congress passed ICRA to address intensifying complaints that "tribal officials were tyrannical and biased; elections were rigged; tribal courts were puppets of the government and issued biased decisions . . . and tribal members, especially those who supported candidates who lost in a tribal election, were being denied their rights under tribal law."[28] In recognition of increasing political corruption and civil rights violations on Indian reservations, including his own, Deloria originally favored ICRA.[29] But over time he resisted rendering any "final judgment" on ICRA's effects, saying in 1984 that the law caused "confusion and injustice" in "the relationship between an Indian tribe and its members."[30]

The congressional record confirms ICRA was intended "to ensure that the American Indian is afforded the broad Constitutional rights secured to other Americans" and "to protect individual Indians from arbitrary and unjust actions of tribal governments."[31] Congress intended to protect the likes of Julia and Audrey Martinez.

The Pueblo attempted to deflect ICRA's application to Julia and Audrey by arguing that the federal district court lacked jurisdiction over intratribal controversies, particularly those involving Tribal membership. US district court Judge Edwin L. Mechem, appointed by President Richard Nixon in 1970, disagreed with the Pueblo on his court's jurisdiction, but ruled that the Pueblo did not violate ICRA's equal protection guarantee.

Judge Mechem held that Julia and Audrey's allegations of Santa Clara's membership ordinance being applied discriminatorily both created a federal question under ICRA and abrogated the Pueblo's sovereign immunity from suit. On the merits, though, he found for the Pueblo, ruling that ICRA's equal protection guarantee "should not be construed in a manner which would require or authorize this Court to determine which traditional values will promote cultural survival and therefore should be preserved and which of them are inimical to cultural survival and should therefore be abrogated."[32] Judge Mechem was persuaded that the Pueblo's fiscal motivations to restrict membership were legitimate, calling per capita preservation a matter "of economic survival of the tribal unit."[33] It appears Judge Mechem had no appreciation that, dating back to the first Indian pay rolls circa 1790, federally authorized monetary payments to Tribal individuals had the effect of destroying the Tribal unit.

Reviewing the trial court's decision, the Tenth Circuit Court of Appeals agreed with Judge Mechem on jurisdiction but not on equal protection. According to the Tenth Circuit, ICRA both afforded federal jurisdiction and limited the Pueblo's immunity. The court reasoned that ICRA was "designed to provide protection against tribal authority," and if that federal statute did not allow suit against a Native nation, "it would constitute a mere unenforceable declaration of principles."[34] The Tenth Circuit then looked to the merits and weighed the individual right to fair treatment under the law against the Pueblo's cultural interests.[35] The appellate panel concluded that because "the ordinance was the product of economics and pragmatics" and not Santa Clara tradition, Julia and Audrey's individual rights necessarily outweighed those of the Pueblo.[36]

The Tenth Circuit declared that if the equal protection clause of the ICRA is to have any consequence, it must operate to ban invidious discrimination of the kind leveled against Julia and Audrey—women "within the cultural group who have been allowed to develop a substantial stake in the life of the Tribe."[37] Emphasizing that the Pueblo's gender discrimination as to Tribal membership originated from "practical economic considerations," the Tenth Circuit deemed it "an arbitrary and expedient solution to the problem" of per capita wealth preservation.[38] The Tenth Circuit saw it all for what it was—a patriarchal cash grab—and ruled accordingly.

On appeal to the US Supreme Court, the Pueblo shifted arguments. First, the Pueblo asserted that ICRA did not authorize federal courts to review Indian civil rights violations except as they might sound in habeas corpus. Second, the Pueblo contended that ICRA failed to waive Tribal sovereign immunity from suit. Julia and Audrey contended that sovereign immunity did not bar their action for equitable relief against future conduct of a government violating basic constitutional rights. They also maintained that the 1939 IRA membership ordinance was not traditional, and it discriminated against women in violation of ICRA's equal protection promise.

In their Supreme Court briefing, Julia and Audrey made clear: "The actual purpose of the Ordinance was to hold down Tribal membership to enlarge the shares of money and land for members, which purpose could have been accomplished without resort to discrimination. . . . The principal concern behind the Ordinance was economic."[39] In oral argument, their counsel described the controversy as "18 years of attempts" by Julia simply to get her children "home."[40]

The Pueblo ignored Julia and Audrey's economic arguments, feigning that per capitalism did not motivate the 1939 membership ordinance. That strategy worked. Supreme Court bench memoranda reveal that the Justices either did not understand Indian per capita distributions, or they did not care that those monies motivated the ordinance. The Pueblo instead focused on Tribal sovereignty, arguing: "Indian tribes are allowed the right to define and protect their cultures as they see fit and to develop their societies as they choose, even if Tribal policies differ from the policies of mainstream America. This is what is meant by the policy of Indian Self-determination."[41] Even if Pueblo membership had become transactional and sexist, related Tribal decision-making was inoculated by nascent federal self-determination policy.

The Supreme Court also ignored the economic reality of Julia and Audrey's situation and agreed with the Pueblo, reversing the Tenth Circuit on purely procedural grounds. The Court held that ICRA did not waive Tribal sovereign immunity and only the statute's habeas corpus provision allowed a federal right of action.[42] Without ruling on whether Audrey belonged to Santa Clara or whether the 1939 membership ordinance violated equal protection as applied to her or her mom, the Court reasoned: "Unless and until Congress makes clear its intention to permit the additional intrusion on tribal sovereignty that adjudication of such actions in a federal forum would represent, we are constrained to find that [ICRA] does not impliedly authorize actions for declaratory or injunctive relief against either the tribe or its officers."[43]

The Supreme Court did not decide the conflict between Tribal sovereignty and equal protection as much as they legislated an outcome. In the 1970s, the Burger Court loathed Indian law cases.[44] The justices were outcome oriented, deciding Indian law cases on "an ad hoc, case-by-case basis."[45] *Santa Clara Pueblo* was no exception. Conference notes reveal Justice William Brennan, Jr. persuaded six colleagues, including Justice Thurgood Marshall, to reverse the Tenth Circuit on the grounds that ICRA afforded "no cause of action."[46] Justice Brennan reportedly rationalized that "Indian Tribes are impoverished—can't afford these suits."[47]

The all-male Burger Court was more concerned with stemming the rise of federal court ICRA suits post-1968 than resolving the merits of the Martinezes' gender discrimination claim.

Justice Marshall did the honors. The Supreme Court's first Black Justice, whose legal career and jurisprudence "reflected a broad approach to . . . 'the fundamental constitutional right of access to the courts,'" penned the opinion that closed federal courthouse doors to Indigenous civil rights plaintiffs.[48] Citing Congress' new policy of furthering Tribal self-government to justify the Court's demurral in *Santa Clara Pueblo*, Justice Marshall was keenly aware of the ramifications of his opinion for Audrey and her siblings: "as a result of their exclusion from membership they may not vote in tribal elections or hold secular office in the tribe; moreover, they have no right to remain on the reservation in the event of their mother's death, or to inherit their mother's home or her possessory interests in the communal lands."[49]

Thirty-seven years after Julia commenced her fight to enroll her daughter, Audrey's belonging was denied. Audrey remained unenrolled when Julia died in 2000.[50]

Over time *Santa Clara Pueblo* has operated throughout Indian Country to deny belonging to thousands more Indigenous persons, especially thanks to two sentences of dicta that Justice Marshall embedded in a footnote to the decision:

> A tribe's right to define its own membership for tribal purposes has long been recognized as central to its existence as an independent political community. Given the often vast gulf between tribal traditions and those with which federal courts are more intimately familiar, the judiciary should not rush to create causes of action that would intrude on these delicate matters.[51]

It is those words that have since operated to close federal courthouses throughout the country to Indigenous civil rights plaintiffs. As Deloria and Lytle were quick to observe, that dicta emboldened Tribal politicians to persecute their political opponents, knowing no federal official or judge would likely intercede in such "delicate matters" to remedy the persecution.[52]

Today, almost every Indigenous human rights concern is dubbed an "internal matter," thus enabling the blind eye and deaf ear of federal lawmakers, judges, and law enforcement agents. Even federal major crimes committed in Indian country are met with federal indifference as soon as they are described as "internal." *Santa Clara Pueblo* has become another excuse for the federal trustee, in all facets, to deflect domestic human rights abuse. Meanwhile, the joint Tribal and federal failure to venerate Indigenous humanity contributes to endemic rates of violence against women, missing and murdered peoples, and youth suicide on reservations.

Deloria and Lytle also correctly explained that Tribal law enforcement systems, including judiciaries formed in response to ICRA, are most likely unable or unwilling to deter or redress human rights abuses.[53] Tribal courts, to the extent they exist, are only as strong and independent as Tribal politicians allow them to be. As Justice Byron White observed in his *Santa Clara Pueblo* dissent, when passing ICRA, Congress could not have "desired the enforcement of these rights to be left up to the very tribal authorities alleged to have violated them."[54]

By 1989, Deloria supported a congressional *Santa Clara Pueblo* fix, which would have restored federal court jurisdiction over ICRA claims following the exhaustion of Tribal court remedies, and waived Tribal sovereign immunity as a defense.[55] A federal court would have been required to adopt any Tribal court findings unless "the tribal court was not fully independent from the tribal legislative or executive authority."[56] It seems Deloria reached "final judgment" on the need for federal Indian civil rights protection, which has yet to and may never be realized.

Now, nearly forty-five years after the *Santa Clara Pueblo* decision, Indigenous human rights violations within Native nations are pervasive and perennial. Indigenous kinship systems, in particular, have eroded. The original ICRA is dead letter. Tribal neocolonialism has emerged, with Tribal politicians perpetuating modes of Indigenous kinship destruction pioneered by settlers centuries ago. Per capita–fueled Tribal disenrollment and enrollment moratoria exemplify those powerful forces. Wilkins incisively describes the "seemingly chronic tribal divisiveness and elite corruption [as] an outcome of the inexorable tide of modernization, a direct or indirect result of colonial and assimilative federal policies aimed at an indigenous absorption, [and] a byproduct of contemporary phenomena like gaming and the tension that capitalism can invoke."[57]

But short of a congressional response to either *Santa Clara Pueblo*[58] or the Tribal neocolonialism that opinion has engendered, Deloria had a solution. He urged that Native nations return "to the Indian way" of governance, where "within the kinship system and the clans you have responsibilities to every person you know and they have responsibilities to you."[59] In other words, Indigenous relational sovereignty.

Indigenous Cultural Renewal and Relational Sovereignty

"A man who has a language consequently possesses the world expressed and implied by that language."

—Frantz Fanon[60]

In 1987, Deloria wrote to Wilkins, explaining that "the proper way to revise tribal governments is to return to forms and structures that are as close to what the people once had as is humanly possible."[61] Deloria "recognized a need for many native Nations to structurally reform their governing institutions, but in a way that supported a strong linkage between traditions in contemporary times."[62] He and Lytle called for "lasting cultural renewal" that would, as Wilkins puts it, allow both "natives to reconcile cultural identity in a contemporary America" and "Native nations to achieve economic stability."[63] Consistent with Deloria's teachings, it is time for Native nations to develop relational sovereignty. Indigenous people must "get emotionally organized around their responsibilities to their relatives," as Deloria urged in 2001.[64]

Indigenous peoples in the United States must renew what Daniel Heath Justice calls "a web of kinship rights and responsibilities" that reconnect the People, land, and cosmos.[65] That starts by recognizing that precontact, most Indigenous societies did not self-identify as nations.[66] Indigenous peoples, both as societies and individuals, originally self-identified through kinship.[67]

Robert Williams, Jr. observes that what today we call a "Tribe" was "a coherent, culturally distinct group constituted by its own language, common territory, and consciously conceived kinship ties of long-established consanguinity."[68] Religion and spiritual tradition also bound the group together.[69] Cornell explains that with few exceptions, Indigenous societies lacked "formally distinct institutional structures in which secular authority in civil affairs is vested."[70] Though self-governing, those societies were generally not centralized or integrated as "nations." They were instead organized through interrelated clans, villages, or bands that adhered to established systems and rules.[71]

Nationhood terminology was superimposed upon Indigenous societies by European colonies and the United States in order to justify settler dispossession of Indigenous homelands under international legal process, particularly treaty-making. Entreating with Tribal "nations" allowed colonial and federal powers to pretend they acquired Indigenous homelands "in perfect good faith."[72] As US Supreme Court justice John Marshall confessed in 1832, in a generally overlooked passage in *Worcester v. Georgia*: "The words 'treaty' and 'nation' are words of *our* own language, selected in *our* diplomatic and legislative proceedings, *by ourselves*, having each a definite and well understood meaning. *We* have applied them to Indians."[73]

The US rounded out its Indian nationhood regime a century later when Tribes adopted federal constitutions and bylaws at the behest of Congress and the BIA, despite lacking any "intelligent understanding" of the IRA.[74] As Nick Estes explains, what IRA Tribes really adopted was "a winner-takes-all" system that "turned relatives against each other" and "broke down the family kinship unit that . . . was fundamental to decision making" in Indigenous societies.[75] Felix Cohen was fully aware that the IRA's version of Tribal "self-government" would foster "graft, corruption, and the making of decisions by inexpert minds . . . [as] in white cities and counties."[76]

To renew expertise rooted in Indigenous kinship custom and develop relational sovereignty, Native Nations should begin by recognizing that words like "Indian,"[77] "tribe,"[78] and "nation"[79] are all products of the imperialist, sociohistorical process that Michael Omi and Howard Winant call "racial formation."[80] Those words were applied to Indigenous peoples when the United States remained a racial dictatorship, with "non-whites firmly eliminated from the sphere of politics."[81] Those imperialist words, and the federal treaties, statutes, and case law that enshrine them—most notably, the US Constitution—have transmuted Indigenous identity over the last several centuries and caused Tribal amnesia regarding kinship custom and tradition.[82]

As Williams urges, Indigenous peoples must now "refrain from using a language of white racial superiority that traces back to the European colonial era's war for America."[83] Williams calls for "a strategy of confrontation and mental correction," which neatly aligns with Deloria's call for cultural renewal according to Indigenous custom and tradition.[84] Inspired by such calls to action, what follows are legal and political ideas for achieving Indigenous relational sovereignty.

- Native Nations should renew their original names.

A great many Indigenous societies originally self-identified through names in their own languages that roughly translate to English as "the People."[85] As Deloria said of those original names in *God Is Red*, they "indicate the fundamental belief that the tribe is a chosen people distinct from other peoples of mankind."[86] To illustrate, the traditional word "Anishinaabe" (now Ojibwe/Chippewa) translates to "the Original People"; Biloxi means "the First People"; Diné (Navajo) means "the People"; Haudenosaunee (Iroquois) means "People Building a Longhouse"; Hidatsa means "People of the Willows"; and Kiowa means "Principal People." Even the IRA's primary architect Felix Cohen wrote that he "expected that an Indian tribe, pueblo, band, or nation will continue to use its traditional name" upon its adoption of the IRA's constitutional regime.[87]

To illustrate, in 1986, the Tohono O'odham—or "Desert People"—of southern Arizona abandoned the Spanish colonial name Papago Tribe, through a federal Secretarial election. In 2015 the former Smith River Rancheria of northern California changed its name from a reference to pioneer Jedediah Smith to Tolowa Dee-ni' Nation, a Tolowa word that encompasses the Nation's peoples and aboriginal lands and waters. In 2017, the Colville Tribes Business Council voted to change the Tribe's name to "The 12 Confederated Tribes of the Big Water," rejecting the namesake Andrew Colville, a Scottish settler and governor of the Hudson Bay Company. The new name, if adopted, would affirm the aboriginal connection between those twelve Columbia Plateau societies and the Columbia River. In 2021, the Yuhaaviatam of San Manuel Band of Mission Indians renamed their business operations, Yaaamava', a Serrano word that means the spring season and serves to honor and remember their "people, community, and ancestors in everything [they] do."[88]

As Robert Hershey teaches, Indigenous renaming is a way of "preserving the Indigenous community's spatial memories."[89] By changing a Native nation's name to reflect a people's original or historical relations, the People's original existence can be less easily forgotten.

- Native Nations should restore kinship systems.

Under the Haudenosaunee kinship system, relationships arose from within the fireside family and emanated outward to one's clan, moiety, longhouse, village, or society.[90] As Williams explains, matrilineal Haudenosaunee social structures were reinforced by a set of relational kinship terms derived from the fireside family, which translate to English as "brother," "grandmother," "grandfather," "nephew," and "uncle."[91] For the Southeastern Cherokee, responsibility was rooted in matrilineal clanship, starting with a member's mother and extending to uncles, siblings, other consanguine relatives, clans, groups, and towns.[92] Cherokee clanship structures included much the same familial terminology as the Haudenosaunee to describe kinship interconnections.[93] According to John Phillip Reid, Cherokee clanship was "the family writ large."[94]

In the Southwest, the Diné's kinship system constituted "a set of categories altogether different from that of white Western culture. The category 'government,' something fixed and powerful to white people, [was] foreign to Navajo thinking."[95] Eastern and Western Pueblo societies in the Southwest were moieties fused into clans.[96] In the Great Plains, Cheyenne society involved camps, bands, subsocieties, and divisions.[97] Algonquin societies of the Great Lakes involved families, clans, and villages.[98] For Indigenous societies in the Pacific Northwest, kinship took shape in longhouses and villages.[99]

A child's birth often determined his or her place of belonging, according to matrilineal, patrilineal, or bilateral family lineage.[100] For the Cherokee, a child belonged to the mother and her clan, not the father or his clan, at birth.[101] As Reid observes, Cherokee "membership was too exact to be challenged."[102] Mirroring Deloria's belief about innate Indigenous belonging, his aunt and prominent Dakota anthropologist Ella Deloria explained: "Everyone who was born a Dakota belonged in it; nobody need be left outside."[103] It would have been inconceivable to self-governing Indigenous societies that a child, like Audrey Martinez, would have been excluded.

Kinfolk typically descended from common ancestors, although that evolved with intermarriage, emigration, or adoption involving European settlers and African and Chinese arrivants.[104] Outsiders were welcomed and adopted into Indigenous societies as kin through ceremony.[105] For the Cherokee, "an alien had no legal security, no rights, privileges or duties until adopted by a clan" but "once adopted, he was equal to any native-born Cherokee."[106] For the Cheyenne, settlers, including war captives, were included through adoption or intermarriage after a period of residence.[107] "Blood" was not a consideration, and although a settler's "previous affiliation remained in collective memory . . . it did not taint their status as Cheyenne"—they were fully Cheyenne.[108] Kinship allowed everyone, no matter how they came to belong, to "rest assured in their collective and personal identities and to not have to wonder about who they were."[109]

Kinship was a matter of reciprocal obligation and duty between the group and the individual.[110] As Deloria and Lytle put it, "kinship ties and responsibilities generally extended to include everyone in the tribe in one way or another."[111] Cherokee clanship, for example, "provided order and security in tribal social life" through "a binding scheme of reciprocal rights and duties upon each relationship a Cherokee might have within the tribe."[112] "To be a good Dakota," as Ella Deloria explained, was "to keep the rules imposed by kinship for achieving civility, good manners, and a sense of responsibility toward every individual dealt with."[113]

Indigenous societies were not void of internal conflict or individual wrongdoing. Fission occurred between clans, which at times caused the secession of clan members and the formation of new villages or bands.[114] Individuals transgressed. Banishment was a sanction reserved for serious wrongs. A banished individual was typically allowed to return home conditionally, after spending time away. Permanent banishments were, as David and Shelly Wilkins explain in *Dismembered*, "rarely practiced since kinship systems were highly effective mechanisms to regulate member conduct and any transgressions that arose."[115] Even so, no relative was excluded through any practice that resembles modern Tribal disenrollment. Nobody involuntarily lost "their everything," meaning "the essence of one's identity, belonging to community, connection to one's heritage, and an affirmation of their human being place in this life and world."[116]

Indigenous kinship persists, albeit imperiled by neocolonial forces. As Yurok Tribal Court chief Judge Abby Abinanti observes: "We're not a rights-based culture; we're a responsibility-based culture."[117] Native nations should shun neocolonial, exclusionary, rights-based practices and restore traditional, inclusionary, duty-based kinship systems.

- Native Nations should replace blood quantum.

Indigenous kinship has been especially decimated by Indian blood quantum, a colonial construct that is devoid of Indigenous origin. As Sterling HolyWhiteMountain explains: "There's no way to talk about blood quantum in Blackfoot, because it's not a concept that belongs to us [or] comes from our cultural history."[118] Yet a great many Tribal citizens now act and speak as if blood quantum has always been Indigenous custom and tradition. Dr. Veronica Tiller puts it wryly: "Today Indian people treat blood quantum almost as a sacred holy decree from the Great Spirit."[119]

Blood quantum is rooted in now-debunked European fractional inheritance theory and eugenics genealogy.[120] Blood quantum is fictional. There are not percentages of racial blood running through Indigenous persons' veins. Yet dating back to the early nineteenth century, the US incorporated the "Indian blood" fiction in federal law in order to eradicate Indigenous peoples. In the 1817 Treaty with the Wyandot, the United States pledged a 640-acre allotment to those children of deceased settler William M'Collock, "who are quarter-blood Wyandot Indians."[121] By the late 1800s, the US recognized "Indians by blood," including "full-blood" and "mixed-blood," in order to assimilate Tribal citizens through reservation land allotment.[122]

In the early 1900s, blood quantum became a proxy for Indian "competence" so allotted land could be taken from Tribal peoples.[123] BIA superintendents caused Tribes to form enrollment councils and identify individuals for federal allotments and benefits, with blood quantum the overriding criterion. As Alexandra Harmon explains: "By emphasizing that aboriginal 'blood' was a sine qua non of entitlement, they also expressed a conception of racial categories that underlay the department's enrollment policies."[124] BIA superintendents also urged that individuals with low blood quantum not be enrolled, to enhance the economic interests of those already enrolled.[125]

The most significant blood law is the IRA of 1934, which defines "Indian" as "persons of one-half or more Indian blood" who reside on a reservation.[126] As US Senator Burton Wheeler of Montana said on the floor of Congress during debate about the IRA: "I do not think the government of the United States should go out there and take a lot of Indians that are quarter bloods and take them in under this act. . . . What we are trying to do is get rid of the Indian problem rather than to add to it."[127] Blood quantum has nevertheless become the single most pervasive and divisive metric of Tribal belonging, with 70 percent of Native Nations using it as some measure of enrollment.[128] Native Nations should no longer perpetuate the colonialist blood quantum lie. If that lie persists, Indigenous peoples will self-extinguish—it is a statistical certainty.[129]

Native nations should instead consider alternative citizenship criteria rooted in traditional kinship, perhaps lineal descent coupled with reciprocal duty (i.e., proven understanding of or commitment to the People). As Deloria espoused, if an Indigenous person is born unto their people, they belong to their people; it is that simple. To that end, enrollment criteria and colonial terminology in Tribal constitutions and membership ordinances should be amended. Customary adoption practices should also be revived for relatives who have been left behind.

In 2020, Alan Parker urged the amendment of IRA constitutions to reestablish citizenship "rules" that "rely on traditional concepts of belonging" and "focus on the goal that there will be future generations."[130] In 2022, Quinault Nation and Minnesota Chippewa Tribe voters each passed constitutional amendments that eliminated blood quantum in favor of lineal descent.[131] Sealaska Corporation shareholders likewise voted to delete blood quantum as a requirement to own shares in the Alaska Native corporation.[132] Bearing in mind their coming generations, a great many more Indigenous peoples should follow suit.

- Native Nations should renew kinship terminology.

As Blackfeet language preservationist Darrell Kipp taught, "The culture comes from the language." Cornell and Dr. Joseph Kalt likewise explain that "language matters to the fabric of a community; it carries lessons and norms of behavior that are repeated over and over."[133] While amending citizenship criteria, words like "citizens" could be amended and infused with kinship terms like "kin" or "relative." Better yet, those definitions could incorporate a people's customary language of kinship. IRA-rooted definitions like "member" should be avoided. "Member"—like disenrollment and enrollment moratoria—smacks of private clubs.

In 2021, the Cherokee Nation eliminated all language in their laws that restricted Tribal citizenship or other rights to Cherokees "by blood," calling that language "a relic of a painful and ugly, racial past."[134] Language changes in Tribal constitutions and other laws can eliminate neocolonial identifiers and help renew Indigenous belonging.

- Native Nations should outlaw disenrollment and bring their relatives home.

As Duane Champagne states: "A constitution must reflect a society's fundamental values if it is truly to serve as its highest law."[135] Tribal constitutions should reflect that disenrollment—a practice that originated in the late 1880s to remove settlers from early Tribal rolls—is antithetical to Indigenous values, particularly kinship.[136]

In 2013, on the heels of opening one of California's largest casinos, the Federated Indians of Graton Rancheria revised its constitution to prohibit disenrollment. According to Graton chairman Greg Sarris: "We saw the money coming. . . . We saw the changes coming. We saw the challenges and we said, 'Let's do something that could prohibit disenrollments in our tribe.'"[137] In 2015, the Spokane Tribe of Indians also banned disenrollment through a constitutional amendment. Likewise, the Passamaquoddy Tribe of the Pleasant Point Reservation amended its constitution to disallow disenrollment. As one of the Passamaquoddy constitutional amendment authors explained: "We felt . . . we had to do this. It wouldn't be right for us to say we have the power to decide who no longer is one of us."[138]

Not only should disenrollment be outlawed, but disenrolled Indigenous relatives should be brought home to their people and reenrolled. In 2016, the Enterprise Rancheria General Council voted to reenroll twenty-five Tribal citizens who were disenrolled in 2003. The following year, the Robinson Rancheria Tribal Council reinstated sixty Tribal citizens who were disenrolled in 2008.[139] In 2021, the Modoc Tribe of Oklahoma restored sixteen Tribal citizens who were disenrolled the previous year.[140] The Confederated Tribes of the Grand Ronde Reservation, who in 2016 threatened to disenroll sixty-six direct lineal descendants of the Tribes' Treaty Chief, amended their constitution in 2022 to generally forbid disenrollment.[141] In 2023, the Cahto Tribe of the Laytonville Rancheria brought home several Tribal citizens who had been disenrolled in 1995.[142]

Tribal politicians must heed the teachings of Billy Frank, Jr., whose own enrollment was once challenged by Nisqually politicians and who often said, "We don't throw our people away." The pervasive practice of discarding Indigenous kinfolk must end. As Patty Krawec teaches in *Becoming Kin*, there is opportunity for Indigenous peoples to listen "to the stories and to the harm . . . to old relationships and memory . . . to how things should be," and to make new offerings and agreements that honor "our place in creation and our responsibilities to each other."[143]

- Native Nations should lift enrollment moratoria and welcome their lost generations.

Twenty years ago, a scholar suggested that "in the view of existing citizens, the proper solution may seem to be closing the rolls."[144] In other words, close Tribal enrollment in order to preserve gaming per capita and other economic benefits for enrolled members, even at the expense of leaving their next generations behind. That is precisely what far too many Tribal politicians have done, with the support of Tribal members and Elders who receive lucrative per capita payments.[145]

Enrollment moratoria, however, are also antithetical to Indigenous kinship. In Indigenous societies, as Champagne explains, "accumulation of wealth on an individual basis is not a primary value; in fact, people who hoarded wealth were considered stingy and often ostracized. Most tribal communities emphasize sharing, exchange, and giveaways, so that wealth is shared throughout the community."[146]

Nobody should go without or be left outside. Practically, Native Nations must remember that there is power in numbers and plenty of resources to share.[147] Culturally, Tribal politicians must remember that Indigenous peoples do not leave each other behind.

- Native Nations should cease per capita payments.

Indigenous societies once sustained themselves through social labor, the underpinning of which was the ethical ideal that the individual should fish, hunt, gather, or farm to benefit the group.[148] Indigenous kinship and reciprocity extended to the land, waters, and animals—to grasslands and buffalo, oak trees and acorns, and rivers and salmon—through environmental stewardship and subsistence. As Cornell observes: "Land, labor, and the productive process [were] inextricably bound up in webs of kinship, ritual, and custom."[149]

Indigenous social labor production began to wane in the early nineteenth century. As Prucha explained: "So long as Indians were assured of receiving their annual stipend, they did not exert themselves to earn a living" by the 1840s.[150] Meanwhile, traditional Indigenous subsistence was "largely destroyed by the encroachment of white civilization."[151] Within a century, Tribal members were no longer surviving through kinship subsistence practices. Settler decimation of buffalo herds in the Great Plains and salmon runs in the Pacific Northwest devastated Indigenous societies. As former Lummi Nation chairman Darrell Hillaire teaches, the devastation of salmon relatives increasingly disrupts Coast Salish kinship customs and traditions.

According to the 1928 Meriam Report, the federal government had instead created a socioeconomic situation where Tribal members felt that "the government owe[d] them a living, having taken their lands, and that they [were] under no obligation to support themselves." Per capita payments "made to the individual from tribal funds" were a particular reason why "the Indian . . . postponed the day when it would be necessary for him to go to work to support himself."[152]

Half a century later, a US Advisory Commission on Indian Reservation Economies described an Indigenous state of "social welfare dependency."[153] As the commission explained in 1983: "There is no difference between a per capita payment from a tribal enterprise [or] judgment fund, a mineral royalty or bonus, and a welfare distribution, where no opportunity exists for individual Indians to self-actualize or to succeed through individual effort."[154]

Indian gaming has not necessarily improved that situation. While member income and employment levels have risen since IGRA's passage in 1988, Tribal unemployment remains more than double national averages and Tribal family poverty rates are three times higher.[155] Many of the same factors that contributed to high Tribal unemployment and poverty rates in 1928 and 1983 persist today, most notably per capita income.

Tribal per capitalism increasingly destabilizes a great many Native Nations in this day and age. A rising number of Tribal members feel entitled to a "per cap" from every large tranche of federal or Tribal money. As Deloria warned decades ago, members demand the money now, without concern for coming generations. Tribal leaders thus face the untenable choice of resisting the per-capita clamors and enduring threats of recall or ouster, or bowing to the political pressure and forgoing Nation-building opportunities by making the per capita distribution.

Gaming per capitalism, in particular, has also catalyzed violent unrest on several reservations as well as Tribal citizenship–related human rights violations on a great many more reservations.[156] As exemplified by enrollment moratoria, gaming per capitalism has rendered Tribal citizenship transactional on far too many reservations. Gaming dollars significantly increase the likelihood of a debilitating political struggle over disenrollment or citizenship denial.[157]

Research also shows that insofar as per-capita distributions dissipate Tribal communal wealth, they defeat "larger goals of community revitalization," including Indigenous kinship renewal efforts.[158] In 2008, the Mashantucket Pequot Tribe began to "slowly ween" its people off of gaming per-capita dependence, and reinvested the savings in programs that establish social "safety nets not only for individual tribal members but for the community at large."[159]

Yet more than 230 years after the first federal Indian payment roll, per-capita distributions permeate a great many reservations in ways that undermine the reciprocal duties intrinsic to Indigenous kinship.[160] While non-Tribal America inches toward a universal basic income system, history suggests such a regime would have uniquely destructive effects on Native Nations. True to Deloria's prediction four decades ago, today's growing Tribal per-capita entitlement reflects the rejection of Indigenous social responsibilities and, therefore, requires careful reconsideration. Individual rights must now be reconciled with a people's obligations and duties to one another.

In 1974, years before the *Santa Clara Pueblo* decision or Indian gaming per capita payments, Deloria called the question: "The gut question has to do with the meaning of the tribe. Should it continue to be a quasi-political entity? [Should] it become primarily an economic structure? Or should it become, once again, a religious community? The future, perhaps the immediate future, will tell."[161] Over the last nearly fifty years, that existential questioning has yet to be answered within a great many Native Nations. The Tribal elitism and corruption propelled by two centuries of federal Indian law and hundreds of billions of gaming dollars have made Deloria's inquiry almost impossible to confront, let alone resolve.[162]

That gut question must now be urgently asked and answered by Native Nations. Answers remain available. They can be found through Indigenous kinship and relational sovereignty. They can be found within us. They can be found within the People.

CHAPTER 31

LIST-MAKING AND THE REAL PANDEMIC

Kiros A. B. Auld

At the end of January 2021, we were mourning the one-year anniversary of our son's wrongful death when a friend informed me that I was named among those on the "Alleged Pretendians List" (hereinafter "The List") as an impliedly "Fake Pamunkey." Seeing my formerly enrolled mother and dead grandmother smeared by outsider falsehoods, bad research, and (at best) half-truths was an almost welcome distraction from sights of blood and gore from our child's body, one year prior. My calls that weekend were first to my mother and then to a Pamunkey Tribal council member, who expressed condolences for our family's loss. The council member also expressed the following sentiment: "*Who*, in the middle of COVID, has time for this?"

In the weeks following our son's January 2020 death, the looming Covid-19 pandemic engulfed America and the world in a tidal wave of ubiquitous trauma, fear, and death—especially my wife's hard-hit Navajo Nation. Despite our fresh Indigenous dead, a vocal minority of Native Academia within "the Ivory Tipi" insisted that the "Other" and somehow "Real" Pandemic was "Ethnic Fraud." We were warned that false claims to Indigeneity by the Ward Churchills and Susan Taffe Reeds were enabling the theft of coveted academic tenureships and speakerships, while the Johnny Depps were stealing entertainment industry opportunities.

Importantly, we were promised that outing these people would somehow trickle down to those scraping for blue-collar and service jobs. The solution? Lists and elevated harassment for those named on them.

I remain skeptical of this being more than the modernized demagoguery of a boutique, white-collar "problem" mostly affecting elites within Indian Country. We're still waiting on totals detailing how much money and opportunities "ethnic frauds" actually steal, as we are more painfully aware of the established infrastructure, health, and safety issues affecting Indian Country. We're still waiting to hear how this supports Land Sovereignty, Language, Faith, and Culture. I'm still waiting to hear how this is anywhere near as real of an issue as our dead baby and the shadow of lawbreaking under which he died.

I appreciate the invitation to submit a meditation on these issues and to offer an informed perspective, being founder and a moderator of /r/ Indian Country: the largest Native American community on Reddit.com (consistently ranking among the Top 10 Websites in US Web Traffic per Alexa rankings). Our mission is to center and elevate Indigenous Voice. I serve alongside Kyle Pittman (Nez Perce/Yakama) and Donovan Pete (Diné); we do so as volunteers. To be clear, "volunteer" means that we do not get paid for this, nor is such expected. We curate our community and protect our users from the lateral violence of bigotry through clear rules and guidelines. Reddit also protects their users through strict prohibitions of "doxing," which is wrongful publication of personally identifiable information (names, addresses, SSNs, etc.) that is a form of harassment itself and can lead to physical, professional, and financial harm. We beheld the development of this present era of digital gatekeeping.

Consistent with my invitation to submit this piece, I will endeavor to not name names or directly draw blood. I leave you, the reader, to your follow-up inquiries as to the "who" would dedicate their energies and platform to racial gatekeeping to the exclusion of saving Native Lives during the COVID-19 Pandemic; the actual challenge of our time still disproportionately impacting Indian Country.

List-Making: Democratizing and Indigenizing Harassment for Profit

In the Digital Age, "clout" or influence is a currency acquired by the cynical through activism, mainstream publication, and sizable social media followings that can transform a failed novelist into a recognized authority within or concerning Indian Country. Our demographics being small, this necessarily requires wider appeal to non-Natives and especially the almighty "White Gaze." Until the 2020 Democratic primaries, attacking the heritage claims of Senator Elizabeth Warren was a limited access path to tangible mainstream success for a select few within Indian Country. The problems with this model include its normalizing invasions of our already diminished privacy rights within Indian Country, incentivizing gatekeeping, and encouraging non-Natives to encroach on self-determination, uninvited. Further, genealogical websites provide tools for amateurish, bad faith, and financially motivated self-made genealogists. The end-result and current challenge is people who were late to the "Liz Warren Pretendian Gravy-Train" realizing they could promote themselves by stuffing its figurative firebox with an alternative fuel source in the form of vulnerable people within Indian Country: Adoptees, Black Natives, Disenrollees, Native Women, and the Unenrolled.

In brief, The List exploits the systemic inequalities and grievances within Indian Country, with the immediate goal of self-promotion by its proponents. There is no higher principle beyond demagoguery and harassment for profit. Anti-Black racism, corruption, enrollment abuses, human rights violations, misogyny, and violence pose challenges to Tribal governance, Tribal law, and Tribal sovereignty, but The List invariably reinforces and highlights these problems within Tribes for the sake of tawdry spectacle. The List includes Tribal citizens enrolled in Federally Recognized Tribes. It usurps the exclusive sovereign Self-Determination prerogative of Native Nations, who neither invited nor authorized the scrutiny of its promoters and "researchers," who have public records of Anti-Black statements and animus. The List provides targets and scripts for harassment, attracting a criminal element whose targeted harassment was actively encouraged by its lead promoter. Its initial iterations included links to pictures of targets' minor children who are otherwise eligible for enrollment in a Federally Recognized Tribe—a fact included knowing that some people value status more than the innocence of children. Internally, The List is driven by deep insecurity, jealousy, and the human dynamic that everyone loves having scapegoats that can be looked down upon.

Successors to Genocide and White Supremacy

What follows is an illustration of a previous iteration of this twenty-first-century gatekeeping as backed by twentieth-century state power. In our part of Indian Country, resting in the shadow of the nation's Capital, we are no stranger to "lists." Among a certain generation, local Tribes (seven now with federal recognition, to the extent that validates our Indigeneity and humanity to some) have visceral and personal memories of this part of the Jim Crow period. In the Mid-Atlantic, "The List" is the spiritual successor to "the Plecker List."[1]

Dr. Walter Ashby Plecker was a prominent and internationally known eugenicist and white supremacist. His professional goal became the administrative annihilation of Indigenous people within Virginia. Those who did not fit or comply walked a fine line with the consequence of felony conviction and imprisonment. This was also an era of forced sterilization that disproportionately impacted Tribal communities. Appointed as the first director and registrar of Virginia's Bureau of Vital Statistics in 1912, Plecker regulated the recording of birth, marriage, and death. Plecker advocated for the Virginia General Assembly to pass the Racial Integrity Act of 1924 and in his official capacity, served as its enforcer.[2]

The Racial Integrity Act outlawed interracial marriage involving whites and codified racial classifications, with exceptions. Of interest to Plecker was closing the infamous "Pocahontas Exception," a loop-hole affording white status to whites of mixed Indian ancestry, such as those among Virginia's "First Families" whose descendants held seats in the general assembly and governorship. It extended whiteness to persons "one sixteenth or less of the blood of the American Indian and have no other non-Caucasian blood [to] be deemed to be white persons." Plecker viewed this loophole as a danger to the purity of the white race, so he used state power to destroy and alter records of persons belonging to local Tribes, forcing those within his purview to identify as Black/Colored.[3] The Racial Integrity Act of 1930 later officially codified the "One-Drop Rule," as to Black/Colored racial status, further prompting some Tribal leaders to (falsely) certify that they had "no Negro blood," further encouraging Tribes to continue the internal purges and exclusion of previous generations.

In a republished and statewide distributed letter including "the Plecker List," he enumerated our families by surname and county, encouraging the identification of us, our associates, and our workplaces; state-sponsored persecution and harassment. The law imposed felony penalties for noncompliance, creating harassment and a state terror regime for Tribes within the commonwealth. During his tenure, Plecker bragged that his methods were superior to those of his Third Reich contemporaries, writing that "Hitler's genealogical study of the Jews is not more complete."[4] Virginia hosted an official delegation from the Reich and Plecker was not shy about sharing his methods of identifying "undesirable" lineages. In a more just world, Plecker would have been tried (and hanged) as a Nazi collaborator at Nuremberg. Instead, he was a figurehead in the now-embarrassing state action that justified congressional action in recognizing six Tribes in Virginia through the Thomasina E. Jordan Indian Tribes of Virginia Federal Recognition Act of 2018.[5]

The full extent of the damage Plecker inflicted upon this part of Indian Country is unknowable, and he was not an anomaly. Federal Indian policy and law have Jeffersonian roots published and documented in his *Notes on the State of Virginia*, as they concerned Powhatan Tribes. I also will not pretend that our challenges are exclusively external. We have internalized far more damaging anti-Black and misogynistic practices and laws in our overlong compliance with this cradle of American slavery and in misguided efforts at self-preservation, long after settler-colonist threats ceased and within our lifetimes. Responsive justice and restoration are retroactive. We have much work to do, much to account for. But today, we will not be baited into turning on each other at the instigation of outsiders.

Real Stakes

The external fear is this animus once again gaining state and institutional power of a kind that it held in Virginia during the Jim Crow Era. The federal government has inflicted enough harm on Native Nations. Higher education institutions have a historically predatory disposition toward Indian Country, and Native academics reinforce that dynamic when they cultivate independent and antagonistic power bases built on embracing and Indigenizing settler-colonist gatekeeping. Indian Country does not need rogue actors exploiting our fault lines and vulnerabilities for personal profit. Further, Indian Country does not need mainstream political partisan coalescence that intrudes on self-determination and valid exercises of sovereignty. Fortunately, this incipient twenty-first-century hate movement has no considerable traction among Tribal governments and Tribal communities at a grassroots level.

The list-bearers have a combination of disqualifying methodological and personal flaws that make their current effort abortive. Disturbingly, some voices wish to preserve "better methods" from "more reputable proponents" as a weapon for future personal use. I prefer deference to the valid citizenship determinations of Tribes and demanding institutional accountability to ensure valid Tribal governmental decisions are respected. This is complicated by blood quantum, lineal descent, and external settler-colonist validation, which limit self-determination and impose subtractive regimes. At threshold, recognition also creates distinct challenges. Congressional recognition is fairly criticized as "rights for recognition," while being hypocritically derided by Tribal representatives whose nations received it. As to the administrative alternative, the federal acknowledgment process is fairly criticized as "whether your white neighbors agree that you're Indian." It also encourages the self-mutilation of our communities, and a petitioner will not be rejected for deliberately excluding the living or the dead (Tribal law be damned). External validation is predicated on surrendering sovereignty. These dynamics and policies were designed to weaken us, and so they have. Uncritically and carelessly advocating for our own destruction, backed by a brown face, enrollment, letters, and/or a list is a distinct, incentivized, and problematic choice.

Indian Country is sufficiently astute as to recognize that taxing alleged ethnic frauds will not provide food/housing security, meaningfully create jobs, or fix roads. Ethnic frauds have nothing to do with affecting quality of water, health care, or governance. Institutions should ensure intended beneficiaries of programs are selected, but safeguarding their fidelity to programming imperatives does not justify self-appointed Pan-Indian enrollment vigilantism and invalidation. Consistently and presently, the gatekeepers dubbed "Karendians" by the Twitter platform's unofficial rez dog account @DeadDogLake,[6] lost the narrative. Individually, we need to understand the combination of demagoguery, grievance, and American exceptionalism that leaves us vulnerable to exploitation within and without. We need to challenge ourselves, our biases, and reevaluate our perspectives.

Writing this, I encourage you to focus on "what is real," which has been a profound challenge during this pandemic. For starters, you are real. Your family is real. Your elders are real. Your job is real. Your Tribal and/or urban Indian community is real. Your Indigenous language, faith, and culture are real. Kinship is real. All of these people and things are real, and THEY NEED YOU. The necessary social distancing and safety protocols of the pandemic amplified online spaces, frustrated responsible social gatherings, and fostered disconnectedness. This has the cumulative effect of amplifying the Toxic Authenticity described herein, but I assure you, Indian Country needs you, regardless of your status. I personally challenge and encourage you to step out into that real world, as you are, and make it better. Volunteer. Give your time to a child and/or Elder. Individually and collectively, we absolutely have to be our own heroes. I wish our Native Nations would be alongside us in this, but we cannot afford to wait for them. Indian Country isn't just Tribal governments, it's people. Be the answer to the challenges of our time. You are needed, you are loved. Anah (Goodbye).

CHAPTER 32

THE MORAL ORDER OF KINSHIP

Thomas Biolsi

What was the role of kinship in traditional Native life, and what could its role be in the twenty-first century? In 1944, Ella C. Deloria, Vine Jr.'s paternal aunt, published *Speaking of Indians*, describing the centrality of kinship in Dakota life, where the aim was to "be a good relative," the practical effect of which was to foster "a minimum of friction and a maximum of good will." Indeed, the production, distribution, and consumption of goods and care-work was organized based on kinship. Kinship was "theoretically all-inclusive and coextensive with the Dakota domain" (in other words, *mitakye oyasin*, we are *all* related). At its broadest, kinship was the foundation of "peace"—*Odakota* [or *Wolakota* in Lakota]. Thus, a moral order that shaped the horizon of thinkable action among the Dakota structured and shaped social relationships and interactions and was the ethical and moral glue of the society.[1]

Vine Deloria, Jr., was of course more than a little aware of this. He often—both in writing, and in public addresses—linked his legal and political analyses back to the base of Native tradition (perhaps most obviously in his *Behind the Trail of Broken Treaties: An Indian Declaration of Independence*, with its emphasis on what young activists and even lawyers had to learn from Elders about treaties.)[2] But Deloria also said or wrote some tantalizing things about Native tradition in general, and about traditional Native kinship in particular—about its potential role in the present and the future. As early as 1969, in *Custer Died for your*

Sins: An Indian Manifesto, Deloria pointed out that "highly organized clans" shaped daily life and "handled specific problems"—he meant by this social tensions and disputes—within Tribes; this allowed Tribal government to attend to "general affairs," although Tribal government could learn from the clans and adopt clan practices "into general tribal usage."[3] Deloria came to call this traditional content of Tribal sovereignty "internal sovereignty,"[4] something akin to what has also been called "cultural sovereignty."[5] Deloria had in mind specifically "traditional mechanisms of reconciliation, traditional ways of child adoption, traditional ways of dealing with spouses, siblings and any other problem that can arise between human beings."[6] He went even further in 2001 in advocating return to grounding Tribal government in kinship—specifically in the *tiyošpaye* (band) among the Lakota, Dakota, and Nakota—and called for "set[ting] up structures where the elders' wisdom can come to the fore," whereby people would be "emotionally organized around their responsibilities to their relatives." In "the Indian way, within the kinship system and the clans you have responsibilities to every person you know and they have responsibilities to you."[7] His Aunt Ella would have agreed wholeheartedly.

This essay will take seriously Deloria's admittedly brief and schematic comments on the practical significance of traditional Indigenous kinship practices for contemporary Native communities and Tribal governments. We will first briefly review some of examples of how kinship systems governed—but not at all in ways that the political philosophers of the European Enlightenment meant by the idea of "government." To govern through a moral order is quite different from governing through enforcement, democratic or otherwise (more on that to follow) (for an insightful analysis of the [related] concept of a moral economy among Diné coal workers, see Curley).[8] Examples of the continuing role of kinship in Native life and the possibilities for deriving "kinship principles" for inclusion in Tribal constitutions or ways of governing are useful.

To understand the significance of kinship in Native societies, it is necessary to delve briefly into one of the questions that has vexed anthropologists for more than a century: How did what we now call "Indigenous" societies differ from other kinds of societies? As one can imagine, there have been all kinds of theories, and Deloria lampooned and lambasted many of them, beginning with his 1969 "Anthropologists and Other Friends."[9] But I would argue that Deloria fundamentally agreed with the premise that there are foundational differences between Native and non-Native societies, and that there was some overlap in his thinking on this issue with that of anthropologists.

Anthropology has, since the nineteenth century, had a core intellectual tenet that human societies are usefully classified, at least for some purposes, into those with centralized, coercive forms of imposing order (states), and those achieving order on the basis of kinship custom and moral systems, rather than by enforcement of law (which would imply the power to compel). The latter kind of society was, unfortunately, long labeled by anthropologists as primitive. I certainly don't expect my readers to be mollified by my pleading that the p-word was—it's no longer used in the field—meant to signify the sense of originary, not backwardness. The anthropological concept of primitive just had too much overlap with mainstream American conceptions of the savagery, the uncivilized, and the inevitability of modernity's "progress"—progress that Indigenous peoples supposedly must keep up with if they plan to survive—at least in the stark (and quite racist) American worldview of "the primitive" and "the civilized." One can easily understand Deloria's abiding conviction that anthropology is beset with a deep, "evolutionary" bias, in which more "advanced" societies are somehow better or preferable to those left behind by the march of progress.[10]

But we might want to take care not to throw out the baby of recognizing a distinctive organizational characteristic of Indigenous societies with the bathwater of ethnocentrism and (racist) social Darwinism. Deloria himself recognized, in his writings cited earlier, the same kind of distinction between Native and non-Native societies that is at the core of the anthropological worldview. In general, the field of anthropology has recognized an important distinction between kin-ordered societies—

societies in which kinship institutions are the most important or even the only kind of institutions that exist—and state societies, where kinship institutions may continue to exist, but are limited in function and relegated to "the private sphere," while "public institutions"—the agencies and authorities of state-organized, formal government—make, interpret, and enforce (deploying the power to use, or threaten to use, physical force or other forms of coercion) legal rules upon the general population.

Another distinctive feature of the state is class stratification—differential access to the basic necessities of life, something unseen in Indigenous societies. The ultimate resort of the state is to take life; as Deloria pointed out, the ultimate resort of Indigenous societies was banishment.[11] The state as a form of social and political organization appeared only about five or six thousand years ago,[12] and it bears noting that surviving Indigenous peoples the world over see their primary political opponent as the nation-states that encompass them (more on this to follow). Again, I want to emphasize that Deloria himself found this distinction—between stateless Indigenous peoples and state-level societies—instructive for thinking about the future of Native communities and Tribal government.

Much of the history of anthropology has been about the study of kin-ordered societies, and until relatively recently most of the major thinkers in the field spent at least part of their careers studying and trying to understand how kinship works in Indigenous societies (concomitantly, kinship has often been one of the central theoretical debates in the field). An apt thinker for present purposes is Eric R. Wolf, whose 1982 *Europe and the People without History* identified crisply what is unique about kin-ordered societies in relation to states.[13] For Wolf kinship—bands, clans, lineages—is the institution by which kin-ordered societies organize work (including both production of food and other necessities, and care-work) and allocate the "product"—all of which is done without markets regulated by supply and demand, or "command" as found in state societies (think of taxation and conscription, even in liberal democracies, and tribute-taking in the "classical civilizations").

More concretely, relations between band or lineage members serve as the basis for cooperative labor and pooling of resources. Let's take a classic example in anthropology, matrilineal lineages, matrilocal households, and matrilineal clans among the Haudenosaunee.

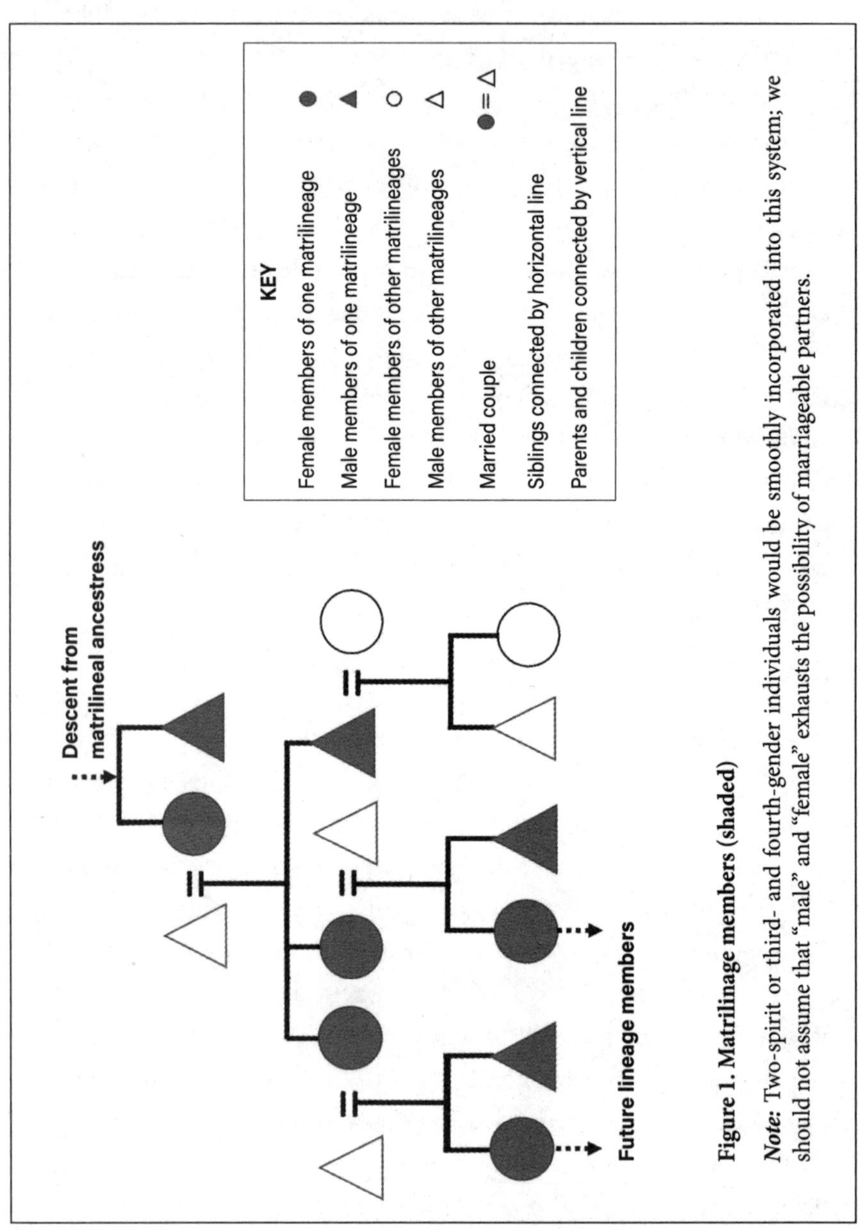

Figure 1. Matrilinage members (shaded)

Note: Two-spirit or third- and fourth-gender individuals would be smoothly incorporated into this system; we should not assume that "male" and "female" exhausts the possibility of marriageable partners.

A matrilineal clan or lineage (lineages are subsets of a larger clan) is based on common descent from a female ancestress. Both girls and boys are born into their mother's clan and lineage, but only women members of the clan or lineage pass on membership to their children. See Figure 1 for a representation of this matrilineage system.

(I have no knowledge of whether two-spirit or third- and fourth-gender members could pass clan or lineage membership to children, but I would bet on the existence of flexibility and accommodation of individuals that went far beyond limiting lineage continuity only to those conforming to a biological definition of sex; this is obviously an important question deserving scholarly attention.)[14] All members of a lineage know each other personally; several closely related lineages (say, the descendants of three grandmothers who were sisters) may have lived in the same village or nearby. But not all members of the lineage lived together. The longhouse—the home base of the lineage—was composed of the adult women of the lineage, their children, and their in-marrying husbands. See Figure 2 for a representation of the matrilocal system.

The technical term for this is a matrilocal household, and it is a textbook case of a society where men were beholden to women—because they were not members of the lineage that fed and housed them—and (senior) women had what we might call executive authority over all residents of the longhouse, including the in-married men who were "outsiders," but with a right to live there by marriage to a lineage member. A younger person called both their mother and the mother's sister "mother," and both father and father's brother were called "father" (more on this to follow). The clan was composed of all the "sister" lineages that traced their descent to an ancestress who lived in the dim past. An individual would know only those fellow clan members with whom they came into daily or regular contact, but the majority of clan "sisters" and "brothers" (and those are the precise terms that would have been used) were not known personally. Nevertheless, when traveling beyond one's village, even in the territory of one of the other Haudenosaunee Six Nations, an individual could count on being treated as a *sister* or a *brother* by fellow clan members she or he had never met before.

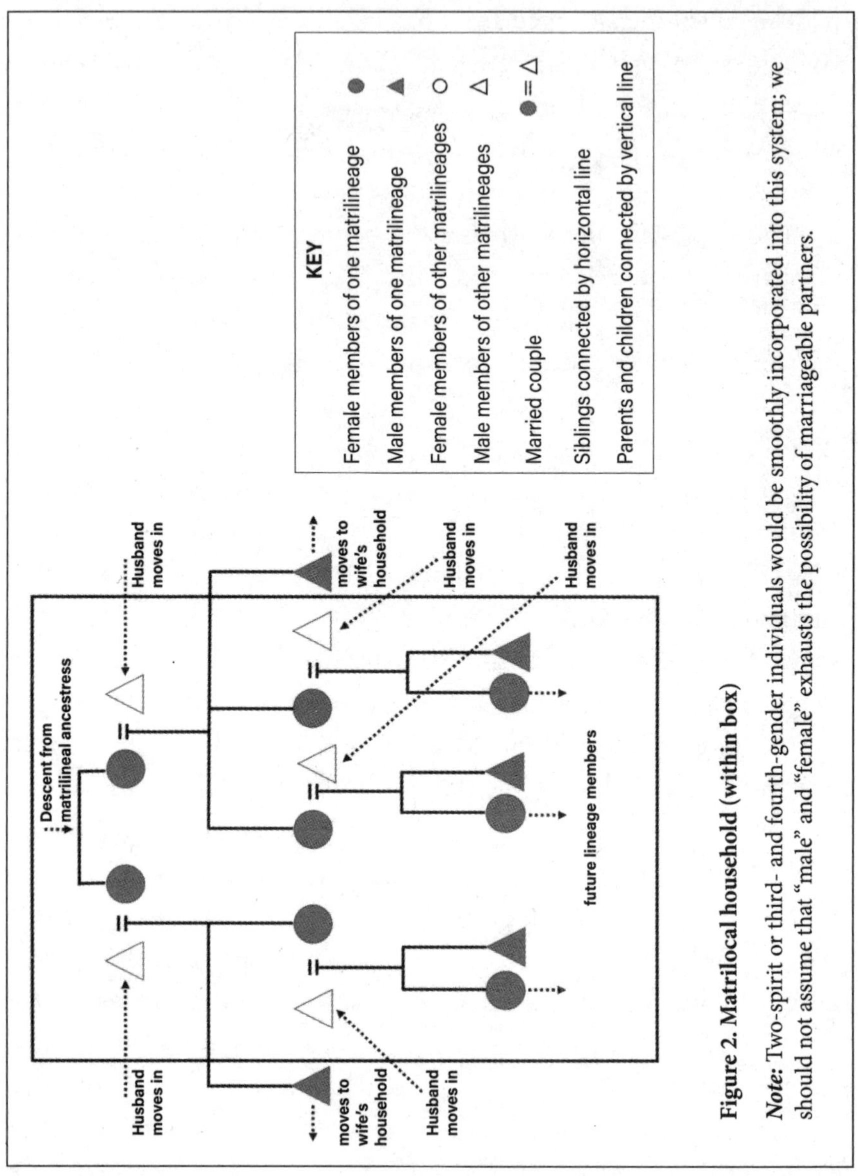

Figure 2. Matrilocal household (within box)

Note: Two-spirit or third- and fourth-gender individuals would be smoothly incorporated into this system; we should not assume that "male" and "female" exhausts the possibility of marriageable partners.

A Haudenosaunee delegation to a United Nations conference in Geneva in 1977 presented a paper titled "Economic History of the Hau De No Sau Nee," in which it pointed out that the Six Nations traditionally had no "economic institutions, nor do we have specifically distinct political institutions" since the only institutions were kinship-based. "Our basic economic unit is the ["extended"] family," and no concept of private property existed.[15] The matrilineage organized the production and distribution of food and care-work, but there were also customs of generosity and hospitality beyond the lineage—which helped to create good will with the members of other lineages, which is also where spouses and alliances between in-laws were sought (one needed to marry outside of one's clan). The Geneva delegates described the organization of Haudenosaunee life as a "Domestic Mode of Production," a concept they borrowed from the anthropologist Marshall Sahlins in which "our people's economy requires a community of people and is not intended to define an economy based on the self-sufficient nuclear family."[16] Critically, the domestic mode of production, "by our cultural definition, is not an economy [regulated by "economic laws"] at all. . . . All had the right to food, clothing and shelter. . . . No one stood in any material relationship of power over anyone else. No one could deny anyone access to the things they needed." What was involved was an all-encompassing "Way of Life" (*Ongwe Honwekah*), something far beyond a mere "economy" and much closer to a total moral order.[17]

The mode of subsistence was based on farming maize, beans, and squash (the three sisters), hunting, and fishing. The longhouse, as mentioned, was matrilocal, and when a couple married, they took up a space in the woman's mother's longhouse. Thus, women lived their whole lives—from birth—with their female lineage mates—sisters, cousins (who were also addressed as "sister"), mothers, aunts (who were also addressed as "mother"), and grandmothers (the term "grandmother" was also applied to one's grandmother's sisters and cousins in the same lineage). A longhouse might include five to twenty nuclear families, all related through the women. "Every household," anthropologist Lewis Henry Morgan wrote in 1881, "was organized under a matron who supervised the domestic economy. It was her duty to divide the food, from the kettle, to the several families according to their respective needs."[18] The principle of allocating food was simple and straightforward, and in keeping with the moral order of kinship: "Whatever was gained by any member of the household on hunting or fishing expeditions [by men], or was raised by cultivation [by women], was made a common stock" of the longhouse. Morgan summarized the system thusly: "Here was communism in living carried out in practical life. . . . In these households, formed on the principle of kin, was laid the foundation for . . . 'mother power.'"[19]

As the 1977 Haudenosaunee delegates to Geneva said, just as there was no distinct economy (market or otherwise), there was no *free-standing* political system among the Six Nations, which is not to say that there was no political order or means for making decisions. Indeed, as is widely recognized and as Morgan wrote, "The Iroquois commended to our [American] forefathers a union of the colonies similar to their own as early as 1755."[20] The Six Nations Confederacy was ultimately rooted in the matrilineal kinship system. Each matrilineal clan was represented by hereditary chiefs "claiming no superiority," since each clan was "a brotherhood bound together by the ties of kin."[21] Doug George-Kanentiio explains that the English word "chief" is a mistranslation, and that "nice people" is the literal translation of the Native terms.[22] These clan chiefs also sat on the council of each nation, and represented each of the six nations in the confederacy council.[23] Each clan chose among the eligible senior men of the clan those who would replace chiefs who had died, but it was the senior women of the clan who chose chiefs and who could depose them.[24] That is still the case among Haudenosaunee people who abide by the traditional Six Nations council, as opposed to the popularly elected Tribal councils in the US and Canada (on the contemporary role of clan mothers, see *Haudenosaunee Confederacy, and Onondaga Nation*).[25] Morgan observed that while the confederacy yielded "the benefits of an alliance," it "had a deeper foundation in the bond of kin." "All the members of the same [clan] . . . were brothers and sisters to each other in virtue of their descent from the same common ancestor, and they recognized each other as such with the fullest cordiality."[26]

There was, of course, tremendous variation in the specific forms of kinship systems and terms of address among Native people in what became the US, and it is not possible to provide a serious overview in a short essay. But having examined how kinship functioned among the Haudenosaunee, a society with farming and highly organized lineages and clans, it is worth looking briefly at a foraging (fishing, gathering, hunting) society with a very different kind of kinship system. A good example is the Sahaptin-speaking people of Yakama, Warm Springs, and Umatilla reservations on the Columbia Plateau in Washington and Oregon, studied by the anthropologist Eugene Hunn and his consultants, James Selam and family of the Yakama Nation. These peoples had winter village sites, but during other seasons the winter villages broke down into extended families that fished (especially species of salmon), gathered (especially bitterroot, camas, and huckleberries), and hunted (especially deer).[27]

As is commonly the case with foraging societies, Sahaptin speakers did not have unilineal (matrilineal or patrilineal) clans or lineages; the winter-village communities had flexible memberships composed of relatives related through either one's mother or father (technically called "bilateral" relations). A key feature of the Sahaptin system of kinship terms is that *all* members of one's own generation are referred to as either elder sister/younger sister, or elder brother/younger brother.[28] This is also a distinctive feature of the Native Hawaiian system of addressing kin, something called a "generational" system, since all members of one's own generation are lumped into the category of siblings. Not surprisingly, given this vision of *close* kinship among all Sahaptin peoples, Hunn describes the system of distributing food, care, and other basic necessities this way: "One shares what one has without (obvious) expectation of return."[29] Hunn draws on Marshall Sahlins's concept of "generalized reciprocity" to name this kind of system, and Sahlins actually suggests that the Hawaiian-type kinship terminology is a kind of template for this kind of open and generous economic cooperation.[30] The point we should draw is that kinship was a way of organizing work and sharing in order to make a collective living. We don't need to separate the "moral" nature of kinship from its economic role in Native society. In fact, we can't.

Importantly, Hunn writes that "despite drastic changes in traditional Columbia River Indians' lives since the first Euro-American influences were felt on the [Columbia] Plateau, this ethical principal [of freely giving without an expectation of return from the recipient] *retains much of its original moral force.*"[31] I venture to say that anyone who has spent any time in a Native community has seen "generalized reciprocity"—or, the moral conviction that "we are all related, and we should act as if we are"—at work. I can certainly attest to its persistence in the community on Rosebud Reservation; sharing food, cash, housing, dependent care, and other resources are everyday occurrences among people—even people who don't *formally* recognize each other as "close kin." Wilkins and Wilkins describe this living kinship as a moral system of relationships.[32]

Generalized reciprocity and widely extended recognition of kinship are two sides of the same Indigenous coin, and they make sense only in societies where the separation of the public realm and the private realm has not advanced to the point that it has in capitalism; in Indigenous societies individuals are not continuously challenged to recognize the difference between "public" and "private" and to carefully behave appropriately in the two very distinct domains. One might even go so far as to say that private interest *coincides* with the public interest in a system of generalized reciprocity. Ella Deloria wrote, Dakota "kinship had everybody in a fast net of interpersonal responsibility and made everybody like it, because its rewards were pleasant."[33] And Vine Deloria, Jr. observed of traditional kinship systems that "because everyone was related to everyone else in some specific manner, by giving to others within the society, a person was enabled to receive what was necessary to survive and prosper."[34]

Of course, this was precisely the moral order that settler colonial society found "immoral," "primitive," and, yes, "communist" or "socialist," targeting it for replacement by "enlightened self-interest," "possessive individualism," and the more-or-less isolated nuclear family; the latter values, of course, are part and parcel of private property. While the project to "civilize" Indigenous peoples never succeeded in eliminating all of traditional Indigenous kinship, both the Bureau of Indian Affairs (BIA) and missionary programs, as well as the general environment of liberal democracy, capitalism, and the dominance of the "free market," had deeply destabilizing effects upon Indigenous communities, including kinship institutions. Think of what boarding schools did to extended families. And this raises the question of whether Deloria meant that Tribes should literally return to the formal organization of clans, *tiyošpaye*, or other traditional kinship institutions. Perhaps he did have this in mind, but given the fact that Deloria was a stubbornly pragmatic thinker, I suspect that he would advocate thinking of traditional Native kinship institutions as *sources of creative inspiration*, rather than as templates to be reinstalled in contemporary Native communities.

A concrete example of what I mean by creative inspiration is Eva Marie Garroutte's method of "allowing the ancestors to speak."[35] She takes on the question of Tribal enrollment, where both the BIA and many Tribes have long relied on blood quantum (even to the point of requiring specified fractions of specific Tribal "blood" for enrollment).[36] While Garroutte recognizes that Native people are right to understand their Native identities as tied to a "physical relationship" with ancestors and with each other, she argues that kinship comes closer to describing that relationship than does "blood quantum," which, after all, was a colonial technique to administratively and legally erase Tribes and Native peoples. A kin-based rule would be consistent with the way that Native communities traditionally defined "membership." Furthermore, Garroutte reasons, kinship in its essence—as opposed to "membership," "enrollment," or even "citizenship"—is not a system of "entitlement" (my terms, not Garroutte's), although non-Natives commonly see it that way, and that's why they're so eager to "enroll."

Admittedly, we could say that a traditional kinship system "allocated rights," but that's only half the story, since it also allocates responsibilities, and rights and responsibilities are part and parcel of a moral order and a worldview of relatedness (that ultimately goes beyond mere human beings). Kinship also "respects the primacy of the collective, the tribal 'we' . . . ; for it reminds [kinspeople] that they enjoy their place in the community only by the community's collective pleasure." It is "grounded in the traditional value of reciprocity," and "tradition is fundamentally a *sacred* concept"—or what I have been calling a moral order.[37] None of this would be simple to institute in the present, of course, and Garroutte is not saying that Native groups that were traditionally matrilineal should simply adopt a matrilineal *rule* for enrollment, since that would leave out the question of one's *obligations* to clan and community and the complex challenge of how those obligations would be *taught, routinized, and perhaps even assessed* by Tribal communities. This is all very thorny, and not easily implemented, but there is no escaping the fact that concerns and contention over blood quantum and enrollment rules are becoming only more heightened for Tribes. In that context, it's a good time to think about Native kinship as an organizing principle.

Another example of harnessing traditional kinship for very contemporary purposes comes from the Diné Nation, famous for its Peacemaker Court that facilitates what Chief Justice Emeritus Robert Yazzie of the Navajo Nation Supreme Court has called *original* dispute resolution. Matrilineal clans and extended families have a critical role in the Peacemaker Court.[38] But there is an even more ambitious initiative to bring traditional justice, and kinship principles in particular, into the present in Diné society. In 2002, the Navajo Nation Council amended the Navajo Nation Code to recognize the Fundamental Laws of the Diné.[39] As Justice Emeritus Raymond D. Austin describes it, a "group of traditionalists who were selected for their fluency in Navajo philosophy, language, culture, spiritualty and sense of place, scrutinized the Navajo Creation Scripture and Journey Narratives and identified several foundational postulates that were appropriate for codification."[40] Austin describes in his book how the Navajo Nation Supreme Court has drawn on kinship principles derived from the Fundamental Laws to decide cases.[41]

For example, the Court has drawn on the Diné concept of matrilineal clan relationships (*k'é*) to render decisions in inheritance cases.[42] But kinship is about more than clan relationships, and Austin describes *k'é* as the "principle of universal kinship," involving not just all human beings but not-humans, as well (more on that follows).[43] A stunning example of the court applying that concept is a 2011 case involving a Diné receptionist of a non-Indian-owned law firm who had been fired for "sending emails containing sexually offensive matters, making demeaning comments about other staff and clients and undermining staff morale and office decorum, being rude and unhelpful to visitors and clients, and failing to perform assigned tasks properly."[44] The former employee appealed the termination to the Navajo Nation Labor Commission, which found in favor of the fired worker, essentially because the law firm had not imposed "progressive sanctions" (a common requirement in American labor law). But the Supreme Court overruled that decision, holding that the law firm had engaged in "sustained *k'é* measures . . . where [the receptionist] was told of the gravity of her violations and expected to be self-accountable." When the law firm "made its concerns about [the worker's] violations known . . . over the course of eight months through personal meetings and emails without imposing punishments [which would have satisfied the progressive sanctions rubric], [the firm] undertook a course of action in keeping with the Diné Fundamental Law, which emphasizes personal accountability through talking out, self-knowledge, and self-correction." It was the Diné former employee who had "show[n] how little respect is accorded *k'e* measures by an employee" without formal sanctions. "The Diné method of dispute resolution is averse to threats of punishment in relationships, while emphasizing accountability and personal responsibility, on the basis of self-respect, self-awareness and respect for others."[45] The "philosophical" basis for this is the conviction of universal relatedness and harmony. The court validated the termination as lawful in its conformity with the Diné Fundamental Laws, and thus traditional concepts prevailed over the (essentially non-Indian) Labor Code that had been adopted by the council.

It would not be difficult to find similar philosophical bases for treating others (even people who are not members of one's Tribe) as related—as kinspersons—for purposes of guiding social relationships in most Native

American communities, even if some degree of revitalization of traditional moral concepts might be necessary. Such re-traditionalization and cultural revitalization is obviously linkable to *Native language* revitalization—something flourishing across Indian Country. There are related moral principles of kinship responsibilities that are also widespread among Indigenous peoples, and the concept of the seventh generation comes to mind. Kinship is obviously not only a set of moral relationships with presently living people (and nonhumans), but also across generations, with ancestors and descendants. As Kyle Whyte writes, *kinship time* entails responsibility not just for the abstraction of "future generations," but for *descendants*—in other words, relatives.[46] Deloria elucidated the point by describing the Native family as "a multigenerational complex of people, and clan and kinship responsibilities extended beyond the grave and far into the future. Remembering a distant ancestor's name and achievements might be equally as important as feeding a visiting cousin or showing a niece how to sew and cook. Children were greatly beloved by most Tribes, and this feeling gave evidence that the future was as important as the present or past, a fact that [US] policy makers and treaty signers have deliberately chosen to ignore as part of the Indian perspective on life."[47]

The 2005 Constitution of the Little Traverse Bay Bands of Odawa Indians provides that "in consideration of the next seven generations, each generation of the Tribal Membership to assert Tribal sovereignty directs" the three branches of Tribal government to preserve the Anishinaabe language and culture; promote the well-being of the people, "especially our children and elders"; work toward the development of jobs, education, and social assistance; and protect the youth and elders against exploitation.[48] The Rosebud Sioux Tribe amended its 1935 IRA Constitution in 2007 to require the council to "develop plans and consider implications of the decisions they make on the next seven generations."[49] And the Constitution adopted by the Nottawaseppi Huron Band of the Potawatomi adopted in 2013 provides "Guiding Principles," including the promotion of "sustainable development strategies and practices to ensure the health and balance of the next seven generations of Tribal Members."[50] *Anyone* is free to remind council representatives in public or in private of these constitutional obligations and in theory might pursue action in Tribal Court to enforce them. What comes of it, we'll have to see, but these seven-generation provisions represent a pointed reminder and political and legal touchstone for all three branches of Tribal government and for Tribal citizens.

Finally, if one takes seriously traditional forms of Indigenous kinship—a maximum expansion of the recognition of relatedness—the question of nonhumans (animals, plants, trees, rivers, indeed, all of creation) and their place in the moral order must be faced; many scholars call this a "more-than-human" understanding of relatedness and relationships, or even of "society" itself. The appropriate concept might be (more-than-human) *persons* fully on a "level" with human beings, the literal *kin* of human beings, and/or members of allied nations of human nations, with the full moral implications such recognition entails.[51] For some Indigenous peoples, this is a no-brainer and is a key tactic in anticolonial resistance and "environmental justice" (the latter cannot be separated from the anticolonial movement for justice).

The 2014 Constitution of the Chippewas of the Thames First Nation, Ontario, Canada, provides that "every member/citizen of the Chippewas of the Thames First Nation is equal before and under the laws of the Chippewas Thames First Nation, without discrimination or prejudice, including the fish."[52] It's not a leap of logic to see that fish can have rights as citizens because they are understood as persons standing in relationship to all other citizens of the First Nation. In 2018, the White Earth Band of Ojibwe adopted a law recognizing that

> Manoomin, or wild rice, within the White Earth Reservation possesses inherent rights to exist, flourish, regenerate, and evolve, as well as inherent rights to restoration, recovery, and preservation. These include, but are not limited to, the right to pure water and freshwater habitat; the right to a healthy

> climate system and a natural environment free from human-caused global warming impacts and emissions; the right to be free from patenting; as well as rights to be free from infection, infestation, or [genetic] drift by any means of genetically-engineered organisms.[53]

In 2019 the Yurok Tribe of California adopted a resolution to recognize the rights of the Klamath River to "exist, flourish, and naturally evolve, to have a clean and healthy environment free from pollutants; to have a stable environment free from human-caused climate change impacts; and to be free from contamination by genetically engineered organisms." The Council codified this five years later by "establishing Tribal law which will grant the Klamath River, its ecosystem, and species the rights of personhood," enabling legal action "against entities inflicting harm in violation of the Klamath River, its ecosystem, and species rights."[54] Again, in theory anyone might file suit on behalf of the Klamath River against any party, government, corporation, or individual. The "rights of nature" is clearly an emerging front that will have important lessons for all Tribes.

In 1985, I was driving in the country on Pine Ridge Reservation, and I happened upon an elderly man standing in the middle of the road, waving his hat at me. When I stopped, he said something to the effect of, "Nephew [he used the English word], drive me to Porcupine." It didn't matter that I'm not Lakota, not even Indian; all that mattered was that I was a (younger) person on the road with a functioning vehicle, and from whom he needed help. In other words, I was a *relative* in precisely the way Ella Deloria described it, and he was calling on me *to be a good relative*. Please, don't reduce this invocation of "we are all related" to the kind of sociality that uttering words like "bro" or "bud" are meant to enact in the mainstream society. In Indigenous communities, even when uttered in English, a kinship term goes far beyond merely being chummy.

With one word, that Elder summoned an entire worldview into immediate, practical presence, and called on a living—if at-risk—moral order. What's more, it is a moral order that is compelling even for many non-Indigenous people, since even though mainstream society has "modernized" kinship to the point that it excludes most human others and all more-than-humans, everybody understands the basic idea "we are all related," and many sense its universal meaning. Even some western philosophers have argued as much.[55] The challenge Vine Deloria, Jr. gave to Native communities is to find practical and concrete ways to *institutionalize* the ability of people to call, and act, on kinship relations, to bring it back from the "informal" or "private" action of people into the center of public life and civic responsibility in Tribes and Native communities. Both the world and our everyday lives would be better if Tribes—and all of us—could make progress on meeting Deloria's challenge. We need it more now than we ever have, just as we have more to learn from the ancestors.

CHAPTER 33

INDIAN CHILD WELFARE, TRIBAL SOVEREIGNTY, AND THE PREEMINENCE OF THE TRIBAL-STATE AXIS

Céline Planchou

"To be an Indian in modern American society is in a very real sense to be unreal and ahistorical."[1] I was a young French student in an English studies department who had just started to specialize in US history and who had recently joined the CSIA-Nitassinan (Comity in Solidarity with the Indigenous Peoples of the Americas) in Paris when I first encountered Vine Deloria, Jr.'s words. Notions of Tribal sovereignty and Tribal self-determination slowly made their way into my mind, yet they did not seem to find echoes in the classes I attended on US contemporary history. If they were mentioned at all, Native peoples only resurfaced in the 1960s and 1970s and were described as another ethnic minority whose members were fighting for integration and equal civil rights within the US constitutional framework. Issues pertaining to treaty rights, Native nationhood, and territories were indeed unreal, and did not seem to exist or matter in modern American society.

As I struggled to grasp the multifaceted and convoluted status of Native Nations and individuals in today's United States (which was not made easy by my upbringing within a highly centralized French Republic model that tends to equate equality with uniformity and does not encourage the expression of collective political rights), Deloria's writings always challenged me and helped flesh out complex legal and political intricacies, making the issues accessible without oversimplification. With his help, I came to enjoy the complexities of dissecting and trying to make sense of federal Indian laws and policies.

This essay will attempt to navigate the legal maze surrounding Indian child welfare. First, I will focus on the maze prior the adoption of the Indian Child Welfare Act (ICWA),[2] exploring how the legal confusion paved the way for the massive removal of Indian children from their families. Then, I will turn to how ICWA as an important piece of legislation favors the expression of Tribal sovereignty. Eventually, drawing from Deloria's recommendation for Tribes to develop more amicable relations with state governments,[3] I will examine the ambivalence of the Tribal-state axis's preeminence in Indian child welfare. I feel honored to have the opportunity to be part of this collection devoted to Vine Deloria's legacy, and I hope these pages will live up to the task I was entrusted with.

The Pre-ICWA Legal Maze: State Institutions' Twisted Path to Steal Native Children

A legal maze has always been at play in the sphere of Indian child welfare—a world of overlapping and confounding legal orders and conflicts between the multiple dimensions of Native children's legal and political status. As US citizens, their well-being depends on the mainstream US child welfare apparatus that involves both the federal government and state institutions. In this way, they are entitled to child welfare funds deriving from the Social Security Act. Yet federal responsibility toward Native American children also derives from their special status as members of nations that have a treaty-based relationship with the United States. In this way, Bureau of Indian Affairs (BIA) child welfare services have their origins in federal trust obligations. Finally, Native American children are also members of Tribal Nations, and, as such, their well-being should primarily rely on Tribal institutions.

To complicate matters further, aside from the complex interplay between these different dimensions of legal and political status, the mainstream US child welfare system is itself quite intricate and involves various governmental actors. According to the division of power between the federal and state governments, child welfare is primarily in the hands of state institutions. Depending on the state, the apparatus is more or less decentralized and thus can also rest on local governments. This added dimension complicates things even more. These agencies exist at the crossroads of social work and justice, and hence they rely on rules and oversight from both the bureaucratic and judicial spheres.

The legal maze of Indian child welfare has been mapped and followed differently across time. Thus, power dynamics within the federal-Tribal-state triangle have constantly been reshaped. The federal government has been instrumental in these ever-changing movements, oscillating between two tendencies. On the one hand, it pushed for the integration of Indian child welfare services within the general apparatus and insisted on the preeminence of state responsibility for Native American children. On the other hand, it recognized the right of Tribal Nations to organize for the welfare of their children. Based on this understanding, it established that some American children have an essential legal tie to their Tribe, thus pushed for the development of specific Indian child welfare services both within reservations and outside Tribal territories.

In the middle of the twentieth century, when the BIA started to articulate a specific policy toward dependent Native children within its newly created branch of welfare, the integration alternative was clearly encouraged. For decades, most minors had been forced into BIA boarding schools. Little more than reeducation and labor camps, by the 1950s most of these so-called schools were closed or in the process of closing. Without these options, BIA social workers sought new placement options for the children who, according to their standards, could not go back "safely" to their homes or who were orphans.[4]

The federal agency chose to align with mainstream child welfare practices by turning to services that supposedly re-created what they deemed a good family life; that is, foster care and adoption. But instead reforming to become a proper placement agency, the BIA decided to take advantage of states' existing resources and encouraged more state intervention into the lives of Native families. To justify this orientation, it insisted on US citizenship as being the prime source of public responsibility toward dependent Native children.[5] In other words, Indian Child Welfare services were to be excluded from the array of federal services that derive from federal trust obligations. Thus, they were gradually integrated into the mainstream system and fell under the responsibility of states.

However, the administrative attempt to further involve state institutions was never statutorily sanctioned by Congress, and the implementation of the new policy proved chaotic. Some states rejected the idea of prime responsibility as they thought it brought a too-heavy financial burden. So they went on considering Indian child welfare as essentially a federal matter.[6] Yet, according to the new rules, as US citizens, Native children were entitled to a share of the money that states received for child welfare services and that flowed through the Social Security Act, even if they resided on reservations.[7] Could states legally exclude themselves from Indian child welfare issues without denying Native children access to these funds? Other states assumed prime responsibility through administrative agreements with the BIA but understood it as de facto overriding Tribal authority; state norms and forums were then used to decide placements.[8]

One may notice that nothing is said in these agreements about federal trust obligations. It seems that the transfer of authority somehow "erased" these obligations, but there was no way to cut the special legal tie that existed between Native children and their Tribal nation. State institutions readily ignored this reality when they made decisions affecting Native American families. Indian child welfare policies in the middle of the twentieth century testify to the inability of US institutions to articulate and reconcile the multiple dimensions of Native individuals' statuses. On the one hand, if states were to recognize the special status of these children and allow Tribal institutions to be involved in their well-being, then they stood to lose access to the federal money that followed the children as US citizens. On the other hand, if states cooperated with the BIA and assumed responsibility over Native children, their special status, along with funding, disappeared. This illustrates the either/or logic that was described by Vine Deloria, Jr. when one aspect of Native-American individuals' multidimensional status is used "as an excuse" to hinder another.[9]

What was clear is the constant disregard for Tribal nations as legitimate actors in the decisions affecting their minor members. Indeed, the inherent right of Tribal nations to organize for the welfare of their children according to their own norms had never been expressly restrained by Congress when the BIA launched its new child welfare policy. Except in the states in which Public Law 280[10] was applied and where civil matters now fell under state jurisdiction, from the moment a child was domiciled on a reservation, he or she should fall under Tribal jurisdiction if intervention in the family seemed necessary. Yet, as we have seen, things were more complex, and Tribal institutions did not necessarily have the means to exercise that right.

In the 1950s, even if some modern Tribal governments had adopted the parens patriae doctrine and established the public responsibility of the Tribe to limit family sovereignty in the interest of children,[11] Tribal child welfare practices remained highly informal and relied heavily on solidarities within extended families. In accordance with Tribal cultural norms, few Tribes had, for instance, adopted procedures that totally severed parent-child relations and "freed" children for full adoptions. Tribal child welfare practices were often rated as inadequate by US institutions, and when the BIA started to align on US mainstream child welfare mechanisms—mechanisms that necessarily involve the judicial sphere—it chose to turn toward the courts, a forum deemed more "capable" to secure placements and terminate parental rights.

In 1951, E. Morgan Pryse, then director of the BIA Portland Area, explained that the BIA relied entirely on Idaho courts for children on the Nez Perce and Kootenai reservations because the two Tribes had no Tribal courts.[12] The absence of a Tribal court was thus considered as a rationale for skirting Tribal authority. However, even the existence of a Tribal court was not enough to ensure that Tribal decisions were enforced. In the same letter, Pryse added that because they lacked resources, different Tribes in the area had tried to place minor members in state group homes. Yet the placement orders were always rejected by states because they emanated from Tribal courts. No legal framework existed at the time to organize Tribal-state relationships, and nothing encouraged state courts to give full faith and credit to Tribal decisions. To lessen the risks of having these decisions rejected, the BIA pushed for referring Native children directly to state courts. Tribal institutions were thus induced to transform and move toward more formalized and more "acceptable" child welfare practices. Yet, this gradual alignment was still not enough to allow Native Nations to exercise their inherent right to organize for the welfare of their children. Tribal sovereignty kept on being eroded while Native American children were increasingly placed in non-Indian foster care and adoptive families by state courts. In this way, the administrative and judicial maze that prevailed in the sphere of Indian child welfare more than seventy years ago paved the way for the massive removal of Native American children.

ICWA: An Important Piece of Legislation in Favor of Tribal Sovereignty

In the late 1960s, families across Indian Country mobilized against the growing number of non-Native placements by state institutions. Led by parents and other relatives contesting placement decisions, a national campaign calling for federal action was launched that led to special hearings in the Senate Subcommittee on Indian Affairs in 1974.[13] In 1976, the Supreme Court asserted Tribal exclusive jurisdiction over adoption proceedings occurring on reservations and involving an Indian child in *Fisher v. District Court*.[14] Two years later, Congress enacted the Indian Child Welfare Act, which recognized the unique and essential legal tie binding Native American children to their Tribal Nation by establishing minimum standards for the removal of children from their families by state institutions.

The purpose of the federal ICWA legislation was twofold. First, it attempted to clarify the jurisdictional framework by establishing that children who reside on reservations fall under exclusive Tribal jurisdiction. While concurrent state and Tribal jurisdiction exists, whenever a procedure of foster care, preadoptive or adoptive placement, or termination of parental rights affecting a Native child living off-reservation is initiated in a state court, if the child is enrolled or eligible for enrollment in a Tribe, that Tribe has the right to be notified, have the case transferred to Tribal court, or intervene in the state procedure. If the case is not transferred, different standards have to be followed by the state, such as respecting ICWA placement preferences or ensuring that "active efforts" were dispensed before moving toward a permanent separation. Second, the 1978 legislation released specific federal funds to encourage the development of Tribal child welfare services.

In many respects, ICWA is an important piece of legislation that helps in maintaining the distinct political existence of Tribal Nations in the United States and favors the expression of Tribal sovereignty.[15] In *The Nations Within*, Deloria explains that "few of the funds and programs that Indians received during the sixties and the seventies were given to them because the government felt the responsibility to fulfill treaty obligations" and because of the special relation between the United States and Native Nations.[16] This clearly established that "Congress, through statutes, treaties, and the general course of dealing with Indian Tribes, has assumed the responsibility for the protection and preservation of Indian Tribes and their resources," and that "there is no resource that is more vital to the continued existence and integrity of Indian Tribes than their children."[17] By granting specific funds to preserve Tribal integrity, ICWA is indeed part of these few attempts. It enabled many Tribes to reaffirm Tribal inherent powers that were de facto overridden and constantly neglected.

The judicial component of child welfare was instrumental in this process. In the case of Tribes that had been impacted by PL 280, child welfare largely contributed to the reestablishment of judicial forums that had collapsed following the federal statute of 1953. Still, as Deloria explains, one must not forget that Tribal courts are forums originally designed by external forces that have overseen necessary acts of transformation but which can be at odds with traditional ways of resolving disputes.[18] Especially after the adoption of the Indian Civil Rights Act of 1968 when "the informality of Indian life that had been the repository of cultural traditions and customs was suddenly abolished, and in its place came the rigid requirements that were necessary to identify those instances in which the actions of the Tribal government impinged upon the rights of Tribal members."[19]

In the sphere of child welfare, Tribal courts clearly became instrumental in maintaining the rights and responsibilities of Native families—mutual responsibilities they traditionally had for one another within Tribal communities. But is the increasing role of Tribal courts enough to conclude that ICWA favored the expression of Tribal sovereignty and enabled Tribes to "act in a national capacity?"[20] As mentioned, the BIA policy launched in the 1950s had already encouraged Tribes to formalize their child welfare practices. ICWA, by placing Tribal courts at the heart of the decisions affecting Native children, reinforced this formalization process. This time, the power of Tribal governments to organize for the welfare of their children is expressly articulated by Congress as stemming from inherent Tribal powers, thus powers that predate the United States and exist to some extent independently of the US constitutional framework.

This means that the laws and norms codified by Tribal governments dealing with child welfare should be able to vary from mainstream US child welfare norms and still be given credit by US institutions. For instance, whereas the Adoption and Safe Families Act (ASFA)[21] requires a state to file a petition to terminate a parent's parental rights to "free" a child for adoption when that child has been in foster care for fifteen of the most recent twenty-one months, this does not apply to Tribes unless they have adopted similar requirements. In the same way, some Tribes have enacted child welfare codes that encourage existing customary practices and rely on extended families' strengths as valuable resources for dependent children.[22] Such evolutions can be interpreted as acts of national capacity and seem to be in keeping with Deloria's remarks that "more extensive development of Tribal customs as the basis for a Tribal court's decision will enable these institutions to draw even closer to the people" and be more effective.[23]

Not only does ICWA favor the expression of Tribal sovereignty, one may even say that, by turning the special status of Native children into a significant element in the shaping of Indian child welfare, it extends Tribal authority outside reservations since Tribes now have the right to intervene in state cases involving their minor members wherever the latter reside in the United States. The legal tie that binds children to their Tribe does not stop being legally significant when they reside off-reservation. In other words, the legal and political attributes of Tribal distinct existence are not confined to reservations.

The issue of adoption is quite telling in this respect. Today, US institutions and non-Indian parents who want to adopt a Native child have to take the distinct political existence of the Tribe to which that child belongs into consideration. Although they are not equated with international procedures, these adoptions still reflect the national dimension of Tribal political entities, which has not been without tensions. The federal legislation has often been under attack, inaccurately accused of creating legal barriers between US citizens—here, parents and an adoptive child on the basis of race—yet the constitutionality of ICWA has so far been upheld by federal courts. In 2021, the Fifth Circuit Court of Appeals reversed a 2018 Texas district court decision that considered that ICWA placement requirements were based on race and as such violated the US Constitution. Although striking down a few important provisions of the federal statute,[24] the decision established that ICWA placement preferences reflect the special legal and political status of Native children and do not amount to a race-based discrimination, thus reaffirming the constitutionality of the 1978 federal legislation.[25] The Supreme Court upheld this decision in *Haaland v. Brackeen* on June 15, 2023. The 7–2 decision, in an opinion authored by Justice Barrett, affirmed ICWAs constitutionality and ensured continued protections.[26]

The Ambivalence of the Tribal-State Axis Preeminence in the Sphere of ICWA

In *The Nations Within*, Deloria recommended that Tribes develop more amicable relations with state governments.[27] This seems particularly relevant to Indian child welfare. Indeed, to be able to exercise the rights established by the 1978 statute, Tribal governments are expressly encouraged to engage in a dialogue with states.[28] Yet, the contours of that dialogue are left unclear. Despite the new jurisdictional framework and the clause that requires states to give full faith and credit to Tribal decisions,[29] much confusion remains in the modern legal maze, and the Tribal-state axis is left to compensate and fill the vacuum of the sometimes-obscure language of the federal law.

Interactions have first been necessary to facilitate the administration of Tribal child welfare services and enable Tribes to have access to federal money flowing through the Social Security Act, especially through Title IV-E, which mainly finances foster care placements and which, up until 2008, Tribes could not receive directly.[30] In 2013, there were ninety-eight Tribal-state agreements that had been signed between 267 Tribes and 16 states.[31] Dialogue has also been instrumental concerning concurrent jurisdiction and the handling of cases initiated by state institutions. How can the latter determine if a child is a member of a Tribe or eligible for membership? How is the Tribe to be notified? How are transfers to Tribal courts organized? If there is no transfer, how is it ensured that Tribes can still intervene in state procedures and that ICWA regulations (the placement preferences or the "active efforts" requirement, for instance) are followed by state social workers and judges? These are only a few questions that were left unclear and that are all the more important to deal with since the federal statute does not articulate any sanctions if states do not comply.

Although necessary, engaging in dialogue is not easy. Both Tribal and state governments must be willing to perceive the other as a legitimate negotiating partner and to move away from a long-established conflictual relational pattern. In many regional contexts, relations have remained antagonistic and issues are often dealt with in courts.[32] In this way, various state courts have used different doctrines or legal exceptions to try and limit the applicability of the federal law, such as the doctrine of substantial compliance[33] or the Existing Indian Family exception.[34] When a more constructive dialogue has been established, it leads to more compliance with ICWA.[35] Six states have so far enacted their own version of the 1978 federal law,[36] while multilateral Tribal/state agreements have been negotiated to try and ease tensions.

An example of such agreements is the Tribal/State Indian Child Welfare Agreement, first signed in 1994 and amended in 2007, between Minnesota and the different Dakota and Ojibwe Tribes in the area. It appears as a compromise intended to clarify ICWA's gray areas and ambiguities in ways that are mutually beneficial.[37] For instance, it enabled Tribes and the state to try and solve the difficult articulation between ICWA's "active efforts" requirement and ASFA's "reasonable efforts" standard. According to the agreement, the different parties agree that "active efforts" means "a rigorous and concerted level of case work that uses the prevailing social and cultural values, conditions and way of life of the Indian child's Tribe to preserve the child's family and to prevent the placement of an Indian child" and that it "sets a higher standard than 'reasonable efforts' to preserve the family, to prevent the break-up of the family, and to reunify the family."[38]

Even when more amicable Tribal-state relations improve compliance with ICWA, the dominance of the Tribal-state axis in the sphere of child welfare is not without drawbacks. It generates disparities and inequalities according to the interactions that exist in the different regional contexts, which lies in opposition to the intent of the 1978 statute. Indeed, shouldn't the minimum standards set in the law be applied to all the procedures involving Native American children, no matter the state they reside in? If not, then Tribal inherent powers, although articulated as such in 1978, are de facto transformed and become contingent upon Tribal-state relations.

The dual component of child welfare, both judicial and administrative, further contributes to maintaining the ambivalence. We have seen earlier that ICWA clearly favors the expression of Tribal sovereignty, even extending it beyond the limits of reservations, especially through the authority of Tribal courts and the adoption of more culturally relevant Tribal child welfare norms. Yet when it comes to the power to administer child welfare services, it appears that decisions are often constrained by a recurring lack of resources, and that Tribal institutions have to accept their sovereignty to be somewhat eroded in order to have access to the necessary funding.

In Title IV-E Tribal/state agreements, for instance, Tribal child welfare services are often described as being considered as an integral part of state welfare systems.[39] Do these services then become an instrumentality of state governments? What standards do they have to meet for the agreement to be renewed? Does it mean that their administrative powers are considered as contractual and delegated powers? Tribal Nations are thus themselves maintained in an ambivalent position, both able to perform acts of national capacity and yet pushed to integrate and "adopt self-government within the existing federal structure,"[40] which, in the sphere of child welfare, necessarily involves state institutions. What's the point in exercising one's authority and developing norms that are more adequate with one's culture if Tribes then do not have the administrative and financial means to apply these norms?

This ambivalence can be interpreted as another attempt by the federal government to make sure that Tribal distinct existence does not elude its control. After having enhanced Tribal sovereignty with the adoption of ICWA, it has limited its expression by confronting it with state powers and "forc[ing] federalism"[41] upon Tribal nations. States now act as counterweights containing Tribes' inherent powers to make sure that the products of these specific powers are "compatible with the goals and policies of the larger political power."[42] This process is even more problematic since the federal government has never established if the intervention of states in Indian child welfare matters meant that the latter consequently inherited federal trust obligations. In regional contexts where more amicable relations have developed, Tribes have sometimes been able to bring states to expressly endorse these obligations, yet this should not be left to the discretion of states.[43] All the more since there is still a fundamental inequality between Tribes and states. Indeed, the permanent status of states is guaranteed by the US Constitution while the existence of Tribes as distinct political entities is extra-constitutional and still subjected to the plenary powers of Congress.

The federal government should deploy more legal means to make sure that the minimum standards established in 1978 are met by state institutions. To reduce tensions and encourage Tribal-state dialogue beyond regional contexts, some inter-Tribal and interstate mechanism might come up with common and concerted ways of resolving issues left unclear by ICWA. Yet such a mechanism could only be beneficial if the federal government clarifies the issue of trust protections in the sphere of Indian child welfare. As David E. Wilkins and K. Tsianina Lomawaima explain, "The privileging of states in the federalist model" must not mean "the treaty and trust commitments of the United States—as a nation—towards Tribes [are] unilaterally terminated simply by delegating those commitments to states."[44] Tribes have to be guaranteed that whenever they deal with a state over the future of their dependent minor members, and no matter the state they deal with, trust protections are not dismissed and their right to maintain a distinct political existence, as "nations within" is respected.

CHAPTER 34

WHY THIS MEMORIAL?

A Statue Dedication Honoring Community and Friendship in Sheridan, Wyoming, October 9, 2023

Vivian Arviso

Today in New Mexico and in several other states, it is Indigenous Peoples' Day. A day recognizing the contributions of Native Americans and the land of their ancestors.

Welcome, everyone, and thank you for attending this dedication of the All American Indian Days Memorial. I lived in this town when I was Miss Indian America in 1960. Jack and Doris Mullinax, and their children Bob, David, and Nancy, became my host family. Jack was a strong supporter of All American Indian Days.

This Memorial site honors the hundreds of people, non-Natives and Native Americans, who worked together in an interracial effort to improve race relations. This is an untold story for all generations.

Sixteen-year-old Lucy Yellowmule, a Crow high school student, entered the contest for Rodeo Queen at the 1951 Sheridan, Wyoming, Rodeo. She won this prestigious title, an unexpected upset for local ranchers' daughters. No doubt the news of the first Native woman to hold this title swept across Indian Country.

Like many border towns to reservations, Sheridan had signs in its stores targeting Indians. "No Dogs or Indians Allowed" turned away a young Santee Sioux Episcopal priest traveling with his pregnant wife seeking lodging in Sheridan after a long day's drive. He later became Bishop Harold Jones, Bishop of the Diocese of South Dakota. This sad memory stayed with him throughout his life as did his skin color.

Although Lucy was the Rodeo Queen, these signs still meant she and Native people could not do business in Sheridan.

Natives were seen as drunks, having poor hygiene, with different ways of dressing, and lacking English-speaking skills. Unfortunately, this negative environment of racial tensions is similar to what we see today on television and social media.

Howard Sinclair, a journalist with the *Sheridan Press*, saw this dilemma. Raised near the Assiniboine Sioux, he had been adopted within their traditions and never forgot this connection with them. He saw the potential to change the negative treatment of Native Americans who came to Sheridan. Don Diers, a photographer, and the Reverend Ray Clark were key supporters. They envisioned a community environment that was welcoming.

Together, Sinclair and Lucy Yellowmule started a campaign for the removal of the offensive signs. Lucy met with people in their homes and at civic clubs. The signs came down.

Since understanding came about through meeting Lucy and listening to her talk, Sinclair consulted people at Crow about his vision to eliminate racial discrimination against Native Americans. Sinclair founded All American Indian Days, but its backbone came from several Crow individuals who helped grow it into a major production over the years. They shared a background of traveling in Europe and the US. They knew Sheridan and knew that non-Natives lacked basic knowledge about their Native American neighbors. Thanks to the success of Lucy Yellowmule, the role of Miss Indian America became a model for positive race relations.

Crow leadership can be credited for the success of the event. Donald Deernose served as chair of the Indian Executive Committee for more than two decades, building a network across Indian Country and bringing thousands of Native people to Sheridan. Dr. Joe Medicine Crow was the program chair incorporating traditional and cultural activities into the program. Thomas Yellowtail was a spiritual leader who supported everyone. His wife, Susie Yellowtail, is distinguished as the first Native American woman to become a registered nurse and who became a beloved chaperone of Miss Indian America, as did Agnes Deernose, wife of Donald.

The Kalif Shriners provided huge support to Sinclair who teamed up with JC Rhodes, a local auto dealer. This first All American Indian Days featured a Miss Indian America pageant at Third and Broadway, just down the street.

All American Indian Days became a celebration of traditions and cultures for Native people. Many camped in the iconic Tipi Village. At least fifty Miss Indian America contestants competed each year, sometimes more than a hundred. An Outstanding Indian of the Year was honored for their work on behalf of Native people. The list includes a congressman, a state Supreme Court judge, a journalist, culture bearers, and many others.

Participants brought amazing energy and enjoyment to social dancing, singing, horsemanship, foot races, artwork, and Tribal storytelling. Contests were held for lance throwing, bow and arrow shooting, tipi races, hide races, and other athletic skills. The oldest Native persons were honored in the parade. Survivors of the Battle of Little Big Horn were also honored. The Sunday religious service invited Native clergy and choirs. To end the story of Bishop Harold Jones, organizers invited him back to Sheridan to conduct one of those services.

My memory of 1960 was riding in the half-mile women's horse race when the Real Birds entered a horse but didn't have a jockey. I also played a memorable game of Indian Football on Barney Old Coyote's team. What fun and enjoyment there was for everyone.

The management of All American Indian Days demonstrated an example of racial harmony unique for its time. The board of directors consisted of non-Natives basically for logistics while the Indian Executive Committee provided the program.

Imagine putting together a production of this scale with an Indian Executive Committee scattered across the US and a local board with volunteers publicizing and preparing the fairgrounds. These unpaid volunteers were key to the success of All American Indian Days. No one had any idea how many tourists or Native people would show up. Each side had to trust the other to do their part.

Emmie Mygatt, a key supporter for Miss Indian America appearances in New York City, wrote an article in 1960 for the *Sheridan Press*. She said "For the last hundred years and on a national basis—experts with theories have bungled the job of bringing the two races together. Now, let's see what a bunch of amateurs can do. Crazy? Maybe, but here in Sheridan, we are willing to take a dare and are right on the edge of making this thing happen."[1]

Sixteen years later, in 1976, Dick Redburn wrote in *The Weekender* about the vision of All American Indian Days. He brought up the dream of Sinclair and how it had not yet been fully realized but the goals remain. He described that the board of directors included Native people along with non-Natives. He ended his article saying, "No matter what the future of Indian Days, its vision will continue. Indian and whites will always try to improve the human relationship no matter what the future of Indian Days."[2] Both writers captured the sentiment of Sheridan and its commitment to support All American Indian Days each year.

Finances were always an issue. The local chapter of the American Association of University Women pledged to pay off nearly $40,000 in debt from the first four years. Contrast this to today's dollars, this committed group of women did it in ten years. Most of the time, a bank balance was less than $10. Loans from individuals and the bank saved the day. Some would pull the plug on such an event. Not Sheridan. The tenacity of this town is noteworthy. They refused to lose their vision to build understanding between races and kept the dream for thirty-one years.

This Memorial honors the people of Sheridan, and those throughout Sheridan and Johnson counties who volunteered year after year. This Memorial also honors the Native American leadership who believed that sharing their culture helped build this understanding. Sheridan was a town that welcomed them. Sheridan became the center of attention for scholars, activists, and Tribal leaders who discussed Native issues. So many of those involved are no longer here, but the town's legacy remains.

I want to acknowledge Sarah Johnson Luther, former Miss Indian America XIV, and a part of the John and Virigina Patton family. After she saw nothing to remind the public about All American Indian Days, she had the vision to initiate this Memorial. Now, this visual public record can speak to this memory.

The Honoring Project is a Wyoming organization. We want to thank the Brinton Museum for being our fiscal agent. We owe so much to our advisors, Kendra Heimbuck, executive director of the Brinton Museum, and Mary Jane Edwards, executive director of the Jentel Foundation. Our beloved advisor, the late Father J. Powell, who passed away recently, was deeply involved with All American Indian Days for fifteen years. We remember him reflecting upon his first time seeing the Tipi Village. There, standing the tallest and largest was a Blackfeet tipi with its vivid colors. This is now part of the tipi panel on the Memorial.

We want to thank Jon DeCelles who brought his skills as a master sculptor to create *Mitakuye Oyasin*. He comes from the Aaniih, the White Clay People, and Assiniboine Sioux. Greg Nickerson, local historian, pointed out that Jon's selection as sculptor brought full circle a connection with Howard Sinclair's adoption by an Assiniboine Sioux.

We invite you to enter the circle and examine this Memorial. The circle opens with sidewalks to the four directions just as Native people came from all directions to Sheridan. The sculpture, *Mitakuye Oyasin*, translates as "We Are All Related." Its hoop and colors reflect the races of humanity. Two other panels tell the story of All American Indian Days through the Outstanding Indian of the Year and the Miss Indian America pageant. The panel facing West honors Donald Deernose who began each evening of All American Indian Days with the pipe ceremony. What better way to honor the friendship and interracial harmony between Native Americans and the people of Sheridan.

Today, across our country, the message of All American Indian Days is just as critical as it was in 1953. The Honoring Project commemorates these extraordinary people. All American Indian Days is an important story for Wyoming and our nation. We see much more to do.

How fitting it is that this Memorial is across from the Sheridan Inn: a historic place for Native people and the Wild West Show of the late 1800s.

How fitting it is that this Memorial is near the street where the first Miss Indian America pageant was held in a parking lot.

How fitting it is that this is near the historic locomotive whose railway system crossed Native American lands. The railroad provided a livelihood for generations of Native families who worked on it.

I want to acknowledge Mr. Drake Hill of the Hill Law Firm in Cheyenne, whose wisdom and guidance were invaluable in this journey. Truly, we would not be here today if not for him.

I also want to acknowledge the individual donors and the foundations who responded to our fundraising efforts. Without their support, we would not be here today.

Lastly, to acknowledge the Rotary Club and the City of Sheridan Mayor Roger Miller and Richard Bridger and both city councils who provided this location for this Memorial.

Our memory of All American Indian Days is now here at this Memorial site. It is a beautiful story of a heroic town that worked with their Native neighbors to eliminate racial discrimination. This Memorial commemorates the many ordinary people who believed in a better world and who gave all they could to make good things happen.

Let's keep their dream alive!

CHAPTER 35

CONTINUOUS KNOWLEDGE

Of Living Stone's Cover Art

James Johnson

Our traditional Tlingit knowledge has been passed down from our ancestors to carry forward. Our art is alive, it tells our history of who we are as a people, and where we come from. This knowledge is in constant movement, passing from generation to generation.

Continuous Knowledge Original Painting—US Department of the Interior Museum, Washington, D.C.—Permanent Collection. The work is used with the kind permission of the leaders of the Central Council of the Tlingit and Haida Indian Tribes of Alaska.

James Johnson is an award-winning Tlingit artist and carver, born and raised in Juneau, Alaska. He belongs to the Dakl'aweidi Clan. His family lineage is from the Xutsnoowu Kwaan.

ACKNOWLEDGMENTS

Each of our contributors is to be commended for their dedication to the ideals of the project and patience with the process. We also deeply appreciate the sound advice, insights, and kindness of Sam Deloria and Vivian Arviso. Many others, including the late Senator John McCoy, Mona M. Smith, Jeffery Veregge, Willie and Peggan Frank, Ginger Awapuhi Dunnill, Tina Delisle, Vince Diaz, Matika Wilbur, Ashley Fairbanks, La quen náay Liz Medicine Crow, Nick Tilsen, Crystal Echo Hawk, Dan Wildcat, Dallas Goldtooth, Wenona Singel, Carmen and Gary "Litefoot" Davis, Patricia Albers, and Tassie Hannah offered ideas and words of encouragement. DeLanna Studi's performance in her play *And So We Walked* on kinship and belonging was inspiring and her company delightful.

Many thanks to the Lummi Nation and Northwest Indian College faculty and staff, Dr. Victoria Walsey, Dr. Emma Norman, Dr. Justin Guillory, and library director Valerie McBeth. They house Vine's personal library just as he left it (including his old recliner and the lingering smell of Pall Malls) and continue to organize and host the annual Vine Deloria, Jr. Indigenous Studies Symposium that has convened at NWIC for nearly twenty years.

We offer gratitude and respect to the leaders of the Central Council of the Tlingit and Haida Indian Tribes of Alaska for allowing James Johnson's *Continuous Knowledge* to grace the cover of this book. They commissioned the work to represent the Generations Southeast Community Learning Center, a school based in traditional values created through an alliance of six nations: Central Council of the Tlingit and Haida Indian Tribes of Alaska, Chilkoot Indian Association, Douglas Indian Association, Hoonah Indian Association, Organized Village of

Saxman, and Skagway (Skaqua) Traditional Council. The Generations Southeast mission statement beautifully expresses the spirit and intent behind this collection of essays: *For us knowledge is a perpetual process that never stops. Today, we acknowledge our communities have changed, but we can never lose our methods of learning.*

The support of family and friends has been essential, including David's little brother, Craig, his aunt Nancy and uncle Don, Cathy Cory and Ruben Rodriguez, Mark and Carla Foreman Maslin, Gene and Alice Sloan, David Gibbs, Élise Marienstras, Céline Piétrois, Terry and Lori Speagle Price, Chris Gleason, Julio and Maralise Hood Quan, Amy Ruble, Rachel Smith, Doug and Laura Birch Marty, Danny Bell, and Harry and Etsuko Locklear. Our grandsons, Kai and Levi, keep us laughing.

We have been welcomed by great folks in a now white-supremacist-monument-free Richmond, including old friends, Matt Latimer and Holly Mortlock, and new ones, Stephanie Trent, Cristina Stanciu, Lucretia McCulley, Dan Ream, Marion and Greg Werkheiser, and the best neighbors anyone could wish for—such fine evenings on Mary Margaret and Bob Bowlings' porch, great suppers with newlyweds Cindy Norwood and Eduardo Marquez, and Mardi Gras celebrations with ever-gracious hosts Wayne Gautier and Gregory Frank.

David Wilkins would also like to thank Vine, and is grateful, too, for the ongoing support of his dean, Sandra Peart, of the Jepson School of Leadership Studies. Finally, he is most appreciative of Shelly's love and writing.

Shelly thanks Sam Deloria for his groundbreaking work on Tribal–state relations that guided and inspired her. Against all odds, she, a Sam-Delorian, fell for David, a Vine-Delorian. She is also grateful for her dear friend and mentor, the late Senator John McCoy, without whom she would never have taken this path. John always took credit for introducing her to David, joking that theirs was the only marriage to result from a shared interest in Public Law 280.

We are fortunate to work together on this and many other projects. The burdens of this world are lighter when one is lucky enough to share them with deep love and respect.

APPENDIX

THE TRIBAL-COMMONWEALTH ACCORD

An Agreement between Tribal Nations & the Commonwealth of Virginia

(2021 Draft Document)

Preamble

This Tribal-Commonwealth Accord affirms government-to-government relations between the Commonwealth of Virginia and the seven federally recognized Indigenous nations located within its present-day boundaries.

These Tribal Nations have wielded sovereign powers since time immemorial. The Chickahominy, Eastern Chickahominy, Monacan, Nansemond, Pamunkey, Rappahannock, and Upper Mattaponi, each a distinct polity, have maintained relations with one another across time. Over the past five centuries, all have sought to institute consistent diplomatic ties with shifting realms of outside governance; first, colonial authorities, followed by the establishment of the Commonwealth of Virginia in 1782 and, more recently, through the exercise of full government-to-government relations with the United States of America.

Tribes have created an enduring web of interrelations with relatives, allies, and neighbors, including the Commonwealth, over issues of common concern. This agreement is an acknowledgment of the sanctity of these bonds.

Although the web is strong, to our unending sorrow, history has shown it is also fragile, torn by forces of conquest, erasure, greed, racism, and injustice. Henceforth, all parties formally pledge to respectfully protect and tend these alliances so that the wrongs of the past can never be repeated.

As independent nations, each sovereign Tribe possesses self-determination, knowledge, perspectives, territory, and resources vital for all who live within the boundaries of Virginia. The Commonwealth protects the well-being of its residents under authority granted by the United States Constitution and by the people of the state through its constitution, state laws, and regulations. This agreement declares the shared intention of the signatories to bring their respective powers to bear for the benefit of current and future generations. Each, herein, commits to the creation and maintenance of an ongoing intergovernmental process designed to identify, address, and resolve issues of concern. Herein, are also set forth essential protocols for commencement and maintenance of effective, amicable, and mutually beneficial relations.

The United Nations Declaration on the Rights of Indigenous Peoples states, "…treaties, agreements and other constructive arrangements, and the relationship they represent, are the basis for a strengthened partnership between indigenous peoples and states."

Therefore, let the Tribal-Commonwealth Accord between these federally recognized Tribal Nations and the modern Commonwealth of Virginia as represented by its Governor establish the basis for lasting government-to-government relations bound by respect, deep understanding, and consent that is free, prior, and informed.

Principles & Protocols

Certain solemn bonds are hallmarks of institutionalized intergovernmental relations. For the purposes of this Tribal-Commonwealth Accord, these include the shared promises of mutual respect, recognition of sovereignty, dedication to good-faith action, resolute cooperation, adherence to processes, assurance of accountability, devotion to justice, and never-ending commitment to the pursuit of understanding.

Mutual Respect & Acknowledgment of Sovereign Authorities

The guiding principles of mutual respect and acknowledgment of sovereignty will frame negotiations, cooperation and agreements between the signatories.

- All departments, agencies, offices, and representatives of the Commonwealth of Virginia shall recognize the unique sovereign powers retained and wielded by Tribal Nations since time immemorial as well as any additional powers emanating from their evolving government-to-government relations with the United States of America.
- Tribal Nations through their departments and representatives shall acknowledge the authority of the Commonwealth over state territory, citizenry, and governmental operations.
- Rights, including treaty rights, immunities, sovereign immunities, or jurisdiction are not waived by this agreement.
- Rights and protections afforded Indigenous persons or entities under state or federal law are not waived by this agreement.
- Each government reserves the right to elevate an issue of importance to any decision-making authority of another party, including, when appropriate, an executive office.

Consultation, Cooperation & Consent

The Commonwealth of Virginia through the official actions of its agents, departments, and representatives shall consult and cooperate in the utmost good faith with the Tribal Nations located within its current borders. Such engagement shall be required in order to obtain full, free, and prior consent from Tribal Nations for actions that will affect, or have the potential to affect, their territory, resources, citizenry, or sovereignty.

These include, but are not limited to, actions that will or might impact territorial integrity, health, religious freedom, exercise of civil rights, sacred and historical sites, Indian child welfare, cultural patrimony, subsistence rights, economic well-being and opportunities, taxation, access to quality education, intellectual property, historical records, and the quality of Tribal land, water, air, and wildlife. All materials, documentation, and research practices involving Tribal communities, individuals, assets, and resources will meet or exceed the highest established professional standards.

- **Consultation** is here defined as timely, meaningful engagement and exchange of information prior to any action or proposed action that might affect Tribal interests, territory, resources, citizenry, or sovereignty. To meet this threshold representatives are required to act in the utmost good faith. They will engage in complete, accurate, and transparent communications that allow the time and capacity to review, understand and react accordingly to any issue under consideration. There must be a reasonable opportunity to respond with insight and recommendations on proposed actions to the governmental officials responsible for final decision-making.
- **Cooperation** is the effort to engage with concerned parties in the utmost good faith regarding an issue of mutual interest through adherence to established protocols.
- **Consent** is the power of Tribes, acting in the utmost good faith, to amend, approve or reject a Commonwealth action that might affect their territories, citizenry, sovereignty or resources. Prior, free, and informed consent may only be given after the requirements for consultation and cooperation have been duly met.

Actions & Responsibilities

Those who make pledges of cooperation are obligated to give life to those promises through actions. This agreement will set forth a means by which all parties affirm their commitment to government-to-government relations through work that will lead to mutual benefits for all communities.

Cooperative Plan of Work

The Commonwealth and Tribal Nations agree to modify elements of their respective governmental structures in order to implement the collaborative protocols established in this agreement.

1. The Governor of the Commonwealth shall create a cabinet-level state agency, the Office of Tribal-Commonwealth Relations, headed by the Secretary of Tribal-Commonwealth Relations, adequately and appropriately authorized, funded and staffed to effectively facilitate the implementation and exercise of meaningful government-to-government relations with federally recognized Tribal Nations with the aims of increasing understanding, obviating litigation, improving shared outcomes, and demonstrating sincere respect.
   a) The Secretary of the Office of Tribal-Commonwealth Relations shall:
      i. Have demonstrated experience regarding Indigenous intergovernmental matters and be chosen in consultation with signatory Tribes;
      ii. Be empowered by the Governor with the authority to advise, direct and oversee the processes necessary for the meaningful exercise of government-to-government-relations within each state agency and department including implementation of protocols, training, reporting outcomes, and accountability;
   b) The authority and purposes of the Office of Tribal-Commonwealth Relations shall include:
      i. Ability to exercise decision-making powers and the authority to enter into contracts and negotiations as required to fulfill the duties of the agency;
      ii. Act as Tribal policy and regulatory advisor to the Governor;
         a. Recommend modifications to existing laws and policies affecting Tribes, including promulgation or vetting

of future policies and regulations that relate, either directly or indirectly, to Tribal affairs;

b. Advocate as appropriate for the rights of Tribal Nations within the executive, judicial, legislative, and bureaucratic decision-making processes;

iii. Serve as principal liaison with signatory Native Nations;

a. Coordinate a Sovereign Nations Commonwealth Council for the purposes of providing direct information and guidance to the Governor:

1) The Council shall be comprised of two Tribal representatives from each signatory nation designated in accordance with their respective processes;

2) Terms will be limited to three years with the option for reappointment;

3) Commonwealth Secretaries, Executive Officers, and others with decision-making authority related to an issue of concern shall be directed by the Governor to respond to Council inquiries in a manner consistent with the good-faith protocols established by this accord;

4) The Council, assisted by agency staff, will communicate with Tribes bi-annually to convey up to date information, progress, and concerns;

iv. Convene and coordinate work of the Truth and Reconciliation Commission (see item 5);

v. Direct and coordinate implementation of the Tribal-Commonwealth Accord with all state departments including, but not limited to, those currently organized under the Secretaries of Administration, Agriculture and Forestry, Commerce and Trade, Education, Finance, Health and Human Resources, Natural Resources, Public Safety and Homeland Security, Transportation, Veterans and Defense Affairs, and the Executive Offices of the Attorney General, Lieutenant Governor, and State Inspector General;

vi. Veterans and Defense Affairs, and the Executive Offices of the Attorney General, Lieutenant Governor, and State Inspector General;

a. Develop interdepartmental policies, guidelines, research and reporting methods in consultation with Tribes, agency secretaries, and executive officers;

b. Conduct mandatory employee trainings within state agencies to educate all staff about the responsibilities and benefits inherent in government-to-government relations and to ensure they have the skills required to fulfill these duties;

c. Coordinate the work of all assigned departmental Tribal liaisons and, in the absence of such liaisons, be responsible for soliciting mandatory reports from each Secretary or Executive Officer that will include data compiled by each departmental lead;

vii. Convene an annual meeting to honor the accord and to hear agency reports on actions taken and the statuses of issues of interest;

viii. Complete an annual review to include annual reporting from agencies, councils, and commissions.

2. The Governor of the Commonwealth shall direct Secretaries and Executive Officers and their staff members to assist in accordance with the protocols contained, herein, the Secretary of the Office of Tribal-Commonwealth Relations in advancing the purposes of that agency and ensuring initiatives of that agency are fully coordinated with their own goals and activities.

a) The Governor will require each state departmental entity to work with the Secretary and staff of the Office of Tribal-Commonwealth Relations in order to implement a comprehensive educational training program designed to promote understanding of the workings of government-to-government relations within their own areas of responsibility, and to enable staff to make informed policy and regulatory decisions that consider real or potential impacts to Tribal Nations and their interests;

b) Secretaries and Executive Officers shall direct their staff to respect and acknowledge the culture, traditions, beliefs, governance processes, laws, codes, regulations, and protocols of Tribes and to comply with applicable Tribal laws, codes, and regulations, providing them the resources needed to fulfill such obligations in a meaningful manner;

c) Departmental leads in coordination with the Office of Tribal-Commonwealth Relations will develop efficient and comprehensive mechanisms for fulfillment of these duties including:

   i. Establishment of and adherence to regulations and protocols with Tribal staff or officials regarding communication, consultation, and consent regarding such actions or potential actions that could affect Tribal Nations or their interests including, but not limited to;

      a. Mandatory usage of ethical research practices that meet or exceed the highest recognized professional standards;

      b. Guidelines for identification of any action or proposed action that have the potential to affect a Tribal Nation located within Virginia;

      c. Mandatory staff reporting of these actions or potential actions to the appropriate supervisor;

      d. Mandatory supervisory review, record of decision-making processes, and reporting of a given issue that has the potential to trigger the process of communication, consultation, and consent with a Tribal entity or entities;

   e. Intake and recording procedures for Tribal responses and additional data.

d) Departmental leads will set guidelines and empower staff to communicate openly and directly with their Tribal counterparts for the purposes of sharing information on potential impacts of an agency decision under consideration;
   i. Departmental leads will design procedures based on the understanding that those responsible for an issue area are the best informed and equipped to work directly with their Tribal counterparts;
   ii. Departmental staff will work with their Tribal counterparts to identify areas of mutual benefit, create strategies for success, and avoid escalation of conflict;

e) Departmental leads will track the progress of their workgroups and document these efforts as part of annual report to be formally presented by Secretaries and Executive Officers to the Governor and Tribal leaders at the annual meeting;

f) Departmental leads will submit a yearly program analysis to their Secretary or Executive Officer for inclusion in the Office of Tribal-Commonwealth Relations annual program review.

3. The Governor of the Commonwealth shall actively and regularly communicate with the state's Attorney General to ensure that all laws, policies, and regulations are consistent, both in letter and in spirit, with existing federal and state laws related to Indian affairs.
   a) In addition to the departmental participation outlined in Comparative Plan of Work section 2, the Attorney General shall work with the Governor and the Secretary of the Office of Tribal-Commonwealth Relations and in ongoing consultation with Tribes to identify legal inconsistencies and improper applications in a manner that is structured, responsive, and transparent as defined by the protocols of this agreement;
   b) The Governor shall require a systemic annual review of rel-

evant state laws, rules and regulations and their applications in order to ensure the Commonwealth's official actions do not conflict with inherent Tribal sovereign rights, federally recognized authority of Tribal Nations, or federal law:

i. The review will be conducted jointly by the Office of the Attorney General and the Office of Tribal-Commonwealth Relations in formal consultation with Tribes;
ii. The review will be based on the cumulative historic record of treaties, laws, policies, rules, and regulations;
iii. The report will document irregularities and propose area-specific remedies;
iv. The Governor will direct all Secretaries and Executive Officers to review the report and create departmental plans for adoption of recommendations outlined in the review;
v. The Governor will take appropriate steps to communicate with the legislative body so that legislators are 1) aware of the need to amend existing statues and 2) have information needed to craft future legislation in a manner that comports with Tribal sovereign authority and federal law.

4. Tribal Governments shall direct their chosen issue area leads to assist the Secretary and staff of the Office of Tribal-Commonwealth Relations in advancing the purposes of that agency and ensuring that activities of the office are fully coordinated with their own issue area goals and activities.
   a) Tribal Nations shall require their departments to implement a comprehensive educational effort to ensure understanding of the government-to-government relations;
   b) Each Tribal agency or department shall be responsible for working with their state counterparts as they identify and report on issues with the potential to affect Tribes;
   c) Tribal agencies will work with their state counterparts to address issues of shared concern;

d) Tribal liaisons or representatives shall assist state departmental directors with compilation of their annual meeting report on Tribal-Commonwealth activities within their issue areas.
e) Tribal issue area experts may assist state departmental directors with completion of an annual departmental analysis as part of the Office of Tribal-Commonwealth Relations annual review.
f) Each Nation shall commit to the establishment of and adherence to ethical research practices that meet or exceed the highest recognized professional standards;

5. The Governor through executive order and in partnership with Tribes shall create a Truth and Reconciliation Commission organized under charter, adequately funded, authorized and tasked over the course of six years to 1) create a better understanding of the Native Nations located with Virginia, 2) correct and bear witness to the historical record, 3) address injustices, and 4) repair relations between those Nations and the Commonwealth.
   a) Authority
      i. Guided by the protocols outlined in this accord, Tribal Nations and the Commonwealth of Virginia shall fully empower, support, protect, and promote the work of this Commission;
      ii. Guided by the protocols outlined in this accord, Tribal and state agencies and offices shall cooperate fully, both in letter and spirit, with this Commission and, upon request, assist in fulfilling its mission and purposes.
      iii. The Commission shall have decision-making powers, including contract-making authority, with the support of the Secretary and staff of the Office of the Tribal-Commonwealth Relations.
   b) Membership
      i. Voting Members

- a. Each federally recognized Tribe shall appoint a voting member;
- b. Voting members will commit to serve a six-year term;

ii. Non-voting members

- a. One alternate Tribal member shall be chosen by each federally recognized nation;
  - 1) Tribal alternates may be designated by their Tribes to act as voting members in the absence of appointed voting members;
  - 2) Tribal alternates will commit to serve a three-year term;
- b. One advisory member may be chosen by each federally recognized nation;
  - 1) Advisory members will be expected to offer relevant expertise or an informed perspective, such as that of an academic, active community member, or stakeholder group representative;
  - 2) Advisory members will serve a one-year term at the discretion of their appointing Tribe with an option for reappointment;

c) Meetings

- i. The Commission shall meet quarterly;
- ii. Meetings will take place in venues across the state and on Tribal lands when possible;
- iii. Commission meetings shall be transparent, accessible, and open to the public;
- iv. Materials and reports shall be posted on the Office of Tribal-Commonwealth Relations website;

d) Organization

- i. Staff of the Office of Tribal-Commonwealth Relations shall coordinate the work of the Commission including development and facilitation of meetings, publication of information and schedules on its public website, and generation of educational materials and reports;

ii. The Secretary or her/his designee shall act as liaison between the Governor, Tribal Nations, administrative agencies, other outside entities as appropriate, and the Commission;

iii. The Commission shall work in consultation with Tribes to shape its agenda, select appropriate venues, conduct its work, and accurately represent the diversity of experiences;

iv. Voting members shall elect officers;

v. Rules and protocols shall be approved by voting members;

e) Reports

i. A year-end executive summary shall be presented to the Governor and Tribal Leaders at each annual Tribal-Commonwealth Accord meeting;

ii. A comprehensive three-year summary and a final six-year report, to include status updates and recommendations for needed action, shall be presented to the Governor and Tribal Leaders at Tribal-Commonwealth Accord meetings;

iii. The Commission shall have the ability to submit special summaries and reports to Tribal Nations, the legislature, judiciary, Congress, or other bureaucratic entities as needed;

f) Duration

i. This Commission shall conclude its business after six years;

ii. The Governor, in consultation with Tribal Nations, shall have the authority to reauthorize the Commission's charter.

Tribal-Commonwealth Accord Annual Meetings and Reports

The Governor shall host an annual Tribal-Commonwealth Accord open gathering where government-to-government relations will be honored and entities tasked with implementation will present annual reports and have the opportunity to address the meeting.

1. The Office of Tribal-Commonwealth Relations will organize an annual meeting:
   a) Leaders and representatives from all elements of Commonwealth and Tribal governments shall attend in order to discuss issues of shared concern;
   b) An annual departmental progress report shall be submitted and presented to the Governor and Tribal Leaders by each Secretary and Executive Officer. The report will provide an overview of the year's issues including shared successes and areas of potential concern. Staff members from each state and Tribal working group will assist with reporting as needed;
   c) Designated Tribal and state staff members representing key issue areas will participate in planning meetings prior to the main gathering in order to develop joint strategies and come to specific agreements regarding outlining tasks, overcoming obstacles and achieving specific goals for the coming year;
   d) The Truth and Reconciliation Commission shall present a report through the Secretary of the Office of Tribal-Commonwealth Relations;
   e) The Sovereign Nations Commonwealth Council may choose to submit remarks through the Secretary of the Office of Tribal-Commonwealth Relations or to make a presentation at the annual meeting.

Accountability

Tribal leaders, elected officials, agency Secretaries, Executive Officers, and staff from all governments will accept the responsibilities inherent in the good-faith operation of intergovernmental relations.

1. The Commonwealth shall develop systems of transparency and accountability:
   a) Secretaries and Executive Officers shall be directly accountable to the Governor;
   b) Secretaries and Executive Officers shall create and implement a documented plan of accountability to be shared with the Governor and the Secretary of the Office of Tribal-Commonwealth Relations;
   c) Each state departmental lead shall be directly accountable to their respective Secretary or Executive Officer for their role in the implementation of government-to-government relations within their given issue areas;
   d) Departmental leads and staff shall document their timely, respectful, and comprehensive communications with Tribal representatives;
   e) Secretaries and Executive Officers shall authorize agency and departmental leads to work with the Office of Tribal-Commonwealth Relations to create and maintain guides for Tribal governments that map their organizational structures, decision-making processes, staff issue assignments, systems of accountability, and any interactions with corresponding state agencies and departments that might be necessary for completion of projects;
   f) An annual review from each Secretary and Executive Officer will include an evaluation of the overall process, recommendations for shared strategies, and agreements to outline tasks, identify shared goals and perceived obstacles.

g) The Sovereign Nations Commonwealth Council and the Truth and Reconciliation Commission shall be accountable to the Governor and Tribes through the Secretary of the Office of Tribal-Commonwealth Relations.

2) Tribal Nations shall develop systems of accountability
   a) Each Nation will establish a documented plan and system of accountability that is the most effective for their priorities and governmental structure;
   b) Tribal Nations shall pledge to share and update pertinent information on their unique organizational structures, decision-making processes, personnel issue assignments, systems of accountability, and other necessary decision-making protocols. This information will be treated as highly confidential and made available only to the Secretary and staff of the Office of Tribal-Commonwealth Relations and appropriate state departmental staff on an as needed basis;
   c) Tribal officials will direct and authorize their staff to communicate with state agency staff responsible for their issue areas and to keep a record of these interactions;
   d) The Sovereign Nations Commonwealth Council will monitor, evaluate and report progress from the Nations' perspectives. Such oversight may include, but is not limited to, an annual intra-Tribal evaluation of the overall process, recommendations for shared strategies, and agreements to outline tasks, identify shared goals and perceived obstacles:
   e) The Truth and Reconciliation Commission shall regularly consult with Tribes.

A Commitment to Just and Honorable Government-to-Government Relations

Let this Tribal-Commonwealth Accord, hereby, represent the enduring commitment of all participating governments to the principles of good faith cooperation as together they shoulder the burdens and share the benefits of this alliance for generations to come.

Date:

Signatures:

Chickahominy,
Eastern Chickahominy,
Monacan,
Nansemond,
Pamunkey,
Rappahannock,
Upper Mattaponi,
Governor of the Commonwealth of Virginia.

NOTES AND BIBLIOGRAPHIES

Introduction

Notes

1. Billy Frank Jr. Statue Project—ArtsWA, https://www.arts.wa.gov/billy-frank-jr/, accessed October 27, 2023.
2. Tom Crash, "First Nations Sculpture Garden Dedicated in Rapid City," *Lakota Times*, November 23, 2017, https://www.lakotatimes.com/articles/first-nations-sculpture-garden-dedicated-in-rapid-city/, accessed October 27, 2023.

Chapter 2

Notes

1. Vine Deloria letter to Sioux Nation Chiefs, May 12, 1992, and Treaty Between the Ottawa and Chippewa and the Sioux Nation, July 12, 1781. Contact author for copies of these documents.
2. Dakota, Lakota, Nakota Unification Accord, June 11, 1992. Contact author for copy of this resolution.
3. Constitution of the Little Traverse Bay Bands of Odawa Indians, Feb. 2, 2005. https://1tbbodawa-nsn.gov/wp-content/uploads/2020/12/LTBB-Constitution.pdf.

Chapter 4

Notes

1. Vine Deloria, Jr., *Custer Died for Your Sins: An Indian Manifesto* (New York: The Macmillan Company, 1969), 180.
2. Deloria, *Custer*, 181.
3. Vine Deloria Jr., *Behind the Trail of Broken Treaties: An Indian Declaration of Independence* (Austin: University of Texas Press, 2000), 2–3.
4. Deloria, *Behind the Trail*, 55.
5. Stokely Carmichael, "The Red and the Black," *Akwesasne Notes*, Winter 1975.
6. Carmichael, "The Red and the Black."
7. Carmichael, "The Red and the Black."
8. Carmichael, "The Red and the Black."

Chapter 5

Notes

1. See Rebecca Tsosie, "Sacred Obligations: Intercultural Justice and the Discourse of Treaty Rights," *UCLA Law Review* 47 (2000): 1615.

2. Treaty of Guadalupe Hidalgo [Exchange copy]; 2/2/1848; Perfected Treaties, 1778–1945; General Records of the United States Government, Record Group 11; National Archives Building, Washington, DC.
3. Erin Stone, Anton L. Delgado, and Ian James, "The Wall's Death Grip," *Arizona Republic*, Sun., Apr. 25, 2021 (describing many of the Tribes and bands in the region that have been impacted by the Wall, and including federally recognized Tribes and those that are not currently recognized).
4. See generally Vine Deloria, Jr., *God Is Red: A Native View of Religion* (Golden, CO: Fulcrum, 1994); *For This Land: Writings on Religion in America* (New York: Routledge,1999).
5. E. Stone, A. L. Delgado and I. James, "Trump's Border Wall Scarred Sacred Lands, Displaced Wildlife and Drained Water. Can It Be Taken Down?" *Arizona Republic*, April 15, 2021, https://www.azcentral.com/in-depth/news/local/arizona-environment/2021/04/15/arizona-mexico-border-calls-removing-wall-and-repairing-environmental-impacts/4589493001/, accessed October 27, 2023.
6. Trump v. Sierra Club, Case No. 19A60 (9th circuit, petition for cert filed in Supreme Court in 2019 and Tohono O'odham Nation sought leave to file an amicus brief).
7. La Posta Band of Diegueno Mission Indians of the La Posta Reservation et al. v. Donald J. Trump et al., Case No. 3:20-CV-01552 (D.Cal. 2020).
8. See Stone, Delgado, and James, supra note 4 (interviews with contemporary descendants of the Chiricahua and Warm Springs bands who escaped capture by the US military in the nineteenth century but lack federal recognition today).
9. R. v. Desautel, 2021 S.C.C. 17 (Can.).
10. United Nations Declaration on the Rights of Indigenous Peoples, Art. 36 (detailing the rights of Indigenous peoples "divided by international borders").
11. See, e.g., United States v. Dion, 476 U.S. 734 (1986) (articulating test for treaty abrogation).
12. The United States Treaty with the Apaches (Treaty of Santa Fe) negotiated on July 1, 1852, 10 Stat. 979 (ratified March 23, 1853).
13. Katherine E. Lovett, "Not All Land Exchanges Are Created Equal: A Case Study of the Oak Flat Land Exchange," *Colorado Natural Resources Energy & Environmental Law Review* 28 (2017): 353.
14. San Carlos Apache Tribe v. United States Forest Service, 2:21-cv-00068-JZB (D. Ariz. Jan. 14, 2021); Apache Stronghold v. United States, 2:21-cv-00050-PHX-SPL (D. Ariz. Jan. 12, 2021); Arizona Mining Reform Coalition v. United States, 2:21-cv-00122-DLR (D. Ariz. Jan. 22, 2021).
15. *United States v. Abeyta*, 632 F. Supp. 1301, 1305 (D.N.M. 2986).
16. See Vine Deloria, Jr., "Laws Founded in Justice and Humanity: Reflections on the Content and Character of Federal Indian Law," *Arizona Law Review* 31, no. 2 (1989): 203 (discussing congressional language in the Northwest Ordinance of 1789 requiring the "utmost good faith" toward Indian Tribes).
17. The ideas in this section of the essay are drawn from several works by Vine Deloria, Jr., including *God Is Red* and *For This Land* (cited supra note 3) and also his earlier books: *American Indians, American Justice* (Austin: University of Texas Press, 1983), *Of Utmost Good Faith* (Straight Arrow Books, 1971), and *We Talk, You Listen: New Tribes, New Turf* (Lincoln: University of Nebraska Press, 2007). Professor Deloria was the only Indigenous

author writing from a self-determination perspective as of the 1970s and 1980s, and his ideas were very influential in the construction of Tribal sovereignty and Indigenous self-determination.

18. See Cherokee Nation v. Georgia, 30 U.S. (5 Pet.) 1 (1831); Worcester v. Georgia, 31 U.S. (6 Pet.) 515 (1832) (designating Tribal governments as "domestic dependent nations" who were under the sole protection of the United States and encompassed within its national boundaries).
19. Oliphant v. Suquamish Tribe, 435 U.S. 191 (1978).
20. Montana v. United States, 450 U.S. 544 (1981).
21. Wallace Coffey and Rebecca Tsosie, "Rethinking the Tribal Sovereignty Doctrine: Cultural Sovereignty and the Collective Future of Indian Nations," *Stanford Law & Policy Review* 12, no. 2 (2001): 191.
22. I made this argument in earlier work. See Rebecca Tsosie, "Sovereigns or Citizens? The Paradox of Indigenous Self-Determination," in *Community as the Material Basis of Citizenship: The Unfinished Story of American Democracy*, ed. Rodolfo Rosales (New York: Taylor & Francis), 2019, 136–137.
23. See Lyng v. Northwest Indian Cemetery Protective Ass'n, 485 U.S. 439 (1988) (holding that Free Exercise balancing test was not applicable to the federal government's land management practices even if the actual effect was to destroy the Indigenous peoples' ability to conduct their place-based ceremony altogether).
24. Vine Deloria, Jr. and David E. Wilkins, *Tribes, Treaties, and Constitutional Tribulations* (Austin: University of Texas Press, 1999).
25. See, supra note 11 (upholding the principle that the US has the political right to unilaterally abrogate an Indian treaty). See, e.g., *Lonewolf v. Hitchcock*, 187 U.S. 553 (1903).
26. See, e.g., Deloria, "Laws Founded in Justice and Humanity," supra note 16 at 219.
27. Deloria, "Laws Founded."
28. Walter R. Echo-Hawk, *In the Light of Justice: The Rise of Human Rights in Native America and the UN Declaration on the Rights of Indigenous Peoples* (Golden, CO: Fulcrum Publishing, 2013).
29. In New Zealand, for example, the Maori people achieved a settlement that resulted in recognition of their ancestral river and mountain as legal "persons," using the Maori understanding of the essence of these places.
30. *McGirt v. Oklahoma*, 591 U.S. ____ (2020).
31. See, e.g., Lonewolf v. Hitchcock, 187 U.S. 553 (1903).

Chapter 6

Notes

1. Vine Deloria, Jr. and David E. Wilkins, *Tribes, Treaties, and Constitutional Tribulations* (Austin: University of Texas Press, 1999), 33–34.
2. Deloria and Wilkins, vii.
3. Deloria and Wilkins, 34.
4. *Johnson v. McIntosh*, 21 U.S. 543 (1823).
5. United Nations Declaration on the Rights of Indigenous Peoples.
6. Thomas McKenney, "Annual Report of the Commissioner of Indian Affairs," Office of the Commissioner of Indian Affairs (Washington, D.C., November 1, 1828), 80.

7. Deloria and Wilkins, 82.
8. Deloria and Wilkins, 83
9. Deloria and Wilkins, 59.
10. Elbert Herbert, "Annual Report of the Commissioner of Indian Affairs," Office of the Commissioner of Indian Affairs (Washington, D.C., 1832).
11. T. Hartley Crawford, "Annual Report of the Commissioner of Indian Affairs," Office of the Commissioner of Indian Affairs (Washington, D.C., 1840).
12. US Congress. United States Code: Ordinance of: The Northwest Territorial Government 1934. 1934. Section 14, Article 3. Periodical. Retrieved from the Library of Congress. www.loc.gov/item/uscode1934-001000009/.
13. Letter from Thomas Jefferson to William Henry Harrison, February 27, 1803. Retrieved from the National Archives. https://founders.archives.gov/documents/Jefferson/01-39-02-0500.
14. Deloria and Wilkins, 33.
15. Papers of William Medill, Commissioner of Indian Affairs (1845–1850). Retrieved from the Library of Congress. https://www.loc.gov/item/mm78032524/.
16. Papers of Luke Lea, Commissioner of Indian Affairs (1852). Library of Congress.
17. Deloria and Wilkins, 162.

Chapter 7

Notes

1. John Kincheloe, *Rediscovering Christanna: Native Worlds and Governor Spotswood's Fort* (Alcalde, NM: Spirit Lines Press, 2020), 12.
2. Kincheloe.
3. Vine Deloria, Jr. "Reserving to Themselves: Treaties and the Powers of Indian Tribes," *Arizona Law Review* 38, no. 3 (1996): 963.
4. Deloria: 971.
5. There are currently eleven state-recognized Tribes in Virginia. The Chickahominy Tribe, Chickahominy Tribe Eastern Division, Monacan Nation, Nansemond Tribe, Pamunkey Tribe, Rappahannock Tribe, and Upper Mattaponi Tribe have been federally recognized since 2018. The others—the Cheroenhaka Nottoway, Mattaponi Tribe, Nottoway Tribe of Virginia, and Pattawomeck Tribe—are not federally recognized to date.
6. David H. DeJong. *American Indian Treaties: A Guide to Ratified and Unratified Colonial, United States, State, Foreign, and Intertribal Treaties and Agreements*, 1607–1911 (Salt Lake City: University of Utah Press), 4.
7. Vine Deloria, Jr. and Raymond J. DeMallie, eds., *Documents of American Indian Diplomacy: Treaties, Agreements, and Conventions, 1775–1979*, 2 vols. (Lincoln: University of Nebraska Press, 1999).
8. Deloria and DeMallie, 3.
9. W. Stitt Robinson, "Tributary Indians in Colonial Virginia," *Virginia Magazine of History and Biography* 67, no. 1 (1959): 49–64.
10. W. Stitt Robinson, ed. *Early American Indian Documents: Treaties and Laws, 1607–1789* vol. 4 (Frederick, MD: University Publications of America, 1983), 220–224.
11. "Treaty of Lancaster," *Virginia Magazine of History and Biography* 13, no. 2 (1905): 142.

12. "The Treaty of Logg's Town, 1752," *Virginia Magazine of History and Biography* 13, no. 2 (1905): 143–174. For a discussion of the negligence of the Ohio Company of Virginia in encroaching on Shawnee lands in particular see Colin G. Calloway, *Shawnees and the War for America* (New York: Penguin Books, 2007); Stephen Warren, *The Worlds the Shawnees Made: Migration and Violence in Early America* (Chapel Hill: University of North Carolina Press, 2014).
13. DeJong, *American Indian Treaties*, 20.
14. Pope Alexander VI "Inter Caetera" May 4, 1493.
15. Vine Deloria, Jr. and Clifford M. Lytle, *American Indians, American Justice* (Austin: University of Texas Press, 1983), 3.
16. Reginald Horsman, "American Indian Policy in the Old Northwest, 1783–1912," *The William and Mary Quarterly* 18, no. 1 (1961): 36–37.
17. George Washington, Letter to James Duane, September 7, 1783, in *The Writings of George Washington*, ed. John C. Fitzpatrick, 27 (Washington, DC: Government Printing Office, 1938), 140.
18. Horsman, "American Indian Policy," 38.
19. Horsman, 39.
20. 7 Stat. 26-27.
21. Francis Paul Prucha, *Documents of United States Indian Policy*, 3rd ed. (Lincoln: University of Nebraska Press, 2001), 7.
22. "Treaty of Lancaster."
23. Horsman, "American Indian Policy," 38.
24. Horsman, 39–40. For a detailed discussion of post-American Revolution turmoil and failed Indian diplomacy in the Northwest see Randolph C. Downes, *Council Fires on the Upper Ohio* (Pittsburgh: University of Pittsburgh Press), 940.
25. Horsman, "American Indian Policy," 42.
26. Prucha, *Documents of United States Indian Policy*, 12; Prucha, 9.
27. Ordinance for the Government of the Territory of the United States North-West of the River Ohio; 7/13/1787; Miscellaneous Papers of the Continental Congress, 1774–1789; Article 3. Records of the Continental and Confederation Congresses and the Constitutional Convention, Record Group 360; National Archives Building, Washington, DC. See e.g., Robert Berkhofer, *The White Man's Indian: Images of the American Indian from Columbus to Present* (New York: Vintage Books, 1979).
28. Deloria and DeMallie, *Documents of American Indian Diplomacy*, 5.
29. Vine Deloria, Jr. and David E. Wilkins, *Tribes, Treaties, and Constitutional Tribulations* (Austin: University of Texas Press, 1999), viii.
30. Francis Paul Prucha, *American Indian Treaties: The History of a Political Anomaly* (Berkeley: University of California Press, 1993).
31. Deloria and DeMallie, *Documents of American Indian Diplomacy*; DeJong, *American Indian Treaties.*
32. Robert A. Williams, Jr. *Linking Arms Together: American Indian Treaty Visions of Law and Peace, 1600–1800* (New York: Oxford University Press, 1997), 14.
33. Williams, 5.
34. Deloria and DeMallie, *Documents of American Indian Diplomacy*, 8.

35. In C. Emanuelli, "State Succession, Then and Now, With Special Reference to the Louisiana Purchase." *Louisiana Law Review* 63, no. 4 (2003): 1278.
36. Emanuelli: 1280.
37. Emanuelli: 1280–1281.
38. E. F., Robinson, ed. *Early American Indian Documents* (Arlington, VA: University Publications of America, 1984), vol. 4, 91, 217, 221.
39. Chief Walt "Red Hawk" Brown, "Ethno-Historical / Current Snapshot of Cheroenhaka (Nottoway) Indian Nation of Southhampton County, Virginia," updated Dec. 31, 2020, https://www.cheroenhaka-nottoway.org/about-us/ethno-historical-current-snapshot-of-the-cheroenhaka-nottoway-indian-nation-of-southhampton-county-virginia/.
40. Public Law 115-121-Jan. 29, 2018, https://www.govinfo.gov/content/pkg/PLAW-115publ121/pdf/PLAW-115publ121.pdf.
41. Virginia's race integrity policies, which were incubated in the larger context of the eugenics movement, essentially declared that the racial designator "Indian" no longer existed in the state, basically making it illegal to self-identify as such. See generally, J. David Smith, *The Eugenic Assault on America: Scenes in Red, White and Black* (Fairfax, VA: George Mason University Press, 1993). For a discussion of how Virginia Indians from various Tribes successfully challenged race integrity laws when they resisted the draft during World War II when denied the right to self-identify as "Indian," see Paul T. Murray, "Who Is an Indian? Who Is a Negro? Virginia Indians in the World War II Draft," *Virginia Magazine of History and Biography* 95, no. 2 (1987): 215–231.
42. Deloria, "Reserving to Themselves," 1996.
43. David E. Wilkins, "Reconsidering the Tribal-State Compact Process," *Policy Studies Journal* 22, vol. 3 (1994): 474–488.
44. Deloria and Lytle, *American Indians, American Justice*, Ch. 5; Jeff Corntassel, "Re-Envisioning Resurgence: Indigenous Pathways to Decolonization and Sustainable Self-Determination," *Decolonization: Indigeneity, Education & Society* 1/1 (2012): 110–128.
45. Jeanette Armstrong, "An Okanagan Worldview of Society," in *Original Instructions: Indigenous Teachings for a Sustainable Future*, ed. Melissa K. Nelson (Rochester, VT: Bear and Co., 2008), 66–74.
46. Commonwealth of Virginia, Office of the Governor, Executive Order Number Eighty-Two (2021) Consultations with Federally Recognized Tribal Nations for Environmental and Historic Permits and Reviews, https://www.governor.virginia.gov/media/governorvirginiagov/executive-actions/EO-82-Consultation-With-Federally-Recognized-Tribal-Nations-For-Environmental-And-Historic-Permits-And-Reviews.pdf.
47. 104 Stat. 2048 (1990).
48. 91 Stat. 685 (1977).
49. Glen Sean Coulthard, *Red Skin, White Masks: Rejecting the Colonial Politics of Recognition* (Minneapolis: University of Minnesota Press, 2014), 3.
50. Edward H. Spicer, "The Nations of a State," in *American Indian Persistence and Resurgence*, ed. Karl Kroeber (Durham, NC: Duke University Press, 1994), 27–49.
51. Deloria, "Reserving to Themselves," 1996.
52. The "Restatement of the Law of American Indians" project is an initiative guided by a

committee of some of the most prominent scholars and practitioners in the realm of Indian law and policy, under the auspices of the American Law Institute. It has become the centerpiece of virtually all Indian law conferences at present. See, https://www.ali.org/projects/show/law-american-indians/#_status. It probably represents the most recent iteration of such movements as Deloria described in "Reserving to Themselves," which have emerged with new generations of Indian law practitioners ever since the publication of Felix Cohen's *Handbook of American Indian Law*. The problem, as Deloria aptly notes, is that these efforts to establish a uniform and coherent canon rely on Cohen's *Handbook* as its foundation, which automatically complicates the possibility of establishing this body of law on Indigenous input.

Chapter 8

Notes

1. Laurence M. Hauptman, "Peacemakers: Leaders Who Fought Against Wars and in Courts to Preserve Native Rights," *National Museum of the American Indian, Commemorative Issue: An Enduring Tribute to Native Veterans* (Fall 2020): 13.
2. I'd like to thank Professor Rob Williams of the University of Arizona Law School for his help on finding information on the Crocker case. See the *Los Angeles Times*, Feb. 7, 1947, 15; *Kansas City Star*, Feb. 7, 1947, 15.
3. *Valley Times* (CA), March 22, 1947, 1; *Los Angeles Times*, March 23, 1947, 4; *Hollywood Citizen News*, March 24, 1947, 7.
4. Donald L. Fixico, *Termination and Relocation: Federal Indian Policy 1945–1960* (Albuquerque: University of New Mexico Press, 1986), 3.
5. Paul C. Rosier, *Saving Their Country: American Indian Politics and Patriotism in the Twentieth Century* (Cambridge, MA: Harvard University Press, 2012), 255.
6. Rosier, 255.
7. Woody Kipp, *Viet Cong at Wounded Knee: The Trail of a Blackfeet Activist* (Lincoln: University of Nebraska Press, 2004).
8. *Akwesasne Notes*, Early Summer, June 1973, 5.
9. Jim Northrup, *The Rez Road Follies: Canoes, Casinos, Computers, and Birch Bark Baskets* (Minneapolis: University of Minnesota Press, 1999), 2.
10. *Leader-Telegram* (Eau Claire, WI), May 2, 1999, 57.
11. Cynthia H. Enloe, *Ethnic Soldiers: State Security in a Divided Society* (New York: Penguin Books, 1980), 36–38.
12. Gwynne Dyer, *War* (Homewood, IL: Dorsey Press, 1985), 9.
13. John P. Brown, *Old Frontiers* (reprint, New York: Arno Press, 1971), 9, footnote.
14. Enloe, *Ethnic Soldiers*, 190–192.
15. Tom Holm, "Strong Hearts: Native Service in the U.S. Armed Forces," in *Aboriginal Peoples and Military Participation: Canadian and International Perspectives*, ed. P. Whitney Lockenbauer, R. Scott Sheffield, and Craig Leslie Mantle (Kingston, Ontario: Canadian Defense Academy Press, 2007), 132–133.
16. Quoted in Ethel Nurge, ed., *The Modern Sioux* (Lincoln: University of Nebraska Press, 1970), 242.

17. Quoted in Tom Holm, *Strong Hearts, Wounded Souls: Native American Veterans of the Vietnam War* (Austin: University of Texas Press, 1996), 192.

Chapter 9

Notes

1. From the video "A Conversation with Vine Deloria, Jr.," as part of the series *Native Literature in the American Southwest*, Larry Evers, producer (University of Arizona Radio-TV-Film Bureau, 1978), https://streaming.oia.arizona.edu/play.php?clipname=/perm/glogoff/a_conversation_with_vince_deloria_jr/web.smil&align=left&autoplay=off&banner=none.
2. Vine Deloria, Jr., "Accountability and Sovereignty in American Indian Education," *Indian Country Today*, Aug. 4, 2005, https://indiancountrytoday.com/archive/accountability-and-sovereignty-in-american-indian-education.
3. "CDC Data Show Disproportionate COVID-19 Impact in American Indian/Alaska Native Populations," Centers for Disease Control press release, Aug. 19, 2020, https://www.cdc.gov/media/releases/2020/p0819-covid-19-impact-american-indian-alaska-native.html, and "American Indians and Alaska Natives are Dying of COVID-19 at Shocking Rates," Brookings Institute report, Feb. 18, 2021, https://www.brookings.edu/research/american-indians-and-alaska-natives-are-dying-of-covid-19-at-shocking-rates/.
4. Megan Hill, "Interview with Dr. Stephanie Carroll about New Research on COVID-19 Spread in Indian Country," May 1, 2020, https://www.youtube.com/watch?v=m26M9O_KUYE.
5. Vine Deloria, Jr. and Clifford M. Lytle, *The Nations Within: The Past and Future of American Indian Sovereignty* (New York: Pantheon Books, 1984), viii.
6. Interview with Vine Deloria, Jr., 2005 https://nnigovernance.arizona.edu/vine-delorias-last-video-interview.
7. "Project Tiwahu: Redefining Tigua Citizenship | Ysleta del Sur Pueblo," Harvard Project on Economic Development (Cambridge, MA, 2016), https://hwpi.harvard.edu/files/hpaied/files/projecttiwahu-final.pdf?m=1639579190.
8. "Citizen Potawatomi Nation Constitution Reform | Citizen Potawatomi Nation," Harvard Project on Economic Development (Cambridge, MA, 2010), https://hpaied.org/publications/citizen-potawatomi-nation-constitution-reform-citizen-potawatomi-nation.
9. Vine Deloria, Jr. and Daniel Wildcat, *Power and Place: Indian Education in America* (Golden, CO: Fulcrum Publishing, 2001), 128.
10. Kerry R. Venegas, "The Ya Ne Dah Ah School: Melding Traditional Teachings with Modern Curricula," John F. Kennedy School of Government, 2005, https://hwpi.harvard.edu/files/hpaied/files/yndas_web_version.pdf?m=1639579315 f.
11. "The Agua Caliente Curriculum," Agua Caliente Band of Cahuilla Indians, July 14, 2021, https://www.youtube.com/watch?v=j4Mw4HcPErk&ab_channel=AguaCalienteBandofCahuillaIndians.
12. "Akwesasne Freedom School | Mohawk Nation at Akwesasne," John F. Kennedy School of Government, 2005, https://hpaied.org/publications/akwesasne-freedom-school-akwesasne-mohawk-nation.

13. Iakionhnhehkwen "Life Sustainers," https://www.oherokon.org/ and https://hpaied.org/publications/oherokon-under-husk-rites-passage-haudenosaunee-confederacy.
14. Santa Fe Indian School Leadership Institute, https://www.sfis.k12.nm.us/leadership_institute and https://hpaied.org/publications/leadership-institute-santa-fe-indian-school-all-indian-pueblo-council.

Chapter 11

Notes

1. Vine Deloria, Jr., *The World We Used to Live In: Remembering the Powers of the Medicine Men* (Golden, CO: Fulcrum Publishing, 2006).
2. In the interest of concision, I give only reductive translations or explanations of most Hawaiian terms. For a better appreciation, readers can look up any of them in Wehewehe Wikiwiki: https://hilo.hawaii.edu/wehe/.
3. Deloria, *The World We Used to Live In*, 214.
4. Manulani Aluli Meyer, Hoʻoulu: *Our Time of Becoming: Collected Early Writings of Manulani Meyer* (Honolulu: ʻAi Pōhaku Press, 2003).
5. This is my English rendition of the formulaic saying expressing the infinite multitude of *akua*. Once instance is found in Pukui and Elbert, *Hawaiian Dictionary*, s.v. melehuka: "ʻo ka lau, ʻo ka mano, ʻo ke kini a me ka lehua o ke akua."
6. See *kuʻualoha hoʻomanawanui, Voices of Fire: Reweaving the Literary Lei of Pele and Hiʻiaka* (Minneapolis: University of Minnesota Press, 2014).
7. Z. P. Kalokuokamaile, "Kekahi Mau Mea Ulu Kahiko o Hawaii," September 18, 1914; Z. P. Kalokuokamaile, "Na Inoa o na Manu, Na Limu ame na I'a Pili Kahakai," *Ka Nupepa Kuokoa*, November 6, 1914; Z. P. Kalokuokamaile, "Hanaia Ka Heiau O Hikiau Ma Ke One O Kealakekua," *Ka Nupepa Kuokoa*, February 16, 1917; Z. P. Kalokuokamaile, "Ke Kalaiwaa ana ame Kona Mau Ano," *Ka Nupepa Kuokoa*, October 26, 1922; Z. P. K. Kawaikaumaiikamakaokaopua, "Ke Kukulu Hale ana o ka Wa Kahiko ame na Loina," *Ka Hoku O Hawaii*, March 18, 1923; Z. P. K. Kawaikaumaiikamakaokaopua, "Na Upena Lawai'a o ka Wa Kahiko ame ka Lakou Hana Pakahi," *Ka Nupepa Kuokoa*, June 22, 1923.
8. Interview with Kaleohano Kalili, Robert Plunkett, Jennie Wilson, Napua Stevens, Kaupena Wong, and Rubellite Kinney, Tape reel 7 in.,¼4 in. tape, May 9, 1956, Audio (Interviews, etc.), Bishop Museum Audio Collection HAW 60.4.
9. Obituary for Robert Plunkett, *Honolulu Advertiser*, Dec. 2, 1969, 28, newspapers.com.
10. Joel Apuakehau, "Ko Na Koolau Mau Luhiehu," *Ka Nupepa Kuokoa*, Oct. 26, 1922, 3.
11. Pualani Kanakaʻole Kanahele, Ka Honua Ola: *ʻEliʻeli Kau Mai (The Living Earth: Descend, Deepen the Revelation)* (Honolulu: Kamehameha Publishing, 2011), 24. Also see Hooulumahiehie, "Ka Moolelo o Hiiaka-i-ka-poli-o-Pele," *Ka Na'i Aupuni*, Sept. 10, 1906, 4.
12. Among these works are: John Dominis Holt, *Waimea Summer: A Novel*, 2nd ed. (Honolulu: Ku Paʻa Publishing Inc., 1998); John Dominis Holt, *Hanai, a Poem for Queen Liliuokalani*, 1st ed. (Honolulu: Topgallant, 1986); John Dominis Holt, *Princess of the Night Rides and Other Tales* (Honolulu: Topgallant, 1977); John Dominis Holt, *Kaulana Na Pua—Famous Are the Flowers: Queen Liliuokalani and the Throne of Hawaii: A Play*

in Three Acts (Honolulu: Topgallant, 1974); John Dominis Holt, *The Art of Featherwork in Old Hawai'i* (Honolulu: Ku Pa'a Publishing Inc., 1997).

13. John Dominis Holt, *On Being Hawaiian* (Honolulu, Hawaii: Ku Pa'a Publishing Inc., 1995).
14. John Dominis Holt, *Recollections: Memoirs of John Dominis Holt*, lst ed. (Honolulu: Ku Pa'a Publishing Inc., 1993), 1.
15. Holt, 6.
16. Holt, 6.
17. Holt, 7.
18. Holt, 8–9.
19. Holt, 9–10.
20. Holt, 10.
21. Holt, 11.
22. Mary Kawena Pukui, "Ke Awa Lau o Pu'uloa: The Many-Harbored Sea of Pu'uloa," *Annual Report of the Hawaiian Historical Society* (Honolulu: Hawaiian Historical Society, 1943).
23. Pukui, 56.
24. Pukui, 57–58.
25. Pukui, 59.
26. Pukui, 59.
27. Pukui, 59.
28. For a cogent description of kākū'ai see Marie Alohalani Brown, *Ka Po'e Mo'o Akua: Hawaiian Reptilian Water Deities* (Honolulu: University of Hawai'i Press, 2022), 142–145.
29. Larry Lindsey Kauanoe Kimura, "Ka Leo Hawai'i," audio/mpeg, Interview of Iokepa Maka'ai (University of Hawai'i at Mānoa, November 9, 1980), Kani'āina in Ulukau, http://ulukau.org/kaniaina/?a=d&d=A-KLH-HV24-246&e=———en-20-A-1—txt-tpIN%7ctpTI%7ctpTA%7ctpCO%7ctpTY%7ctpLA%7ctpKE%7ctp-PR%7ctpSG%7ctpTO%7ctpTG%7ctpSM%7ctpTR%7ctpSP%7ctpCT%7ctpET%7ct-pHT%7ctpDT%7ctpOD%7ctpDF-maka%ca%bbai——————. There are at least three other discussions of 'aumākua in the Ka Leo Hawai'i archives: Interview of Helen Wahineokai, no. 247, which has two discussions; and Interview of Kalāhikiola Nāli'i'elua, no. 166.
30. Kalei Nu'uhiwa, "Makahiki—Nā Maka o Lono: Utilizing the Papakū Makawalu Method to Analyze Mele and Pule of Lono and the Makahiki," (Ph.D. diss., University of Waikato, Hamilton, New Zealand, 2020), 189.
31. Nu'uhiwa, 122.
32. Nu'uhiwa, 234.
33. Brown, *Ka Po'e Mo'o Akua*, 142; Kimura, "Ka Leo Hawai'i." Interview with Jonah Kamālani.
34. Brown, 172.
35. Brown, 174–175.
36. Noelani Goodyear-Ka'opua, "On the Cattle Guard," *Biography* 43, no. 3 (2020): 527–529.

Bibliography

Brown, Marie Alohalani. *Ka Poʻe Moʻo Akua: Hawaiian Reptilian Water Deities*. Honolulu: University of Hawaiʻi Press, 2022.

Deloria, Vine. *The World We Used to Live In: Remembering the Powers of the Medicine Men*. Golden, CO: Fulcrum Publishing, 2006.

Goodyear-Kaʻopua, Noelani. "On the Cattle Guard." *Biography* 43, no. 3 (2020): 527–529.

Holt, John Dominis. *Hanai, a Poem for Queen Liliuokalani*, 1st ed. Honolulu: Topgallant, 1986.

———. *Kaulana Na Pua—Famous Are the Flowers: Queen Liliuokalani and the Throne of Hawaii : A Play in Three Acts*. Honolulu: Topgallant, 1974.

———. *On Being Hawaiian*. Honolulu: Ku Paʻa, 1995.

———. *Princess of the Night Rides and Other Tales*. Honolulu: Topgallant, 1977.

———. *Recollections: Memoirs of John Dominis Holt*, 1st ed. Honolulu: Ku Paʻa, 1993.

———. *The Art of Featherwork in Old Hawaiʻi*, 2nd ed. Honolulu: Ku Paʻa, 1997.

———. *Waimea Summer: A Novel*, 2nd ed. Honolulu: Ku Paʻa, 1998.

hoʻomanawanui, kuʻualoha. *Voices of Fire: Reweaving the Literary Lei of Pele and Hiʻiaka*. Minneapolis: University of Minnesota Press, 2014.

Interview with Kaleohano Kalili, Robert Plunkett, Jennie Wilson, Napua Stevens, Kaupena Wong, and Rubellite Kinney. Tape reel 7 in.,¼4 in. tape, May 9, 1956. Audio (Interviews, etc.). Bishop Museum Audio Collection.

Kalokuokamaile, Z. P. "Hanaia Ka Heiau O Hikiau Ma Ke One O Kealakekua." *Ka Nupepa Kuokoa*, Feb. 16, 1917.

———. "Ke Kalaiwaa ana ame Kona Mau Ano." *Ka Nupepa Kuokoa*, Oct. 26, 1922.

———. "Kekahi Mau Mea Ulu Kahiko o Hawaii," September 18, 1914.

———. "Na Inoa o na Manu, Na Limuesista Iʻa Pili Kahakai." *Ka Nupepa Kuokoa*, Nov. 6, 1914.

Kanahele, Pualani Kanakaʻole. *Ka Honua Ola: ʻEliʻeli Kau Mai (The Living Earth: Descend, Deepen the Revelation)*. Honolulu: Kamehameha Publishing, 2011.

Kawaikaumaiikamakaokaopua, Z. P. K. "Ke Kukulu Hale ana o ka Wa Kahikoesista Loina." *Ka Hoku O Hawaii*, March 18, 1923.

———. "Na Upena Lawaiʻa o ka Wa Kahiko ame ka Lakou Hana Pakahi." *Ka Nupepa Kuokoa*, June 22, 1923.

Kimura, Larry Lindsey Kauanoe. "Ka Leo Hawaiʻi." Audio/mpeg. Interview of Iokepa Makaʻai. University of Hawaiʻi at Mānoa, Nov. 9, 1980. Kaniʻāina in Ulukau, http://ulukau.org/kaniaina/?a=d&d=A-KLH-HV24-246&e=———en-20-A-1—txt-tpIN%7ctpTI%7ctpTA%7ctpCO%7ctpTY%7ctpLA%7ctpKE%7ctpPR%7ctpSG%7ctpTO%7ctpTG%7ctpSM%7ctpTR%7ctpSP%7ctpCT%7ctpET%7ctpHT%7ctpDT%7ctpOD%7ctpDF-maka%ca%bbai——————.

Meyer, Manulani Aluli. *Hoʻoulu: Our Time of Becoming: Collected Early Writings of Manulani Meyer*. Honolulu: ʻAi Pōhaku Press, 2003.

Nuʻuhiwa, Kalei. "Makahiki—Nā Maka o Lono: Utilizing the Papakū Makawalu Method to Analyze Mele and Pule of Lono and the Makahiki." Ph.D. diss., University of Waikato, 2020.

Pukui, Mary Kawena. "Ke Awa Lau o Puʻuloa: The Many-Harbored Sea of Puʻuloa." *Annual Report of the Hawaiian Historical Society*. Honolulu: Hawaiian Historical Society, 1943.

Chapter 12

Notes

1. Vine Deloria, Jr., *Red Earth, White Lies: Native Americans and the Myth of Scientific Fact* (Golden, CO: Fulcrum Publishing, 1997), 7.
2. V. Gewin, "Respect and Representation: Indigenous Scientists Seek Inclusion for Knowledge and for Themselves," *Nature* 589 (2021): 315–317; D. J. Nelson and L. D. Madson, "Representation of Native Americans in US Science and Engineering Faculty," *MRS Bulletin* 43 (2018): 379-383, https://doi.org/10.1557/mrs.2018.108; R. E. Bernard and E. H. G. Cooperdock, "No Progress on Diversity in 40 Years," *Nature Geoscience* 11 (2018): 292–295.
3. Sandra Harding, *Sciences from Below: Feminisms, Postcolonialities, and Modernities* (Durham, NC: Duke University Press, 2008), 283.
4. R. Levins and R. Lewontin, "Applied Biology in the Third World: The Struggle for Revolutionary Science," in *The Dialectical Biologist* (Cambridge, MA: Harvard University Press, 1988), 225–237; Vine Deloria, Jr., *Evolution, Creationism, and Other Modern Myths: A Critical Inquiry* (Golden, CO: Fulcrum Publishing, 2002), 274.
5. H. Branswell, "The World Needs Covid-19 Vaccines: It May Also Be Overestimating Their Power," *STAT* (May 22, 2020), https://www.statnews.com/2020/05/22/the-world-needs-covid-19-vaccines-it-may-also-be-overestimating-their-power/; Franklin Foer, "What Big Tech Wants Out of the Pandemic," *The Atlantic* (July–August 2020), https://www.theatlantic.com/magazine/archive/2020/07/big-tech-pandemic-power-grab/612238/; G. F. Kileen and S. S. Kiware, 2020 "Why Lockdown? Why National Unity? Why Global Solidarity? Simplified Arithmetic Tools for Decision-Makers, Health Professionals, Journalists and the General Public to Explore Containment Novel Coronavirus," *Infectious Disease Modeling* 5 (2020): 442–548.
6. Gewin, "Respect and Representation"; D. J. Nelson and L. D. Madson, "Representation of Native Americans in US Science and Engineering Faculty," *MRS Bulletin* 43 (2018): 379–383.
7. E. M. O'Brien, "American Indians in Higher Education, Research Briefs, Division of Policy Analysis and Research," *American Council on Education* 11, no. 3 (1992), Washington, DC.
8. National Science Board, "The Skilled Technical Workforce: Crafting America's Science and Engineering Enterprise," Report NSB-2019-23 (2019).
9. Center for Science and Democracy, "Science under Trump, Voices of Scientists across 16 Federal Agencies" (2018), Union of Concerned Scientists, accessed April 4, 2021, www.ucsusa.org/2018survey.
10. E. Yen-Kohl and The Newtown Florist Club Writing Collective, 2016, "We've Been Studied to Death, We Ain't Gotten Anything: (Re)claiming Environmental Knowledge Production through the Praxis of Writing Collectives," *Capitalism Nature Socialism* 27 (2016): 52–67; Sandra Harding, "Introduction: Eurocentric Science Illiteracy—A Challenge for the World Community," in *The Racial Economy of Science, Toward a Democratic Future*, ed. S. Harding (Bloomington: Indiana University Press, 1993), 1–29.
11. P. Cochran, O. H. Huntington, C. Pungowiyi, S. Tom, F. S. Chapin III, H. Huntington, N. G. Maynard, and S. F. Trainor, 2013, "Indigenous Frameworks for Observing and

Responding to Change in Alaska," *Climatic Change*, DOI: 10.1007/s10584-013-0735-2; S. Gearhead, M. Pocernich, R. Stewart, J. Sanguya, and H. P. Huntington, 2010, "Linking Inuit Knowledge and Meteorological Station Observations to Understand Changing Wind Patterns at Clyde River, Nunavut," *Climatic Change*, 100 (2010): 267–294; A. Marin, "Riders under Storms: Contributions of Nomadic Herders' Observations to Analyzing Climate Change in Mongolia," *Global Environmental Change*, 20, no. 1 (Feb. 2010): 162–176; H. P. Huntington, T. Callaghan, S. Fox, and I. Krupnik, "Matching Traditional and Scientific Observations to Detect Environmental Change: A Discussion on Arctic Terrestrial Ecosystems," *Ambio* 13 (2004): 18–23.

12. C. Lipo, T. Hunt, R. Horneman, and V. Bonhomme, 2016, "Weapons of War? Rapa Nui Mata'a Morphometric Analyses," *Antiquity* 90, no. 349 (2016): 172–187, DOI:10.15184/aqy.2015.189.
13. Vine Deloria, Jr., *Red Earth, White Lies: Native Americans and the Myth of Scientific Fact* (Golden, CO: Fulcrum Publishing, 1997), 7.
14. Deloria, *Red Earth, White Lies*, 376.
15. Deloria, *Red Earth, White Lies*.
16. J. M. Adovasio and J. Page, *The First Americans: In Pursuit of Archaeology's Greatest Mystery* (New York: Random House Publishing, 2003), 328.
17. Vine Deloria, Jr., *Evolution, Creationism, and Other Modern Myths*.
18. David E. Wilkins, *Red Prophet: The Punishing Intellectualism of Vine Deloria, Jr.* (Golden, CO: Fulcrum Publishing, 2018), 188.
19. M. H. Redsteer, K. Bemis, K. D. Chief, M. Gautam, B. R. Middleton, and R. Tsosie, "Unique Challenges Facing Southwestern Tribes: Impacts, Adaptation and Mitigation," in *Assessment of Climate Change in the Southwest United States: A Technical Report* prepared for the US NCA, ed. Greg Garfin, Angie Jardine, and Jonathan Overpeck (Washington, DC: Island Press, 2013), 385–404; M. H. Redsteer, K. B. Kelley, H. Francis, and D. Block, "Increasing Vulnerability of the Navajo People to Drought and Climate Change in the Southwestern United States: Accounts from Tribal Elders," in *Indigenous Knowledge for Climate Change Assessment and Adaptation*, ed. D. Nakashima, J. Rubis, and I. Krupnik (Cambridge, UK: Cambridge University Press, 2018), 171–187.
20. Redsteer et al., in *Indigenous Knowledge for Climate Change Assessment and Adaptation*, ed. D. Nakashima, J. Rubis, and I. Krupnik (Cambridge, UK: Cambridge University Press, 2018); M. H. Redsteer, K. B. Kelley, H. Francis, and D. Block, "Disaster Risk Assessment Case Study: Recent Drought on the Navajo Nation, Southwestern United States," in Annexes and Papers for the *Global Assessment Report on Disaster Risk Reduction* (New York, United Nations, 2011), 19, http://www.preventionweb.net/english/hyogo/gar/2011/en/what/drought.html; J. T. Doyle, M. H. Redsteer, and M. J. Eggers, "Exploring Effects of Climate Change on Northern Plains American Indian Health," *Journal of Climatic Change*, 2013 special issue: 135–148; J. K. Maldonado, R. E. Pandya, and J. C. Benedict, eds. *Climate Change and Indigenous Peoples in the United States: Impacts, Experiences and Actions* (New York: Springer, 2014), 643–655; M. H. Redsteer, and S. M. Wessells, "A Record of Change: Science and Elder Observations on the Navajo Nation," U.S. Geological Survey General Information Product 181, 2017.

21. Svante Arrhenius, "On the Influence of Carbonic Acid in the Air upon the Temperature of the Ground," *The London, Edinburgh and Dublin Philosophical Magazine and Journal of Science*, 1896, Series 5L: 237–276.
22. Deloria, *God Is Red*, 294
23. Ben Orlove, Heather Lazrus, Grete K. Hovelsrud, and Alessandra Giannini, "Recognitions and Responsibilities: On the Origins and Consequences of the Uneven Attention Climate Change around the World," *Current Anthropology* 55 (2014): 249–261; D. J. Nakashima, K. Galloway McLean, H. D. Thulstrup, A. Ramos Castillo, and J. T. Rubis, *Weathering Uncertainty: Traditional Knowledge for Climate Change Assessment and Adaptation* (Paris, UNESCO, and Darwin, Australia: United Nations University, 2012), https://collections.unu.edu/eserv/UNU:1511/Weathering-Uncertainty_FINAL_12-6-2012.pdf.
24. C. Farbotko and H. Lazrus, "The First Climate Refugees? Contesting Global Narratives of Climate Change in Tuvalu," in *Global Environmental Change* 22, no. 2 (May 2012): 382–390.
25. Tsosie, Rebecca, "Indigenous People and Environmental Justice: The Impact of Climate Change," *University of Colorado Law Review* 78 (2007): 1625-1677.
26. United Nations Framework Convention on Climate Change, 1992, 8–9.
27. J. Maldonado, T. M. B. Bennett, K. Chief, P. Cochran, K. Cozzetto, B. Gough, M. H. Redsteer, K. Lynn, and N. Maynard, "Engagement with Indigenous Peoples and Honoring Traditional Knowledge Systems," *Journal of Climatic Change* 135 (2015): 111–126.
28. Technical Summary of the IPCC Working Group II Climate Assessment Report 2014, p. 53.
29. Technical Summary of the IPCC Working Group II Climate Assessment Report 2014, p. 53.
30. Maldonado et al., "Engagement with Indigenous Peoples": 1–16.
31. Wilkins, *Red Prophet*, 188.
32. Kyle Whyte, "Critical Investigations of Resilience: A Brief Introduction to Indigenous Environmental Studies and Sciences," *Daedalus* 147, no. 2 (2018): 136–147.
33. J. Rockstrom, W. L. Steffan, K. Noone, A. Persson, F. S. Chapin, T. M. Lambin, M. Lenton, C. Scheffer, H. Folke, B. Schellnhuber, C. A. Nykvist, T. De Wit, S. Hughes, H. van der Leeuw, S. Rodhe, P. K. Sorlin, R. Snyder, U. Costanza, M. Svedin, L. Falkenmark, R. W. Karlberg, V. J. Corell, J. Fabry, B. Hansen, D. Walker, K. Liverman, K. Richardson, P. Crutzen, and J. Foley, "Planetary Boundaries: Exploring the Safe Operating Space for Humanity," *Ecology and Society* 14, no. 2 (2009): Article 32.
34. Vine Deloria, Jr., *Spirit and Reason: The Vine Deloria, Jr. Reader* (Golden, CO: Fulcrum Publishing, 1999), 84.

Chapter 14

Notes

1. Maya Angelou, "America's Renaissance Woman," interview on January 22, 1997, www.achievement.org.
2. Vine Deloria, Jr., *God Is Red: A Native View of Religion*, 30th Anniversary Edition (Golden, CO: Fulcrum Publishing, 2003), 80.

3. Deloria, *God Is Red*.
4. Deloria, 77.
5. Richard H. Pratt, "Education on Native Americans." Speech given at George Mason University, 1892, http://carlisleindian.dickinson.edu/teach/kill-indian-and-save-man-capt-richard-h-pratt-education-native-americans.
6. J. R. Miller, *Shingwauk's Vision: A History of Native Residential Schools* (Ontario: University of Toronto Press, 1996).
7. See Royal Commission on Aboriginal Peoples, "Report of the Royal Commission on Aboriginal Peoples." Full text of "Royal Commission on Aboriginal Peoples, Vol. 1—Looking Forward Looking Back" (Ottawa, ON: Royal Commission on Aboriginal Peoples, 1996).
8. Royal Commission on Aboriginal Peoples, "Report of the Royal Commission."
9. The National Native American Boarding School Healing Coalition, "US Indian Boarding School History," accessed 2022 from https://boardingschoolhealing.org/education/us-indian-boarding-school-history/.
10. Beverly Jacobs, "Indigenous Lawyer: Investigate Discovery of 215 Children's Graves in Kamloops as a Crime against Humanity," *The Conversation*, National Public Radio, June 8, 2021, accessed 2022 from https://theconversation.com/indigenous-lawyer-investigate-discovery-of-215-childrens-graves-in-kamloops-as-a-crime-against-humanity-161941.
11. Deloria, *God Is Red, 189.*
12. Deloria.
13. Deloria, 243.
14. Deloria, 67.
15. Luke Baker and Pascale Denis, "As Notre-Dame Money Rolls in, Some Eyebrows Raised over Rush of Funds," Reuters, April 17, 2019, accessed 2021 from https://www.reuters.com/article/us-france-notredame-donations/as-notre-dame-money-rolls-in-some-eyebrows-raised-over-rush-of-funds-idUSKCN1RT28Q.
16. Deloria, *God Is Red*, 285.

Bibliography

Angelou, Maya. "America's Renaissance Woman." January 22, 1997, interview. www.achievement.org

Baker, Luke, and Pascale Denis. "As Notre-Dame Money Rolls in, Some Eyebrows Raised over Rush of Funds." Reuters, April 17, 2019. Accessed 2021 from https://www.reuters.com/article/us-france-notredame-donations/as-notre-dame-money-rolls-in-some-eyebrows-raised-over-rush-of- funds-idUSKCN1RT28Q.

Deloria, Vine, Jr., *God Is Red: A Native View of Religion*. Golden, CO: Fulcrum Publishing, 2003.

Garnett, Stephen T., Neil D. Burgess, John E. Fa, Álvaro Fernández-Llamazares, Zsolt Molnár, Cathy J. Robinson, James E. M. Watson, et al., "A Spatial Overview of the Global Importance of Indigenous Lands for Conservation." *Nature Sustainability* 1, no. 7. (2018): 369–374. DOI:10.1038/s41893-018-0100-6.

Jacobs, Beverly, "Indigenous Lawyer: Investigate Discovery of 215 Children's Graves in Kamloops as a Crime against Humanity." *The Conversation*, National Public Radio, June

8, 2021. Accessed 2022 from https://theconversation.com/indigenous-lawyer-investigate-discovery-of-215-childrens-graves-in-kamloops-as-a-crime-against-humanity-161941.

Miller, J. R. *Shingwauk's Vision: A History of Native Residential Schools.* Ontario: University of Toronto Press, 1996.

Pratt, Richard H. "Education on Native Americans." Speech given at Georgia Mason University, 1892. http://carlisleindian.dickinson.edu/teach/kill-indian-and-save-man-capt-richard-h-pratt- education-native-americans.

Royal Commission on Aboriginal Peoples. "Report of the Royal Commission on Aboriginal Peoples." "Royal Commission on Aboriginal Peoples, Vol .1—Looking Forward Looking Back." Ottawa, ON: Royal Commission on Aboriginal Peoples, 1996.

Chapter 15

Notes

1. Vine Deloria, Jr., *The World We Used to Live In: Remembering the Powers of the Medicine Men* (Golden, CO: Fulcrum Publishing, 2006), xviii.
2. Linda Tuhiwai Smith, *Decolonizing Methodologies: Research and Indigenous Peoples* (London: Zed Books, 2012).
3. Nelson Maldonado-Torres, "Race, Religion, and Ethics in the Modern/Colonial World," *Journal of Religious Ethics* 42, no. 4 (2014): 691–711, https://doi.org/10.1111/jore.12078.
4. Deloria, *The World We Used to Live In*, xviii.
5. Vine Deloria, Jr. and Daniel Wildcat, *Power and Place: Indian Education in America* (Golden, CO: Fulcrum Publishing, 2001), 2.
6. *Power and Place*, 28.
7. Deloria, *The World We Used to Live In*, 195.
8. Deloria and Wildcat, *Power and Place*, 25.
9. Renya Ramirez, *Native Hubs: Culture, Community and Belonging in Silicon Valley and Beyond* (Durham, NC: Duke University Press, 2007).
10. Maria Yellow Horse Brave Heart, "The Return to the Sacred Path: Healing the Historical Trauma and Historical Unresolved Grief Response Among the Lakota Through a Psychoeducational Group Intervention," *Smith College Studies in Social Work* 68, no. 3 (1998): 287–305.
11. Leanne Betasamosake Simpson, *Dancing on Our Turtle's Back: Stories of Nishnabeg Re-Creation, Resurgence and a New Emergence* (Winnipeg, Manitoba: Arbeiter Ring Publishing, 2011).
12. Portions of this essay draw on a previously published work. See Natalie Avalos, Sandy Grande, and Jason Mancini, "Red Praxis: Lessons from Mashantucket to Standing Rock," in *Standing with Standing Rock: Voices From the #NoDAPL Movement*, ed. Jaskiran Dhillon and Nick Estes (Minneapolis: University of Minnesota Press, 2019).
13. See Natalie Avalos, *The Metaphysics of Decoloniality: Transnational Indigeneities and Religious Refusal*, *The CLR James Journal* 27, nos. 1–2 (2021): 81–99.

Bibliography

Avalos, Natalie, and Molly Basset, eds. *Indigenous Religious Traditions in 5 Minutes*. Sheffield, UK: Equinox Publishing, 2022.

Brave Heart, Maria Yellow Horse. "The Return to the Sacred Path: Healing the Historical Trauma and Historical Unresolved Grief Response Among the Lakota Through a Psychoeducational Group Intervention." *Smith College Studies in Social Work* 68, no. 3 (1998): 287–305.

Deloria, Vine, Jr. *The World We Used to Live In: Remembering the Powers of the Medicine Men*. Golden, CO: Fulcrum Publishing, 2006.

Deloria, Vine, Jr., and Daniel Wildcat. *Power and Place: Indian Education in America*. Golden, CO: Fulcrum Publishing, 2001.

Maldonado-Torres, Nelson. "Race, Religion, and Ethics in the Modern/Colonial World." *Journal of Religious Ethics* 42, no. 4 (2014): 691–711, https://doi.org/10.1111/jore.12078.

Ramirez, Renya. *Native Hubs: Culture, Community and Belonging in Silicon Valley and Beyond. Durham*, NC: Duke University Press, 2007.

Chapter 16

Notes

1. There is growing public awareness of the appropriation of Indigenous identities by non-Indigenous individuals and groups who co-opt such identities for personal or collective gain. Terms such as "pretendians" (pretend Indians) and other portmanteaus accompany discussions across social media and news outlets. Indigenous identity appropriation is not new by any stretch of the imagination; Philip Deloria covers its long history within the United States in *Playing Indian* (New Haven, CT: Yale University Press, 1998), and Indigenous communities throughout the world continue to experience identity appropriation. I do not address this topic here, just as Vine Deloria, Jr. did not address it in calls for recognition of unrecognized Tribal communities. He understood that bona fide but unrecognized Tribes existed within the United States, especially on the East Coast. His publications and letters cited throughout this essay clarify his understanding of bona fide but unrecognized Tribes.
2. See, for example, Vine Deloria, Jr., *Custer Died for Your Sins: An Indian Manifesto* (Norman: University of Oklahoma Press, 1969), 52, 246; and Vine Deloria, Jr., *Spirit and Reason: The Vine Deloria, Jr., Reader* (Golden, CO: Fulcrum Publishing, 1999), 266, 267.
3. Lumbee Recognition—Testimony & Materials (Folder title), Vine Deloria Papers, WA MSS S-2661, Box 58f, Yale Collection of Western Americana, Beinecke Rare Book and Manuscript Library, Yale University.
4. Lumbee Recognition—Testimony & Materials, Vine Deloria Papers. See also Vine Deloria, Vine, Jr. *A Better Day for Indians* (New York: The Field Foundation, 1977).
5. Deloria describes sovereignty as an act of developing, sustaining, and transforming Tribal traditions for collective survival in "Self-Determination and the Concept of Sovereignty" in *Economic Development in American Indian Reservations*, ed. Roxanne Dunbar-Ortiz, University of New Mexico Native American Studies Development Series No. 1 (Albuquerque: University of New Mexico, 1979), 22–28. For other discussions of

inherent sovereignty see, for example, Stephen Cornell and Joseph P. Kalt, "American Indian Self-Determination: The Political Economy of a Policy That Works," HKS Faculty Research Working Paper Series RWP10-043, (John F. Kennedy School of Government, Harvard University, 2010), 3; Brian Klopotek, *Recognition Odysseys: Indigeneity, Race, and Federal Tribal Recognition Policy in Three Louisiana Indian Communities* (Durham, NC: Duke University Press, 2011), 21.

6. Deloria, "Self-Determination and the Concept of Sovereignty," 26.
7. Cornell and Kalt, "American Indian Self-Determination." See also research produced by Indigenous-serving initiatives such as the Harvard Project on American Indian Economic Development (https://hpaied.org) and the University of Arizona's Native Nations Institute (https://nni.arizona.edu).
8. See, for example, Kyle P. Whyte, "Settler Colonialism, Ecology, and Environmental Injustice," *Environment and Society* 9, no. 1 (2018).
9. Actions by Indigenous people to protect and steward their sacred places are not separate from economic expressions of sovereignty. For example, if Indigenous lands and waters are polluted, and if Indigenous communities are unhealthy because of exposure to pollution and environmental hazards, then economic possibilities become fewer. The trade-off between environmental harm and economic possibility is widely recognized, evidenced by the fact that governments and corporations offer financial incentives for Indigenous peoples to store toxic waste or host hazardous infrastructure on their lands. See Tracylee Clarke, "An Ideographic Analysis of Native American Sovereignty in the State of Utah: Enabling Denotative Dissonance and Constructing Irreconcilable Conflict," *Wicazo Sa Review* 17, no. 2 (2002).
10. L. D. Jantarasami, R. Novak, R. Delgado, E. Marino, S. McNeeley, C. Narducci, J. Raymond-Yakoubian, L. Singletary, and K. P. Whyte, "Tribes and Indigenous Peoples," in *Impacts, Risks, and Adaptation in the United States: Fourth National Climate Assessment, Volume II*, ed. D. R. Reidmiller, C. W. Avery, D. R. Easterling, K. E. Kunkel, K. L. M. Lewis, T. K. Maycock, and B. C. Stewart, U.S. Global Change Research Program, Washington, DC, 572–603.
11. For decades leading up to the 1970s, scholarly consensus on Lumbee identity aligned with the findings of anthropologist John Swanton, who described them as the descendants of fragmented Indigenous communities and various other non-Indigenous peoples who amalgamated into a unified group during the colonial era. Lumbee people generally agreed with the scholarly consensus, although some families and individuals identified culturally with specific colonial era Tribes and rejected Lumbee as an overarching cultural identity. See John R. Swanton, "Probable Identity of the 'Croatan Indians,'" US Dept. of Interior, Office of Indian Affairs, Washington, DC, 1933. Historians, anthropologists, and ethnographers have filled in additional details in the decades since the 1970s, but Swanton's general findings still hold in academic circles today. Today, the Lumbee Tribal government and most Lumbee citizens agree with Swanton's general conclusion that the Tribe is an amalgamation of colonial-era Native peoples.
12. See Ryan E. Emanuel, "Water in the Lumbee World: A River and Its People in a Time of Change," *Environmental History* 24, no. 1 (2019), 25–51. For a broader history of Lumbee people (including a history of Tribal names) see Malinda Maynor Lowery, *Lumbee*

Indians in the Jim Crow South: Race, Identity, and the Making of a Nation (Chapel Hill: University of North Carolina Press, 2010).

13. For a detailed discussion of forced assimilation during the termination era, see Stephen J. Herzberg, "The Menominee Indians: Termination to Restoration," *American Indian Law Review* 6, no. 1 (1978): 143–186.
14. United States Statutes at Large, 67: B132.
15. Public Law 84-570, An Act relating to the Lumbee Indians of North Carolina (70 Stat. 254).
16. Deloria quoted in letter from Senator Daniel Inouye to Tribal Leaders, Lumbee (Folder title), Vine Deloria Papers.
17. Letter from Vine Deloria to Sam Ervin, Lumbee Resolution Controversy (Folder title), Vine Deloria Papers.
18. Letter from Howard Tommie to US Department of Labor and attached position paper. Lumbee Resolution Controversy, Vine Deloria Papers. The phrase "possibly non-Indian" appears several times in the lobbying materials, suggesting that one purpose of USET's campaign may have been to manufacture doubt among Tribes nationally about Lumbee indigeneity. By the 1970s, Lumbee people were already known among Tribal nations. Lumbee judge Lacy Maynor had delivered a keynote address at the National Congress of American Indians (NCAI) convention in 1958 so popular that NCAI printed and distributed copies of the address nationally following the convention. Lumbees Brantley Blue and Helen Maynor Scheirbeck served in prominent federal roles—Blue on the Indian Claims Commission and Scheirbeck in several roles, including director of the Office of Indian Education. In a 1974 interview, Scheirbeck claimed to have helped launch USET by encouraging the formation of an intertribal council and negotiating funds from the Association on American Indian Affairs to launch the initiative. Interview by Lew Barton with (Commissioner) Brantley Blue and Helen Maynor Schierbeck, November 4, 1974, University of Florida Digital Collections, https://ufdc.ufl.edu/UF00006825/00001.
19. Letter from Howard Tommie to US Department of Labor and attached position paper, Lumbee Resolution Controversy, Vine Deloria Papers.
20. This claim was based on a misinterpretation of fieldwork conducted in the 1930s by anthropologist Carl Seltzer. The 1930 Census, which took place a few years before Seltzer's visit to Robeson County, listed more than twelve thousand people in the county who were enumerated as "other than White or Negro." Undoubtedly, the vast majority of these individuals were Native Americans. USET's claim of twenty-two was, instead, based on Seltzer's conclusion that twenty-two of two hundred physical examinees were Native Americans. Census data from Steven Manson, Jonathan Schroeder, David Van Riper, Tracy Kugler, and Steven Ruggles, IPUMS National Historical Geographic Information System: Version 15.0 [dataset], Minneapolis: IPUMS. 2020, http://doi.org/10.18128/D050.V15.0.
21. For a detailed chronology and analysis of USET's activities related to the Lumbee Tribe during this period, see Harold W. Elliott, "The Colorblind Turn in Indian Country: Lumbee Indians, Civil Rights, and Tribal State Formation," (PhD diss. University of Michigan, 2019).

22. American Indian Press Association News Service Document Lumbee—N0011, Lumbee Resolution Controversy, Vine Deloria Papers.
23. Letter from Howard Tommie to US Department of Labor, Vine Deloria Papers. USET materials played up a paucity of historical documentation about Lumbees; however, Lumbee ancestors lived in a region that was poorly mapped and documented by outsiders prior to 1800, which makes a lack of historical documentation unsurprising. See Emanuel, "Water in a Lumbee World," and note Francis Jennings's caution, "The blank places in the histories do not represent a paucity of events," in "The Indian Trade of the Susquehanna Valley," *Proceedings APS*, 1966, 406.
24. Letter from James H. Woods to anonymous, Lumbee Resolution Controversy, Vine Deloria Papers.
25. Letter from Vine Deloria to Sam Ervin, Lumbee Resolution Controversy, Vine Deloria Papers.
26. Deloria, *A Better Day for Indians*, 20.
27. Deloria's papers include a manuscript copy of "Comments on the Lumbee of North Carolina," a 1992 report by Kenneth H. Carleton, Tribal anthropologist and ethnohistorian for the Mississippi Band of Choctaw Indians, as well as printed reactions to the report from several academic scholars with expertise on Native Americans of the eastern United States. Sturtevant was not the only one of these academics to criticize Carleton's report. William Starna (SUNY Oneonta) summarized Carleton's work as a "racist tract" and Jack Campisi (Wellesley College) called it a "diatribe against the Lumbees" by a "hired gun of extremely low calibre." Raymond Fogelson (University of Chicago) observed "serious flaws" in Carleton's work, including overreliance on outdated research on tri-racial isolates, a mid-twentieth century term applied to Lumbee and other racially marginalized groups in the southeastern United States. Science historian Veronika Lipphardt highlights some of the scientific and moral challenges of tri-racial isolate research and traces its roots in eugenics. In a bizarre example of sloppy research built atop dubious scholarship, Carleton's report not only relied on outdated tri-racial isolate research, but it mistakenly cited "blood" and "race" statistics from an entirely different research study that did not involve Lumbee people at all; Carleton had taken results from the wrong study by a team of researchers that had studied blood characteristics of several different communities in North and South Carolina. See Lumbee, Vine Deloria Papers and Veronika Lipphardt, "'Geographical Distribution Patterns of Various Genes' Genetic Studies of Human Variation after 1945," *Studies in History and Philosophy of Science Part C: Studies in History and Philosophy of Biological and Biomedical Sciences* 47 (2014).
28. Lumbee Resolution Controversy, Vine Deloria Papers.
29. Lumbee Resolution Controversy, Vine Deloria Papers.
30. Leaders of USET and individual Tribes have maintained political opposition to Lumbee recognition from the 1970s to this day. For example, during the Lumbee Tribe's 2020 bid to amend the 1956 Lumbee Act in Congress, Eastern Band principal Chief Richard Sneed told newspaper reports that "the group of people calling themselves Lumbees have never provided any substantial evidence of descendancy from any of the historical Tribes." In a joint letter to Congress, Sneed and Mississippi Band of Choctaw Tribal

Chief Cyrus Ben wrote, "Other tribal leaders have expressed similar opposition, including the Cherokee Nation and the United South and Eastern Tribes (USET), representing over 30 Tribes." See "US House OK of Lumbee Recognition Act Celebrated Locally," *The Robesonian*, November 20, 2020. In 2021, at my own university, a representative of a USET-affiliated Tribe opined to a group of undergraduate students that federally unrecognized Tribes had no languages, no historical evidence of indigeneity, and shorter durations of connection to the landscape than federally recognized Tribes. The guest speaker's opinion might have been taken as an established fact by the entire group of students, except that one of the students belonged to a federally unrecognized Tribe and challenged the assertions. The instructor allowed time for a nuanced discussion and gave me an opportunity to provide students with additional context. This story is anecdotal, but it highlights the pervasiveness of ideas that decades ago were criticized by Deloria and debunked by others. See note 27, above.

31. 1988 Testimony to US Senate, Lumbee Recognition—Testimony & Materials, Vine Deloria, Jr. Papers.
32. Letter from Vine Deloria to Hank Brown, Lumbee Recognition Testimony & Materials, Vine Deloria, Jr. Papers.
33. Deloria Papers.
34. See, for example, Angela Gonzales, Judy Kertész, and Gabrielle Tayac, "Eugenics as Indian Removal: Sociohistorical Processes and the De(con)Struction of American Indians in the Southeast," *The Public Historian* 29, no. 3 (2007): 53–67.
35. Deloria, *Spirit and Reason*, 267; For a detailed account of Carl Seltzer's 1936 visit and problematic methods, see Lowery, *Lumbee Indians in the Jim Crow South,* 181–212. See also Note 18, above.
36. David E. Wilkins, *Red Prophet: The Punishing Intellectualism of Vine Deloria, Jr.* (Golden, CO: Fulcrum Publishing, 2018), 25.
37. Kyle P. Whyte, "Justice Forward: Tribes, Climate Adaptation and Responsibility," *Climatic Change*, DOI:10.1007/S10584-013-0743-2, 2013.
38. Ryan E. Emanuel and David E. Wilkins. "Breaching Barriers: The Fight for Indigenous Participation in Water Governance," *Water* 12, no. 8 (2020): 2113.
39. See Debra Utacia Krol, "Can Native American Tribes Protect Their Land if They're Not Recognized by the Federal Government?" *The Revelator*, March 19, 2019, https://therevelator.org/native-american-Tribes-protect-land/.
40. In particular, federal statutes such as the National Historic Preservation Act and the Native American Graves Protection and Repatriation Act include legal protections that apply to federally recognized Tribes.
41. Daniel R. Wildcat, *Red Alert! Saving the Planet with Indigenous Knowledge* (Golden, CO: Fulcrum Publishing, 2009), 19.
42. See "End of Mission Statement by the United Nations Special Rapporteur on the Rights of Indigenous Peoples, Victoria Tauli-Corpuz of Her Visit to the United States of America," United Nations OHCHR, March 3, 2017, http://www.ohchr.org/EN/NewsEvents/Pages/DisplayNews.aspx?NewsID=21274.
43. Todd A. Mitchell, N. J. Casper, L. T. Logan, E. Colclazier, and K. J. R. Mitchell, "Using Traditional Ecological Knowledge to Protect Wetlands: The Swinomish Tribe's Wetlands

Cultural Assessment Project" (unpublished manuscript, 2020).

44. Consider the politicization of recent fossil fuel projects such as the Dakota Access Pipeline and the Atlantic Coast Pipeline. Tribes with active bids for recognition may be wary of becoming involved in controversies that could jeopardize political support for their administrative or legislative petition. See Emanuel and Wilkins, "Breaching Barriers."
45. See note 27, above.
46. Gonzales, et al., "Eugenics as Indian Removal."
47. Emanuel, "Water in a Lumbee World"; Emanuel and Wilkins, "Breaching Barriers."
48. Jantarasami et al., "Tribes and Indigenous Peoples," 2018.
49. See Emanuel, "Water in a Lumbee World"; Emanuel and Wilkins, "Breaching Barriers."
50. See Emanuel, "Water in a Lumbee World."
51. I generated this result by first searching the US legislative record for bills containing the phrase "extend federal recognition" plus the term "Tribe." I included variants. The search returned 188 bills, an overestimate that includes legislation unrelated to federal Tribal recognition (e.g., omnibus bills with no recognition riders but containing variants of search phrases). I then added "environment" to the list of search terms, which left only the Mono Lake Kutzadikaª recognition bill. I conducted the search at http://congress.gov.
52. See, for example, efforts by the Duwamish Tribe (Washington) and the Isle de Jean Charles Band of Biloxi-Chitimacha-Choctaw Indians (Louisiana), both of whom have centered environmental issues in their arguments for federal recognition. Adam Crepelle, "The United States First Climate Relocation: Recognition, Relocation, and Indigenous Rights at the Isle de Jean Charles," *Belmont Law Review* 6, no. 1 (2018): 1–40; Rebecca M. Mitchell, "People of the Outside: The Environmental Impact of Federal Recognition of American Indian Nations," *Boston College Environmental Affairs Law Review* 42, no. 2 (2015): 507–540.
53. Deloria, "Self-Determination and the Sovereignty," 26.

Bibliography

Clarke, Tracylee. "An Ideographic Analysis of Native American Sovereignty in the State of Utah: Enabling Denotative Dissonance and Constructing Irreconcilable Conflict." *Wicazo Sa Review* 17, no. 2 (2002).

Cornell, Stephen, and Joseph P. Kalt. "American Indian Self-Determination: The Political Economy of a Policy That Works." HKS Faculty Research Working Paper Series RWP10-043, John F. Kennedy School of Government, Harvard University, 2010.

Crepelle, Adam. "The United States First Climate Relocation: Recognition, Relocation, and Indigenous Rights at the Isle de Jean Charles." *Belmont Law Review* 6, no. 1 (2019): 1–40.

Deloria, P., *Playing Indian*. New Haven, CT: Yale University Press, 1998.

Deloria, V., Jr., *Custer Died for Your Sins: An Indian Manifesto*. Norman: University of Oklahoma Press, 1969.

———. *A Better Day for Indians*. New York: The Field Foundation, 1977.

———. "Self-Determination and the Concept of Sovereignty." In *Economic Development in*

American Indian Reservations, ed. Roxanne Dunbar-Ortiz. University of New Mexico Native American Studies Development Series No. 1, Albuquerque: University of New Mexico, 1979, 22–28.

———. *Spirit and Reason: The Vine Deloria, Jr., Reader*. Golden, CO: Fulcrum Publishing, 1999.

Elliott, H. W. "The Colorblind Turn in Indian Country: Lumbee Indians, Civil Rights, and Tribal State Formation." PhD diss. University of Michigan, 2019.

Emanuel, R. E., "Water in the Lumbee World: A River and Its People in a Time of Change." *Environmental History* 24, no. 1 (2019): 25–51.

Emanuel, R. E, and D. E. Wilkins. "Breaching Barriers: The Fight for Indigenous Participation in Water Governance." *Water* 12, no. 8 (2020).

Gonzales, A., J. Kertész, and G. Tayac. "Eugenics as Indian Removal: Sociohistorical Processes and the De(con)Struction of American Indians in the Southeast." *The Public Historian* 29, no. 3 (2007).

Herzberg, Stephen J. "The Menominee Indians: Termination to Restoration." *American Indian Law Review* 6, no. 1 (1978).

Jantarasami, L. C., R. Novak, R. Delgado, E. Marino, S. McNeeley, C. Narducci, J. Raymond-Yakoubian, L. Singletary, and K. Powys Whyte. "Tribes and Indigenous Peoples." In *Impacts, Risks, and Adaptation in the United States: Fourth National Climate Assessment, Volume II*, ed. D. R. Reidmiller, C. W. Avery, D. R. Easterling, K. E. Kunkel, K. L. M. Lewis, T. K. Maycock, and B. C. Stewart. U.S. Global Change Research Program, Washington, DC, 572–603.

Jennings, F. "The Indian Trade of the Susquehanna Valley." *Proceedings APS*, 1966.

Klopotek, B. *Recognition Odysseys: Indigeneity, Race, and Federal Tribal Recognition Policy in Three Louisiana Indian Communities*. Durham, NC: Duke University Press, 2011.

Krol, D. U. "Can Native American Tribes Protect Their Land if They're Not Recognized by the Federal Government?" *The Revelator*, March 19, 2019.

Lipphardt, Veronika. "'Geographical Distribution Patterns of Various Genes: Genetic Studies of Human Variation after 1945." *Studies in History and Philosophy of Science Part C: Studies in History and Philosophy of Biological and Biomedical Sciences* 47, 2014.

Lowery, M. M. *Lumbee Indians in the Jim Crow South: Race, Identity, and the Making of a Nation*. Chapel Hill: University of North Carolina Press, 2010.

Manson, S., J. Schroeder, D. Van Riper, T. Kugler, and S. Ruggles. IPUMS National Historical Geographic Information System: Version 15.0 [dataset]. Minneapolis: IPUMS, 2020.

Mitchell, R. M. "People of the Outside: The Environmental Impact of Federal Recognition of American Indian Nations." *Boston College Environmental Affairs Law Review* 42, no. 2 (2015).

Mitchell, T. A., N. J. Casper, L. T. Logan, E. Colclazier, and K. J. R. Mitchell. "Using Traditional Ecological Knowledge to Protect Wetlands: The Swinomish Tribe's Wetlands Cultural Assessment Project." Unpublished manuscript, 2020.

Vine Deloria Papers, WA MSS S-2661, Box 58f, Yale Collection of Western Americana, Beinecke Rare Book and Manuscript Library, Yale University.

Whyte, Kyle P. "Justice Forward: Tribes, Climate Adaptation and Responsibility." *Climatic Change* (2013).

Wildcat, D. R. *Red Alert! Saving the Planet with Indigenous Knowledge.* Golden, CO: Fulcrum Publishing, 2009.

Wilkins, David E. *Red Prophet: The Punishing Intellectualism of Vine Deloria, Jr.* Golden, CO: Fulcrum Publishing, 2018.

Chapter 17

Notes

1. E. H. Erikson, *The Life Cycle Completed* (New York: Norton, 1982).
2. Oren Lyons, "An Iroquois Perspective," in *American Indian Environments: Ecological Issues in Native American History*, ed. C. Vecsey and R. W. Venables (Syracuse, NY: Syracuse University Press, 1980), 173–174; M. Verma, S. Seth, and N. K. Chadha, "Intergenerational Familial Relationships from the Lens of Generativity," *Indian Journal of Positive Psychology* 8, no. 4 (2017): 554–557.
3. J. P. Lewis and J. Allen, "Alaska Native Elders in Recovery: Linkages between Indigenous Cultural Generativity and Sobriety to Promote Successful Aging," *Journal of Cross-Cultural Gerontology* 32 (2017): 209–222.
4. Erikson, *The Life Cycle*, 276.
5. F. Villar and R. Serrat, "A Field in Search of Concepts: The Relevance of Generativity to Intergenerational Relationships," *Journal of Intergenerational Relationships* 12 (2014): 381–397.
6. J. Hofer, H. Busch, I. P. Solcova, A. Au, and P. Tavel, "For the Benefit of Others: Generativity and Meaning in Life in the Elderly in Four Cultures," *Psychology and Aging* 29, no. 4 (2014): 764–775; Villar and Serrat, "A Field in Search of Concepts."
7. D. McAdams, E. de St. Aubin, and R. L. Logan, "Generativity Among Young, Midlife, and Older Adults," *Psychology and Aging* 8 (1993): 221–230.
8. Erikson, The Life Cycle.
9. Villar and Serrat, "A Field in Search of Concepts."
10. M. W. Pratt, "Forum Response: Erikson's Stage: Fostering Adults' Intergenerational Programs," *Journal of Intergenerational Relationships* 11 (2013): 97–100.
11. M. Tabuchi and A. Miura, "Young People's Reactions Change Elderly People's Generativity and Narratives: The Effects of Intergenerational Interaction on the Elderly," Journal of Intergenerational Relationships 13 (2015): 118–133.
12. J. D. Anderson, *The Four Hills of Life: Northern Arapaho Knowledge and Life Movement* (Lincoln: University of Nebraska Press, 2001).
13. Hofer et al., "For the Benefit of Others."
14. Tabuchi and Miura, "Young People's Reactions."
15. J. Kotre, *Make It Count: How to Generate a Legacy That Gives Meaning to Your Life* (New York: Free Press, 1999); Tabuchi and Miura, "Young People's Reactions"; Villar and Serrat, "A Field in Search of Concepts."
16. Verma, Seth, and Chadha, "Intetergenerational Familial Relationships."
17. J. Warburton and D. McLaughlin, "Passing on Our culture: How Older Australians from Diverse Cultural Backgrounds Contribute to Society," *Journal of Cross Cultural Gerontology* 22, no. 1 (2007): 47–60.
18. Tabuchi and Miura, "Young People's Reactions."

19. M. F. Tanaka, M. Glasser, T. Supahan, and J. Vater, "Giving Back to Get Back: Assessment of Native and Non-Native American Perceptions of Generativity," *Journal of Health Care for the Poor and Underserved* 31 (2020): 1427–1439.
20. Tabuchi and Miura, "Young People's Reactions."
21. Villar and Serrat, "A Field in Search of Concepts."
22. E. H. Erikson, J. M. Erikson, and H. Q. Kivnick, *Vital Involvement in Old Age* (New York: Norton, 1986), https://hpaied.org/publications/leadership-institute-santa-fe-indian-school-all-indian-pueblo-council.
23. J. D. Anderson, "Space, Time and Unified Knowledge: Following the Path of Vine Deloria, Jr." in *Counterpoints* 379 (2011): 92–108.
24. Villar and Serrat. "A Field in Search of Concepts."
25. Villar and Serrat.
26. C. L. Bradley, "Generativity-Stagnation: Development of a Status Model" in *Developmental Review* 17 (1997): 262–290; Erickson, *The Life Cycle.*

Chapter 19

Notes

1. White Swan Negotiation Team records in possession of author.
2. White Swan records.
3. White Swan records.
4. Tribal records in possession of author.
5. Water Resources Development Act of 1999–2000, https://www.congress.gov/106/plaws/publ53/PLAW-106publ53.pdf.
6. Peter Capossela, *The Ongoing Saga of The Sioux Land Claim, 1851–2012* (Sioux Falls, SD: Mariah Press, 2015).
7. Indian Sacred Sites: A Presidential Document by the Executive Office of the President on 05/29/1996. E.O. 13007 of May 24, 1996. 61 FR 26771, 26771-26772. Document Number: 96-13597, https://www.federalregister.gov/documents/1996/05/29/96-13597/indian-sacred-sites.

Chapter 20

Notes

1. United Nations Declaration on the Rights of Indigenous Peoples, accessed March 15, 2022, from https://www.un.org/development/desa/indigenouspeoples/declaration-on-the-rights-of-indigenous-peoples.html.
2. From their website: "International Committee for the Indigenous Peoples of the Americas: Since 1974, the Swiss human rights organization Incomindios has campaigned for the rights of the Indigenous peoples worldwide. With a special focus on North, Central and South America. Since 2003, Incomindios has been adviser to the UNO (ECOSOC), accessed March 15, 2022, from https://www.incomindios.ch/en/.
3. Vine Deloria, Jr., *Peau-Rouge*, préface de Yves Berger, traduit de l'américain par Nathalie Savary et Anne-Marie Savarin (Paris: Edition Speciale), 197.

4. Michel Davaud, X. Vauthrin, and R. Jaulin, *Nous Parlons, Vous Écoutez* (Institut National de l'Audiovisuel, Paris), 1978, accessed March 17, 2022, from https://en.unifrance.org/movie/52453/nous-parlons-vous-ecoutez.
5. Vine Deloria, Jr., *Singing for a Spirit* (Santa Fe, NM: Clear Light Publishers, 1999).
6. Jean-François Graugnard, E. Patrouilleau, and S. Eimeo a Raa, *Nations Indiennes, Nations Souveraines* (Paris: Editions François Maspero, 1977).
7. International Treaty Council's final report on the International NGO Conference on Discrimination Against Indigenous Populations in the Americas, held at United Nations' offices in Geneva on September 20–23, 1977. Accessed March 15, 2022, from https://ipdpowwow.org/%201977_conference%20ITTC%20Report%20copy.pdf.
8. WARN was founded in 1974 by Lorelei DeCora Means (Ho-Chunk), Madonna Thunder Hawk (Oohenumpa Lakota), Phyllis Young (Standing Rock), and Janet McCloud (Tulalip) to bring attention to women's issues in Indian Country.
9. Édith Patrioulleau and J. Menier, *Les Chemins de la Survie* (Paris: Self-published, 1980), https://www.amazon.fr/Chemins-survie-%C3%89dith-patrouilleau/dp/B0014KYHJA.
10. Vine Deloria, Jr., *God Is Red: A Native View of Religion* (Golden, CO: Fulcrum Publishing, 1994).
11. Deloria, *God Is Red*, 97.
12. Deloria, *Custer Died for Your Sins: An Indian Manifesto* (Norman, University of Oklahoma Press, 1988), 79.
13. Édith Patrioulleau and Aurélie Journée-Duez, excerpt from conversations in January 2022.
14. Kim O'Bomsawin, director, *Quiet Killing* (Longueuil, Quebec: Wabanok, 2018).
15. Benjamin Brookwell, "Remembering Joyce Echaquan: Systemic Racism and Indigenous Deaths in Health Care," in the *Toronto Star*, Fri., Oct. 15, 2021, accessed March 15, 2022, from https://www.thestar.com/opinion/contributors/2021/10/15/remembering-joyce-echaquan-systemic-racism-and-indigenous-deaths-in-health-care.html.
16. Eve Tuck and K. W. Yang, "Decolonization Is Not a Metaphor," *Decolonization: Indigeneity, Education, & Society* 1, no. 1 (2012).

Chapter 21

Notes

1. Brian Stelter, "Rick Santorum Departs CNN after Criticism of Native American comments," CNN, last modified May 22, 2021, https://www.cnn.com/2021/05/22/media/rick-santorum-cnn-departure-native-americancriticism/index.html.
2. Alex Wilson, Bronwyn Carlton, and Acushla Sciascia, "Reterritorialising Social Media: Indigenous People Rise Up," *Australasian Journal of Information Systems* 21 (2017): 2.
3. Marisa Duarte, "Connected Activism: Indigenous Uses of Social Media for Shaping Political Change," *Australasian Journal of Information Systems* 21 (2017): I .
4. Duarte: 4.
5. Duarte: 4.
6. Leanne Betasamosake Simpson, *As We Have Always Done: Indigenous Freedom through Radical Resistance* (Minneapolis: University of Minnesota Press, 2017), 222.

7. Simpson, 223, viii, 221.
8. Simpson, 220.
9. Simpson, 220.
10. Simpson, 220.

Chapter 22

Note

1. California v. Cabazon Band of Mission Indians, 480 U.S. 202 (1987). This decision effectively overturned existing state laws that restricted gaming in Indian Country. Congress responded the following year by enacting the Indian Gaming Regulatory Act, which created a national framework for how gaming could be operated by Native Nations.

Chapter 23

Notes

1. Gregory A. Cajete, *Look to the Mountain: An Ecology of Indigenous Education* (Skyland, NC: Kivaki Press, 1994).
2. Vine Deloria, Jr., *Spirit and Reason: The Vine Deloria, Jr. Reader* (Golden, CO: Fulcrum Publishing, 1999).
3. David E. Wilkins, "Forging A Political, Educational, and Cultural Agenda for Indian Country," in *Destroying Dogma: Vine Deloria, Jr. and His Influence on American Society,* ed. Steve Pavlik and Daniel Wildcat (Golden, CO: Fulcrum Publishing, 2006), 186–187.
4. Wilkins, 188–189.
5. Vine Deloria, Jr, *God Is Red: A Native View of Religion* (Golden, CO: Fulcrum Publishing, 1994).
6. Deloria in Cajete, *Look to the Mountain*, 11–13.
7. Deloria in Cajete, 11–12.
8. Vine Deloria, Jr., "The Perpetual Indian Education Message," *Winds of Change* (Washington, DC: American Indian Higher Education Consortium, 1992).
9. Deloria, *Spirit and Reason,* 139.
10. Edward T. Hall, *Beyond Culture* (New York: Anchor Books/Doubleday, 1976), 28–29.
11. P. V. Beck and A. L. Walters, *The Sacred* (Tsaile, AZ: Navajo Community College Press, 1977), 84.
12. Deloria, *Spirit and Reason*, 139.
13. Michelle Sam, "Indigenous Peoples' Transformative Research Framework," in *Native Minds Rising: Exploring Transformative Indigenous Education*, ed. G.A. Cajete (Vernon, BC: John Charlton Publishing, 2019), 24–41.
14. Vine Deloria, Jr., *The Metaphysics of Modern Existence* (New York: Harper & Row, 1979), vii.
15. Deloria, viii.
16. Nicholas C. Peroff, "Doing Research in Indian Affairs: Old Problems and a New Perspective," unpublished paper, University of Missouri (Kansas City: L. P. Cookingham Institute of Public Affairs, 1989).
17. Thomas Berry, *The Dream of the Earth* (San Francisco: Sierra Club Books, 1988), 3.

Chapter 24

Notes

1. David E. Wilkins, *Red Prophet: The Punishing Intellectualism of Vine Deloria, Jr.* (Golden, CO: Fulcrum Publishing, 2018).
2. Wilkins.
3. Vine Deloria, Jr. *Custer Died for Your Sins: An Indian Manifesto* (Norman: University of Oklahoma Press, 1969), 79.
4. Deloria, 79.
5. Deloria, 82.
6. Deloria, 82.
7. Deloria, 83.
8. Wilkins, *Red Prophet*, 126.
9. Wilkins, 128.
10. Vine Deloria, Jr., *Indian Education in America* (Denver, CO: American Indian Science and Engineering Society [AISES], 1991), 11.
11. Bryan McKinley Jones Brayboy, Amy J. Fann, Angelina E. Castagno, and Jessica A. Solyom, *Postsecondary Education for American Indian and Alaska Natives: Higher Education for Nation Building and Self-Determination*, ASHE Higher Education Report: 37/5. Kelly Ward and Lisa E. Wolf-Wendel, series editors (JB, 2012), 29.
12. Wilkins, *Red Prophet*, 126–127.
13. Vine Deloria, Jr and Daniel R. Wildcat, *Power and Place: Indian Education in America* (Golden, CO: Fulcrum Publishing, 2001), 43.
14. Gregory Cajete, *Look to the Mountain: An Ecology of Indigenous Education* (Skyland, NC: Kivaki Press, 1994).
15. Wilkins, *Red Prophet*, 127.
16. Tiffany S. Lee, "Native American Studies: A Place of Community," *AlterNative: An International Journal of Indigenous Peoples* 13, no. 1 (2017): 18–25.
17. Linda Tuhiwai Smith, *Decolonizing Methodologies: Research and Indigenous Peoples* (London: Zed Books, 1999), 25.
18. Audra Simpson and Andrea Smith, eds., *Theorizing Native Studies* (Durham, NC: Duke University Press, 2014), 3.
19. NATV 590 Syllabus, UNM.

Chapter 25

Notes

1. Steve Pavlik and Daniel Wildcat, *Destroying Dogma: Vine Deloria Jr. and His Influence on American Society* (Golden, CO: Fulcrum Publishing, 2006), 185.
2. David E. Wilkins, *Red Prophet: The Punishing Intellectualism of Vine Deloria, Jr.* (Golden, CO: Fulcrum Publishing, 2018), 12–17 (all recommendations come from Wilkins's list).
3. Rosebud Sioux Tribe Education Code, retrieved July 10, 2021, from edu.pdf (narf.org).
4. Vine Deloria, Jr. and Daniel R. Wildcat, *Power and Place: Indian Education in America* (Golden, CO: Fulcrum Publishing, 2001).
5. Richard Simonelli, "Vine Deloria, Jr.: Education in the Next Millennium," *Tribal College*

Journal 11, no. 2. (1999), retrieved May 20, 2021, from https:///vine-deloria-jr-education-millennium/.
6. Wilkins, *Red Prophet*, 14.
7. Cheryl Crazy Bull and Justin Guillory, "Revolution in Higher Education: Identity and Cultural Beliefs Inspire Tribal Colleges and Universities," *Daedalus, Journal of the American Academy of Arts and Sciences* 147, no. 2 (2018): 95–105.
8. Vine Deloria, Jr., "Tribal Colleges and Traditional Knowledge" *Tribal College Journal* 5, no. 2 (1993). Retrieved May 20, 2021, from Tribal Colleges and Traditional Knowledge, https://Tribalcollegejournal.org/tribal-colleges-traditional-knowledge/.
9. Cheryl Crazy Bull and Cynthia Lindquist, "In the Spirit of Our Ancestors," *Tribal College Journal* 30, no. 2. (Winter 2018). Retrieved July 14, 2021, from "In the Spirit of Our Ancestors," https://Tribalcollegejournal.org/in-the-spirit-of-our-ancestors/.

Chapter 26

Notes

1. Vine Deloria, Jr., *Custer Died for Your Sins: An Indian Manifesto* (New York: Avon Books: 1969), 23.
2. "Final Report," American Indian Policy Review Commission, Submitted to Congress on May 17, 1977, Vol. 1, 573.
3. American Indian Policy Review Commission, May 17, 1977. Vol. 1. 43 USC Ch. 33: Alaska.
4. Native Claims Settlement Act: http://www.alaskool.org/projects/ancsa/reports/rs-jones1981/ancsa_history71.htm; United States v. State of Washington, 384 F. Supp. 312 (W.D. Wash. 1974).
5. Peter H. Jackson, "Lloyd Meeds: A Man Who Got Things Done," *The Everett Herald* (Washington), Sept. 17, 2005; Associated Press, "Rep. Meeds Bowing Out," *Spokane Daily Chronicle* (Washington), Dec. 29, 1977, 1, accessed Feb. 2, 2022.
6. Chris Eyre, director, *Smoke Signals* (United States: Miramax, 1998).
7. American Indian Policy Review Commission, Final Report, submitted to Congress on May 17, 1977, Volume 1 of 2 Volumes, enacted on Jan. 2, 1975, Public Law 29-580, 88 Stat. 1910. The commission, by statute, had to have five of the eleven commissioners be American Indian and each three-member task force had to have a majority of American Indians serving in these capacities.
8. "From the earliest history of our country the federal government has had the authority over Indians and Indian Tribes. The relationship established from the inception of this country, however, has no exact counterpart in the history of international or domestic law. This unique relationship has never been exactly defined." The Indian Policy Review Commission, Congressman Lloyd Meeds, 1976.
9. The Meriam Report, though impactful in changing the direction of Federal-Indian interactions, was still a report void of any Indian voice, providing solutions solely from a non-Indian perspective.
10. Jens Bartelson, *A Genealogy of Sovereignty* (Cambridge, UK: Cambridge University Press, 1995), 239.

11. The debate was part of a forum organized by John Rouillard, chair of the American Indian Studies Department. A transcript was published later that year in a collection of the event's presentations: "Sovereignty, Fact or Fiction? A Debate between Vine Deloria, Jr., Author, Visiting Professor of Political Science at the University of Arizona, and Congressman Lloyd Meeds, Democrat from the State of Washington," in *Indian Tribal Sovereignty and Treaty Rights* (Albuquerque, NM: La Confluencia), 1978, S33–S45.
12. Deloria, "Sovereignty, Fact or Fiction?" S34, S37.
13. Worcester v. Georgia, 31 U.S. 515, 1932 (emphasis in original).
14. Deloria, *Custer Died for Your Sins*, 23.
15. Final Report, 573.
16. Vine Deloria, Jr. and Clifford Lytle, *The Nations Within: The Past and Future of American Indian Sovereignty* (Austin: University of Texas Press, 1988), 244.
17. Seminole Tribe v. Butterworth, 491 F. Supp. 1015, S.D. Fla. 1980, aff'd, F.2d. The State of Florida has a history of gambling; in 1932, sports betting was legalized, in 1935, Jai-Alai was permitted. That same year, the state legalized slot machines, but that law was repealed in 1973. In 1984, casino cruises ("cruises to nowhere") commenced and two years later, Florida legalized their lottery.
18. Oneida Tribe of Indians v. Wisconsin, 518 F. Supp. 712, 719 W.D. Wis. 1981. The Wisconsin lottery commenced in 1988. Barona Group of Capitan Band of Mission Indians v. Duffy, 649 F.2d 1185, 1189, 9th Cir, 1982. The California lottery commenced in 1984.
19. David E. Wilkins and Heidi Kiiwetinepinesiik Stark, *American Indian Politics and the American Political System* (Lanham, MD: Rowman and Littlefield), 121–122. "The Federal government responded to this activism by enacting several laws and initiating policies that recognized the distinctive group and individual rights of indigenous peoples. In some cases the law supported Tribal sovereignty; in other cases they acted to erase or diminish Tribal sovereignty."
20. Deloria and Lytle, *The Nations Within*, 256.
21. Jessica R. Cattelino, *High Stakes: Florida Seminole Gaming and Sovereignty* (Durham, NC: Duke University Press, 2008), 96.
22. Wilkins, *American Indian Politics and the American Political System*, 123. "Self-Governance is fundamentally designed to provide Tribal Governments with control and decision-making authority over the Federal financial resources provided for the benefit of Indian people. More importantly, Self-Governance fosters the shaping of a 'new partnership' between Indian Tribes and the United States in their government-to-government relationships. . . . Self-Governance returns decision-making authority and management responsibilities to Tribes."
23. Deloria and Lytle, *The Nations Within*, 259.
24. Michael D. Cox, "The Indian Gaming Regulatory Act: An Overview," *St. Thomas Law Review* (1994–1995): 772. "The Interior Department's policy of support was reflected in BIA approval of loans and loan guarantees for the construction of bingo halls. The Department's support for Indian bingo enterprises was not shared by the Criminal Division of the Justice Department."
25. The Fifth Circuit Court of Appeals was augmented in 1981, and the Eleventh Circuit Court of Appeals was created that included Alabama, Georgia and Florida.

26. Deloria and Lytle, *The Nations Within*, 260.
27. Deloria and Lytle, 260.
28. Vine Deloria, Jr., "Rethinking Tribal Sovereignty," paper presented to the American Indian Research and Policy Institute, St. Paul, MN, May 25–26, 1995, 1. Internal sovereignty is the Tribal political activities within the "borders and with their own people." External is the political actors outside the borders.
29. Bartelson, *A Genealogy of Sovereignty*, 2.
30. Deloria, "Rethinking Tribal Sovereignty." Here, Deloria stresses the importance of understanding sovereignty as a tool for dealing with the challenges of the future.
31. The first attempt—Proposition 5 in 1999—was ruled unconstitutional by the California Supreme Court because the language did not alter the constitution, even though the proposition was passed with more than 60 percent of the vote. Proposition 1A in 2000, with the correct language to amend the constitution, was also approved with over 60 percent of the vote. In 2002, Tribal governments in Arizona succeeded by passing Proposition 202, with approved, via compact, continuation of current gaming activities on reservations.
32. Vine Deloria, Jr., "The Indian World Today," *American Indian Culture*, Center Journal (Winter 1973): 3.
33. Deloria, "Rethinking Tribal Sovereignty," 2.
34. Vine Deloria, Jr., "The Next Three Years: A Time For Change," *The Indian Historian* 7 (1974): 27.
35. Vine Deloria, Jr., "Self-Determination and the Concept of Sovereignty," in *Economic Development in American Indian Reservations*, ed. Roxanne Dunbar Ortiz (Albuquerque: University of New Mexico Press, 1979), 27.
36. Robert Jackson, *Sovereignty: The Evolution of an Idea* (New York: Polity, 2007), 5–6.
37. E. H. Carr, *The Twenty Years Crisis: 1919–1939* (NY: Harper Perennial, 1964), 230–231.
38. Deloria, "Rethinking Tribal Sovereignty," 1.
39. Deloria, *Custer Died for Your Sins*, 205.
40. Deloria, 205.
41. Jonathan Wacks, director, *Pow Wow Highway* (London: HandMade Films, 1989).
42. Deloria, "The Indian World Today," 4. Walt Kelly. *Pogo: We Have Met the Enemy and He Is Us* (New York: Simon and Schuster, 1972).
43. Deloria, "The Indian World Today," 4.
44. Deloria, 4.

Chapter 28

Notes

1. Donald D. Stull. "Review of *Indians and Anthropologists: Vine Deloria, Jr. and the Critique of Anthropology*," ed. Thomas Biolsi and Larry J. Zimmerman (Tucson: University of Arizona Press, 1999).
2. Chris Eyre, director, *Smoke Signals* (United States: Miramax, 1998).
3. Vine Deloria, Jr., *Red Earth, White Lies: Native Americans and the Myth of Scientific Fact* (Golden, CO: Fulcrum Publishing, 1997); *Custer Died for Your Sins: An Indian Manifesto*

(New York: Avon Books, 1969); *God Is Red: A Native View of Religion* (New York: Grosset and Dunlap, 1973); *Spirit and Reason, The Vine Deloria, Jr. Reader* (Golden, CO: Fulcrum Publishing, 1999).

4. Deloria, *Red Earth, White Lies*, 9.
5. Vine Deloria, Jr., "Indians, Archaeologists, and the Future," *American Antiquity* (1992): 595–598.
6. Deloria, *Red Earth, White Lies.*
7. Steve R. Holen, T. A. Deméré, D. C. Fisher, R. Fullagar, J. B. Paces, G. T. Jefferson, and K. A. Holen, "A 130,000-Year-Old Archaeological Site in Southern California, USA," *Nature*, 544, no. 7651 (2017): 479-483.
8. Deloria, *Custer Died for Your Sins.*
9. Native American Graves Repatriation and Protection Act of 1990, 25 U.S.C. ch. 32 § 3001 et seq (1990), accessed June 25, 2022, from https://www.congress.gov/bill/101st-congress/house-bill/5237#:~:text=Passed%20Senate%20amended%20(10%2F26,on%20Federal%20or%20tribal%20lands.
10. James Adovasio and Jake Page, *The First Americans: In Pursuit of Archaeology's Greatest Mystery* (New York: Random House, 2002); Tom Dillehay, "The Late Pleistocene Cultures of South America," *Evolutionary Anthropology* 7, no. 6 (1999): 206–216; C. Gnecco and P. Ayala, eds., *Indigenous Peoples and Archaeology in Latin America* (New York: Routledge, 2001); Ian J. McNiven and Lynette Russell, "Appropriated Pasts: Indigenous Peoples and the Colonial Culture of Archaeology," *Canadian Journal of Archaeology / Journal Canadien d'Archéologie* 31, no. 2 (2007): 274–277.
11. Deloria, *Red Earth, White Lies.*
12. Paulette F. Steeves, *The Indigenous Paleolithic of the Western Hemisphere* (Lincoln: University of Nebraska Press, 2021).
13. Wildcat, Daniel. R. "Indigenizing the Future: Why We Must Think Spatially in the Twenty-First Century," *American Studies* 46, nos. 3–4 (2005): 417–440.

Chapter 29

Notes

1. Vine Deloria, Jr., *Peau-Rouge* (Paris: Edition spéciale, 1972), back cover (my translation).
2. Vine Deloria, Jr., *Custer Died for Your Sins: An Indian Manifesto* (Norman: University of Oklahoma Press, 1988), 8.
3. Gerald Vizenor, *Manifest Manners: Narratives on Postindian Survivance* (Lincoln: University of Nebraska Press, 1994), 7.
4. Deloria, *Peau-Rouge*, preface, Yves Berger.
5. Deloria, *Custer Died for Your Sins.*
6. Deloria, xi.
7. There are a lack of sources on the number of exemplars sold in France, and nothing was found on the publisher and the translators of the French edition; there's also an unknown number of exemplars sold in the US between its first publication in 1970 and the date when the French translation was published in 1972.
8. Interview with activist Marcel Canton, July 1989.

9. Interview with Élise Marienstras, July 2021.
10. See, for instance, Francis Jennings, *The Invasion of America: Indians, Colonialism, and the Cant of Conquest* (Berkeley: University of California Press, 1975).
11. Elise Marienstras, *La Résistance Indienne aux États-Unis, XVIe-xXe siècle* (Paris : Gallimard, 1980; rev. ed. 2014).
12. Deloria, *Peau-Rouge*, 23–24.
13. On the *coureurs de bois*, see p. xxx in this essay.
14. Vine Deloria, Jr., *Singing for a Spirit: A Portrait of the Dakota Lakota* (Santa Fe, NM: Clear Light, 1999), 7.
15. Marc Bloch, *Apologie pour L'histoire ou Métier D'historien* (posthumous) (Paris: Armand Colin, 1949).
16. Richard White, *The Middle Ground: Indians, Empires, and Republics in the Great Lakes Region, 1650–1815* (New York: Cambridge University Press), 1991.
17. With British takeover in 1763, land became the focus of colonization, but French-Canadians and other Euro-Americans continued trading with the Indians on the frontier well into the twentieth century.
18. On the contrary, the distant British fur trade Hudson's Bay Company's board of directors in London prohibited marriages between their employees and Native women in the name of morality, but without much success since intermarriage was necessary to seal commercial alliances with the Natives.
19. Gilles Havard, *L'Amérique Fantôme: Les Aventuriers Francophones du Nouveau Monde*, (Paris: Flammarion, 2019).
20. Philippe Jacquin, *Les Indiens Blancs: Français et Indiens en Amérique du Nord, XVIe-XVIIIe siècle* (Paris: Payot, 1987).
21. Deloria "Índio Blanco," Marine Le Puloch, field survey in the Guarani reservation of Dourados, Brazil, August 2016.
22. Deloria, *Singing for a Spirit*, 30.
23. *Report of the Royal Commission on Aboriginal Peoples* (1996), vol. 1 (Looking Forward, Looking Back), 33.
24. Delgamuukw v. British Columbia, [1997] 3 S.C.R. 1010, paragraph 87.
25. Havard, *L'Amérique Fantôme*.

Chapter 30

Notes

1. Frantz Fanon, *The Wretched Of the Earth* (1961), 239, quoted by Julia Wright, Preface, in Mumia Abdul Jamal, *Death Blossoms: Reflections From a Prisoner of Conscience* (1996), xviii.
2. Vine Deloria, Jr. and Clifford M. Lytle, *American Indians, American Justice* (1983), xii.
3. Vine Deloria, Jr. and Clifford M. Lytle, *The Nations Within: The Past and Future of American Indian Sovereignty* (1984), 200–201.
4. Deloria and Lytle, *American Indians, American Justice*, supra note 2, at 15.
5. 436 U.S. 49, 62–64 (1978).
6. Deloria and Lytle, *The Nations Within*, supra note 3, at 206.
7. David E. Wilkins, *Red Prophet: The Punishing Intellectualism of Vine Deloria, Jr.* (2018), 105.

8. Id. at 18.
9. Deloria and Lytle, *American Indians, American Justice*, supra note 2, at 196; Wilkins, *Red Prophet*, supra note 7, at 91.
10. Vine Deloria, Jr., "Like the Victory Over Custer, the Sioux's Win May Mean Defeat," *Los Angeles Times*, July 6, 1980.
11. Gabriel S. Galanda, "Tribal Per Capitas and Self-Termination," Indian Country Today Media Network, Aug. 13, 2014.
12. Gabriel S. Galanda, "Tribal Neocolonialism: Disenrollment, Enrollment Moratoria, and Per-Capitalism," Critical Race Theory Summer School: Teaching Truth to Power, *African-American Policy Forum* (July 21, 2022).
13. Marilyn Norcini, "The Political Process of Factionalism and Self-Governance at Santa Clara Pueblo," *Proceedings of the American Philosophical Society* 149, no. 4 (2005): 546, 561–562.
14. Martinez v. Santa Clara Pueblo, 402 F. Supp. 5, 12 (D.N.M. 1975).
15. See, e.g., Treaty with Oneida et al., 1794, Art. I; Kent Carter, *The Dawes Commission and the Allotment of the Five Civilized Tribes* (1999), 12 ("Indian agents had been making census and payment rolls since 1789 . . ."); see generally *Cohen's Handbook of Federal Indian Law* 16.04[2], ed. Nell Newton et al. (2005) ("Most Indian Treaties ceded tribal land in return for payment in money . . . and some directed distributions to members either as annuities or single payments."); id. ("The U.S. government had approved and made payments based on tribal rolls since 1790.").
16. See id.
17. Treaty with Cherokee, December 29, 1835, 7 Stat., 478, Art. 12.
18. Act of March 3, 1847, 9 Stat. 203 (1847); 25 U.S.C. § 111; Francis Paul Prucha, *The Great Father: The United States Government and the American Indians* (1984), 106.
19. 25 U.S.C. § 119.
20. See Prucha, *The Great Father*, supra note 18, at 106.
21. Martinez v. Santa Clara Pueblo, 540 F.2d 1039, 1040-41 (10th Cir. 1976), *rev'd*, 436 U.S. 49 (1978).
22. Oral Argument at 28:09, 47:41, Santa Clara Pueblo v. Martinez, 436 U.S. 49 (No. 76-682), https://www.oyez.org/cases/1977/76-682.
23. Martinez v. Santa Clara Pueblo, 402 F. Supp. at 18.
24. Id. at 11.
25. Deloria and Lytle, *The Nations Within*, supra note 3, at 200–201.
26. Stephen E. Cornell, *The Return of the Native: American Indian Political Resurgence* (1988), 85.
27. Prucha, *The Great Father*, supra note 18, at 94–95.
28. Stephen Pevar, *The Rights of Indians and Tribes*, 4th ed. (2012), 242.
29. Email from Stephen Pevar to Gabriel S. Galanda (Aug. 8, 2021, 10:51 a.m.) (on file with author).
30. Deloria and Lytle, *The Nations Within*, supra note 3, at 214; see also Vine Deloria, Jr. and David E. Wilkins, *Tribes, Treaties, and Constitutional Tribulations* (1999), 158.
31. S. Rep. No. 90-841, at 6 (1967).
32. Martinez v. Santa Clara Pueblo, 402 F. Supp. at 18.

33. Id. at 15; see also id. at 16 ("The ability of the Pueblo to control the use and distribution of its resources enhances its ability to maintain its cultural autonomy.")
34. Martinez v. Santa Clara Pueblo, 540 F.2d at 1042.
35. Id. at 1045.
36. Id. at 1047.
37. Id. at 1048.
38. Id.
39. Respondent's Brief, Santa Clara Pueblo v. Martinez, 436 U.S. 49 (No. 76-682), 1977 WL 189106, at *8, 39; see also id. at *34 ("The intent and purpose of the 1939 Ordinance were to hold down the size of tribal membership so there would be plenty of money and land for the members.").
40. Oral Argument at 56:49, Santa Clara Pueblo v. Martinez, 436 U.S. 49 (No. 76-682), https://www.oyez.org/cases/1977/76-682.
41. Reply Brief, Santa Clara Pueblo v. Martinez, 436 U.S. 49 (No. 76-682), 1977 WL 204931, at *15.
42. US courts have since required that Tribal habeas corpus remedies be exhausted prior to the filing of any ICRA habeas corpus action in federal district court. See *Nat'l Farmers Union Ins. Co. v. Crow Tribe of Indians*, 471 U.S. 845 (1985). In practice, that Tribal court exhaustion requirement defeats federal court review (see infra n. 54), rendering the original "Indian Bill of Rights" dead letter *en toto*. See, e.g., *Chegup v. Ute Indian Tribe of the Unitah and Ouray Indian Reservation*, 28 F.4th 1051 (10th Cir. 2022) *remanded to* 2022 WL 4359260 (D. Utah 2022); *Adams v. Dodge*, 2022 WL 458394 (9th Cir.) *cert. denied*, 142 S.Ct. 2839 (2022).
43. Santa Clara Pueblo v. Martinez, 436 U.S. at 71.
44. Matthew L. M. Fletcher, *The Supreme Court Indian Problem*, 59, *Hastings Law Journal* 579, 604 (citing Bob Woodward and Scott Armstrong, *The Brethren: Inside The Supreme Court* [1979]), 57–58.
45. John R. Herman and Karen O'Connor, "American Indians and the Burger Court," *Social Science Quarterly* 77, no. 1 (1996): 127, 140–141.
46. Santa Clara Pueblo v. Martinez Supreme Court Case Files Collection, Box 45, Powell Papers, Lewis J. Powell, Jr. Archives, Washington and Lee University School of Law 45 (manuscript collection).
47. Id.
48. Stephen L. Carter, "What Thurgood Marshall Taught Me," *The New York Times Magazine*, July 14, 2021 (quoting Bounds v. Smith, 430 U.S. 817, 828 [1977]).
49. Santa Clara Pueblo v. Martinez, 436 U.S. at 59.
50. See Gloria Valencia-Weber, "Three Stories in One: The Story of Santa Clara Pueblo v. Martinez," in *Indian Law Stories*, ed. Carole Goldberg, Kevin Washburn, and Phillip Frickey (2011), 465, 480.
51. Id. at 65 n.32 (citation omitted).
52. See Deloria and Lytle, *The Nations Within*, supra note 3, at 206.
53. Id. at 211.
54. Santa Clara Pueblo v. Martinez, 436 U.S. at 264 (White, B. dissenting).

55. Letter from Vine Deloria, Jr., University of Arizona, to Stephen Pevar, American Civil Liberties Union, June 9, 1989 (on file with author).
56. Indian Civil Rights Act Amendment of 1989, S. 517, 101st Cong. (1989).
57. David Wilkins, "Seasons of Change," in *American Indian Constitutional Reform and the Rebuilding of Native Nations*, ed. Eric D. Lemont (2006), 45.
58. For example, Congress has recently taken steps to fix the Tribal criminal jurisdiction void created by another disastrous US Supreme Court decision 1978, *Oliphant v. Suquamish Indian Tribe*, 435 U.S. 191 (1978). See e.g., Violence Against Women Reauthorization Act of 2013, Pub. L. No. 113-4, § 906, 127 Stat. 54, 124 (codified at 18 U.S.C. § 113); Violence Against Women Act Reauthorization Act of 2022, Pub. L. No. 117-103, 136 Stat. 840.
59. Vine Deloria, Jr., untitled essay, in *We, The People: Of Earth and Elders*—Vol. II, ed. Serle L. Chapman (2001), 296.
60. Frantz Fanon, *Black Masks, White Skins* (1952), 9.
61. Wilkins, *Red Prophet*, supra note 7, at 120.
62. Id. at 118.
63. Id.
64. Deloria, untitled essay, supra note 59, at 295.
65. Yael Ben-Zvi, *Native Land Talk: Indigenous and Arrivant Rights Theories* (2018), 123.
66. *Cohen's Handbook of Federal Indian Law*, supra note 15, 3.03[2] ("Before contact with Europeans . . . the constituent social units of most native communities were clans or extended kinship groups"); Robert A. Williams, Jr., *Linking Arms Together: American Indian Treaty Visions of Law and Peace 1600–1800* (1997), 63 ("Indigenous tribal peoples such as those encountered by Europeans in eastern North America during the colonial period [were] bound together by 'kinship'"); Shelly Hulse Wilkins and David E. Wilkins, *Dismembered: Native Disenrollment and the Battle for Human Rights* (2017), 3 ("Historically, lands, languages, kinship systems, and spiritual values and traditions" formed the basis for Indigenous "collective and personal identities").
67. Raymond D. Fogelson, "Perspectives on Native American Identity," in *Studying Native America: Problems and Prospects*, ed. Russell Thornton (1998), 44–45 ("Kinship not only included [individuals] with whom one could trace familiar common descent, but could be extended to include more ramifying groups like clans, moieties, and even nations").
68. Williams, *Linking Arms Together*, supra note 66, at 70; *Cohen's Handbook of Federal Indian Law*, supra note 15, 3.02[2] (Indigenous group existence "turns on shared language, rituals, narratives, kinship or clan ties, and a shared relationship to specific land").
69. Williams, supra note 66, at 34; Wilkins and Wilkins, *Dismembered* supra note 66, at 3 ("Historically, lands, languages, kinship systems, and spiritual values and traditions provided the most recognized framework" for Indigenous belonging).
70. Cornell, *The Return of the Native*, supra note 26, at 7. Id. at 73, 75; Matthew L. M. Fletcher, *Federal Indian Law* (2016 ed.), 238 ("A formalized, hierarchical government was anathema to many American Indian communities"); Deloria and Lytle, *American Indians, American Justice*, supra note 2, at 83–84 ("With the exception of the Iroquois, Cherokee, Creeks, and perhaps Choctaw-Chickasaws, few tribes attempted to form a large encompassing form of government").

71. Id. at 75; Williams, *Linking Arms Together*, supra note 66, at 34, 64; Ella Deloria, *Speaking of Indians* (1944), 24–25, 30, 32; Cornell, *The Return of the Native*, supra note 26, at 73, 81, 99; see also Fletcher, supra note 70, at 238 ("Traditional Indian governments ruled by consensus and permission").
72. Tee-Hit-Ton Indians v. United States, 348 U.S. 272 (1955).
73. Worchester v. Georgia, 31 U.S. (6 Pet.) 515 (1832) (emphasis added); see also Brackeen v. Haaland, 599 U.S., No. 21-276 slip op. at 13-14 (2023) (Gorsuch, N., dissenting). (In early America, "the 'settled state of things' reflected the British view that Tribes were 'nations capable of maintaining the relations of peace and war; [and] of governing themselves'") (citation omitted; original alteration).
74. Felix S. Cohen, "On the Drafting of Tribal Constitutions," David E. Wilkins (2006), xxiv–xxv; Prucha, *The Great Father*, supra note 18, at 324.
75. Nick Estes, *Our History Is the Future* (2019), 37.
76. Felix C. Cohen, "Indian Self-Government," in *Red Power: The American Indians' Fight for Freedom*, ed. Alvin M. Josephy, Jr. (1971), 30.
77. Cornell, *The Return of the Native*, supra note 26, at 106 ("When Christopher Columbus, sailing westward in 1492, concluded that he had struck the Indies and accordingly designated the peoples he encountered 'los Indios,' he gave birth to a misnomer—'Indians' in English—that soon came to embrace all of the native inhabitants of the Western Hemisphere. It was a label at odds not only with geographical facts, but also . . . with the subjective perceptions and sociological realities of the inhabitants themselves"); Robert F. Berkhofer Jr., *The White Man's Indian: Images of American Indians from Columbus to the Present* (1968), 4 ("The term 'Indians' stems from the faulty geography of Columbus. . . . Under the impression he had landed among the islands off Asia, he called the peoples he met *los Indios*. Although he quite self-consciously gave new names to islands upon his first voyage, his application of the term *Indios* seems to have been almost casual. The word was introduced to the public in the offhand manner of an aside through his oft-reprinted letter of 1493").
78. David Sneath, "Tribe," *Cambridge Encyclopedia of Anthropology* (2016), ("The word 'tribe' itself is derived from the Latin term *tribus*, the administrative divisions and voting units of ancient Rome. It came to be used in biblical texts for the thirteen divisions of the early Israelites and appears with this meaning in Middle English in the thirteenth century. By the sixteenth century it was being applied to non-biblical contexts in ways that resembled concepts such as race and lineage").
79. Worcester, 31 U.S. (6 Pet.) at 516; see e.g., Treaty with Delawares, U.S.—Delaware Nation, Sept. 17, 1778, 7 Stat. 13 at Art. III; Act of July 22, 1790, 1 Stat. 137 (1790).
80. Michael Omi and Howard Winant, *Racial Formation in the United States* (1994), 65–66.
81. Id.
82 Any English word to describe the People is problematic. In this essay the term "Indigenous" is used to hearken the People's original existence and place. See Vine Deloria, Jr., *God Is Red*, 3rd ed. (2003), 58 ("The Indian is indigenous . . . to the land in the deep emotional sense of knowing that he or she belongs there"). Consider Dr. Paulette Steeves's explanation of the term "Indigenous" as a paradigm that "turns a tool of oppression (cultural homogenization) into one of liberation (cultural unity) to support

contemporary human rights struggles on a global scale." Paulette F. C. Steeves, *The Indigenous Paleolithic of the Western Hemisphere* (2021), 15. "People" is used to connote traditional Indigenous existence and belonging, in keeping with Article 9 of the United Nations Declaration on the Rights of Indigenous Peoples. "Indian" is used as a colonial or federal term of art. "Nation" or "Tribe" are used to connote modern or neocolonial existence.

83. Robert A. Williams, Jr., *Like a Loaded Weapon* (2005), 164.
84. Id.
85. Cornell, *The Return of the Native*, supra note 26, at 106 ("Many groups identified themselves with names that mean simply 'persons,' 'people,' or 'human beings'").
86. Vine Deloria, Jr., *God Is Red* (1973), 210.
87. "On the Drafting of Tribal Constitutions," supra note 74, at 5.
88. Kim Guimarin, "San Manuel Name Change to Yaamava' Aims to Unify Voice and Identity," *The Sun*, Oct. 1, 2021.
89. Robert Hershey, Jennifer McCormack, and Gillan Newell, "Mapping Intergenerational Memories (Part I): Proving the Contemporary Truth of the Indigenous Past," Arizona Legal Studies Discussion Paper No. 14-01, Jan. 10, 2014.
90. Williams, *Linking Arms Together*, supra note 66, at 63–66.
91. Id. at 65.
92. John Phillip Reid, *A Law of Blood: The Primitive Law of the Cherokee Nation* (1970), 38–41.
93. Id. at 47, 89; Williams, *Linking Arms Together*, supra note 66, at 65.
94. Reid, A *Law of Blood*, supra note 92, at 37.
95. Cornell, *The Return of the Native*, supra note 26, at 73 (brackets in original).
96. Florence M. Hawley, "Pueblo Social Organization," *American Anthropologist* 39 (1937): 504, 505.
97. Christina Gish Hill, "Kinship as an Assertion of Sovereign Nationhood," in *Tribal Worlds*, ed. Brian Hosmer and Larry Nesper (2013), 19.
98. Heidi Bohaker, "'Nindoodemag:' The Significance of Algonquian Kinship Networks in the Eastern Great Lakes Region, 1600–1701," *William and Mary Quarterly* 63 (2006): 23, 33.
99. Deloria and Lytle, *American Indians, American Justice*, supra note 2, at 83.
100. Williams, *Linking Arms Together*, supra note 66, at 64–66; Reid, *A Law of Blood*, supra note 92, at 38–39; Hill, *Kinship as an Assertion of Sovereign Nationhood*, supra note 97, at 19 (Cheyenne "band identity was determined at birth").
101. Reid, *A Law of Blood*, supra note 92, at 39.
102. Id. at 38.
103. E. Deloria, Speaking of Indians, supra note 71, at 25.
104. Williams, *Linking Arms Together*, supra note 66, at 64; Wilkins and Wilkins, *Dismembered*, supra note 66, at 27 ("Historically, Native nations were inclusive sociocultural communities that incorporated not only mixed bloods but other Indigenous racial, and ethnic groups"); id. at 29 (discussing "tribal adoption of non-Indians and intermarried whites" and African Americans); Carter, *The Dawes Commission*, supra note 15, at 39 (discussing Chinese citizens of the Creek Nation).

105. Wilkins and Wilkins, *Dismembered*, supra note 66, at 27; see also Alexandra Harmon, "Tribal Enrollment Councils: Lessons on Law and Indian Identity," *Western Historical Quarterly* 32 (2001): 193 ("Aboriginal villages had readily incorporated migrants who showed a desire to live with established residents, according to local mores").
106. Reid, *A Law of Blood*, supra note 92, at 37.
107. Hill, *Kinship as an Assertion of Sovereign Nationhood*, supra note 97, at 20.
108. Id.
109. Wilkins and Wilkins, *Dismembered*, supra note 66, at 3.
110. Williams, *Linking Arms Together*, supra note 66, at 63; E. Deloria, *Speaking of Indians*, supra note 71, at 21.
111. Deloria and Lytle, *American Indians, American Justice*, supra note 2, at 196.
112. Reid, *A Law of Blood*, supra note 92, at 67; see also id., at 37 ("For the Cherokees, as for most American Indians . . . the clan . . . was woven together through viable interrelationship of consanguinity which created legal rights and duties, both individual and collective").
113. E. Deloria, *Speaking of Indians*, supra note 71, at 25.
114. Cornell, *The Return of the Native*, supra note 26, at 84; Graham D. Taylor, *The New Deal and American Tribalism* (1980), 45.
115. Wilkins and Wilkins, *Dismembered*, supra note 66, at 20.
116. Gabriel S. Galanda and Ryan D. Dreveskracht, "Curing the Tribal Disenrollment Epidemic: In Search of a Remedy," *Arizona Law Review* 57, no. 2 (2015): 383, 390; Samuelson v. Little River Band of Ottawa Indians-Enrollment Com'n, 2007 WL 6900788, at *1 (Little River Ct. App. Jun. 24, 2007).
117. *American Diagnosis Podcast*, "Tribal Values, Tribal Justice," July 14, 2022, https://khn.org/wp-content/uploads/sites/2/2022/07/ADXs4e8-TRANSCRIPT.pdf.
118. Matt Strohl, Sterling HolyWhiteMountain on Blood Quantum, Native Art, and Cultural Appropriation, interview, Jan. 31, 2019, https://aestheticsforbirds.com/2019/01/31/sterling-holywhitemountain-on-blood-quantum-native-art-and-cultural-appropriation/.
119. Comments from Veronica Tiller to Gabriel S. Galanda, Feb. 1, 2022 (on file with author).
120. Jill Doerfler, *Those Who Belong: Identity, Family, Blood, and Citizenship Among the White Earth Anishinaabeg* (2015), xxvi; see also Kim Tallbear, *Native American DNA* (2013), 47.
121. Treaty with the Wyandot etc. 1817, U.S.—Wyandot, Seneca, Delaware, Shawnee, Potawatomie, Ottawas and Chippewa Tribes of Indians, Sept. 20, 1817, 7 Stat. 160, Art. 8.
122. Paul Spruhan, "A Legal History of Blood Quantum in Federal Indian Law to 1935," *South Dakota Law Review* 51: 41–44; Carter, *The Dawes Commission*, supra note 15, at 49.
123. John P. LaVelle, "The General Allotment Act 'Eligibility Hoax': Distortions of Law, Policy, and History in Derogation of Indian Tribes," *Wicazo Sa Review* 14 (1999): 251.
124. Harmon, "Tribal Enrollment Councils, supra note 105, at 185.
125. Id. at 179.
126. 25 U.S.C. § 479 (current version at 25 U.S.C. § 5129 [2016]).
127. David E. Wilkins and Shelly Hulse Wilkins, "Blood Quantum and the Mathematics of Ethnocide," in *The Great Vanishing Act: Blood Quantum and the Future of Native Nations*, ed. Kathleen Ratteree and Norbert Hill (2017), 210, 219 (quoting *To Grant*

to Indians Living under Federal Tutelage the Freedom to Organize for Purposes of Local Self-Government and Economic Enterprise: Hearing Before the Committee on Indian Affairs United States Senate, 73rd Cong. (1934), 263–264 [statement of Sen. Wheeler]).

128. Felix S. Cohen, "On The Drafting of Tribal Constitutions," supra note 74, at 113; Wilkins and Wilkins, "Blood Quantum and the Mathematics of Ethnocide," supra note 127, at 210, 220 (citing Kirsty Gover, *Tribal Constitutionalism* 83 [2010], 83).
129. See Barbara Anne Henderson, "Division by Blood: Examining a History of Political and Racial Clashes Underlying American Indian Identity" (2004); see e.g., Nicole Martin Rogers et al., "Red Lake Nation: Population Projections" (2022), 3, https://www.wilder.org/wilder-research/research-library/red-lake-nation-population-projections.
130. Alan Parker, *Compare Paradigms: Tribal Citizenship v. Tribal Membership* (2020), 10 (on file with author) (emphasis added).
131. Jennifer Scott, "Constitutional Amendment Changes Enrollment Criteria," *Nugguam*, Oct. 2022; "MN Chippewa Tribe Votes to End Blood Requirement for Members," *U.S. News & World Report*, July 7, 2022.
132. Angela Denning, "Blood Quantum Requirement Dropped for Sealaska Corporation Enrollment," KTOO, July 2, 2022.
133. Stephen Cornell and Joseph P. Kalt, "From Tribal Members to Native Nations Citizens," in Ratteree and Hill, *The Great Vanishing Act*, supra note 127, at 296.
134. *In re: Effect of Cherokee Nation v. Nash and Vann v. Zinke*, Case No. SC-17-07, Final Order (Cherokee Sup. Ct. Feb. 22, 2021), 8.
135. Duane Champagne, "Remaking Tribal Constitutions," in *American Indian Constitutional Reform*, ed. Eric D. Lemont (2006), 11, 23.
136. Stephens v. Creek Nation, 174 U.S. 445, 488 (1899); see generally Galanda and Dreveskracht, "Curing the Tribal Disenrollment Epidemic," supra note 116.
137. Jeremy Hay, "Graton Rancheria's Disenrollment Rules Defy Trend," *Press Democrat*, April 5, 2013.
138. Cornell and Kalt, "From Tribal Members to Native Nations Citizens," in *The Great Vanishing Act*, supra note 127, at 131; see also Galanda and Dreveskracht, "Curing the Tribal Disenrollment Epidemic," supra note 116, at 451.
139. Glenda Anderson, "Lake County's Robinson Rancheria Re-enrolls Almost 70 Former Members," *The Press Democrat*, Feb. 19, 2017; Jaime Dunaway, "The Fight Over Who's a 'Real Indian,'" *Slate*, June 18, 2022.
140. Lee Juillerat, "Cheewa James and Family Reinstated to Modoc Tribe," *Klamath Herald and News*, May 1, 2021.
141. Chris Aadland, "Grand Ronde Members Disenrollment," Oregon Public Broadcasting, Dec. 9, 2022.
142. Special General Council Meeting Minutes, Cahto Tribe of the Laytonville Rancheria, Jan. 22, 2023.
143. Patty Krawec, *Becoming Kin: An Indigenous Call to Unforgetting the Past and Reimagining Our Future* (2022), 172–173.
144. Carole Goldberg, "Members Only? Designing Citizenship Requirements for Indian Nations," *University of Kansas Law Review* 50 (2002): 437, 464.
145. See Alan Parker, *Fractions: The Politics of Blood Quantum* (2010), 9, 14 (on file with

author); see, e.g., Tom Gorman and Dan Morain, "Gaming Profits Stir Fights Over Tribal Membership," *Los Angeles Times*, Feb. 28, 2000.

146. Champagne, "Remaking Tribal Constitutions," supra note 136, at 17.
147. Id. Jana Berger and Paula Fisher, "Navigating Tribal Membership Issues," in *Emerging Issues in Tribal-State Relations* (2013), 61; Parker, *Compare Paradigms*, supra note 130, at 9.
148. Williams, *Linking Arms Together*, supra note 66, at 64–65; 162 n.7; Rennard Strickland, *Fire and the Spirits: Cherokee Law from Clan to Court* (1975), 196.
149. Cornell, *The Return of the Native*, supra note 26, at 38.
150. Prucha, *The Great Father*, supra note 18, at 106.
151. Institute for Government Research, *The Problem of Indian Administration* (1928), 6.
152. Id. at 7, 8; see also id. at 5 ("He generally seeks out an existence through unearned income from leases of his land, the sale of land, per capita payments from tribal funds, or . . . ratios given him by the government"); id. at 19 ("They will hardly knuckle down to work while they still hope the government will pay what they believe is due them"); id. at 434 ("They are depending too largely on unearned income from the use or sale of their property, managed for them as a rule by the national government, and not enough on earned income derived from their own efforts").
153. Presidential Advisory Commission on Indian Reservation Economies, *Report and Recommendations to the President of the United States*, pt. 1 (1983), 36.
154. Id. pt. 1 at 41.
155. Thaddieus W. Connor and Aimee L. Franklin, "20 Years of Indian Gaming: Reassessing and Still Winning," *Social Science Quarterly* 100 (2019): 793, 805.
156. Randall K. Q. Akee, Katherine A. Spilde, and Jonathan B. Taylor, "The Indian Gaming Regulatory Act and Its Effects on American Indian Economic Development," *Journal of Economic Perspectives* 29 (2015): 185, 199; Kathryn R. L. Rand and Steven A. Light, "Virtue or Vice? How IRGA Shapes the Politics of Native American Gaming, Sovereignty, and Identity," *Virginia Journal of Social Policy & the Law* 4 (1997): 381, 422.
157. See Anna Malinovskaya, "Understanding the Native American Tribal 'Disenrollment Epidemic': An IV Approach" (May 1, 2021): 2 (draft).
158. Eric C. Henson, Megan M. Hill, Miriam R. Jorgensen, and Joseph P. Kalt, *Policy Brief No. 6, Recommendations for the Allocation and Administration of American Rescue Plan Act Funding for American Indian Tribal Governments,* Harvard Project on American Indian Economic Development and Native Nations Institute, April 9, 2021, 16–17.
159. Harvard Ash Center, *Navigating the American Rescue Plan Act: A Series for Tribal Nations, Session 7*, at 30:30, YouTube, Sept. 8, 2021, https://youtu.be/V15ZCcoOrl0.
160. Carter, *The Dawes Commission*, supra note 15, at 12.
161. Vine Deloria, Jr., *For This Land: Writings on Religion in America* (1999), 43.
162. The multibillion-dollar influence of Indian gaming presently disincentivizes almost every Tribal rights and social justice organization in the country from helping Native Nations confront and correct the existential threats identified in this chapter. Gabriel S. Galanda, "Into the Void: American Indigenous Civil Rights," *Trial News*, Feb. 2022.

Chapter 31

Notes

1. Letter from Walter A. Plecker to Local Registrars et al. (January 1943), *Encyclopedia of Virginia*, https://encyclopediavirginia.org/entries/letter-from-walter-a-plecker-to-local-registrars-et-al-december-1943/#:~:text=In%20our%20January%201943%20annual, into%20the%20white%20race%20by.
2. "The New Virginia Law to Preserve Racial Integrity," Library of Virginia, https://lva.omeka.net/items/show/62.
3. Circular Letter to "Local Registrars, Clerks, Legislators, and Others Responsible for, and Interested in, the Prevention of Racial Intermixture," from Walter A. Plecker, State Registrar of Vital Statistics, Richmond, Library of Virginia, https://lva.omeka.net/items/show/63.
4. W. A. Plecker to the Honorable John Collier, Commissioner, Office of Indian Affairs, April 6, 1943 TLS, 3 pp. Papers of John Powell, 1888–1978, n.d., Accession #7284, 7284-a, box-folder 42:31, Special Collections, University of Virginia Library, Charlottesville, VA.
5. 132 Stat. 40 (January 29, 2018).
6. Rez dog's tweet.

Chapter 32

Notes

1. Ella Deloria, *Speaking of Indians* (Vermillion, SD: State Publishing, 1983), 17, 18, 22.
2. Vine Deloria, Jr., *Behind the Trail of Broken Treaties: An Indian Declaration of Independence* (Austin: University of Texas Press, 1985).
3. Vine Deloria, Jr., *Custer Died for Your Sins: An Indian Manifesto* (Norman: University of Oklahoma Press, 1988), 232.
4. Vine Deloria, Jr., "Rethinking Tribal Sovereignty" (summary), 1995 keynote address at the American Indian Policy Center, St. Paul, MN.
5. Wallace Coffey and Rebecca Tsosie, "Rethinking the Tribal Sovereignty Doctrine: Cultural Sovereignty and the Collective Future of Indian Nations," *Stanford Law and Policy Review* 12 (2001): 191–222; Rebecca Tsosie, "Introduction: Symposium on Cultural Sovereignty," *Arizona State Law Journal* 34, no. 1 (2002): 1–14.
6. Deloria, "Rethinking Tribal Sovereignty."
7. Vine Deloria, Jr., Contribution to *We, the People: Of Earth and Elders—Volume II*, ed. by Serle L. Chapman (Missoula, MT: Mount Press Publishing), 295, 296.
8. Andrew Curley, "*T'áá Hwó Ají T'éego* and the Moral Economy of Navajo Coal Workers," *Annals of the American Association of Geographers* 109, no. 1 (2019): 71–86.
9. Vine Deloria, Jr., "Anthropologists and Other Friends," *Custer Died for Your Sins: An Indian Manifesto*, 2nd ed. (Norman: University of Oklahoma Press, 1988), 78–100; Vine Deloria, Jr., *Red Earth, White Lies: Native Americans and the Myth of Scientific Fact* (Golden, CO: Fulcrum Publishing, 1997); Vine Deloria, Jr., "Conclusion: Anthros, Indians, and Planetary Reality," in *Indians and Anthropologists: Vine Deloria, Jr., and the Critique of Anthropology*, ed. Thomas Biolsi and Larry J. Zimmerman (Tucson: University of Arizona Press, 1997), 209–222.

10. Deloria, "Conclusion: Anthros, Indians, and Planetary Reality."
11. Vine Deloria, Jr. and Daniel R. Wildcat, *Power and Place: Indian Education in America* (Golden, CO: Fulcrum Publishing, 2001); for more on banishment, see Chapter 1 in David E. Wilkins and Shelly Hulse Wilkins, *Dismembered: Native Disenrollment and the Battle for Human Rights* (Seattle: University of Washington Press, 2017); for a classic, but not outdated, anthropological analysis of stateless and state societies see Morton Fried, *The Evolution of Political Society: An Essay in Political Anthropology* (New York: Random House, 1967).
12. States appeared in numerous places across the planet, including Mesopotamia (approximately 6,000–5,000 years ago), the lower Nile Valley in Egypt (approximately 5,550–5,100 years ago), the Indus Valley in Pakistan (approximately 5,600–5,000 years ago), the Yellow River Valley in China (approximately 3,900–3,500 years ago), the Oaxaca Valley in Mexico (approximately 2,300–2,200 years ago), and the Valley of Mexico (Teotihuacan, approximately 2,200 years ago). Archaeologists and anthropologists do not attribute the rise of the state to "progress" but instead to the emergence in specific places of a pressing need to solve "management" challenges associated with rising population, such as irrigation, facilitation of long-distance trade, and so on; states are good at administering large organizations and projects involving dense populations. In terms of human cultural history, states invented writing, law, and centralized command and control, and advanced math, astronomy, engineering, and military science (as anyone who has taken world history in high school will recall). The price that human beings have paid for this "civilization"—something *not* taught in high school—was tribute, conscription, taxation, class inequality and exploitation of others' labor (including slavery), and large-scale warfare and conquest (see note 2).
13. Eric R. Wolf, *Europe and the People without History* (Berkeley: University of California Press, 1982), 89–99.
14. For important interpretations, see Wesley Thomas, "Navajo Cultural Constructions of Gender and Sexuality," in *Two Spirit People: Native American Gender Identity, Sexuality, and Spirituality*, ed. Sue-Ellen Jacobs, Wesley Thomas, and Sabine Lang (Urbana: University of Illinois Press, 1997), 156–173; Mark Rifkin, *When Did Indians Become Straight: Kinship, the History of Sexuality, and Native Sovereignty* (New York: Oxford University Press, 2017); Leanne Betasamosake Simpson, *As We Have Always Done: Indigenous Freedom through Radical Resistance* (Minneapolis: University of Minnesota Press, 2017), 128–129.
15. *Basic Call to Consciousness*, ed. *Akwesasne Notes* (Summertown, TN: Book Publishing Company, 1991), 12. The original documents were published in *Akwesasne Notes*, Dec. 31, 1977.
16. Marshall Sahlins, *Stone Age Economics* (Chicago: Aldine Publishing Company, 1972), Chapters 2, 3.
17. *Akwesasne Notes*, 1977, 92, 94, 95.
18. Lewis H. Morgan, "Houses and House Life of the American Aborigines," in *U.S. Geographical and Geological Survey of the Rocky Mountain Region* (Washington, DC: Government Printing Office, 1881), 65.

19. Morgan, "Houses and House Life," 64, 121: By "communism," Morgan did not mean to denigrate Haudenosaunee society. His meaning was closer to Marshall Sahlins's concept of "generalized reciprocity" (see below). Frederick Engels devoted a chapter in *The Origin of the Family, Private Property and the State* to "The Iroquois Gens [Clan]." He wrote that classless (commonly called egalitarian, in anthropology) societies like the Haudenosaunee were aggressively subdued by states; stateless societies were "broken by influences which from the very start appear as a degradation, a fall from the simple moral greatness of the old gentile [clan-based] society. The lowest interests—base greed, brutal appetites, sordid avarice, selfish robbery of the common wealth—inaugurate the new, civilized class society. It is by the vilest means—theft, violence, fraud, treason—that the old classless gentile society is undermined and overthrown. And the new society itself during all of the 2,500 years of its existence [Engels was a little off on dating the origin of the state] has never been anything else but the development of the small minority at the expense of the great exploited and oppressed majority; today it is so more than ever." Frederick Engels, *The Origin of the Family, Private Property and the State*, ed. and introduced by Eleanor Leacock (New York: Int'l Publishers, 1972). While it is true that Engels and Marx saw the Haudenosaunee as *primitive* communists—they were revolutionaries, but with an evolutionary bias about the necessity of technological "progress"—we should not ignore their insights about the moral and humane features of Indigenous societies, especially in comparison to "civilization."
20. Morgan, "Houses and House Life," 32.
21. Morgan, 2.
22. Doug George-Kanentiio, "Why Do We Need Chiefs?" Indianz.com, Jan. 4, 2021, accessed June 2022 from https://www.indianz.com/News/2021/01/04/doug-george-kanentiio-why-the-mohawk-people-never-had-chiefs/ (document accessed June 2022).
23. Morgan, "Houses and House Life," 28.
24. Elizabeth Tooker, "The League of the Iroquois: Its History, Politics, and Ritual," in *Handbook of North American Indians, Vol. 15, Northeast,* ed. by Bruce G. Trigger (Washington, DC: Smithsonian Institution), 425–426; and Nancy Shoemaker, "The Rise and Fall of Iroquois Women," *Journal of Women's History* 2, no. 3 (1991): 39–57. Morgan did not report this political authority on the part of women and wrote that the widely known authority of women in the longhouse "did not reach outward to the affairs of the [clan] or tribe, but seems to have commenced and ended with the household" (Morgan, "Houses and House Life," 122). This omission is likely an effect of Morgan's Victorian-era patriarchal biases, as well as the fact that he likely consulted primarily Haudenosaunee men in his ethnographic research, perhaps, again, because of his own biases.
25. Haudenosaunee Confederacy, "Current Clan Mothers and Chiefs," https://www.haudenosauneeconfederacy.com/government/current-clan-mothers-and-chiefs/; and Onondaga Confederacy, "Clan Mothers," accessed June 2022 from https://www.onondaganation.org/government/clan-mothers/.
26. Morgan, "Houses and House Life," 33.
27. Eugene S. Hunn with James Selam and Family, *Nch'i-Wána, The Big River: Mid-Columbia Indians and their Land* (Seattle: University of Washington Press, 1990), 177.

28. Hunn et al., *Nch'i-Wána*, 207.
29. Hunn et al., 219.
30. Sahlins, *Stone Age Economics*, 193–194, 123–124.
31. Hunn et al., *Nch'i-Wána*, 219, emphasis added.
32. See Wilkins and Wilkins, *Dismembered.*
33. E. Deloria, *Speaking of Indians*, 21.
34. Deloria and Wildcat, *Power and Place*, 44.
35. Eva Marie Garroutte, *Real Indians: Identity and the Survival of Native America* (Berkeley: University of California Press, 2003), Chapter 6.
36. For a good overview, see Kathleen Ratteree and Norbert Hill, eds., *The Great Vanishing Act: Blood Quantum and the Future of Indian Nations* (Golden, CO: Fulcrum Publishing, 2017).
37. Garroutte, *Real Indians*, 135, 137, emphasis in original.
38. Court TV's *Instant Justice*, "Navajo Peacemaking," YouTube video accessed June 2022, https://www.youtube.com/watch?v=zJp_RMYKx9k&t=3006s; see also Robert Yazzie, "Life Comes from It: Navajo Justice Concept," *New Mexico Law Review* 24 (1995): 175–190; Marianne O. Neilsen and James W. Zion, eds., *Navajo Peacemaking: Living Traditional Justice* (Tucson: University of Arizona Press, 2005); Larry W. Emmerson, "Diné Sovereign Action: Rejecting Colonial Sovereignty and Invoking Diné Peacemaking," in *Navajo Sovereignty: Understandings and Visions of the Diné People*, ed. Lloyd L. Lee (Tucson: University of Arizona Press, 2017), 160–178; and Native American Rights Fund Indigenous Peacemaking Initiative, accessed June 2022 from https://www.narf.org/category/indigenous-peacemaking-initiative/.
39. Navajo Nation Council, Amending Title 1 of the Navajo Nation Code to Recognize the Fundamental Laws of the Dine. Resolution CN-69-02, accessed June 2022 from http://www.courts.navajo-nsn.gov/Resolutions/CN-69-02Dine.pdf.
40. Raymond D. Austin, *Navajo Courts and Navajo Common Law: A Tradition of Tribal Self-Governance* (Minneapolis: University of Minnesota Press, 2009).
41. Austin, *Navajo Courts*, Chapter 2.
42. Austin, Chapter 5.
43. Austin, 83.
44. Rosenfelt & Buffington v. ____ [party name redacted to protect privacy—Biolsi], No. SC-CV-34-08, Supreme Court of the Navajo Nation, 1.
45. Rosenfelt & Buffington v. ____, 7, 8
46. Kyle Whyte, "Time as Kinship," in *The Cambridge Companion to Environmental Humanities*, ed. Jeffrey Cohen and Stephanie Foote (Cambridge, UK: Cambridge University Press, 2021), xx.
47. Deloria and Wildcat, *Power and Place*, 44.
48. Little Traverse Bay Bands of Odawa Indians 2005 Constitution, Article 1, Section B, accessed June 2022 from https://ltbbodawa-nsn.gov/wp-content/uploads/2020/12/LTBB-Constitution.pdf.
49. Rosebud Sioux Tribe 1935 [as amended] Constitution and By-Laws, Article IV, Section 1, Sub-Section V, accessed June 2022 from https://narf.org/nill/constitutions/rosebud-const/constitution.pdf.

50. Nottawaseppi Huron Band of the Potawatomi, Michigan 2013 Constitution, Article II, Section 2, Sub-section b[2]), accessed June 2022 from https://ecode360.com/NO3539. I thank my friend and colleague David Wilkins for pointing me to these Tribal seventh-generation provisions. David E. Wilkins, "How to Honor the Seven Generations," *Indian Country Today*, June 18, 2015 (updated Sept. 2018), accessed June 2022 from https://indiancountrytoday.com/archive/how-to-honor-the-seven-generations. A provision in the juvenile justice chapter of the Nottawaseppi Tribal code is also relevant here: "Bode'wadmi traditions and values recognized the interconnectedness of every person and everything in the world and that the actions of one individual, or a group of individuals, will have an impact on the whole of our community. In all things we do as a government, it is our obligation to promote Bode'wadmi traditions and values by seeking consensus so that decisions that are made will benefit the whole of our community for this and the next seven generations," Nottawaseppi Huron Band of the Potawatomi 2014:Title VII, Article III, Section 7.3-4.
51. See Hunn et al, *Nch'i-Wána*, 230–235; Harold L. Harrod, *The Animals Came Dancing: Native American Sacred Ecology and Kinship* (Tucson: University of Arizona Press, 2000); Deloria and Wildcat, *Power and Place*; Julie Cruikshank, *Do Glaciers Listen? Local Knowledge, Colonial Encounters and Social Imagination* (Vancouver: University of British Columbia Press, 2005); Paul Nadasdy, "The Gift in the Animal: The Ontology of Hunting and Human-Animal Sociality," *American Ethnologist* 34, no. 1 (2007): 25-43; Enrique Salmón, *Eating the Landscape: American Indian Stories of Food, Identity, and Resilience* (Tucson: University of Arizona Press, 2012); Simpson, *As We Have Always Done*, 2014; Zoe Todd, "Fish Pluralities: Human-Animal Relations and Sites of Engagement in Paulatuuq, Arctic Canada," *Études/Inuit/Studies* 38, no. 1–2 (2014): 217–238; Christopher J. Pexa, "More Than Talking Animals: Charles Alexander Eastman's Animal Peoples and Their Kinship Critiques of United States Colonialism," *PMLA* 13, no. 3 (2016): 652–667; and "Citizen Kin: Charles Eastman's Reworking of US Citizenship," *Studies in American Indian Literatures* 29, no. 3 (2017): 1–28; Nicole J. Wilson and Jody Inkster, "Respecting Water: Indigenous Water Governance, Ontologies, and the Politics of Kinship on the Ground," *Environment and Planning E: Nature and Space* 1, no. 4 (2018): 516–538; Nick Estes and Jaskiran Dhillon, "Introduction: The Black Snake, #NoDAPL, and the Rise of a People's Movement," in *Standing with Standing Rock: Voices from the #NoDAPL Movement*, ed. Nick Estes and Jaskiran Dhillon (Minneapolis: University of Minnesota Press, 2019), 1–10; Kim TallBear, "Badass Indigenous Women Caretake Relations: #Standingrock, #IdleNoMore, #BlackLivesMatter," in Ester and Dhillon, *Standing with Standing Rock*, 13–18; Edward Valandra, "Mni Wiconi: Water Is [More Than] Life," in Ester and Dhillon, *Standing with Standing Rock*, 81–89; Anja Kanngieser and Zoe Todd, "From Environmental Case Study to Environmental Kin Study," *History and Theory* 59, no. 3 (2020): 385–393; Kyle Whyte, "Indigenous Environmental Justice: Anti-Colonial Action through Kinship," in *Environmental Justice: Key Issues*, ed. Brendan Coolsaet (London: Routledge, 2020), 266–278.
52. Chippewas of the Thames First Nation 2014 Constitution, Article 4.3, accessed June 2022 from https://www.cottfn.com/chief-council/committee/cottfn-constitution/.

53. White Earth Band of Ojibwe, Resolution No. 001-19-009 and attached Rights of Manoomin, 2018, accessed June 2022 from https://whiteearth.com/assets/files/public_documents/Letter%20to%20Tim%20Walz%20re%20Rights%20of%20Manoomin.pdf. An identical law was adopted by the 1855 Treaty Authority (a board representing all the individual treaty beneficiaries in Minnesota) applying to all lands ceded in the treaty (now outside the reservation, but still subject to Native rights to fish and gather) by the Anishinaabe, Ojibwe, or Chippewa. Both the White Earth Band and the Treaty Authority worked with the NGOs Community Development Legal Defense Fund and Honor the Earth in drafting the laws as described in "Chippewa Establish *Rights of Manoomin* White Earth Reservation and Throughout 1855 Ceded Territory," document accessed June 2022 from https://whiteearth.com/assets/files/public_documents/Letter%20to%20Tim%20Walz%20re%20Rights%20of%20Manoomin.pdf. See also Jens Camp, "A Movement in Indian Country Toward Legal Rights for Nature," *Law Journal for Social Justice at Arizona State University* (March 10, 2020), accessed June 2022 from https://lawjournalforsocialjustice.com/2020/03/10/a-movement-in-indian-country-toward-legal-rights-for-nature/.
54. See "Resolution Establishing the Rights of the Klamath River," Resolution 19-40, 9 (May 2019), Yurok Tribal Council; "Tribe Passes Powerful Resolution," *Yurok Today*, May 2019; and Geneva Thompson, "Codifying the Rights of Nature," *Judges' Journal* 59, no. 2 (2020): 12–15.
55. See, for example, Judith Butler, *Precarious Life: The Powers of Mourning and Violence* (London and New York: Verso, 2006), Chapter 5 on the European philosopher Emanuel Levinas who wrote of our moral responsibility for "the other."

Chapter 33

Notes

1. Vine Deloria, Jr., *Custer Died for Your Sins: An Indian Manifesto* (Norman: University of Oklahoma Press, 1988), 2.
2. Public Law 95-608, §§1901-63, 1978.
3. Vine Deloria, Jr. and Clifford M. Lytle, *The Nations Within: The Past and Future of American Indian Sovereignty* (Austin: University of Texas Press, 1984), 263.
4. See Melvin Glasser's October 10, 1953, memorandum entitled "Relations with the Bureau of Indian Affairs—Branch of Welfare and Placement," records of the Children's Bureau, RG 102, Central File, Box 351, Folder Indians, National Archives at College Park.
5. See, for example, the "Agreement for Child Welfare Services for Indians of Nevada," signed on August 1, 1950, between the BIA and the Nevada State Welfare Department, Records of the Children's Bureau.
6. The letters exchanged at the time between the BIA, the Children's Bureau, and different state agencies testify to the efforts deployed by the BIA to try and induce states to get involved in Indian child welfare and to the various reactions of state governments. These letters are accessible in the Records of the Children's Bureau.
7. In an opinion rendered on April 22, 1936, on the applicability of the Social Security Act, the solicitor of the Department of the Interior established that, as US citizens, all

Native Americans were taken into consideration into the figures used to calculate the allocation of federal funds per state. They were thus entitled to a share of that money, even if they resided on reservations.

8. See the agreement signed with Nevada in 1950 (note 5).
9. Deloria and Lytle, *The Nations Within*, 4.
10. Public Law 83-280, 18 U.S.C., §1162, 25 U.S.C. §§1321-1326, 28 U.S.C. §1360, 1953.
11. In *The Legal Universe*, Deloria and Wilkins explain that this doctrine, along with the "best interests of the child," are "undeterminate and jurisprudentially unsound," "not unlike the doctrine of plenary power as applied to Indian Tribals" as they rely on a lot of discretionary power. Vine Deloria, Jr. and David E. Wilkins, *The Legal Universe: Observations on the Foundations of American Law* (Golden, CO: Fulcrum Publishing, 2011), 333.
12. E. Morgan Pryse, Letter to the Children's Bureau, October 22, 1951, Records of the Children's Bureau.
13. U.S. Congress, Senate, Subcommittee on Indian Affairs of the Committee on Interior and Insular Affairs, "Hearings on Problems That American Indian Families Face in Raising Their Children and How These Problems Are Affected by Federal Action or Inaction," 93rd Cong., 2d sess., April 8–9, 1974.
14. Fisher v. District Court, 424 U.S. 382, 96 S. Ct. 943, 47 L. Ed. 2d 106 (1976).
15. On this subject see, for instance, Pauline Turner Strong, "What Is an Indian Family? The Indian Child Welfare Act and the Renascence of Tribal Sovereignty," *American Studies* 46, no. 3/4 (2005–2006): 205–223; Terry L. Cross and Robert J. Miller, "The Indian Child Welfare Act and Its Impact on Tribal Sovereignty and Governance," in *Facing the Future: the Indian Child Welfare Act at 30*, ed. Matthew L. M. Fletcher, Wenona T. Singel, and Kathryn E. Fort (East Lansing: Michigan State University Press, 2009), 13–27.
16. Deloria and Lytle, *The Nations Within*, 216.
17. Public Law 95-608, §1901.
18. Deloria and Lytle, *The Nations Within*, 212–214.
19. Deloria and Lytle, 213.
20. Deloria and Lytle, 212.
21. Public Law 105-89, 111 Stat. 2115, 1997.
22. For instance, the Oglala Sioux Tribal has established the possibility for extended families to designate a *tiyospaye* interpreter who, after receiving special training, will act as an intermediary between the Tribe and members of the extended family (*Wakanyeja na Tiwahe ta Woope*, Oglala Sioux Tribal Child and Family Codes, 401-412, 2007). The Law and Order Code of the Pawnee Tribe of Oklahoma established that family ties created between adults through a customary adoption are recognized by the Tribal court and constitute rights and responsibilities over the children of both adoptees. Section 1103 of the code reads: "Tribal Custom Adoptions shall continue to be recognized and shall be fully recognized by the Court, without the necessity of filing any document, when proven for the purpose of establishing extended family status in child custody actions, determining child custody, the obligation to support children, and other family matters."

23. Deloria and Lytle, *The Nations Within,* 248.
24. The active effort and the qualified expert witness requirements were found in violation of the commandeering doctrine of the U.S. Constitution, which prohibits the federal government from "taking control" of the resources of state governments for federal purposes.
25. Brackeen v. Haaland, No. n18-11479, F.3d 406, 5th Cir. (2021).
26. 21-376 Haaland v. Brackeen (06/15/2023).
27. Deloria and Lytle, *The Nations Within,* 263.
28. Public Law 95-608, § 1919.
29. Public Law 95-608, § 1911.
30. In 2008, an amendment to the Social Security Act authorized the federal government, through the Administration for Children and Families (ACF), to directly allocate Title IV-E money to Tribal governments (Public Law 110-351, 122 stat. 3949, 2008). Six years later, the ACF indicated that seventeen Tribes had then decided to take advantage of this option, while many continued to rely on the agreements they had negotiated with states to access these funds, www.acf.hhs.gov/cb/grant-funding/Tribals-approved-title-iv-e-plans.
31. Jack Thorpe and Shannon Keller O'Loughlin, "A Survey Analysis of Select Title IV-E Tribal-State Agreements," Association on American Indian Affairs, Casey Family Programs (March 2014): 2–3.
32. This is often the case in states with a low Native American population. South Dakota—where, on the contrary, Native Americans make up nearly 9 percent of the state population—is another example. Between 1978 and 2008, the South Dakota Supreme Court rendered forty-two decisions in relation with ICWA. For further information on the subject, see Lorinda Mall, "Keeping It in the Family: The Legal and Social Evolution of ICWA in State and Tribal Jurisprudence," in Fletcher et al., *Facing the Future: The Indian Child Welfare Act at 30,* 164–220.
33. See In re S.Z. and C.Z., 325 N.W.2d.53 (S.D. 1982).
34. In 1982, the Kansas Supreme Court created this exception that holds that ICWA does not apply in adoption procedures when the child does not have adequate ties with his Indian family (and thus his Tribe). See In re Baby Boy L., 643 P.2d 168, 206 (Kan. 1982). Other state courts have used the exception since then. See, for example, In re Bridget R., 49, Cal. Rptr.2d.507, Ct (Cal.1996).
35. See CSR Incorporated, Three Feathers Associates, "Indian Child Welfare Act: A Status Report, Final Report of the Survey of Indian Child Welfare" and "Implementation of the Indian Child Welfare Act and Section 428 of the Adoption Assistance and Child Welfare Act of 1980" (Washington, DC: Government Printing Office, 1988); Andrea Wilkins, "State-Tribal Cooperation and the Indian Child Welfare Act," NCSL State-Tribal Institute (July 2008), www.ncsl.org/print/stateTribal/ICWABrief08.pdf.
36. Oklahoma Indian Child Welfare Act, Ok. Stat. §10.40, 1982; Minnesota Indian Family Preservation Act, Min. Stat. §§260.751-835, 1985; Nebraska Indian Child Welfare Act, Neb. Stat. §§43.1501-1516, 1986; Iowa Indian Child Welfare Act, Iowa Code §232B, 2003; Michigan Indian Family Preservation Act, Public Act 565, MCL 712 B.1-712 B.41, 2012; Washington State Indian Child Welfare Act, Wash. Revised Code, §13.38.010, 565, 2013.

37. "Tribal/State Indian Child Welfare Agreement as amended in 2007," Minnesota Department of Human Services, https://edocs.dhs.state.mn.us/lfserver/Legacy/DHS-5022-ENG. The different signatory entities acknowledge that "as sovereigns, they may disagree as to the extent of each other's authority, power and jurisdiction in such proceedings. [They] agree, however, that the fundamental purpose for making this Agreement is to secure and to preserve an Indian child's sense of belonging to her or his family and Band or Tribal. They agree that cooperating to combine their abilities and resources to provide effective assistance to Indian children and their families is the best means to reach this shared goal," 4.
38. Minnesota Department of Human Services, 9.
39. For instance, the Red Lake Nation and Minnesota Department of Human Services Title IV-E Foster Care Agreement signed in January 2008 explains that "the Nation's Family & Children Services Division is considered part of the state welfare system," 2.
40. Deloria and Lytle, *The Nations Within*, 13.
41. I am using Jeff Corntassel and Richard C. Witmer's expression found in *Forced Federalism: Contemporary Challenges to Indigenous Nationhood* (Norman: University of Oklahoma Press, 2008).
42. Corntassel and Witmer, *Forced Federalism*, 14.
43. See, for instance, the Leech Lake Band of Ojibwe and the Minnesota Department of Human Services Title IV-E Foster Care Maintenance, Administrative and Training Agreement, signed in 2007 and amended in 2014, which states, page 2, that "the department understands that the federal government is bound to the Trust Responsibility Doctrine, and that, by entering this agreement, the department is carrying out a program of the federal government. Nothing in this agreement shall abrogate that trust responsibility."
44. David E. Wilkins and K. Tsianina Lomawaima, *Uneven Ground: American Indian Sovereignty and Federal Law* (Norman: University of Oklahoma Press, 2001), 188.

Bibliography

Bureau of Indian Affairs, Nevada State Welfare Department. "Agreement for Child Welfare Services for Indians of Nevada," August 1, 1950. Records of the Children's Bureau, RG 102, Central File, Box 351, Folder Indians, National Archives at College Park.

Corntassel, Jeff, and Richard C. Witmer II, *Forced Federalism: Contemporary Challenges to Indigenous Nationhood*. Norman: University of Oklahoma Press, 2008.

Cross, Terry L., and Robert J. Miller, "The Indian Child Welfare Act and Its Impact on Tribal Sovereignty and Governance." In *Facing the Future: the Indian Child Welfare Act at 30*, ed. Matthew L. M. Fletcher, Wenona T. Singel, and Kathryn E. Fort. East Lansing: Michigan State University Press, 2009, 13–27.

CSR Incorporated, Three Feathers Associates. "Indian Child Welfare Act: A Status Report." Final Report of the Survey of Indian Child Welfare and Implementation of the Indian Child Welfare Act and Section 428 of the Adoption Assistance and Child Welfare Act of 1980. Washington, DC: Government Printing Office, 1988.

Deloria, Vine, Jr., *Custer Died for Your Sins: An Indian Manifesto*. Norman: University of Oklahoma Press, 1988.

Deloria, Vine, Jr., and Clifford M. Lytle, *The Nations Within: The Past and Future of American Indian Sovereignty*. Austin: University of Texas Press, 1984.

Deloria, Vine, Jr., and David E. Wilkins. *The Legal Universe: Observations on the Foundations of American Law* (Golden, CO: Fulcrum Publishing, 2011).

Glasser, Melvin. "Relations with the Bureau of Indian Affairs-Branch of Welfare and Placement," Memorandum. Records of the Children's Bureau, RG 102, Central File, Box 351, Folder Indians, National Archives at College Park.

Leech Lake Band of Ojibwe. Minnesota Department of Human Services, Title IV-E Foster Care Maintenance, Administrative and Training Agreement, 2014. Accessed Aug. 13, 2021, from https://www.dhs.state.mn.us/main/groups/county_access/documents/pub/dhs16_142484.pdf.

Mall, Lorinda. "Keeping It in the Family: The Legal and Social Evolution of ICWA in State and Tribal Jurisprudence." In *Facing the Future: the Indian Child Welfare Act at 30*, ed. Matthew L. M. Fletcher, Wenona T. Singel, and Kathryn E. Fort. East Lansing: Michigan State University Press, 2009, 164–220.

Minnesota Department of Human Services. "Tribal/State Indian Child Welfare Agreement, as amended in 2007." Accessed Aug. 18, 2021, from https://edocs.dhs.state.mn.us/lfserver/Legacy/DHS-5022-ENG (accessed August 18, 2021).

Morgan Pryse, E. "Letter to the Children's Bureau," October 22, 1951, Records of the Children's Bureau, RG 102, Central File, Box 351, Folder Indians, National Archives at College Park.

Public Law 95-608, §§1901-63, 1978.

Red Lake Nation. Minnesota Department of Human Services, Title IV-E Foster Care Agreement, 2008. Accessed Aug. 13, 2021, from https://www.narf.org/nill/resources/title-iv-e/minnesota/minnesota-red-lake.pdf.

Thorpe, Jack, and Shannon Keller O'Loughlin. Association on American Indian Affairs, Casey Family Programs, "A Survey Analysis of Select Title IV-E Tribal-State Agreements," March 2014.

Turner Strong, Pauline. "What Is an Indian Family? The Indian Child Welfare Act and the Renascence of Tribal Sovereignty." *American Studies* 46, no. 3/4 (2005–2006): 205–231.

US Congress, Senate, Subcommittee on Indian Affairs of the Committee on Interior and Insular Affairs. "Hearings on Problems That American Indian Families Face in Raising Their Children and How These Problems Are Affected by Federal Action or Inaction." 93rd Cong., 2d sess., April 8–9, 1974.

Wilkins, Andrea. *State-Tribal Cooperation and the Indian Child Welfare Act*, National Conference of State Legislatures, State Tribal Institute, July 2008. Accessed Aug. 15, 2021, from http://www.ncsl.org/print/stateTribe/ICWABrief08.pdf.

Wilkins, David E., and K. Tsianina Lomawaima. *Uneven Ground: American Indian Sovereignty and Federal Law*. Norman: University of Oklahoma Press, 2001.

Chapter 34

1. Mygatt, Emmie D. Papers, 1886–1973 (bulk 1950–1973), American Heritage Center, University of Wyoming.
2. Dick Redburn, *Sheridan Press Weekender*, 1976, copy with author.

CONTRIBUTORS

Vivian Arviso (Diné) is an educator, administrator, consultant, writer, and a specialist in curriculum development. Her early teaching years were spent at Red Cloud Indian School on the Pine Ridge Indian Reservation where she developed the yearlong curriculum, "Oglala Sioux History and Culture." Funded by the US Office of Education in 1971, it was the first Native curriculum to test the change in self-image of Oglala Lakota students as they studied their own history and culture. While at Black Hills State College she assisted with the development of Oglala Lakota College. Upon returning to the Navajo Nation, Dr. Arviso served as vice president at Navajo Community College (now Diné College), then as the executive director of Tribal education for the Navajo Nation.

In 2011, she initiated the annual Hero Twins Conference for Navajo boys in partnership with the Miss Navajo Council, Inc. She is former chair of the board of directors of the Southwestern Association on Indian Arts and former president of the Navajo Nation Women's Commission. She received an honorary doctorate as Defender for the Lakota Way of Life and Wisdom from Sinte Gleska University.

Dr. Arviso is married to Sam Deloria (Standing Rock), who first laid eyes upon her when she, as Miss Indian America 1960, waved to parade-goers from the official pageant float. He remembers thinking, "That's the one I have in mind." They married thirty-five years later.

Kiros A. B. Auld is of Miles lineage, his grandmother and mother's generation were enrolled in the Pamunkey Indian Tribe, the leading nation of the historic and local Powhatan Paramount Chiefdom that contended and treated with the first British Colonies. His maternal grandfather is of the Doeg-Tauxenants, Powhatan Tributaries in its Northernmost Homelands of modern Fairfax County and Washington, D.C. This is how he is Pamunkey. Auld graduated Phi Beta Kappa, summa cum laude with honors from Howard University, receiving his bachelor's of arts degree in history; he earned his Juris Doctor degree from the Howard University School of Law, focusing on Federal Indian Law and International Law. Auld founded and moderates /r/IndianCountry, the largest Native American community on Reddit.com and is consistently among the top ten viewed websites in the US. He recently concluded his leadership and service on the board of directors for Native American LifeLines, which provides contracted Urban Indian Health services for the Baltimore and Boston Service Areas. He previously provided professional and personal services to help secure Federal Acknowledgment for the seven recognized Tribal Nations in Virginia.

Natalie Avalos is an assistant professor in the Department of Ethnic Studies and affiliate faculty in the Religious Studies and Women and Gender Studies Departments at the University of Colorado–Boulder. She is an ethnographer of religion whose work in comparative Indigeneities explores urban Indian and Tibetan refugee religious life as decolonial praxis. She received her doctorate from the University of California–Santa Barbara in religious studies with a special focus on Native American and Indigenous religious traditions and Tibetan Buddhism. She is currently working on her manuscript titled *The Metaphysics of Decoloniality: Transnational Indigeneities and Religious Refusal.* It argues that the reassertion of land-based logics among Native and Tibetan peoples not only de-centers settler colonial claims to legitimate knowledge but also articulates forms of sovereignty rooted in interdependent relations of power among all persons, both human and other-than-human. She is a Chicana of Apache descent, born and raised in the Bay Area.

Thomas Biolsi is professor of ethnic studies at the University of California–Berkeley, where he teaches courses in Native American studies and comparative ethnic studies. Most of his archival and ethnographic research is focused on the political and legal history of Rosebud Reservation. He is the author of *Power and Progress on the Prairie: Governing People on Rosebud Reservation* (University of Minnesota Press, 2018), *Deadliest Enemies: Law and Race Relations on and off Rosebud Reservation* (University of Minnesota Press, 2007), and *Organizing the Lakota: The Political Economy of the New Deal on Pine Ridge and Rosebud Reservations* (University of Arizona Press, 1992). He edited *Companion to the Anthropology of American Indians* (Blackwell Publishers, 2004), and coedited (with Larry J. Zimmerman) *Indians and Anthropologists: Vine Deloria, Jr., and the Critique of Anthropology* (University of Arizona Press, 1997).

Gregory A. Cajete, a native of Santa Clara Pueblo, is professor emeritus of Native American studies and language, literacy, and sociocultural studies at the University of New Mexico. He has served as a New Mexico Humanities scholar in ethno-botany of northern New Mexico and is a member of the New Mexico Arts Commission. A former dean, department chair, and professor at the Institute of American Indian Arts in Santa Fe, he organized and directed the first National Native American Very Special Arts Festival in the 1990s. He earned his bachelor's in biology and sociology with a minor in secondary education from New Mexico Highlands University, a master's in adult and secondary education from UNM, and a PhD from International College–Los Angeles New Philosophy Program in social science education with an emphasis in Native American studies. He has authored ten books on Indigenous education and community.

Tantoo Cardinal (Cree-Metis) is a writer, activist, and performer known for her dedication to the protection of Indigenous lands and traditions, and for iconic television and movie roles including *Smoke Signals*, *Westworld*, *Legends of the Fall*, *Dances with Wolves*, *Falls Around Her*, and *Killers of the Flower Moon*.

Canada honored her in 2009, when she was made a member of the Order of Canada for her contributions to the arts, and again in 2021 with the Governor General's Performing Arts Award.

In 2023, she was inducted into the Canadian Walk of Fame.

Her many professional awards include the Academy of Canadian Cinema and Television's Earle Grey Award for lifetime achievement, First Americans in the Arts Award for Outstanding Performance for *The Education of Little Tree*, and a Gemini Award. In 1993, she became the first recipient of the American Indian Film Festival's Rudy Martin Award for Outstanding Achievement by a Native American in Film.

She holds honorary doctorates from the University of Rochester, St. Lawrence University, the University of Calgary, and the University of Fraser Valley.

Martin Case is an Irish American researcher and writer. His research focuses on political and economic networks that shaped US relationships with Indigenous nations and on "dominant culture" narratives that feed the American Myth. He was on the design team for *Why Treaties Matter*, a collaboration of the Minnesota Indian Affairs Council, the Minnesota Humanities Center, and the Smithsonian's Museum of the American Indian. Case is the author of *The Relentless Business of Treaties: How Indigenous Land Became US Property* (Minnesota Historical Society Press, 2018).

Samuel R. Cook is an associate professor in the Department of History and the director of American Indian Studies. His research interests include Indigenous political economies and ecologies, American Indian law and policy, Indigenous knowledge systems, Appalachian cultures, and human ecology and sustainability.

Cheryl Crazy Bull, Wacinyanpi Win (They Depend on Her), a member of the Sicangu Lakota Nation, is president and CEO of the American Indian College Fund, a role she has held since 2012. A lifelong educator and community activist, Cheryl is an advocate for self-determination focused on Native voice, philosophy, and traditions as the heart of the people's work in building prosperity for current and future generations. She served as a faculty member, department chair, dean of academic affairs, and vice president of administration at Sinte Gleska University on her home reservation; chief educational officer at Francis Indian School; and president of Northwest Indian College. She is also a member of the boards of IllumiNative, an organization that focuses on a widespread accurate narrative about Indigenous people; the Native Ways Federation, a national association of Native nonprofits; the State Higher Education Executive Officers Organization Equity Advisory Committee; and the Brookings Institution. She has an honorary cultural degree from Sinte Gleska University, an honorary doctorate from Seattle University, and other awards for her leadership as a Native educator and Native woman.

Cheryl has received many awards and honors throughout her long career. In 2015 she was named by *Indian Country Today* magazine as one of the fifty most influential people in Indian Country. In 2017, she was one of two American Indian women leaders honored by National Indian Women's "Supporting Each Other" group. The Native American Finance Officers Association honored her with a Lifetime Achievement Award in October 2019. In March of 2020, CBS paid tribute to Crazy Bull, along with six other women, as an example of what it means to challenge and overcome stereotypes and biases in their industries as part of a series of CBS CARES public service announcements. Other awards include the 2020 Working Mother Media Legacy Award and the 2021 Mitchell Museum of the American Indian Elizabeth Seabury Mitchell Award for exemplary service and philanthropic giving in promoting American Indian culture. Global MindED, a nonprofit organization dedicated to closing the equity gap by creating a diverse talent pipeline through role models, mentors, and internships, named her as its 2021 Inclusive Leader Awardee.

Sarah Deer is a citizen of the Muscogee (Creek) Nation of Oklahoma and a University Distinguished Professor at the University of Kansas. Her

2015 book, *The Beginning and End of Rape: Confronting Sexual Violence in Native America*, is the culmination of more than twenty-five years of working with survivors and has received several awards, including the Best First Book award from the Native American and Indigenous Studies Association. A lawyer by training but an advocate in practice, Deer's scholarship focuses on the intersection of federal Indian law and victims' rights, using Indigenous feminist principles as a framework. Deer is a coauthor of four textbooks on Tribal law and has been published in a wide variety of law journals, including the *Harvard Journal of Law and Gender*, the *Yale Journal of Law and Feminism*, and the *Columbia Journal of Gender and Law*. Her work to end violence against Native women has received national awards from the American Bar Association and the Department of Justice. She has testified before Congress on four occasions regarding violence against Native women and was appointed by Attorney General Eric Holder to chair a federal advisory committee on sexual violence in Indian Country. Professor Deer was named a MacArthur Foundation Fellow in 2014. In 2019, she was inducted into the National Women's Hall of Fame. She currently teaches at the University of Kansas (her alma mater), where she holds a joint appointment in women, gender, and sexuality studies and the School of Public Affairs and Administration. Professor Deer is also the chief justice for the Prairie Island Indian Community Court of Appeals.

Ryan E. Emanuel (Lumbee) is an associate professor in the Nicholas School of the Environment at Duke University. Trained as an interdisciplinary environmental scientist with an emphasis on water, Emanuel studies the flow and status of water in a variety of landscapes and ecosystems. He works to elevate Indigenous perspectives on water and the environment in scholarly discussions and in decision-making spaces through partnerships with Tribes and Indigenous organizations in North Carolina and elsewhere. He is the recipient of North Carolina State University's annual sustainability award and the North Carolina Environmental Justice Network's annual award for academic research. Emanuel advises the North Carolina Commission of Indian Affairs on environmental justice policy, and he has held positions on local and statewide advisory boards for American Indian education. He serves on the academic advisory council of the American Indian Science and Engineering Society and on the diversity and inclusion advisory committee of the American Geophysical Union. He formerly served on the education and outreach committee of CUAHSI, the Consortium of Universities for the Advancement of Hydrologic Science, Inc. He is the author of *On the Swamp: Fighting for Indigenous Environmental Justice* (2024). Emanuel holds a PhD and MS in environmental sciences from the University of Virginia and a BS in geology from Duke University.

Frank Ettawageshik lives in Harbor Springs, Michigan, with his wife, Rochelle. He served in Tribal elected office for sixteen years, fourteen as the Tribal chairman of the Little Traverse Bay Bands of Odawa Indians in Harbor Springs, Michigan. He is the executive director of the United Tribes of Michigan. He also serves on several nonprofit boards, including as president of the Association on American Indian Affairs, the oldest nonprofit organization serving Indian Country.

Gabriel S. Galanda belongs to the Round Valley Indian Tribes and descends from the Nomlaki and Concow Peoples. As Managing Lawyer at Galanda Broadman, PLLC, an Indigenous rights law firm in Seattle, he focuses on complex, multiparty litigation and crisis management, representing Indigenous nations, businesses, and citizens. Gabe has been named to Best Lawyers in America in the fields of Native American Law and Gaming Law from 2007 to 2024 and was dubbed a Super Lawyer by his peers from 2013 to 2024. He was a 2022 recipient of the American Bar Association's Spirit of Excellence Award, presented to lawyers who personify excellence on the national, state, or local level and have demonstrated a commitment to racial and ethnic diversity in law. The Washington State Bar Association honored him with the 2014 Excellence in Diversity Award for his "significant contribution to diversity in the legal profession." For his staunch Indigenous human rights advocacy, the University of Arizona College of Law awarded him the Professional Achievement Award, and Western Washington University named him a Distinguished Alumnus in 2018. *Indian Country Today* recognized Gabe as one of "five people rocking the world with their forward thinking, innovation and commitment to social justice" in 2013, and as one of "Fifty Faces of Indian Country" in 2017. Gabe also operates Huy, a 501(c)(3) nonprofit organization he founded that is dedicated to enhancing religious, cultural, and other rehabilitative opportunities for American Indian prisoners. As Chair of the Huy Board of Advisors, he has led the organization's amicus curiae efforts before the US Supreme Court and federal and state appellate courts across the country.

Doug George-Kanentiio of the Mohawk Bear Clan is an award-winning freelance Native American author and activist. His books include *Iroquois Culture & Commentary; Iroquois on Fire: A Voice from the Mohawk Nation*, with a foreword by Vine Deloria, Jr.; and *Skywoman: Legends of the Iroquois*, coauthored with his late wife, Joanne Shenandoah. For many years he was a land rights negotiator for the Mohawk Nation Council. From 1986 to 1992, he was the editor for *Akwesasne Notes*. In 1994, the Native American Journalists Association recognized George-Kanentiio's dedication with the Wassaja award for Journalism Excellence, their highest honor. He was an Olympic torch carrier for the 2002 Winter Games, and he currently serves as vice president of the Hiawatha Institute for Indigenous Knowledge.

Wendy S. Greyeyes (Diné) is an assistant professor of Native American studies at the University of New Mexico. Dr. Greyeyes received her MA and PhD in sociology from the University of Chicago and BA in Native American studies from Stanford University. Her research is focused on political sociology, organizational analysis, Indigenous education, Tribal sovereignty, and Nation Building. Dr. Greyeyes formerly worked for the Arizona governor as a Tribal liaison for the Arizona Teacher Excellence Program and Homeland Security, a grassroots manager for the Indian

Self Reliance Initiative in Arizona, a statistician/demographer for the Department of Diné Education, and a program analyst/chief implementation officer for the Bureau of Indian Education. She formerly served as the cochair for the National Indian Education Association's Advocacy Committee and is a former faculty for the Institute for American Indian Education. She currently serves as the Navajo representative member for the New Mexico Indian Education Advisory Council; president for the Diné Studies Conference, Inc.; a member of the American Indian Studies Association; faculty advisor for the University of New Mexico Native American Alumni Chapter; and faculty advisor for Kiva Club. Recent publications include an article for *Wicazo Sa Review* titled "The Paradox of Tribal Community Building: The Roots of Local Resistance to Tribal State Craft" (2021) and a book titled *A History of Navajo Education: Disentangling Our Sovereign Body* (2022). She currently is a coeditor with Dr. Lloyd L. Lee for University of New Mexico Press's Studies in Indigenous Community Building. Her favorite hobbies are teaching Navajo and ribbon skirt making classes, running, and cooking.

Megan Minoka Hill (Oneida) is the program director of the Harvard Project on American Indian Economic Development and the director of the Honoring Nations program at the Harvard Kennedy School, Harvard University. She serves on the Native American Graves Protection Repatriation Act Committee at the Peabody Museum of Archaeology and Ethnology, on the board of the Sustainable Native Communities Collaborative, and as board secretary for the Dr. Rosa Minoka Hill Fund board. Previously, she worked as the director of development for the University of New Mexico College of Arts and Sciences, senior program officer at the Institute of American Indian Arts, and director of Individual Giving at the American Indian College Fund. Megan graduated from the University of Chicago with a master of arts in the social sciences and received a bachelor of arts in international affairs, with an emphasis on Latin America and economics from the University of Colorado–Boulder.

Norbert S. Hill, Jr. (Oneida) serves on the Oneida Nation Trust and Enrollment Committee at the Oneida Nation of Wisconsin. His most recent appointments include area director of education and training at the Oneida Nation and vice president of the College of Menominee Nation. Previously, Norbert served as executive director of the American Indian Graduate Center (AIGC) in New Mexico, a nonprofit organization providing funding for American Indian and Alaskan Natives to pursue graduate and professional degrees; the executive director of the American Indian Science and Engineering Society; the assistant dean of students at the University of Wisconsin–Green Bay; and the director of the American Indian Educational Opportunity Program at the University of Colorado–Boulder. He founded *Winds of Change* and *The American Indian Graduate* magazine publications of AISES and AIGC, respectively. Norbert holds two honorary doctorates from Clarkson University and Cumberland College. Past board appointments include Environmental Defense Fund, chair and board member of the Smithsonian National Museum of the American Indian, and the Wisconsin Historical Society. In 1989, Norbert was awarded the Lifetime Achievement Award from the National Action Council for Minorities in Engineering. Norbert has three children and resides on the Oneida reservation with his wife.

Tom Holm (Cherokee Nation) holds the title of professor emeritus at the University of Arizona. He was a member of the Cherokee Nation's Sequoyah Commission. Holm served with Bravo Company, 1st Battalion, 3rd Marines in Vietnam. He holds a PhD from the University of Oklahoma. Tom served on two Native American commissions for the Department of Veterans Affairs in the 1980s. In 1996, his book *Strong Hearts, Wounded Souls* was a finalist for the Victor Turner prize. "His books include *Ira Hayes: The Akimel O'odham Warrior, World War II, and the Price of Heroism* (2023), *The Great Confusion in Indian Affairs* (2005), and *Warriors and Code Talkers: Native Americans and World War II* (2007). He has written two novels, *The Osage Rose* (2008) and *Anadarko* (2015). With Steve Pavlik and M. Elise Marubbio, he edited *Native Apparitions: Critical Perspectives on Hollywood's Indians* (2018).

James Johnson (Tlingit) is an award-winning artist and carver. Born and raised in Juneau, Alaska, he belongs to the Tlingit Ch'áak' Dakl'aweidi Clan (Eagle Killerwhale). James's great-great-grandfather was Chief Gusht'eiheen (Spray off the Dorsal Fin) of the Dakl'aweidi of the Xutsnoowú Kwáan (Angoon, Alaska) and his great-grandfather was Chief Jimmy Johnson. He was named James Peter in honor of his grandfather Chief Peter Johnson. This strong ancestral history led him to purse the Tlingit art form. His late father, Franklin Johnson, first encouraged him to begin carving, and James has now dedicated his life to perpetuating the Tlingit art form, honoring his ancestors through his work.

Aurélie Journée-Duez holds a PhD in social anthropology and ethnology from the EHESS (Paris, France). She recently contributed to the book *Subjective Constellations: Pour une histoire féministe de l'art* (2020) by Editions X, with a chapter dedicated to the artist Wendy Red Star (Crow). Her latest paper focuses on Indigenous comics and their use in addressing the global health crisis. Her dissertation, "Indigenous Women and Queer Artists facing their images" offers an intersectional and decolonial history of Indigenous contemporary arts in the US and Canada, 1969–2019, under the direction of Marie Mauzé (CNRS) and Michel Poivert (Paris 1 Pantheon-Sorbonne University), EHESS, Paris, 2020.

Tiffany S. Lee is Dibé Łizhiní (Blacksheep) and born for Naałaní (Oglala Lakota). She is from Crystal, New Mexico, located on the Navajo Nation, on her mother's side, and Pine Ridge, South Dakota, on her father's side. Dr. Lee is professor and chair of Native American studies at the University of New Mexico. She earned her doctorate in sociology of education from Stanford University. Her research examines Native youth perspectives with regard to language reclamation and identity. She also investigates socioculturally centered educational approaches. In 2016, she was awarded a grant from the Spencer Foundation to examine the impact of Indigenous language immersion schools on Native American student achievement. Some of her publications include "Critical Language Awareness among Native Youth in New Mexico" in *Indigenous Youth and Multilingualism: Language Identity, Ideology, and Practice in Dynamic Cultural Worlds* and "You Should Learn Who You Are through Your Culture: Transformative Educational Possibilities for Native American Youth in New Mexico" in *Cultural Transformations: Youth and Pedagogies of Possibility*. She is the former president of the Navajo Studies Conference, Inc. and a former high school social studies and language arts teacher at schools on the Navajo Nation and at Santa Fe Indian School. She is also a member of the New Mexico Indian Education Advisory Council for the New Mexico Office of Indian Education.

Marine Le Puloch, associate professor at the Université de Paris, teaches North American and Indigenous Studies. She is the author of *Le piège colonial: Histoire des traités de colonisation au Canada* (2007) and various papers on the past and present colonization of western Canada and its effects on the sovereignty of Indigenous peoples. Using a transdisciplinary approach—historical, judicial, political, and ethnographical—she considers the response of Native peoples as they sometimes negotiate with the colonial authorities, sometimes seek redress in its courts of justice, and sometimes turn to civil disobedience as a last resort. Using exemplary test cases in northern Alberta, she examines Indigenous opposition to the exploitation of nonrenewable resources on their traditional territory and their efforts to prevent irreversible environmental damage, and to pass down a viable means of existence to the next generations.

Jordan P. Lewis (Aleut) is a Department of Family Medicine and biobehavioral health professor. His expertise is in Indigenous successful aging, rural community health, generativity and healthy aging, and cultural constructions of Alzheimer's disease and related dementias. During the past decade, Dr. Lewis's research agenda has significantly contributed to the field with community-based research and discussions on culture-specific approaches in Alaska Native (AN) successful aging and

Alzheimer's disease and related disorders (ADRD) among AN Elders, including the development of a model of AN successful aging, the theory of AN healthy aging, the concept of Indigenous cultural generativity, and cultural understandings and construction of ADRD among AN caregivers. His research has identified Indigenous cultural generativity as a critical ingredient to healthy aging, a resilience resource, and has important implications for the well-being of Alaska Native and American Indians, including those with ADRD, their caregivers, and family and community members.

Cannupa Hanska Luger is a multidisciplinary artist and an enrolled member of the Three Affiliated Tribes of Fort Berthold (Mandan, Hidatsa, and Arikara and Lakota). Through monumental installations and social collaboration, he activates speculative fiction and communicates stories about twenty-first-century Indigeneity, combining critical cultural analysis with dedication and respect for the diverse materials, environments, and communities he engages. He lectures and produces large-scale projects around the globe and his works are in many public collections.

Notable works include *Sweet Land* (2020), an award-winning multi-perspectival and site-specific opera produced through The Industry and staged at the State Historical Park in downtown Los Angeles, for which he was codirector and costume designer; The MMIWQT Bead Project (2018), a social collaboration resulting in the monumental sculptural installation *Every One*, composed of more than four thousand individual handmade clay beads created by hundreds of communities across the US and Canada to rehumanize the data of missing and murdered Indigenous women, girls, queer, and trans community members; and The Mirror Shield Project (2016), a social engagement work that invited the public to create mirrored shields for water protectors at Standing Rock and which has since been formatted and used in various resistance movements across the nation.

Luger is a 2023 SOROS Arts Fellow, 2022 Guggenheim Fellow, recipient of the 2021 United States Artists Fellowship Award for Craft, and was named a Grist 50 Fixer for 2021, a list which includes emerging leaders in climate, sustainability, and equity who are creating change across the nation.

He has exhibited nationally and internationally, including venues such as the Metropolitan Museum of Art, Gardiner Museum, Kunsthal KAdE, Washington Project for the Arts, Art Mûr, Crystal Bridges Museum of American Art, and the National Center for Civil and Human Rights, among others. He holds a BFA in studio arts from the Institute of American Indian Arts.

Deron Marquez (Yuhaaviatam of San Manuel Nation) served as chairman of the San Manuel Nation from 1999 through April 2006. In addition to leading the seven-member Business Committee, he was instrumental in designing and directing a progressive agenda of social, economic, and governance development for the Tribal government and community. Under his leadership, the Tribe has entered into successful business ventures with the goal of securing critical government revenues well into the future. The Tribe also enhanced its governance capabilities, instituted public services for Tribal members, and solidified intergovernmental relations at the local, state, and national levels under his leadership. Marquez is a nationally recognized speaker and lecturer on such issues as economic development, Tribal governance, and Tribal sovereignty. He is the cofounder and director of the Tribal Administration Certificate Program at Claremont Graduate University, a certificate program providing instruction on Tribal sovereignty, Tribal law, and management. Marquez earned his undergraduate degree from the University of Arizona as well as a master's degree and PhD in politics from Claremont Graduate University.

Kyle T. Mays (Saginaw Chippewa) is an assistant professor of African American studies, American Indian studies, and history at the University of California–Los Angeles. He is a transdisciplinary scholar of urban history and studies, Afro-Indigenous Studies, and contemporary popular culture. He is the author of *City of Dispossessions: African Americans, Indigenous*

Peoples, and the Creation of Modern Detroit (University of Pennsylvania Press, 2022), *An Afro-Indigenous History of the United States* (Beacon Press, 2022), and *Hip Hop Beats, Indigenous Rhymes: Modernity and Hip Hop in Indigenous North America* (SUNY Press, 2018). Dr. Mays has received numerous fellowships, including a Newberry Library Research Fellowship and Carolina Diversity Postdoctoral Fellowship at the University of North Carolina at Chapel Hill. During the 2019–2020 academic year, he was a Mays Mellon Visiting Scholar at the James Weldon Johnson Institute for the Study of Race and Difference at Emory University. Mays received his BA from James Madison College at Michigan State University and his PhD in US history from the University of Illinois–Urbana-Champaign.

Édith Patrouilleau earned her research master's degree in Anglo-American Studies at the University of Paris–Nanterre in 1974, focusing on Indian government policy and Indian nationalism in the US. In 1977, she coauthored with Jean-François Graugnard and Eiméo A. Raa *Nations Indiennes, Nations Souveraines* (Éditions François Maspéro). Other publications and films include *Les Chemins de la Survie*, codirection of two documentaries, *Lakota Land* in 2005 and *Black Indians: African-American Masking in New Orleans* in 2018 (Lardux Films).

In 1978, she and Danielle Faure cofounded the Committee in Solidarity with the Indians of the Americas (CSIA-Nitassinan), an organization created at the request of Indigenous delegates who met at the 1977 United Nations meeting in Geneva, Switzerland. Considered the first official UN diplomatic gathering of representatives of Earth's Indigenous peoples, it was here that delegates formally reaffirmed Indigenous existence, reclaimed and defended their rights in international institutions, and requested global solidarity. Nearly half a century later, the members of CSIA-Nitassinan continue to support their ongoing struggles.

Migizi Pensoneau (Ponca/Ojibwe) is a screenwriter and performer known for his work on *Barkskins*, an original series by Fox and NatGeo, and *Reservation Dogs*, an award-winning comedy on FX. He also starred as Roy Crooks in the *Rutherford Falls* series. Migizi was born and raised in Minnesota and attended Wesleyan University. He received his MFA in screenwriting at the Institute of American Indian Arts in Santa Fe. He continues to write and tour for the 1491s, the popular comedy troupe he cofounded.

Céline Planchou is an associate professor of US Studies at the University of Sorbonne Paris Nord (Paris 13 Villetaneuse—France) and a member of PLÉIADE (Centre de recherche pluridisciplinaire en Lettres, Langues, Sciences Humaines et des Sociétés). Her research focuses on the legal and political status of Native peoples in the United States, with a focus on child welfare. She has published several articles in France and coedited with Marine Le Puloch an issue of the French Journal of American studies on "The Nations Within" (*Revue française d'études américaines* 144.3, 2015). Her current work, a collaborative project, deals with the political and spatial dynamics of Indigenous visibility in Rapid City, South Dakota. Her latest article, coauthored with Sandrine Baudry and entitled "Urban Economic Development and Indigenous Cultures: The Case of the Lakota Sioux in Rapid City" was published in the online journal of the Institute of the Americas (*IdeAs-Idées d'Amériques* 17, 2021).

Margaret Hiza Redsteer (Crow) is an assistant professor in the School of Interdisciplinary Arts and Sciences at the University of Washington Bothell Indigenous Knowledge for Climate Assessment and Adaptation. She is a former research scientist for the US Department of the Interior and USGS based in the Flagstaff Science Center. She has also worked on water issues for the Navajo Nation, melding scientific data with traditional knowledge to discover the ties between these problems and climate change. Her work examines aspects of global change that include interactions of different landscape processes, including erosion by wind and water and how changing vegetation communities and climate can influence these processes and exacerbate geologic hazards. In the Southwest, she has studied aspects of drought and increasing aridity that have not been well quantified, including seasonal changes to surficial processes and ecologic conditions. This work requires detailed geomorphologic mapping, sediment sampling, seasonal vegetation surveys, and meteorological monitoring but also requires investigations of land use history and policy. Incorporating Indigenous knowledge from Tribal Elders about the changes they have observed has aided her research in elucidating the effects of increasing temperatures in poorly monitored regions of the US and communicates the relevance of ecosystem change to the livelihoods of those who are most vulnerable. Increasing aridity and its alteration of ecosystem services has serious consequences for marginalized populations, agriculture, grazing, and infrastructure.

Lauren Schad (Cheyenne River Lakota) is an artist, model, activist, and former professional volleyball player. She received a degree in anthropology from the University of San Diego, where she helped lead the volleyball team to the NCAA tournament three years in a row. In 2015, she was selected to play with the US National Team and was also an AVCA All-American Honorable Mention. During her time as a professional player with Volleyball Nantes-Pro, Nantes, the team received silver medals in both the French Cup and French Championship. In 2023, she was inducted into the North American Indigenous Athletics Hall of Fame.

Lauren uses her platform to create awareness around issues critical to youth in Indian Country. She is a member of the Red Ribbon Skirt Society and an MMIWC2S Ambassador. She also volunteers her time to coach Tribal youth athletic programs. In 2018, the Nike corporation chose her to be a Nike Ambassador recognizing her as an athlete who reflects the Native community and influences Native youth. She recently designed the N7 Air Zoom Type athletic shoe featuring colors of the medicine wheel.

Noenoe K. Silva (Kanaka ʻŌiwi Hawaiʻi) is a keiki of Keahupuaʻanui in Kailua, Koʻolaupoko, Oʻahu. She is professor of Hawaiian and Indigenous politics in the Department of Political Science and ʻŌlelo Hawaiʻi in Kawaihuelani Center for Hawaiian Language, both at the University of Hawai'i at Mānoa. She is the author of *Aloha Betrayed: Native Hawaiian Resistance to American Colonialism* and *The Power of the Steel-Tipped Pen: Reconstructing Native Hawaiian Intellectual History.*

Faith Spotted Eagle (Yankton Sioux Nation) is a founder of the Brave Heart Society, an organization dedicated to the revival of a traditional cultural society for Indigenous women. She is a fluent speaker of the Dakota Language and a member of the Ihanktonwan. Faith is a leader in the resistance against tar sands pipelines including DAPL, Line 3 and the Keystone XL pipelines. As the chair of the Ihanktonwan Treaty Committee and Brave Heart Society Grandmother, she helped bring forth the International Treaty to Protect the Sacred against the KXL Pipeline and the Tar Sands. Faith attended college at American University in Washington, D.C., and Black Hills State College, Spearfish, South Dakota, and earned a master's in guidance and counseling in her early twenties at the University of South Dakota. She has been active in teaching the Dakota language and is a twenty-year member and coordinator of a revived traditional Brave Heart Society that operates a multipurpose lodge. She has been a delegate of the Treaty Committee NGO at the United Nations. Faith's priority, beyond stopping risky pipelines, has been to battle for the preservation of Sacred Sites through Brave Heart Society support of the World Peace and Prayer Day. In the 2016 presidential election, she became the first Native American to receive an electoral vote for president of the United States as well as one of the first two women to receive an electoral vote for president of the United States. Spotted Eagle's single vote came from Robert Satiacum, Jr. (Puyallup), a faithless elector in Washington, who cast it for her instead of Hillary Clinton.

Paulette F. C. Steeves (Cree-Metis) is an associate professor in sociology and anthropology at Algoma University in Ontario where she holds a Canada Research Chair Tier II in Indigenous History, Healing, and Reconciliation. She is an Indigenous archaeologist with a focus on the Pleistocene history of the Western Hemisphere. In her research, Steeves argues that Indigenous peoples were present in the Western Hemisphere as early as 100,000 years ago, and possibly much earlier. She has created a database of hundreds of archaeology sites in both North and South America that date from 250,000 to 12,000 years before present, which challenges the Clovis First dogma of a post-12,000-year-before-present initial migrations to the Americas. Dr. Steeves received her BA honors cum laude in 2000 at the University of Arkansas at Fayetteville. In 2008, she was awarded the Clifford D. Clark fellowship to attend graduate studies at Binghamton University in New York state where she earned her master's and doctorate in anthropology. During her doctoral studies, she worked with the Denver Museum of Nature and Science to carry out work in the Great Plains on mammoth sites that contained evidence of human technology on the mammoth bone, thus showing that humans were present in Nebraska more than 18,000 years ago. Dr. Steeves has taught anthropology courses with a focus on Native American and First Nations histories and studies, and decolonization of academia and knowledge production at Binghamton University, Selkirk College, Fort Peck Community College, the University of Massachusetts at Amherst, and Mount Allison University. Her book, *The Indigenous Paleolithic of the Western Hemisphere*, was published by the University of Nebraska Press in 2022.

Mark Trahant (Shoshone-Bannock) is editor-at-large of *Indian Country Today*, a daily digital news platform covering the Indigenous world of American Indians, Alaska Natives, and First Nation peoples reaching some eight hundred thousand readers a month. He is known for his election reporting in Indian Country and for developing the first comprehensive database of American Indians and Alaska Natives running for public office. His research has been cited in publications ranging from the *New York Times* to *The Economist* to *Teen Vogue*. Previous work includes reporting for PBS Frontline. A recent piece, "The Silence," focused on abuse by priests in an Alaska Native village. He was the editorial page editor of the *Seattle Post-Intelligencer* and has worked for *The Arizona Republic*, *Salt Lake Tribune*, *The Seattle Times*, the *Navajo Times Today*, and the *Sho-Ban News*. Trahant currently is working on an Indigenous economics project—a comprehensive examination of the contributions made by Tribes to regional economies—as well as a look at how the new standards of the ESG (Environmental, Social, Governance) investing tool impact both extractive resource development and climate change.

Rebecca Tsosie is a Regents Professor at the James E. Rogers College of Law at the University of Arizona, and she serves as a faculty cochair for the Indigenous Peoples' Law and Policy Program at the University of Arizona. Professor Tsosie, who is of Yaqui descent, is widely known for her work in the fields of federal Indian law and Indigenous peoples' human rights. Prior to joining the U of A faculty, Professor Tsosie was a Regent Professor and vice provost for inclusion and community engagement at Arizona State University. Professor Tsosie was the first faculty executive director for ASU's Indian Legal Program and served in that position for fifteen years. Professor Tsosie has published widely on sovereignty, self-determination, cultural pluralism, environmental policy, and cultural rights. She teaches in the areas of federal Indian law, property, constitutional law, critical race theory, and cultural resources law. Professor Tsosie is a member of the Arizona Bar Association and the California Bar Association. She serves as a Supreme Court justice for the Fort McDowell Yavapai Nation and as an associate judge on the San Carlos Tribal Court of Appeals. She received her BA and JD degrees from the University of California–Los Angeles.

Kyle Whyte (Citizen Potawatomi) is George Willis Pack Professor of Environment and Sustainability at the University of Michigan. Kyle's research addresses moral and political issues concerning climate policy and Indigenous peoples, the ethics of cooperative relationships between Indigenous peoples and science organizations, and problems of Indigenous justice in public and academic discussions of food sovereignty, environmental justice, and the Anthropocene. Dr. Whyte currently serves on the White House Environmental Justice Advisory Council. He was an author for the US Global Change Research Program and is a former member of the Advisory Committee on Climate Change and Natural Resource Science in the US Department of Interior and of two environmental justice work groups convened by past state governors of Michigan. He is also involved with organizations that advance Indigenous research and education methodologies and environmental justice, including the Climate and Traditional Knowledges Workgroup, the Sustainable Development Institute of the College of Menominee Nation, the Affiliated Tribes of Northwest Indians, Michigan Environmental Justice Coalition, Pesticide Action Network, and Ngā Pae o te Māramatanga, New Zealand's Māori Centre of Research Excellence. He received the Bunyan Bryant Award for Academic Excellence from Detroiters Working for Environmental Justice, Michigan State University's Distinguished Partnership and Engaged Scholarship awards, and grants from the National Science Foundation.

Melanie K. Yazzie is an assistant professor in the Departments of Native American Studies and American Studies at the University of Minnesota. She specializes in Navajo/American Indian history, political ecology, Indigenous feminisms, queer Indigenous studies, and theories of policing and the state. She also organizes with The Red Nation, a grassroots, Native-run organization committed to the liberation of Indigenous people. She is lead editor of *Decolonization: Indigeneity, Education & Society*, an international journal committed to public intellectualism and social justice. Yazzie is a citizen of the Navajo Nation.

INDEX

Please note page numbers with *t* indicate tables; page numbers with *f* indicate figures; page numbers with n indicate endnotes; page numbers in bold indicate defined terms.

Abeyta case, 35–36
Abinanti, Abby, 338
aboriginal rights, 31–32
accreditation, 148, 271–72
acculturation, 272, 306, 308
activism: African American, 21, 23; cornerstone of, 67; in eugenics era, 70; in France, 209; of Frank, 78; NAGPRA by, 190; in 1960s and 1970s, 13, 273; Red Power-era, 158; rights for, 288; on social media, 222, 223, 348; twentieth-century, 15; twenty-first century, 18, 298; for unrecognized Tribes, 169; veteran, 80, 84
Adams, Hank, xvii, 78
Administration for Children and Families (ACF), 461n30
Administration for Native Americans (ANA), 7–8
adoption: for Cheyenne, 379–80; with child welfare, 374, 376–77, 380; family ties by, 460n22, 461n34; for kinship, 337; revival of practices, 340; of Sinclair, 389; as social practice, 319
Adoption and Safe Families Act (ASFA), 379, 382
Advisory Council on Historic Preservation (ACHP), 190, 198
Africa, 22
African America, 20–24
Age of Enlightenment, 145
aging population, 93
agreements: after 1871, 40; compacts *vs*., 55, 292; failure of, 85; grants or, 144; NAGPRA as, 38, 73, 190–95, 198–99, 308, 310; PA as, 190, 199; records of, 66; spitting for, 54; and transfer of authority, 375; treaties vs., 39–40, 58, 292; Tribal-Commonwealth Accord as, 71–75, 395–411; Tribal-state, 381, 382; Tribal/State Indian Child Welfare, 382–83
Agua Caliente Band of Mission Indians' People Curriculum, 96
Agua Caliente Indian Reservation, 16
Ahtna Athabascan cultural practices, 95–96
Akimel O'odham, 79, 80, 86
aku, 105
akua, **105**, 106, 109–11, 115, 116
akua nui, **106**
Akwesasne, 205, 301
Akwesasne Freedom School, 96
Akwesasne Notes, 81, 301, 302
Akwesasronon, **301**
Alaska Native Claims Settlement Act of 1971, 284
Alaska Natives, 18, 179, 181, 183
Alcatraz, 13, 15, 80–81, 315
alcoholism, 240
Alfred P. Murrah federal building, 215
Algonquian Nations, 59, 62
Ali, Muhammad, 76
All American Indian Days Memorial, 385–90
Allen, Richard, 82
alternative schools, 270
American Civil Liberties Union, 274
American Confederation, 60–61
American Indian Citizens' League (AICL), 79
American Indian Graduate Student organization, 76
American Indian Languages Preservation and Revitalization Act, 233
American Indian Movement (AIM), 13, 22, 23, 157, 158, 202, 204
American Indian Museum (AIM), 302
American Indian National Bank Project, 13
American Indian Policy and Law, 77
American Indian Policy Review Commission, 283, 284, 441n7
American Indian Religious Freedom Act, 38, 272
American Indians, American Justice (Deloria and Lytle), 14, 321
American Indian Studies Association conference, 267
American Indian Studies program, 76
American Law Institute, 419n52
American Relief Plan Act (ARPA), 90, 92, 93, 95, 97
American Revolution, 58, 61

Amnesty International Report, 18
ANA. see Administration for Native Americans (ANA)
analog politics, 213–19
ancestors: connecting to, 119; defending, 190–201; deified, 105, 109; and dreams, 106; and education, 277; and identity, 365; and kinfolk, 337; preparing to walk with, 193–94; understanding, 105
ancestral rights, 31, 38
ancestral traditions, 251
Angelou, Maya, 141
Anishinaabe, 209, 222, 303, **335**, 368, 459n53
Anishinaabeg at Michilimackinac, 9
Annual American Indian Week, 228
anthropology, 135–36, **254–55**, 356–58, 456n19
Apache, 27, 28, 32–34
Apache Stronghold, **34**
Apache-US conflicts, 33
Apensanakwat (Marine Vietnam veteran), 82
Archaeological Resources Protection Act, 38
archaeology, 131, 138, 310–11
Archambeau, Madonna, 194–96, 199, 201
Archambeau, Ron, 194
Arizona, 27, 28, 30, 33, 34, 127, 336, 443n31
Arizona–Mexico border, 29
Arizona Mining Reform Coalition, 34
Arizona Republic, 225
Arrhenius, Svante, 128
Articles of Confederation, 68
Arviso, Vivian, 385
ASFA. see Adoption and Safe Families Act (ASFA)
assimilation, 47–48, 51, 95, 111, 144, 163, 188, 203, 231, 272–74, 294, 320, 431n12
Association on American Indian Affairs, 431n18
As We Have Always Done: Indigenous Freedom through Radical Resistance (Simpson), 222
Atlantic Coast Pipeline, 174, 434n44
Atwood, Margaret, 16
Auld, Kiros A. B., 346
ʻaumākua, **105**, 111, 115–18
Austin, Raymond D., 366
Australia, 47
Austria, 208
autonomy, 36, 271
Avalos, Natalie, 151
axiology, **242**

bands, 334
banishment, **338**, 357
Banks, Dennis, xvii
Barrett, Amy Coney, 381
Bartelson, Jens, 285, 291
Barton, Lew, 431n18
Bataan Death March, 79
Bears Ears National Monument, 40
Becoming Kin (Krawec), 342
Behind the Trail of Broken Treaties: An Indian Declaration of Independence (Deloria), 14, 21, 89, 354
Bellecourt, Clyde, xvii, 23–24
Bellecourt, Vernon, xvii, 76
belonging, xix, 102–3, 322, 331, 337, 340–41
Ben, Cyrus, 433n30
Bennett, Ramona, xvii
Berger, Yves, 315
Bering Land Bridge theory, 309
Bering Strait theory, 303
Berry, Thomas, 246–47
Better Day for Indians, A (Deloria), 172
Bible, 142
Biden administration, 30, 35
bilingual education, 271
Biloxi, **335**
bingo operation, 288
biology, 136
Biolsi, Thomas, 354
birth, 337, 349
birth certificates, 172
birth rates, 93
Bishop Museum Association, 110, 113
Blackbird, Andrew, 6
Black Elk, Nicholas, xv
Blackfeet Community College, 81
Black labor, 21
Black Lives Matter, 250
Black power, 21
Black radicals, 21, 23
blood quantum, 93, 94, 186, 187, 338–40, 351, 365–66
Blue, Brantley, 431n18
BNP Paribas Bank, 211
boarding schools, 15, 83, 95, 144, 365, 374
Boatman, John, 76
Boldt Decision, 79, 284
borderlands, 26, 28, 33, 36–38, 40, 41
borders: Arizona–Mexico, 29; imagined, 25–41; international, 29; introduction to, 25–26; Northern, 31–32; and sacred places, 32–36; Southern, 27–31, 32; US–Mexico, 25, 26, 27, 28, 32
border wall, 28–30
Bowron, Fletcher, 80
Boyd, Margaret, 6

Brackeen, Haaland v., 380
Brando, Marlon, 78–79
Brave Heart Society, 196, 199, 200
Bread, Jerry, 76
Brennan, William, Jr., 330
Bridges, Maiselle, xvii
British Columbia, 31, 126
Brown, Hank, 168
Brown, Marie Alohalani, 117, 118, 119
Buffalo Women's Society, 197
Bureau of Indian Affairs (BIA): AIM taking over, 13, 22; Alaska Native villages in, 18; and blood quantum, 339; and coal, 125; constitutions for, 10, 334; denominations working for, 47; and Hayes, 80; and ICWA, 373–77; inefficiency in, 168; and Pueblo, 324; and Red Power, 315; and settler colonial society, 365; and Tribal gaming, 289; Tribal schools from, 273
Bureau of Indian Affairs (BIA) occupation, 14, 15, 22
Bureau of Indian Education, 271
burial sites, 28–30, 34, 39, 125

Cabazon Band of Mission Indians, California v., 225–26, 439n1
Cabeza Prieta National Wildlife Refuge, 29
cacique, 324
Cahto Tribe of the Laytonville Rancheria, 342
Cajete, Gregory A., 228
California: and border wall, 29; casino in, 341; environmental law in, 170; gaming in, 283, 288, 290, 291; name changes in, 336; Pueblo in, 86; rights in, 370; Tribal Law and Policy Institute in, 16; Tribally controlled institutions in, 273; and US expansion, 27, 29
California Supreme Court, 443n31
California v. Cabazon Band of Mission Indians, 225–26, 439n1
Calloway, Colin G., 417n12
Cal State–Sacramento, 228
Campbell, Ben Nighthorse, 302
Camp, Carter, 76
Campisi, William, 432n27
Canada, 31–32, 40, 47, 144–46, 204, 212, 222, 306, 318, 362, 369
Canada's Constitution Act of 1982, 31
canoes, 107
capitalism, 23, 212, 323, 325, 330, 344, 364–65
capitalists, 21, 112
Caposello, Peter, 200
carbon dioxide, 128
Carleton, Kenneth H., 432n27
Carlisle Indian Industrial School, 143
Carmichael, Stokely, 21–22
Carpio, Luzmila, 206
Carr, E. H., 293
Carter, Jimmy, 16
casino cruises, 442n17
casinos, 12, 191, 194, 195, 226, 288, 341
Catholic Church, 144, 146, 273, 319
ceremonial life, 151–59
ceremonies. *see also* rituals: for adoption, 337; and ancestors, 200; defined, **236–37**; initiation, 235; knowledge through, 250; by medicine men, 230; as monetized industry, 147; powers available by, 106; regaining land for, 201; today, 116–19; for traditional life, 236; for war and peace, 86, 87; for women, 200
Cesaire, Aimé, 152
Champagne, Duane, 341
checks and balances, 65
Cheroenhaka Nottoway Tribe, 68, 416n5
Cherokee Nation: Allen serving, 82; Blue as, 79; clanship structures of, 336–38; as identifier for Lumbee, 162; language of, 341; Noble serving, 82; settlers encroaching on, 59; treaties with, 62–63, 324
Cheyenne, 337
Chiapas, 207, 209
Chich'il Bilda-gotee, 33. *see also* Oak Flat
Chickahominy Tribe, 69, 70, 416n5
Chickahominy Tribe Eastern Division, 69, 416n5
Chickaloon Native Village, 95
Chickasaws, 62, 93
chiefs, 74, 111, 362
child abuse, 240
child rearing, 15
children: assimilation of, 144; in boarding schools, 144; education of, 276, 278, 280; finding remains of, 144–45; of French fur traders, 317–19; and ICWA, 296, 297, 373–84, 461n32, 461n34; and identity, 274; land to M'Collock, 339; from mixed unions, 93, 325–26; during 1960s and 1970s, 15; number forcibly removed, 144; separating, 30, 32, 95, 144, 297; and seventh generation, 175–78; socialization of, 236, 272; stealing, 373–77; violence to, 211
Chile, 206
Chippewas of the Thames First Nation, 369
Chippewa Tribe, 451n121, 459n53
Chiricahua Apaches, 33
Choctaws, 62, 335, 369
Christian churches, 273
Christianity, 47–48, 140, 191, 231

churches, 47–48
Churchill, Ward, 346
Citizen Potawatomi Nation, 94
citizens: amended, 340; benefiting, 90; and blood quantum, 339; children as, 373, 375; disenrollment of, 322, 345; in federally recognized Tribes, 348; government assistance for, 40; Indigenous groups as, 37; for Little Traverse Bay Bands of Odawa Indians, 8; needs of, 91, 373; qualifications for, 93; reinstatement of, 341–42; rights for, 26, 322; safety of, 91; and sovereignty, 37, 93; as term, 340; on US–Canada border, 31, 38; on US–Mexico border, 27, 28
citizenship: blood quantum for, 93, 94; for children, 375; criteria for, 94, 97, 340, 351; and gaming, 344; and ICWA, 375; kinship *vs*., 365; as metaphor, 93; rights for, 38; on US–Canada border, 31–32; on US–Mexico border, 27–28, 30, 31
civilization, 47, 48, 85, 254, 262, 301, 455n12
civilization programs, 47
civil rights: for African Americans, 20–21; and borders, 26–27, 30; and diplomacy, 70; and education, 270, 272, 275; and Indian child welfare, 372; and kinship, 322; for Lumbees, 165; in *Santa Clara Pueblo v. Martinez*, 327–29, 331–32; and unrecognized tribes, 165
Civil Rights Act of 1964, 272
Civil Rights Act of 1968, 379
civil rights movement, 80, 327
Civil War, 85
clans, 240, 324, 334, 336–38, 355, 357–59, 363, 365–66, 448n66
classless societies, 456n19
class stratification, **357**
Clean Air Act, 73, 171
Clean Slate Doctrine, 68
Clean Water Act, 171
climate change: as catastrophe, 161–62, 169–71, 179, 250; and environment, 149, 370; and reservations, 127–33, 173; and science, 122–23, 128; and territory, 40
climate change research, 123
Climate Coalition, 211
climate crisis, 122, 123, 128
Clinton, Bill, 6, 10
clout, **348**
Clovis people, 309–10
CNN, 217, 220
Cocopah, 28
Cohen, Felix S., 55, 334, 335, 419n52
collaborative governance, 36–38, 40, 41
Collier, John, 70
colonial aggression, 217
colonialism, 24, 65, 74, 81, 91, 113, 139, 152, 157, 159, 170, 216
colonization, 163, 211–12, 218, 229, 241, 248, 306–7, 311, 313, 316
Colorado, 27, 168, 204, 303
Columbia Plateau societies, 336, 363
Columbus, Christopher, xiii, 449n77
Columbus Day, 218
Colville, Andrew, 336
Colville Tribe, 31, 166, 336
Comanche Indians, 27, 218
Committee in Solidarity with the Indigenous Peoples of America (CSIA-Nitassinan), 205, 208, 210, 211, 372
communism, 456n19
communication, in education, 243–44
community, pedagogy of, 264–67
community-based scholarship, **260–61**
community engagement, **260**, 261
compacts, 55, 63, 72, 289, 292
Confederated Tribes of the Grand Ronde Reservation, 342
Congress: authority over Indian affairs, 72; Continental, 60–61; and education, 230; federally recognized Tribes in, 174; and gaming, 225, 226, 283; ICRA by, 327–28; and ICWA, 375, 377, 384; and IRA, 339; and Little Traverse Bay Bands of Odawa Indians, 8–9, 12; Lumbee Act in, 162–63, 167; and nationhood, 334; and Northwest Ordinance, 50, 64; and Oak Flats, 34–36; and Pueblo, 324–25, 331, 332; and science, 126; and self-rule, 272, 282; and settler privilege, 65; and sovereignty, 284, 287, 290, 322; and treaties, 41; on tribal criminal jurisdiction void, 448n58
constitutional rights, 32, 65, 328, 329
Continental Congress, 60–61
Cook-Lynn, Elizabeth, xv
Cook, Michelle, 211
Cook, Samuel R., 54
copper deposit, 34
copper mine, 35
Cornell, Stephen, 327, 334, 340, 343, 449n77
coronavirus, 91
Coronavirus Aid, Relief, and Economic Security Act, 90
Coulthard, Glen, 74, 222
counselors, 178
counting coup, 305–13
COVID-19, 25, 90, 91, 92, 120, 212, 346, 347
Crash, Tom, xv

Crawford, T. Hartley, 49
Crazy Bull, Cheryl, 268, 279, 280
Cree-Metis, 306
crimes against humanity, 147
critical race theory, 42–44, 218
Crocker, Harry, 79, 80
Crocker, Isabel, 79, 80
Crowe, John, 166, 167, 169
CSIA-Nitassinan. *see* Committee in Solidarity with the Indigenous Peoples of America (CSIA-Nitassinan)
Cultural Bioregion, 201
cultural conservation, 76–88
cultural generativity, **178–79**
cultural preservation, 78, 80, 161
cultural purposes, 35
cultural renewal, 333–45
cultural rights, 30, 31
cultural sovereignty, 36-39, 41, 355. *see also* internal sovereignty
culture: as battleground, 218; and education, 251; news on social media, 220; study of, 254 (*see also* anthropology)
Curran, Tom, 196
Custer Died for Your Sins: An Indian Manifesto (Deloria): Biolsi on, 354–55; Deer on, 14, 15; Ettawageshik on, 6, 7; George-Kanentiio on, 301; Hill on, 89; Lee on, 254; Le Puloch on, 314, 315; Luger on, 102; Marquez on, 282, 285, 286, 287, 294; Mays on, 21; Minoka on, 89; Patrouilleau on, 203, 209; Steeves on, 308; Trahant on, 225; Whyte on, 134
Custer, George Armstrong, 11

Dakota Access Pipeline, 149, 158, 434n44
Dakota Nation, 9, 158, 159, 191, 309, 317–20, 354, 355, 364, 382
dances, 157–58
Dawes Act, 325
decolonization, 96, 152, 157, 159, 211–12, 219–20, 222, 311
Deer, Ada, xvii, 18
Deer, Kenneth, 207
Deer, Montie, 13
Deer, Sarah, 13
Deer, Tom, 208
defamation, 217
dehumanization, 311
deified ancestors, 105, 109
deities, 86, 115, 117, 142
DeJong, David, 56
DeLaCruz, Joe, xvii
Delaware, 126
Delaware Tribe, 451n121
Delgamuukw case, 318
Deloria, Ella, 167, 309, 337, 338, 354, 364, 370
Deloria, Philip J., 10, 308, 429n1
Deloria, Sam, xvii
Deloria, Vine, Jr.: and African American problem, 20–24; Avalos on, 151–59; commitment to education, 268; counting coup with, 305–13; Deer on, 13–19; and Deloria, 354–71; on diplomacy, 55, 56, 67, 69; Emanuel on, 160–74; and French, 314–20; George-Kanentiio's memories of, 301–4; Hill on, 89–97; Holm on, 77–88; on Identity appropriation, 429n1; on Indian educaiton, 228–52; on Indian education, 268–81; on Indigenous peoples and borders, 25–41; international reach of, 202–12; in introduction, xiii–xx; Journée-Duez on, 202–12; on kinship renewal, 321–45; Le Puloch on, 314–20; letter from Luger to, 101–4; on Little Traverse Bay Bands of Odawa Indians, 6–12; Marquez on, 282–98; Mays on, 20–24; on media plight, 225–27; on "More Ivory Than Red" chapter, 253–67; on nationhood, 42–53; on negotiation, 71, 75; Patrouilleau on, 202–12; Pensoneau on, 185–89; philosophy of (pseudo)science, 134–39; Planchou on, 372–84; on race, 42–53; Redsteer on, 120–33; on relational sovereignty, 321–**23**, 333–45; on "Restatement of the Law of American Indians" project, 419n52; roles of, 268; round dancing with, 305–13; Schad on, 140–50; and science, 121–33; on settler privilege, 65; on seventh generation, 176, 177–78, 182; Silva on, 105–19; Spotted Eagle on, 190–201; Steeves on, 305–13; Tantoo Cardinal, 3–5; Trahant on, 225–27; on treaty-making, 61; as truth-teller, 90; Whyte on, 134–39; writings in 1970s and 1980s, 414n17
DeMallie, Raymond J., 56, 65, 67, 69
Department of Interior, 58, 130, 271
Department of Justice, 16
Department of the Interior, 7, 271
Desautel, R. v., 31, 32
Deski, Wopida, 190
Diana (Princess of Wales), 215
digital politics, 219–23
Diné, **335**
Diné kinship system, 337
Diné Nation, 253, 266, 365–68
dinosaurs, 135
diplomacy, 54–75, 417n24. *see also* treaty-making; treaty process

discrimination, 120, 160, 165, 170, 172, 211, 329, 331, 369, 380, 386, 390
disenrollment, 187, **296–97**, 322–23, 332, 338, 341–42, 344
Dismembered: Native Disenrollment and the Battle for Human Rights (Wilkins and Wilkins), 338
District Court, Fisher v., 377
diversity, 97, 121, 142, 240, 251, 281
DNA testing, 197
Doctrine of Discovery, 45–48, 60, 67
doctrine of universal succession, 68
Documents of American Indian Diplomacy (Deloria and DeMallie), 67
Dolezal, Rachel, 185
domestic treaties, 39–41
Dominic, Bob, 6
Dominic, Juanita, 6
doxing, **347**
Drapeau, Galen, Jr., 195
Drapeau, Glenn, 195
Drapeau, Sharon, 196
dreams, 106, 151, **236**, 309
drug abuse, 240
Duane, James, 62
Duarte, Marisa, 220
Duez-Alesandrini, Sylvain, 206
Duwamish Tribe, 434n52
Dyer, Gwynne, 86

early childhood education, 268, 276–79
Earth, 122, 127–28, 131, 135
Eastern Band of Cherokee Indians, 166
Eastern Pueblo society, 337
Eastman, Charles, xv
Échanges Solidaire, 207
Echaquan, Joyce, 211–12
ecology, 136, 138
economic development, and education, 274
education: adapting to, 251; basis of, **238**; bilingual, 271; in crisis, 249, 250; defined, **252**; of Deloria, 95; early childhood, 268, 276–79; and economic development, 274; forced, 152; higher, 248, 255, 256, 258, 265, 268, 269, 272, 276–81; holistic, 237; ideal of, 250; for identity, 269, 273; Indian (*see* Indian education); K-12 systems in, 276–79; legacy of, 249; Native teacher, 279; Navajo, 262; programs for, 96; radical ideas in, 218; role of, 277; as social activity, 244; Tribally controlled, 268–80; at UNM, 264
educational reform, 263, 281
egalitarian societies, 456n19
1855 Treaty Authority, **459n53**
1852 Treaty of Santa Fe, 32, 34, 36, 41
1848 Treaty of Guadalupe Hidalgo, 27, 30, 32, 35, 41, 67
1817 Treaty with the Syandot, 339
1830 Indian Removal Act, 48
Eisenhower, Dwight, 163
Ejercito Zapatista de Liberación Nacional (EZLN), 220, 223
Elder councils, 177
Elders: access to, 274; for battle with Army Corps of Engineers, 195; and education, 230, 275; and generativity, 178–81; knowledge from, 277; learning from, 175, 354; listening to, 210; observing, 229; per capita payments for, 342; protection for, 368; roles of, 175; values for, 175; for Yankton, 197, 198
Elliott, Harold W., 431n21
Emanuel, Ryan E., 160, 432n23
Encounter Era, 67
endangered species, 28
Engels, Frederick, 456n19
English as a second language programs, 271
Enloe, Cynthia, 84, 87
enrollment, 323, 325–27, 333, 340–44, 348–49, 365–66, 378
enslavement, 23
Enterprise Rancheria General Council, 341
environmental crises, 160–74
environmental harms, 29–30, 430n9
environmental issues, 127, 162, 172, 174, 434n52
environmental justice, 250, 369
environmental permits, 170
environmental protection, 170, 171, 174
environmental racism, xix, 191
environmental rights, 30
environmental stewardship, 161, 176, 343
epistemology, 117, 139, 152, **242**, 258–61
erasure, 65, 168, 217, 307, 311
Erikson, Erik, 175, 176, 178, 179, 182
Ervin, Sam, 164, 165, 166, 169
Esther Martinez Native Languages Preservation Act, 271
ethnic frauds, 352
Ethnic Soldiers: State Security in a Divided Society (Enloe), 84, 87
ethnocentrism, 356
Ettawageshik, Frank, 6
eugenics, 172, 339, 432n27
eugenics era, 70
eugenics movement, 418n41
European Alliance for the Self Determination of Indigenous Peoples, 208

Europe and the People without History (Wolf), 357
Executive Order 82, 73
expansion, 47, 50, 51, 53, 58–61
experiential learning, **236**
external sovereignty, 291
extraction technologies, 122
extractivism, 170

Facebook, 219
families: in boarding school era, 95; fragmentation of, 240; immigrant, 30; interpreter for, 460n22
family relationships, 274
Fanon, Frantz, 152, 321, 333
farming, 361
Farrakhan, Louis, 120
Faure, Danielle, 205
federal detention centers, 32
federal government, role in education, 270, 271
federally recognized Tribes: Alaska Native list of, 18; and border, 29, 30, 33–39, 414n3; and diplomacy, 70–74; and disenrollment, 322; and environment, 171; and The List, 348, 349; list of, 7, 18, 348; in 1977, 165; number of, 148; and sovereignty, 297; support from, 9, 10; unrecognized tribes as, 160–74; in US, 72; of USET, 164, 433n30; in Virginia, 56, 71, 416n5
federal prisons, 33
federal recognition process, 10
federal-state binary framing, 285
Federated Indians of Graton Rancheria, 341
Feyerabend, Paul, 135
Field Foundation, 165
Fifth Assessment Report, 129
Final Environmental Impact Statement (FEIS), 34, 35
First Nations, 144, 157
First People of the Western Hemisphere, 309
Fisher v. District Court, 377
fishing rights, 78, 288
500 Years of Indigenous, Black and Popular Resistance campaign, 209
Five Nations of Haudenosaunee, 58
Five Nations of Iroquois, 58
Florida, 33, 288, 442n17
Floyd, George, xiii, 120
Flute, Jerry, 197
Fogelson, Raymond, 432n27
Fontaine, John, 54
football players, 16
Forbes, 226
Force, Rolland, 302
Fort Christanna, 54, 58
Fort Finney Treaty, 63
Fort McIntosh, 62
Fort Sill Apache Tribe, 33
fossil fuel projects, 434n44
fossil fuel resources, 122
Fourteenth Amendment, 79, 80
Fox, 220
France, 202, 204, 205, 208, 314–20, 444n7
Frank, Billy, Jr., xiv, xvii, 12, 78, 79, 342
Frederick, Tom, 197
Freedmen of the Five Tribes, 22
Free Exercise balancing test, 415n23
French activism, 209
French and Indian War, 59
full-blooded, 326, 339

Gaddafi Prize for Human Rights, 23
Gadsden Purchase, 27, 32
Galanda, Gabriel S., 321
gambling, 226, 442n17
gaming, 225–28, 226, 282–83, 286–90, 292, 295, 323, 342, 344–45, 453n162
Ganienkeh, 205
Garcia, Anthony, 80
Garroutte, Eva Marie, 365
gender, 15
gender discrimination, 329, 331
generalized reciprocity, 363–64, 364, 456n19
generations, lost, 342–43
generation X, **13**, 14
generativity: cultural, **178**; defined, **178**; and Erikson, 176; and Indigenous communities, 178–80; key to, 182; and seventh generation, 180–81
Geneva Conference, 204–6, 360, 361, 362
genocide, 66, 144, 156, 214–15, 217, 314, 349–51
gen X, 219
George-Kanentiio, Doug, 362
Georgia, Worcester v., 286, 334
Germany, 208
Geronimo (Apache leader), 33
Ghost Dance, 157
Gila River Indian Community, 79
Gingrich, Newt, 302
global heating, 122
global warming, 122
God Is Red (Deloria), 14, 125, 140, 147, 203, 210, 230, 308, 315, 335
Goldbert-Hillder, Jonathan, 119
Gonzales, Ben, 191
Goodyear-Ka'opua, Noelani, 118
Google, 219

governance: collaborative, 36–38; role of, 36–38; of sacred places, 38–39
governors, 324
grandchildren, 175, 178
Graugnard, Jean Francois, 204
Gray, Terry, 197
Great Law of the Iroquois, 176
Great Plains Tribes, 9
Great Treaty of 1722, 58
greenhouse gases, 122
Greenland, 40
Greyeyes, Wendy S., 253, 261, 262, 264
Guatemala, 206, 209, 301
Guillory, Justin, 279
Gurkha experience, 87

Haaland v. Brackeen, 380
Haley, Alex, 16
half-breed, 319
Handbook of American Indian Law (Cohen), 55, 419n52
Handbook of North American Indians (Sturtevant), 166
harassment, 347–50
Harjo, Micco Efau, 87
Harjo, Suzan Shown, xvii, 191
Harmon, Alexandra, 339
Harris, Ladonna, 13
Harrison, William Henry, 51
Harvard, Gilles, 319
Haudenosaunee (Iroquois), 59, **336**; clans, 205, 358; and communism, 456n19; Confederacy, 67, 303; defined, **335**; delegates, 362; delegation, 360; diplomacy, 67; kinship system, 336, 337, 363; leaders, 63; life, 361; passports, 208; sachems, 62; seventh-generation principle, 90
Haudenosaunee Six Nations, 359
Haudenosaunee Thanksgiving Address, 96
Hayes, Ira, 79, 80
Head Start, 233
healers, traditional, 178
Hefner, Hugh, 16
heiau, **107**
Helms, Jesse, 164, 167
Herring, Elbert, 49
Hershey, Robert, 336
heuristics, 262–63
higher education, 248, 255, 256, 258, 265, 268, 269, 272, 276–81
Hiʻiakaikapoli-pele, 106
Hillaire, Darrell, 343
Hill, Charlie, 93
Hill, Megan Minoka, 89
Hill, Norbert S., Jr., 89
historical trauma, 147, 152, 156
history, and education, 251
hōʻailona, **111**
Holen, Steve, 309, 310
holistic education, 237
holistic teaching and learning, 234
hollow sovereignty, **293**
Holm, Ina, 77
Holm, Tom, 76
Holt, John Dominis, 111, 112
HolyWhiteMountain, Sterling, 339
Hopi people, 86, 125
Horsman, Reginald, 63
Houska, Tara, 211
Howe, Oscar, xv
Hudson Bay Company, 336, 445n18
humanitarian impulse, **47**
human rights: and borders, 25, 30–32, 35–36, 38, 40–41; and diplomacy, 66; international, 202, 207–9; and kinship, 321–22; in *Santa Clara Pueblo v. Martinez*, 322, 327, 332–33
Human Rights Council, 206
Hunn, Eugene S., 363, 364
Hutchins Commission, 227

Idaho, 126, 376
identity: and assimilation, 51; blood shaping, 94; component of, 153; cornerstone of, 38; criteria for, 164; damaging, 254; and diplomacy, 74; education focus on, 230, 249, 269, 273–76, 280, 281; generalizing culture for, 254; and genocide, 144; Lumbee, 166, 430n11; maintaining, 82, 156; masking, 306; political, 29, 70, 186, 286; and race, 44, 186; reclaiming, 141; and sovereignty, 43, 286; spiritual power for, 153; as steward, 155
identity appropriation, 429n1
Idle No More movement, 157, 158, 222
idols, xiii–xiv
Ihanktonwan, 190, 191, 194, 195, 197
Illinois, 61
imagined borders, 25–41
immigrants: families, 30; illegal, 28; Mexican, 32
immigration, 41, 250
immigration enforcement, 30
Incomindios, 437n2
India, 84
Indian, as term, 335, 450n82
Indiana, 61
Indian Affairs Sub-Committee, 285

Indiana Territory, 51
Indian Child Welfare Act (ICWA), 296, 297, 373–84, 461n32, 461n34
Indian Citizenship Act of 1934, 272
Indian Civil Rights Act (ICRA), 327, 328, 329, 330, 332, 379
Indian Country Today, xiii, 91
Indian education: contemporary, 248–51; contexts of, 246; defined, **252**; Deloria on, 228–52; dilemma of, 237–41; exploration of, 245; expressions of, 238–39; federal government in, 270; final thoughts on, 251–52; foundation of, 249; future of, 247–48; Indigenous studies for, 255–58, 257*t*; introduction to, 228–29; philosophy of, 243; purpose of, 245, 258; relational, 241–47; roles of, 246; thoughts on, 229; traditional, 234–37
Indian Education for All in the State of Montana, 274
Indian education revolution, 268–81
Indian Gaming Regulatory Act, 82, 225, 323
Indian Health Service facilities, 15
Indian Historian, The (Deloria), 217
Indian rights, 15
Indian rights movement, 19
Indian Scouting Service, 85, 86
Indian Self-Determination and Education Assistance Act, 233
Indian Self-Determination and Education Assistance Act (PL-638), 90
Indian Time, 301
Indigeneity, **28**
Indigenous, as term, 449n82
Indigenous Australians, 181
Indigenous Environmental Network, 211
Indigenous media, 213–24
Indigenous Paleolithic of the Western Hemisphere, The (Steeves), 312
Indigenous peoples: and Borderlands, 26, 28, 33, 36–38, 40, 41; and imagined borders, 25–41; and Northern Border, 31–32; and Southern Border, 27–31
Indigenous Peoples' Center for Documentation, Research and Information (DOCIP), 208
Indigenous Peoples' Day, 218, 385
Indigenous religion, 48, 140, 142, 143, 147, **148**
Indigenous rights, 31, 32, 36
Indigenous studies, 257*t*, 258, 259, 267–68
Indigenous-US diplomacy, 66–69
Indigenous worldviews, 95, **242**
individual rights, 73, 329, 345, 442n19
inherent rights, 8, 12, 203, 270, 272, 281, 376, 377
Inouye, Daniel, 191, 302
Inslee, Jay, xv
Institute of American Indian Arts, 210–11, 228
Institutions of Higher Education (IHE), 259, 260
Intergovernmental Panel on Climate Change (IPCC), 122, 128, 129
intermarriages, 317, 337, 445n18
internal sovereignty, 291, 292, 355, **443n28**. *see also* cultural sovereignty
international border, 29
International Center of Popular Culture, 207
international law, 60–61, 67
International Solidarity Day, 206, 207
international treaties, 39–41
interracial marriage, 349
intractable conflict, 239, 242
Introduction to Tribal Law (Deer and Richland), 18
Inuit, 303
Inuit Circumpolar Conference, 40
Inuit people, 40, 303
IRA. see 1934 Indian Reorganization Act (IRA)
Iraq, 214
Ironshield, George, 198
Iroquois, 59, 176, 303, **335**
Iroquois diplomacy, 67
Iroquois on Fire (George-Kanentiio), 304
Isle de Jean Charles Band of Biloxi-Chicimacha-Choctaw Indians, 434n52
Isnati Awica Dowanpi ceremony, 200

Jackson, Robert, 293
Jacquin, Philippe, 318
JaiAlai, 442n17
Jandreau, Mike, 197
Janklow, Bill, 199
Jaulin, Robert, 202, 203
Jefferson, Thomas, 51
Jennings, Francis, 432n23
Jim Crow Era, 351
Jim Crow period, 349
job security, 270
John, Clint, 120
Johnson, James, 391
Johnson, Rubellite Kawena, 110
Johnson v. M'Intosh, 45, 46
Joseph, Victor, 292
Journée-Duez, Aurélie, 202, 209–10
justice: environmental, 250, 369; as foundation for treaties, 26; and law, 26; movements for, 219; for removal of children, 144; treaty-making process for, 39; uneven, 120; for unrecognized tribes, 160
Justice, Daniel Heath, 333

K-12 systems, 268, 276–79
Kai'a, 112, 113
Kalili, Kaleohano, 111
Kali'na peoples, 207
Kalokuokamaile, Z. P., 106, 107, 109, 111
Kalt, Joseph, 340
Kamohoali'i, 111
Kamploops Indian school, 144
kānaenae, **106**
Kānaka Hawai'i, 105, 106, 109, 115, 119
Kānaka 'Ōiwi, **105**
Kansas, 13, 27
Kansas Supreme Court, 461n34
Ka Po'e Mo'o Akua: Hawaiian Reptilian Water Deities (Brown), 117
kapu aloha, 119
k'e, **366–67**
Kelly, Walt, 296
Keneenaw Bay Indian Tribal Center, 7
Kennedy, Patrick J., 196
Kerry, John, 76
Keway, Charlie, 6
Keway, Sam, 6
Kickapoo, 28
Kildee, Dale, 9
Killers of the Flower Moon (Scorsese), 218
Kimura, Larry Lindsey Kauanoe, 115
King, Martin Luther, Jr., 16
Kinney, Rubellite Kawena, 110
kinship: bonds, 320; as debate, 357; and education, 274–76; history, 167; moral order of, 354–71; patterns, 256; principles, 366; reality of, 352; regaining, 297; relationships, 49, 268; renewal, 321–45; role of, 354, 355; significance of, 355; systems, 336–38; terminology, 340–41
Kiowa, **335**
Kipp, Darrell, 340
Kipp, Woody, 81, 82
knowledge: defined, **xiv**; and Indian education, 235, 250, 255–59, 276, 280; storytelling for, 262; woodstove, 259–61, 267
knowledge production, 137, 153, 309, 311
knowledge systems, 136–37, 139, 254, 260
Knox, Henry, 63
Kosovo, 215
Kotre, J., 181
Kraemer, Shelley v., 80
Krawec, Patty, 342
Kugler, Tracy, 431n20
Kumeyaay Indians, 28, 29
kūpuna o ka pō, **105**
Lakota Nation, xx, 9, 158, 159, 206, 250, 315, 354, 355
Lakota Times, xv
Lamont, Buddy, 81
land: copper mine, 34; protection of, 157; religion and, 148; sacred relationships to, 159
land allotment, 339
Landback movement, xix, xx
land expropriation, 23, 162
land rights, 27, 31, 32, 472
land tenure, 49
land titles, 49
land trust, 74
language: Cherokee Nation eliminating, 341; Dakota, 191; English as a second, 271; forbidden to speak, 95; Hawaiian, 106, 111, 113; and kinship, 275, 341; Lumbee, 164; Mohawk, 96; Ojibwe, 82, 83; preservation of, 233, 268, 271, 273, 277–81, 340, 368; in ritual and ceremony, 237; schools around, 239; stories as base for, 259
language immersion schools, 270
La Posta Band of Diegueno Mission Indians, 29
La Posta case, 39
La Résistance Indienne aux Etats-Unis (Marienstras), 316
law: human rights, 31, 35; inconsistency of, 42; international, 60–61, 67; and justice, 26; for Oak Flat, 36; PL 103-324, 6, 12; and race, 44; sacred sites under, 39
law enforcement reform, xix
Leacock, Eleanor, 456n19
leadership, goal of, 294
Lea, Luke, 52
learning: activities for, 248; by artistic creation, **236**; by ceremony, **236**; defined, **252**; by dreaming, **236**; experiential, **236**; lifelong, 236; by master/apprentice, **236**; by ritual, **236**; by storytelling, **236**; teaching and, 234–36, 244, 249, 259, 278, 280
Lee, Robert E., xiii
Lee, Tiffany S., 253, 259
legal foundations, 60–61
legal issues, 36
legal rights, 39
legal system, 42
legal traditions, 56, 65, 73
Le Guin, Ursula, 16
Lekanoff, Debra, xv
Le Puloch, Marine, 314
Les Chemins de la Survie (Paths of Survival) (Menier), 205
letter, from Luger to Deloria, 101–4
Lewis, Jordan P., 175

LGBTQIA2S+ rights, xix
Libya, 23
Life, as metaphor, 249
lifelong learning, 236
Lindquist, Cynthia, 280
lineages, 363
lineal descent, 351
Linking Arms Together (Williams), 66
Lipphardt, Veronika, 432n27
list-making, 346–53
List, The, 348–49
Little River Band of Ottawa Indians, 7, 10
Little Thunder, Rosalie, 198
Little Traverse Bay Bands of Odawa Indians, 6–12, 11, 368
logic, **242**
Lokono peoples, 207
Lomawaima, K. Tsianina, 384
Lono, 117, 118
Looking Horse, Arvol, 197
Look to the Mountain: An Ecology of Indigenous Education (Deloria), 228, 231, 232
Loomis, Lorraine, xvii
Los Angeles Times, 15, 323
lottery, 442n17, 442n18
Louisiana, 434n52
Louisiana Purchase, 51, 67
Lower Brule Sioux Cultural Resource Elder Advisory Committee, 197
Luger, Cannupa Hanska, 101, 211
Lumbee Act of 1956, 162–65, 167, 172, 174, 432n30
Lumbee identity, 166, 430n11
Lumbee Regional Development Association, 165
Lumbee Resolution Controversy, 431n18
Lumbee Tribe, 162–74, 431n18, 431n21, 432n23, 432n27, 432n30
Lummi Nation, 343
Lyons, Oren, xvii, 176, 177, 182, 303
Lytle, Clifford M., 14, 61, 287, 321, 322, 327, 331, 332, 333, 338

Mack, Irene, 76
Mad Bear Camp, 200
Maine, 288
mainstream media, 227
Makaʻai, Joseph, 115, 116
Makahiki, 116, 117
mākaʻikaʻi, **106–7**, 110, 111
Makaliʻi, 117
Malcolm X, 120, 121
Malo, David, 117
Mandela, Nelson, 215
Manifest Destiny, 27
Mankiller, Wilma, 82
Mann, Henrietta, xvii
Manson, Steven, 431n20
Manuel, Kanahus, 211
Maori people, 415n29
Mapuche, 206
Marienstras, Elise, 316
Marine Vietnam veterans, 82
Marquez, Deron, 282
marriages, 320, 325–27, 349, 359, 445n18
Mars, 132
Marshall, John, 45–49, 334
Marshall Plan for Indian Country, 92
Marshall, Thurgood, 286, 330, 331
martial race, **84**
Martinez, Audrey, 326–31, 337
Martinez, Julia, 326–31
Martinez, Myles, 326
Martinez, Santa Clara Pueblo v., 322–33
Marx, Karl, 456n19
Maryland, 13, 126, 303
masculine movement, 15
Mashantucket Pequot Tribe, 344
Maspero, François, 204
materialism, 121, 152
matrilineal clan or lineage, 336, 358, 358*f*, 359, 361, 362, 366, 367
matrilineal kinship system, 362
matrilocal household, 358, 359, 360*f*
Mattaponi Tribe, 69, 74, 416n5
Maunakea, 105, 118, 119, 217
Maya K'iche peoples, 206
Mayans, 301
Maya peoples, 303
Maynor, Lacy, 431n18
McCain, John, 34, 191
McCloud, Janet, xvii
McGirt v. Oklahoma, 41
McKenney, Thomas L., 48
M'Collock, William, 339
mea Hawaiʻi, 107
Means, Nataani, 211
Means, Russell, xvii
Mechem, Edwin L., 328
media: and economic stability, 290–91; and education, 65; and French, 203–5; and Hawaiians, 112; Indigenous, 213–24; Red, 219, 224; and science, 132; social, xviii, 95, 120, 145, 158, 219–24, 298, 348, 386, 429n1; and Wounded Knee, 158

media plight, 225–27
medicine people, 151, 178
Medill, William, 51
Meeds, Lloyd, 283, 284, 285, 287, 297
member, as IRA-rooted definition, 341
membership, 325–31, 337, 340, 359, 363, 365, 368, 381
men, xvi, 15, 16, 359
Menchu Tum, Rigoberta, 209
Menominee Nation, 82
Mentz, Alma, 198
Mentz, Tim, 191, 198
Meriam Report, 441n9
Mestanapeu, Matthieu André, 206
metaphysics, 26, 28
Metaphysics of Modern Existence, The (Deloria), 10, 14, 241
métchif, **319**
Métis, **319**
metissesés, **319**
Mexican-American War, 67, 85
Mexican government, 27, 28
Mexican immigrants, 32
Mexican Jaguar, 28
Mexican nationals, 31
Mexico, 27, 28, 32, 33
Michigan, 7, 11, 61
Michigan State University, 11
Midthunder, Amber, 218
migrant workers, 207
military, 50, 78, 81, 84, 86, 87, 414n8
military campaigns, 34
military coalitions, 317
military control, 33
military tradition, 85
millennials, 219
Minnesota, 22, 61, 205, 382, 459n53
Minnesota Chippewa Tribe, 340
M'Intosh, Johnson v., 45, 46
Miskitos, 301
missionaries, xv, 48, 309, 365
missionization, 152
Mississippi Band of Choctaw Indians, 166, 432n27
mixed-blood, **319**, 339
mixed marriages, 320, 325–26
MNI WIZIPAN WAKAN, **201**
Modoc Tribe, 342
Mohawk Nation Council, 301
Mohawks, 96, 207, 209
moieties, 323–24
Momaday, Scott, 77
Mombasa Times, 204
Monacan Alliance, 54, 55, 69
Monacan Nation, 416n5
Mono Lake Kutzadika, 174, 434n51
Montana, 127, 274, 339
monuments, xiv, xvi, xx, 40–41, 149, 218, 394
moʻo, **105**, 105, 117, 118
moʻolelo, **106**
Morales, Evo, 206
morality, 152
Morgan, Lewis Henry, 361, 362, 456n19, 456n24
mortality rates, 93
Mother Earth, 141, 207
Mount Rushmore, xx
movement building, **223**
movement-oriented media, 223
Murdered and Missing Indigenous Women, 211
Murray, Paul T., 418n41
Muscogee Creek Nation, 41
Museum of Contemporary Native Arts, 209

Nagiksapa, **191**
Nakota Nation, 9, 355
Nansemond Tribe, 69, 416n5
Nation, as term, 335, 450n82
National Congress of American Indians (NCAI), 77, 164, 431n18
National Historic Preservation Act, 36, 38
National Indian Youth Council (NIYC), 76
nationalism, 20, 204
National Museum of the American Indian (NMAI), 302, 303
National Press Club, 18
National Science Foundation, 126
national security, 30
National Tribal Chairman's Association, 8
nationhood: issues of, 372; race and, 42–53; recognition of Indigenous, 39–41; terminology, 334
Nation of Islam, 120, 121
Nations Indiennes Nations Souveraines (Graugnard and Raa), 204, 205
Nations Within, The (Vine and Lytle), 8, 91, 287, 322, 378, 381
Native American Graves Protection and Repatriation Act (NAGPRA), 38, 73, 190–95, 198, 199, 308, 310
Native American Research Institute, 123
Native American Rights Fund, 274
Native Americans: connection to African Americans, 23; drafted for war, 84; goal of, 21; as martial race, 84; military tradition of, 84–86; population of, 85, 156; in science, 130; as veterans, 76–88; as warriors, 88

Native American Student Association, 306
Native American Studies (NAS), 253, 259–67
Native Hawaiians, 105, 363
Native language resources, 280
Native language restoration, 279
Native language revitalization, 368
Native Nations: cease per capita payments, 343–45; lift enrollment moratoria, 342–43; outlaw disenrollment, 341–42; renew kinship terminology, 340–41; renew original names, 335–36; replace blood quantum, 338–40; restore kinship systems, 336–38; welcome lost generations, 342–43
Native survivance, **314**
Native teacher education, 279
Native veterans, 76–88
naturalization, 93, 285
Navajo, **335**
Navajo Community College, 273
Navajo Nation, 120, 121, 125, 127, 130, 216, 261, 262, 326, 346
Navajo Nation Board of Education, 261
Navajo Nation Code, 366
Navajo Nation Council, 366
Navajo Nation Labor Commission, 367
Navajo Nation Supreme Court, 365
Navajo Reservation, 273
Nebraska, 197
neocolonialism, 322, 333
Nepal, 87
Nevada, 27
Newberry Library, 225, 227
New Mexico, 27, 28, 33, 35, 126, 156, 209, 323, 327, 385
New York, 58
New York Times, 194
New Zealand, 47, 415n29
Nicaragua, 301
1977 Final Report, 287, 290, 292, 297
1973 Indian Self-Determination and Education Assistance Act, 272
1934 Indian Reorganization Act (IRA), 94, 272, 321, 324, 325, 329, 334, 335, 336, 339–41
1928 Meriam Report, 285, 343
Nisqually Nation, 78
Nitassinan, **206**
Nixon, Richard, 163
NIYC. *see* National Indian Youth Council (NIYC)
NMAI. *see* National Museum of the American Indian (NMAI)
Nobel Peace Prize, 209
Noble, Rogan, 82
#NoDAPL movement, 158
Northam, Ralph, 73
North Carolina, 162, 164, 165, 432n27
North Dakota, 158, 200
Northrup, Jim, 82, 83
Northwest Ordinance, 50, 51, 63, 64, 415n16
Northwest Territory, 50, 61
Notre Dame, 149
Nottawaseppi Huron Band of the Potawatomi, 368, 456n50
Nottoway Tribe of Virginia, 416n5
Nu'uhiwa, Kalei, 116, 117, 119

oak, in section 1, 1
Oak Flat, 32–36, 39, 217
Oates, Joyce Carol, 16
Obama, Barack, 34, 79
objectivism, **243**
O'Bomsawin, Kim, 211
O'Brien, E. M., 122
Oceti Sakowin, 158, 196–201
Odakota, **354**
Office for Tribal Relations, 72
Of Utmost Good Faith (Deloria), 203
Oglala Sioux Tribal, 460n22
Ohio, 61, 62, 64, 126
Ohio Company of Virginia, 417n12
Ohio Land Company, 59
Ojibwe, 459n53
Ojibwe language, 82, 83
Ojibwe Tribe, 382
Oka/Kanesatake crisis, 209
okicize, **190**
Oklahoma, 27, 33, 41, 198, 306, 308, 342
Oklahoma, McGirt v., 41
Old Coyote, Barney, 13
Oliphant v. Suquamish Indian Tribe, 448n58
Omi, Michael, 335
Oñate, Juan de, xiii
On Being Hawaiian (Holt), 112
One-Drop Rule, 350
Onondaga Nation, 176, 303
"On the Cattle Guard" (Goodyear-Ka'opua), 119
ontology, 117
O'odham people, 27, 28, 29
oppression, 23, 141, 145, 211, 239, 315
oral traditions, 277, 311, 318
Oregon, 126, 363
Organ Pipe Cactus National Monument, 29
Origin of the Family, Private Property and the State (Morgan), 456n19
origin places, 28, 33

Osage Nation, 218
Ottawa Tribe, 451n121
oyakapi, **190**

PA. *see* programmatic agreement (PA)
Pace University, 177
paleontology, 136
Pamunkey Tribe, 69, 74, 75, 346, 416n5
Papago Tribe, 336. *see also* Tohono O'odham Nation
Papa'I'i, John, 117
Paris Climate Conference, 209, 210
Parker, Alan, 340
Passamaquoddy Tribe, 341
Patrouilleau, Édith, 202
Pattawomeck Tribe, 416n5
Pawnee Tribal of Oklahoma, 460n22
Paykweneh peoples, 207
Peacemaker Court, 365
Peace of Paris, 59, 68
Pearl Harbor, 113
Pearson, Maria, 194
Peau-Rouge (Deloria), 314, 315, 316, 320
Pele, **105**, 106–11, 115
Peltier, Leonard, 206
Pennsylvania, 58, 62, 79
Penobscot, 288
Pensoneau, Migizi, 185
people: place and, 28, 38; as term, 449n82
People of the Dark Water, 174. *see also* Lumbee Tribe
per capita payments, 92, 323–30, 333, 342–45
Pershing, John, 85
Pete, Donovan, 347
Peter Parker Principle, 296
Pevar, Stephen, 327
Philadelphia Inquirer, 226
Phillips, Patsy, 209
philosophy: ecological, 241; educational, 232, 243–45, 263, 268; Indigenous relational, 232; of land-based learning, 267; of nature, 241; Navajo, 366; research, 263–64; role of Native, 229; of (pseudo)-science, 134–39; of sovereign responsibility, 57; teaching, 264; theology *vs.*, 26
physics, 136
Piersol, Lawrence, 195
Pilot, Gilbert, 205
Pimatisiwin, **307**, 313
Pine Ridge Reservation, 206, 370
Pipestone Indian School, 83
Pittman, Kyle, 347
place: for community, 264; and education, 251; and people, 28, 38; relationship to, 240
Planchou, Céline, 372
Playboy, 16
Playing Indian (P. Deloria), 429n1
Pleasant Point Reservation, 341
Plecker List, 349, 350
Plecker, Walter, 172, 349, 350
Pleiades, 117
plight, **225**
Plunkett, Robert Kamohoali'i, 110, 111
Pogo comic strip, 296–97
policing, 120
political discourse, 73
political goals, of African Americans, 21
political identity, 29, 70, 186, 286
political motivations, 60–61
political participation, 76–88
political rights, 36, 37, 42, 373, 415n25
political sovereignty, 37
political stakes, 139
politics: analog, 213–19; and analog news, 224; digital, 219–23; Ettawageshik in, 7; and Indigenous art, 211; Navajo, 216; self-preservation in, 295; on Southern Border, 32; Tribes playing, 291
pollution, 161, 162, 169–71, 174, 430n9
Ponca Tribe, 197
Poor Bear, Enos, 81
population: aging, 93; Lumbee, 164; Native Americans in, 156–57, 461n32
Porter, Robert Odawi, 14
Portland Army Corps of Engineers, 200
positionality, **263–64**
post-traumatic stress disorder (PTSD), 78, 156
Potawatomie Tribe, 451n121
poverty, 11, 85
poverty rates, 344
Power and Place: Indian Education in America (Deloria and Wildcat), 153, 276, 278
Powhatan Tribe, 350
Pratt, Richard A., 95, 143, 144, 231
prayers, 103, 106, 118, 119
predominately white institutions (PWIs), 268, 275, 279, 280
president, 64
Presidential Executive Order 13007, 200
pretendians, **429n1**
Prey (Trachtenberg), 218
principle of consent, 39
prisoners of war, 33
private schools, 239
privilege: disparity of, 185; settler, 65–66
process, **242**
programmatic agreement (PA), 190, 198

Project of Excellence (POE), 265, 266
property rights, 27, 36, 80
property system, 45, 47, 48
property titles, 45, 47
Proposition 5, 443n31
Proposition 1A, 443n31
Proposition 202, 443n31
protests, 80, 149, 302
Prucha, Francis Paul, 325, 343
Pryse, E. Morgan, 376, 377
public hearings, 261–63
public lands, 32–36, 38
Public Law 84-570, 162
Public Law 280, 376
public relations campaigns, 290
public schools, 270
Pueblo Council, 326
Pueblo Indians, 35, 323
Pueblo Lands Act, 324
Pueblo Nations, 27, 35, 86
Pukui, Mary Kawena, 113, 114, 118
PWIs. see predominately white institutions (PWIs)
Pyawasit, Wallace, 76

quantum physics, 154
Quapaw Tribe, 308
Quiet Killing (O'Bomsawin), 211
Quigno, Ben, 11
Quinault Nation, 340

race: and adoption, 380; and diplomacy, 74; formation, 44; and law, 44; martial, **84**; and nationhood, 42–53; Plecker on, 350; and property rights, 80; property rights on, 80; statistics, 432n27; Tribes as, 297
race integrity laws, 418n41
race integrity policies, 418n41
race relations, 385
race science, 172
racial classifications, 349
racial formation, **335**
Racial Integrity Act of 1924, 349
Racial Integrity Act of 1930, 350
racial restrictions, 28
racism: in critical race theory, 42; in Crocker case, 79; defined, **44**; Echaquan on, 212; environmental, xix, 191; and federal-state binary framing, 285; and gaming, 290; and Lumbee, 165; Steeves on, 306, 307, 313; and unrecognized tribes, 165, 172; in US-Indian relations, 44
racist language, 52
radio show, 115
Ramirez, Renya, 156
Rappahannock Tribe, 69, 416n5
reaffirmation legislation, 7
reburials, 193, 197, 199, 200
Recollections: Memoirs of John Dominis Holt 1919–1935 (Holt), 111–12
Red Bow, Buddy, 296
Red Cloud, Henry, 207
Reddit.com, 347
Red Earth, White Lies (Deloria), 125, 134, 308, 309, 311
Red Media, 219, 224
Red Power movement, 15, 158, 204, 217, 315
Red Prophet (Willkins), xviii, 276
Redsteer, Margaret Hiza, 120
Reed, Henry, 79
refugees, 156
Reid, Joan Phillip, 337
relational education, 241–47
relational sovereignty, 321–23, 333–45
relationship: between all things, 153; completion of, 151; with places, 161; with social group and natural world, 249–50; understanding, 250
religion: analysis of, 230; Christianity as, 48; and civilization, 47; defined, **141, 148**; following one, 142; Indigenous, 48, 140, 142, 143, 147, **148**; interpretation of, 141; and land, 148; for meaning, 150; more than one, 142, 143; and spirituality, 140, 142; and traditions, 148; western, 141–47; and Williams, Jr., 334
religious action, 157
religious expression, 151
religious freedom, 28, 30, 35, 39, 101, 398
religious lifeways, 159
religious practices, 34, 38
religious praxis, 158
religious purposes, 35
religious rights, 35
religious worlds, 152
relocation, 33, 80
removal: and assimilation, 51; of children, 373, 377; and civilization, 48; as goal, 48; legacy of, 44; of offensive signs, 386; people and place concept, 28; of Western Apache, 33
repudiation, **46**
research: community-based, 259, 261, 264, 265; on COVID-19, 91; and education, 243–44; for knowledge, 255; on per-capita distribution, 345; role of, 274; and science, 121, 123, 127–28, 131, 136; on veterans, 77

researcher philosophy, 263–64
Reservation Dogs show, 218
reservations: age of, 69; in Arizona, 33, 127; bonds on, 275; and borders, 29, 41, 72, 121, 127; and climate change, 127, 130; human rights violations on, 327; land ownership on, 188; observation of, 254; in Oklahoma, 41; and politics, 80; and refugees, 156; and relocation, 33; schools on, 273; Tohono O'odham Nation, 29
Resolution Copper Corporation, 34
responsibility, rights *vs.*, 73
responsible sovereignty, **293–94**
"Restatement of the Law of American Indians" project, 419n52
Return of the Native (Cornell), 327, 449n77
Revolutionary War, 60, 68, 85
Richardson, Anne, 71
Richland, Justin, 18
right of dominion, 45
right of occupancy, 45
rights: aboriginal, 31–32; activism, 288; ancestral, 31, 38; civil (*see* civil rights); constitutional, 32, 65, 328, 329; cultural, 30, 31; environmental, 30; fishing, 78, 288; gaming, 288; human (*see* human rights); to hunt, 31; Incomindios on, 203, 437n2; Indigenous, 31, 32, 36; individual, 73, 329, 345, 442n19; inherent, 8, 12, 203, 270, 272, 281, 376, 377; of Inuit people, 40; land, 27, 31, 32, 472; legal, 39; of minorities, 316; political, 36, 37, 42, 373, 415n25; property, 27, 36, 80; religious, 35; to religious freedom, 28; responsibility *vs.*, 73; of self-determination, 25, 36–39, 41; sovereign, 75, 203; through treaties, 56; transborder, 38; of transborder Indigenous peoples, 31; treaty, 25, 31, 32, 36–39, 79, 80, 284, 372, 397; usufructuary, 32; water, 32, 80, 228
/r/Indian Country, 347
Rio Tinto/BHP, 34
rituals. *see also* ceremonies: blood, 103; defined, **236–37**; of diplomacy, 67; knowledge through, 250; military, 87; powers available by, 106; purpose of, 236; spitting as, 54; for traditional life, 236
Robesonian, The, 433n30
Robinson Rancheria Tribal Council, 342
Rogers, Will, Jr., 79
Romania, 211
Roosevelt, Teddy, 85
Rosebud Sioux Tribe, 275, 368
Rose, Charlie, 164
Rosenthal, Joe, 79
Rosier, Paul C., 80
Rostkowski, Joelle, 209
Rough Rock Demonstration School, 273
Rouillard, John, 442n11
round dancing, **305**–13
Ruggles, Steven, 431n20
Rutherford Falls show, 218
R. v. Desautel, 31, 32
Rwandan genocide, 214

sacred places: and borders, 25, 30; existence of, 28; governance of, 38–39; and Hawaii, 105; loss of, 173; protecting, 158, 161, 171, 173; on public lands, 32–36; stewardship of, 430n9
Sacred Runs for Land and Life, 209
Sacred Stone Camp, 158
Saginaw Chippewa Tribe, 11
Sahaptin speakers, 363
Sahlin, Marshall, 363, 456n19
Sam, Michele, 239
San Carlos Apache Tribe, 34
San Diego State University, 285
San Manuel Band of Mission Indians, 288
Santa Clara Pueblo v. Martinez, 322–33, 345
Santa Fe Indian School, 96
Santorum, Rick, 217
Saponi, 54
Sarris, Greg, 341
Save the Man, Kill the Indian (Pratt), 95
Schad, Lauren, 140
Scheirbeck, Helen, xvii, 431n18
Schmidt, Ruben S., 79
schools: alternative, 270; American Indian students in, 238; and Black Lives Matter, 250; boarding, 15, 83, 95, 144, 365, 374; in Canada, 144, 145; by Catholic Church, 144; children's remains at, 145; and Christianity, 231; closure of, 144; community, 230, 239; and COVID-19, 91; genocide in, 144; K–12, 268, 276–79; language immersion, 270; modern, 230; in 1960s and 1970s, 273; pedagogical style of, 235; Pratt in, 231; private, 239; public, 270; survival, 205; Tribally controlled, 270, 271, 273–75, 277, 281
school system, 143, 203, 261, 280
Schroeder, Jonathan, 431n20
science: and academe, 256; and knowledge, 301, 311; race, 172; Redsteer on, 120–33; Whyte on, 134–39
Scorsese, Martin, 218
Sealaska Corporation, 340
Selam, James, 363
self-actualization, 147

self-determination: and African Americans, 21; and borders, 26; and decolonization, 222; defined, **36**; Deloria on, 26, 247, 414n17; education focus on, 245, 247, 269, 271, 272, 275–77, 279, 281; exercising, 92, 95; federal laws for, 272; innovations for, 269; kinship for, 275; Kipp on, 81; and The List, 351; for 1956 Lumbee Act, 163; and Planchou, 372; Pueblo on, 330; right of, 25, 36–39, 41; and self-government, 287, 289; social movements for, 219; and Warren, 348; Wilkins on, 288
self-government: Cohen on, 334; Cornell on, 334; Marshall on, 331; and self-determination, 287
self-preservation, 71, 295, 351
self-rule, 272, 285, 289
Selkirk (Lord), 319
Seltzer, Carl, 168, 431n20
Seminole Tribe, 198, 288, 289
Seminole Tribe v. Butterworth, 442n17
Senate Committee on Interior and Insular Affairs, 163
Seneca Tribe, 14, 79, 451n121
Sequoyah Club, 76
Serbia, 214
Serra, Junípero, xiii
settler colonialism, 24, 65, 113, 152, 157, 159, 216
settler privilege, 65–66
settlers, 59, 62, 152, 309, 319, 332, 337
1784 Fort Stanwix Treaty, 62
1752 Logg's Town Treaty, 59
1744 Treaty at Lancaster, 58, 59
seventh generation: concept of, 177, 281; conclusion to, 182; Deloria on, 176, 177–78, 182; generativity in, 178–81; introduction to, 175–76; meaning of, 176–77; origins of, 176–77
Seventh Generation Fund, 198
Seven Years War, 59
sexism, 16
sexual assaults, 16
sexuality, 15
sharks, 105, 111–16
Shawandase, Jonas, 6
Shawnee Tribe, 59, 62, 63, 417n12, 451n121
Shelley v. Kraemer, 80
Siberia, 301
sicun, **191**
Sierra Club, 29
Silko, Leslie, 77
Silva, Noenoe K., 105
Simpson, Audra, 262
Simpson, Leanne Betasamosake, 221, 223
Since Time Immemorial: Tribal Sovereignty in Washington legislation, 274
Singing for a Spirit (Deloria), 204, 317
Sinixt people, 31
Siouan settlement, 58
Six Grandfathers, xx
Six Nations, 62
Six Nations Confederacy, 362
1677 Treaty of Middle Plantation, 68, 69
sky, in section 3, 183
slavery, 351
Smith, Andrea, 262
Smith, Houston, xvii
Smith, Jedediah, 336
Smith, Linda Tuhiwai, 152, 262
Smith River Rancheria, 336
Smithsonian Institution, 165–66, 302
Sneed, Richard, 432n30
Snyder Act, 272
social Darwinism, 356
social equity movement, 250
socialism, 23
socialization, 234, 236, 276
social media, xviii, 95, 120, 145, 158, 219–24, 298, 348, 386, 429n1
social relevance, 139
Social Security Act, 373, 375, 381, 461n30
solidarity, 22–24, 121, 156, 158, 198, 202–12, 220, 305–6
South Africa, 215
South Carolina, 62, 432n27
South Dakota, 158, 191, 195, 197, 200, 205, 275, 461n32
South Dakota Supreme Court, 461n32
Southeast Arizona Land Exchange and Conservation Act, 34
Southeastern Cherokee, 336
Southern Border, 27–31, 32
Sovereign Nations of Virginia Conference, 71
sovereign rights, 75, 203
sovereignty: and activism, 80; Articles of Confederation on, 68; Carr on, 293; conference on, 12; cultural, 36–39, 41, 355 (*see also* internal sovereignty); Dakota Access Pipeline for, 158; defined, **429n5**; Deloria on, 26, 78, 414n17; education for, 273; exercising, 90, 260–61; external, 291; hollow, **293**; and ICWA, 373, 376, 377–84; innovations for, 269; internal, 291, 292, 355, **443n28** (*see also* cultural sovereignty); Kipp on, 81; Marquez on, 282–98; Marshall on, 286; and media, 226; Native Americans for, 20, 24; of Native American Tribes, 160–61; #NoDAPL movement for, 158; and Planchou, 372; political, 37; protection of, 157; and race, 43, 44; relational,

321–**23**, 333–45; respect for, 21; responsible, **293**; role of, 36–39; of sacred lands, 26; and science, 139; surrendering, 352; treaty-making for, 49; Ture on, 22, 23; and unrecognized tribes, 173, 174; US Constitution on, 9
Spain, 27
Speaking of Indians (Deloria), 354
Spicer, Edward, 74
Spirit and Reason (Deloria), 168, 308
spiritualism, 315
spirituality: expressions of, 251; in *God Is Red*, 140; percentage practicing, 142, 148; priority of, 141; sustaining, 280
spiritual power, 151–54, 159
spiritual tradition, 334
spirit world, 105, 111, 151, 153, 154, 158, 159, 191
spitting, for agreements, 54
Spokane Tribe of Indians, 341
Sports betting, 442n17
Spotswood, Alexander, 54, 68
Spotted Eagle, Blanche Oldman, 193
Spotted Eagle, Faith, 190, 195
stages of growth and maturation, 235
Stahlins, Marshall, 361
Standing Rock International Treaty Conference, 202
Standing Rock Reservation, 158, 198, 200, 211, 216, 217, 309
Stanfield, Allan, 198
Starna, William, 432n27
states: defined, **293**; on planet, 455n12
state succession, **67**
Steeves, Paulette F. C., 305, 449n82
stereotypes, 86, 89, 217, 254, 255, 308, 315
sterilization, 15, 349
stewardship: and Elders, 179; environmental, 161, 176, 343; as teleology, 151–59
Stillaguamish, 168
storytelling, 138, **236**, 262–63, 265, 387
Stovall Museum, 76
St. Philip's Episcopal Church Cemetery, 197
Strong Hearts, Wounded Souls: Native American Veterans of the Vietnam War (Holm), 86
Stull, Don, 305
Sturtevant, William, 165–66, 432n27
succession, 68, 95–97
Summer People, 323
Supreme Court of Canada, 31, 40, 318
Surplus Property Act, 200
Swanton, John, 430n11
Swinomish Indian Tribal Community, 171
Switzerland, 208
Syracuse University, 303
Taffe Reeds, Susan, 346
TCUs. *see* Tribal Colleges and Universities (TCUs)
teaching and learning, 234–36, 244, 249, 259, 278, 280
Teko peoples, 207
teleology, stewardship as, 151–59
Teresa, Mother, 215
termination, 38, 51, 64, 80, 162–63, 188, **296**, 367, 378
Tewa, 303
Texas, 27, 30, 126, 380
theology, 26
Theorizing Native Studies (Simpson and Smith), 262
Thomasina E. Jordan Federal Recognition Act of 2017, 69
Thomasina E. Jordan Federal Recognition Act of 2018, 350
Thomas, Robert K., xvii, 77, 81
Thunder Hawk, Madonna, xvii
Tiller, Veronica, 339
timekeeping, 117
tiyoŝpaye, **365**
Tk'emlúps te Secwépemc First Nation, 144
Tohono O'odham Nation, 29, 336
Tolowa Dee-ni' Nation, 336
Tommie, Howard, 431n18, 432n23
Tonasket, Mel, xvii
Traditional Cultural Property, 36, 38
Trahant, Mark, 225
Trail of Broken Treaties, 13, 80, 315
Trail of Broken Treaties, The (Deloria), 203
transborder rights, 38
treaties: agreements *vs*., 39–40, 58, 292; Cherokee, 62; Deloria on, 26; domestic, 39–41; and education, 270; honoring, 21; international, 39–41; issues of, 372; for land titles, 49; for Little Traverse Bay Bands of Odawa Indians, 7, 9, 10; for monetary payments, 324; of peace and friendship, 36; of Pueblo Nations, 35; respect for, 204; from 1781, 9; with Six Nations, 62; unilateral interpretation of, 65–66; US Constitution and, 9; Virginia, 67
treaty claims, 36
treaty-making: and diplomacy, 64; end of, 40, 77; evolution of, 57–60; legal foundation for, 60–61; and nationhood terminology, 334; political motivations for, 60–61; records of, 56; for sovereignty, 49
Treaty of Albany, 58
Treaty of La Mesilla, 27
treaty process: conclusion to, 73–75; diplomacy in, 56–57; introduction to, 54–56; modern nation-to-nation relations in, 69–70; revitalizing

Indigenous-US diplomacy in, 66–69; settler privilege in, 65–66; twenty-first-century relations in, 71–73
treaty rights, 25, 31, 32, 36–39, 79, 80, 284, 372, 397
Tribal Coalition, 40
Tribal College Journal, 278, 280
Tribal Colleges and Universities (TCUs), 258, 268, 271, 272, 275, 277, 279, 280
Tribal-Commonwealth Accord, 71–75, 395–411
Tribal Criminal Law and Procedure (Deer and Garrow), 18
Tribal Education Codes, 275
Tribal General Council, 193
Tribal governments: Bears Ears National Monument, 40; defined, **8–9**, **415n18**; Deloria support of, 12, 97, 290; difficulties of, 291; and education, 272, 275, 277, 281; gaming for, 289; and Lumbee, 167, 173; responsibilities of, 72; and self-determination, 95; and seventh generation, 177; sovereignty of, 37–38, 72, 286, 288, 291–92; and US, 39; and veterans, 77, 83
Tribal Law and Policy Institute, 16
Tribally Controlled Community College Assistance Act, 233
Tribally controlled education, 268–80
Tribally controlled schools, 270, 271, 273–75, 277, 281
Tribal Nations-Commonwealth Sovereignty Accord, 56, 70
Tribal-state agreements, 381, 382
Tribal-state axis, 372–73, 381–84
Tribal/State Indian Child Welfare Agreement, 382
Tribe: defined, 334; as term, 335, 450n82
Tribes, Treaties, and Constitutional Tribulations (Deloria), 39, 42–53
Trudeau, Justin, 146
Trudell, John, xvii, 76
Trump administration, 28, 34
Trump, Donald, xx, 220, 221
Tsosie, Rebecca, 25
Tukano, Daiara, 211
Tunica-Biloxi, 168
Ture, Kwame, 21, 22, 23. *see also* Carmichael, Stokely
12 Confederated Tribes of the Big Water, The, 336. *see also* Colville Tribe
21st Conference of the Parties, 209, 210
2018 Union of Concerned Scientists Report, 126

Umatilla Reservation, 363
UN Conference on Environment and Development, 128
UNDRIP. *see* United Nations Declaration on the Rights of Indigenous Peoples (UNDRIP)
UN Educational, Scientific, and Cultural Organization, 207
unemployment rates, 344
UN Framework Convention on Climate Change (UNFCCC), 128–29
UN General Assembly, 36
Union of Concerned Scientists, 122
Unist'ot'en movement, 217
United Nations, 46, 47, 176, 360
United Nations Declaration on the Rights of Indigenous Peoples, 36, 46–47
United Nations Declaration on the Rights of Indigenous Peoples (UNDRIP), 31, 35, 36, 40, 41, 47, 202, 208, 450n82
United Nations Framework Convention on Climate Change, 211
United Southeastern Tribes (USET), 164–66, 431n18, 431n20, 431n21, 432n23, 432n30, 433n30
United States: acquiring Mexican land, 27; bombing Iraq, 214; bombing Serbia, 214; borders in, 26; children forcibly removed in, 144–45; Clean Slate Doctrine in, 68; and college campuses, 6; dances in, 158; in 1817 Treaty with the Wyandot, 339; engagement with, 61–65; expanding territory, 27, 53, 62; funding into Indian Country, 92; goals of education in, 272; Great Plains Tribes and, 9; groups forced into, 24; higher education in, 279; human rights abuses in, 30; and ICWA, 373; inconsistency by, 42; Indigenous rights structure in, 32; invading Kosovo, 215; military in, 50; PhD program in NAS, 267; political rights in, 37; reasons for treaties, 60; recognized tribes in, 8; religious freedom in, 35; sacred lands in, 26; scientific workforce in, 122; territories for, 60; treaty history in, 39; treaty obligations in, 67–68; Tribal social-economic status in, 297; unrecognized tribes in, 160, 161, 162, 171, 429n1; USET in, 164; and Viet Cong, 81
United States Codes, 57
United States v. Washington, 79
Université Paris 7 (Diderot), 202
Université Paris Cité, 202
University of Alaska–Fairbanks, 267
University of Arizona, 77, 81, 89, 267
University of Arkansas, 306, 308
University of California, 267
University of Colorado, 16
University of Hawai'i, 115
University of Kansas, 14
University of Michigan, 6, 10

University of New Mexico (UNM), 253, 258, 260, 264, 267
University of New York, 308
University of Oklahoma, 76
University of Wisconsin–Milwaukee, 76
unrecognized Tribes, 160–74, 416n5, 429n1
unsustainable development, 161
Upper Mattaponi Tribe, 69, 416n5
USACOE, Yankton Sioux Tribe vs., 190
US Advisory Commission on Indian Reservation Economics, 344
US armed forces, 88
US Army, 33, 79, 85, 87, 190, 192
US Army Corps of Engineers, 193, 194, 195–96, 197, 198, 199
US Congress, 8
US Constitution, 9, 26, 39, 43, 48, 50, 63, 64, 65, 72, 79, 80, 284, 384, 461n24
US Customs and Border Protection Department, 29
US democracy, 22
US democratic project, 20, 23
US Department of Education, 271
US Department of Labor, 431n18, 432n23
US education system, 95
USET. *see* United Southeastern Tribes (USET)
US Forest Service, 34–35
US Geological Survey, 127–28
US Global Change Research Act of 1990, 128
US House of Representatives, 7, 9, 10, 163, 164, 168
US Indian Affairs, 47
US Indian policy, 43, 47, 48, 51
US Marine Corps, 76–79
US-Mexico Border, 25–28, 32
US-Mexico War, 27
US National Climate Assessments, 129
US Navy, 76, 115
US policy, 21, 40, 78
US Senate, 10, 67, 77, 162–68, 377, 433n31
US State Department, 57–58
US Supreme Court, 37, 41, 45, 46, 65, 322, 326, 329, 334, 367, 380, 448n58
US Treasury, 92
usufructuary rights, 32
Utah, 27, 40

Van Riper, David, 431n20
Venezuela, 206
veteran activism, 80
veterans, 76–88, 156, 196, 199
Veterans' Administration Commissions, 77
Vienna Convention on the Succession of States in Respect of Treaties, 67
Viet Cong at Wounded Knee (Kipp), 81
Vietnam, 76, 81, 82
Vietnam veterans, 81
Vietnam Veterans Against the War, 76
Vietnam War, 80, 84
villages: fission forming, 338; Gurkhas in, 87; on list of federally recognized Tribes, 18; moieties into, 324; societies into, 334
Villa, Pancho, 85
Vine Deloria Papers, 431n18, 432n23
violence: academic, 310; of bigotry, 347; against the Earth, 211; of Indigenous children, 211; and PTSD, 156; and stereotypes, 86, 308; systemic hierarchical, 192–93; against women, xix, 211, 332
Violence Against Women Reauthorization Act of 2013, 448n58
Virginia, 54–59, 67–75, 172, 349–51, 395–411, 416n5, 418n41
Virginia General Assembly, 349
Vitoria, Francisco de, 60, 61
Vizenor, Gerald, 314
volcano, 106, 107

Waganakising, Odawak Tribe, 6, 12. *see also* Little Traverse Bay Bands of Odawa Indians
Walker, Linda, 200
Walker, Tillie, xvii
Warm Springs Apaches, 33
Warm Springs Reservation, 363
War of 1812, 85
Warren, Elizabeth, 348
Warrior, Clyde, xvii
warriorhood, 86
warriors, 88, 103–4, 305, 320
warrior societies, 256
warrior traditions, 86
Washington, 79, 126, 164, 274, 283, 303, 363, 434n52
Washington, D.C., 13, 18, 80, 205, 315
Washington football team, 218
Washington, George, 62
Washington State, 78
Washington, United States v., 79
water: and border wall, 28–29; and mining, 34; in section 2, 99
Water Resources Development Act, 200
water rights, 32, 80, 228
Wayampi peoples, 207
Wayana peoples, 207
Wayuu peoples, 206

Westerman, Floyd, xvii
Western Apache people, 27, 28, 32–36
Western Pueblo society, 337
western religion, 141–47
West, Richard, 302
We Talk, You Listen (Deloria), 14, 203
Wheeler, Burton, 339
Whitebear, Bernie, xvii
White, Byron, 332
White Earth Band of Ojibwe, 369, 459n53
white feminists, 15
white leaders, xv
white racial superiority, 335
whites, xvi, 14, 23, 85, 89, 120, 121, 185–87, 189, 337, 349–50
white society, 47–48
white supremacy, xiii, xix, 24, 44–46, 349–51
White Swan, 190–201
White Swan Negotiation Team, 194, 196, 198
White Swan Spiritual Camp, 197, 198
Whitman, Marcus, xv
Whyte, Kyle, 131, 134, 368
Wildcat, Daniel, 153, 276, 312
Wilkins, David: on allegiance vs disciplines, 253, 255, 256, 258; on banishments, 338; on child welfare, 384; on Deloria in France, 202; on education, 269, 270, 276, 278, 288, 289; on kinship, 364; on Lumbee Tribe, 169; in *Red Prophet*, xviii; on rights, 65; on *Santa Clara Pueblo* decision, 333; on sovereignty, 322; on Tribal-Commonwealth Accord, 71, 395; in *Tribes, Treaties, and Constitutional Tribulations*, 39, 42–53
Wilkins, Shelly Hulse, 71, 119, 338, 364, 395
Williams, Robert A., 66
Williams, Robert, Jr., 334, 336
Wilson, Carrie, 308
Winant, Howard, 335
Winnebago Tribe, 198
Winter People, 323
Wisconsin, 61, 76, 88, 288
Wolakota, **354**
Wolf, Eric R., 357
women: and border, 30, 32; from Brave Heart Society, 196, 197, 199; ceremonies for, 200; Deer on, 13–19; and list-making, 348; in matrilineal clan, 359, 362; in matrilocal clan, 361; of mixed marriages, 317, 325; and political authority, 456n24; power of, 211; role of, 205; in *Santa Clara Pueblo v. Martinez*, 329, 332; violence against, xix, 211, 332
Women of All Red Nations, 205
Women's Earth and Climate Action Network, 211
Woods, James H., 165
woodstove knowledge, 259–61, 267
Worcester v. Georgia, 286, 334
"Words and Place: A Conversation with Vine Deloria, Jr." (discussion), 89
worldviews, Indigenous, 242
World War I, 86
World War II, 87, 113
World We Used to Live In, The (Deloria), xiv, 105, 151, 152, 154, 155, 159
Wounded Head, Marilyn, xv
Wounded Knee, 14, 15, 80–81, 158, 204
Wyandot Tribe, 451n121
Wynne, Mary, 195–96
Wyoming, 27, 385, 389, 390

Xennial generation, 219

Yaaamava', **336**
Yakama Reservation, 363
Ya Ne Dah Ah School, 95
Yankton band of the Dakota Nation, 309
Yankton Cultural Committee, 200
Yankton Sioux Tribe, 194–200
Yankton Sioux Tribe vs. USACOE, 190
Yaqui, 28
Yazzie, Melanie K., 213
Yazzie, Robert, 366
Young, John, 111
Youngkin, Glen, 74
Ysleta del Sur Pueblo, 94
Yuhaaviatam of San Manuel Nation, 288, 336
Yurok Tribe, 338, 370

Zapatista, 207, 209
Zaragoza, Raye, 211
Zuni, 86

ABOUT THE EDITORS

David E. Wilkins (Lumbee Nation) is the E. Claiborne Robins Distinguished Professor in Leadership Studies at the University of Richmond Jepson School of Leadership Studies. He is also professor emeritus at the University of Minnesota where he held the McKnight Presidential Professorship in American Indian Studies with appointments in law, political science, and American studies. He earned his PhD in political science from the University of North Carolina–Chapel Hill in December 1990.

He is the author or editor of more than twenty books, including *Indigenous Governance: Clans, Constitutions, and Consent* (2024), *Documents of Native American Political Development* (2019), and *Hollow Justice* (2013). *The Legal Universe* (2011) and *Tribes, Treaties, and Constitutional Tribulations* (2000) were coauthored with Vine Deloria, Jr. His articles have appeared in a range of social science, law, history, and ethnic studies journals.

Shelly Hulse Wilkins is an analyst and consultant with the Wilkins Forum, LLC. She holds an MPA with an emphasis in Tribal-state relations and has worked on issues of importance to Native governments for twenty-five years. Before convening the Wilkins Forum with her partner, David, she worked as a state legislative caucus liaison, senior analyst for the Washington State Senate, and program principal for the State-Tribal Institute at the National Conference of State Legislatures. With David Wilkins, she coauthored *Dismembered: Native Disenrollment and the Battle for Human Rights* (2017).